Property of
FAMILY OF FAITH
LIBRARY

FUNDAMENTALS OF OPERATIONS MANAGEMENT

FUNDAMENTALS OF OPERATIONS MANAGEMENT

Nicholas J. Aquilano
University of Arizona

Richard B. Chase
University of Southern California

IRWIN

Homewood, IL 60430
Boston, MA 02116

Sponsoring editor: *Richard T. Hercher, Jr.*
Developmental editor: *James Minatel*
Project editor: *Susan Trentacosti*
Production manager: *Ann Cassady*
Designer: *Maureen McCutcheon*
Artist: *Art Force*
Compositor: *Better Graphics, Inc.*
Typeface: *10/12 Bembo*
Printer: *R. R. Donnelley & Sons Company*

Library of Congress Cataloging-in-Publication Data

Aquilano, Nicholas J.
Fundamentals of operations management / Nicholas J. Aquilano, Richard B. Chase.
p. cm.
Includes indexes.
ISBN 0–256–02830–3 —0–256–11399–8 (International ed.)
1. Production management. I. Chase, Richard B. II. Title.
TS155.A58 1991
658.5—dc20 90–25951

Printed in the United States of America
3 4 5 6 7 8 9 0 DOC 8 7 6 5 4 3 2 1

To our wives
Nina and Harriet
and to our children
Don, Kara, and Mark
Laurie, Andy, Glenn, and Rob

Preface for the Student
(By a student)

The study of Operations Management is in large part the study of how the world around us functions. If you are waiting in line at a restaurant, deciding on how much food to purchase at the supermarket, or scheduling your own study time, the basic principles of OM give insights into how these day-to-day activities are carried out. If you have ever wondered why something is done the way it is, there is probably a good "OM reason" to be found in this book to help explain it. The reason you can see the concepts and techniques all around is because they are so heavily used by organizations of all kinds, be they manufacturing firms making "things" or firms providing intangibles. OM brings together the areas of marketing, engineering, accounting, finance, and general management to the study of problems of running an organization.

This book gets across the basics of OM with some of the most up-to-date information available. Since the world is constantly changing, the way OM is studied and practiced is changing as well. Dr. Aquilano and Dr. Chase have presented the practical side of such state-of-the-art concepts and issues as total quality management, service operations management, Just-in-Time production systems, and synchronous manufacturing.

As you study the areas of OM, take time out to look around you and see where the ideas could be applied. By noting applications of OM as they appear in the news and in your daily life, you'll enhance your understanding of the material, and, if you're like me, you'll enjoy the subject much more.

Joseph Pope
Student, College of Business
and Public Administration
University of Arizona

Preface

Never before has the field of production and operations management been as important as it is right now. The loss of U.S. manufacturing markets to foreign competition is staggering. First it was steel, then autos, then electronics, then small appliances, and the list goes on. Now the United States is also losing the battle in services. Even if the manufacturing sector was lost, the United States had believed it could retain superiority in services which would become the new building base providing jobs to maintain a high standard of living. This is not happening. Among financial institutions, for example, the United States does not have a firm in the world's top ten—not even close! Citibank, the nation's largest financial institution, places number 33 worldwide. In terms of per capita income, the United States is now sixth, falling behind Norway, Sweden, and Finland. The United States is becoming a "hollow" country by purchasing and subcontracting manufacturing and services from foreign producers. Some experts have argued that a nation cannot retain economic and world power superiority without its own industrial base.

As authors, we present this bit of gloom to encourage both faculty and students to take a greater interest in the future of this country and in the means to reverse what may seem to be the inevitable. Operations management is extremely important in this effort because operations management is the core of this entire process of managing resources and converting them efficiently into desirable goods and services.

This textbook presents the best and latest in current operations management practice. We, as authors, have drawn upon much of the material in our other book *Production and Operations Management* and have added new material. We reduced the level of quantitative treatment and are combining the latest practice with theory.

There have been major changes in manufacturing and services recently. Terms such as Just-in-Time and computer-integrated manufacturing have become household words. We discuss these and also cover synchronous production, service management, service quality, and flexible manufacturing systems. In the field of quality, we've gone beyond the usual quality control considerations and entered the Baldrige phase of the quality movement which views quality as an organizational measure and not just a product measure.

We've targeted this book for an audience of students and faculty who need a good and current book in the field. We pride ourselves in being active developers of concepts and in being able to present the material at a suitable level. We welcome your comments and suggestions.

Teaching aids available for this text include:

- *Study Guide,* by Aquilano and Agrawal.
- *Instructor's Manual and Transparency Masters.*
- *Test Bank and CompuTest,* by Delurgio, Foster, Aquilano, and Chase.
- *Lotus Spreadsheets,* by Aquilano and Pope.

Acknowledgments

Since we have included much of the material in our *Production and Operations Management* text, naturally all of the reviewers of that text rightfully need to be recognized. We would like to specifically thank the reviewers who participated in evaluating and making suggestions for this text. These include: D. Keith Denton, Southwest Missouri State University; Frank G. Forst, Loyola University of Chicago; Charles W. Lackey, Jr., University of Texas at El Paso; Ann Marucheck, University of North Carolina—Chapel Hill; Roger Shoenfeldt, Murray State University; and V Sridharan, Clemson University.

Additionally we would like to thank Joe Pope of the University of Arizona for his help both on the text and in the Lotus Spreadsheets for the Student Guide. We would also like to thank Jim Minatel, Susan Trentacosti, Dick Hercher and the rest of the Richard D. Irwin staff for Irwin's usual very high level of assistance.

Nicholas J. Aquilano
Richard B. Chase

Contents

FUNDAMENTALS OF OPERATIONS MANAGEMENT

Chapter 1

Introduction and Overview

EPIGRAPH

The mechanics of running a business are really not very complicated, when you get down to essentials. You have to make some stuff and sell it to somebody for more than it cost you. That's about all that there's to it, except for a few million details.

John L. McCaffrey, "What Corporation Presidents Think about at Night."

CHAPTER OUTLINE

KEY TERMS

Five P's of Operations Management
Transformation Process
Scientific Management
Just-in-Time (JIT)
Total Quality Control (TQC)
Computer-Integrated Manufacturing (CIM)

Just a few years ago, the average person knew very little about the production of goods or services. Now, it is amazing how many people can discuss terms such as Japanese competition, Just-in-Time manufacturing, total quality control, turnaround cycle times, inventory control, and so on.

American firms are realizing that we have been running our companies wrong. Firms underestimated the customer, assuming that all products would be purchased—the good as well as the not so good. Customers have become more sophisticated.

Accounting procedures, especially cost accounting, have been used as the basic measure of performance in our firms. We know now that was a grave mistake. Cost accounting has been blamed as a major cause of our poor performance and the loss of our manufacturing base to foreign competition. The argument is that cost accounting has not been measuring the right things, nor in the right way. Inventories, for example, are now considered bad. Financial reports have always carried inventory as an asset. Now, from a management standpoint, inventory is often considered a sunk cost. In many cases, it's worse than a sunk cost. A sunk cost can usually be done away with and forgotten with a one-time write-off. Inventory, in contrast, continues to need space, care, and a list of ongoing costs. The accounting profession has responded impressively. Major efforts are now in process to develop new techniques and procedures.

Marketing, also, had been blamed for our poor performance because of its attitude toward production—"We'll tell you what to produce, you just produce it."

We've lost a great deal of our manufacturing jobs and there is a strong argument that we should get them back. A lot of our services are lost as well. The United States does not have a bank within the world's top 10. In fact, our largest bank is number 28 on the list!

The game has changed dramatically. Product cycles are very short; customers want high quality; workers want more control over their work and a piece of the action in the way of bonuses and profit sharing. It's an exciting time because everyone realizes we have problems and we're in this together. All of the functional areas of the firm are concerned. Marketing, finance, and operations have never worked together more closely.

This book discusses the basic concepts of operations management, which is responsible for making the products and services that the firm sells. It is important to learn about operations management for a number of reasons:

1. International competition, especially from the Japanese, has compelled North American companies to "raise the level of their game" to remain competitive in world markets. Producing high-quality products that can be sold at competitive prices is the basic responsibility of the operations area.

2. New operations technologies and control systems are significantly affecting the way firms conduct their businesses. No matter what the business specialty happens to be, a knowledge of operations is critical in making informed managerial decisions.
3. Operations management is critical to service companies as well as manufacturing firms. Take a look at the Fortune 500 service businesses; the vast majority achieved their success through well-run operations. Indeed, no service firm can be called "excellent" without superior operations management.
4. Entrepreneurs, if they are to survive, must have a thorough knowledge of how their organizations make their products. This is particularly true for new service businesses, where quality of operations is frequently the only thing that separates one firm from another.
5. The concepts and tools of operations management (OM) are widely used in managing other functions of the business as well. For example, every manager is concerned with quality and productivity issues—topics which are presented in this book.

The Christian Science Monitor, November 24, 1987. Danziger © 1987. Reprinted with permission.

6. Operations management offers an interesting and rewarding career. It requires a broad set of skills that, if mastered, makes you a very attractive candidate for jobs in a wide range of organizations.

1.1 SPECIFIC OBJECTIVES OF THE BOOK

The specific objectives of the book are: (1) to explain how the operations function is managed; (2) to introduce some standard tools and techniques used by production (or operations) managers; (3) to help you develop an appreciation for the interaction of this management activity with other management systems within the organizations; (4) to introduce some *new* concepts in the field; and (5) to provide an understanding of the field as a totality.

With respect to the last objective, we intend to show that operations management is not just a loosely knit aggregation of tools but rather a *synthesis* of concepts and techniques that relate directly to productive systems and enhance their management. This point is important because operations management (OM) is frequently confused with operations research (OR) (or its synonym, management science [MS]), and with industrial engineering (IE). The critical difference is this: OM is a field of management, whereas OR is a branch of applied mathematics and IE is an engineering discipline. Thus, while operations managers use the tools of OR (such as linear programming) in decision making, and are concerned with many of the same issues as IE (such as factory automation), OM has a distinct management role in managing resources to produce a product or service. When a problem arises that requires a more specialized knowledge of a mathematical or statistical technique, the OM person may submit it to an OR specialist for analysis and solution.

1.2 OPERATIONS MANAGEMENT DEFINED

Operations management (or *production management,* as it is often called) may be defined as the management of the direct resources required to produce the goods and services provided by an organization. Exhibit 1.1 presents a summary model of the field in a broad business context.

The marketplace—the firm's customers for its products or services—drives the corporate strategy of the firm. This strategy is based on the corporate mission, and in essence reflects how the firm plans to use all its resources and functions (marketing, finance, and operations) to gain competitive advantage. The operations strategy specifies how the firm will employ its production capabilities to support its corporate strategy. (The extent to which operations influences corporate strategy will be discussed in subsequent chapters.)

Operations management deals with the direct production resources of the firm. These resources may be thought of as the **Five P's of operations**

EXHIBIT 1.1

Summary Model of the Field

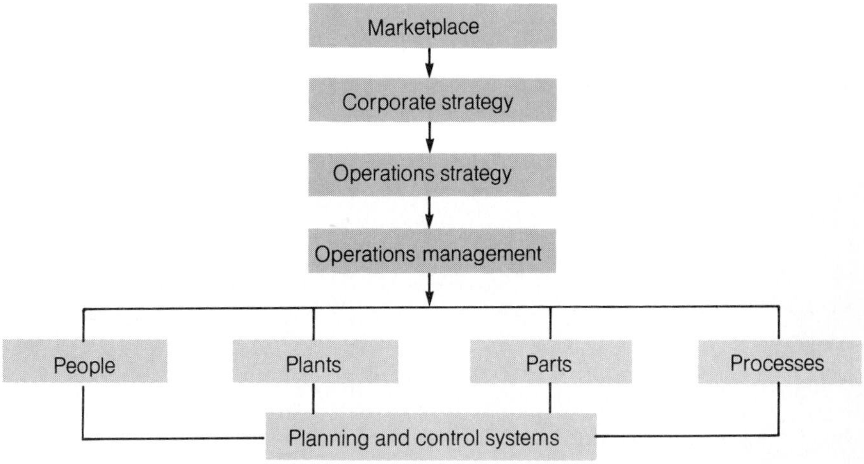

management—People, Plants, Parts, Processes, and Planning and control systems. The people are the direct and indirect work force; the plants include the factories or service branches where production is carried out; the parts include the materials (or in the case of services, the supplies) that go through the system; the processes include the equipment and the steps by which production is accomplished; and the planning and control systems are the procedures and information used by management to operate the system.

1.3 THE OPERATIONS FUNCTION AND ITS ENVIRONMENT

In most organizations, operations is an internal function that is buffered from the external environment by other organizational functions.

Consider the relationship between the operations and other organization functions and the environment shown in Exhibit 1.2. Orders are received by the sales department, which is an arm of the marketing function; supplies and raw materials are obtained through the purchasing function; capital for equipment purchases comes from the finance function; the labor force is obtained through the personnel function; and the product is delivered by the distribution function. Thus, while there may be a good deal of interaction between the firm and its environment, the production function is rarely involved in it directly.

Buffering the production function (or, as it is sometimes called, the *technical core*) from direct environmental influence has been traditionally seen as desirable, for several reasons:

EXHIBIT 1.2 **Relationship between the Operations Function, Other Organization Functions, and the Environment**

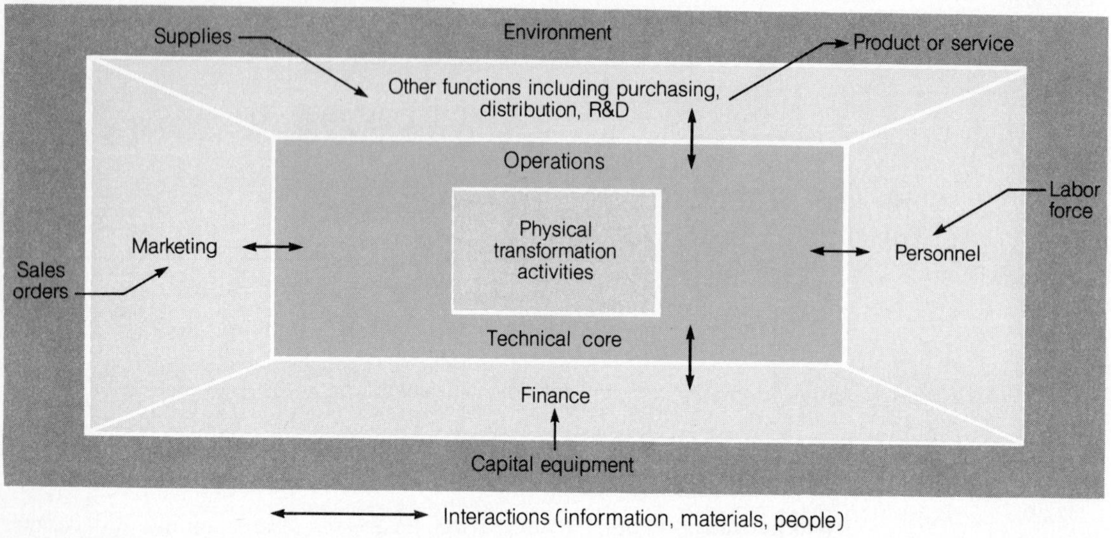

1. Interaction with environmental elements (e.g., customers and salespeople on the production floor) can be a disturbing influence on the production process.
2. The direct production process is often more efficient than the processes required for obtaining inputs and disposing of finished goods.
3. In certain technologies (for example, assembly lines and petroleum refining), maximum productivity can be achieved only by operating as if the market could absorb all the product being manufactured and at a continuous rate. This means that the production process must shift at least some of the input and output activities to other parts of the firm.
4. The managerial skills required for successful operation of the production process are often different from those required for successful operation of the boundary systems of marketing and personnel, for example.

However, such buffering should *not* be used as a rationale for inflexibility to the changing demands of the marketplace. As Goldhar states,

> All production activities start with the marketplace—what the customer values. This knowledge is converted into information for product design, which in turn is translated into a three-dimensional specification for a manufactured product, or a

EXHIBIT 1.3 **Sample Organization Charts of Four Diverse Firms**

Chart (A) : Airline

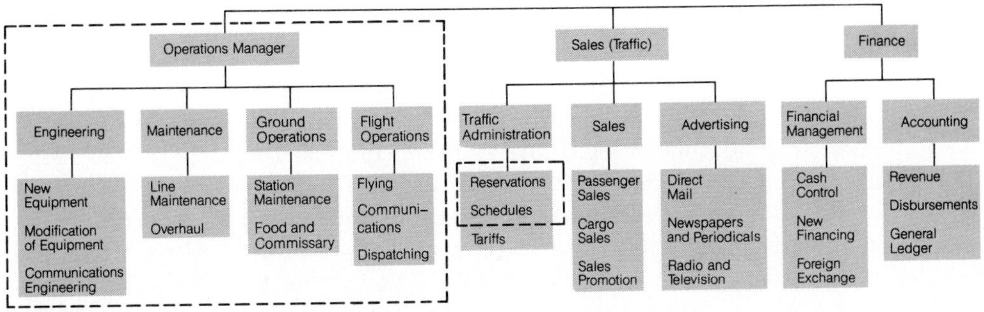

Chart (B) : Commercial bank branch

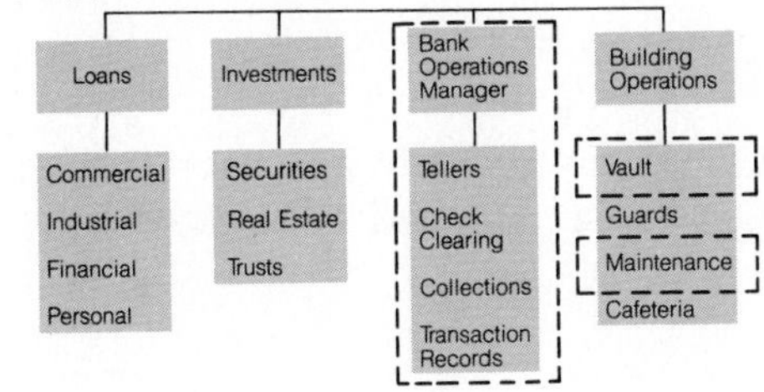

Chart (C): Manufacturing firm

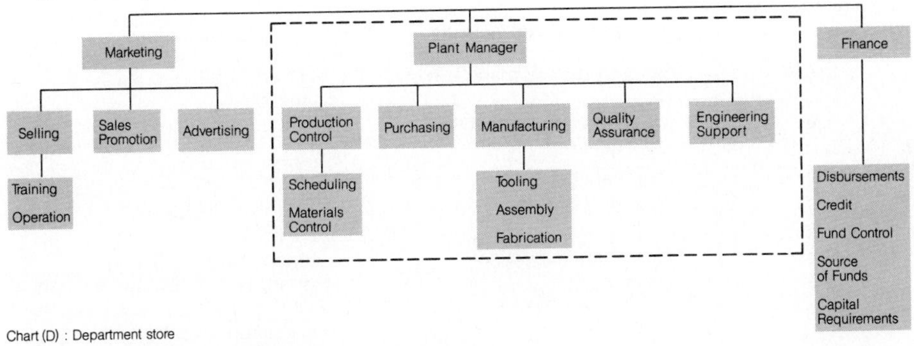

Chart (D) : Department store

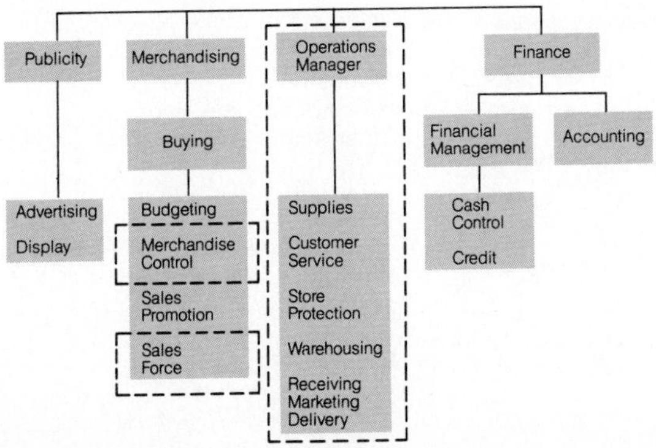

conceptual specification for a service. Spanning the boundary between the technical core and the marketplace in a fast, efficient manner is now "the name of the game" for most producers.[1]

We have identified the location of "production" activities in four different types of organizations in Exhibit 1.3: three service firms (A, B, and D) and one manufacturing company (C). Aside from differences in terminology, the non-manufacturing organizations also differ from the manufacturing firm in structure. In the manufacturing company, production functions are grouped in one department. In the service firms, certain production activities are scattered throughout the organization. This does not mean that the activity is any less a production one, but only that it is deemed best performed under the aegis of a different department. Note also that the position of plant manager is used in manufacturing to administer the various support activities required for production.

Jobs Related to the Operations Function

Exhibit 1.4 lists some line and staff jobs that are frequently viewed as relating to the operations function. The focus on materials in manufacturing gives rise

EXHIBIT 1.4

Line and Staff Jobs in Operations Management

Organizational Level	Manufacturing Industries	Service Industries
Upper	Vice president of manufacturing	Vice president of operations (airline)
	Regional manager of manufacturing	Chief administrator (hospital)
Middle	Plant manager	Store manager (department store)
	Program manager	Facilities manager (wholesale distributor)
Lower	Department supervisor	Branch manager (bank)
	Foreman	Department supervisor (insurance company)
	Crew chief	Assistant manager (hotel)
Staff	Production controller	Systems and procedures analyst
	Materials manager	Purchasing agent
	Quality controller	Inspector
	Purchasing agent	Dietician (hospital)
	Time-study analyst	Management consultant
	Maintenance manager	
	Process engineer	

[1] Joel Goldhar, speech before the University of Arizona–Honeywell Manufacturing Strategy Seminar, Spring 1984.

to more staff specializations than for service organizations, such as banks and hospitals. The Insert on nuts-and-bolts bosses indicates that the operations route is not a bad career path to the top of the organization.

INSERT Nuts-and-Bolts Bosses

"Graduates are definitely moving toward line jobs and away from staff positions," says Placement Director Parker Llewellyn. Why? That's where the opportunities are.

This change of emphasis mirrors a similar trend at corporate headquarters. "In the last two or three years, the bloom has come off the highflying marketing guy or financial type," says David Smith, managing director of Korn/Ferry International, an executive recruiting firm. "Companies have had to cut costs and focus on how they make their products. Operations people control that process, so they seem to be in greater demand today."

An informal survey illustrates the trend dramatically. Officials at Chicago-based Heidrick & Struggles, another executive recruiter, kept a record of high-level promotions at major corporations during the first six months of last year. Of 74 individuals promoted to top positions, 60 came up through operations, versus 11 in finance, 2 in sales and marketing, and 1 in law.

"We were shocked," says William Bowen, chief executive of Heidrick & Struggles. "We expected that the traditional routes to the top, like finance and marketing, would still dominate." In comparison, a similar study by H&S three years ago found that nearly 28 percent of the executives who made it to the top rose through sales and marketing. Manufacturing and operations men were second at 27 percent, while 23 percent had financial backgrounds and 8 percent were lawyers. "The fast track often fits the squeaky-wheel analogy," says Harvard professor Robert Hayes. "The squeaky wheel today is the operations function."

Source: Extracted from John A. Byrne, "Nuts-and-Bolts Bosses," *Forbes*, September 26, 1983.

1.4 OPERATIONS OBJECTIVES

The general objectives of operations management are to produce a specified product, on schedule, at minimum cost. Most organizations, however, use additional criteria for purposes of evaluation and control. Typical criteria for a manufacturing firm include:

1. Volume of output.
2. Cost (materials, labor, delivery, scrap, etc.).
3. Utilization (equipment and labor).
4. Quality and product reliability.
5. On-time delivery.
6. Investment (return on assets).

7. Flexibility for product change.
8. Flexibility for volume change.

Several of these measures are internally oriented, and thus are of little concern to the customer. However, Schoenberger observes that the very best companies (he calls them "world-class manufacturers") use customer-oriented performance measures at the corporate level. These are typically summarized as cost (to the customer), lead time, quality, and flexibility.[2]

In actually applying these objectives, it is necessary to recognize that not all of them can be achieved with the same level of success. In many cases, low cost must be sacrificed for the flexibility necessary to customize products, or to deliver products within a very short lead time. Even quality, which has reached the level of a religious commandment in many firms, sometimes must be sacrificed to meet lead-time pressures. A case in point would be a hospital supplier delivering a state-of-the-art laboratory device for analyzing blood samples. The hospital may insist on having it immediately, even though it has scratches or minor operating problems. Thus, despite the laudable goal of wanting to excell on all objectives, situations can force trade-offs and priorities, at least in the short run.

Operations objectives are cascaded through the organization and are translated into measurable terms that become part of the operating goals for production-related departments and their managers.

Most companies also have developed a statement of corporate philosophy, or mission, to which operating objectives are closely tied. IBM's corporate philosophy centers on the concept of "customer service," Hewlett-Packard emphasizes "customer satisfaction." A company that describes its objectives as "success factors" is Allen-Bradley, known for state-of-the-art industrial control equipment (see Insert).

INSERT Success Factors at Allen-Bradley Industrial Control Group

What are the key success factors in manufacturing? What should a company point toward in its strategic planning of the manufacturing function? What goals should it set to indicate where it wants manufacturing to be so that it can best serve the overall business objectives? [The vice president of the Industrial Control Group, Larry Yost] lists them as follows:

- Competitive delivery.
- Asset utilization.
- Quality.
- Cost.

[2] Richard J. Schoenberger, *World Class Manufacturing, The Lessons of Simplicity Applied* (New York: Free Press, 1986), p. 205.

- New product introduction.
- Business systems.
- Human resources.

Competitive delivery means that promised dates are met. Lead times must accurately reflect manufacturing requirements. And delivery compliance must be effected in this post-mass-production age, where manufacturing capability is a hybrid of volume output and flexible product mix.

Asset utilization has become a key indicator in evaluating the performance of a company, right up there with market share, sales volume, and profits. While the "hot buttons" seem to change weekly in industry—inventory is too high, profits are too low, and so forth—return on assets is an approach that keeps everything balanced. If that is in fact the focus, then what manufacturing can do to help the company is optimize its inventory and the utilization of its fixed assets.

Element number three, quality, must be approached from two angles: customer perception and the internal cost of maintaining quality. As for cost, manufacturing must contribute to a cost equation that is competitive worldwide as well as manageable throughout the different phases of the business cycle. Anyone can make money when business is good; the trick is to be able to do it during a downturn.

New product introductions are an extremely important gauge of a successful manufacturing operation. In the good old days, five to eight years would transpire from the marketing idea to the sale of the first product. That product in turn would have a 20-year life cycle.

Now, product life cycles can be less than two years. There is no future without new products, and manufacturing's role within the division is to deliver them in a timely manner, to the planned volumes, with respect to both the introduction process and the actual production cost of the item itself.

Finally, manufacturing must be effectively integrated within the business systems and must successfully manage its human resources, including both hiring and training its people for the current and future skills that will be required to fulfill the strategic plan.

Source: Extracted from John M. Martin, "Strategic Planning for Manufacturing," *Manufacturing Engineering,* November 1987, pp. 45–50.

1.5 PRODUCTION SYSTEMS

Operations management manages production systems. A production system may be thought of as a set of components whose function is to convert a set of inputs into some desired output through what we call a **transformation process.** A component may be a machine, a person, a tool, or a management system. An input may be a raw material, a person, or a finished product from another system. Some transformations that take place are:

- Physical, as in manufacturing.
- Locational, as in transportation.
- Exchange, as in retailing.

EXHIBIT 1.5

Input–Transformation–Output Relationships for Typical Systems

System	Primary Inputs	Components	Primary Transformation Function(s)	Typical Desired Output
Hospital	Patients	MDs, nurses, medical supplies, equipment	Health care (physiological)	Healthy individuals
Restaurant	Hungry customers	Food, chef, waitress, environment	Well-prepared food, well served; agreeable environment (physical and exchange)	Satisfied customers
Automobile factory	Sheet steel, engine parts	Tools, equipment, workers	Fabrication and assembly of cars (physical)	High-quality cars
College or university	High school graduates	Teachers, books, classrooms	Imparting knowledge and skills (informational)	Educated individuals
Department store	Shoppers	Displays, stock of goods, sales clerks	Attract shoppers, promote products, fill orders (exchange)	Sales to satisfied customers
Distribution center	Stockkeeping units (SKUs)	Storage bins, stockpickers	Storage and redistribution	Fast delivery, availability of SKUs

- Storage, as in warehousing.
- Physiological, as in health care.
- Informational, as in telecommunications.

These transformations, of course, are not mutually exclusive. For example, a department store is set up to enable shoppers to compare prices and quality (informational), to hold items in inventory until needed (storage), and to sell goods (exchange). Exhibit 1.5 presents sample input–transformation–output relationships for typical systems. Note that only the direct production components are listed; a complete system description would, of course, also include managerial and support functions.

1.6 THE FIRM'S LIFE CYCLE

The Operations Management Association has defined subject areas of OM, as listed in Exhibit 1.6. Although it is useful as a topical checklist, an organizing structure for teaching purposes is needed to (1) allow us to view the field of OM as more than a collection of loosely related topics and (2) mirror the

EXHIBIT 1.6

Subject Areas in Operations Management

1. Operations strategy.
2. Inventory control.
3. Aggregate planning.
4. Forecasting.
5. Scheduling.
6. Capacity planning.
7. Purchasing.
8. Facility location.
9. Facility layout.
10. Process design.
11. Maintenance and reliability.
12. Quality control.
13. Work measurement.

Source: Modified from Operations Management Association, *The Operations Management Newsletter* 1, no. 1 (May–June 1979), p. 14.

decision hierarchy and sequence actually used in the practice of OM. The structure we have adopted for this book seems to meet these requirements in a straightforward way. This life cycle structure follows the progress of the productive system from its inception to its termination—a concept that we feel reflects the true breadth of the area. The following discussion illustrates how a productive system evolves through its life cycle.

Let us assume that an idea for a product or service is proposed. Questions of marketability, producibility, capital requirements, and so on are examined. If the decision is made to produce this good or service, then the final form of the product, the location of the producing facility, the building, and the floor layout all must be specified. The required equipment must be purchased and the production, inventory, and quality control systems designed. The particular tasks to be done must be designed, the functional groups staffed, and production initiated. Quite likely, there will be problems in this startup phase requiring design changes, re-layout, and personnel adjustments. Once the facility is in operation, problems become more of the day-to-day type, requiring decisions on scheduling priorities, minor changes to remove inefficiencies, and maintenance to ensure continued operation. We term this stage the *steady state*.

This steady-state operating condition may be changed in a number of ways: new products may come into the system or a new service may be offered; new developments may cause significant changes in methods; markets may shift or even cease to exist. If these changes are moderate, a slight revision may be all that is necessary to bring the system into line. At times, though, the needed revisions are of such magnitude that certain phases of the life cycle must be repeated, probably calling for new designs, more or less extensive restaffing, and restarting the revised system. If the system cannot adjust to the stimulus that has generated the need for revision, then, in the extreme case, the enterprise will die (through liquidation) or cease to exist as a separate entity (through sale or merger).

In reality, most enterprises operate within this dynamic life cycle. A system, whether it is a manufacturing firm, service facility, or government agency, is born of an idea, passes through a growth stage, and continually changes to meet new demands. And sometimes, of course, it is deliberately terminated.

Some of the key decision areas at the various stages in a system's life cycle, and the chapter where each is emphasized, are shown in Exhibit 1.7. Remember that this is a dynamic process, and several phases in the life cycle may occur simultaneously. Indeed, many firms allocate a large portion of their resources to foster a continual rebirth or rejuvenation program through research and development staffs. Further, although no interconnections are shown in the exhibit, in actuality such interconnections are common. The introduction of a new product, for example, might cause the system to loop back to basic product design, followed by the activities of process selection, new system design, staffing, and startup.

It should also be emphasized that this text is not built around the life cycle of any one system. On the contrary, we have intentionally sought illustrations from a variety of products and services. By doing this, we hope to emphasize

EXHIBIT 1.7 **Key Decisions in the Life of a Productive System**

Stages	Key Decision	
BIRTH of the system	What are the goals of the firm?	Chapters 1, 2
	What product or service will be offered?	Chapters 1, 2
PRODUCT DESIGN and PROCESS SELECTION	What is the form and quality of the product?	Chapters 3, 4, 5
	Technologically, how should the product be made?	Chapters 3, 4, 5
DESIGN of the system	How do you determine demand for the product or service?	Chapter 6
	What capacity do you need?	Chapters 6, 7
	Where should the facility be located?	Chapter 7
	What physical arrangement is best to use?	Chapter 8
	What job is each worker to perform?	Chapter 9
	How will the job be performed and measured?	Chapter 9
	How will the workers be compensated?	Chapter 9
STARTUP of the system	How do you get the system into operation?	Chapter 10
	How long will it take to reach desired rate of output?	Supplement 10
The system in STEADY STATE	How do you manage day-to-day activities?	Chapters 11–14
	How can you improve the system?	Chapters 15–17
	How do you revise the system in light of changes in corporate strategy?	Chapter 18

PRODUCT DESIGN AND PROCESS SELECTION—MANUFACTURING

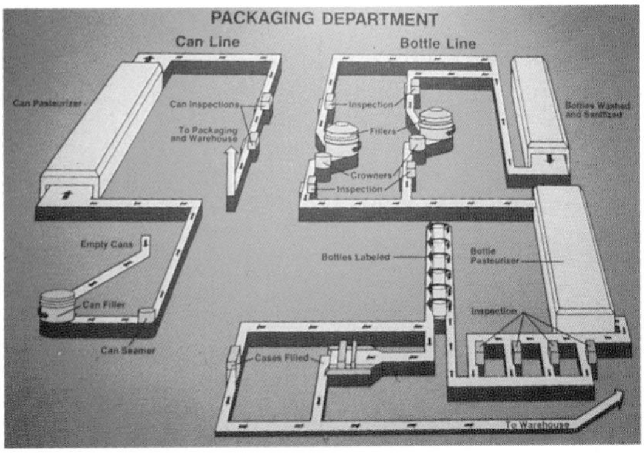

Courtesy of Stroh Brewery Company.

Above: Stroh's packaging department layout. Top right: Stroh Brewery Company—continuous flow operation. Middle right: Stroh's bottling facility. Bottom right: Stroh's packing facility.

Courtesy of Stroh Brewery Company.

Courtesy of Stroh Brewery Company.

Courtesy of Stroh Brewery Company.

COMPUTER-INTEGRATED MANUFACTURING

Below: These are the machines with control systems that take instructions and translate them into machine operations at Northrop. Bottom left: Computer-aided design. Right: Automated body shop at Ford's St. Louis, Missouri, assembly plant, which builds Ford Aerostars.

Courtesy of Northrop Corporation.

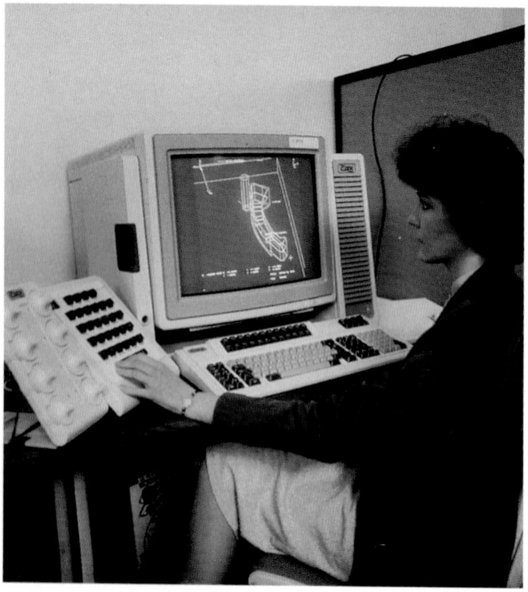

Courtesy of Northrop Corporation.

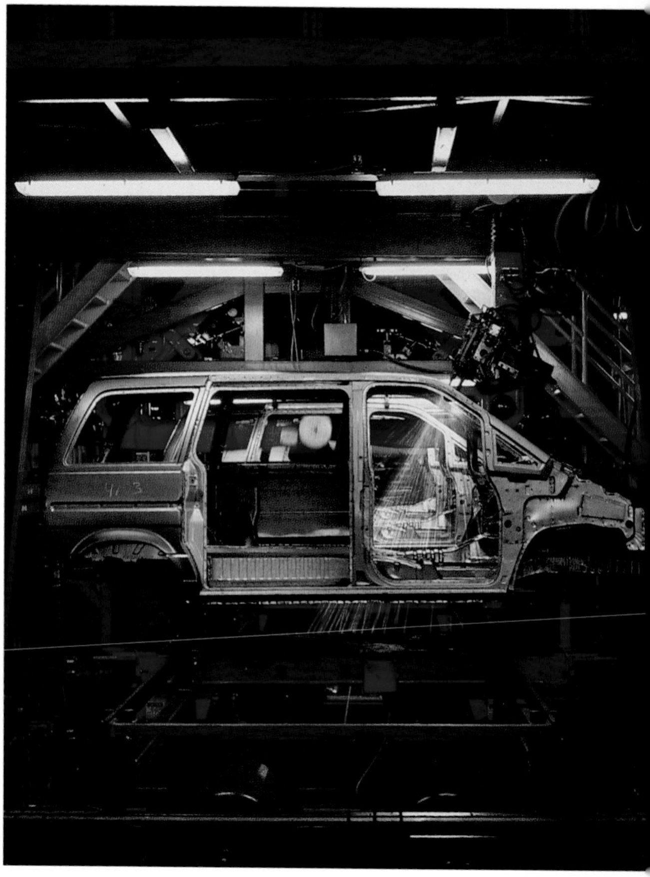

Courtesy of Ford Motor Company.

Courtesy of AT&T.

Courtesy of AT&T.

Above: Plating requirements are maintained with tight tolerances at AT&T. Left: An AT&T product checker examines the laser-produced negative of a multilayer board.

DESIGN OF THE QUALITY CONTROL SYSTEM

Courtesy of Hewlett-Packard.

Courtesy of Hewlett-Packard.

Above: Quality circles at Hewlett-Packard. Left: Hewlett-Packard's quality control for printed circuit boards.

Courtesy of Northrop Corporation.

Courtesy of Northrop Corporation.

Above: Northrop facility. Left: A typical Northrop employee during World War II (Marilyn Monroe). Below: Northrop facility design.

Courtesy of Northrop Corporation.

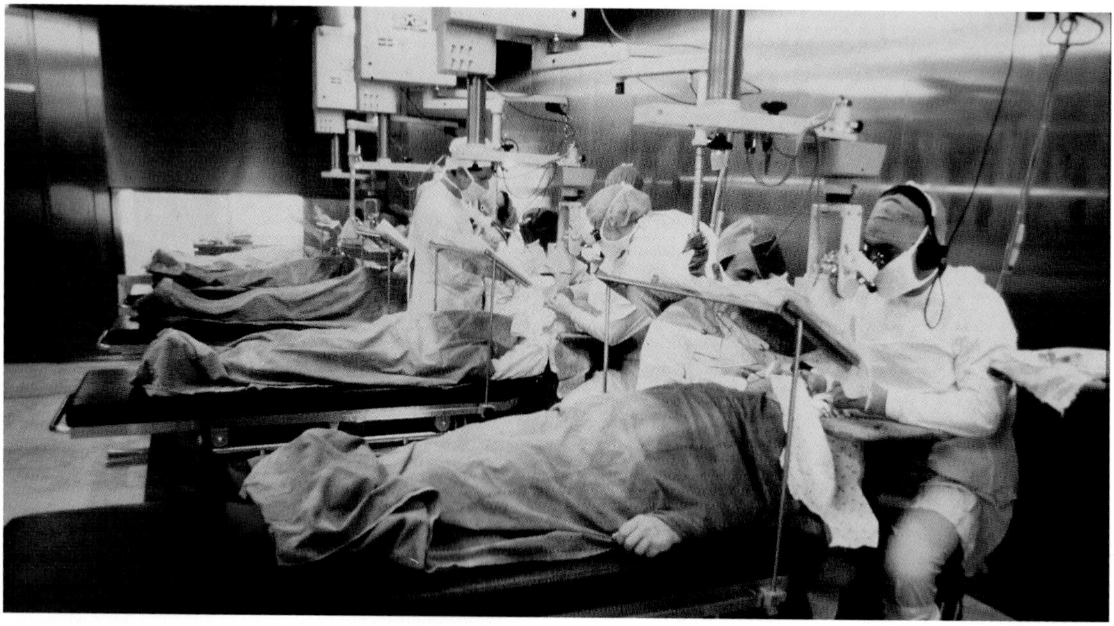

Tass from Sovfoto.

Courtesy of Volvo.

Courtesy of Volvo.

Top: Russian cataract surgery is performed in assembly-line fashion. Above and right: As early as 1973, Volvo's Kalmar plant had done away with the traditional assembly line.

INVENTORY SYSTEMS FOR DEPENDENT DEMAND

Below: Plant photo of materials handling using a Crown Turret Sideloader.

JIT FOR SERVICES

Below: JIT at Federal Express—superhub in Memphis, where more than 650,000 packages are sorted and dispatched each night.

JUST-IN-TIME PRODUCTION SYSTEMS

Courtesy of Hewlett-Packard.

Courtesy of Saturn Corporation.

Courtesy of Hewlett-Packard.

Courtesy of Saturn Corporation.

Left and top left: Here at Hewlett-Packard's Cupertino facility, employees assemble computers using the Just-in-Time (JIT) procedures—keeping just enough parts on hand to complete an order—to reduce costs and increase productivity. At the Saturn Corporation, the Just-in-Time manufacturing philosophy is an integral part of the overall corporate strategy. Top right: A large fleet of trucks is required to make frequent shipments of finished parts to dealers and service centers, thus avoiding the need for these retail outlets to carry unnecessarily large inventories. Bottom right: A vacancy on a subassembly shelf generates a purchase order to the vendor to resupply.

the fact that production and operations management is essential in such diverse systems as hospitals, supermarkets, banks, universities—and, of course, factories.[3]

1.7 OPERATIONS MANAGEMENT AND OTHER BUSINESS SPECIALTIES

Operations management is a required course in many business schools not only because it deals with the basic question of how products and services are created but because it affects every other field of business in the real world.

Accountants, be they internal or external to the firm, need to understand the basics of inventory management, capacity utilization, and labor standards to develop accurate cost data, perform audits, and prepare financial reports. Cost accountants in particular must be aware of how Just-in-Time (JIT) and computer-integrated manufacturing (CIM) work.

Financial managers can use inventory and capacity concepts in judging the need for capital investments and forecasts of cash flow and in the management of current assets. Further, there is a mutual concern between OM and finance in specific decisions such as make-or-buy and plant expansion.

Marketing specialists need an understanding of what the factory can do relative to meeting customer due dates, product customization, and new product introduction. In service industries, marketing and production often take place simultaneously, so a natural mutuality of interest should arise between marketing and OM.

Personnel specialists need to be aware of how jobs are designed, the relationship of standards to incentive plans, and the skills required of the direct work force.

MIS specialists often install manufacturing information systems that they themselves design or that are developed as off-the-shelf software by computer companies. Moreover, a major application of computers in business is in the area of production control.

1.8 HISTORICAL DEVELOPMENT OF OM

Exhibit 1.8 gives a timeline of the history of the field of OM. We will now highlight some of the major concepts and their developers.

---

[3] See Roger W. Schmenner, "Every Factory Has a Life Cycle," *Harvard Business Review* 61, no. 2 (March–April 1983), pp. 121–29.

EXHIBIT 1.8

Historical Summary

Year	Concept or Tool	Originator or Developer
1911	*Principles of Scientific Management*; formalized time-study and work-study concepts	Frederick W. Taylor (United States)
1911	Motion study; basic concepts of industrial psychology	Frank and Lillian Gilbreth (United States)
1913	Moving assembly line	Henry Ford (United States)
1914	Activity scheduling chart	Henry L. Gantt (United States)
1917	Application of economic lot size model for inventory control	F. W. Harris (United States)
1931	Sampling inspection and statistical tables for quality control	Walter Shewhart, H. F. Dodge, and H. G. Romig (United States)
1927–33	Hawthorne studies' new light on worker motivation	Elton Mayo (United States)
1934	Activity sampling for work analysis	L. H. C. Tippett (England)
1940	Team approaches to complex system problems	Operations research groups (England)
1947	Simplex method of linear programming	George B. Dantzig (United States)
1950s–60s	Extensive development of OR tools of simulation, waiting line theory, decision theory, mathematical programming, computer hardware and software, project scheduling techniques of PERT and CPM	United States and Western Europe
1970s	Development of a variety of computer software packages to deal with routine problems of shop scheduling, inventory, layout, forecasting, and project management; rapid growth of MRP	Computer manufacturers, researchers, and users in the United States and Western Europe Joseph Orlicky and Oliver Wight (United States)
1980s	Extensive use of JIT, TQC, and factory automation (CIM, FMS, CAD/CAM robots, etc.)	Tai-ichi Ohno of Toyota Motors (Japan), A. V. Faigenbaum, W. E. Deming, J. M. Juran (United States); engineering disciplines
	Service quality and productivity; introduction of mass production in the service sector	McDonald's restaurants

Scientific Management

Although operations management has existed since man started to engage in production, the advent of **scientific management** around the turn of the century is probably the major historical landmark for the field. This concept was developed by Frederick W. Taylor, an imaginative engineer and insightful observer of organizational activities.

The essence of Taylor's philosophy was that scientific laws govern how much a man can produce per day and that it is the function of management to discover and use these laws in the operation of productive systems (and the function of the worker to carry out management's wishes without question). This philosophy was not greeted with approval by all his contemporaries. On the contrary, some unions resented or feared scientific management—and with some justification. In too many instances, managers of the day were quick to embrace the "mechanisms" of Taylor's philosophy—time study, incentive plans, and so forth—but ignored their responsibility to organize and standardize the work to be done. Hence, there were numerous cases of rate cutting (reducing the payment per piece if the production rate were deemed too high), overwork of labor, and poorly designed work methods. Such abuses resulted in overreaction, leading to the introduction of a bill in Congress in 1913 to prohibit the use of time study and incentive plans in federal government operations. The unions advocating the legislation claimed that Taylor's subject in several of his time-study experiments, a steelworker called "Schmidt," had died from overwork as a result of following Taylor's methods (in evidence whereof they even distributed pictures of Schmidt's "grave"). It was later discovered that Schmidt (whose real name was Henry Nolle) was alive and well and working as a teamster.[4] Ultimately, the bill was defeated.

It is interesting to note that Taylor's ideas were widely accepted in contemporary Japan, and a Japanese translation of Taylor's book, *Principles of Scientific Management* (was titled *The Secret of Saving Lost Motion*), sold over two million copies. To this day, there is a strong legacy of Taylorism in Japanese approaches to manufacturing management.[5]

Notable co-workers of Taylor were Frank and Lillian Gilbreth (motion study, industrial psychology) and Henry L. Gantt (scheduling, wage payment plans). Their work is well known to management scholars. However, it is probably not well known that Taylor, a devout Quaker, requested "cussing lessons" from an earthy foreman to help him communicate with workers; that Frank Gilbreth defeated younger champion bricklayers in bricklaying contests by using his own principles of motion economy; or that Gantt won a Presidential citation for his application of the Gantt chart to shipbuilding during World War I.

Moving Assembly Line

The year 1913 saw the introduction of one of the machine age's greatest technological innovations—the moving assembly line for the manufacture of Ford automobiles.[6] Before the line was introduced, in August of that year,

[4] Milton J. Nadworny, "Schmidt and Stakhanov: Work Heroes in Two Systems," *California Management Review* 6, no. 4 (Summer 1964), pp. 69–76.

[5] Charles J. McMillan, "Production Planning in Japan," *Journal of General Management* 8, no. 4, pp. 44–71.

[6] Ford is said to have gotten the idea for an assembly line from observing a Swiss watch manufacturer's use of the technology. Incidentally, all Model-T Fords were painted black. Why? Because black paint dried fastest.

each auto chassis was assembled by one man in about 12½ hours. Eight months later, when the line was in its final form, with each worker performing a small unit of work and the chassis being moved mechanically, the average labor time per chassis was 93 minutes. This technological breakthrough, coupled with the concepts of scientific management, represents the classic application of labor specialization and is still common today.

Hawthorne Studies

Mathematical and statistical developments dominated the evolution of operations management from Taylor's time up to around the 1940s. An exception was the Hawthorne studies, conducted in the 1930s by a research team from the Harvard Graduate School of Business Administration and supervised by the sociologist Elton Mayo. These experiments were designed to study the effects of certain environmental changes on the output of assembly workers at the Western Electric plant in Hawthorne, Illinois. The unexpected findings, reported in *Management and the Worker* (1939) by F. J. Roethlisberger and W. J. Dickson, intrigued sociologists and students of "traditional" scientific management alike. To the surprise of the researchers, changing the level of illumination (for example) had much less effect on output than the way in which the changes were introduced to the workers. That is, reductions in illumination in some instances led to increased output because workers felt an obligation to their group to keep output high. Discoveries such as these had tremendous implications for work design and motivation and ultimately led to the establishment of personnel management and human relations departments in most organizations.

Operations Research

World War II, with its complex problems of logistics control and weapons-systems design, provided the impetus for the development of the interdisciplinary, mathematically oriented field of operations research. Operations research (OR) brings together practitioners in such diverse fields as mathematics, psychology, and economics. Specialists in these disciplines customarily form a team to structure and analyze a problem in quantitative terms so that a mathematically optimal solution can be obtained. As mentioned earlier in the chapter, operations research, or its approximate synonym management science, now provides many of the quantitative tools used in operations managements as well as other business disciplines.

OM Emerges as a Field

In the late 1950s and early 1960s, scholars began to write texts dealing specifically with operations management as opposed to industrial engineering or operations research. Writers such as Bowman and Fetter (*Analysis for Produc-*

tion and Operations Management [1957]) and Elwood S. Buffa (*Modern Production Management* [1961]) clearly noted the commonality of problems faced by all productive systems and emphasized the importance of viewing production operations as a system. In addition, they stressed the useful applications of waiting line theory, simulation, and linear programming, which are now standard topics in the field. In 1973, Chase and Aquilano [*Production and Operations Management: A Life Cycle Approach*] stressed the need "to put the management back into operations management" and suggested the life cycle as a means of organizing the subject.

Computers and the MRP Crusade

The major development of the 1970s was the broad use of computers in operations problems. For manufacturers, the big breakthrough was the application of materials requirements planning (MRP) to production control. This approach ties together in a computer program all the parts that go into complicated products. This program then enables production planners to quickly adjust production schedules and inventory purchases to meet changing demands for final products. Clearly, the massive data manipulation required for changing schedules on products with thousands of parts would be impossible without such programs and the computer capacity to run them. The promotion of this approach (pioneered by Joseph Orlicky of IBM and consultant Oliver Wight) by the American Production and Inventory Control Society (APICS) has been termed *the MRP Crusade.*

JIT, TQC, and Factory Automation

The 1980s have seen a revolution in the management philosophies and the technologies by which production is carried out. **Just-in-Time (JIT)** production is clearly the major breakthrough in manufacturing philosophy. Pioneered by the Japanese, JIT is an integrated set of activities designed to achieve high-volume production using minimal inventories of parts that arrive at the workstation "just-in-time." This philosophy, coupled with **total quality control (TQC)** which aggressively seeks to eliminate causes of production defects, is now a cornerstone in the production practices of many manufacturing firms.

Synchronous production focuses on creating product and output while preventing in-process inventory and finished goods inventory from building up within the system. The primary focus is on identifying the specific operations that lack capacity or are operated incorrectly, thereby slowing the product flow. Synchronous manufacturing is new, so we will see much more of it applied in the future.

Factory automation in its various forms promises to have great impact on operations management in the decades beyond. Such terms as **Computer-Integrated Manufacturing (CIM),** Flexible Manufacturing Systems (FMS), and Factory of the Future (FOF) are already familiar to many readers of this book and are becoming everyday concepts to practitioners of OM.

Service Quality and Productivity

Quality and productivity represent challenges to today's service firms; whatever new tools are developed to meet these challenges will take their place in the history of OM. The great diversity of service industries—ranging from airlines to zoos, with about 2,000 different types in between—precludes identifying any single pioneer or developer that has made a major impact across the board in these areas. However, there is one service company whose unique approach to quality and productivity has been so successful that it stands as a reference point in thinking about how high-volume standardized services can be delivered: McDonald's. In fact, so successful is McDonald's operating system that the president of Chaparral Steel used it as a model in planning the company's highly efficient mini-mills.

1.9 CONCLUSION: CURRENT ISSUES IN OPERATIONS MANAGEMENT

We will conclude our introduction with a listing of some of the major current issues that face operations management executives today. Many of these issues will be addressed as we move through the system life cycle.

1. Integrating new technology into the production system.
2. Working effectively with suppliers.
3. Managing international production and service.
4. Obtaining and training qualified workers and managers for operations.
5. Working effectively with other business functions in new-product introduction and day-to-day operations.
6. Dealing with a changing external business environment, including government regulations, inflation, and tax laws.
7. Continuously improving operations.

1.10 REVIEW AND DISCUSSION QUESTIONS

1. What is the difference between OM and OR? Between OM and IE?
2. How would you distinguish OM from management and organizational behavior as taught at your college?
3. Why might "buffering the technical core" be an undesirable strategy for a manufacturing firm?

4. Take a look at the want ads in *The Wall Street Journal* and evaluate the opportunities for an OM major with several years of experience.
5. What are the major factors leading to the resurgence of interest in OM today?
6. What operations objectives seem to drive your university?
7. Using Exhibit 1.5 as a model, describe the input–transformation–output relationships found in the following types of systems:
   a. An airline.
   b. A state penitentiary.
   c. A branch bank.
   d. The home office of a major banking firm.
8. What is the life cycle approach to production/operations management? Does it make sense to you? Could it be applied to any other fields you are studying?
9. Suppose that *Variety*, the Hollywood trade paper noted for its colorful jargon, presented the following headlines relating to OM. What particular historical events or individuals would they be referring to?

   FRED RISKS X-RATING TO GET ACROSS PRINCIPLES
   HAWTHORNE WORKERS DO IT FASTER IN THE DARK
   STEEL KING VISITS GOLDEN ARCHES
   MATERIALS MANAGEMENT MAVENS GET WITH THE PROGRAM
   INVENTORY–OH NO!
   FRANKY BURIES YOUNG STUDS AT BRICKOFF
   CLOCKWISE HENRY BECOMES MARVEL OF MOTOWN
   P.S.M. TOPS CHARTS IN GINZA
   HERO MEDAL FOR HANK AS BOAT BIZ BOOMS

1.11 RECOMMENDED PERIODICALS

The following periodicals are listed according to a rough estimate of the number of OM-related articles found in a typical issue. They, of course, vary in their emphasis and degree of technical sophistication.

Journal of Operations Management
Operations Management Review
International Journal of Operations and Production Management
Production and Inventory Management
Industrial Engineering
IIE Transactions
International Journal of Production Research
Management Science
Interfaces

Decision Sciences
Harvard Business Review

1.12 SELECTED BIBLIOGRAPHY

Bowman, Edward H., and Robert B. Fetter. *Analysis for Production and Operations Management.* 3rd ed. Homewood, Ill.: Richard D. Irwin, 1957.

Buffa, Elwood S. *Modern Production Management.* New York: John Wiley & Sons, 1961.

———. "Research Operations Management." *Journal of Operations Management* 1, no. 1 (August 1980), pp. 1–7.

Deming, W. Edwards. *Out of the Crisis.* Cambridge, Mass.: Massachusetts Institute of Technology Center for Advanced Engineering Study, 1986.

Drucker, Peter F. "The Emerging Theory of Manufacturing." *Harvard Business Review,* May–June 1990, pp. 94–102.

Singhal, Kalyan; Charles H. Fine; Jack R. Meredith; and Rajan Suri. "Research and Models for Automated Manufacturing." *Interfaces* 17, no. 6 (November–December 1987), pp. 5–14.

Skinner, Wickham. "Manufacturing—Missing Link in Corporate Strategy." *Harvard Business Review*, May–June 1969, pp. 136–45.

———. "The Focused Factory." *Harvard Business Review*, May–June 1974, pp. 113–21.

Chapter 2

Productivity and Competitiveness

EPIGRAPH

The wealth and power of the United States depends upon maintaining mastery and control of production.

Stephen S. Cohen and John Zysman, *Why Manufacturing Matters: The Myth of the Post-Industrial Economy* (New York: Basic Books, 1987).

In the next century, the United States will be our farm and Western Europe our boutique.

Attributed to a Japanese minister of trade in Gore Vidal, "Rebirth of a Nation: Why Italy Works," *Los Angeles Times*, May 1, 1988.

CHAPTER OUTLINE

KEY TERMS

Competitiveness

Productivity

Competitive Priorities of Manufacturers

Outsourcing

Hollow Corporations

Commercialization

Competitiveness refers to the relative position in the marketplace and productivity usually refers to output per unit input. This chapter will discuss the interrelationship of competitiveness and productivity.

2.1 COMPETITIVENESS DEFINED

Competitiveness is a recurring topic in business, government, and academic circles. Business managers talk of discovering and strengthening competitive advantages, the United States bemoans its lack of competitiveness in world markets, and instructors ponder how to prepare their students for the increasingly competitive future. **Competitiveness** can be defined at different levels. Individual firms are competitive if the goods and service they offer have the features, quality, and price that make them desirable in the marketplace. Typically a business strives to excel in at least one of those areas, thus assuring sales. If a firm can remain competitive, it will produce profits and be a viable concern into the future.

At a national and international level, the definition becomes a little more complex. In 1985 the President's Council on Industrial Competitiveness offered this definition:

> Competitiveness for a nation is the degree to which it can, under free and fair market conditions, produce goods and services that meet the test of international markets while simultaneously maintaining and expanding the real incomes of its citizens.

As can be seen in Exhibit 2.1, international competitiveness results in more than a positive trade balance. Improved domestic performance increases competitiveness in world markets—which also increases the number and quality of jobs, the domestic standard of living, and improves the national budget and national security.

Productivity is often discussed with competitiveness. Productivity plays a role in achieving competitiveness and will be the major statistic used in talking about competitiveness in this chapter. However, it must be emphasized that productivity is but *one* measure by which nations gauge their relative competitive positions. Other measures include wage growth, returns on capital employed in industry, and position in the world marketplace. Regarding this last measure, consider Exhibit 2.2, which demonstrates one disturbing aspect of the competitive position of the United States.

Some measures that are used to determine a nation's competitive position have familiar counterparts at the individual-firm level. Businesses routinely use return on investment (ROI), which is equivalent to returns on capital employed in industry. Market share is equivalent to position in the world marketplace. Wage growth would be similar, although not equivalent, to earnings ratios or other measures of increases to shareholder wealth. The only

EXHIBIT 2.1

Benefits of Competitiveness

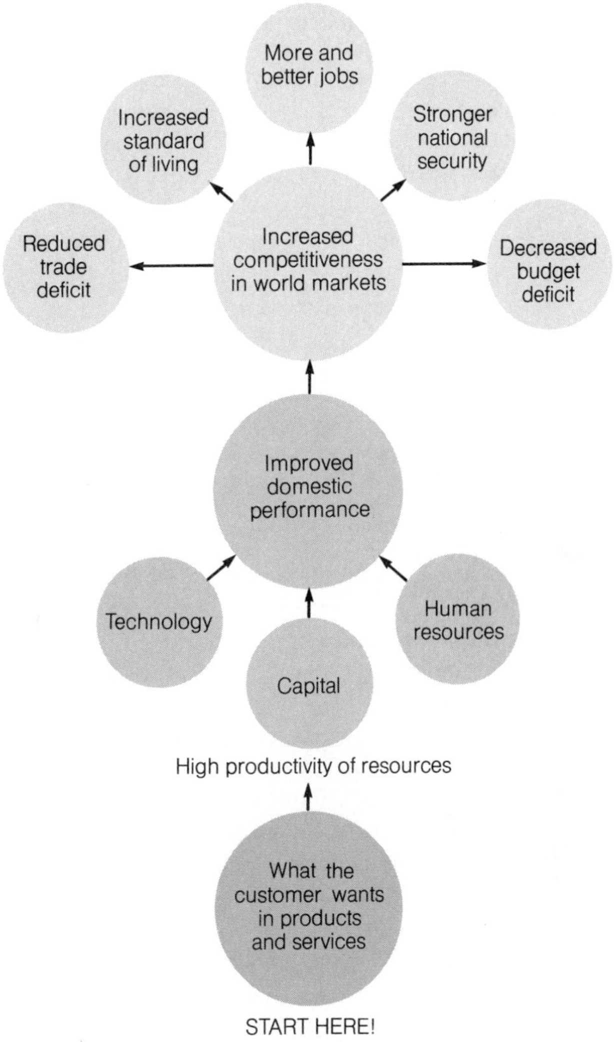

measure that is not always routinely followed is productivity. Most businesses use profitability measures instead. However, this might not be wise, as profitability is often affected by forces that are not under managerial control, such as inflation. Productivity *is* under management control and hence is a key concept in evaluating performance of a firm and the operations function within it.

EXHIBIT 2.2

What Do These U.S. Industries Have in Common?

Automobiles	Food processors
Cameras	Microwave ovens
Stereo equipment	Athletic equipment
Medical equipment	Computer chips
Color television sets	Industrial robots
Hand tools	Electron microscopes
Radial tires	Machine tools
Electric motors	Optical equipment

Answer: They are some of the industries and products that lost 50 percent or more of their share of world markets since 1960.

Source: Attributed to Steven Wheelwright, March 20, 1984.

2.2 THE HOLLOWED MANUFACTURING FIRM

Some people believe a manufacturing firm should subcontract, or **"outsource,"** a major part of its manufacturing requirements. The firm can then operate as a service-type business because the service functions are essentially all that remain.

We will present this side of the argument for hollowed manufacturing, but we want to point out that many experts argue exactly the opposite—that the manufacturing part of the firm is, in fact, its competitive weapon. Rather than be subordinate to other functions, manufacturing should be brought to the forefront.

A **"hollow"** manufacturing firm is one that designs, markets, and does some manufacturing. While a hard product is delivered to the customer, most of the production is outsourced. *Business Week* gives an excellent summary of the operations of hollowed corporations.[1]

The following argument for outsourcing is from a recent *Harvard Business Review* article.

Strategic Focus on Service Activities[2]

We think about companies as manufacturing firms, but most of them are, in a sense, service firms. Most people who work in manufacturing firms actually

[1] "Special Report," *Business Week,* March 3, 1986, pp. 56–85.

[2] James Brian Quinn, "Beyond Products: Services-Based Strategy," *Harvard Business Review,* March–April 1990, pp.58–67.

do service jobs. In fact, 65 to 75 percent of those working in manufacturing perform service jobs such as marketing, accounting, financing, research product design, logistics, and maintenance.

The value added to a product from the services is now higher than the value added through production. Consider the manufacturing value added through changing sheet metal into a fender, and compare this to the service value of the fender design, styling, advertising, image, market distribution, and so on. Profits of drug companies come from the service activities of product research, development, patents, clinical testing, marketing, and distribution. As most of us are aware, the production cost of many expensive pills is often trivial.

Strategic hollowing, or outsourcing much of the production, avoids the clumsiness of vertical integration, decreases total investment, and reduces risk. Further, a firm that outsources has the world's best talent available, because the firm, as a customer, can choose from the world's best talent (better than its own in-house personnel). The firm also has available all of the R&D departments of companies with which it does business. Relieved of burdensome production, the firm can focus its efforts where it wishes.

With a meaner and leaner organization, the firm presents a formidable barrier to competition. It can move faster and be more innovative because of its reduced size and orientation.

Producing parts and components on a global basis offers more advantages than domestic outsourcing for a variety of reasons, such as nearness to the raw material, low wage rates, low transportation costs, availability of labor talent, nearness to major markets, and so on.

Quinn lists Honda, Apple, Merck, Glaxo, and SCI Systems among the companies that fall into this hollowed outsourcing approach.

Sourcing on an international basis has been around for years. Open your personal computer case and note the number of countries' names on the components. In discussing outsourcing with students several years ago, one of the authors of this text opened the cases of two computers: an IBM PC and an IBM clone. Students were amazed that the IBM PC had even more foreign parts than the clone. We need to add, however, that IBM has made a complete reversal in its PS/2 and produces almost every part and component itself.

2.3 COMMERCIALIZING TECHNOLOGY

We usually think of firms as marketing products or services. We could, instead, consider that a firm markets its technology, which appears in the marketplace in the form of products and services. For firms that operate in sophisticated technologies, their success or failure will depend on their ability to **commercialize** their technology; in other words, to use their technology to produce successful products.

One study examined companies in the United States, Europe, and Japan to try to find the differences between the leaders and laggards.[3] That study found the leading companies

1. Create two or three times as many new products as their competitors.
2. Incorporate two or three times as many technologies into their products.
3. Bring their products to market in less than half the time.
4. Compete in twice as many product and geographic markets.

The study also found that such performance of the leading companies was consistent over a number of years, and that these differences existed between competitive companies whether they were American, European, or Japanese. The successful companies viewed the commercialization of their technology as a highly disciplined system. They view it as a top priority, set measurable goals, develop the necessary organizational skills, and encourage managers to take aggressive action. They are also dedicated to improving the process. Industry leadership in commercializing technology is particularly crucial in product markets such as copiers, facsimile machines, computers, automobiles, semiconductor production equipment, and pharmaceuticals. Companies first to market gain higher profits and greater market share.

The Insert shows Hewlett-Packard's success in printers.

INSERT The Commercialization Process

Commercialization begins when a business identifies a way to use scientific or engineering advances to meet a market need. The process continues through design, development, manufacturing ramp-up, and marketing, and includes later efforts to improve the product. While it is often viewed as a linear process—a series of steps performed by people in different functions—companies with strong commercialization capability see the process as a series of overlapping phases that involve many business functions simultaneously.

Take Hewlett-Packard's development of the DeskJet printer. In the mid-1980s, H-P's Vancouver, Washington, division, which specializes in printers for personal computers, needed a blockbuster. Market research had shown that PC users would welcome a relatively slow-speed device that printed as clearly as a laser printer but sold for less than half the $2,000 price. In late 1985, a team of researchers, engineers, and marketers formed to explore the feasibility of such a product.

In conceptualizing the product, the team defined customers' needs precisely and clarified the drawbacks of existing low-cost printers. It sized up the proposed product's technical feasibility by reviewing H-P's thermal-ink-jet technology, which uses electrical current to vaporize ink and shoot it onto paper in patterns of microscopic dots. Although earlier printers using that technology required specially

---

[3] T. Michael Nevens, Gregory L. Summe, and Bro Uttal, "Commercializing Technology: What the Best Companies Do," *Harvard Business Review* 68, No. 3, May–June 1990, pp. 154–63.

coated paper and created narrow, blurred characters, the DeskJet team concluded that given sufficient resources, H-P's InkJet Components Operation in Corvallis, Oregon, could refine the technology enough to produce patterns as dense and clear as those from a laser printer.

Still in the concept-generation phase, the team brought manufacturing engineers into the process to verify that the company could produce the print head and the printer. Then the team submitted a formal plan, which Vancouver management approved.

Next, the team had to design a manufacturing prototype that could be tested for performance, reliability, producibility, and product cost. It started with a breadboard prototype, an assemblage of components handwired to printed circuit boards that represented the technical core of the printer. As soon as the breadboard proved technically feasible and appropriate for the market, H-P augmented its project team with specialists in component sourcing, mechanical design, and control software. Six months later, the expanded group released several working prototypes, complete with cabinet, control software and panel, and paper-handling mechanism, and let consumers try them. The team improved print quality based on feedback from the trials, and the DeskJet was ready for manufacture.

While the DeskJet team was designing and developing the product, the printer factory in Vancouver and the print-head factory in Corvallis had been constructing pilot production lines. At the same time, marketing had developed distribution, promotion, sales, and service plans and had primed the sales force and scheduled an advertising blitz.

H-P officially launched the DeskJet in February 1988—just 26 months after the Vancouver division first explored the idea. It rang up strong sales almost immediately.

Most DeskJet team members transferred to other projects after the launch, but several key engineers and marketers stayed on to oversee ongoing improvements. As customers asked for greater printing speed and more typefaces, the team went back to the concept-generation stage and executed a short version of the commercialization effort. In April 1989, they launched a faster, more flexible, less expensive version of the original printer, and in July 1989, a model that would work with Apple's Macintosh.

Source: Reprinted by permission of *Harvard Business Review*. An excerpt from "Commercializing Technology: What the Best Companies Do" by T. Michael Nevens, Gregory L. Summe, and Bro Uttal, 68, no. 3 (May–June 1990).

2.4 PRODUCTIVITY MEASUREMENT AND TRENDS

Productivity Measurement

Productivity in its broadest sense is defined as follows:

$$\text{Productivity} = \frac{\text{Outputs}}{\text{Inputs}}$$

Obviously, for any situation, you want that ratio to be as large as possible; that would indicate that you are getting more out of what you put in. The units used in productivity measurement for output may be, for example, dollars generated, goods produced, or customers served; measurements for inputs may include dollars invested, machine hours used, or labor hours used. In discussions of productivity across countries or industries, the most common measure is output in goods and services per labor hour. Because of problems in adjusting for changing values in currencies, productivity comparisons, where possible, should use tangible output measures such as units produced rather than dollars. Examples of productivity measures are shown in Exhibit 2.3.

Productivity Trends

The United States has shown a good productivity recovery, in general terms, since 1983. However, long-term productivity has been flat since the highs and lows in total-factor productivity have balanced out.

While productivity has been positive for the past decade, it hasn't been performing as well as it should. The Insert shows that improvement rates are declining for larger (Fortune 500) companies.

INSERT Not Working Harder and Not Working Smarter Either

Despite heavy payroll cuts at Fortune 500 industrial companies, the rate of productivity improvement in manufacturing declined from 1984 to 1988 and rose only slightly last year. In services, where employment has increased, productivity growth has been consistently poor. Meanwhile, companies have cut muscle, not just fat. Corporate R&D spending, languid since 1985, will likely fall in real terms in 1989, the first such drop in 15 years.

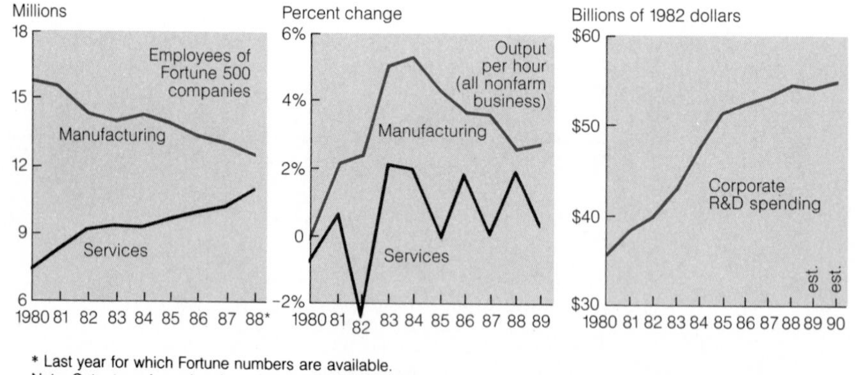

* Last year for which Fortune numbers are available.

Note: Output per hour data from the Bureau of Labor Statistics; corporate R&D spending data from the National Science Foundation.

Source: Ronald Henkoff, "Cost Cutting: How to Do It Right," *Fortune*, April 9, 1990, p. 43.

EXHIBIT 2.3

Examples of Productivity Measures

Partial measure	$\frac{\text{Output}}{\text{Labor}}$ or $\frac{\text{Output}}{\text{Capital}}$ or $\frac{\text{Output}}{\text{Materials}}$ or $\frac{\text{Output}}{\text{Energy}}$
Multifactor measure	$\frac{\text{Output}}{\text{Labor + Capital + Energy}}$ or $\frac{\text{Output}}{\text{Labor + Capital + Materials}}$
Total measure	$\frac{\text{Output}}{\text{Inputs}}$ or $\frac{\text{Goods and services produced}}{\text{All resources used}}$

Source: Reprinted from David J. Sumanth and Kitty Tang, "A Review of Some Approaches to the Management of Total Productivity in a Company/Organization," *Institute of Industrial Engineering Conference Proceedings*, Fall 1984, p. 305. Copyright Institute of Industrial Engineers, 25 Technology Park/Atlanta, Norcross, Georgia 30092.

EXHIBIT 2.4

Trends of Manufacturing Productivity Growth Rates in Output per Labor Hour

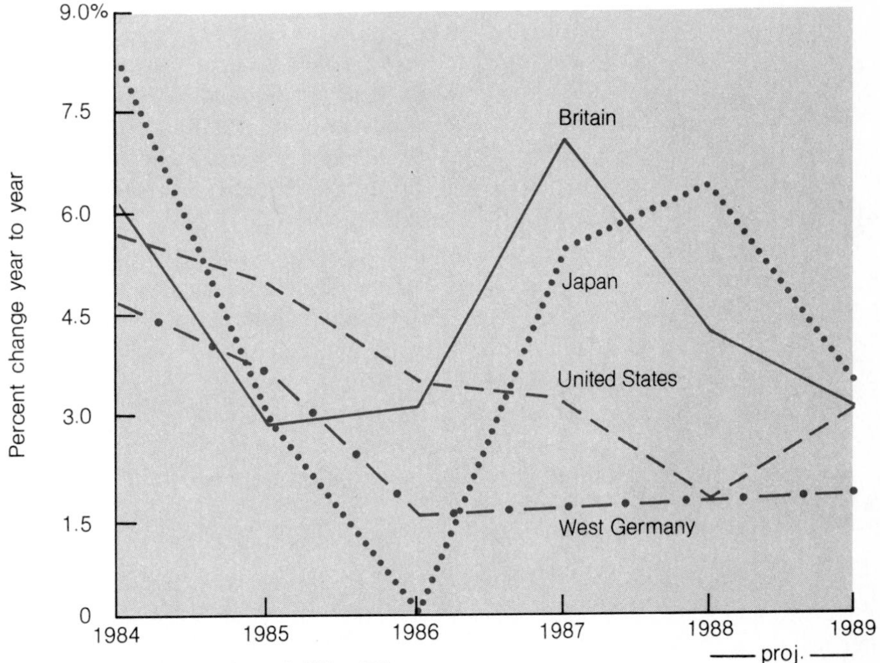

Source: Adapted from *Fortune*, August 1, 1988, p. D50.

International Productivity Performance

Very few consistent statistics are available to compare productivity among various nations. When the comparisons are based on manufacturing productivity growth, overall the United States's performance is encouraging (Exhibit 2.4). The U.S. rate of improvement for 1988 is climbing faster than the

International Monetary Fund had predicted. Germany's achievement is surprisingly low, given its history as a leader in European productivity growth. In the United Kingdom, much of the increase came from decreases in the labor force rather than increases in output.

Not shown are the East Asian countries (Hong Kong, Singapore, South Korea, and Taiwan); their growth rates in manufacturing output from 1970 to 1980 average around 12 percent per year overall. During that time, U.S. manufacturing output averaged 2.9 percent and Japan's, 6.4 percent. A major reason for the high growth rate of these Asian countries is a "hungry" work force, willing to put in long hours. Workers at Hyundai, for example, are said to be motivated to work 12 hours a day not only for the money but also, for obvious historical reasons, "to beat the Japanese."

2.5 GENERAL CAUSES AND SOLUTIONS TO THE COMPETITIVENESS PROBLEM

Taken together, productivity data, market-share loss, and trade deficits indicate rather clearly that the United States has a serious competitiveness problem. Rationalizations abound. Blame is frequently put on the relative strength of the dollar against foreign currencies. However, the U.S. trade deficit increased during the 1970s when the dollar depreciated by 15 percent. Thus, although the current (1988) weakness in the dollar has stimulated exports, long-term reliance on a cheaper dollar is a risky solution at best.

Some say that reliance on manufacturing is outdated and given our shift to services, there *is* no problem. And, indeed, exported services have produced a surplus in the trade-balance equation. However, even here, the trend has been moving toward a deficit, as shown in Exhibit 2.5. While business services do not constitute all services, they do include the major services that are traded in international markets, such as travel, transportation (both passenger and cargo), construction, engineering, consulting, banking, communications, and insurance.

Moreover, those who see a shift to the service economy as a salvation miss two crucial points. First, service and manufacturing are linked. Many services are purchased by manufacturing firms, for example, advertising, legal, health care, and accounting services. The United States cannot be supported only by a strong service sector. Second, although foreign purchase of services is high at the present time, it is naive to believe that foreign manufacturers and the societies that are developing around them will forever rely on U.S. services. Japan is building a strong financial base that is already competing with the United States in both the world and domestic marketplaces. For example, the ten largest banks (in terms of asset base) in the world are Japanese-owned. In fact, the United States has no institutions in the top 25, with Citibank, the nation's largest, having fallen from 17th in 1986 to 28th (according to a survey published in the *American Banker,* July 1988).

EXHIBIT 2.5

Business Services—Imports and Exports

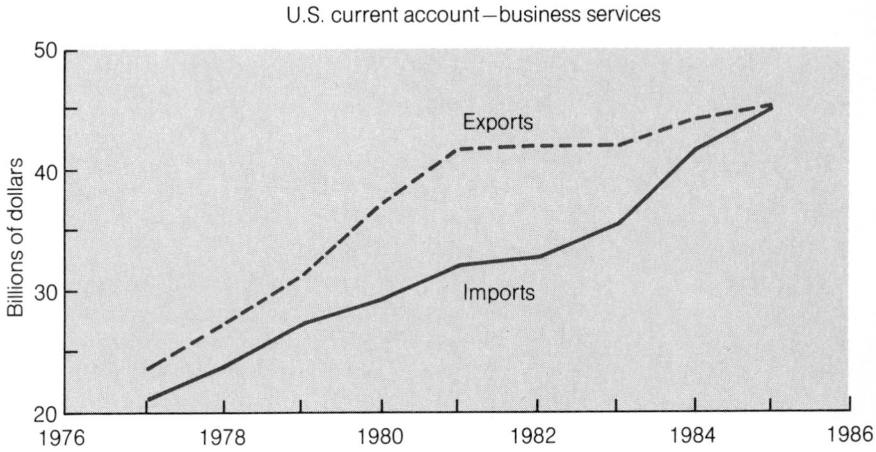

Source: U.S. Department of Commerce, *Monthly Labor Review*, January 1988.

Another rationalization for the disappointing performance of the United States in the global marketplace is that the poor performers are just isolated industries and that overall performance is what really matters. This might be true; a dollar's worth of exported wheat has the same value as a dollar's worth of electronics. Unfortunately, the poor performance is not isolated in just a few industries. Portfolio theory has taught us the benefits of diversification. The United States needs a diversified picture in exports, and an increasing number of U.S. goods are not competitive.

U.S. business leaders and policymakers have been slow to recognize that the superiority of industry cannot be taken for granted. The global marketplace is a reality, and we are not competitive. According to the MIT Commission on Industrial Productivity, there are five basic causes of this:[4]

> *1.* American business decisions have been frequently characterized by *short time horizons,* and a related tendency to give excessive weight to financial relative to other criteria. This preoccupation with short-term financial results has had among its consequences a lack of staying power on the part of affected firms, reflected in underinvestment in R&D [research and development] and the physical and human capital needed to maintain technological leadership in a field once the first big returns have been captured. A related tendency has been to diversify away from established businesses in which expertise has been accumulated over a long period into activities that are more profitable in the short term.

[4] Lester Thurow et al., "Interim Results of the MIT Commission on Industrial Productivity," AAAS Annual Meeting, Boston, February 15, 1988.

> 2. *Strategic weaknesses* among American companies have arisen particularly as a consequence of parochial attitudes, which have frequently led these firms to pay insufficient attention to the capabilities and intentions of foreign competitors, and to the opportunities presented by foreign markets. Intensifying international competition has forced U.S. companies in a broad range of industries to become less insular, but many firms still seem to be poor imitators even when imitation would be advantageous. Neglect of the manufacturing function relative to other functional areas has been another area of strategic weakness. Despite the strategic benefits conferred by manufacturing excellence, many firms have underinvested in both the human and physical capital needed to build up and sustain a competitive manufacturing capability.
>
> 3. *A lack of cooperation* in individual and organizational relationships within and among U.S. firms has been another key barrier to improved productivity performance. Within firms there are often organizational "walls" separating product design, process design, manufacturing, marketing and R&D; and individuals, often highly trained professionals, have frequently been unable to work in teams. Decisions which should have been unified have instead been subdivided and made sequentially, resulting in delay and inefficiency. Similarly, arms-length contractual relationships with a minimum of information flow between the parties have typically been favored over long-term, cooperative relations between companies and their suppliers. As a result, feedback about market preferences has been inhibited and the introduction of new product and process technologies impeded. Very often the obstacles to closer cooperation seem to have resulted from an excessively narrow or short-term perception of self-interest. In some cases the problem has been aggravated by excessive specialization and compartmentalization of individual and departmental functions.
>
> 4. *Weaknesses in human resource management and organization* have prevented the full benefits of technical change from being realized. Firms have tended to view labor more as a cost factor to be minimized than as a productive, evolving resource. The importance of a well-trained, well-motivated, and adaptable work force to firm performance has frequently been underestimated.
>
> 5. The commission has also found evidence of *recurring weaknesses in technological practice*. While U.S. companies in many industries have made key technological advances, weaknesses in designing simple, reliable, and manufacturable products, failures to build quality into products at the design stage, weaknesses in the design of manufacturing processes and in production operations, and a related tendency to overinnovate on product but underinnovate on process have often led to a loss of market position, or in some cases an inability to establish one. The inventiveness of American industry has rarely been in question. But technical abilities to reduce new concepts to commercial practice quickly and efficiently, and in embodiments that are responsive to customer demands, have fallen behind international standards of best practice in a number of industries.

The solutions to the competitiveness problem appear to lie in reversing the attitudes and strategies enumerated in the MIT Commission report. That is,

1. Place less emphasis on short-term financial payoffs and invest more in R&D.

2. Revise corporate strategies to include responses to foreign competition. This in turn calls for greater investment in people and equipment to improve manufacturing capability.
3. Knock down communication barriers within organizations and recognize mutuality of interests with other companies and suppliers (the former relative to international competition, in particular).
4. Recognize that the labor force is a resource to be nurtured, not just a cost to be avoided.
5. Get back to basics in managing production operations. Build in quality at the design stage. Place more emphasis on process innovations rather than focusing sole attention on product innovations.

In sum, we must become better at managing our productive capabilities in all dimensions—in strategy and in the five P's of operations: people, plants, parts, processes, and planning and control systems.

2.6 COMPETITIVE PRIORITIES

In the preceding section, we discussed the MIT Commission's priorities for becoming competitive as a nation in manufacturing. In this section, we present **competitive priorities of manufacturers:** what manufacturing executives themselves see as priorities for their firms.

In a 1986 survey by Boston University, senior manufacturing executives were asked to indicate on a scale from 1 (no effect) to 5 (very critical) the degree of importance of eight designated manufacturing capabilities. In Exhibit 2.6 the average scores for each competitive priority are given.

By contrast, a 1985 survey of competitive priorities in Europe, North America, and Japan (also by Boston University) yielded the results shown in

EXHIBIT 2.6

Competitive Priority Scores, 1983–1986

Priority	1983	1984	1985	1986
Consistent quality	4.47	4.50	4.50	4.54
High-performance products	4.21	4.13	4.05	4.08
Dependable delivery	4.02	4.05	4.18	4.06
Low price	3.55	3.72	3.67	3.81
Fast delivery	3.63	3.58	3.69	3.65
Design flexibility	3.47	3.62	3.50	3.57
After-sales service	3.57	3.57	3.62	3.52
Rapid volume change	3.37	3.28	3.31	3.23

Source: Jeffrey G. Miller and Aleda V. Roth, "Report on the 1986 North American Manufacturing Futures Survey," *The Boston University Manufacturing Roundtable* (Boston, June 1986), p. 10.

EXHIBIT 2.7 **Comparative Competitive Priorities**

Europe	North America	Japan
Consistent quality (1)(1)	Consistent quality (1)(1)	Low prices (1)(1)
High-performance products (3)(2)	Dependable deliveries (3)(3)	Rapid design changes (2)(2)
Dependable deliveries (2)(3)	High-performance products (2)(2)	Consistent quality (3)(3)
Low prices (4)(4)	Fast deliveries (4)(4)	High-performance products (4)(4)
Fast deliveries (6)(6)	Low prices (6)(5)	Dependable deliveries (5)(5)
Rapid design changes (5)(5)	After-sales service (5)(7)	Rapid volume changes (6)(6)
After-sales service (8)(8)	Rapid design changes (7)(5)	Fast delivery (8)(7)
Rapid volume changes (7)(7)	Rapid volume changes (8)(8)	After-sales service (7)(8)

( ) ( ) Rank in 1983 and 1984 surveys.

Source: Jeffrey Miller, Jinchiro Nakane, and Thomas Vollmann, "The 1985 Global Manufacturing Futures Survey," *Manufacturing Roundtable Research Series*, Boston University, 1986.

Exhibit 2.7. Note that Japan listed "low prices" as first priority rather than "consistent quality" as listed by Europe and North America. The reason: The Japanese have already achieved consistent quality and are now looking toward the next level of challenge—low prices.

2.7 CONCLUSION

Competitiveness and productivity are what operations management is all about. Whether American industry settles for niche markets, catch-up strategies, and "hollow corporations," or decides to get back into the production game and play it well, will ultimately depend on its operations capability. The next chapter discusses the process technology that is a central part of this capability.

2.8 REVIEW AND DISCUSSION QUESTIONS

1. What is productivity?
2. What is competitiveness?
3. How can the United States become more competitive in the national and international marketplace?
4. During 1988, the dollar showed relative weakness with respect to foreign currencies, such as the yen, mark, and pound. This stimulated exports. Why would long-term reliance on a lower-valued dollar be at best a short-term solution to the competitiveness problem?
5. The MIT Commission on Industrial Productivity identified "preoccupation with short-term financial results" as one of five recurring weaknesses leading to the

decline in competitiveness of U.S. industry. If you assume that every U.S. firm's existence is dependent on its financial survival, would the MIT Commission's conclusion lead to the demise of American industry?

6. When you purchase (*a*) a new car from a dealer, (*b*) a personal computer, and (*c*) tickets to a baseball game, what qualities are you looking for? Categorize these desired qualities in terms of the competitive priorities in Exhibit 2.7.

2.9 PROBLEMS

1. A manufacturing company that produces furniture has provided the following data. Compare the labor, raw materials and supplies, and total productivity of 1984 and 1987.

		1984	1987
Output:	Sales value of production	$22,000	$35,000
Input:	Labor	10,000	15,000
	Raw materials and supplies	8,000	12,500
	Capital equipment depreciation	700	1,200
	Other	2,200	4,800

2. You would like to organize your firm as suggested in the hollowed manufacturing section of this chapter—as a service-oriented firm geared to outsourcing most of the manufacturing. Pick a product line and create a list of what you would do.

2.10 SELECTED BIBLIOGRAPHY

Cohen, Stephen S., and John Zysman. *Why Manufacturing Matters: The Myth of the Post-Industrial Society*. New York: Basic Books, 1987.

Edosomwan, Johnson A. "A Program for Managing Productivity and Quality." *Industrial Engineering,* January, 1987, pp. 64–69.

Hayes, Robert H.; Steven Wheelwright; and Kim B. Clark. *Dynamic Manufacturing: Creating the Learning Organization*. New York: Free Press, 1988.

Henkoff, Ronald. "Cost Cutting: How to Do It Right." *Fortune,* April 9, 1990, pp. 40–49.

Miller, Jeffrey G., and Aleda V. Roth. "Report on the 1986 North American Manufacturing Futures Survey." *Boston University Manufacturing Roundtable,* Boston, June 1986.

Miller, Jeffrey G.; Jinchiro Nakane; and Thomas Vollmann. "The 1985 Global Manufacturing Futures Survey." *Manufacturing Roundtable Research Series,* Boston University, Boston, 1986.

Productivity Perspectives. Houston, Tex.: American Productivity Center, January 1985.

Quinn, James Brian; Thomas L. Doorley; and Penny C. Paquette. "Beyond Products: Services-Based Strategy." *Harvard Business Review* 68, no. 2, March–April 1990, pp. 58–67.

Skinner, Wickham. *Manufacturing: The Formidable Competitive Weapon*. New York: John Wiley & Sons, 1985.

———. "The Productivity Paradox." *Harvard Business Review* 64, no. 4 (July–August 1986), pp. 55–59.

Starr, Martin K. *Global Competitiveness: Getting the U.S. Back on Track*. New York: W. W. Norton & Co., 1988.

Wheelwright, Steven C., and Robert H. Hayes. "Competing through Manufacturing." *Harvard Business Review* 65, no. 1, January–February 1985, pp. 99–109.

Chapter 3

Product Design and Process Selection—Manufacturing

EPIGRAPH

Manufacturing Is in Flower. After years of neglect, America's factories are taking on a fresh allure.

Time, March 26, 1984, p. 50.

And God said unto Noah, . . .
Make thee an ark of gopher wood; rooms shalt thou make in the ark, and shalt pitch it within and without with pitch. And this is the fashion which thou shalt make it of: The length shall be three hundred cubits, the breadth of it fifty cubits, and the height of it thirty cubits.

Genesis 6.

CHAPTER OUTLINE

KEY TERMS

Product Specifications
Compatibility
Simplification
Continuous Processes
Repetitive Processes
Intermittent Processes
Machining Centers
Numerically Controlled (NC) Machines
Industrial Robots
Computer-Aided Design and Manufacturing (CAD/CAM)
Flexible Manufacturing System (FMS)
Computer-Integrated Manufacturing (CIM)
Islands of Automation
Break-Even Analysis
Process Flow Design
Manufacturing Cycle
Computer-Aided Design (CAD)
Group Technology (GT)
Manufacturing Planning and Control Systems (MP&CS)
Automated Materials Handling Systems (AMH)
Computer-Aided Manufacturing (CAM)
Robotics
Computing Technology

The recognized importance of manufacturing operations as a competitive weapon for the firm, coupled with breakthroughs in hard and soft technology, have made the understanding of manufacturing essential for most students of business. In this chapter, we present some of the basics of manufacturing technology and material flow processes, and sample some of the latest approaches to the design of products and processes. We also take a brief look at how various parts of a manufacturing organization interrelate during the manufacturing cycle. We begin our discussion with the product design and development sequence.

3.1 PRODUCT DESIGN AND DEVELOPMENT SEQUENCE

Every new product starts with an idea. The steps leading from the idea stage to actual production product are outlined in Exhibit 3.1.

Origin of the Product Idea

Where do product ideas come from? In their book *In Search of Excellence*, Peters and Waterman argue that in excellent companies new-product ideas come primarily from listening to the customer. In addition to traditional market research, such listening may take the form of managers and engineers visiting users of the company's existing products or going into production on inventions and prototypes developed by users (with their concurrence, of course). While these companies have extensive R&D functions, they also encourage their own employees to generate new product ideas and to contribute to the development of those currently being investigated. In Hewlett-Packard, for example, product design engineers leave whatever they are working on out on their desks so that others may come by and tinker with them.

Choosing among Alternative Products

The idea-gathering process will often lead to more ideas than can be translated into producible products, so a screening procedure is instituted to eliminate those ideas that clearly are infeasible. In this screening process, some ideas are rejected because they do not meet the company's objectives or its marketing, operations, or financial criteria. Marketing criteria include competition, ability to cross sell, promotional requirements, and distribution considerations. Operational criteria include compatibility with current processes, equipment, facilities, and suppliers. Financial criteria combine marketing and operational concerns and focus on risk, investment requirements, cost accounting, anticipated profit margin, and length of life cycle. An effective screening device is the project value index (PVI), shown in Exhibit 3.2. It displays decision factors based on quantitative comparisons (i.e., best estimates) of one project to

EXHIBIT 3.1 **Product Design and Development Sequence**

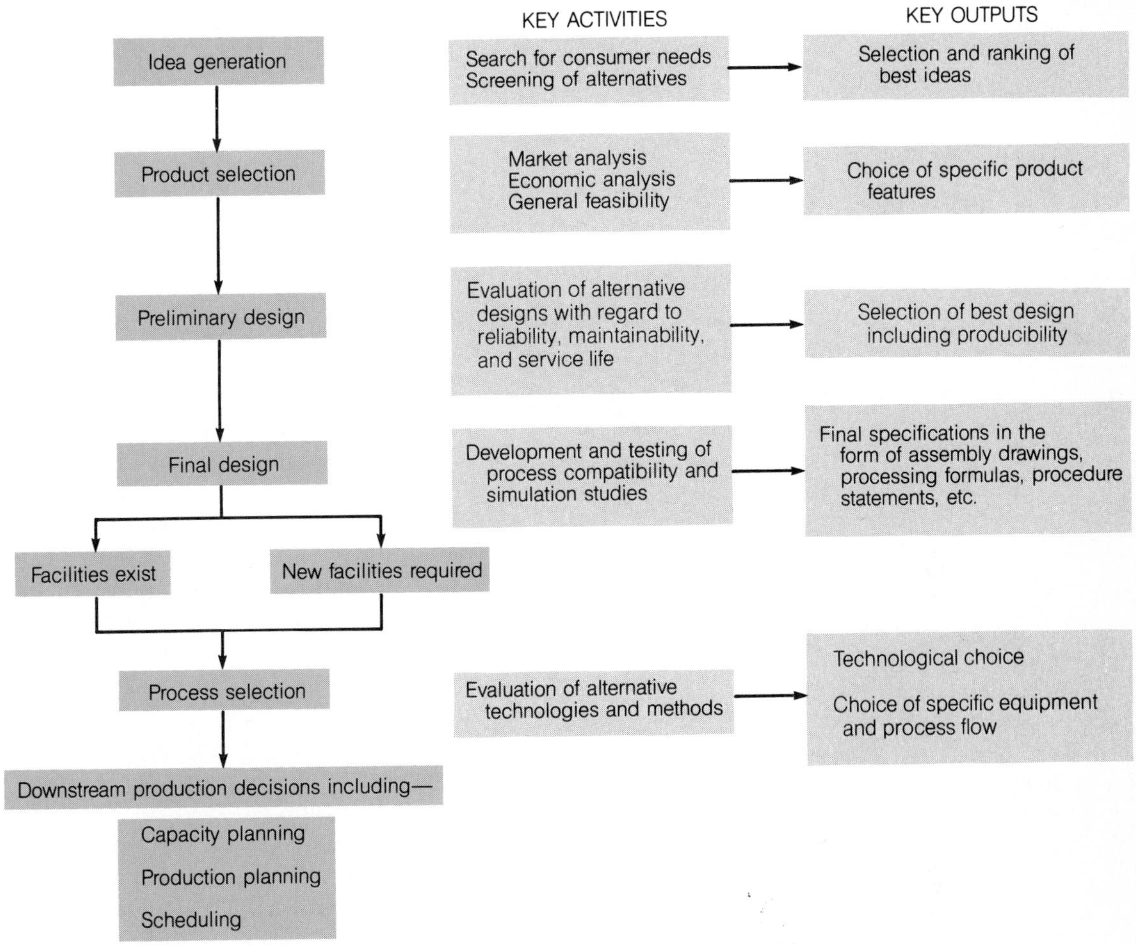

another. (Note that all costs are fully loaded, meaning that all relevant costs, such as cost of goods and materials, selling costs, and administrative expenses, are taken into consideration.)

If the product passes the screening procedure, more rigorous analysis of its cost and revenue characteristics is undertaken. It is here that the tools of financial analysis—break-even charts and rate-of-return calculations—come into play. The major problem associated with these tools is that their value is limited to short-run evaluation of the product alternatives, since long-term developments in costs, the competition, and the economy make the numerical inputs inaccurate (in many cases) within a year.

EXHIBIT 3.2

Project Value Index

$$PVI = \frac{CTS \times CCS \times AV \times P \times L}{TPC}$$

where

PVI = Project value index
CTS = Chances for technical success on an arbitrary rating scale, say 0 to 10
CCS = Chances for commercial success on an arbitrary rating scale, say 0 to 10
AV = Annual volume (total sales of product in units)
P = Profit in dollars per unit (i.e., price minus cost)
L = Life of product in years
TPC = Total project cost in dollars

Financial analysis generally yields information on how many units must be sold. Meanwhile the marketing department runs studies of potential demand to determine how many units are *likely* to be sold, and conducts marketing-mix analyses, which attempt to determine *how* they are to be sold. This process can be quite involved, however. Peters and Waterman include a diagram of the new-product introduction process in one firm; it shows 223 formal linkages among departments and standing committees, all of whom must sign off on each new product. Some recent thinking has raised the point that existing organizations and procedures stifle creativity and new product development. We need a new way of thinking on how new product development can best be done.

3.2 PRODUCT DESIGN AND SELECTION

From the production manager's point of view, the critical output of the product design activity is the **product's specifications**. These specifications provide the basis for a host of production-related decisions the manager must make, including the purchase of materials, selection of equipment, assignments of workers, and often even the size and layout of the productive facility.

Product specifications, while commonly thought of as blueprints or engineering drawings, may take a variety of other forms, ranging from highly precise quantitative statements to rather fluid guidelines. A sampling of specifications along a continuum ranging from the exact to the general is provided in Exhibit 3.3.

Preliminary Design

Whether or not it is a separate phase in the sequence of design activities, preliminary design is usually devoted to developing several alternative designs that meet the conceptual features of the selected product. If, for example, a

EXHIBIT 3.3

Specifications Continuum

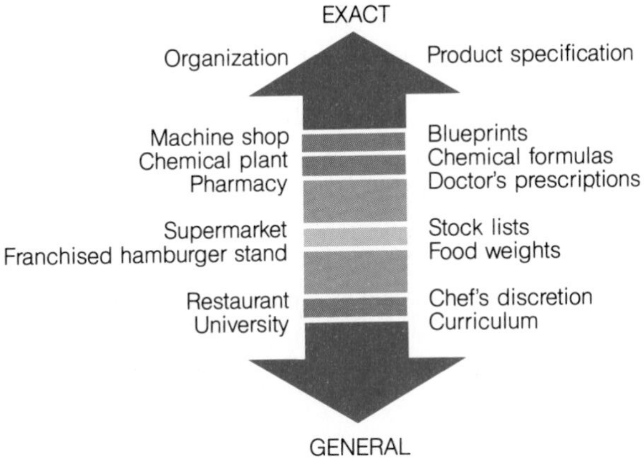

refrigerator manufacturer decides to manufacture freezers, questions of style, storage capacity, size of motor, and so forth, will likely be encountered here. During preliminary design, it also is common to specify the key product attributes of reliability, maintainability, and service life. For a freezer, these would involve decisions about frequency of breakdown of component parts (reliability), the ease of repair and general maintenance (maintainability), and the anticipated useful performance period (service life).

Final Design

During the final design phase, product prototypes are developed and "bugs" are worked out so that the product is sound from an engineering standpoint. Thus, ultimate output of the final design includes the complete specification of the product and its components, and assembly drawings, which provide the bases for its full-scale production.

At this point, too, the effectiveness of alternative designs must be balanced with cost considerations, and inevitably compromises must be made. This is especially true in selecting the configuration and material for manufactured items. The complexity of this trade-off can be seen when we consider that even such a relatively unsophisticated product as a home freezer has roughly 500 components, each of which could conceivably be subjected to an alternative cost analysis. Typical considerations that must enter the analysis are component *compatibility* and *simplification*.

Compatibility refers to the fitting together and proper articulation of parts during operation. Problems of compatibility arise not only with parts that must mesh, such as freezer door latches, but also with parts that must respond similarly to conditions of stress. Drawbridge components must of course fit together, but they must also have similar tensile strength to accommodate high winds and similar expansion coefficients to adjust equally to variations in temperature. **Simplification** refers to the exclusion of those features that raise production costs. Lack of simplification might be evident where such seemingly innocuous features as rounded edges or nonstandard hole sizes create bottlenecks in production and repair problems for the consumer.

During the final stage, most organizations also engage in rather formalized product-testing programs and redesign activities. Product testing may take the form of test marketing in the case of consumer products or test firing of a weapons system in the case of the military. Product redesign generally takes place after the prototype has been tested and may be major or minor in scope. If the redesign is major, the product may be recycled through the preliminary design phase; if the change is minor, the product will probably be carried through to production. Note, however, that there are minor changes and "minor changes"; an apparently slight modification to some component can greatly alter the integrity of the entire product.

Life Cycle Involvement with Products

A major trend in manufacturing is early and continuing involvement with new products by production, materials planning, and engineering support groups to ensure that the products are effectively managed throughout their life cycles. At Hewlett-Packard, this responsibility is seen as carrying through product development, transition to manufacturing, volume production, and obsolescence (see Exhibit 3.4).

One of the keys to making early involvement effective is simply daily contact between engineering and production groups.

> Consider, for example, the case of Ampex, an early leader in the production of video broadcast recorders. At first, design engineers and manufacturing people were located in the same facility, shared comparable goals, and kept in close touch. As volume grew and as the need to lower costs grew with it, manufacturing not only physically moved away from the development center; its objectives and priorities changed as well. To maintain the smooth transfer of products from development to production, the company tried a number of organizational expedients (pilot plants, new product groups, and so on), but in a company as engineering-driven as Ampex no such after-the-fact device could circumvent the barriers of distance and altered priorities. Cut off from immediate daily contact with production, engineering became so involved with the ramifications of product technology that it lost touch with the manufacturing process.[1]

---

[1] William J. Abernathy, Kim B. Clark, and Alan M. Kantrow, *Industrial Renaissance* (New York: Basic Books, 1983), p. 121.

EXHIBIT 3.4

Hewlett-Packard Life Cycle Involvement Activities

DEVELOPMENT | TRANSITION TO MANUFACTURING | VOLUME PRODUCTION | OBSOLESCENCE | END SUPPORT LIFE

Product development	We're responsible for design of the product →
Manufacturing engineering	We're responsible for design and support of the processes →
Materials/ materials engineering	We're responsible for sourcing/ management of vendor resources →
Production	We're responsible for building the product →
Marketing	We're responsible for support of the product →

Computer-Aided Design

One of the major contemporary approaches to the product design process is computer-aided (or -assisted) design (CAD). *CAD* may be defined as carrying out all structural or mechanical design processes of a product or component at a specially equipped computer terminal. Engineers design through a combination of console controls and a light pen that draws on the computer screen or electronic pad. Perspectives can be visualized by rotating the product on the screen, and individual components can be enlarged to examine particular characteristics. Depending on the sophistication in software, on-screen testing may replace the early phases of prototype testing and modification.

CAD has been used to design everything from computer chips to potato chips. Frito-Lay, for example, used CAD to design its O'Grady's double-density, ruffled potato chip. The problem in designing such a chip is that if it is cut improperly, it may be burned on the outside and soggy on the inside, it may be too brittle (and shatter when placed in the bag), or display other characteristics that make it unworthy for, say, a guacamole dip. However, through the use of CAD, the proper angle and number of ruffles were determined mathematically, and the O'Grady's model passed its stress test in the infamous Frito-Lay "crusher" and is now on your grocer's shelf.

A general rule is "the more parts a product is made of, the greater the chance of failure." IBM designed a printer with few parts and is realizing many benefits (see the Insert).

INSERT IBM Discovers a Simple Pleasure

Manufacturers are just beginning to realize the enormous potential of simplifying design. The advantages are so obvious that hardly anyone noticed them until the Japanese began using simplicity as a competitive weapon.

As IBM advanced from one generation of printer to another, it formed teams of design and manufacturing engineers to reduce the number of parts. Using a computer-aided design and manufacturing system (CAD/CAM), the teams could quickly test their new concepts for printers. Their goal was to combine multiple parts into one and substitute snap-on fastenings for screws and bolts—without sacrificing quality or changing the look of the printer.

IBM's success is evident when the parts of its new LaserPrinter (below right) are laid out next to components from Hewlett-Packard's comparable LaserJet III. Not only does the IBM machine have fewer parts; the number of screws to hold them together has been reduced from dozens to a handful as well. So far, however, H-P's printers dominate the market.

IBM had expected to assemble its printers with robots. Instead, engineers found that simplicity yielded yet another extra dividend: It turned out to be cheaper and easier to make them by hand.

Hewlett-Packard's LaserJet III (left) Has Many More Parts Than IBM's LaserPrinter

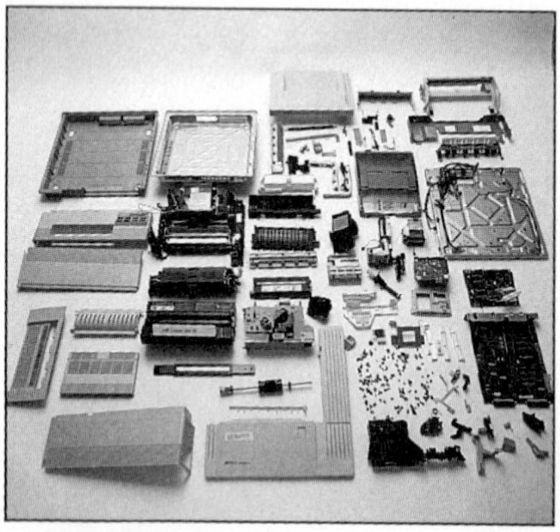

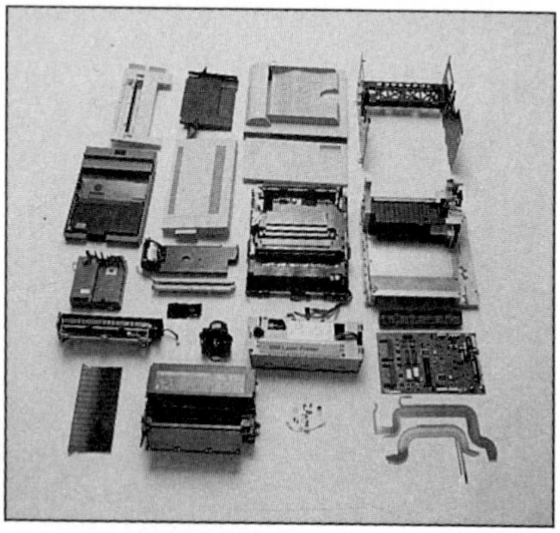

Source: Jeremy Main, "Manufacturing the Right Way," *Fortune*, May 21, 1990, p. 6.

A practical limitation of CAD at the present time is the extensive programming time required to introduce all parts of a complicated product into the database program. Still, virtually every major manufacturer, from cars to computers, has CAD as one of its priority areas of technical development.[2]

3.3 PROCESS SELECTION

Process Structures

Manufacturing operations, in the general sense of transforming some material input into some material output, can be categorized into three types of process structures.

Continuous processes. Those that must be carried out 24 hours a day to avoid expensive shutdown and startups. These are typified by *process industries* such as steel, plastics, chemicals, beer, and petroleum.

Repetitive processes. Those in which items are produced in large lots following the same series of operations as the previous items. These are typified by *mass production* using production lines in such industries as automobiles, appliances, electronic components, ready-to-wear clothing, and toys.

Intermittent processes. Those in which items are processed in small lots or *batches,* often to a customer's specifications. These are typified by *job shops,* which in turn are characterized by individual orders taking different workflow patterns through the plant and requiring frequent starting and stopping. Common examples are repair facilities, capital-equipment manufacture, and custom clothing. Also under the heading of intermittent is *unit* production: one-of-a-kind items or items made one by one. Unit production is typified by large turbine, airplane, and ship manufacture, and by major *projects* such as found in construction.

Continuous-process industries *generally* provide fewer operations options since the technology is often analogous to one big machine, rather than a linkage of several individual machines. Intermittent and some repetitive processes often can be decoupled into discrete processing stages and, as a result, present management with more production alternatives.

---

[2] A "CAD" on the beach? CAD is now being used to custom design swimsuits. Measurements of the wearer are fed into the CAD program, along with the style of suit desired. Working with the customer, the designer modifies the suit design as it appears on a human-form drawing on the computer screen. Once the design is decided upon, the computer prints out a pattern, and the suit is cut and sewn on the spot.

Product-process matrix
The relationship between process structures and volume requirements is often depicted on a matrix such as shown in Exhibit 3.5. The way to interpret this matrix is that as volume increases and the product line narrows, (the horizontal

EXHIBIT 3.5 **Matching Major Stages of Product and Process Life Cycles**

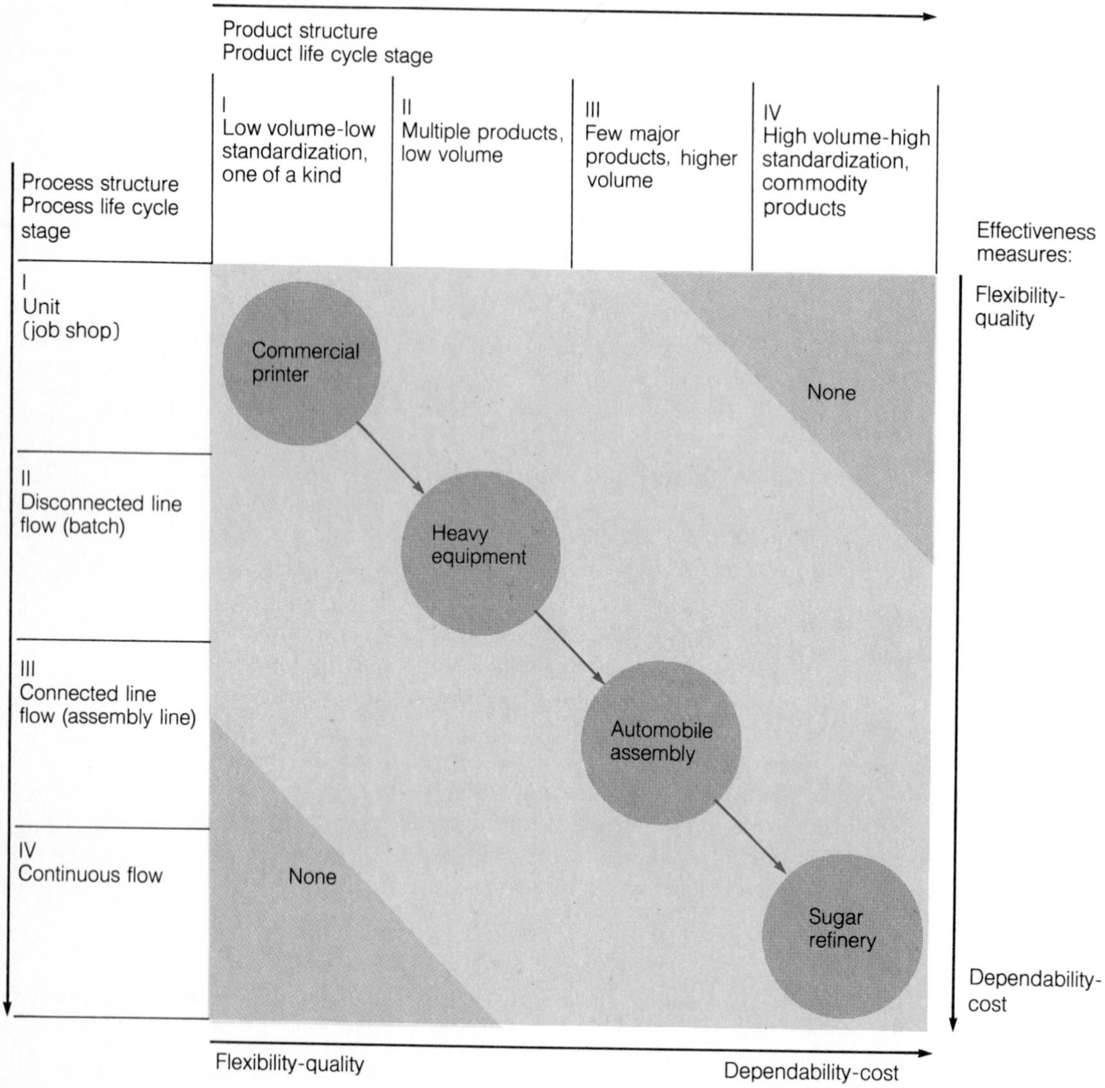

Source: Robert Hayes and Steven Wheelwright, *Restoring Our Competitive Edge: Competing through Manufacturing* (New York: John Wiley & Sons, 1984), p. 209.

dimension), specialized equipment and standardized material flows (the vertical dimension) become economically feasible. Since this evolution in process structure is frequently related to the product's life cycle stage (introduction, growth, and maturity), it is termed a *product-process matrix*.

The industries listed within the matrix are presented as ideal types that have found their process niche. It certainly is possible for an industry member to choose another position on the matrix, however. For example, Volvo makes cars on movable pallets rather than an assembly line. Thus, on the matrix it would be at the intersection of process stage II and product stage III. Volvo's production rate is lower than its competitors because it is giving up the speed and efficiency of the line. On the other hand, the Volvo system has more flexibility and easier quality control than the classic automobile production line. Similar kinds of analysis can be carried out for other types of process-product options through the matrix.[3]

Specific Equipment Selection

The choice of specific equipment follows the selection of the general type of process structure. Some of the key factors that should be considered in the selection decision are shown in Exhibit 3.6.

Firms may have both general-purpose equipment and special-purpose equipment. For example, a machine shop would have lathes and drill presses (general-purpose) and could have transfer machines (special-purpose). An electronics firm may have a single-function test module to perform only one test at a time (general-purpose) and may have a multifunction test unit to perform multiple tests at the same time (special-purpose). As computer-based technology evolves, however, the general-purpose/special-purpose distinction becomes blurred, since a general-purpose machine has the capability to produce just as efficiently as many special-purpose ones.

In choosing production equipment, the ability to maintain consistent performance is very important. Variability is undesirable. Note Exhibit 3.7. Do you agree that Sam is the better shot? His shooting is consistent and predictable. A small adjustment in his sights will give him many bull's-eyes next time.

Process Technology Evolution

Soon after the Industrial Revolution, machines were substituted for human labor, and mechanized technology replaced many manual tasks. As the volume of standardized products grew, it became more economical to design special-purpose machines dedicated to the production of a single part or product. Ultimately, in discrete-parts manufacturing, these machines became

---

[3] See R. H. Hayes and S. Wheelwright, "The Dynamics of the Product-Process Life Cycle," *Harvard Business Review*, March-April 1979, pp. 127–36.

EXHIBIT 3.6

Major Decision Variables in Equipment Selection

Decision Variable	Factors to Consider
Initial investment	Price Manufacturer Availability of used models Space requirements Need for feeder/support equipment
Output rate	Actual versus rated capacity
Output quality	Consistency in meeting specs Scrap rate
Operating requirements	Ease of use Safety Human factors impact
Labor requirements	Direct to indirect ratio Skills and training
Flexibility	General-purpose versus special-purpose equipment Special tooling
Setup requirements	Complexity Changeover speed
Maintenance	Complexity Frequency Availability of parts
Obsolescence	State of the art Modification for use in other situations
In-process inventory	Timing and need for supporting buffer stocks
Systemwide impacts	Tie-in with existing or planned systems Control activities Fit with manufacturing strategy

EXHIBIT 3.7

Who's the Better Shot?

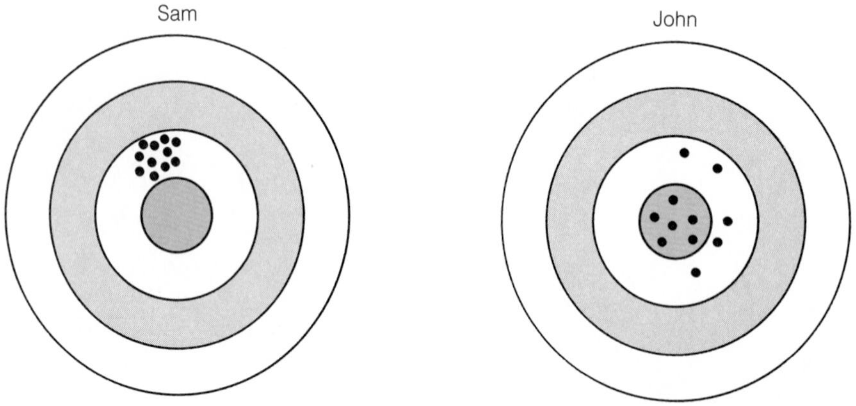

Source: Genichi Taguchi and Don Clausing, "Robust Quality," *Harvard Business Review*, January–February 1990, p. 67.

linked through material-handling devices. Now, both material movement and direct production can be performed automatically through automation.

Before the 1960s, the state of the art in manufacturing was the mechanized assembly line used by automobile manufacturers. Now, although many car companies still use many of the same processes, leading-edge applications of technology are found in other industries. This is particularly true in metal fabrication and electronic component manufacturing, where the objective is to approach the flexibility and speed of process industries such as chemicals and foods. Process industries are held up as a model because their processes require no hands-on production by workers. All operations are built into the "machine" and can be changed by turning a dial or altering a computer code.

3.4 AUTOMATION

The term *automation* is familiar to all, but a commonly agreed-upon definition still eludes us. Some authorities view automation as a totally new set of concepts that relate to the automatic operation of a production process; others view it as simply an evolutionary development in technology in which machinery performs some or all of the process-control function. Automation is a new set of concepts, but it is also evolutionary in the sense that it is a logical and predictable step in the development of equipment and processes.

Some major developments in manufacturing automation include machining centers, numerically controlled machines, industrial robots, computer-aided design and manufacturing systems, flexible manufacturing systems, computer-integrated manufacturing, and islands of automation.

Machining centers not only can provide automatic control of a machine, but can carry out automatic tooling changes as well. For example, a single machine may be equipped with a shuttle system of two worktables that can be rolled into and out of the machine. While work is being done at one table, the next part can be mounted on the second table. Then, when machining on the first table is complete, it is moved out of the way and the second part is moved into position.

Numerically controlled (NC) machines are under the control of a digital computer. Feedback control loops determine the position of the machines during the work, constantly compare the actual location with the programmed location, and correct as needed. This eliminates time lost during setups, and applies to both high-volume, standardized types of products and low-volume, customized products.

Industrial robots are substitutes for human manipulation and other highly repetitive functions. A robot can be seen as a reprogrammable machine with multiple functions that can move devices through specialized motions in order to perform any number of tasks. It is essentially a mechanized arm that can be fitted with a variety of handlike fingers or grippers, vacuum cups, or a tool such as a wrench. Robots are capable of performing many factory operations

EXHIBIT 3.8

The FMS Components—Workstations, Automated Transport, and Computer Control

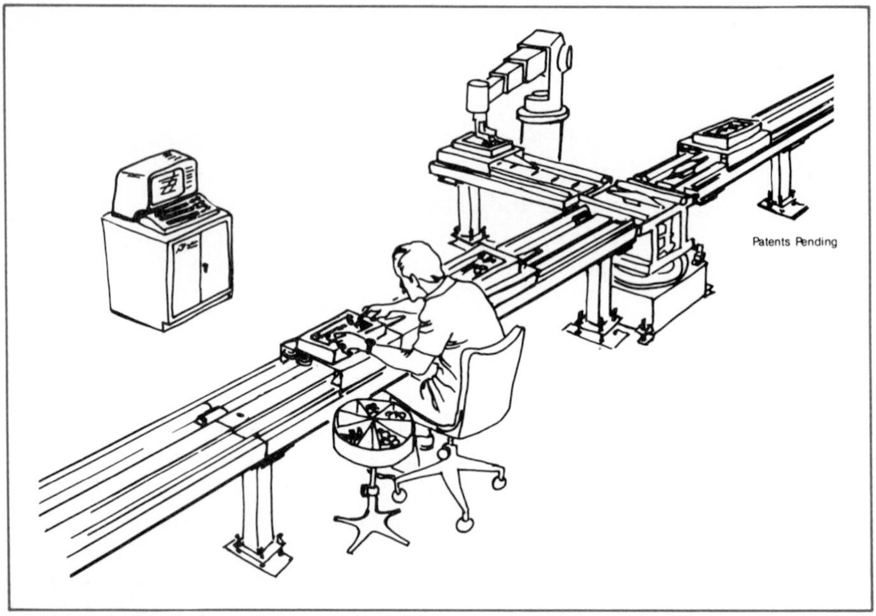

Source: Courtesy of SI Handling Systems, Inc., Easton, Pa.

ranging from machining processes to simple assembly. Exhibit 3.8 depicts how robots fit with people as part of a flexible manufacturing system.

Exhibit 3.9 examines the human motions a robot can reproduce. Advanced capabilities have been designed into robots to allow vision, tactile sensing, and hand-to-hand coordination. In addition, some models can be "taught" a sequence of motions in a three-dimensional pattern. A worker moves the end of the robot arm through the required motions, and the robot records this pattern in its memory and repeats them on command.

Robots are expensive but usually can be economically justified, because production time is decreased as accuracy and consistency are increased. (See the Insert for a formula to evaluate a robot investment.) At the Fort Worth General Dynamics plant, the computerized Milicron T-3 drills holes at a rate of 24 to 30 parts per shift with no defects. A human worker can produce only 6 parts per shift, with a 10 percent rejection rate. Even though the robot cost $60,000, it saved the company $90,000 the first year.

As productivity increases with robots, workers can be eliminated. Current estimates set worker displacement at anywhere from 1.7 to 6.0 employees per robot; the potential is especially high in the metalworking industry. It seems just a matter of time before sophisticated robots with vision systems will be

EXHIBIT 3.9

Typical Robot Axes of Motion

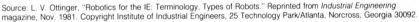

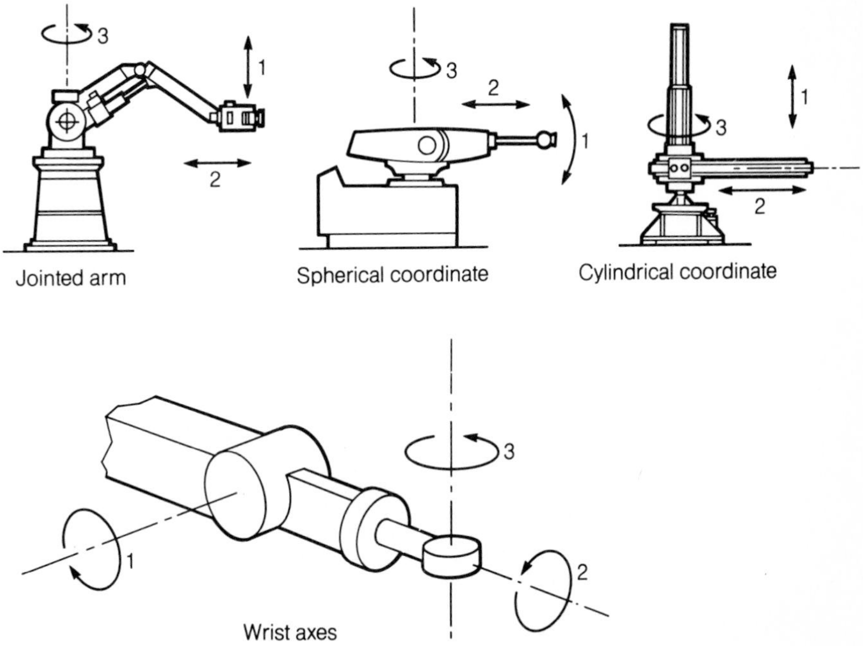

Source: L. V. Ottinger, "Robotics for the IE: Terminology, Types of Robots." Reprinted from *Industrial Engineering* magazine, Nov. 1981. Copyright Institute of Industrial Engineers, 25 Technology Park/Atlanta, Norcross, Georgia 30092.

viable for assembly and sensitive-touch jobs in other industries. Some experts estimate these robots of the future could replace as many as 3.8 million workers. There are, however, some things a robot will probably never be able to do (see Exhibit 3.10).

INSERT Formula for Evaluating a Robot Investment

The following modification of the basic payback formula is used by many companies in deciding if a robot should be purchased:

$$P = \frac{I}{L - E + q(L + Z)}$$

where

P = Payback period in years

I = Total capital investment required in robot and accessories

EXHIBIT 3.10

Tasks That Robots Can Do and May Be Able to Do

Things Present (or Past) Robots Can Do	Things Next Generation Robots Will Be Able to Do	Things a Very Sophisticated Future Robot May Be Able to Do	Things No Robot Will Ever Be Able to Do (Probably)
Play the piano	Vacuum a rug (avoiding obstructions)	Set a table	Cut a diamond
Load/unload CNC machine tools	Load/unload a glass blowing or cutting machine	Clear a table	Polish an opal
Load/unload die casting machines, hammer forging machines, molding machines, etc.	Assemble large and/or complex parts, TVs, refrigerators, air conditioners, microwave ovens, toasters, automobiles	Juggle balls	Peel a grape
Spray paint on an assembly line	Operate woodworking machines	Load a dishwasher	Repair a broken chair or dish
Cut cloth with a laser	Walk on two legs	Unload a dishwasher	Darn a hole in a sock/sweater
Make molds	Shear sheep	Weld a cracked casting/forging	Play tennis or Ping Pong at championship level
Deburr sand castings	Wash windows	Make a bed	Catch a football or a Frisbee at championship level
Manipulate tools such as welding guns, drills, etc.	Scrape barnacles from a ship's hull	Locate and repair leaks inside a tank or pipe	Pole vault
Assemble simple mechanical and electrical parts: small electric motors, pumps, transformers, radios, tape recorders	Sandblast a wall	Pick a lock	Dance a ballet
		Knit a sweater	Ride a bicycle in traffic*
		Make needlepoint design	Drive a car in traffic*
		Make lace	Tree surgery
		Grease a continuous mining machine or similar piece of equipment	Repair a damaged picture
		Tune up a car	Assemble the skeleton of a dinosaur†
		Make a forging die from metal powder	Cut hair stylishly
		Load, operate, and unload a sewing machine	Apply makeup artistically
		Lay bricks in a straight line	Set a multiple fracture
		Change a tire	Remove an appendix
		Operate a tractor, plow, or harvester over a flat field	Play the violin‡
		Pump gasoline	Carve wood or marble
		Repair a simple puncture	Build a stone wall
		Pick fruit	Paint a picture with a brush
		Do somersaults	Sandblast a cathedral
		Walk a tightrope	Make/repair leaded glass windows
		Dance in a chorus line	Deliver a baby
		Cook hamburgers in a fast-food restaurant	Cut and trim meat
			Kiss sensuously

*Assuming the other vehicles are not robot controlled.
†Admittedly a computer could provide very valuable assistance.
‡But it could "synthesize" violin music.

Source: Robert U. Ayres and Steven M. Miller, *Robotics: Applications and Social Implications* (Cambridge, Mass.: Ballinger Publishing, 1983), p. 25.

L = Annual labor costs replaced by the robot (wage and benefit costs per worker times the number of shifts per day)
E = Annual maintenance cost for the robot
q = Fractional speedup (or slowdown) factor
Z = Annual depreciation

Example:

I = \$50,000
L = \$60,000 (two workers @ \$20,000 each working one of two shifts; overhead is \$10,000 each)
E = \$9,600 (\$2/hour × 4,800 hours/year)
q = + 150% (robot works half again as fast as a worker)
Z = \$10,000

then

$$P = \frac{\$50{,}000}{\$60{,}000 - \$9{,}600 + 1.50\ (\$60{,}000 + \$10{,}000)} = \tfrac{1}{3}\ \text{year}$$

Computer-aided design and manufacturing (CAD/CAM) uses a computer to join part design and processing instructions. In current CAD/CAM systems, the product designer can draw on a data bank of existing part designs and view them in any orientation, scale, or cross section. With the computer, several alternatives can be analyzed without building a prototype. When the design is finalized, the link to CAM is made by producing the manufacturing instructions. Because of the efficiency of CAD/CAM systems, design and manufacture of small lots can be low in cost.

Even though CAD/CAM systems are usually limited to larger companies because of the high cost, they do increase productivity and quality dramatically. More alternative designs can be produced, and the specifications can be more exact. Updates can be readily made, and cost estimates can be drawn easily. In addition, computer-aided process planning (CAPP) can shorten or in some cases eliminate traditional process planning.

A flexible manufacturing system (FMS) combines the elements of machining centers and robots with computerized parts transfer, to create an "automatic factory." When combined with CAD, it gives manufacturers the opportunity to go from a new design to full-scale production virtually overnight. The implications of this capability are profound, especially because most machined products are produced in batches of 50 or less, and assembled products are becoming more and more customized to satisfy particular market segments. In addition, the trend toward shorter product life cycles is accommodated by the responsiveness of FMS.

Computer-integrated manufacturing (CIM) integrates all aspects of production into one automated system. Design, testing, fabrication, assembly, inspection, and materials handling may all have automated functions within the area. However, in most companies, communication between departments still flows by means of paperwork. In CIM, these islands of automation are integrated, thus eliminating the need for the paperwork. A computer links all sectors together, resulting in more efficiency, less paperwork, and less manpower expense. (See the section later in this chapter for further development of this idea.)

Islands of automation refers to the transition from conventional manufacturing to the automated factory. Typical islands of automation include numerically controlled machine tools, robots, automated storage/retrieval systems, and machining centers.

Choosing among Alternative Processes and Equipment

A standard approach to choosing among alternative processes or equipment is **break-even analysis.** A break-even chart visually presents alternative individual and relative profit and losses as a function of number of units produced or sold. The choice obviously depends on anticipated demand. The method is most suitable when processes or equipment entail a large initial investment and fixed cost, and when variable costs are reasonably proportional to the number of units produced. By way of example, suppose a manufacturer has identified the following options for obtaining a machined part: It can buy the part at $200 per unit (including materials), it can make the part on a numerically controlled semiautomatic lathe at $75 per unit (including materials), or it can make the part on a machining center at $15 per unit (including materials). There is negligible fixed cost if the item is purchased; a semiautomatic lathe costs $80,000, and a machining center costs $200,000.

Whether we approach the solution to this problem as a cost minimization or as profit maximization really makes no difference, as long as the relationships remain linear; that is, variable costs and revenue are the same for each incremental unit. Exhibit 3.11 shows the break-even points for each of the processes. If demand is expected to be more than 2,000 units (point A), the machine center is the best choice since this would result in the lowest total cost. If demand is between 640 (point B) and 2,000 units, the NC lathe is the cheapest. If demand is less than 640 (between 0 and point B), the most economical course is to buy the product.

Consider the effect of revenue, assuming the part sells for $300 each. As Exhibit 3.11 shows, profit (or loss) is the distance between the revenue line and the alternative process cost. At 1,000 units, for example, maximum profit is shown as the difference between the $300,000 revenue (point C) and the semiautomatic lathe cost of $160,000 (point D). For this quantity the semiautomatic lathe is the cheapest of the alternatives available. The optimal choices for both minimizing cost and maximizing profit are the lowest segments of lines: origin to B, to A, and to the right side of the exhibit.

EXHIBIT 3.11 Break-Even Chart of Alternative Processes

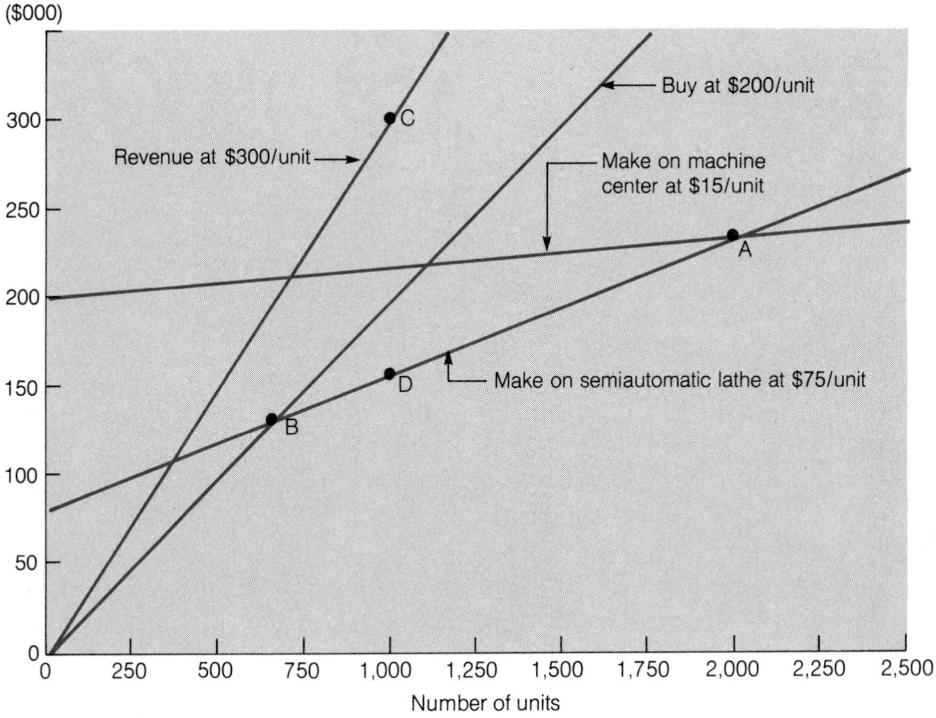

3.5 PROCESS FLOW DESIGN

Process flow design focuses on the specific processes that raw materials, parts, and subassemblies follow as they move through the plant. Several production management tools are used in planning the process flow; the most common are assembly drawings, assembly charts, route sheets, and flow process charts. Each of these charts is a useful diagnostic tool and can be used to improve operations during the steady state of the productive system. Indeed, the standard first step in analyzing any production system is "to map the flows and operations" using one or more of these techniques. These are the "organization charts" of the manufacturing system.

An *assembly drawing* (see Exhibit 3.12) is simply an exploded view of the product showing its component parts. An *assembly chart*[4] (Exhibit 3.13) uses

[4] Also called a *Gozinto chart*, named, so the legend goes, after the famous Italian mathematician Zepartzat Gozinto.

EXHIBIT 3.12

Plug Assembly Drawing

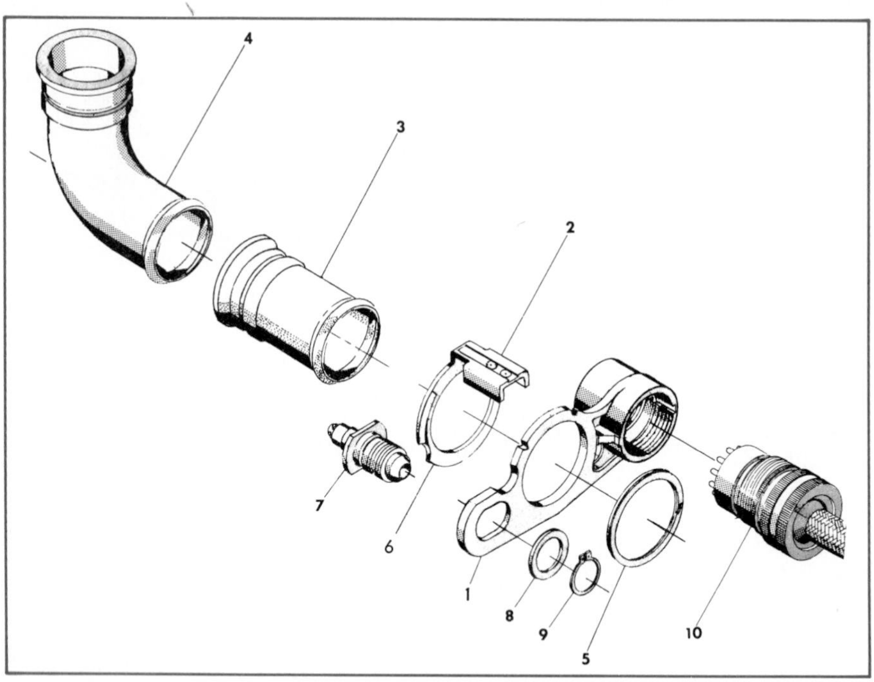

the information presented in the assembly drawing and defines (among other things) how parts go together, their order of assembly, and often the overall material flow pattern. An *operation and route sheet* (as in Exhibit 3.14), as its name implies, specifies operations and process routing for a particular part. It conveys such information as the type of equipment, tooling, and operations required to complete the part.

A flow process chart such as Exhibit 3.15 typically uses standard American Society of Mechanical Engineers (ASME) symbols to denote what happens to the product as it progresses through the productive facility. The symbols for the various processes are explained at the bottom of the chart. As a rule, the fewer the delays and storages in the process, the better the flow.

The Manufacturing Cycle

During the **manufacturing cycle,** the production function interacts with virtually every other function of the enterprise (see Exhibit 3.16). Because we examine the activities that take place during the cycle throughout this text, we

EXHIBIT 3.13 **Assembly (or Gozinto) Chart for Plug Assembly**

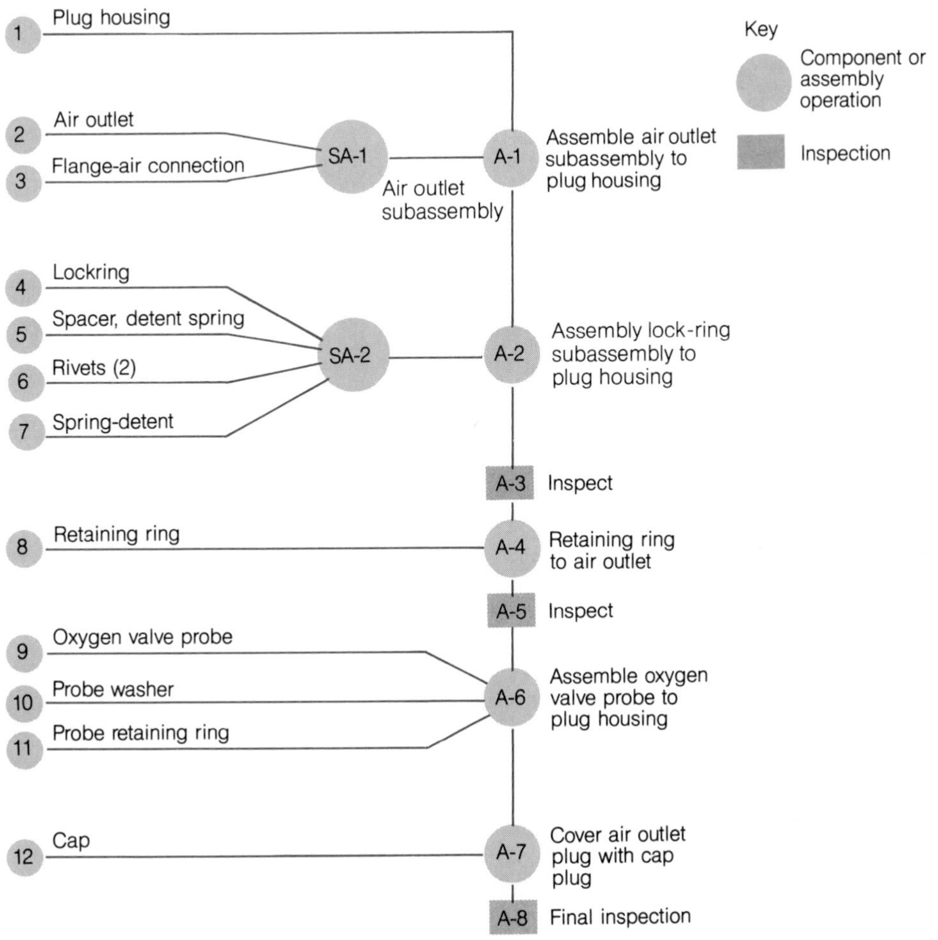

won't explain all of them here. It is desirable at this point, however, to highlight some of the major organizational interrelationships that have an ongoing impact on production.

First, there are two engineering groups—manufacturing engineering and industrial engineering. Manufacturing engineering's major responsibilities typically include (1) advising the product design group on producibility of the product, (2) planning process flow along the lines mentioned above, (3) specifying the tooling and equipment required, and (4) updating the bill of

EXHIBIT 3.14

Operation and Route Sheet for Plug Assembly

Material Specs. ____	Part Name: Plug Housing	Part No. TA 1274
Purchased Stock Size ____	Usage: Plug Assembly	Date Issued ____
Pcs. Per Pur. Size ____	Assy. No. TA 1279	Date Sup'd. ____
Weight ____	Sub. Assy. No. ____	Issued By ____

Oper. No.	Operation Description	Dept.	Machine	Set Up Hr.	Rate Pc/Hr.	Tools
20	Drill 1 hole .312 +.015 −.005	Drill	Mach 513 Deka 4	1.5	254	Drill Fixture L-76, Jig #10393
30	Deburr .312 +.015 −.005 Dia. Hole	Drill	Mach 510 Drill	.1	424	Multi-Tooth Burring Tool
40	Chamfer .900/.875, Bore .828/.875 dia. (2 Passes), Bore .7600/.7625 (1 Pass)	Lathe	Mach D109 Lathe	1.0	44	Ramet-1, TPG 221, Chamfer Tool
50	Tap Holes as designated - 1/4 Min. Full Thread	Tap	Mach 514 Drill Tap	2.0	180	Fixture #CR-353, Tap, 4 Flute Sp.
60	Bore Hole 1.133 to 1.138 Dia.	Lathe	H & H E107	3.0	158	L44 Turrent Fixture, Hartford
						Superspacer, pl. #45, Holder #L46,
						FDTW-100, Inser #21, Chk. Fixture
70	Deburr .005 to .010, Both Sides, Hand Feed To Hard Stop	Lathe	E162 Lathe	.5	176	Collect #CR179, 1327 RPM
80	Broach Keyway To Remove Thread Burrs	Drill	Mach. 507 Drill	.4	91	B87 Fixture, L59 Broach, Tap. . 875120 G-H6
90	Hone Thread I.D. .822/.828	Grind	Grinder		120	
95	Hone .7600/.7625	Grind	Grinder		120	

materials (BOM, the listing of parts that make up the product). Industrial engineering's major responsibilities typically include (1) determining work methods and time standards, (2) developing the specifics of the plant layout, (3) conducting cost and productivity improvement studies, and (4) implementing operations research projects.[5]

Second, it is common to refer to all functions shown in the exhibit, other than sales and marketing, product design, and production per se, as "manufacturing support groups." This conveys the idea that the role of these activities is, quite simply, to help in the frequently complicated task of manufacturing.

Finally, the plant manager is responsible for coordinating these groups, the production manager is responsible for coordinating the direct production work force, and, in multisite firms, the vice president of manufacturing is responsible for coordinating the manufacturing activities throughout the plant network.

3.6 COMPUTER-INTEGRATED MANUFACTURING

As we discussed in Chapter 2, international and domestic competition is becoming more intense with each passing day. Product life cycles now average

[5] M. P. Groover, *Automation, Production Systems, and Computer-Aided Manufacturing* (Englewood Cliffs, N.J.: Prentice-Hall, 1980), pp. 15–18.

EXHIBIT 3.15

Flow Process Chart
of Plug Housing from
Plug Assembly

Feet moved	Dec. Min.		Description
		▽	Materials received from supplier
	0.250	■	Inspect
95	1.500	●	To finish dept.
	0.060	⬤	Apply corrosive previous treatment
60	1.000	●	To raw stores
		▽	In raw stores
40	1.000	●	To drill press
	90.000	▽	Wait for drill operator (setup)
	0.236	⬤	Drill holes
94	1.500	●	To finish drill press
	6.000	▽	Wait for operator (setup)
	0.142	⬤	Deburr
65	1.000	●	To lathe

Key

⬤ Operation

● Transportation

▽ Storage or delay

■ Inspection

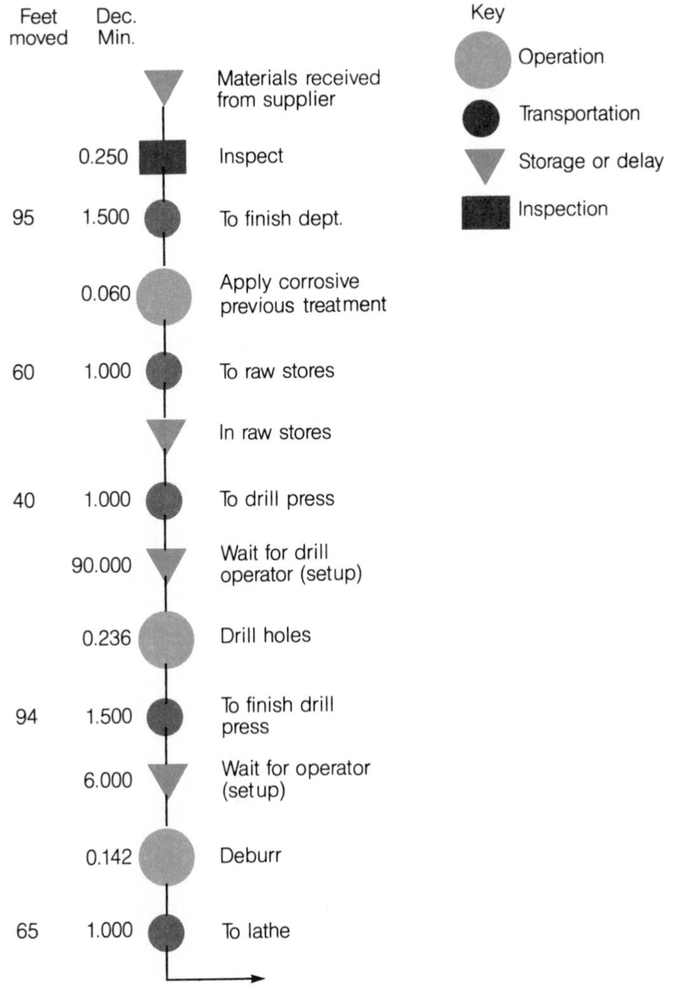

Note: These production times were based on a run of 500 items.
Source: Arizona Gear & Manufacturing Company.

12 to 18 months,[6] and they continue to get shorter. Consumers and end users of manufactured products are demanding more individually customized products to suit their own needs. With these pressures facing them, manufacturers are searching out new ways to improve their competitive position.

[6] James R. Koelsch, "Robots: The Keystone of Flexible Assembly," *Production Engineering,* February 1986, pp. 36–40.

EXHIBIT 3.16 **The Manufacturing Cycle**

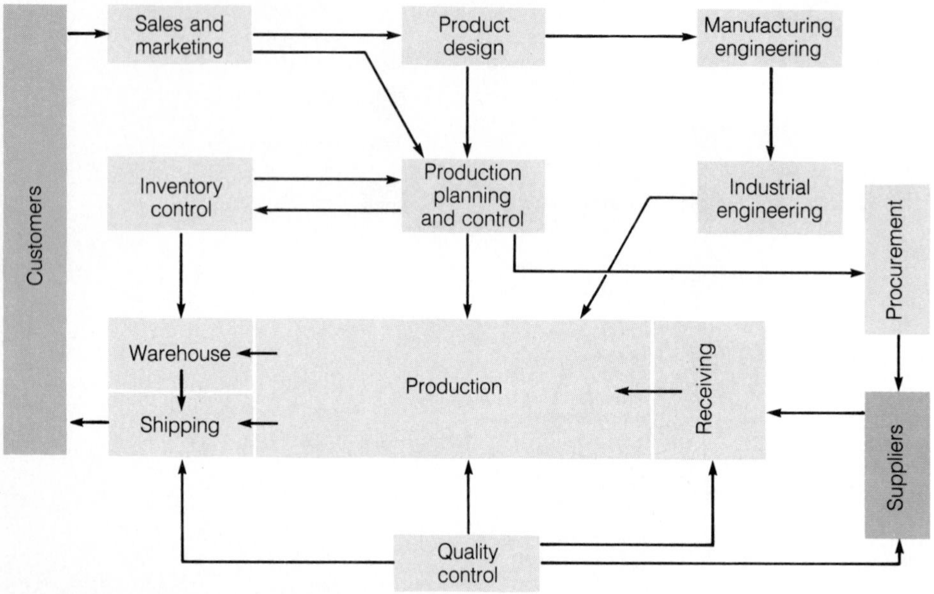

Source: Modified from Mikell P. Groover, *Automation, Production Systems, and Computer-Aided Manufacturing* (Englewood Cliffs, N.J.: Prentice-Hall, 1980). p. 16.

The answer for many companies lies in automation technologies. Automated manufacturing systems have the potential for providing a heretofore unmatched level of manufacturing performance along the four strategic dimensions of cost, quality, delivery, and flexibility.[7] In the 1960s, manufacturers began using computers to automate financial transactions and later to control inventory, production scheduling, and parts routing. The earliest applications of computers to the actual manufacturing process were the computer-aided design (CAD) systems first introduced in the aerospace and defense industries. Computer automation then moved to the machines used in the manufacturing process to create computer-aided manufacturing (CAM). Automation has now created a host of systems and devices to improve the effectiveness of the entire manufacturing process.

In addition to improving productivity, automation has also improved product quality and made possible rapid design and manufacture of new products.

[7] Kalyan Singhal, "Introduction: The Design and Implementation of Automated Manufacturing Systems," *Interfaces* 17, no. 6 (November–December 1987), p. 1.

EXHIBIT 3.17

Computer-Integrated Manufacturing

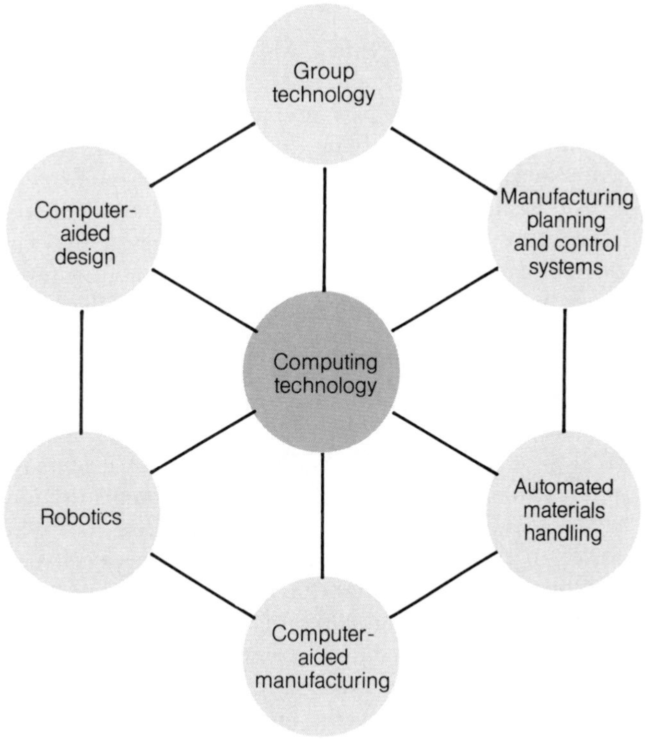

However, automation by itself is not sufficient to assure a competitive manufacturing system. While computer automation alone can make improvements through so-called islands of automation, it is not until these islands are linked and coordinated that an automated system achieves its maximum potential. The approaches taken to achieve such linkages go under several names: *total factory automation*, the *factory of the future*, and *computer-integrated manufacturing*.

Computer-integrated manufacturing (CIM) has six functional areas: computer-aided design, group technology, manufacturing planning and control systems, automated materials handling, computer-aided manufacturing, and robotics. (See Exhibit 3.17.)

Computer-aided design (CAD) covers several automated technologies in addition to the computer graphics systems used to design geometric specifications of a part. CAD includes computer-aided engineering (CAE), used to evaluate and conduct engineering analyses on a part. CAD also includes two technologies associated with manufacturing process design. CAD can be used to design numerically controlled part programs, which give instructions to computer-controlled tools, and to design the use and sequence of machine centers.

Closely associated with CAD in the process design is **group technology (GT),** a production methodology that uses a computer system for classifying, coding, and grouping parts and processes based on the geometry of parts. It is widely used in identifying cells of groups of machinery that are closely associated with each family of parts (see Chapter 8).

Automated **manufacturing planning and control systems (MP&CS)** are simply computer-based information systems. They plan and schedule operations, compare alternatives, update data continuously, monitor operations, and project operating results. More sophisticated manufacturing planning and control systems also include order-entry processing, shop floor control, purchasing, and cost accounting.

Closely related to MP&CS are **automated materials handling (AMH)** systems. These systems include automated storage and retrieval systems (ASRS) in which computers direct automatic loaders to pick items from bulk and return remainders to storage. AMH systems also include automatic guided vehicle (AGV) systems, which use embedded floor wires to direct unmanned trucks to various locations around the factory, delivering materials.

Computer-aided manufacturing (CAM) includes several technologies used in manufacturing: computer-run machine tools, flexible manufacturing systems (FMS), and computer-aided inspection. Computer-run machine tools include numerically controlled machine tools, which can be programmed to perform tasks either directly, on the shop floor, or with a disc or tape. FMS is an integrated system using several automation technologies to create the flexibility of a job-shop operation with the low costs of mass production. FMS links together the machine centers and materials handling system, limiting human involvement to part fixturing and system maintenance. Computer-aided inspection automatically collects and analyzes quality control information and can be used to establish a statistical database and to isolate production process problems.

Robotics is closely associated with CAM. A robot is a reprogrammable, multifunctional manipulator with an end effector (such as a gripper, welder, or sprayer) used in a variety of factory tasks that can be segmented as stand-alone operations. Robots are often used for spot welding and assembly.

All these CIM technologies are tied together in a communications link made possible by **computing technology.** The emphasis here is on linking databases of the different components together, since this is where the power of CIM is unleashed. With data integration, CAD systems can be linked to CAM numerical-control parts programs, and MP&CS can be linked to AMH systems to further enhance parts pick-list generation. In a fully integrated system, each automated technology will be able to interface with each of the other technologies through advanced computing technology. (See Exhibit 3.18, which sketches the physical features of a CIM factory.)

EXHIBIT 3.18 The Automated Factory

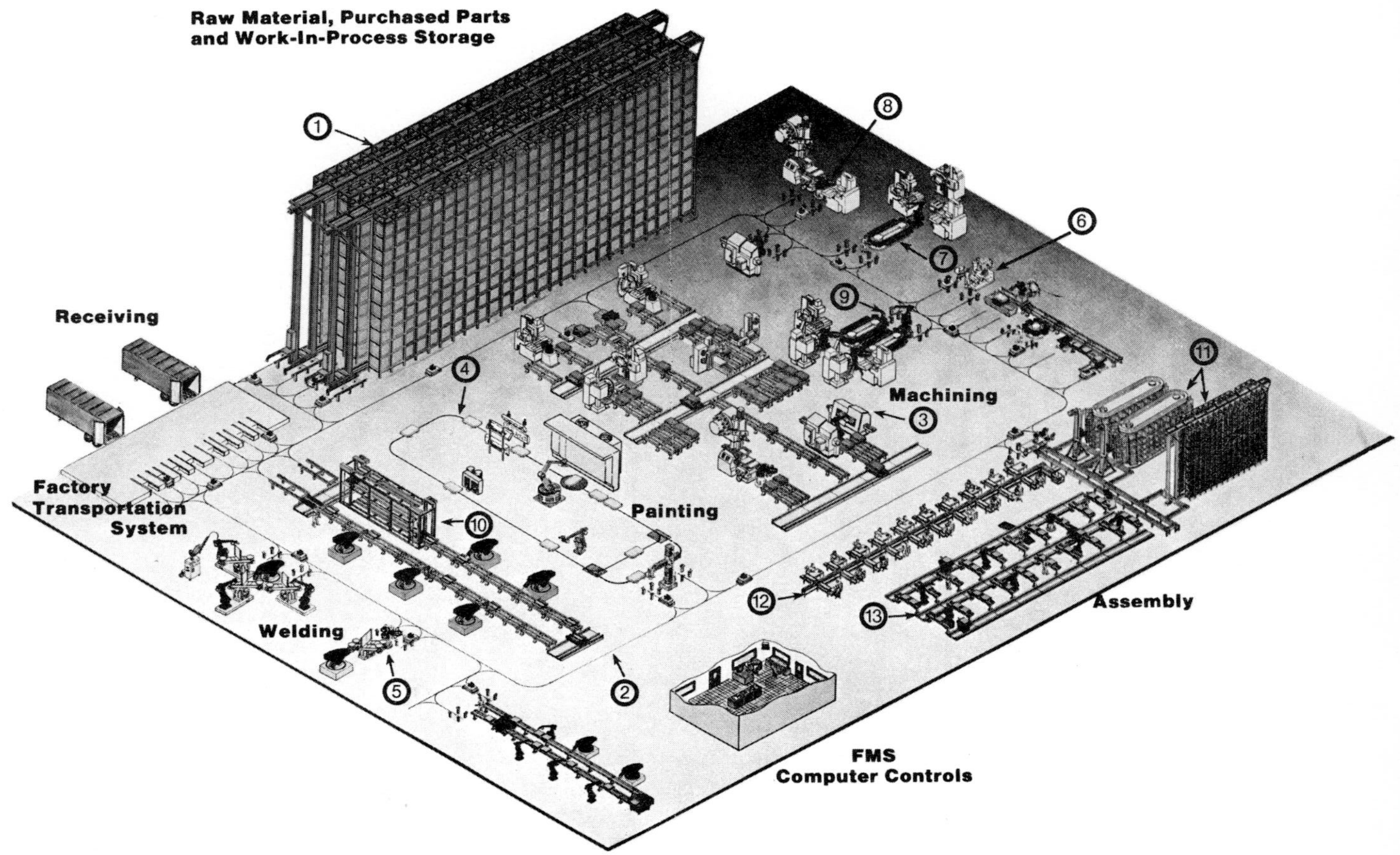

Source: Courtesy SI Handling Systems, Inc.

EXHIBIT 3.19

Number of Companies Identified through Literature Search Implementing Key CIM Areas and Technologies

CIM Area or Technology	Number (and Percentage) of Companies*
CAD/CAE/CAM	39 (37%)
Enterprise-integrated information systems	31 (29%)
Just-in-time manufacturing	29 (27%)
Manufacturing automation	28 (26%)
Robotics	28 (26%)
Computer or direct numerical control machines	25 (24%)
Automated materials-handling systems	25 (24%)
Flexible manufacturing systems	23 (22%)
Shop floor scheduling systems	21 (20%)
Factory communications systems	19 (18%)
Materials requirements planning	18 (17%)
Coordinate measuring machine or optical inspection	16 (15%)
Bar coding and automated parts identification	12 (11%)
Total quality management	12 (11%)
Artificial intelligence and expert systems	8 (8%)
Statistical process control	8 (8%)
Computer-automated process planning	8 (8%)
Concurrent engineering	6 (6%)
Group technology	5 (5%)
Manufacturing simulation	5 (5%)

* The total sample consisted of 106 companies; however, many companies implemented more than one area or technology.

Source: Frederick J. Michel and Mark D. Pardue, "Survey of World-Class CIM Planning: Information Architecture First," *CIM Review*, Summer 1990, p. 18.

CIM Implementation

With rare exceptions, CIM is an evolutionary process wherein various parts of the production system are added piece by piece. The degree of computer integration grows over time. Exhibit 3.19 shows a survey of companies and the areas they had implemented into their systems.

3.7 BENEFITS OF CIM

The benefits of the six CIM technologies are too numerous to discuss in detail. However, a brief overview of the major advantages would be useful.

The primary benefit of a CAD system is higher design productivity. However, CAD can result in many other benefits, such as better design quality, significantly less time spent on prototypes (parts fit can be verified by computer), and an engineering database with an accurate description of each part. The advantages of group technology include reduction of the number of parts

EXHIBIT 3.20

Qualitative Benefits of MP&CS

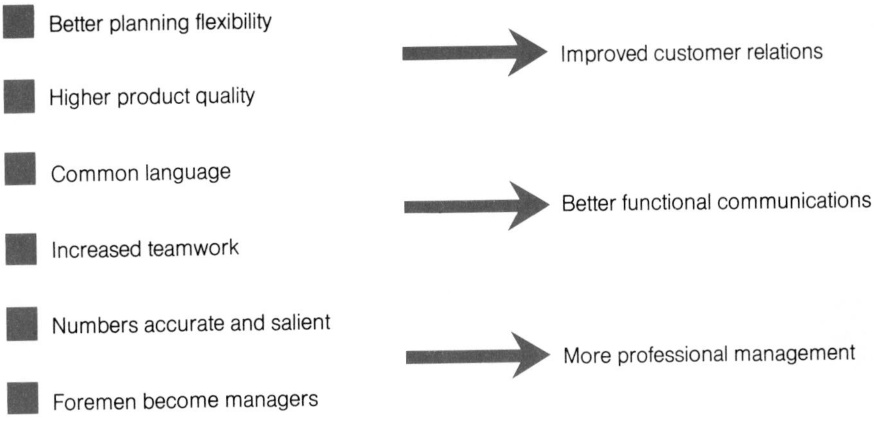

in a database, reduced parts introduction costs, higher machine use factors, and reduced overall setup time.

MP&CS produces quantitative and qualitative benefits. Typical quantitative benefits include reduction of inventory errors, overall inventory reductions, higher productivity, fewer late shipments, shorter delivery lead times, and fewer stockouts. Qualitative benefits include improved customer relations, better functional communications, and more professional management (Exhibit 3.20). Typical automated materials handling benefits include higher inventory record accuracy, reduced storage space requirements, higher labor productivity, increased safety and stockroom security, reduced product damage, and the coordination of material movement with material handling equipment.

CAM systems have many benefits similar to those already mentioned, such as increased labor productivity, increased product quality, and less setup time. Robotics provides many of these same benefits as well, but also substitutes for humans at dirty, dangerous, and dull tasks. In addition, robots can provide higher flexibility, higher reliability, and significant savings in space, materials, heating, and lighting.

The real advantages of CIM, however, are not in the sum of the benefits of each separate technology, although that sum is very significant. The real advantage of CIM lies in the integration of these component technologies. The long-term benefits of a data-integrated system like CIM are the individual benefits amplified geometrically by the benefits of integrating each component into a common system (see Exhibit 3.21). Integration leads to better management of the flow of manufacturing data, better interdepartmental communications, and better resource utilization, all of which can result in major gains in

EXHIBIT 3.21

Synergistic Effects of a CIM System

CIM benefits = Benefits of each separate technology × Benefits of data integration

product quality and production efficiency. Following are examples of benefits achieved by partial implementation of CIM in five companies:[8]

Achievement	Range of Improvement
Reduction in engineering design cost	15–30%
Reduction in overall lead time	30–60%
Increased product quality as measured by yield of acceptable product	2–5 times previous level
Increased capability of engineers as measured by extent and depth of analysis in same or less time than previously	3–35 times
Increased productivity (complete assemblies)	40–70%
Increased productivity (operating time) of capital equipment	2–3 times
Reduction of work-in-process	30–60%
Reduction of personnel costs	5–20%

3.8 EXAMPLES OF CIM

While CIM is a trend for the factory of the future, some companies have already installed integrated systems in their manufacturing facilities. The benefits of CIM are best illustrated by the three companies described below that have CIM systems already in place.

IBM's University Research Park Proprinter Plant

In 1983, IBM designed a highly automated facility to use computer-integrated manufacturing to produce printers that would be cost competitive with foreign manufacturers. IBM designed its printer with automated assembly in mind, so that the factory could be designed around the assembly process. Of the nine assembly stations along the assembly lines that build and test a printer, seven are robotic systems. IBM also uses an automated inventory storage and retrieval system and an automated materials handling system, and ties everything together with its own manufacturing, accounting, production, and inventory control system (MAPICS) software.

[8] Thomas G. Gunn, *Manufacturing for Competitive Advantage* (Cambridge, Mass.: Ballinger, 1987), p. 171.

By removing much of the direct labor, using the automated technologies of CIM, and designing its product with simplicity of manufacturing in mind, IBM was able to build a factory of the future that is able to compete on an international level. IBM's proprinter has only about one third the parts of the competition's printers, which means it can be produced from raw materials in one day and assembled from parts in 20 minutes. With the communication and coordination benefits of CIM, IBM has been able to minimize the number of its vendors and use the concept of Just-in-Time manufacturing to cut inventory inside the factory to about a day and a half's worth of production.

Westinghouse's College Station Electronic Assembly Plant

Westinghouse committed to investing in CIM after discovering that only 15 to 20 percent of its printed circuit boards were ready for shipping after only one pass through the manufacturing loop, as contrasted to 98 to 100 percent in the plants of its Japanese competition. Westinghouse implemented a sophisticated computing network that tied together several levels of computing technologies in a hierarchical data system. This data system is accessed by a central control system that manages one integrated database. A CAD/CAM subsystem was installed to generate machine data and speed up the assembly process. Westinghouse's own engineers developed six different robots that can perform variable sequential tasks in assembling a circuit board.

The resulting gains in efficiency are impressive. The percentage of printed circuit boards that are ready to be shipped after only one pass through the manufacturing loop has risen to 95 percent. The amount of time from receipt of order to shipment of product is down from 12 weeks to 2. In all, the improvements in quality and efficiency have saved Westinghouse an estimated $19 million and have saved the Air Force (one of its important customers) an estimated $37 million.

Fujitsu Fanuc Robot Factory

Fujitsu Fanuc has put into operation an entire factory for producing robots, small machining centers, and wire-cut electrodischarge machines. The machining section of the factory operates almost wholly unattended on the night shift. (See Exhibit 3.22.)

There are 29 machining cells (22 machining centers served by automatic pallet changes and 7 robot-served cells), each consisting of one or more NC machine tools and a robot or pallet changer to keep the machine or machines loaded with parts during the night. Workpieces on pallets are transported to and from the cells and to and from computer-controlled automatic stacker cranes by computer-controlled, wire-guided carts.

During the day there are 19 workers on the machining floor. On the night shift no one is on the machining floor, and there is only one worker in the control room. ("I had some difficulty scheduling a time to visit the

EXHIBIT 3.22

Ghost Shop: Fanuc, Co.

Fanuc, Co. is the world leader in developing fully automated factories like the one shown. Working three shifts a day, the robots produce various machines—and other robots. Human workers appear only to service the machines.

Courtesy of Fanuc Co.

plant . . . because the company's managers were concerned about protocol: There would be no one senior enough to receive a visitor on the site during 10 of its 15 operating shifts.")[9] In a 24-hour period, machine availability is running close to 100 percent, and machine use is averaging 65 to 70 percent. As a result, this 2,050-square-meter factory is producing 100 robots, 75 machining centers, and 75 electrodischarge machines each month.

3.9 CONCLUSION

It is becoming more and more apparent that successful manufacturing firms are not simply a collection of vaguely related activities, but rather well-

[9] Gerald K. O'Neill, "Robots Who Reproduce," *Across the Board*, June 1984, p. 37.

integrated "production machines." Indeed, just like a physical machine, each part of the manufacturing system—labor, equipment, and management—has an important role to play in achieving that success. It is also apparent that computer-based technology will be altering the ways products and factories are designed and manufacturing processes are carried out. How much of an impact such innovations will have across *all* industries is one of the most intriguing questions to be answered in the coming years. CAD/CAM investments offer excellent opportunity to improve labor productivity. However, if labor cost savings is the primary objective, consider robotics.[10]

3.10 REVIEW AND DISCUSSION QUESTIONS

1. What factors in the economy have led to the renewed interest in manufacturing technology, in your opinion?
2. What is the primary production document derived from the product design process? What other types of document does one require to make a product?
3. Why is daily contact between engineering and production groups so important in making early involvement effective?
4. Dennis Heard, Frito-Lay's vice president of R&D, though pleased with O'Grady's, is still seeking to develop the ultimate potato chip. Develop a list of characteristics that would define the perfect chip from your perspective.
5. What is the product-process matrix telling us? How does automation change its basic premise?
6. Why is manufacturing management more than simple production management?
7. With reference to Exhibit 3.3, what form does the product specification take for the following organizations: a wine company, a book publisher, and a baseball-card manufacturer?
8. Discuss your business specialty's role in the manufacturing cycle of a company producing disposable lighters.
9. What are the advantages and disadvantages of CIM?
10. Is CIM appropriate mainly for products that have short life cycles and that are constantly changing?
11. Automation is replacing workers. How should these workers be retrained so that they can cope effectively in a new environment?
12. By implementing CIM, Westinghouse's probability of shipping PCBs after one pass of the manufacturing loop had risen to 95 percent from 15 to 20 percent. The time taken from order to shipment had decreased from 12 weeks to 2 weeks. Calculate separately the productivity gain for assembly and production.

---

[10] Gary S. Vasilash "Which Technologies Are the Best Investments," *Production*, January 1990, pp. 65–67.

3.11 PROBLEMS

1. A computer manufacturer is considering using a robot to spray paint side panels of its tape drives. Given the following information, should the company make the investment if it requires a payback period of one year or less?

   Cost of robot and accessories is $75,000.

   Annual cost of manual spray painting (by one person) is $20,000.

   Annual robot maintenance cost is $10,000.

   A robot spray painting works about 25 percent faster than a human. Annual depreciation on the robot is $12,000.

2. PROJECT VALUE INDEX
   The manager of the New Wave Food Company, A. Gormay, is trying to decide which of two products should be developed by his firm. One is *huevos rapidos* (instant eggs), which would be made by flash freezing and drying chicken eggs and then mixing them with a combination of chili peppers specially grown for this purpose. The end result would be a Mexican omelet for use by campers and harried cooks. The other product is a chili bagel, which, according to a local delicatessen owner, "when topped with smoked salmon and cream cheese will become a new taste sensation that will displace both corned beef sandwiches and tamales as the standard lunch of the Southwest."

   Gormay figures that the probability of being able to produce *huevos rapidos* is 80 percent, the chances of it being a success in the market are 60 percent, and annual sales should be about 500,000 pounds for the next nine years. He figures that by selling the product to retailers for $0.75 per pound, he will realize a profit of $0.45 per pound. He estimates that the cost of developing the process and the new chili will be about $20,000 and that modifications of existing equipment to produce *huevos rapidos* at full-scale production levels will cost about $2,000.

   Gormay estimates that the probability of producing a satisfactory chili bagel, or "chigel" as the boys in R&D refer to it, is 90 percent. He figures that the probability of its being a success in the market is 70 percent, with annual sales being about 550,000 pounds for the next four years. Chigels should cost about $0.50 a pound for material and sell for $1.00 a pound to retailers, yielding a profit of $0.50 per pound. The cost of developing the chigel process is $2,000, and a high-speed bagel press and special packaging line will have to be purchased at a total cost of $50,000.

   The work force required for *huevos rapidos* is projected as five full-time operators at $5 per hour, 50 weeks per year, and seven full-time operators at $6 per hour, 50 weeks per year for chigels.

   Gormay estimates his cost of capital as 10 percent.

   Given the above information, choose between the products using the project value index formula.

3. Mary Entrepreneur is considering introducing a new novelty item for sale to summer visitors in the Catskill Mountains in upstate New York: a wraparound belt with pockets in which vacationers could carry their suntan lotion, playing cards, and snacks. The belt, which she will market as the "Borscht Belt," was greeted with great enthusiasm by members of a local health club.

The prototype model consists of six identical naugahyde pockets sewn onto a terrycloth belt, and a metal buckle available in the shape of different astrological signs. Once production begins, Mary will obtain naugahyde and terrycloth in bulk rolls, and buckles will be supplied by a local machine shop. Mary has two heavy-duty sewing machines and a stud-riveting machine (left over from her Bruce Springsteen Levi pants production) to attach the belt buckles. Before entering production, she would like to know:

a. What an assembly chart for the belts would look like.

b. What a flow process chart for the entire operation, from raw materials receipt to final inspection, would look like.

3.12 SELECTED BIBLIOGRAPHY

Addler, Paul S., Henry E. Riggs; and Steven C. Wheelwright. "Product Development Know-How: Trading Tactics for Strategy." *Sloan Management Review,* Fall 1989, pp. 7–17.

Alden, P. S. "Managing Flexibility." *California Management Review,* Fall 1988.

Avishai, Bernard. "A CEO's Common Sense of CIMS." *Harvard Business Review,* January-February 1989, pp. 110–18.

Ayers, Robert U., and Steven M. Miller. *Robotics: Applications and Social Implications.* Cambridge, Mass.: Ballinger Publishing, 1983.

Bergstrom, Robin P. "Why Nothing Runs like a Deere." *Production,* December 1989, pp. 70–74.

Browne, Jimmy; John Harhen; and James Shiunan. *Production Management Systems: A CIMS Perspective.* Reading, Mass.: Addison-Wesley, 1988.

"Costing the Factory of the Future." *The Economist,* March 3, 1990, pp. 61–64.

Cusumano, Michael A. "Manufacturing Innovation: Lessons from the Japanese Auto Industry." *Sloan Management Review,* Fall 1988, pp. 29–39.

Dhavale, Dileep G. "Indirect Costs Take on Greater Importance, Require New Accounting Methods for CIMS." *Industrial Engineering,* July 1988, pp. 41–44.

Gomory, Ralph E., and Roland W. Schmitt. "Step-by-Step Innovation." *Across the Board,* November 1988, pp. 52–57.

Groover, M. P., and E. W. Zimmers, Jr. *CAD/CAM: Computer-Aided Design and Manufacturing.* Englewood Cliffs, N.J.: Prentice-Hall, 1984.

Haas, E. "Breakthrough Manufacturing." *Harvard Business Review* 2 (March/April 1987), pp. 75–81.

Hales, H. L. "How Small Firms Can Approach, Benefit from Computer-Integrated Manufacturing Systems." *Industrial Engineering,* June 1984, pp. 43–51.

Harrington, Joseph J. *Understanding the Manufacturing Process.* New York: Marcel Dekker, Inc., 1984.

Hayes, R. H., and S. Wheelwright. "The Dynamics of Process-Product Life Cycles." *Harvard Business Review,* March-April, 1979, pp. 127–36.

________. Hayes, R. H., and S. Wheelwright. *Restoring Our Competitive Edge: Competing through Manufacturing.* New York: John Wiley & Sons, 1984.

Koenig, Daniel T. *Computer Integrated Manufacturing: Theory and Practice.* New York: Hemisphere Publishing Company, 1990.

Kusiak, A. *Artificial Intelligence: Implications for CIMS.* Bedford, Mass.: IFS, 1988.

Michel, Frederick J., and Mark D. Pardue. "Survey of World-Class CIM Planning: Information Architecture First." *Computer Integrated Manufacturing Review,* Summer 1990, pp. 17–24.

Monden, Yasuhiro. *Toyota Production System.* Norcross, Ga.: Industrial Engineering and Management Press, Institute of Industrial Engineers, 1983.

Peters, T. J., and R. W. Waterman. *In Search of Excellence: Lessons from America's Best Run Companies:* New York: Harper & Row, 1982.

Ranky, Paul G. *Computer Integrated Manufacturing: An Introduction with Case Studies.* Englewood Cliffs, N.J.: Prentice-Hall, 1985.

Sheridan, John H. "State of the Art CIM in 18 Months? Motorola's 'Operation Bandit'." *Industry Week,* December 5, 1988, pp. 76–78.

Singhal, K.; C. H. Fine; J. R. Meredith; and R. Suri. "Research and Models for Automated Manufacturing," *Interfaces* 17, no. 6 (November–December 1987), pp. 5–14.

Chapter 4

Product Design and Process Selection—Services

EPIGRAPH

Often, the product is the smallest part of what the customer buys. It's the service, or manner in which the product is delivered.

CHAPTER OUTLINE

KEY TERMS

Service Package
Facilities-Based Services
Field-Based Services
Pure Service
Quasi-Manufacturing Service
Mixed Service
Service-System Design Matrix
Service Blueprint

Why do we go out for breakfast and pay $4.75 for eggs, toast, and coffee, when we can make this at home for 75 cents? Obviously, what we are really buying is 75 cents worth of product and $4.00 worth of service. Recognize, though, that the service includes the environment, waiters and waitresses, other customers, and so on. Albrecht and Zemke's *Service America!* gets to the heart of the issue of managing service operations in stating: Every time a customer comes into contact with any aspect of the company it is a "moment of truth," and it can create either a positive or a negative impression about the company.[1] How well these moments of truth are managed depends on a carefully designed service delivery system.

In this chapter, we address the issue of service design, using the notion of customer contact as a way of distinguishing important operational features of any service organization. Specifically, we look at differences between high- and low-contact systems, the operations manager's job within high-contact systems, and a service system design matrix that shows how different forms of contact affect production efficiency and sales opportunity. We also present a tool for designing the detailed steps of a service—the service blueprint—and present three contrasting service design options. At the end of this chapter we present a discussion of a service organization that is familiar to many readers of this book—Kinko's Copier Stores.

4.1 THE NATURE AND IMPORTANCE OF SERVICES

Our study of the nature of services leads to seven generalizations about what must be considered a vast topic.

1. Everyone is an expert on services. We all think we know what we want from a service organization and, by the very process of living, we have a good deal of experience with the service creation process.
2. Services are idiosyncratic—what works well in providing one kind of service may prove disastrous in another. For example, consuming a restaurant meal in less than half an hour may be exactly what you want at Jack-in-the-Box but be totally unacceptable at an expensive French restaurant.
3. Quality of work is not quality of service. An auto dealership may do good work on your car, but it may take a week to get the job done.
4. Most services contain a mix of tangible and intangible attributes that

---

[1] Jan Carlzon, president, Scandinavian Airlines, quoted in Karl Albrecht and Ron Zemke, *Service America! Doing Business in the New Economy* (Homewood, Ill.: Dow Jones-Irwin, 1985), p. 19.

constitute a **service package,** and this package requires different approaches to design and management than the production of goods.

5. High-contact services (described later) are *experienced,* whereas goods are *consumed.*
6. Effective management of services requires an understanding of marketing and personnel, as well as operations.
7. Many services are heavy users of automated technologies (see Exhibit 4.1).

Exhibit 4.2 presents some assorted facts about the impact of services on our economy.

EXHIBIT 4.1

Examples of Automation in Service Industries

Service Industry	Example
Financial services	Electronic funds transfer systems Automatic teller machines MasterCard II—the electronic checkbook IBM 3890 encoded cheque processor machine Pneumatic delivery systems Automated trust portfolio analysis
Utility / government services	Automated one-person garbage trucks Optical mail scanners Electronic computer-originated mail Mail sorting machines Electric power generating plants Airborne warning and control systems
Communication / electronic services	Information systems Two-way cable television Teleconferencing / picturephone Telephone switching systems Phone answering machines Word processing Photocopiers Voice-actuated device
Transportation services	Air traffic control systems Auto-pilot Boeing 747 Automatic toll booths Space shuttle Containerization France's RTV trains Ship navigation systems Bay Area Rapid Transit system
Health care services	CAT scanners Pacemakers Fetal monitors Ambulance electronic dispatching systems Electronic beepers Dentists' chair system Medical information systems

EXHIBIT 4.1

Concluded

Service Industry	Example
Education services	Personal / home computers Audiovisual equipment Speak and Spell / Speak and Read Electronic calculators Language translation computers Library cataloging systems
Restaurant / food services	Supermarket optical checkout scanners Assembly line / rotating service cafeterias Automatic french fryer Vending machines
Wholesale / retail trade	Telemarketing Point-of-sale electronic terminals Dry cleaner's conveyors Automatic window washers Newspaper dispenser Automatic car wash Automated distribution warehouse Automated security systems
Hotel / motel services	Electronic reservation systems Elevators / escalators / conveyors Automatic sprinkler systems Electronic key / lock system
Leisure services	Television games Video disc machines Movie projectors Disney World (Hall of Presidents, Country Bear Jamboree, Circle-Vision 360) Beach surf rake

Source: David A. Collier, "The Service Sector Revolution: The Automation of Services," *Long Range Planning* 16, no. 6 (December 1983), p. 11–13.

Cycle of Good Service

What is good service? Good service often means doing something extra. The Insert suggests how a customer who feels hassled can be treated.[2]

Providing good service gives many benefits throughout the entire firm. Exhibit 4.3, for example, shows that good service leads to employee retention and customer retention and also generates higher profits. Happy employees help create happy customers, which, in the next cycle reinforce the happy employees, and so on.

[2] Timothy W. Firnstahl, "My Employees Are My Service Guarantee," *Harvard Business Review*, July–August 1989, pp. 28–32.

EXHIBIT 4.2

Some Facts about Services

- In 1985, 69 percent of the U.S. GNP resulted from services—a 4 percent increase in 10 years. During the same time the contribution from manufacturing decreased by 2 percent.
- In 1986, the number of persons employed increased by 2.5 million; 87 percent of this increase was in services.
- In 1986, 75 percent of all U.S. workers were employed in service-producing jobs.
- Services have increased their employment share 6 percent between 1975 and 1985.
- More than half of all U.S. service workers are employed in white-collar, often highly skilled, occupations.
- Foreign trade in 1986:
  - The United States reported $133.8 billion of service trade.
  - Services netted a $33.1 billion surplus.
  - The trade surplus in services has grown by 200 percent since 1976.
- Of the total investment in new plants and equipment made in 1985, 73 percent was from the service sector.
- In 1986, the number of service companies rose by 2.4 percent and accounted for every one of the 10 fastest-growing business categories. The top five were health clubs (28 percent increase), beauty shops (16 percent), doctors/health services (15 percent), investment management/other (14 percent), and hotels/lodging (12 percent).
- Mac attack (some statistics on McDonald's):
  - Average number on payroll: 500,000 people.
  - Number of workers employed over past 30 years: 8 million (7 percent of the entire U.S. work force, or 1 out of every 15 American workers).
  - Largest job training organization in the United States (the U.S. Army is number two).

INSERT The Hassle Factor

Imagine you've bought a new pair of shoes at a downtown store. A week later, one sole starts to come off, so you take them back. You drive downtown through heavy traffic and spend 15 minutes finding a parking place. You explain the problem to the salesman, who says, "We stand behind our merchandise." He gives you a new pair of shoes.

Question One: Are you happy?

Answer: Well, no, you're not. Sure, you got a new pair of shoes, and the salesman was pleasant enough, but you had to take time out of your day and go to a lot of trouble to get what you should have gotten in the first place. In short, the whole transaction was a hassle, and neither the salesman nor the store did anything to make it up to you.

Question Two: What should they have done?

Answer: Replace plus one. Besides giving you a new pair of shoes, the salesman should have thrown in a pair of socks or stockings to repay you for your hassle. Instead of, "We'll replace inferior merchandise whenever a customer complains," the store's message should be, "We really regret your inconvenience and want to make you happy."

Like the shoe store, we stand behind our products and services. Unlike the shoe store, we'll do more than the customer demands to make it right. If a guest doesn't like her salad, don't charge her for it. But what about the Hassle Factor?

Replace plus one. By all means, give her the salad free of charge. But buy her a drink or dessert as well—or whatever else it takes to make her happy.

Source: Adapted from the restaurant training manual.

EXHIBIT 4.3

The Cycles of Good and Poor Service

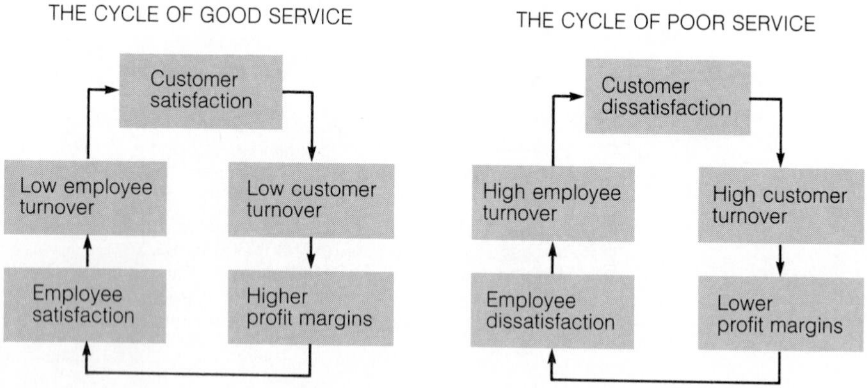

Source: Patricia Sellers, "What Customers Really Want," *Fortune*, June 4, 1990, p. 59.

Service Businesses and Internal Services

Service Operations management issues exist in two broad organizational contexts:

1. *Service business,* the management of organizations whose primary business requires interaction with the customer to produce the service. These include such familiar services as banks, airlines, hospitals, law firms, retail stores, restaurants, and so on. Within this category, we can make a further major distinction: **facilities-based services,** where the customer must go to the service facility, and **field-based services,** where production and consumption of the service take place in the customer's environment (e.g., cleaning and repair services).

Technology has allowed for the transfer of many facility-based services to field-based services. Dental vans bring the dentist to your home. Some auto repair services have repair-mobiles. Telemarketing brings the shopping center to your TV screen.

2. *Internal services,* the management of services required to support the activities of the larger organization. These services include such functions as

data processing, accounting, engineering, and maintenance. Their customers are the various departments within the organization that require such services. Incidentally, it is not uncommon for an internal service to start marketing its services outside the parent organization and become a service business itself.

Our emphasis in this chapter is on service businesses, but most of the ideas apply equally well to internal services.

Service Product Design and Development Sequence

Starting a new service business typically entails the following sequence:

1. *Idea generation.* What niche in the market is not being filled?
2. *Definition of service package.* What tangible and intangible features define the service?
3. *Process selection.* How is the service package to be produced?
4. *Worker requirements.* What jobs and skills are needed?
5. *Facilities requirements.* How many facilities are needed and where are they to be located?

Several major factors distinguish the sequence of developing a service product from manufacturing. First, the process and the product must be developed simultaneously; indeed, in services, the product *is* the process. Second, although equipment and software that support a service can be protected by patents and copyrights, a service operation itself lacks the legal protection commonly available to goods production. Third, the service package, rather than a definable good, constitutes the major output of the development process. Fourth, many parts of the service package are often "defined" by the training individuals receive before they become part of the service organization. In particular, in professional service organizations (PSOs) such as law firms and hospitals, prior certification is necessary for hiring. Fifth, many service organizations can change their service offerings virtually overnight. Routine service organizations (RSOs) such as barbershops, retail stores, and restaurants, have this flexibility.

4.2 AN OPERATIONAL CLASSIFICATION OF SERVICES

Services systems are generally classified according to the service they provide (financial services, health services, transportation services, and so on). These groupings, though useful in presenting aggregate economic data, are not particularly appropriate for OM purposes because they tell us little about the process. In manufacturing, by contrast, there are fairly evocative terms to classify production activities (such as *intermittent* and *continuous production*); when applied to a manufacturing setting, they readily convey the essence of the process. While it is possible to describe services in these same terms, we need one additional item of information to reflect the fact that the customer is involved in the production system. That item, which we believe operationally distinguishes one service system from another in terms of its production function, is the extent of customer contact in the creation of the service.

Service can extend from a **pure service**, where the customer is continuously part of the service system (e.g., barber shop or beauty salon), to the other extreme where most of the service is performed without the customer (e.g., insurance home office, mail services). This latter case closely resembles manufacturing and is therefore termed **quasi-manufacturing service**. In between are the **mixed services**, where customer interaction occasionally occurs for clarification and/or authorization (e.g., auto repair shops).

Customer contact refers to the physical presence of the customer in the system, and *creation of the service* refers to the work process that is involved in providing the service itself. *Extent of contact* here may be roughly defined as the percentage of time the customer must be in the system relative to the total time it takes to perform the customer service. Generally speaking, the greater the percentage of contact time between the service system and the customer, the greater the degree of interaction between the two during the production process.

From this conceptualization, it follows that service systems with a high degree of customer contact are more difficult to control and more difficult to rationalize than those with a low degree of customer contact. In high-contact systems, such as those listed in Exhibit 4.4, the customer can affect the time of demand, the exact nature of the service, and the quality of service since the

EXHIBIT 4.4

Service Systems Classified by Extent of Customer Contact Required to Create Service Product

Pure Services (typically high contact)	Mixed Services (typically medium contact)	Quasi-manufacturing (typically low contact)
Entertainment centers	"Branch" offices of:	"Home" offices of:
Health centers	Financial institutions	Financial institutions
Hotels	Government	Government
Public transportation	Computer firms	Law firms
Retail establishments	Law firms	Ad agencies
Schools	Ad agencies	Real estate firms
Personal services	Real estate firms	Wholesale houses
Jails	Park service	Postal service
Copy centers	Police and fire departments	Mail order services
	Janitorial services	News syndicates
	Moving companies	Research laboratories
	Repair shops	
	Funeral homes	

Increasing freedom in designing efficient production procedures →

customer tends to become involved in the process itself. In low-contact systems, by definition, customer interaction with the system is infrequent or short and hence affects the system little during the production process.

Technical Core

One way to conceive of high- versus low-contact business is that a low-contact system has the capability of decoupling operations and sealing off the "technical core" from the environment, while the high-contact system does not. Indeed, decoupling production from outside influences (for example, via inventory buffers) is a common objective in designing manufacturing systems.

Effect on Operations

Why is it important to determine how much customer contact is required to provide a service? Because it has an effect on every decision that production managers must make. Exhibit 4.5 lists some of the key decisions of system design. The points made in this exhibit lead to four generalizations about the two classes of services systems.

First, high-contact systems have more uncertainty about their day-to-day operations, since the customer can always make an input to (or cause a disruption in) the production process. Even in high-contact systems with relatively specified products and processes, customers can "have it their way." McDonald's will fill special orders, a hospital operating-room schedule will be disrupted for emergency surgery, and so on.

Second, unless the system operates on an appointment-only basis, it is only by happenstance that the capacity of a high-contact system will match the demand on that system at any given time. The manager of a supermarket, branch bank, or entertainment facility can predict only statistically the number of people that will be in line demanding service at, say, 2:00 on Tuesday afternoon. Hence, employing the correct number of staff (neither too many nor too few) must also depend on probability.

Low-contact systems, on the other hand, have the potential to more closely match supply and demand for their services since the work to be done (forms to be completed, credit ratings analyzed, or household goods shipped) can be carried out following a resource-oriented schedule that permits a direct equivalency between producer and product.

Third, by definition, the required skills of the work force in high-contact systems are characterized by a significant public relations component. Any interaction with the customer makes the direct workers in fact part of the product and, therefore, their attitude can affect the customer's view of the service provided.

Finally, high-contact systems are at the mercy of time far more than low-contact systems. Batching of orders for purposes of efficient production sched-

EXHIBIT 4.5

Major Differences between High- and Low-Contact Systems

Decision	High-Contact System	Low-Contact System
Facility location	Operations must be near the customer	Operations may be placed near supply, transport, or labor
Facility layout	Facility should accommodate the customer's physical and psychological needs and expectations.	Facility should focus on production efficiency.
Product design	Environment as well as the physical product define the nature of the service.	Customer is not in the service environment so the product can be defined by fewer attributes.
Process design	Stages of production process have a direct, immediate effect on the customer.	Customer is not involved in majority of processing steps.
Scheduling	Customer is in the production schedule and must be accommodated.	Customer is concerned mainly with completion dates.
Production planning	Orders cannot be stored, so smoothing production flow will result in loss of business.	Both backlogging and production smoothing are possible.
Worker skills	Direct work force constitutes a major part of the service product and so must be able to interact well with the public.	Direct work force need only have technical skills.
Quality control	Quality standards are often in the eye of the beholder and hence variable.	Quality standards are generally measurable and hence fixed.
Time standards	Service time depends on customer needs, and therefore time standards are inherently loose.	Work is performed on customer surrogates (e.g., forms), thus time standards can be tight.
Wage payment	Variable output requires time-based wage systems.	"Fixable" output permits output-based wage systems.
Capacity planning	To avoid lost sales, capacity must be set to match peak demand.	Storable output permits capacity at some average demand level.
Forecasting	Forecasts are short-term, time-oriented.	Forecasts are long-term, output-oriented.

uling is rarely possible in high-contact operations since a few minutes' delay or a violation of the law of the queue (first-come, first-served) has an immediate effect on the customer. Indeed, "unfair" preferential treatment in a box office line often gives rise to some of the darker human emotions, which are rarely evoked if the same unfair preferential treatment is employed by a distant ticket agency where the preference goes unobserved by the customer.

Implications for Operations

Several implications may be drawn from the differences between high-contact and low-contact systems. First, rationalizing the operations of a high-contact system can be carried only so far. While technological devices can be substituted for some jobs performed by direct-contact workers, the workers' attitude, the environment of the facility, and the attitude of the customer will determine the ultimate quality of the service experience.

Second, the often-drawn distinction between for-profit and not-for-profit services has little, if any, meaning from a production management standpoint. A not-for-profit home office can be operated as efficiently as a for-profit home office; conversely, a high-contact, for-profit branch is subject to the same inherent limitations on its efficiency as its not-for-profit counterparts.

Third, wherever possible a distinction should be made between the high-contact and low-contact elements of a service system. This can be done by a separation of functions: all high-contact activities should be performed by one group of people, all low-contact activities by another. This minimizes the influence of the customer on the production process and provides opportunities to achieve efficiency where it is actually possible.

Fourth, separation of functions enhances the development of two contrasting classes of worker skills and orientations: public relations and interpersonal attributes for high-contact purposes, and technical and analytical attributes for low-contact purposes. While some writers have urged mixing of duties under the general heading of job enrichment, a careful analysis before doing so seems warranted when one recognizes the considerable differences in the skills required.

Application of the Concept

Typical service organizations have been placed under headings of *pure service, mixed service,* or *quasi-manufacturing,* according to their dominant service product. However, since most service systems are really a mixture of high and low contact, the following four steps can be used to analyze any service organization.

1. Identify those points in the service system where decoupling is possible and desirable. (It will be necessary to trade off cost savings from operations improvement against marketing losses that result from changes in the nature of the service.)
2. Employ contact-reduction strategies where appropriate.
3. Employ contact-enhancement strategies where appropriate.
4. Employ traditional efficiency improvement techniques (production control, industrial engineering, etc.) to improve low-contact operations.

EXHIBIT 4.6

Contact Reduction and Improvement Strategies

Contact reduction strategies

- Handle only exceptions on a face-to-face basis; all other transactions by phone, or better yet by mail.
- Use reservations or appointments-only systems.
- Decentralize using kiosks with one person for information handling (this takes pressure off the main facility).
- Use drop-off points such as automatic teller machines.
- Bring service to customer through postal rounds or mobile offices.
- Use a roving greeter or signs outside facility to act as buffers and information providers.

Contact improvement strategies

- Take-a-number systems.
- Assign contact workers who are people-oriented and knowledgeable about service system processes and policies.
- Maintain consistent work hours.
- Partition back office from the public service counter; do not permit work breaks in front of the customer.
- Provide queueing patterns and signs to indicate standardized and customized service channels.

Low-contact improvement strategies (for back office or home office)

- Establish control points for items entering and leaving departments (log times and quantities to control work in process and provide a basis for capacity planning).
- Process standard items in an assembly-line mode; customized items as whole tasks.
- Utilize manufacturing-based concepts such as standard times, cost centers, acceptance sampling techniques, and resource-oriented scheduling and dispatching criteria.

Source: Richard B. Chase, "The Customer Contact Approach to Services: Theoretical Bases and Practical Extensions," *Operations Research* 29, no. 4 (1981), p. 704.

In carrying out Steps 2, 3, and 4, a number of widely used, common-sense heuristics come to mind (Exhibit 4.6). The interesting thing is that a "contact" view of the world will lead the system designer or manager directly to them. On the other hand, without this perspective few organizations are likely to apply them all, or seek out others.

4.3 A SYSTEMS VIEW OF HIGH-CONTACT SERVICES

Exhibit 4.7 illustrates the major components and activities of a high-contact service operation and the role of the service operations manager in their coordination. Starting at the bottom of the figure, we see the service package—that combination of tangible and intangible elements and benefits that work together to specify the service. The service package derives from the company's business strategy and should reflect the company's quality and cost

EXHIBIT 4.7 **A Systems View of High-Contact Service Operations**

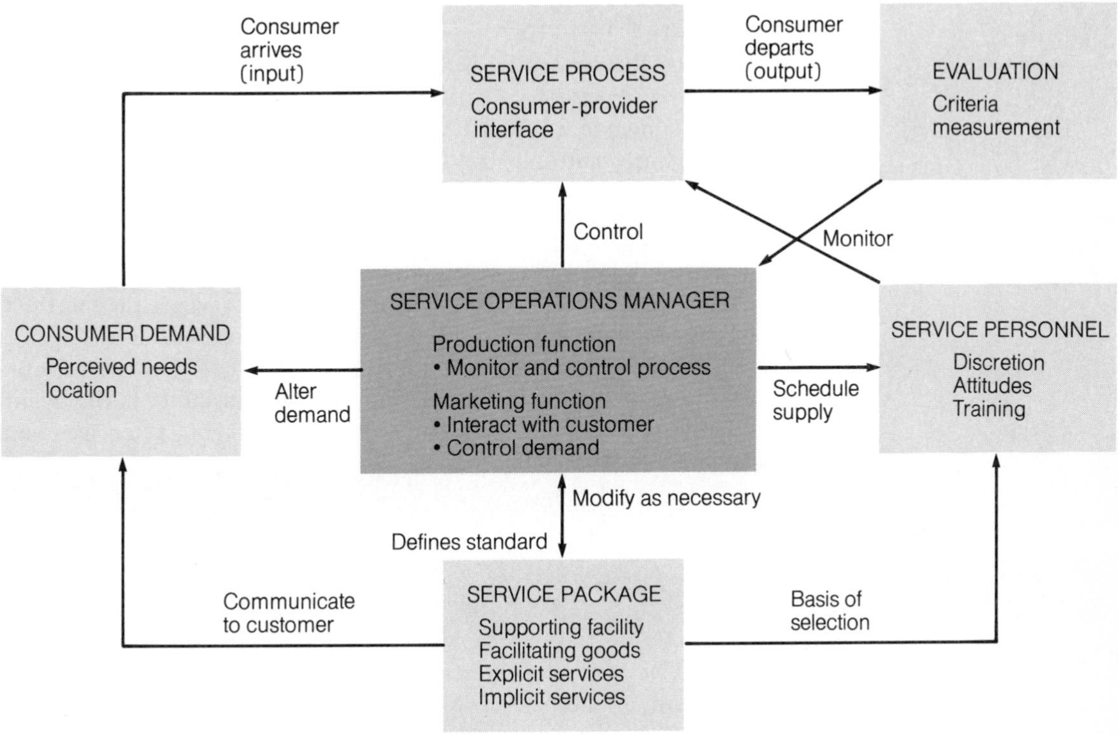

Source: Modified from James A. Fitzsimmons and Robert S. Sullivan, *Service Operations Management* (New York: McGraw-Hill, 1982), p. 27.

objectives. Fitzsimmons and Sullivan define the specific features of the service package as follows:[3]

1. *Supporting facility*. The physical resources that must be in place before a service can be offered. Examples are a golf course, ski lift, hospital, or airplane.
2. *Facilitating goods*. The material purchased or consumed by the buyer or items provided by the consumer. Examples are golf clubs, skis, food items, replacement auto parts, legal documents, or medical supplies.

[3] James A. Fitzsimmons and Robert S. Sullivan, *Service Operations Management* (New York: McGraw-Hill, 1982), pp. 17–19.

3. *Explicit services.* The benefits that are readily observable by the senses and that consist of the essential or intrinsic features of the service. Examples are the quality of instruction, smoothness of ride, or response time of the fire department.
4. *Implicit services.* Psychological benefits which the consumer may sense only vaguely or extrinsic features ancillary to the service. Examples are the status of a degree from an Ivy League school, privacy of a loan office, or worry-free auto repair.

The service package is communicated to the consumer and is used as the basis for selecting service personnel. The consumer's perceived needs and the locational availability of the service generate demand for the service. This demand results in consumers entering the service process, where they interact with service personnel to create the service. The service operations manager is at the center of things—carrying out both a production management function and a marketing management function. This dual responsibility is the major distinction between managing manufacturing or low-contact services and managing high-contact services.

4.4 SERVICE-SYSTEM DESIGN MATRIX

Customer contact with the service system can be configured in a number of different ways. The **service-system design matrix** shown in Exhibit 4.8 identifies six common alternatives.

The top of the matrix shows the degree of customer/server contact: the *buffered core,* which is physically separated from the customer; the *permeable system,* which is penetrable by the customer via phone or face-to-face contact; and the *reactive system,* which is both penetrable and reactive to the customer's requirements. The left-hand side of the matrix shows what we believe to be a logical marketing proposition, namely, that the greater the amount of contact, the greater the sales opportunity; the right-hand side shows the impact on production efficiency as the customer exerts more influence on the operation.

The entries within the matrix list the ways in which service can be delivered. At one extreme, service contact is by mail; customers have little interaction with the system. At the other extreme, customers "have it their way," through face-to-face contact. The remaining four entries in the exhibit contain varying degrees of interaction.

As one would guess, production efficiency decreases as the customer has more contact (and therefore more influence) on the system. To offset this, however, the face-to-face contact provides high sales opportunity to sell additional products. Conversely, low contact, such as mail, allows the system to work more efficiently because the customer is unable to significantly affect (or disrupt) the system. However, there is relatively little sales opportunity for additional product sales.

EXHIBIT 4.8 **Service-System Design Matrix**

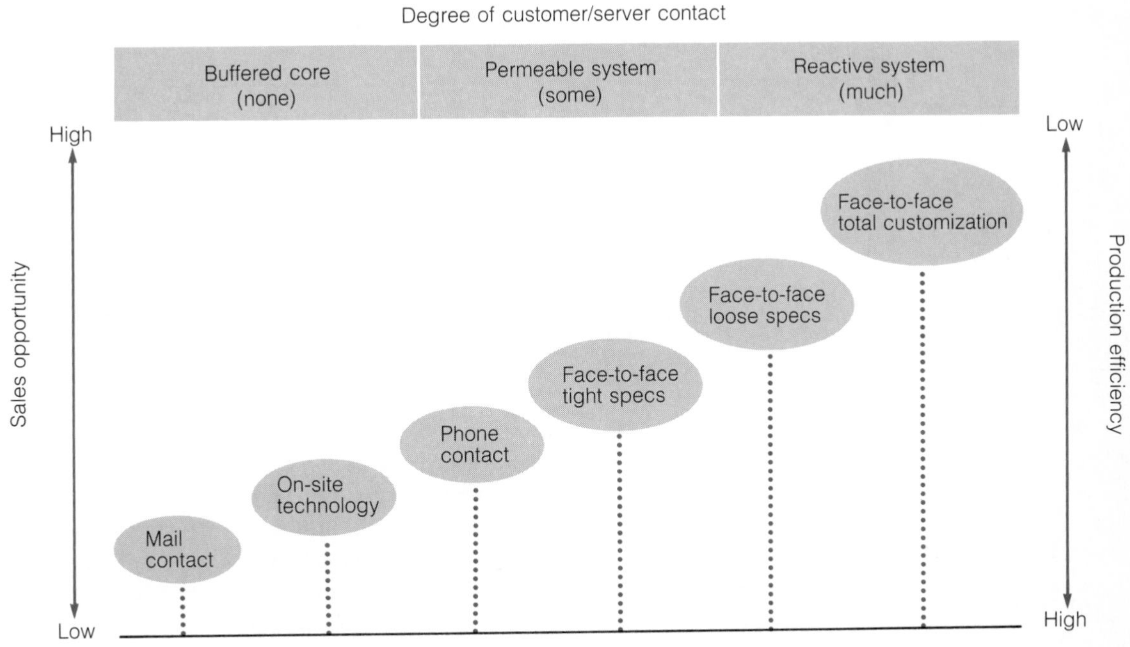

There can be some shifting in the positioning of each entry. Consider the Exhibit 4.8 entry "face-to-face tight specs." This refers to those situations where there is little variation in the service process—neither customer nor server has much discretion in creating the service. Fast-food restaurants and Disneyland come to mind. Face-to-face loose specs refers to situations where the service process is generally understood but there are options in the way it will be performed or the physical goods that are a part of it. A full-service restaurant or a car sales agency are examples. Face-to-face total customization refers to service encounters whose specifications must be developed through some interaction between the customer and server. Legal and medical services are of this type, and the degree to which the resources of the system are mustered for the service determines whether the system is reactive or merely permeable. Examples would be the mobilization of an advertising firm's resources in preparation for an office visit by a major client, or an operating team scrambling to prepare for emergency surgery.

Exhibit 4.9 extends the design matrix. It shows the changes in workers, operations, and types of technical innovations as the degree of customer/service system contact changes. For worker requirements, the relationship between mail contact and clerical skills, on-site technology and helping skills,

EXHIBIT 4.9 **Characteristics of Workers, Operations, and Innovations Relative to the Degree of Customer/Service Contact**

Degree of customer/server contact

Low ← → High

Worker requirements	Clerical skills	Helping skills	Verbal skills	Procedural skills	Trade skills	Diagnostic skills
Focus of operations	Paper handling	Demand management	Scripting calls	Flow control	Capacity management	Client mix
Technological Innovations	Office automation	Routing methods	Computer databases	Electronic aids	Self-serve	Client/worker teams

and phone contact and verbal skills, are self-evident. Face-to-face tight specs requires procedural skills in particular, because the worker must follow the routine in conducting a generally standardized, high-volume process. Face-to-face loose specs frequently calls for trade skills (shoemaker, draftsperson, maitre d', dental hygienist) to "finalize" the design for the service. Face-to-face total customization tends to call for diagnostic skills of the professional to ascertain the needs or desires of the client.

4.5 SERVICE BLUEPRINTING

A useful tool for specifying the precise details of a service is the **service blueprint** developed by G. Lynn Shostack. She describes the steps involved:[4]

1. *Identifying processes.* The first step in creating such a blueprint is mapping the processes that constitute the service. Exhibit 4.10 maps a shoeshine parlor. As the service is simple and clear-cut, the map is straightforward.

2. *Isolating fail points.* Having diagrammed the processes involved, the designer can now see where the system might go awry. The shoeshiner may pick up and apply the wrong color wax. So the designer must build in a subprocess to correct this possible error. The identification of fail points and the design of fail-safe processes are critical. The consequences of service failures can be greatly reduced by analyzing fail points at the design stage.

3. *Establishing time frame.* Since all services depend on time, which is usually the major cost determinant, the designer should establish a standard execution time.

[4] G. Lynn Shostack, "Designing Services That Deliver," *Harvard Business Review* (January/February 1984), p. 135.

EXHIBIT 4.10 **Blueprint for a Corner Shoeshine**

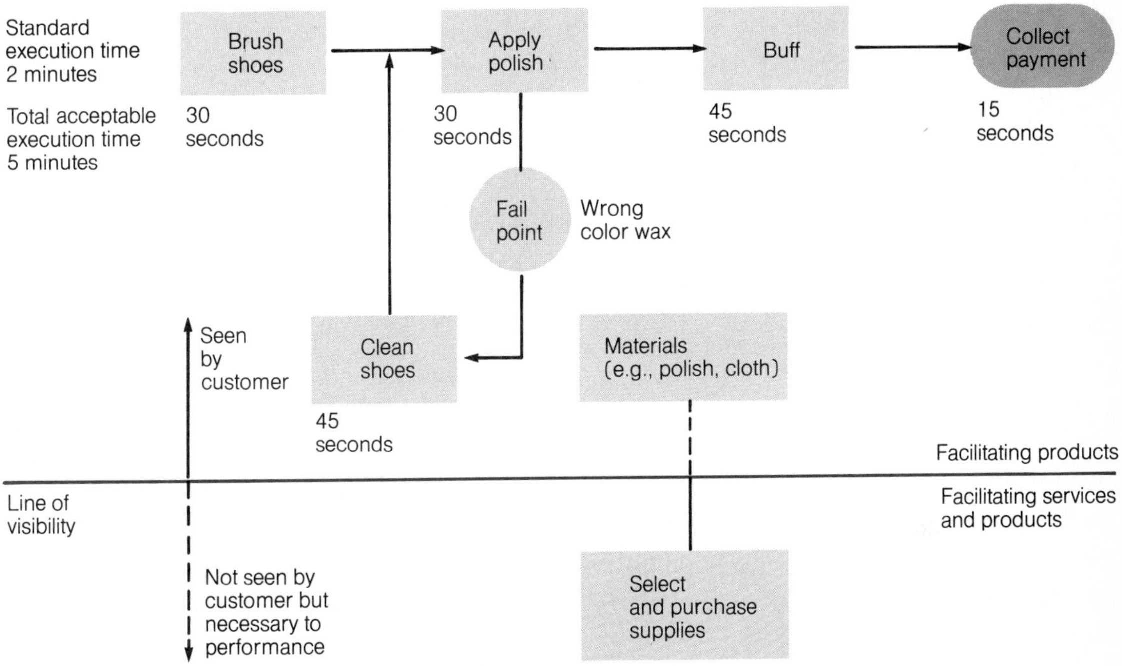

Source: G. Lynn Shostack, "Designing Services That Deliver," *Harvard Business Review* (January/February 1984), p. 134.

EXHIBIT 4.11

Shoeshine Profitability Analysis

		EXECUTION TIME		
		2 minutes	3 minutes	4 minutes
Price		$.50	$.50	$.50
Costs	Time @ $.10 per minute	.20	.30	.40
	Wax	.03	.03	.03
	Other operating expenses	.09	.09	.09
Total costs		$.32	$.42	$.52
Pretax profit		$.18	$.08	($.02)

Source: G. Lynn Shostack, "Designing Services That Deliver," *Harvard Business Review* (January/February 1984), p. 135.

In the shoeshine example, the standard execution time is two minutes. Research showed that the customer would tolerate up to five minutes of performance before lowering his or her assessment of quality. Acceptable execution time for a shoeshine is then five minutes.

4. *Analyzing profitability.* The customer can spend the three minutes between standard and acceptable execution time at the corner parlor waiting in line or during service, if an error occurs or if the shoeshiner does certain things too slowly. Whatever its source, a delay can affect profits dramatically. Exhibit 4.11 quantifies the cost of delay; after four minutes the proprietor loses money. A service designer must establish a time-of-service-execution standard to assure a profitable business.

4.6 IDENTIFYING SALES OPPORTUNITIES

Blueprinting is useful for explicitly describing the production activities of a service process. However, to get the most out of the service encounter, the sales side should also be studied.

Exhibit 4.12 lists some guidelines for identifying sales opportunities.

4.7 THREE SYSTEM DESIGN OPTIONS

Although the scope of design alternatives is limitless, this section provides examples of three different design options. Each involves certain trade-offs in production efficiency and sales opportunity and each results in different operations management concerns.

Substitute Technology for People

The product design and selection process for retail service has been revolutionized by the McDonald's hamburger chain. In an insightful article, Theodore Levitt suggests that an essential feature of McDonald's success is its treating the delivery of fast food as a manufacturing process rather than a service process.[5] The value of this philosophy is that it overcomes many of the problems inherent in the concept of service itself. That is, service implies subordination or subjugation of the server to the served; manufacturing, on the other hand, avoids this connotation because it focuses on things rather than people. Thus in manufacturing and in the case of McDonald's, "the orientation is toward the efficient production of results not on the attendance on others." Levitt notes that besides McDonald's marketing and financial skills, the company carefully controls "the execution of each outlet's central function—the rapid delivery of a uniform, a high-quality mix of prepared foods in an environment of obvious cleanliness, order, and cheerful courtesy. The

[5] Theodore Levitt, "Production-Line Approach to Service," *Harvard Business Review* 50, no. 5 (September/October 1972), pp. 41–52.

EXHIBIT 4.12

General Guidelines for Looking for Sales Opportunities

Look for Sales Opportunities Where. . .

1. *Boy meets girl.*
   Customers are likely to buy more from an attractive server; in other words, sex sells. "Let's see how this necktie goes with your eyes . . . a little closer, please."
2. *Quality of the service is in the eye of the beholder.*
   The virtues of more expensive services can be advocated. "For a really unobtrusive crown, we recommend the porcelain over the gold."
3. *Expected service time is slow.*
   Customers who are more willing to listen to a sales pitch. "What do you think about our new brochure? You're the first to see it."
4. *Service time must take some minimum duration to be credible.*
   Sales pitches can be interspersed with the service. "Let me tell you about a very intelligent customer I had this morning."
5. *Customers have a favorite server.*
   There is an implicit obligation to pay for one's preferences. "Ramon is the only person I allow to cut my hair."
6. *Customization is perceived as necessary.*
   When a standardized service *looks* customized, *this* is the best of all possible worlds. "Do you want the regular Camaro logo on your pit jacket or the embroidered . . . while you wait, of course."
7. *The customer is uncertain about his/her need for the service.*
   "Ramon, do you think I need a permanent?"
8. *Price reductions can be made on the spot.*
   "For you, a very special deal today only."
9. *Excess capacity exists.*
   "My next appointment didn't come in yet, so let's go ahead and do a treadmill test."
10. *Possibility of emergency situations exists.*
    (Not advocated, but universal nonetheless.) "As long as we're replacing the muffler which fell off while you were driving, you can save time and nuisance by replacing your worn out shocks."
11. *Customer's uncertainty about the required procedure necessitates interaction.*
    "Let's go through Form A7X . . . you know, many people are combining their NOW accounts with IRAs or Keoghs."
12. *Consumption potential of involved customer is very large.*
    "Hey big spender, spend a little time with me."

systematic substitution of equipment for people, combined with the carefully planned use and positioning of technology, enables McDonald's to attract and hold patronage in proportions no predecessor or imitator has managed to duplicate."

Levitt cites several aspects of McDonald's operations to illustrate the concepts:

- The McDonald's french fryer allows cooking of the optimum number of french fries at one time.
- A wide-mouthed scoop is used to pick up the precise amount of french fries for each order size. (The employee never touches the product.)

- Storage space is expressly designed for a predetermined mix of prepackaged and premeasured products. There is no space for any foods that were not designed into the system at the outset.
- Cleanliness is pursued by providing ample trash cans in and outside each facility (and the larger outlets have motorized sweepers for the parking area).
- Hamburgers are wrapped in color-coded paper and boxes.
- Through painstaking attention to total design and facilities planning, everything is built integrally into the (McDonald's) machine itself, into the technology of the system. The only choice available to the attendant is to operate it exactly as the designers intended.

Increase Customer Involvement

In contrast to Levitt's approach, Lovelock and Young propose that the service process can be enhanced by having the customer take a greater role in the production of the service.[6] Automatic teller machines, self-service gas stations, direct long-distance dialing, and in-room coffee-making equipment in motels are approaches by which the service burden is shifted to the consumer. Obviously, this philosophy requires some selling on the part of the service organization to convince customers that this is beneficial to them. To this end, Lovelock and Young propose a number of steps, including developing customer trust, promoting the benefits in terms of cost, speed, and convenience, and following up to make sure that the procedures are being effectively used.

Put the Customer First

This is both a design option and a philosophy that can be applied with the other approaches. The following example by Tom Peters describes how Nordstrom's department store operationalizes its customer-first philosophy.[7]

> After several visits to a store's men's clothing department, a customer's suit still did not fit. He wrote the company president, who sent a tailor to the customer's office with a new suit for fitting. When the alterations were completed, the suit was delivered to the customer—free of charge.
>
> This incident involved the $1.3 billion, Seattle-based Nordstrom, a specialty clothing retailer. Its sales per square foot are about five times that of a typical department store. Who received the customer's letter and urged the extreme (by others' standards) response? Co-chairman John Nordstrom.
>
> The front-line providers of this good service are well paid. Nordstrom's salespersons earn a couple of bucks an hour more than competitors, plus a 6.75 percent

---

[6] C. H. Lovelock and R. F. Young, "Look to Customers to Increase Productivity," *Harvard Business Review* 57, no. 2, pp. 168–78.

[7] Tom Peters, *Quality!* (Palo Alto, Calif.: TPG Communications, 1986), pp. 10–12.

commission. Its top salesperson moves over $1 million a year in merchandise. Nordstrom lives for its customers and salespeople. Its only official organization chart puts the customer at the top, followed by sales and sales support people. Next come department managers, then store managers, and the board of directors at the very bottom.

Salespersons religiously carry a "personal book," where they record voluminous information about each of their customers; senior, successful salespeople often have three or four bulging books, which they carry everywhere, according to Betsy Sanders, the vice president who orchestrated the firm's wildly successful penetration of the tough southern California market. "My objective is to get one new personal customer a day," says a budding Nordstrom star. The system helps him do just that. He has a virtually unlimited budget to send cards, flowers, and thank-you notes to customers. He also is encouraged to shepherd his customer to any department in the store to assist in a successful shopping trip.

He also is abetted by what may be the most liberal returns policy in this or any other business: Return *anything,* no questions asked. Sanders says that "trusting customers," or "our bosses" as she repeatedly calls them, is vital to the Nordstrom philosophy. President Jim Nordstrom told the *Los Angeles Times,* "I don't care if they roll a Goodyear tire into the store. If they say they paid $200, give them $200 (in cash) for it." Sanders acknowledges that a few customers rip the store off—"rent hose from us," to use a common insider's line. But this is more than offset by goodwill from the 99 percent-plus who benefit from the "No Problem at Nordstrom" logo that the company lives up to with unmatched zeal.

No bureaucracy gets in the way of serving the customer. Policy? Sanders explains to a dumbfounded group of Silicon Valley executives, "I know this drives the lawyers nuts, but our whole 'policy manual' is just one sentence, 'Use your own best judgment at all times.'" One store manager offers a translation, "Don't chew gum. Don't steal from us."

4.8 CONCLUSION

Service design is still pretty much of an art, requiring an understanding of marketing, human relations, and technology, as well as operations. The future development of services appears to lie in information technology, since information exchange of one sort or another is the common thread that binds virtually all services. There is also a blurring between what we think of as manufacturing firms and what we think of as service firms. Indeed, companies such as Bally Manufacturing, RCA, Turner Construction, and Exxon Pipeline, which started out manufacturing products, are now listed among the Fortune 500 service companies.[8]

Moreover, if we reflect on the manufacturing side of such businesses, we find that the new technologies (FMS, CIM) permit the factory to compete

[8] For further discussion of applying service notions to factories see Richard B. Chase and Warren K. Erikson, "The Service Factory," *Academy of Management Executive* 2, no. 3 (August 1988), pp. 191–96.

very directly on fast, customized service. In fact, we predict that the next "hot topic" among manufacturers will be service, supplanting even quality.

4.9 REVIEW AND DISCUSSION QUESTIONS

1. Who is the "customer" in a jail? A cemetery? A summer camp for children?
2. Give examples of service firms that use the three design alternatives discussed in Section 4.7.
3. Is it possible for a service firm to substitute technology for people or use a self-serve design and still keep a high customer focus (put the customer first)? Explain and support your answer with examples.
4. Explain why a manager of a bank home office should be evaluated differently than a manager of a bank branch.
5. Identify the high-contact and low-contact operations of the following services:
   a. A dental office.
   b. An airline.
   c. An accounting office.
   d. An automobile agency.
6. It has been suggested that customer expectation is the key to service success. Give an example from your own experience to support or refute this assertion.
7. Where would you place an Automat, a campus food vending machine, and a bar's automatic mixed drink machine on the service-system design matrix?
8. What do customer expectations have to do with service system quality?

4.10 PROBLEMS

1. Place the following functions of a department store on the service-system design matrix:

   Mail order (i.e., catalog), phone order, hardware, stationery, apparel, cosmetics, customer service (i.e., complaints).
2. Do the same as in the previous problem for a hospital with the following activities and relationships:

   Physician/patient, nurse/patient, billing, medical records, lab tests, admissions, diagnostic tests (e.g., X rays).
3. The service designer for the shoeshine shop of Exhibits 4.10 and 4.11 has decided to study the following changes:
   - Add a premium two-coat service, which will repeat Steps 2 and 3 (Apply polish and Buff). The price of the premium service will be set at $.70.
   - Provide each customer (both regular and premium) with a receipt and a sample of shoe polish imprinted with the shop's name. This will add $.01 to operating expenses and 0.5 minutes to the execution time but will provide the customer with some tangible evidence of the service.

Both of these changes are to be made simultaneously. Answer the following questions:

a. Draw the blueprint for the premium service.
b. Provide a profitability analysis for the premium service.
c. Provide an updated profitability analysis for the regular service.

4. SYSTEM DESCRIPTION EXERCISE
The first step in studying a productive system is to develop a description of that system. Once a system is described, we are better able to determine why the system works well or poorly and to recommend production-related improvements. Since we are all familiar with fast-food restaurants, try your hand at describing the production system employed at, say, a McDonald's. In doing so, consider Exhibit 4.7 and organize your answer as follows:
a. What are the important aspects of the service package? What are the explicit and implicit services?
b. What skills and attitudes are needed of the service personnel?
c. How can customer demand be altered?
d. Provide a rough-cut blueprint of the delivery system. (It is not necessary to provide execution times, just diagram the basic flow through the system.) Critique the blueprint. Are there any unnecessary steps or can fail points be eliminated?
e. Can the customer/provider interface be changed to include more technology? More self-serve?
f. What measures are being used to evaluate and measure the service? What could be used?

4.11 CASE: KINKO'S COPIER STORES*

"We're not your average printer," says Annie Odell, Kinko's regional manager for Louisiana. She's right. She may have the only printshops in town where customers come as much for the company as for the copies. It's a free-wheeling, hi-tech operation that marches to the beat of a different drum machine. It looks chaotic; it is chaotic. Yet it produces profit as well as fun.

Odell's copy shop empire has grown from one to seven in six years, including five in the greater New Orleans area.

Kinko's keeps its sales figures a secret, but Odell estimates her New Orleans stores make about 40 million copies a year. At the firm's advertised 4½ cents-per copy price, that would mean around $1.8 million a year in sales, or an average of over $300,000 per shop. The New Orleans operations rank among Kinko's top 25 percent nationally, reports Becky Barieau of Kinko's of Georgia.

Sales in New Orleans have climbed even while the marketplace has been sinking. At the Carrollton store, revenues increased 10 percent over last year, an excellent showing considering the 4½ cents-per copy rate has not budged since 1980.

---

* Source: Mark Ballard, "Working in a Fishbowl," *Quick Printing* (May 1987), pp. 30–32. Reprinted by permission.

"Depression seems to generate more need for copies," says Wallis Windsor, manager of the Carrollton store, "There are bankruptcies, legal documents and resumes—hundreds of people who want 50 copies of their resumes on specialty paper."

Printers Sneer

Kinko's is unique. For one thing, it doesn't do a lick of offset printing. It makes copies, copies, and almost nothing but copies. On the side it binds, folds, staples, collates, makes pads, and takes passport photos.

Kinko's is also unique among quick printing chains in that it doesn't franchise. All 300 or so Kinko's stores are divided among a few closely held corporations, and founder Paul Orfalea holds a piece of virtually all of them. Odell explains that the company avoids franchising to ensure tight control over quality at its outlets.

Others attribute the structure to a desire to avoid the legal restrictions and paperwork demanded by setting up franchises in different states. How it's been kept together is a management feat in itself.

Even the name sticks out. The Yellow Pages list dozens of quick printers with some reference to speed in their names, often intentionally misspelled. "Kinko's" denotes a place that's . . . well, a little kinky. For the record, Orfalea, who plugged in his first photocopier when he was in college, was nicknamed by classmates as "Kinko" for his curly head of hair.

Broadway and Benihana

Kinko's management style draws on both the restaurant business and the stage. Fast copies are like fast food, say the managers. It's not just that every Big Mac is a copy of every other one. Images of eating come up again and again as they try to explain what keeps their customers coming back.

"Making copies is addictive," says Windsor, and points to her clientele of "regulars," who "have made this their office. They will spend four or five hours here although they don't spend more than $5 or $6. People have suggested we open a bar in here."

"Instant gratification is what Kinko's is offering," says another manager.

The last time managers from around the country huddled in Santa Barbara for the company "picnic," they studied looseleaf binders crammed full of floor plans for McDonald's and Benihana of Tokyo—a variation on the acclaimed art of Japanese management.

"You'd find it hard to believe," says Odell, "but Benihana is a lot like Kinko's. They're masters of efficiency. We'll try to set up the floor to get one person operating two copiers, just like Benihana puts one cook between two tables. Our paper is centrally located, just as they have all the chopping prepared ahead of time. Then there's the floater, who floats around and pops in wherever he's needed."

Both Kinko's and Benihana's use theater to attract clients, charging their employees with putting on a good show as well as putting out good service. At the Japanese restaurant, the show is the cook, who sizzles a sukiyaki right in front of your table. At Kinko's, it's the clatter of copy machines and the Charlie Chaplinlike spectacle of operators running back and forth between them.

"They do it right in front of you and you get instant quality control," says Odell, "There's no way you're going to drop that document with the customer watching you."

She deliberately displays all her machines and personnel in one big room. "We work out with the public. That's why it's fun," says Odell, "The other guys are behind closed doors.

Windsor enjoys working in a fishbowl. "My personality changes," she says. "I'll be a little more dramatic and louder than I would be in a closed group. I walk quickly. I'll wad up and throw papers a lot."

She believes customers unconsciously get into the act. "Some of the mildest-mannered people get aggressive in here. I've seen a little old lady elbow her way in ahead of people, where if she were in a bank she'd stand in line neatly."

Kinko's does no broadcast and little print advertising, counting on price and word-of-mouth to draw customers, and ambience doesn't hurt. Each Kinko's has its "regulars," who get friendly with particular operators and who favor particular machines. The area in front of the counter is strewn with typewriters, lettering machines and light tables, all the better to hook people into making themselves comfortable and coming back.

A recent addition to that melange is the customer comment form. The customer mails the postage-paid form straight to headquarters in Santa Barbara, where senior management review it and send a thank-you note to the author before routing it back to the shop manager for action. Odell has several inches of forms on file, along with notes on the follow-up calls she made to the customers.

"We don't choose our market so much as our market chooses us," she says. Each shop keeps a different mix of machines, depending on the needs of its patrons. An operator learns quickly that the Xerox 1000 series picks up blue but not yellow, while the 9000 series picks up yellow and black but not blue. Thus, the store adjoining the Tulane campus does not have a 9000 because students tend to bring in notes and books highlighted with yellow markers.

Another adaptation to the market is "Professor Publishing," a service which lets professors excerpt chapters from several books and print them up together as a single textbook. During the first two weeks of every semester, the Broadway office works virtually around-the-clock on this specialty.

Odell maintains that her managers clear all material with publishers before printing a professor's anthology. Indeed, Kinko's says it is one of the most scrupulous of the copy chains about observing copyright laws.

* * * * *

Printing in a Fishbowl

If working at the Kinko's shops in New Orleans is like working in a fishbowl, it's a two-way fishbowl where the fish are always peering back at their audience. The crazy-quilt mix of customers provides endless entertainment and a fund of oddball stories to exchange over beers. A sampling:

- One woman insisted that the manager throw away the ribbon on the self-service typewriter she'd just used, fearing that someone might try to use it to recreate her document. Another customer wanted several confidential pages typed, and asked, "Can you get me a typist who won't read them?"
- Some artists enjoy using the photocopiers for the oddest things. One woman brings in stuffed dead birds for reproduction. Another brought in a box of pecans purported to be from the backyard of a house where Tennessee Williams once lived.

- A tipsy woman, about 25 years of age, meandered in from a Mardi Gras parade, curled up next to a window, and fell asleep. There she remained for four hours, while the copiers and binding machines pounded and rattled. Manager Raynell Murphy called the home office. "What should I do?" she asked.

  "Get a picture," came the word from California, "We can use it as a promotion, you know, to show what a relaxed atmosphere we have at Kinko's."

  Finally, a hulking woman who had just bought some copies walked over to the sleeper, kicked her a couple of times, and asked, "Are you ready yet?" The sleeper arose and groggily headed out the door.

QUESTION

If you were president of Kinko's, what would you do to improve the profitability of your stores?

4.12 SELECTED BIBLIOGRAPHY

Bitran, Gabriel R., and Johannes Hoech. "The Humanization of Service: Respect at the Moment of Truth." *Sloan Management Review,* Winter 1990, pp. 89–96.

Chase, R. B. "The Customer Contact Approach to Services: Theoretical Bases and Practical Extensions." *Operations Research* 21, no. 4 (1981), pp. 698–705.

Cohen, Morris A., and Hau L. Lee. "Out of Touch with Customer Needs?" *Sloan Management Review*, Winter 1990, pp. 55–66.

Collier, D. A. *Service Management: The Automation of Services.* Reston, Va.: Reston Publishing, 1986.

Farsad, Behshid, and Ahmad K. Elshennawy. "Defining Service Quality Is Difficult for Service and Manufacturing Firms." *Industrial Engineering*, March 1989, pp. 17–20.

Firnstahl, Timothy W. "My Employees Are My Service Guarantee." *Harvard Business Review,* July–August 1989, pp. 28–33.

Fitzsimmons, J. A., and R. S. Sullivan. *Service Operations Management.* New York: McGraw-Hill, 1982.

Flint, Jerry, and William Heuslein. "An Urge to Service." *Forbes,* September 18, 1989, pp. 172–174.

Hackett, Gregory P. "Investment in Technology: The Service Sector Sinkhole?" *Sloan Management Review,* Winter 1990, pp. 97–103.

Heskett, J. L. *Managing in the Service Economy*. Cambridge, Mass.: Harvard University Press, 1986.

Peavey, Dennis E. "It's Time for a Change," *Management Accounting,* February 1990, pp. 31–35.

Shapiro, Benson P.; V. Kasturi Rangan; Rowland T. Moriarty; and Elliot B. Ross. "Manage Customers for Profits, Not Just Sales." *Harvard Business Review,* September–October 1987, pp. 101–08.

Sonnenberg, Frank K. "Service Quality: Forethought, Not Afterthought." *Journal of Business Strategy*, September–October 1989, pp. 54–57.

Wagner, William B. "Customer Service: A Competitive Covenant." *Management Decision* no. 1, pp. 5–9.

Supplement

Waiting Line Theory

EPIGRAPH

No matter which line you get in, the other line will move faster.

That the other lines move faster is known as Ettore's observation (*Harpers,* August 1974). The full version is: "The Other Line Moves Faster. This applies to all lines—bank, supermarket, toll booth, and so on. And don't try to change lines. If you do, the other line—the one you were in originally—will then move faster."

SUPPLEMENT OUTLINE

KEY TERMS

Exponential Distribution

Queue

Arrival Rate

Service Rate

After doing your shoppng at the market or department store, you proceed to the cashier area. You're shocked to find a large number of cashiers. In fact, there are more cashiers than there are customers in the store! You have no problem finding an idle cashier, so you immediately go there and do not wait in line.

While this is a great situation for you, operating a store with so many cashiers would not make good business sense. While customers may be happy, the cost of the cashiers would likely be too high because their average utilization throughout the day would be low.

Thus, we can see the basic elements that make up the waiting line problem. An excessive amount of servers eliminates waiting lines, but cost of the servers is high. If there are too few servers and the waiting lines are too long, there is a cost for the customer waiting in line. If you always had to wait a long time in a market, you would probably start going elsewhere and the store would lose your business. The key problem in waiting line analysis, then, is to decide on that delicate balance between the costs associated with the service and the costs associated with those in line waiting to be served.

When the waiting line consists of inanimate objects (such as materials, parts, or components) waiting for some sort of processing (say, on a machine), this is primarily a cost balancing problem: how long the line should be, how much in-process inventory is acceptable, how much equipment should be purchased, and so on.

To introduce you to the topic of waiting lines, we discuss the basic elements of waiting line problems and provide formulas to solve two simple (though real) types of problems. Waiting line theory is a very broad topic and applies to such diverse situations as airplanes in a holding pattern waiting permission to land to picking up a telephone and finding the line busy. Waiting line theory is used extensively in industry and is a standard tool of operations management in such areas as scheduling, machine loading, and inventory control.

A waiting line is also called a *queue*, and waiting line theory is also called *queuing theory*. Modern waiting line (or queuing) theory is based on studies during the early part of this century by A. K. Erlang, a Danish telephone engineer. In studying applications of automatic telephone switching, Erlang was concerned with the capacities and utilization of the equipment and lines.

S4.1 ECONOMICS OF THE WAITING LINE PROBLEM

As we stated above, the central problem in virtually every waiting line situation is a trade-off decision. The planner must weigh the added cost of providing more rapid service (more traffic lanes, additional landing strips, more checkout stands) against the inherent cost of waiting. Neither people nor products arriving for service are spaced evenly in time. Arrivals sometimes will be close together and other times far apart. Therefore, there will be times when a server will have several in line and other times when the server is idle.

Consider, for example, a service-yourself four-island gas station with enough pumps (servers) to accommodate an average of 220 cars per hour. Even if the average number of cars is only 160 per hour at this particular station, the system can still be saturated at times. In a gas station, as in many other facilities, service capabilities are based on the *average* number of arrivals in a given time and the *average* time needed per customer. But in practice, arrivals appear at a random rate subject to local traffic patterns, and the time needed per customer varies with the quantity of gas pumped, the dexterity of the customer, and so on. This variability in arrival rates and serving times may also have the opposite effect, resulting in periods where there are neither waiting lines nor customers at the pumps.

Frequently the cost trade-off decision is straightforward. For example, if we find that the total time our employees spend in line waiting to use a copying machine would otherwise be spent in productive activities, we could compare the cost of installing one additional machine to the value of employee time saved. The decision could then be reduced to dollar terms and the choice easily made.

On the other hand, suppose that our waiting line problem centers on demand for beds in a hospital. We can compute the cost of additional beds by summing the costs for building construction, additional equipment required, and increased maintenance. But what is on the other side of the scale? Here we

EXHIBIT S4.1

Service Capacity versus Waiting Line Trade-Off

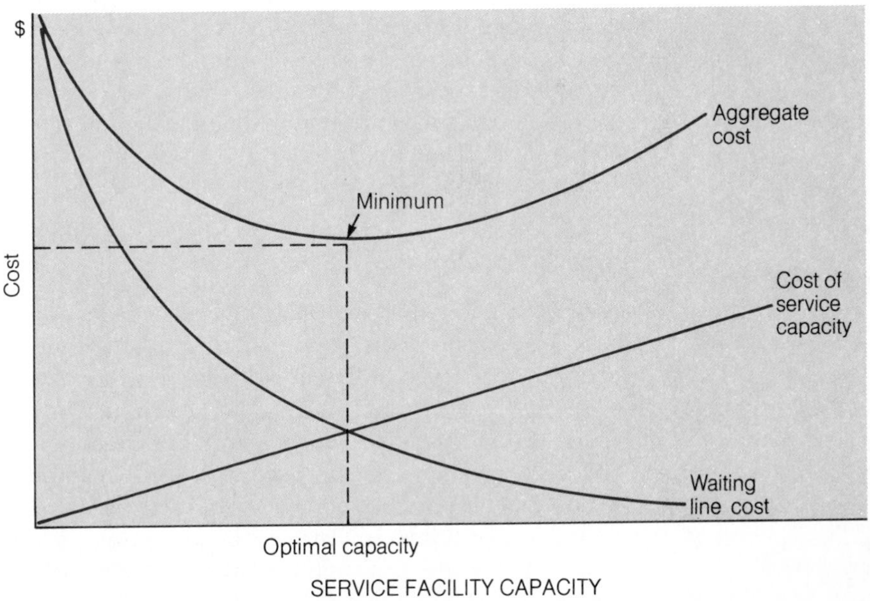

are confronted with the problem of trying to place a dollar figure on a patient's need for a hospital bed that is unavailable. While we can arrive at an estimate of lost hospital income, what about the human cost arising from this lack of adequate hospital care?

Cost Effectiveness Balance

The ultimate objective of waiting line analysis is to achieve acceptable (minimal) levels in service capacity and in costs of customer waiting time. Exhibit S4.1 illustrates the essential trade-off relationship under typical (steady-state) customer traffic conditions. Initially, with minimal service capacity, the waiting line cost is at a maximum. As service capacity is increased, there is a reduction in the number of customers in the line and in their waiting times, resulting in a decreased waiting line cost. The variation in this function is often represented by the negative exponential curve. The cost of installing service capacity is shown simplistically as a linear rather than step function. The aggregate or total cost is shown as a U-shaped curve, a common approximation in such equilibrium problems. The idealized optimal cost is found at the crossover point between the service capacity and waiting line curves.

S4.2 WAITING LINE CHARACTERISTICS

The waiting line (or queuing) phenomenon consists essentially of six major components: the source population, the way customers arrive at the service facility, the physical line itself, the way customers are selected from the line, the characteristics of the service facility itself (such as how the customers flow through the system and how much time it takes to serve each customer), and the condition of the customer exiting the system (back to the source population or not?). These six areas are shown in Exhibit S4.2 and will be discussed separately in following sections.

Population Source

Arrivals at a service system may be drawn from a *finite* or an *infinite* population. The distinction is important, since the analyses are based on different premises and require different equations for their solution.

A *finite population* refers to the limited sized "customer" pool which is the source that will use the resource, and at times form a line. The reason this finite classification is important is because when a customer leaves its position as a member of the potential population of users (by breaking down and requiring service, for example), the size of the user group is therefore reduced by one, which reduces the probability of the next breakdown. Conversely, when a customer is serviced and returns to the user group, the population increases

EXHIBIT S4.2 **Framework for Viewing Waiting Line Situations**

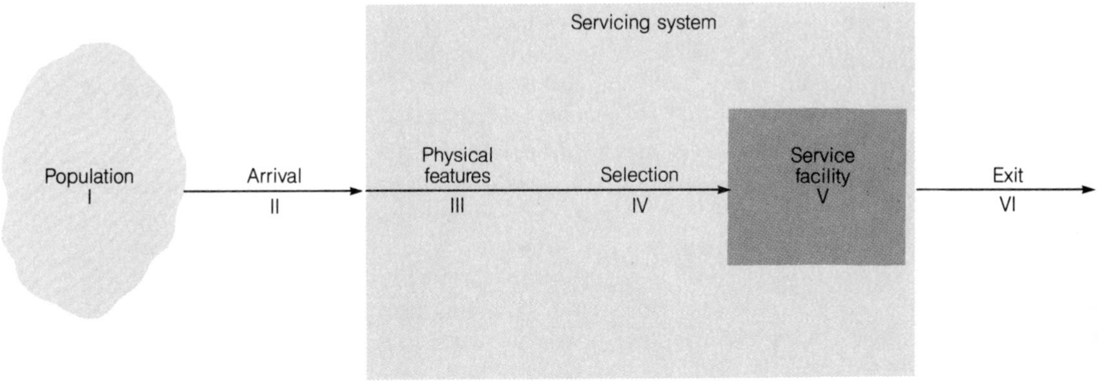

and the probability of a user requiring service also increases. This finite class of problems requires a separate set of formulas from the infinite population class.

An *infinite population* is one that is large enough in relation to the service system so that the changes in the population size caused by subtractions or additions to the population (a customer needing service or a serviced customer returning to the population) does not significantly affect the system probabilities. If, there are one hundred machines and one or two machines break down, the probabilities for the next breakdowns would not be very different and the assumption could be made without a great deal of error that the population (for all practical purposes) was infinite.

Arrival Characteristics

Another determinant in the analysis of waiting line problems is the *arrival characteristics* of the queue members. There are four main descriptors of arrivals: the *pattern of arrivals* (whether arrivals are controllable or uncontrollable); the *size of arrival units* (whether they arrive one at a time or in batches); the *degree of patience* (whether the arrival stays in line or leaves); and the *distribution pattern* (whether the time between arrivals is constant or follows a statistical distribution such as a Poisson, or exponential). We will describe each of these in more detail.

Arrivals at a system are far more *controllable* than is generally recognized. Barbers may decrease their Saturday arrival rate (and supposedly shift it to other days of the week) by charging an extra $1 for adult haircuts or charging adult prices for children's haircuts. Department stores run sales during the off season or "one-day-only" sales in part for purposes of control. Airlines offer excursion and off-season rates for similar reasons. The simplest of all arrival-control devices is the posting of business hours.

Some service demands are clearly *uncontrollable,* such as emergency medical demands on a city's hospital facilities. However, even in these situations, the arrivals at emergency rooms in specific hospitals are controllable to some extent by, say, keeping ambulance drivers in the service region informed of the status of their respective host hospitals.

A *single arrival* may be thought of as one unit (a unit is the smallest number handled). A single arrival on the floor of the New York Stock Exchange (NYSE) is 100 shares of stock; a single arrival at an egg-processing plant might be a dozen eggs or a flat of two and a half dozen.

A *batch arrival* is some multiple of the unit, as a block of 1,000 shares on the NYSE, a case of eggs at the processing plant, or a party of five at a restaurant.

A *patient* arrival is one who waits as long as necessary until the service facility is ready to serve him or her. (Even if arrivals grumble and behave impatiently, the fact that they wait is sufficient to label them as patient arrivals for purposes of waiting line theory.)

There are two classes of *impatient* arrivals. Members of the first class arrive, survey both the service facility and the length of the line, and then decide to leave. Those in the second class arrive, view the situation, and join the waiting line, and then, after some period of time, depart. The behavior of the first type is termed *balking,* and the second is termed *reneging.*

A *constant* arrival distribution is periodic, with exactly the same time period between successive arrivals (see Exhibit S4.3). In productive systems, about the only arrivals that truly approach a constant interarrival period are those that are subject to machine control. Much more common are *variable* (random) arrival distributions.

In observing arrivals at a service facility, we can look at them from two viewpoints: We can analyze the time between successive arrivals to see if the times follow some statistical distribution, or we can set some time length (T) and try to determine how many arrivals might enter the system within T. (See Exhibit S4.4.) Patterns that occur most frequently in system models are described by the *negative exponential* and *Poisson* distributions.

Exponential Distribution

In the first case, when arrivals at a service facility occur on a purely random fashion, a plot of the interarrival times yields an *exponential* distribution such as that shown in Exhibit S4.5. The probability function is

$$f(t) = \lambda e^{-\lambda t} \tag{1}$$

The cumulative area underneath the curve in Exhibit S4.5 is the summation of Equation (1) over its positive range, which is $e^{-\lambda t}$. This integral allows us to compute the probabilities of arrivals within a specified time. For example, for the case of single arrivals to a waiting line ($\lambda = 1$), the following table can be

EXHIBIT S4.3

Constant Arrival Pattern with Time Interval = *t* and Variance = 0

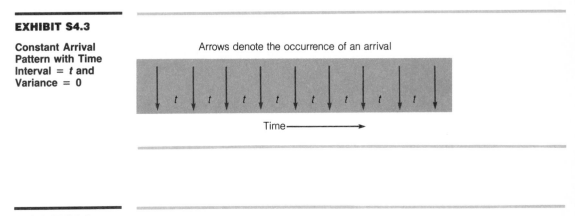

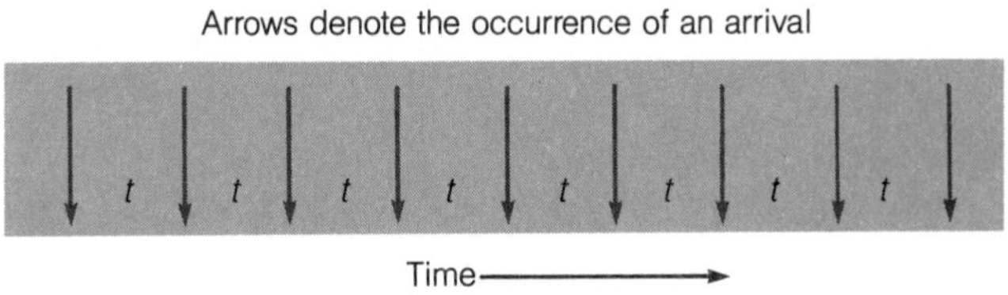

EXHIBIT S4.4

Variable Arrival Pattern

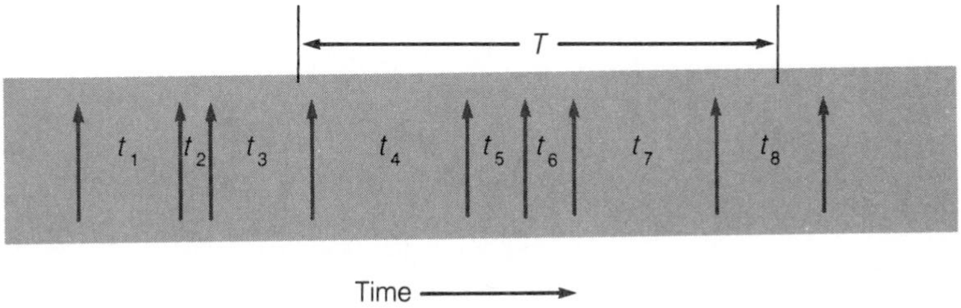

EXHIBIT S4.5

Exponential Distribution

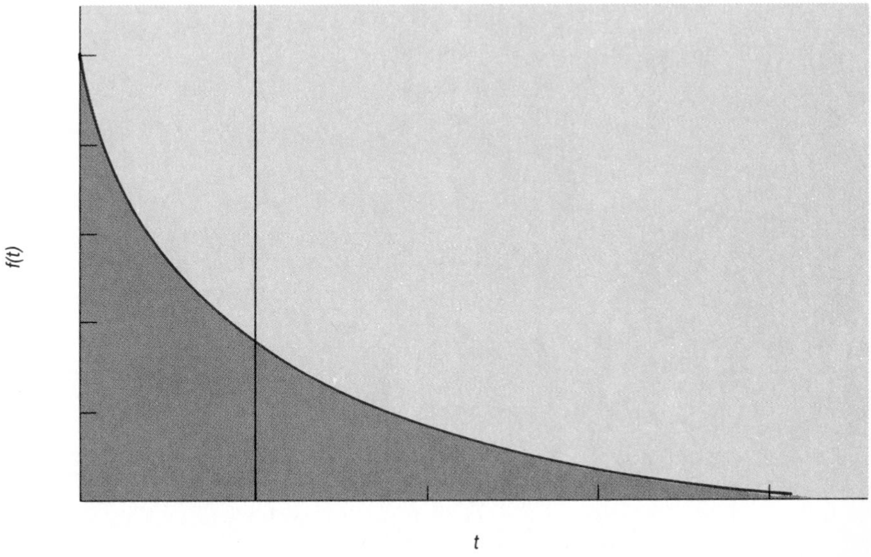

derived by solving $e^{-\lambda t}$. Column 2 shows the probability that it will be more than t minutes until the next arrival. Column 3 shows the probability of the next arrival within t minutes (computed as 1 minus Column 2).

(1) t (minutes)	(2) Probability that the next arrival will occur in t minutes or more (from solving e^{-t})	(3) Probability that the next arrival will occur in t minutes or less [1 − Column (2)]
0	1.00	0
0.5	0.61	0.39
1.0	0.37	0.63
1.5	0.22	0.78
2.0	0.14	0.86

Poisson Distribution

In the second case, where one is interested in the number of arrivals during some time period T, the distribution appears as in Exhibit S4.6 and is obtained by finding the probability of n arrivals during T. If the arrival process is random, the distribution is the *Poisson*, and the formula is:

$$P_T(n) = \frac{(\lambda T)^n e^{-\lambda T}}{n!} \qquad (2)$$

Equation (2) shows the probability of exactly n arrivals in time T. For example, if the mean arrival rate of units into a system is three per minute ($\lambda = 3$) and we want to find the probability that exactly five units will arrive within a one-minute period ($n = 5$, $T = 1$), we have

$$P_1(5) = \frac{(3 \times 1)^5 e^{-3\times 1}}{5!} = \frac{3^5 e^{-3}}{120} = 2.025e^{-3} = 0.101$$

That is, there is a 10.1 percent chance that there will be five arrivals in any one-minute interval.

Although often shown as a smoothed curve, as in Exhibit S4.6, the Poisson is a discrete distribution (the curve becomes smoother as n becomes larger). The distribution is discrete because n refers, in our example, to the number of arrivals in a system, and this must be an integer (for example, there cannot be 1.5 arrivals).

Physical Features of Lines

Length. In a practical sense, an infinite line is very long in terms of the capacity of the service system. Examples of *infinite potential length* are a line of vehicles backed up for miles at a bridge crossing, and customers who must form a line around the block as they wait to purchase tickets at a theater.

EXHIBIT S4.6 Poisson Distribution for $\lambda T = 3$

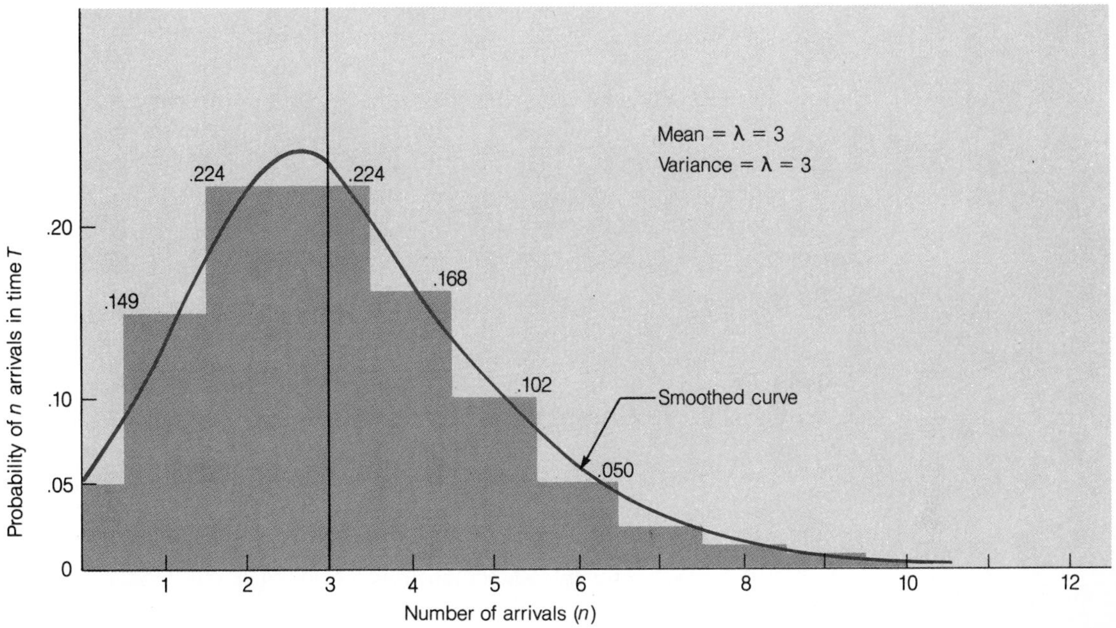

Gas stations, loading docks, and parking lots have *limited line capacity* caused by legal restrictions or physical space characteristics. This complicates the waiting line problem not only in terms of service system utilization and waiting line computations but in terms of the shape of the actual arrival distribution as well.

Number of lines. A *single line* or single file is, of course, one line only. The term *multiple lines* refers either to the single lines that form in front of two or more servers or to single lines that converge at some central redistribution point. The disadvantage of multiple lines in a busy facility is that arrivals often will shift lines if several previous services have been of short duration or if those customers currently in other lines appear to require a short service time.

Selection from the Waiting Line

Queue discipline. A queue discipline is a priority rule, or set of rules, for determining the order of service to customers in a waiting line. The rules selected can have a dramatic effect on the system's overall performance. The number of customers in line, the average waiting time, the range of variability in waiting time, and the efficiency of the service facility are just a few of the factors that are affected by the choice of priority rules.

Probably the most common priority rule is *first come, first served* (FCFS). This rule states that the customers in line are served on the basis of their chronological arrival; no other characteristics have any bearing on the selection process. This is popularly accepted as the fairest rule, even though in practice, it discriminates against the arrival requiring a short service time.

Reservations first, emergencies first, highest-profit customer first, largest orders first, best customers first, longest waiting time in line, and *soonest promised date* are other examples of priority rules. Each has attractive features as well as shortcomings.

Service Facility

The physical flow of items to be serviced may go through a single line, multiple lines, or some mixtures of the two. The choice of format depends partly on the volume of customers served and partly on the restrictions imposed by sequential requirements governing the order in which service must be performed.

A *constant* service time rule states that each service takes exactly the same time. As in constant arrivals, this characteristic is generally limited to machine-controlled operations.

The *exponential* distribution is frequently used to approximate the actual service distribution. This practice, however, may lead to incorrect results; relatively few service situations are closely represented by the exponential function since the service facility must be able to perform services much shorter than the average time of service. Telephone usage (the original subject of queuing theory) is one of the few systems that embodies this feature, and therefore, it is well approximated by the exponential. Telephone usage may range from a few seconds—where the user picks up the receiver and replaces it, having changed his or her mind about making the call, or where the user dialed the first number wrong and starts over again—to a conversation of an hour or more.

Most other types of services also have some practical minimum time. A clerk in a checkout line may have a three-minute average service time but a one-minute minimum time. This is particularly true where another checkout aisle provides a quick service. Likewise in a barbershop, while the average service time of a barber may be 20 minutes, the barber rarely cuts hair or gives a shave in less than 10 or more than 45 minutes.

Hence, these and similar types of services that have strong time dependency are poorly characterized by the exponential curve. Unfortunately, data collectors on a given problem frequently group their data in increments so that, when they are plotted as a histogram, the exponential approximation seems valid. If smaller time increments were taken, however, the inapplicability of the distribution would be obvious at the lower time values.

Exit

Once a customer is served, two exit fates are possible: (1) the customer may return to the source population and immediately become a competing candidate for service again or (2) there may be a low probability of reservice. The first case can be illustrated by a machine that has been routinely repaired and returned to duty but may break down again; the second can be illustrated by a machine that has been overhauled or modified and has a low probability of reservice over the near future. In a lighter vein, we might refer to the first as the "recurring-common-cold case" and to the second as the "appendectomy-only-once case."

It should be apparent that when the population source is finite, any change in the service performed on customers who return to the population will modify the arrival rate at the service facility. This, of course, will alter the characteristics of the waiting line under study and necessitate reanalysis of the problem.

S4.3 TWO TYPICAL WAITING LINE SITUATIONS

Problem 1: Customers in Line

A bank wants to know how many customers are waiting for a drive-in teller, how long they have to wait, the utilization of the teller, and what the service rate would have to be so that 95 percent of the time there will not be more than three cars in the system at any one time.

This waiting line example has a single line, uses first-come first-served criteria on who to serve next, assumes that the line can become very long, and assumes that the teller processes customers with an exponential time pattern (i.e., most customers take a short time but a few can be quite long).

The appropriate equations are included in the example and the definitions of the symbols are as follows:

λ = arrival rate

μ = service rate

ρ = potential utilization of the facility (equal to λ/μ)

$\bar{n}_l$ = average number waiting in line

$\bar{n}_s$ = average number in the system (including any being served)

$\bar{t}_l$ = average time waiting in line

$\bar{t}_w$ = average time in the system (including the time to be served)
n = the number of units in the system
P_n = the probability of exactly n units in the system

Western National Bank is considering opening a drive-in window for customer service. Management estimates that customers will arrive at the rate of 15 per hour. The teller who will staff the window can service customers at the rate of one every three minutes.

Assuming Poisson arrivals and exponential service, find

1. Utilization of the teller.
2. Average number in the waiting line.
3. Average number in the system.
4. Average waiting time in line.
5. Average waiting time in the system, including service.

Solution

1. The average utilization of the teller is

$$\rho = \frac{\lambda}{\mu} = \frac{15}{20} = 75 \text{ percent}$$

2. The average number in the waiting line is

$$\bar{n}_l = \frac{\lambda^2}{\mu(\mu - \lambda)} = \frac{(15)^2}{20(20 - 15)} = 2.25 \text{ customers}$$

3. The average number in the system is

$$\bar{n}_s = \frac{\lambda}{\mu - \lambda} = \frac{15}{20 - 15} = 3 \text{ customers}$$

4. Average waiting time in line is

$$\bar{t}_l = \frac{\lambda}{\mu(\mu - \lambda)} = \frac{15}{20(20 - 15)} = 0.15 \text{ hour, or 9 minutes}$$

5. Average waiting time in the system is

$$\bar{t}_s = \frac{1}{\mu - \lambda} = \frac{1}{20 - 15} = 0.2 \text{ hour, or 12 minutes}$$

Because of limited space availability and a desire to provide an acceptable level of service, the bank manager would like to ensure, with 95 percent confidence, that not more than three cars will be in the system at any one time. What is the present level of service for the three-car limit? What level of teller use must be attained and what must be the service rate of the teller to assure the 95 percent level of service?

Solution
The present level of service for three cars or less is the probability that there are 0, 1, 2, or 3 cars in the system.

$$P_n = \left(1 - \frac{\lambda}{\mu}\right)\left(\frac{\lambda}{\mu}\right)^n$$

$$\begin{aligned}
&\text{at } n = 0 \quad P_0 = (1 - 15/20) \quad (15/20)^0 = 0.250\\
&\text{at } n = 1 \quad P_1 = (1/4) \quad (15/20)^1 = 0.188\\
&\text{at } n = 2 \quad P_2 = (1/4) \quad (15/20)^2 = 0.141\\
&\text{at } n = 3 \quad P_3 = (1/4) \quad (15/20)^3 = \underline{0.106}\\
&\qquad\qquad\qquad\qquad\qquad\qquad\qquad 0.685, \text{ or } 68.5 \text{ percent}
\end{aligned}$$

The probability of having more than three cars in the system is 1.0 minus the probability of three cars or less (1.0 − 0.685 = 31.5 percent).

For a 95 percent service level to three cars or less, this states that $P_0 + P_1 + P_2 + P_3 = 95$ percent.

$$0.95 = \left(1 - \frac{\lambda}{\mu}\right)\left(\frac{\lambda}{\mu}\right)^0 + \left(1 - \frac{\lambda}{\mu}\right)\left(\frac{\lambda}{\mu}\right)^1 + \left(1 - \frac{\lambda}{\mu}\right)\left(\frac{\lambda}{\mu}\right)^2 + \left(1 - \frac{\lambda}{\mu}\right)\left(\frac{\lambda}{\mu}\right)^3$$

$$0.95 = \left(1 - \frac{\lambda}{\mu}\right)\left[1 + \frac{\lambda}{\mu} + \left(\frac{\lambda}{\mu}\right)^2 + \left(\frac{\lambda}{\mu}\right)^3\right]$$

We can solve this by trial and error for values of λ/μ. If $\lambda/\mu = 0.50$:

$$0.95 \stackrel{?}{=} 0.5(1 + 0.05 + 0.25 + 0.125)$$
$$0.95 \neq 0.9375$$

With $\lambda/\mu = 0.45$,

$$0.95 \stackrel{?}{=} (1 - 0.45)(1 + 0.45 + 0.203 + 0.091)$$
$$0.95 \neq 0.96$$

With $\lambda/\mu = 0.47$,

$$0.95 \stackrel{?}{=} (1 - 0.47)(1 + 0.47 + 0.221 + 0.104) = 0.95135$$
$$0.95 \approx 0.95135$$

Therefore, with the utilization $\rho = \lambda/\mu$ of 47 percent, the probability of three cars or less in the system is 95 percent.

To find the rate of service required to attain this 95 percent service level, we simply solve the equation $\lambda/\mu = 0.47$, where λ = number of arrivals per hour. This gives $\mu = 32$ per hour.

That is, the teller must serve approximately 32 people per hour—a 60 percent increase over the original 20-per-hour capability—for 95 percent confidence that not more than three cars will be in the system. Perhaps service may be speeded up by modifying the method of service, adding another teller, or limiting the types of transactions available at the drive-in window. It should also be noted that, with the condition of 95 percent confidence that three or fewer cars will be in the system, the teller will be idle 53 percent of the time.

Problem 2: Equipment Selection

A franchisee for Jiffy Carwash must decide which equipment to purchase out of a choice of three. Larger units cost more, but wash cars faster. To make the decision, costs are related to revenue.

This waiting line example is similar to the previous one except that the service time (time to wash each car) is constant. Cars are washed on a first-come first-served basis and the line can be long, but the customers will wait only a certain length of time or else they will leave.

The appropriate equations differ somewhat from the previous example because the service time is constant.

Jiffy Carwash franchises car wash stations throughout the United States. These are usually leased by service stations and installed on service station property. They consist of a single automatic system wherein customers drive their cars through while remaining inside. The system is quite simple but does a fair job for the price. A wash costs the customer $2.00, and the operating cost for materials, soap, water, power, and so on is $1.10 per wash.

Jiffy has three wash units, and the franchisee must choose one. Unit I can wash a car in 5 minutes and is leased for $30 per day. Unit II, a larger unit, can wash a car in 4 minutes but costs $40 per day. Unit III, the largest, can wash a car in 3 minutes and leases for $50 per day.

The franchisee is open 15 hours per day and assumes customers will wait in line no more than 5 minutes before they will go somewhere else. The franchisee also assumes that, on the average, 10 customers per hour will come in for car washes.

Solution

Using Unit I, calculate the average waiting time of customers in the wash line (μ for Unit I = 12 per hour).

$$\bar{t}_l = \frac{\lambda}{2\mu(\mu - \lambda)} = \frac{10}{2(12)(12 - 10)} = 0.208 \text{ hour, or } 12\tfrac{1}{2} \text{ minutes}$$

For Unit II at 15 per hour,

$$\bar{t}_l = \frac{10}{2(15)(15 - 10)} = 0.067 \text{ hour, or 4 minutes}$$

If waiting time is the only criterion, Unit II should be purchased. However, before we make the final decision, we must look at the profit differential between both units.

With Unit I, some customers would balk and renege because of the 12½-minute wait. And although this greatly complicates the mathematical analysis, we can gain some estimate of lost sales with Unit I by inserting i = 5 minutes or 1/12 hour (the average length of time customers will wait) and solving for λ. This would be the effective arrival rate of customers:

$$\bar{t}_l = \frac{\lambda}{2\mu(\mu - \lambda)}$$

$$\lambda = \frac{2\bar{t}_l\mu^2}{1 + 2\bar{t}_l\mu}$$

$$\lambda = \frac{2(1/12)(12)^2}{1 + 2(1/12)(12)} = 8 \text{ per hour}$$

Therefore, since the original estimate of λ was 10 per hour, an estimated 2 customers per hour will be lost. Lost profit of 2 customers per hour for 15 hours is 2 × 15 × ($2.00 − $1.10) = $27 per day.

Since the additional cost of Unit II over Unit I is only $10 per day, the loss of $27 profit obviously warrants the installation of Unit II.

The original constraint of a five-minute maximum wait is satisfied by Unit II. Therefore Unit III is not considered unless the arrival rate is expected to increase in the future.

S4.4 COMPUTER SIMULATION OF WAITING LINES

Some waiting line problems seem very simple on first impression, but turn out to be extremely difficult or impossible to solve. Several more complicated models exist that may solve other types of waiting line problems. However, when a waiting line consists of multiple lines or where there are flows of operations performed in series, then a simulation program on a computer may be the only way to solve the problem. Simulation is covered in the Supplement to Chapter 8.

S4.5 CONCLUSION

Waiting line problems present both a challenge and frustration to those who try to solve them. The basic objective is to balance the cost of waiting with the cost of adding more resources. For a service system this means that the utilization of a server may be quite low in order to provide a short waiting time to the customer. One of the main concerns in dealing with waiting line problems is in deciding which procedure or priority rule to use in selecting the next product or customer to be served.

Many queuing problems appear simple until an attempt is made to solve them. This supplement has dealt with two simple cases to give the reader a feel for waiting line problems.

S4.6 REVIEW AND DISCUSSION QUESTIONS

1. How might waiting line theory apply to plant layout?
2. What is the major cost trade-off that must be made in managing waiting line situations?
3. In what way might the first-come first-served rule be "unfair" to the customers waiting for service in a bank or hospital?
4. Define, in a practical sense, what is meant by an *exponential service time.*
5. Would you expect the exponential distribution to be a good approximation of service times for
   a. Buying an airline ticket at the airport?
   b. Riding a merry-go-round at a carnival?
   c. Checking out of a hotel?
   d. Completing a midterm exam in your OM class?
6. Would you expect the Poisson distribution to be a good approximation of
   a. Runners crossing the finish line in the Boston Marathon?
   b. Arrival times of the students in your OM class?
   c. Arrival times of the bus to your stop at school?

S4.7 PROBLEMS

*1. Quick Lube Inc. operates a fast lube and oil change garage. On a typical day, customers arrive at the rate of three per hour, and lube jobs are performed at an average rate of one every 15 minutes. The mechanics operate as a team on one car at a time.

Assuming Poisson arrivals and exponential service, find

a. Utilization of the lube team.
b. The average number of cars in line.
c. The average time a car waits before it is lubed.
d. The total time it takes to go through the system (i.e., waiting in line plus lube time).

*2. American Vending Inc. (AVI) supplies vended food to a large university. Since, out of anger and frustration, students kick the machines at every opportunity, management has a constant repair problem. The machines break down at an average of three per hour, and the breakdowns are distributed in a Poisson manner. Downtime costs the company $25/hour per machine, and each maintenance worker gets $4 per hour. One worker can service machines at an average rate of five per hour, distributed exponentially; two workers, working together, can service seven per hour, distributed exponentially; and a team of three workers can do eight per hour, distributed exponentially.

What is the optimum maintenance crew size for servicing the machines?

3. To support National Heart Week the Heart Association plans to install a free blood pressure testing booth in El Con Mall for the week. Previous experience

---

* Problems 1 and 2 are completely solved in Appendix D.

indicates that, on the average, 10 persons per hour will request a test. Assume arrivals are Poisson from an infinite population. Blood pressure measurements can be made at a constant time of five minutes each. Assume the queue length can be infinite with FCFS discipline.

a. What average number in line can be expected?
b. What average number of persons can be expected to be in the system?
c. What is the average amount of time that a person can expect to spend in line?
d. On the average, how much time will it take to measure a person's blood pressure, including waiting time?
e. On weekends, the arrival rate can be expected to increase to nearly 12 per hour. What effect will this have on the number in the waiting line?

4. A cafeteria serving line has a coffee urn from which customers serve themselves. Arrivals at the urn follow a Poisson distribution at the rate of three per minute. In serving themselves, customers take about 15 seconds, exponentially distributed.
a. How many customers would you expect to see on the average at the coffee urn?
b. How long would you expect it to take to get a cup of coffee?
c. What percentage of time is the urn being used?
d. What is the probability that there would be three or more people in the cafeteria?

If the cafeteria installs an automatic vendor that dispenses a cup of coffee at a constant time of 15 seconds, how does this change your answers to *a* and *b?*

5. Customers enter the camera department of a department store at the average rate of six per hour. The department is staffed by one employee, who takes an average of six minutes to serve each arrival. Assume this is a simple Poisson arrival exponentially distributed service time situation.
a. As a casual observer, how many people would you expect to see in the camera department (excluding the clerk)?
b. How long would a customer expect to spend in the camera department (total time)?
c. What is the utilization of the clerk?
d. What is the probability that there are *more than* two people in the camera department (excluding the clerk)?

6. Arrivals at a free beer dispensing station at an "after finals" party come at the rate of one thirsty student or faculty member every 15 seconds. The bartender can pour one beer every 10 seconds.
a. How many thirsty beer drinkers would you expect to see in the *line?*
b. What is the probability that there will be two or more people in line?
c. How long would you expect to wait to get a beer?

7. Kenny Livingston, bartender at the Tucson Racquet Club, can serve drinks at the rate of one every 50 seconds. During a hot evening recently, the bar was particularly busy and someone was at the bar asking for a drink every 55 seconds.
a. Assuming that everyone in the bar drank at the same rate and that Kenny served people on a first-come first-served basis, how long would you expect to have to wait for a drink?
b. How many people would you expect to be waiting for drinks?
c. What is the probability that three or more people are waiting for drinks?
d. What is the utilization of the bartender; how busy is he?

e. If the bartender is replaced with an automatic drink dispensing machine, how would this change *a* above?

8. A study-aid desk manned by a graduate student has been established to answer students' questions and help in working problems in your OM course. The desk is staffed eight hours per day. The dean wants to know how the facility is working. Statistics indicate that students arrive at a rate of four per hour, and the distribution is approximately Poisson. Assistance time averages 10 minutes, distributed exponentially. Assume population and line length can be infinite and queue discipline is FCFS. For the report to the dean, calculate:
   a. The percent of utilization of the graduate student.
   b. The average number of students in the system.
   c. The average time in the system.
   d. The probability of four or more students being in line or being served.
   e. Before a test, the arrival of students increases to six per hour on the average. What does this do to the average length of the line?
9. Consider a service system staffed by a person who takes 10 minutes to satisfy a customer's needs. Customers arrive at this system at the rate of five per hour.
   a. How many customers would you expect to find in *line* waiting?
   b. What total time would you expect a customer to spend in the *system?*
   c. What is the probability that there are three or more customers in the system?
10. The Holland Tunnel under the Hudson River in New York collects tolls for its use. For a portion of a particular day, only one toll booth was open. Automobiles were arriving at this gate at the rate of 750 per hour. The toll collector took an average of four seconds to collect the fee.
   a. What was the utilization of the toll booth operator?
   b. How much time would you expect to take to arrive, pay your toll, and move on?
   c. How many cars would you expect to see in the system?
   d. What is the probability that there will be more than four cars in the system?
11. Since it is getting close to flu season, the university is considering setting up a station to dispense flu shots free to all students, staff, and faculty. There is a question of staffing for a variety of possible demands. One option is to hire just one nurse. Assume that the nurse can give 120 shots per hour, exponentially distributed. People arrive about every 36 seconds, on the average.
   a. What is the utilization of the nurse?
   b. How many people would you expect to find in the system (excluding the nurse)?
   c. How long would it take if you just joined the line to get completely through the system (with shot)?
   d. What is the probability that there will be more than three people in the system (excluding the nurse)?

S4.8 SELECTED BIBLIOGRAPHY

Cooper, Robert B. *Introduction to Queuing Theory*. 2nd ed. New York: Elsevier-North Holland Publishing, 1980.

Gorney, Leonard. *Queuing Theory: A Solving Approach*. Princeton, N.J.: Petrocelli, 1981.

Griffin, Walter C. *Queuing: Basic Theory and Application*. Columbus, Ohio: Grid, 1978.

Hillier, Frederick S., et al. *Queuing Tables and Graphs*. New York: Elsevier-North Holland Publishing, 1981.

Newell, Gordon F. *Applications of Queuing Theory*. New York: Chapman and Hall, 1982.

Newell, Gordon F. *Approximate Behavior of Tandem Queues*. New York: Springer-Verlag, 1980.

Solomon, Susan L. *Simulation of Waiting Lines*. Englewood Cliffs, N. J.: Prentice-Hall, 1983.

Srivastava, H. M., and B. R. Kashyap. *Special Functions in Queuing Theory: And Related Stochastic Processes*. New York: Academic Press, 1982.

Chapter 5

Design of the Quality Control System

EPIGRAPH

To achieve competitiveness, total quality must permeate the organization. Those who adopt and adapt, prosper. Those who do not, disappear.

John F. Gilks, "Total Quality: Wave of the Future," *Canadian Business Review*, Spring 1990, p. 17.

A manager who trades away quality to save a little manufacturing expense is "worse than a thief." When a thief steals from a company, there is no loss in wealth, just a change in ownership of assets. Decisions that create quality losses throw away social productivity—the wealth of society.

Genichi Taguchi and Don Clausing, "Robust Quality," *Harvard Business Review*, January–February 1990, p. 75.

CHAPTER OUTLINE

KEY TERMS

Total Quality Control (TQC)

Statistical Quality Control (SQC)

Acceptance Sampling

Process Control

Sampling by Attributes

Sampling by Variables

Taguchi Methods

Continuous Improvement

Today customers want more than just a product or service. They want good design, good performance, reliability, maintainability, long product life, and good value. In service, the customer demands quality not only in the service received, but also in the manner in which it is delivered.

Today's focus on quality has broadened beyond the simple acceptance sampling plans and control charts of years ago. Quality today refers to every level—from the actions of the top corporate level in long-term planning to how production workers or service personnel accept their responsibilities in producing a top-quality product or in delivering top-notch service.

In this chapter we will present the broader quality issues first, referred to as *total quality* or *total quality control,* and how they permeate the organization. Section 5.2 presents a lightly edited version of a paper by John F. Gilks. This is an excellent summary of the importance of total quality throughout the organization. He also writes of four types of business processes and their particular total quality needs, and five elements for successful total quality programs. The second part of the chapter focuses on sampling plans and statistical control charts which are the heart of quality process control.

5.1 ROLE OF THE QUALITY CONTROL FUNCTION

The philosophical orientation and role of the quality control function has changed radically in the past few years. Traditionally manufacturing QC was operated as a gatekeeping activity; the objective was to control product quality at the output stage through inspection. The issue was whether to pass on to the customer products that were on the margin in quality. Here, natural adversarial relationships developed between manufacturing units and production control people, who wanted to "ship them critters" to meet their output goals, and QC personnel, who wanted to "maintain our quality standards." Resolving such conflicts usually came down to a question of who had the most power in the organization. Frequently, output objectives triumphed over quality, since the marketplace accepted imperfect products.

The game has changed, however. The marketplace now demands high quality, and foreign competitors are supplying it—at competitive prices. The Japanese in particular have demonstrated that high quality, and the high productivity needed to offer low prices, are not mutually exclusive. (The logic is simple: products that are made right the first time don't have to be reworked or scrapped, which means that extra materials and workers are not needed, and hence productivity is higher.)

The new game calls for QC to work with all aspects of the organization in the development of a **total quality control** (TQC) system and philosophy. This notion holds that quality must be approached systematically throughout each function and activity of the firm. In the words of Feigenbaum, "Total quality control is an effective system for integrating the quality development, quality-maintenance, and quality-improvement efforts of various groups in an organization so as to enable marketing, engineering, production and service at the most economical levels which allow for full customer satisfaction."[1]

Every step and every phase of the production system consults with other areas of the system with which it interacts. When a designed product is released for production, for example, there are no surprises. Production has already worked with engineering to assure that equipment is available and specifications can be met.

5.2 TOTAL QUALITY: WAVE OF THE FUTURE[2]

Once in a generation, perhaps, something happens that profoundly changes the world and how we look at it. Business is no different. From time to time, someone develops a new way of operating that spreads from industry to industry. Those who adopt and adapt, prosper; those who do not, disappear. Well-known examples of such processes include the adoption of the factory system in the 18th century and the assembly line in the 20th.

Is total quality (TQ) an innovation on this scale? Although its full impact is not yet being felt, total quality has already become essential to success in some manufacturing-intensive industries. The automotive industry best illustrates this point. The impact on North American manufacturers of high quality competition from Honda Canada Inc., Toyota Canada Inc., and others has been enormous. Between 1978 and 1988, Honda tripled its share of the North American market from 2.4 percent to 7.2 percent while Toyota increased its share from 3.9 percent to 6.5 percent. The Japanese inroads were made through reliability and high resale value not flashy features. So dramatic has their impact been that most consumers instinctively associate "Japanese" with "high quality"—a complete reversal of attitudes 20 years ago.

Manufacturing sector

The fight back has been led by Ford Motor Company of Canada, Ltd., with its consistent theme of "Quality is Job #1." For Ford and its suppliers, this has been more than an advertising slogan. Ford's own quality program, Q101, set up in response to the import threat, has changed conventional thinking in every area of manufacturing, engineering, and design. As a result, Ford has stabilized its position in the market and restored profitability. Ford's market share dropped from 23.5 percent in 1978 to a low of 16.6 percent in 1981. By 1988, Ford's share had recovered to 21.5 percent. Two processes used by Ford to expedite this recovery were participative management and employee in-

---

[1] Armand V. Feigenbaum, *Total Quality Control,* 3rd ed. (New York: McGraw-Hill, 1986), p. 6.

[2] John F. Gilks, "Total Quality: Wave of the Future," *Canadian Business Review,* Spring 1990, pp. 17–20. Used with permission from the *Canadian Business Review* and The Conference Board of Canada.

volvement. In contrast, General Motors of Canada Ltd. has been much slower to react and continues to see its market position eroded. Its share fell from 47.8 percent in 1978 to 35.9 percent in 1988. Is it unreasonable to ask whether there will be room for a non-TQ company in this industry by the turn of the century?

The experience of other manufacturing-based industries has been similar. Motorola in Canada and Mitel Corporation, among others in the electronics industry, and Milliken Industries of Canada Ltd. and Collins & Aikman Inc. in textiles have shown that consistently high product quality is one of the keys to competitive advantage in their industries.

Service sector

A second group of companies that have adopted the concept and implemented the process of total quality is now apparent in the service sector. Four Seasons Hotels Inc., America Express Canada, Inc., and several airlines (Scandinavian Airlines Systems, British Airways, and most recently, Air Canada) have shown that focusing on customers and their needs can build a position of leadership in an industry. Now we are beginning to see the emergence of a third group of companies, primarily in the consumer packaged goods industry, along with some in the legal and consulting world. Examples of companies in this group would include Unilever Canada Ltd., H. J. Heinz Company of Canada Ltd. and our own company, A. T. Kearney.

In the summer of 1989, we became convinced that total quality was a profound and powerful idea that was changing the business world. We undertook some research to see what was happening in Canada, and it quickly became apparent that there had been failures as well as successes and that penetration of the TQ idea varied widely from industry to industry. It also became evident that successful application of the process in one area of a company could be leveraged across the business.

Critical processes

When we examined what had happened in more depth, we first concluded that in any given industry certain business processes are more critical than others to the central missions of satisfying customer requirements. TQ programs had been most successful where the major effort had been focused on these critical processes. For example, in relatively technical manufacturing industries (e.g., automotive, electronics) what really matters to customers is "the product in the box." Therefore, total quality has had the most impact here when it's been applied to the manufacturing and design processes. Consumer service industries (e.g., airlines, hotels) are different. What matters here is the experience of the customer at the actual time of interaction with the supplier: the "moment of truth." The critical processes in these industries are those that allow the front-line service worker to satisfy the customer. In the consumer packaged goods industries, the product itself is often difficult to differentiate from the competition. Creating extra value for the consumer then turns to the intangible benefits of buying the product, or the "feel good" issue. In this type of business, the marketing processes are most important.

In addition, we observed that where TQ programs had not achieved the expected result it was often because TQ thinking had not been applied to the processes that were critical in that particular business. This was particularly evident in situations where a company had attempted to set up total quality as a manufacturing initiative in a marketing-intensive business.

Four waves of total quality

Our findings led us to develop a model for understanding total quality. We concluded that in any business there are four basic types of business processes and that each demands a different emphasis in the way total quality is applied. This means, essentially, that there are four types of total quality. Because TQ thinking has tended to spread sequentially through these four types of processes, we refer to them as the four "waves" of total quality:

1. Engineered quality—total quality applied to the product itself.
2. Repetitive service quality—focus on the service delivery process.
3. Creative quality—when the ouputs are unique.
4. Quality in strategic asset deployment—when assets are intensive.

The first wave we have called *engineered quality*. It is total quality applied to the product itself. Usually heavily focused in the manufacturing area, such programs are the most straightforward to implement. They involve applying a new well-developed and sophisticated set of tools (examples include Statistical Process Control and Design of Experiments) in a controlled environment. These tools are applied to processes that produce the same output (for which a clear specification can be written) many times. Furthermore, in these areas people expect to work to defined standards and have their performance measured. Manufacturing has long been subject to formal quality control. Thus, we concluded that if the consistency of the product itself is critical to your competitive advantage, this type of program will yield major dividends.

The second wave we have called *repetitive service quality*. The differences here are twofold. First, it is much harder to measure whether service (as seen by the customer) meets a specification or not. Second, the environment is much less controllable than a manufacturing plant—customers are less tractable than components. TQ programs of this type concentrate on the service delivery process and the capabilities and the powers of the people with direct customer contact to ensure consistently excellent quality. Developing a second wave TQ program requires greater commitment from management because the process and culture changes required to empower employees who have customer contact cut deeply into traditional management prerogatives.

The third wave is the application of TQ principles to processes that have a unique output. Examples include advertising, development, consulting studies, and legal briefs. We call this *creative quality*. Total quality applied to these processes is in its infancy. There is not much experience to go on, and we do not have the formidable array of techniques available in the manufacturing area. Nonetheless, we are convinced that, given some flexibility in application, TQ principles can be applied to these processes. Further, if these processes are critical to your business, the success of a TQ program will trigger success in this area.

The existence of a fourth wave of total quality is, at this stage, pure speculation. Although we know of no examples, we believe that it ought to be possible to apply total quality to decision processes surrounding strategic asset deployment, as an example. We would expect such an approach to pay its greatest dividends in companies where these processes are key (e.g., management and holding companies and asset-intensive industries like heavy chemicals). Interestingly, some of the most successful companies of this type, such as Berkshire Hathaway Inc., have structured their critical decision processes around clearly defined subprocesses, outputs, roles, and accountabilities. This practice resembles total quality, although Berkshire Hathaway would probably not see it in that light.

Success and failure

The wave theory appears to be one of the keys to understanding why some TQ programs have succeeded and others have failed. We believe that companies are successful when they apply total quality to the processes that are key in their business, regardless of difficulty. For example, in our own business we have begun with what seems most important to our clients; how we manage consulting studies (the process not the results). We chose this rather than the easy-to-define area of document production. Similarly, Chesebrough Ponds (Canada) Inc. has attacked the process of brand development before manufacturing.

In contrast, we have seen several examples of companies that have confined total quality to noncritical areas of their business, usually manufacturing or internal administrative processes. These companies have, of course, benefited from their efforts, but the programs have neither become a way of life in the organization nor yielded the kind of competitive breakthrough that the most successful programs have achieved. We conclude that recognition of which processes are most critical to your business and consequently, which type of TQ program you should apply is essential to launching a successful TQ program.

Once launched, of course, the momentum and experience generated can and should be leveraged right across the business. Milliken has shown how this can be done. Starting classically, and appropriately for it in manufacturing, total quality has now migrated into the "service" areas of its business. This has allowed it, for example, to offer packages such as a 48-hour design and build service for industrial carpeting that would not previously have been conceivable. Similarly AMP of Canada, Ltd., an electrical products distributor, has channeled its original TQ program from the customer service area, a second wave type process, into both manufacturing and sales and marketing. Thus, we can see that there is an underlying logic both for the migration of total quality across industry groups and within individual companies.

Five key elements for successful total quality programs

Recognizing where you fit in the wave model is important but not sufficient. We also have identified five key elements that were present in the most successful TQ programs.

1. Total focus on customers and their needs.
2. Quality improvement techniques applied throughout the business regardless of difficulty or organizational lines.
3. Employee empowerment—to make decisions in customer interactions and in improving the process.
4. Elimination of waste—material, time, effort, and potential.
5. Continuous improvement. Total quality is a way of life.

The first and most important element is total focus on customers and their needs. TQ companies attach great importance to finding out what their customers really want and need. They are open, direct, and honest with their customers. They ask them what they want and how they, as a supplier, are performing. This process is seen as vital and nonthreatening. After getting close to their customers, TQ companies go to great lengths to stay close on a day-to-day basis. At Ford, for example, all managers from the president down take a monthly turn on the 1-800 lines. AMP of Canada has an even more radical approach. All managers, regardless of their function, are assigned a portfolio of customers for whom they act as a contact whenever there is a problem. Naturally information about customers is not enough. Successful companies act on the information and provide the products and services their customers want first time, every time. TQ companies are passionate about meeting commitments and never supplying defective products. Long-term customer relationships are not put at risk for short-term expediency.

Second, the successful TQ companies apply process management principles and improvement techniques to all processes in their businesses regardless of difficulty or organizational lines. As one moves into third wave quality processes, this becomes more difficult. Whereas one can easily specify the characteristics of a washing machine, for example, and its associated manufacturing process, it is much harder to write a specification for a good television commercial. It is possible though, as Unilever has done, to write coherent and useful guidelines for how to create a good commercial. Such guidelines might specify who is to be included at each stage of the process, final and intermediate deliverable formats and timing, as well as general guidelines on what has and hasn't worked in the past. Once documented in this way, any process can be analyzed for weaknesses in the same way as a manufacturing process and, similarly, lessons learned can be continuously incorporated.

The process management approach has its problems, especially in "creative" processes. Workers in these areas are usually not accustomed to having what they do analyzed closely. Further, workers in the critical areas of a business often believe, perhaps with some justification, that they are the key to the company's success and that this places them beyond analysis. Winning over such key workers to the TQ approach is vital to success. Computing Devices Company, a division of Control Data Canada, Ltd., designs and makes highly sophisticated military electronics. Here, winning over the design engineers to the process management approach has been a top priority for the TQ program management.

The third key to total quality is employee empowerment. This comes in two forms. First is the power to meet customer needs. The customer-driven organization inverts the conventional management-employee-customer power relationship and moves from a philosophy of "do what I (management) tell you" to one of "do what I (customer) need." A good example is a service worker faced with a potentially disgruntled customer. The employee must have the power to remedy the situation on the spot without referring to multiple layers of bureaucracy. Anyone who has been presented with a meal voucher to tide one over a flight delay will recognize this. This is the logical extension of "power to stop the line" in a second wave environment.

The second element of employee empowerment is the power to improve processes, again without seeking approval from multiple levels of bureaucracy. This is a form of empowerment that moves beyond "employee participation" in which management seeks input on process improvement from those who know the process best but reserves decision making for itself. TQ companies trust their employees to do the right thing.

Empowerment is addictive and it is a powerful motivator. At Mitel's plant in Renfrew, Ontario, the drive for process improvement even survived plant closure. Laid-off Renfrew workers recalled to the Kanata, Ontario, location quickly wanted to know how they could put their improvement skills to work in their new location.

A fourth key to total quality is the drive to eliminate waste in all its many forms—material, time, effort, and, perhaps most crucially in third wave companies, potential. The drive to eliminate wasted time, for example has led Computing Devices toward a Just-in-Time manufacturing concept while the drive to eliminate wasted sales potential is what motivates the TQ marketers at Chesebrough Ponds.

A final key for all the successful companies we examined is continuous improvement. For these companies, total quality is a way of life—a never-ending journey. Total quality is not the latest "flavor of the month" management fad but a philosophy that has become deeply embedded in their corporate cultures. Milliken employees, for example, may not know what their company will be doing in five years' time, but they know whatever it is will be done in a TQ manner.

Summary

Total quality is a tough concept to come to grips with and tougher still to implement. It gets even tougher to implement as one moves through the four waves of quality, but the rewards also increase. Companies that have already fully committed themselves to total quality have been highly successful, as the example of Computing Devices illustrates. Its long-range strategic plan states "with TQMP . . . we will maintain our vitality, improve our productivity, and continue to offer value to our customers." The results bear out this statement. In three years, profits have risen by more than 117 percent. As we move into the 1990s, third wave companies are beginning to make the same commitment. As Mark Landry, vice president commercial at Chesebrough Pond's (Canada) puts it, "the ultimate winner will be the company that consistently delights the consumer and, for us, that's what total quality is all about."

5.3 MEASURING THE QUALITY OF A COMPANY

There seems to be a high correlation between quality as it permeates the entire firm and quality as it pertains to the firm's products and services. How can we encourage firms to improve quality? One way is to give an award and public recognition.

The Baldrige Award

In 1987, Congress created the Malcolm Baldrige National Quality Award. It has become the standard of excellence in U.S. business. Winning this award means a winner is producing goods or services equal to any in the world, and the quality continues to improve. Not many U.S. companies can now meet the high standards of the Baldrige judges. There have been eight winners so far. The 1988 winners were Motorola, the Nuclear Fuel Division of Westinghouse, and Globe Metallurgical in Cleveland. The 1989 winners were Milliken and Company and Xerox Business Products Division. Winners in 1990 were the Cadillac Division of General Motors and IBM in Rochester, Minnesota.

Service firms are also eligible for the Baldrige Award. While there were no 1988 nor 1989 winners in this category, Federal Express succeeded in being the first service firm to win this coveted award in 1990.

Curt W. Reimann, director of the Malcolm Baldrige National Quality Award, lists eight critical factors that the examiners and judges look for:[3]

1. A plan to keep improving all operations continuously.
2. A system for measuring these improvements accurately.
3. A strategic plan based on bench-marks that compare the company's performance with the world's best.
4. A close partnership with suppliers and customers that feeds improvements back into the operation.
5. A deep understanding of the customers so that their wants can be translated into products.
6. A long-lasting relationship with customers, going beyond the delivery of the product to include sales, service, and ease of maintenance.
7. A focus on preventing mistakes rather than merely correcting them.
8. A commitment to improving quality that runs from the top of the organization to the bottom.

5.4 MEANING AND MEASUREMENT OF QUALITY IN A PRODUCT OR SERVICE

The quality of a product or service may be defined in terms of the quality of its design and the quality of its conformance to that design. *Design quality* refers to the inherent value of the product in the marketplace, and is thus a strategic decision for the firm. The common dimensions of design quality are listed in Exhibit 5.1.

Conformance quality refers to the degree to which the product or service design specifications are met. It too has strategic implications, but the execution of the activities involved in achieving conformance are of a tactical day-to-day nature. It should be evident that a product or service can have high design quality but low conformance quality, and vice versa.

The operations function and the quality organization within the firm are primarily concerned with quality of conformance. Achieving all the quality specifications is typically the responsibility of manufacturing management where a product is involved and branch operations management in a service industry. Exhibit 5.2 shows two examples: one of a stereo amplifier that meets the signal-to-noise ratio standard, and the second a checking account transaction in a bank.

Both quality of design and quality of conformance should provide products that meet the customer's objectives for those products. This is often termed the product's *fitness for use,* and it entails identifying the dimensions of the

[3] Jeremy Main, "How to Win the Baldrige Award," *Fortune,* April 23, 1990, pp. 101–16.

EXHIBIT 5.1

The Dimensions of Quality

Dimension	Meaning
Performance	Primary product or service characteristics
Features	Added touches, "bells and whistles," secondary characteristics
Reliability	Consistency of performance over time
Durability	Useful life
Serviceability	Resolution of problems and complaints
Response	Characteristics of the human-to-human interface like timeliness, courtesy, professionalism, etc.
Esthetics	Sensory characteristics like sound, feel, look, etc.
Reputation	Past performance and other intangibles

Source: Modified from Paul E. Plsek, "Defining Quality at the Marketing/Development Interface," *Quality Progress*, June 1987, pp. 28–36.

EXHIBIT 5.2

Examples of Dimensions of Quality

Dimension	Product Example: Stereo Amplifier	Service Example: Checking Account at Bank
Performance	Signal-to-noise ratio, power	Time to process customer requests
Features	Remote control	Automatic bill paying
Reliability	Mean time-to failure	Variability of time to process requests
Durability	Useful life (with repair)	Keeping pace with industry trends
Serviceability	Ease of repair	Resolution of errors
Response	Courtesy of dealer	Courtesy of teller
Esthetics	Oak-finished cabinet	Appearance of bank lobby
Reputation	*Consumer Reports* ranking	Advice of friends, years in business

Source: Modified from Paul E. Plsek, "Defining Quality at the Marketing/Development Interface," *Quality Progress*, June 1987, pp. 28–36.

product (or service) that the customer wants and developing a quality control program to ensure these dimensions are met.

5.5 COST OF QUALITY

There are a number of definitions and interpretations of the term *cost of quality*. From the purist's point of view, it means all the costs attributable to the production of quality that is not 100 percent perfect. A less stringent definition considers only those costs that are the difference between what can be expected from excellent performance and the current costs that exist.

How significant is the cost of quality? It has been estimated at between 15 and 20 percent of every sales dollar—the cost of reworking, scrapping, repeated service, inspections, tests, warranties, and other quality-related items.

Crosby states that the correct cost for a well-run quality management program should be under 2.5 percent.[4]

There are three basic assumptions needed to justify an analysis of the costs of quality:[5]

1. That failures are caused.
2. That prevention is cheaper.
3. That performance can be measured.

The *costs of quality* are generally classified into four types:

1. Appraisal costs: the costs of the inspection, testing, and other tasks to ensure that the product or process is acceptable.
2. Prevention costs: the sum of all the costs to prevent defects: the costs to identify the *cause* of the defect, to implement corrective action to eliminate the cause, to train personnel, to redesign the product or system, and for new equipment or modifications.
3. Failure costs.
   a. Internal. The costs incurred within the system: scrap, rework, repair.
   b. External. The costs for defects that pass through the system: customer warranty replacements, loss of customer or goodwill, handling complaints, and product repair.[6]

Exhibit 5.3 conveys the message: Spend more money on prevention and you should be able to reduce appraisal and failure costs. The rule of thumb says that for every dollar you spend in prevention, you can save 10 in failure and appraisal costs.

Often, increases in productivity occur as a byproduct of efforts to reduce the cost of quality. A bank, for example, set out to improve quality and reduce the cost of quality and found that it had also boosted productivity. The bank developed this productivity measure for the loan processing area: the number of tickets processed divided by the resources required (labor cost, computer time, ticket forms). Before the quality improvement program, the productivity index was 0.2660 [2,080/($11.23 × 640 hours + $0.05 × 2,600 forms + $500 for systems costs)]. After the quality improvement project was completed, labor time fell to 546 hours and the number of forms to 2,100 for a change in the index to 0.3088, or an increase in productivity of 16 percent.[7]

---

[4] Philip B. Crosby, *Quality Is Free* (New York: New American Library, 1979), p. 15; and "The Push for Quality," *Business Week,* June 8, 1987, p. 132.

[5] Frank Scanlon, "Quality Costs in a Non-Manufacturing Environment," *ASQC Quality Congress Transactions,* 1983, pp. 296–300.

[6] For a description of reports that Honeywell created to state these four costs by department, see Vyasaraj V. Murthy, "Managing Cost of Quality at Honeywell," *ASQC Quality Congress Transactions,* 1983, pp. 463–65.

[7] Charles A. Aubrey II and Debra A. Zimbler, "The Banking Industry: Quality Costs and Improvements," *Quality Progress,* December 1983, pp. 16–20.

EXHIBIT 5.3

Prevention Costs Reduce Total Costs

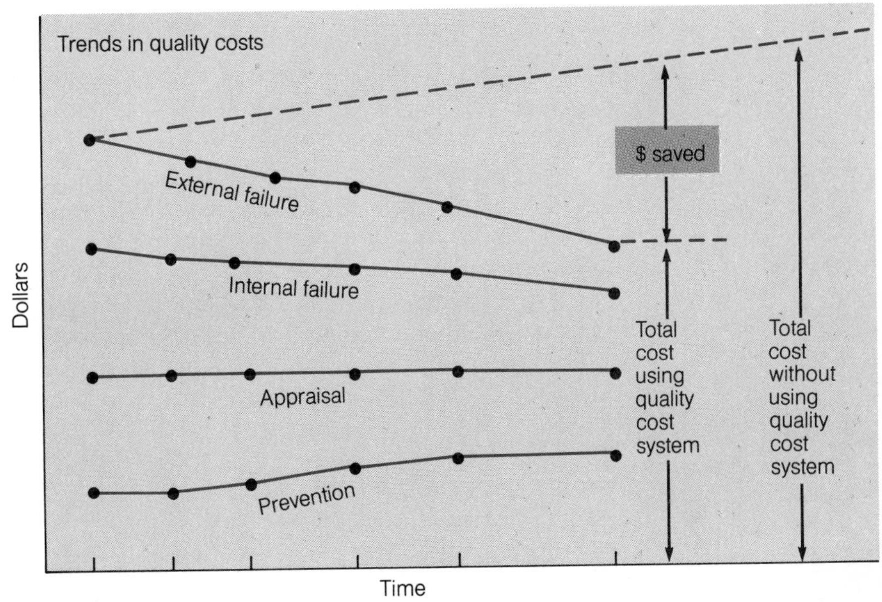

5.6 STATISTICAL QUALITY CONTROL (SQC)

The subject of **statistical quality control** can be divided into *acceptance sampling* and *process control*. **Acceptance sampling** involves testing a random sample of existing goods and deciding whether to accept an entire lot based on the quality of the random sample. **Process control** involves testing a random sample of output from a process to determine whether the process is producing items within a preselected range. When the tested output exceeds that range, it is a signal to adjust the production process to force the output back into the acceptable range. This is accomplished by adjusting the process itself. Acceptance sampling is frequently used in a purchasing or receiving situation, while process control is used in a production situation of any type.

Quality control for both acceptance sampling and process control measures either attributes or variables. Goods or services may be observed to be either good or bad, or functioning or malfunctioning. For example, a lawnmower either runs or it doesn't; it attains a certain level of torque and horsepower or it doesn't. This type of measurement is known as **sampling by attributes.** Alternatively, a lawnmower's torque and horsepower can be measured as an amount of deviation from a set standard. This type of measurement is known as **sampling by variables.**

The following sections describe some standard approaches to developing acceptance sampling plans and process control procedures.

5.7 ACCEPTANCE SAMPLING

Design of a Single Sampling Plan for Attributes

Recall that acceptance sampling is performed on goods that already exist to determine what percentage of products conform to specifications. These products may be items received from another company and evaluated by the receiving department or they may be components that have passed through a processing step and are evaluated by company personnel either in production or later in the warehousing function. Whether inspection should be done at all is addressed in the Insert entitled "Costs to Justify Inspection."

Acceptance sampling is executed through a sampling plan. In this section, we illustrate the planning procedures for a single sampling plan—that is, a plan in which the quality is determined from the evaluation of one sample. (Other plans may be developed using two or more samples; more about this later.)

INSERT Costs to Justify Inspection

Total (100 percent) inspection is justified when the cost of a loss incurred by not inspecting is greater than the cost of inspection. For example, suppose a faulty item results in a \$10 loss. If the average percentage of defective items in a lot is 3 percent, the expected cost of faulty items is 0.03 × \$10, or \$0.30 each. Therefore, if the cost of inspecting each item is less than \$0.30, the economic decision is to perform 100 percent inspection. Not all defective items will be removed, however, since inspectors will pass some bad items and reject some good ones.

The purposes of a sampling plan are to test the lot to either (1) find its quality or (2) ensure that the quality is what it is supposed to be. Thus, if a quality control supervisor already knows the quality (such as the 0.03 given in the example above), he or she does not sample for defects. Either all of them must be inspected to remove the defects or none of them should be inspected, and the rejects pass into the process. The choice simply depends on the cost to inspect and the cost incurred by passing a reject.

A single sampling plan is defined by n and c, where n is the number of units in the sample and c is the acceptance number. The size of n may vary from one up to all the items in the lot (usually denoted as N) from which it is drawn. The acceptance number c denotes the maximum number of defective items that can be found in the sample before the lot is rejected. Values for n and c are determined by the interaction of four factors that quantify the objectives of the product's producer and its consumer. The objective of the producer is to ensure that the sampling plan has a low probability of rejecting good lots. Lots are defined as good if they contain no more than a specified level of defectives, termed the *acceptable quality level* (AQL). The objective of the consumer is to ensure that the sampling plan has a low probability of accepting bad lots. Lots are defined as bad if the percentage of defectives is greater than a specified amount, termed *lot tolerance percent defective* (LTPD). The probability associated with rejecting a good lot is denoted by the Greek letter alpha (α) and is termed the *producer's risk*. The probability associated with accepting a bad lot is denoted by the letter beta (β) and is termed the *consumer's risk*. The selection of particular values for AQL, α, LTPD, and β is an economic decision based on a cost trade-off or, more typically, on company policy or contractual requirements.

There is a humorous story supposedly about Hewlett-Packard during its first dealings with Japanese vendors, who place a great deal of emphasis on high-quality production. HP had insisted on 2 percent AQL in a purchase of 100 cables. During the purchase agreement some heated discussion took place wherein the Japanese vendor did not want this AQL specification; HP insisted that they would not budge from the 2 percent AQL. The Japanese vendor finally agreed. Later, when the box arrived, there were two packages inside. One contained 100 good cables. The other package had 2 cables with a note stating: "We have sent you 100 good cables. Since you insisted on 2 percent AQL, we have enclosed 2 defective cables in this package, though we do not understand why you want them."

The following example, using an excerpt from a standard acceptance sampling table, illustrates how the four parameters—AQL, α, LTPD, and β—are used in developing a sampling plan.

Example

Hi-Tech Industries manufactures Z-Band radar scanners used to detect speed traps. The printed circuit boards in the scanners are purchased from an outside vendor. The vendor produces the boards to an acceptable quality level (AQL) of 2 percent defectives and is willing to run a 5 percent risk (α) of having lots of this level or fewer defectives rejected. Hi-Tech considers lots of 8 percent or more defectives (LTPD) unacceptable and wants to ensure that it will accept such poor-quality lots no more than 10 percent of the time (β). A large shipment has just been delivered. What values of n and c should be selected to determine the quality of this lot?

Solution. The parameters of the problem are: AQL $= 0.02$, $\alpha = 0.05$, LTPD $= 0.08$, and $\beta = 0.10$. We can use Exhibit 5.4 to find c and then n.

First divide LTPD by AQL ($0.08 \div 0.02 = 4$). Then find the ratio in column 2 that is equal to or just greater than that amount (i.e., 4). This value is 4.057, which is associated with $c = 4$.

Finally, find the value in column 3 that is in the same row as $c = 4$, and divide that quantity by AQL to obtain n ($1.970 \div 0.02 = 98.5$).

The appropriate sampling plan is: $c = 4$, $n = 99$.

EXHIBIT 5.4

Excerpt from a Sampling Plan Table for $\alpha = 0.05$, $\beta = 0.10$

c	$LTPD \div AQL$	$n \cdot AQL$
0	44.890	0.052
1	10.946	0.355
2	6.509	0.818
3	4.890	1.366
4	4.057	1.970
5	3.549	2.613
6	3.206	3.286
7	2.957	3.981
8	2.768	4.695
9	2.618	5.426

Operating Characteristic Curves

While a sampling plan such as the one just described meets our requirements for the extreme values of good and bad quality, we cannot readily determine how well the plan discriminates between good and bad lots at intermediate values. For this reason, sampling plans are generally displayed graphically through the use of operating characteristic (OC) curves. These curves, which are unique for each combination of n and c, simply illustrate the probability of accepting lots with varying percent defectives. The procedure we have followed in developing the plan, in fact, specifies two points on an OC curve—one point defined by AQL and $1 - \alpha$, and the other point defined by LTPD and β. Curves for common values of n and c can be computed or obtained from available tables.[8]

Shaping the OC Curve

A sampling plan which discriminates perfectly between good and bad lots will have an infinite slope (vertical) at the selected value of AQL. In Exhibit 5.5, percent defectives to the left of 2 percent would always be accepted and to the right, always rejected. However, such a curve is possible only with complete inspection of all units and thus not a possibility with a true sampling plan.

An OC curve should be steep in the region of most interest (between the AQL and the LTPD), which is accomplished by varying n and c. If c remains constant, increasing the sample size n causes the OC curve to be more vertical. While holding n constant, decreasing c (the maximum number of defective units) also makes the slope more vertical, moving closer to the origin.

[8] See, for example, H. F. Dodge and H. G. Romig, *Sampling Inspection Tables—Single and Double Sampling* (New York: John Wiley & Sons, 1959), and *Military Standard Sampling Procedures and Tables for Inspection by Attributes* (MIL-STD-105D) (Washington, D.C.: U.S. Government Printing Office, 1963).

EXHIBIT 5.5 **Operating Characteristic Curve for AQL = 0.02, α = 0.05, LTPD = 0.08, β = 0.10**

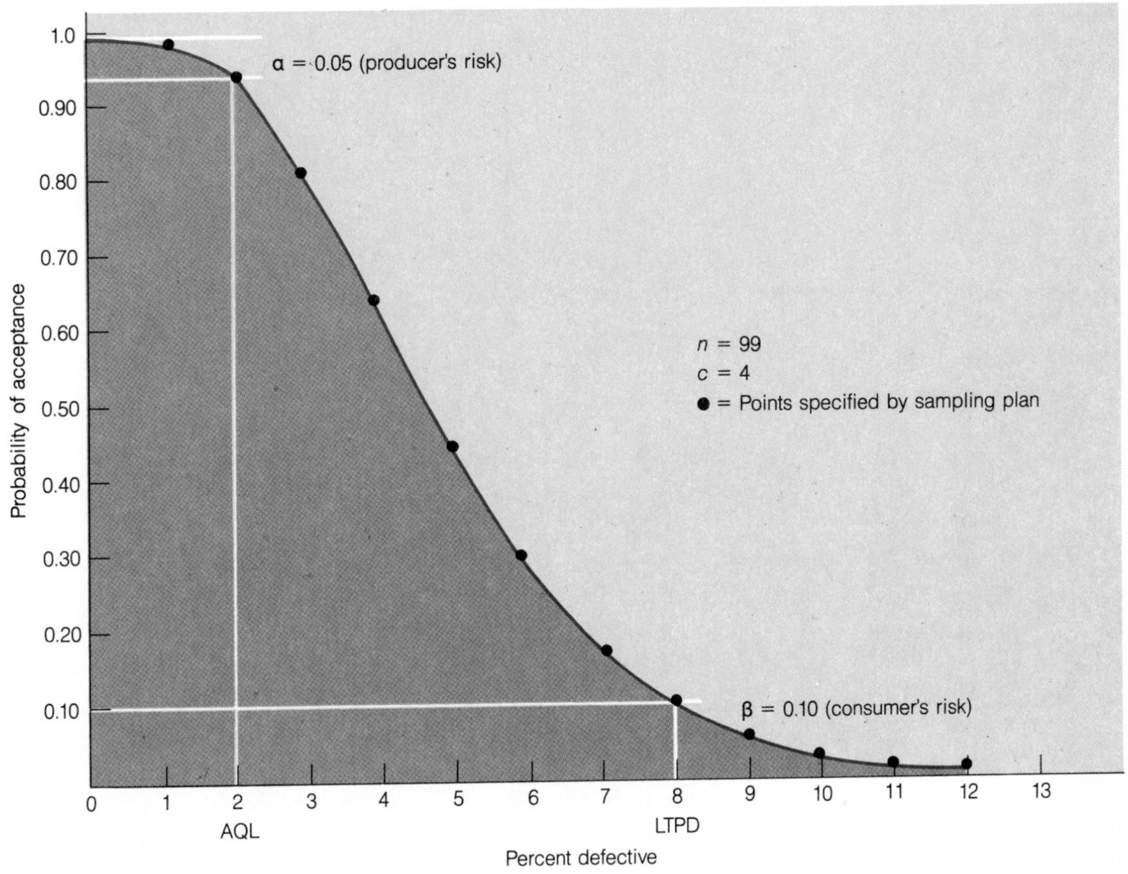

The Effects of Lot Size

The size of the lot the sample is taken from has relatively little effect on the quality of protection. Consider, for example, that samples—all of the same size of 20 units—are taken from different lots ranging from a lot size of 200 units to a lot size of infinity. If each lot is known to have 5 percent defectives, then the probability of accepting the lot based on the sample of 20 units ranges from about 0.34 to about 0.36. What this means is that so long as the lot size is several times the sample size, it makes very little difference how large the lot is. It seems a bit difficult to accept, but statistically (on the average in the long run) whether we have a carload or box full, we'll get about the same answer. It just seems that a carload should have a larger sample size.

EXHIBIT 5.6

Sequential Sampling Plan with $\alpha = 0.05$ at $p_1' = 0.01$ and $\beta = 0.10$ at $p_2' = 0.06$

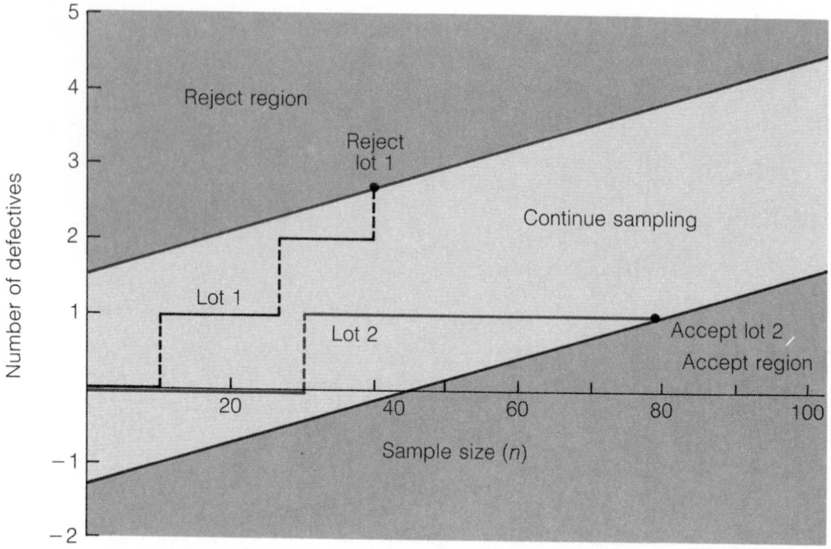

Sequential Sampling Plans

The most efficient sampling technique to test the fewest number of products is called *sequential sampling.* This is used when destructive testing is involved and the product is in short supply. Rather than selecting a sample from a lot and inspecting all items in the sample to make the accept-reject decision, units are tested one at a time. Under sequential sampling fewer items are tested for the same degree of accuracy. In a sequential sampling plan, the results are accumulated and a decision is made to (1) reject the lot, (2) accept the lot, or (3) inspect another item.

Exhibit 5.6 is an example of a sequential sampling plan. It shows that we would have to sample at least 44 items before accepting the lot, but we could reject the lot much sooner.

5.8 PROCESS CONTROL PROCEDURES

Process control is concerned with monitoring quality *while the product or service is being produced.* Typical objectives of process control plans are to provide timely information on whether currently produced items are meeting design specifications, and to detect shifts in the process that signal that future products may not meet specifications. The actual control phase of process control occurs when corrective action is taken, such as a worn part replaced, a machine overhauled, or a new supplier found. Process control concepts, especially statistically based control charts, are being used in services as well as in manufacturing.

Process Control Using Attribute Measurements

Measurements by attributes means taking samples and using a single decision—the item is good, or it is bad. Because it is a yes-no decision, we can use simple statistics to create an upper control limit (UCL) and a lower control limit (LCL). We can draw these control limits on a graph and then plot the fraction defective of each individual sample tested. The process is assumed to be working correctly when the samples, which are taken periodically during the day, continue to stay between the control limits.

$$\bar{p} = \frac{\text{Total number of defects from all samples}}{\text{Number of samples} \times \text{Sample size}}$$

$$s_p = \sqrt{\frac{\bar{p}(1 - \bar{p})}{n}}$$

$$\text{UCL} = \bar{p} + zs_p$$

$$\text{LCL} = \bar{p} - zs_p$$

where p is the fraction defective, s is the standard deviation, and z is the number of standard deviations for a specific confidence. Typically, $z = 3$ (99.7 percent confidence) or $z = 2.58$ (99 percent confidence) are used.

Exhibit 5.7 shows information that can be gained from control charts. We will not give an example of attribute process control here but in the next section we will demonstrate $\overline{X}$ and R charts, which tend to have wider application in process control.

Process Control with Variable Measurements Using $\overline{X}$ and *R* Charts

$\overline{X}$ and R (range) charts are widely used in statistical process control.

In attributes sampling, we determine whether something is good or bad, fit or didn't fit—it is a go/no-go situation. In variables sampling, we measure weight, volume, number of inches, or other variable measurements, and we develop control charts to determine the acceptability or rejection of the process based on those measurements.

There are four main issues to address in creating a control chart: the size of the samples, the number of samples, frequency of samples, and the control limits.

EXHIBIT 5.7 **Control Chart Evidence for Investigation**

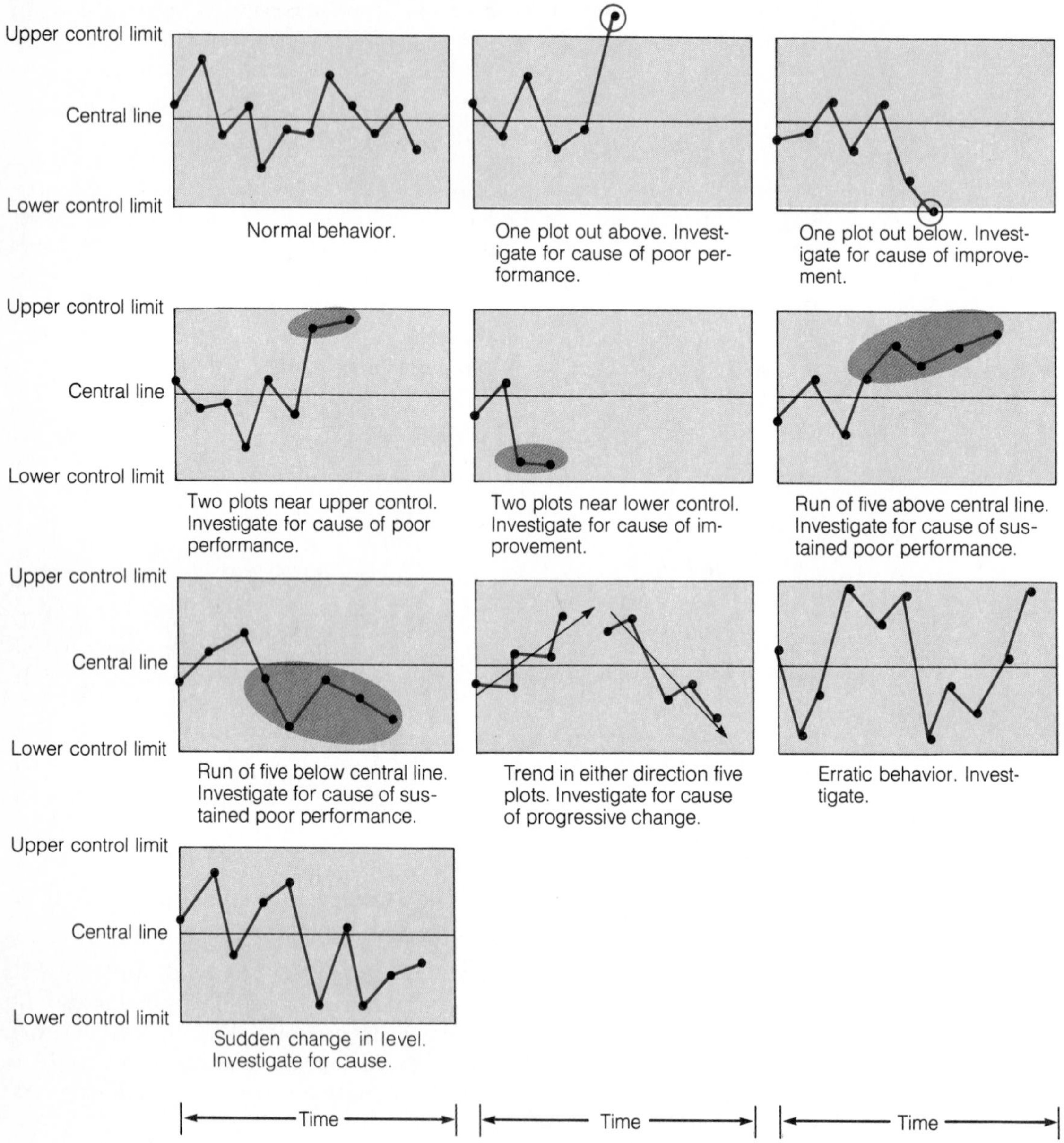
Upper control limit
Central line
Lower control limit
Normal behavior.
One plot out above. Investigate for cause of poor performance.
One plot out below. Investigate for cause of improvement.
Two plots near upper control. Investigate for cause of poor performance.
Two plots near lower control. Investigate for cause of improvement.
Run of five above central line. Investigate for cause of sustained poor performance.
Run of five below central line. Investigate for cause of sustained poor performance.
Trend in either direction five plots. Investigate for cause of progressive change.
Erratic behavior. Investigate.
Sudden change in level. Investigate for cause.
Time
Time
Time

Source: Bertrand L. Hansen, *Quality Control: Theory and Applications*, © 1963, p. 65. Reprinted by permission of Prentice-Hall, Inc., Englewood Cliffs, N.J.

Size of samples

For industrial applications in process control it is preferable to keep the sample size small. There are two main reasons: first, the sample needs to be taken within a reasonable length of time, otherwise the process might change while the samples are taken. Second, the larger the sample, the more it costs to take.

Sample sizes of four or five units seem to be the preferred numbers. The *means* of samples of this size will have an approximately normal distribution, no matter what the distribution of the parent population looks like. Sample sizes greater than five will give narrower control limits and thus more sensitivity. For detecting finer variations of a process, it may be necessary, in fact, to use larger sample sizes. However, when sample sizes exceed 15 or so, it would be better to use the standard deviation σ and $\overline{X}$ charts rather than R and $\overline{X}$ charts.

Number of samples

Once the chart has been set up, each sample taken can be compared to the chart and a decision made about whether the process is acceptable. In order to set up the charts, however, prudence (and statistics) suggests that 25 or so samples be taken.

Frequency of samples

How often to take a sample is a trade-off between the cost of sampling (along with the cost of the unit if it is destroyed as part of the test), and the benefit of adjusting the system. Usually, it is best to start off with frequent sampling of a process and taper off as confidence in the process builds. For example, one might start with a sample of five units every half hour and end up feeling that one sample per day is adequate.

Control limits

Standard practice in statistical process control for variables is to set control limits three standard deviations above the mean and three standard deviations below. This means that 99.7 percent of the sample means are expected to fall within these control limits (that is, within a 99.7 percent confidence interval). Thus, if one sample mean falls outside this obviously wide band, we have strong evidence that the process is out of control.

How to Construct $\overline{X}$ and R Charts

An $\overline{X}$ chart is simply a plot of the means of the samples that were taken from a process. An $\overline{\overline{X}}$ is the average of the means.

An R chart is a plot of the range within each sample. The range is the difference between the highest and the lowest number in that sample. R values provide an easily calculated measure of variation that is used like a standard deviation. An $\overline{R}$ chart is the average of the range of each sample. More specifically defined, these are:

$$\overline{X} = \frac{\sum_{i=1}^{n} X_i}{n}$$

where

$\overline{X}$ = Mean of the sample
i = Item number
n = Total number of items in the sample

$$\overline{\overline{X}} = \frac{\sum_{j=1}^{m} \overline{X}_j}{m}$$

where

$\overline{\overline{X}}$ = The average of the means of the samples
j = Sample number
m = Total number of samples
R = Difference between the highest and lowest measurement in the sample
$\overline{R}$ = Average of the measurement differences R for all samples, or

$$\overline{R} = \frac{\sum_{j=1}^{m} R_j}{m}$$

Grant and Leavenworth computed a table that allows us to easily compute the upper and lower control limits for both the $\overline{X}$ chart and the R chart.[9] These are defined as:

Upper control limit for $\overline{X} = \overline{\overline{X}} + A_2\overline{R}$
Lower control limit for $\overline{X} = \overline{\overline{X}} - A_2\overline{R}$
Upper control limit for $R = D_4\overline{R}$
Lower control limit for $R = D_3\overline{R}$

[9] E. L. Grant and R. Leavenworth, *Statistical Quality Control* (New York: McGraw-Hill, 1964), p. 562. Reprinted by permission.

Example

We would like to create an $\overline{X}$ and an R chart for a process. Exhibit 5.9 shows the measurements that were taken of all 25 samples. The last two columns show the average of the sample $\overline{X}$ and the range R.

Values for A_2, D_3, and D_4 were obtained from Exhibit 5.8.

$$\text{Upper control limit for } \overline{X} = \overline{\overline{X}} + A_2\overline{R}$$
$$= 10.21 + .58(.60) = 10.56$$

$$\text{Lower control limit for } \overline{X} = \overline{\overline{X}} - A_2\overline{R}$$
$$= 10.21 - .58(.60) = 9.86$$

$$\text{Upper control limit for } R = D_4\overline{R}$$
$$= 2.11(.60) = 1.26$$

EXHIBIT 5.8

Factors for Determining from $\overline{R}$ the 3-Sigma Control Limits for $\overline{X}$ and R Charts

Number of Observations in Subgroup n	Factor for $\overline{X}$ Chart A_2	FACTORS FOR R CHART: Lower Control Limit D_3	FACTORS FOR R CHART: Upper Control Limit D_4
2	1.88	0	3.27
3	1.02	0	2.57
4	0.73	0	2.28
5	0.58	0	2.11
6	0.48	0	2.00
7	0.42	0.08	1.92
8	0.37	0.14	1.86
9	0.34	0.18	1.82
10	0.31	0.22	1.78
11	0.29	0.26	1.74
12	0.27	0.28	1.72
13	0.25	0.31	1.69
14	0.24	0.33	1.67
15	0.22	0.35	1.65
16	0.21	0.36	1.64
17	0.20	0.38	1.62
18	0.19	0.39	1.61
19	0.19	0.40	1.60
20	0.18	0.41	1.59

$$\text{Upper control limit for } \overline{X} = UCL_{\overline{X}} = \overline{X} + A_2\overline{R}$$
$$\text{Lower control limit for } \overline{X} = LCL_{\overline{X}} = \overline{X} - A_2\overline{R}$$
$$\text{Upper control limit for } R = UCL_R = D_4\overline{R}$$
$$\text{Lower control limit for } R = LCL_R = D_3\overline{R}$$

Note: All factors are based on the normal distribution.

Source: E. L. Grant, *Statistical Quality Control*, 6th ed. (New York: McGraw-Hill, 1988). Reprinted by permission of McGraw-Hill, Inc.

EXHIBIT 5.9

Measurements in Samples of Five from a Process

Sample Number	Each Unit in Sample					Average $\overline{X}$	Range R
1	10.60	10.40	10.30	9.90	10.20	10.28	.70
2	9.98	10.25	10.05	10.23	10.33	10.17	.35
3	9.85	9.90	10.20	10.25	10.15	10.07	.40
4	10.20	10.10	10.30	9.90	9.95	10.09	.40
5	10.30	10.20	10.24	10.50	10.30	10.31	.30
6	10.10	10.30	10.20	10.30	9.90	10.16	.40
7	9.98	9.90	10.20	10.40	10.10	10.12	.50
8	10.10	10.30	10.40	10.24	10.30	10.27	.30
9	10.30	10.20	10.60	10.50	10.10	10.34	.50
10	10.30	10.40	10.50	10.10	10.20	10.30	.40
11	9.90	9.50	10.20	10.30	10.35	10.05	.85
12	10.10	10.36	10.50	9.80	9.95	10.14	.70
13	10.20	10.50	10.70	10.10	9.90	10.28	.80
14	10.20	10.60	10.50	10.30	10.40	10.40	.40
15	10.54	10.30	10.40	10.55	10.00	10.36	.55
16	10.20	10.60	10.15	10.00	10.50	10.29	.60
17	10.20	10.40	10.60	10.80	10.10	10.42	.70
18	9.90	9.50	9.90	10.50	10.00	9.96	1.00
19	10.60	10.30	10.50	9.90	9.80	10.22	.80
20	10.60	10.40	10.30	10.40	10.20	10.38	.40
21	9.90	9.60	10.50	10.10	10.60	10.14	1.00
22	9.95	10.20	10.50	10.30	10.20	10.23	.55
23	10.20	9.50	9.60	9.80	10.30	9.88	.80
24	10.30	10.60	10.30	9.90	9.80	10.18	.80
25	9.90	10.30	10.60	9.90	10.10	10.16	.70
				$\overline{\overline{X}}$ =		10.21	
				$\overline{R}$ =			.60

$$\text{Lower control limit for } R = D_3\overline{R}$$
$$= 0(1.27) = 0$$

Exhibit 5.10 shows the $\overline{X}$ chart and R chart with a plot of all the sample means and ranges of the samples. All the points are well within the control limits, although sample 23 is close to the $\overline{X}$ lower control limit.

Process Capability

Control charts are of little value if the process itself is not capable of making products that are within design specification (or tolerance) limits. In Section A of Exhibit 5.11, we see a process that on average is producing items within the control limits but its variation is such that it can't meet specifications for all items. Exhibit 5.11 (B) shows reduction in this variability, but the process is

EXHIBIT 5.10

$\bar{X}$ Chart and *R* Chart

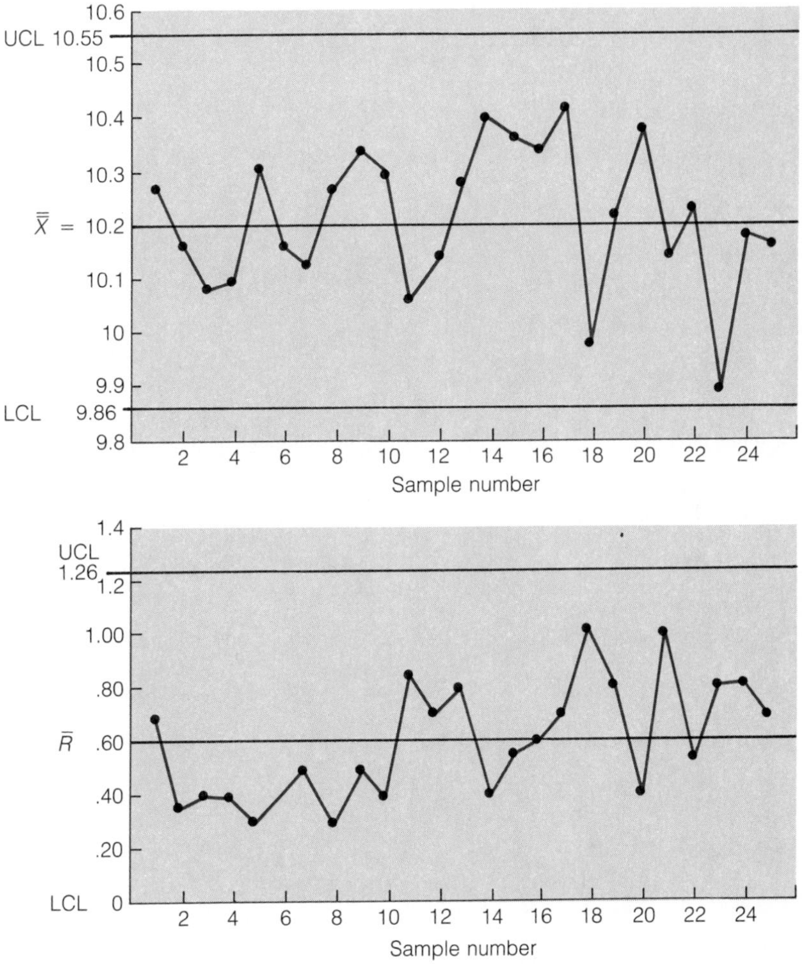

still deficient. Finally, in Exhibit 5.11 (C), we see that the process variability has been brought under control. How is this accomplished? By working to improve the performance of each source of variance: workers, machine, tooling, setup, material, and the environment. Tools (such as fishbone diagrams) for pinpointing the basic causes of variability are discussed in the chapter on Just-in-Time production.

EXHIBIT 5.11 **Reducing Process Variance So That All Parts Are in Tolerance**

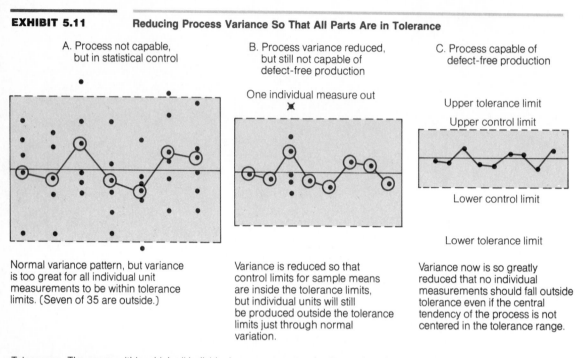

A. Process not capable, but in statistical control

B. Process variance reduced, but still not capable of defect-free production

C. Process capable of defect-free production

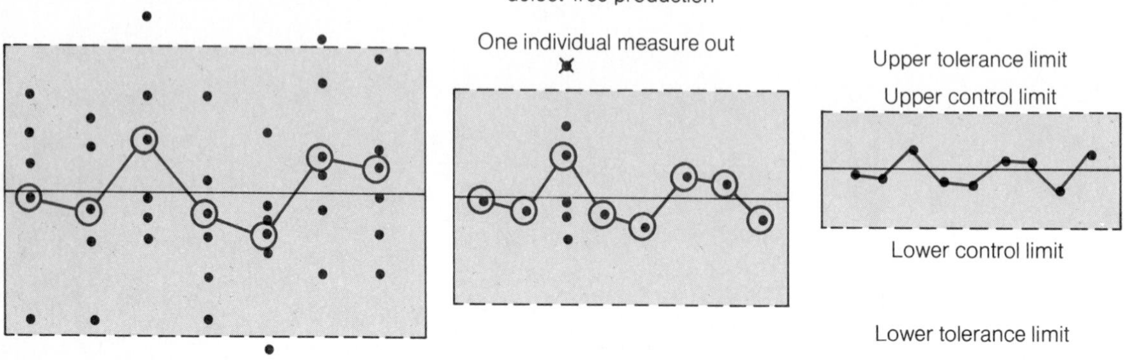

Normal variance pattern, but variance is too great for all individual unit measurements to be within tolerance limits. (Seven of 35 are outside.)

Variance is reduced so that control limits for sample means are inside the tolerance limits, but individual units will still be produced outside the tolerance limits just through normal variation.

Variance now is so greatly reduced that no individual measurements should fall outside tolerance even if the central tendency of the process is not centered in the tolerance range.

Tolerance: The range within which all individual measurements of units produced is desired to fall.

Source: Robert W. Hall, *Attaining Manufacturing Excellence: Just-in-Time Manufacturing, Total Quality, Total People Involvement* (Homewood, Ill.: Dow Jones-Irwin, 1987), p. 66.

5.9 TAGUCHI METHODS

Throughout the chapter we have discussed quality control from the point of view of process adjustments. In what many have termed a revolution in quality thinking, Genichi Taguchi of Japan has suggested the following: Instead of constantly fiddling with production equipment to ensure consistent quality, design the product to be robust enough to achieve high quality despite fluctuations on the production line. This simple idea has been employed by such companies as Ford, ITT, and IBM, and as a result they have saved millions of dollars in manufacturing.

Taguchi methods are basically statistical techniques for conducting experiments to determine the best combinations of product and process variables to make a product. *Best* means lowest cost with highest uniformity. This can be a complicated, time-consuming process. For example, in designing the process for a new product, one might find that a single processing step with only eight process variables (machine speed, cutting angle, and so on) could be combined in up to 5,000 different ways. Thus, finding the combination that will make the product with the highest uniformity at the lowest cost can't be done by trial and error. Taguchi has found a way around this problem by focusing on only a few combinations that represent the extremes of product/process outcomes.

In addition to statistical experimentation, Taguchi also relies on the concept of a quality loss function (QLF) to tie cost of quality directly to variation in a process. The idea here is that deviation from a product's ideal specification has a direct cost penalty that cannot be measured using control charts. That is, control charts treat all items that fall within control limits as being equally good, even though their actual dimensions may differ substantially. The impact of this may be seen in manufacturing a car door and its frame: Both parts may be within their individual specification limits, yet the door may not fit perfectly when closed. The QLF puts a whole new economic perspective on quality by clearly specifying what less than perfect quality costs the company.

5.10 QUALITY MEASUREMENT IN SERVICE INDUSTRIES

Health Care

Nearly all quality control procedures may be used in the health care industry, where one still hears such comments as "Traditional scientific methods do not apply when a human life is at stake," or "No price can be placed on human life." Statements like these have no rhyme or reason. Indeed, the fact that this industry *does* deal with human life makes it all the more important to use the best available techniques to determine and ensure acceptable quality levels. Exhibit 5.12 lists some essential features of a hospital quality measurement system. Remember, though, the key is to control the process.

Banking

In many banks, sampling is periodically performed on savings and checking accounts. The quality of a loan portfolio, however, is observed primarily by examining the larger loans, usually those over 0.1 percent of the total loan portfolio. Exhibit 5.13 lists some essential features of a bank quality measurement system.

EXHIBIT 5.12

Some Essential Features of a Hospital Quality Measurement System

Points of Inspection	Examples of What to Look for	Consequences of Deviations	Possible Method of Measurement
Lab tests	Accuracy in reading	Inaccurate diagnosis, possibly serious consequences	Chief lab technician samples completed tests. Automatic equipment checked for reasonable readings and tests on known samples
Pharmacy	Expiration dates of medications; accuracy in requests	Ranging from minor to fatal	Complete recheck. Pharmacist fills prescriptions, checks, and packages; questions MD on large dosages
Housekeeping	Cleanliness	Dirty areas increase likelihood of infection	Supervisor checks against standards
Operating rooms	Sterile conditions; correct equipment, surgical procedures, scrubbing, attire	Lawsuits, malpractice, possible death or injury, loss of image	Armband verifies correct patient for surgery; verify chart and surgical procedure; sponge and instrument count
Admissions	Verify information with patient; forms all filled in	Usually minor inconveniences or later questions	If computerized, verified by techniques such as format of insurance numbers, age of children versus age and marital status of patient
Billing	Insurance claims filed, late billings, accuracy in amount	Lost money or late receipts	Compare patients' stay with billing date and insurance filing

EXHIBIT 5.12

Concluded

Points of Inspection	Examples of What to Look for	Consequences of Deviations	Possible Method of Measurement
Nursing service	Up-to-date charts, medication on time, correct medication, temperature and pulse readings on time, progress reports	Discomfort, delayed patient recovery, degrading to image	Supervisor checks work; incident reports reviewed daily
Laundry	Cleanliness, on-time schedule	Degrades image, possible contamination	Supervisor inspects linen
Food service	Quality of precooked food, method of preparation, meals on time and satisfactory	Patient satisfaction, hospital's image	Dietician inspects all food; prepackaged frozen food sampled for diet constraints and quality; patient complaints observed
Outpatient	Available facilities, degree of usage	Crowding or underutilization	Perhaps emergency room department may review
Central supply	Stocking of linens, surgical instruments, syringes; sterility of supplies	Delays, infection from unsterilized items	Tapestrip indicating sterilization performed. Indicator to determine if packages opened or leaking; packages dated
Medical staff	Competence, accuracy in diagnosis, acceptable surgery or service	Lawsuits, malpractice suits, hospital image, patient death or injury	Adequate observation by specialists before hospital privileges granted. Analysis of procedures reviewed on all difficult cases. Tissue committee previews all charts for pathology reports

EXHIBIT 5.13

Some Essential Features of a Bank Quality Measurement System

Points of Inspection	Examples of What to Look for	Consequences of Deviations	Possible Method of Measurement
Loan ratio	Too low or too high	Loss of profit, inadequate funds	Complete tabulation, compared to standard
Equity base	Small or large	Committed to lower yield, less risky use of funds; high equity permits greater risk	Routine reports
Liquidity ratio	Ratio of short term to total	High-ratio loss of potential profit; Low-ratio inability to meet withdrawals or make new loans	Tabulation compared to norm
Loan portfolio	Collateral backing, degree of risk, term length	Possible defaults	Internal audits, also audits by Federal Reserve and state for some banks
Margin	Adequate reserves	Violation of regulation	Routine observation
Savings accounts	Accuracy	Not serious to bank but creates unhappy customers, loss of prestige and business	Sampling of accounts
Checking accounts	Accuracy, overdrawn accounts	As above, plus possible losses on overdrafts if honored	Routine sampling plus flagged accounts
Savings to total deposits	Ratio	High ratio results in higher interest costs	Occasional observation
Teller operations	Shortages, overages, neatness, manners	Loss of prestige	Daily tally sheets, general subjective observation

5.11 CONCLUSION

The importance of quality shows signs of continued rapid increase in the present and the foreseeable future. Corporate management is becoming committed to introducing quality programs into their firms. The objective of error-free work through management commitment and employee involvement is part of the total quality approach.

A large part of the Japanese success in producing high-quality products is a result of their mastery of QC techniques. Japanese foremen and workers use statistical control charts, histograms, and other such aids with ease.

What of the future in quality control? It appears that statistical procedures and routines will have less emphasis on sampling. This is especially true as inspection and manufacturing processes become automated and the number of defects becomes very small.

Even more profound is the likely impact of Taguchi methods whose ability to link quality and cost at the design stage will force changes in the financial practices of manufacturing firms.

Total quality has become the modus operandi for the entire firm and may be fast becomming "a way of life."

5.12 REVIEW AND DISCUSSION QUESTIONS

1. What is the difference between the traditional role of the quality control department in the American firms and the new role? Why is a new role for quality control necessary?
2. What are the quality characteristics, as defined in Exhibit 5.1, for each of the following:
   a. IBM personal computer.
   b. School registration process.
   c. Steakhouse.
3. An agreement is made between a supplier and a customer such that the supplier must ensure that all parts are within tolerance before shipment to the customer. What is the effect on the cost of quality to the customer?
4. In the situation described in Question 3, what would be the effect on the cost of quality to the supplier?
5. Identify the type of sampling technique which would be appropriate for the following and justify your answer:
   a. Receipt of food products at a warehouse.
   b. Software system's fitness to users' specifications.
   c. Oil refining.
6. If line employees are required to assume the quality control function, their productivity will decrease. Discuss this.
7. "You don't inspect quality into a product; you have to build it in." Discuss the implications of this statement.
8. "Before you build quality in, you must think it in." How do the implications of this statement differ from those of Question 7?
9. The coordination among marketing, manufacturing, and design engineering to address and resolve quality concerns is particularly important to improving the quality of production and service. What perspective does each of these organizations have with respect to quality?

10. Discuss the trade-off between achieving a zero AQL (acceptable quantity level) and a positive AQL, e.g., an AQL of 2 percent.

5.13 PROBLEMS

*1. Management is trying to decide whether Part A, which is produced with a consistent 3 percent defective, should be inspected. If it is not inspected, the 3 percent defectives will go through a product assembly phase and have to be replaced later. If all Part A's are inspected, one third of the defectives will be found, thus raising the quality to 2 percent defectives.
   a. Should the inspection be done if the cost of inspecting is \$0.01 per unit and the cost of replacing a defective in the final assembly is \$4.00?
   b. Suppose the cost of inspecting is \$0.05 per unit rather than \$0.01. Would this change your answer in *a*?

2. A company currently using an inspection process in its material receiving department is trying to install an overall cost reduction program. One possible reduction is the elimination of one of the inspection positions. This position tests material that has a defective content on the average of 0.04. By inspecting all items, the inspector is able to remove all defects. The inspector can inspect 50 units per hour. Hourly rate including fringe benefits for this position is \$9. If the inspection position is eliminated, defects will go into product assembly and will have to be replaced later at a cost of \$10 each when they are detected in final product testing.
   a. Should this inspection position be eliminated?
   b. What is the cost to inspect each unit?
   c. Is there benefit (or loss) from the current inspection process? How much?

3. Output from a process contains 0.02 defective units. Defective units that go undetected into final assemblies cost \$25 each to replace. An inspection process, which would detect and remove all defectives, can be established to test these units. However, the inspector, who can test 20 units per hour, is paid a rate of \$8 per hour, including fringe benefits. Should an inspection station be established to test all units?
   a. What is the cost to inspect each unit?
   b. What is the benefit (or loss) from the inspection process?

4. There is a 3 percent error rate at a specific point in a production process. If an inspector is placed at this point, all the errors can be detected and eliminated. However, the inspector is paid \$8 per hour and can inspect units in the process at the rate of 30 per hour.

   If no inspector is used and defects are allowed to pass this point, there is a cost of \$10 per unit to correct the defect later on.

   Should an inspector be hired?

---

* Problem 1 is solved in Appendix D.

5. Resistors for electronic circuits are being manufactured on a high-speed automated machine. The machine is being set up to produce a large run of resistors of 1,000 ohms each.

   To set up the machine and to create a control chart to be used throughout the run, 15 samples were taken with 4 resistors in each sample. The complete list of samples and their measured values are as follows:

Sample Number	Readings (in ohms)			
1	1010	991	985	986
2	995	996	1009	994
3	990	1003	1015	1008
4	1015	1020	1009	998
5	1013	1019	1005	993
6	994	1001	994	1005
7	989	992	982	1020
8	1001	986	996	996
9	1006	989	1005	1007
10	992	1007	1006	979
11	996	1006	997	989
12	1019	996	991	1011
13	981	991	989	1003
14	999	993	988	984
15	1013	1002	1005	992

   Develop an $\overline{X}$ chart and an R chart and plot the values. From the charts, what comments can you make about the process? (Use 3 sigma control limits as in Appendix B.)

6. In the past, Alpha Corporation has not performed incoming quality control inspections but has taken the word of its vendors. However, Alpha has been having some unsatisfactory experience recently with the quality of purchased items and wants to set up sampling plans for the receiving department to use.

   For a particular component, X, Alpha has a lot tolerance percent defective of 10 percent. Zenon Corporation, from whom Alpha purchases this component, has an acceptable quality level in its production facility of 3 percent for component X. Alpha has a consumer's risk of 10 percent and Zenon has a producer's risk of 5 percent.

   a. When a shipment of X is received from Zenon Corporation, what is the sample size that the receiving department should test?

   b. What is the allowable number of defects in order to accept the shipment?

7. A company is producing component parts that are used later in its production process. The department producing the products has defined its acceptable quality as 3 percent defective. For later installation, the department has a lot-tolerance percent defective of 8 percent.

   a. Specify the sampling plan; that is, what is the c and n?

   b. Interpret your results for an inspector—explain the plan in terms of the inspector's duties.

8. Parts are produced in one part of a production process to be used later in the assembly of the final product. If items are inspected, the cost of the inspector's wages, fringe benefits, and materials total $10 per hour. The inspector can inspect 10 units per hour, and units are produced at a 95 percent yield (i.e., 0.05 defectives). Defective units that pass on through the system must be replaced later at a cost of $12 each.

   Assuming that the inspector could detect all the existing defects, should an inspector be retained at point A?

5.14 SELECTED BIBLIOGRAPHY

Deming, W. Edwards. *Out of the Crisis.* Cambridge, Mass.: MIT Press, 1986.

Dreyfus, Joel. "Victories in the Quality Crusade." *Fortune*, October 10, 1988, pp. 80–84.

Feigenbaum, Armand V. *Total Quality Control.* 3rd ed. New York: McGraw-Hill, 1986.

Garvin, David A. "Competing on the Eight Dimensions of Quality." *Harvard Business Review*, November–December 1987, pp. 101–108.

________. *Managing Quality: The Strategic and Competitive Edge.* New York: Free Press, 1987.

Gilks, John F. "Total Quality: Wave of the Future." *Canadian Business Review*, Spring 1990, pp. 17–20.

Grant, Eugene L., and Richard S. Leavenworth. *Statistical Quality Control.* 6th ed. New York: McGraw-Hill, 1988.

Juran, Joseph M. *Juran on Planning for Quality.* New York: Free Press, 1988.

Knowlton, Christopher. "What America Makes Best." *Fortune*, March 1988, pp. 40–48.

Pfau, Loren D. "Total Quality Management Gives Companies a Way to Enhance Position in Global Marketplace." *Industrial Engineering*, April 1989, pp. 17–20.

Ross, Philip J. *Taguchi Techniques for Quality Engineering.* New York: McGraw-Hill, 1988.

Saraph, Jayant V.; P. George Benson; and Roger G. Shroeder. "An Instrument for Measuring the Critical Factors of Quality Management." *Decision Sciences* 20 (Fall 1989), pp. 810–29.

Sullivan, Lawrence P. "The Power of Taguchi Methods." *Quality Progress,* June 1987, pp. 76–79.

Suzaki, Kiyoshi. *The New Manufacturing Challenge: Techniques for Continuous Improvement.* New York: The Free Press, Macmillan, 1987.

Taguchi, Genichi; Don Clausing; Connie Dyer; and Lance A. Ealey. "Robust Quality; Design Products Not to Fail in the Field; You Will Simultaneously Reduce Defects in the Factory." *Harvard Business Review*, January–February 1990, pp. 65–75.

Total Quality: An Executive's Guide for the 1990's / Ernst & Young Quality Improvement Consulting Group. Homewood, Ill.: Dow Jones-Irwin, 1990.

Townsend, Patrick L., and Joan A. Gebhardt. *Commit to Quality.* New York: John Wiley & Sons, 1990.

Chapter 6

Forecasting

EPIGRAPH

"If I had only known that would happen I would have . . ."

CHAPTER OUTLINE

KEY TERMS

Time Series Analysis
Causal Relationships
Moving Averages
Exponential Smoothing
Smoothing Constant Alpha
Trend Effects
Seasonal Factors
Mean Absolute Deviation (MAD)
Tracking Signal

One of the authors of this text gave a class lecture on forecasting on the Thursday before the stock market's Black Monday, October 19, 1987. Before covering the formal approaches explained in this chapter, he discussed the logic behind a very common—and very simple—forecasting method: drawing high and low lines containing plots of the existing data and projecting a trend line approximately through the center. This gives an upper and lower boundary for expected future plots. To demonstrate this technique (and some of its problems), he showed three slides depicting stock market data.

The first slide was the *daily* Dow Jones average for January through the first week of October, 1987. The author drew in lines bounding the highest and lowest points (see Exhibit 6.1A) and asked the students to forecast future averages, using this data as a base. This was October 15 and, as expected, students' responses tended to fall in the 2500–2750 range for the immediate future, rising within the boundary lines with the passage of time.

The second slide showed the *weekly* Dow Jones averages for 1983 to 1987 (Exhibit 6.1B). Once again students estimated that future averages would be around a general trend line drawn through the center of the high and low points. The author drew in lines bounding the data for the most recent three years. He asked the specific question: "If the stock market were to fall, how far do you think it would drop?" They forecasted lows at around 2200. The third slide showed monthly Dow Jones averages (see Exhibit 6.1C). Based on the data since 1982, students decided future lows would be around 1500. After some discussion about this monthly data, a set of boundary lines were drawn to include the years from 1974, excluding about one year which contained the recent dramatic rise. After some discussion, students came to a consensus that from this longer-term viewpoint, a Dow Jones average from 1350 down to a low of 1000 would be quite reasonable. Thus, using the same logic and same data, though different time periods, we had derived four possible low points: 2500, 2200, 1500, and 1000. Which one were we to believe?

Then, in an ironic twist, Black Monday occurred before our next class session, and we had an opportunity to review our forecasts and the logic behind them. As it happened, the market fell 500 points, to just above 1700—not unexpected. From Exhibit 6.1C, it could have been much worse.

The point of this discussion is to stress the susceptibility of forecasts to be biased by the views of the forecaster and to rapidly undergo changes. Illustrating the stock market example showed two main points: first, that simply plotted data and drawing lines forces the forecaster to think about what he or she is doing and to get some ball park estimates; and second, forecasts can be very wrong and the system should be prepared to accept this and to respond.

Of course, most businesses use much more sophisticated forecasting techniques, but even basic procedures like simply drawing lines are quite useful.

In this chapter we look at *qualitative* and *quantitative* forecasting and concentrate primarily on quantitative time series techniques.

EXHIBIT 6.1

Daily, Weekly, and Monthly Dow Jones Industrial Averages

A.

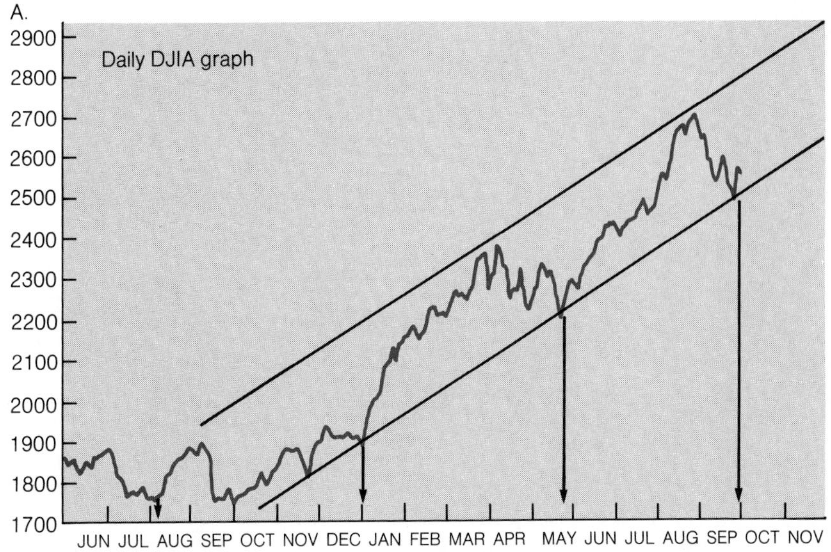

B.

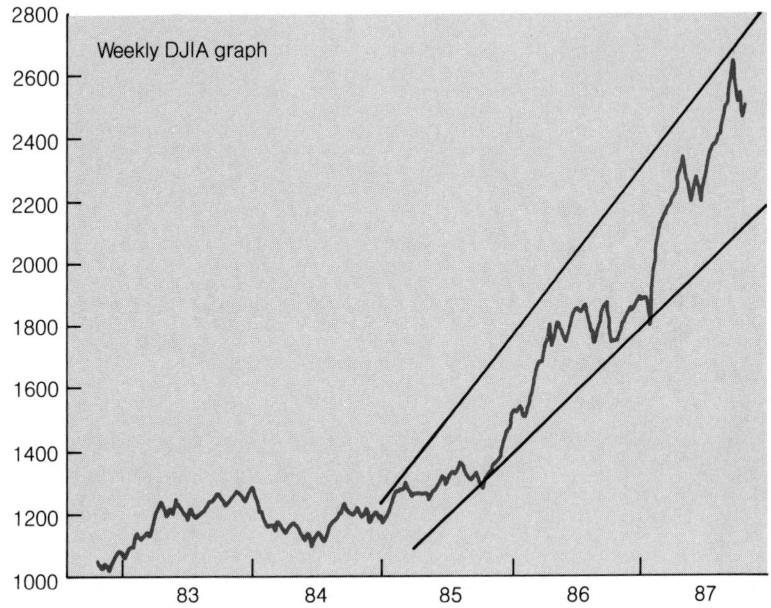

EXHIBIT 6.1

Concluded

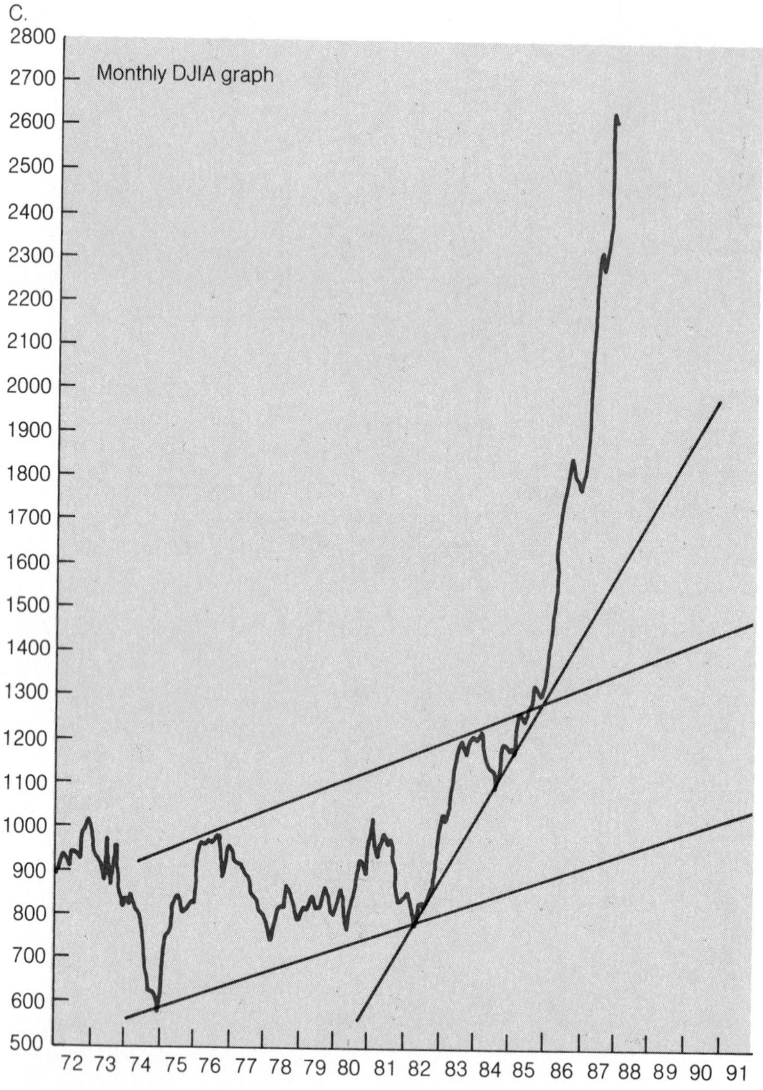

Before we begin, however, we want to stress the importance of forecasting—not only to every business organization, but to virtually every significant management decision. Forecasting is the basis of corporate long-run planning. In the functional areas of finance and accounting, forecasts provide the basis for budgetary planning and cost control. Marketing relies on sales forecasting to plan new products, compensate sales personnel, and make other key decisions. Production and operations personnel use forecasts to make periodic decisions involving process selection, capacity planning, facility layout; and for continual decisions about production planning, scheduling, and inventory.

We must bear in mind that a perfect forecast is usually an impossibility. There are simply too many factors in the business environment that cannot be predicted with certainty. Therefore, rather than search for the perfect forecast, what is far more important is to establish the practice of continual review of forecasts and to learn to live with inaccurate forecasts. This is not to say that we should not try to improve the forecasting model or methodology, but that we should try to find and use the best forecasting method available, *within reason*.

When forecasting, a good strategy is to use two or three methods and look at them from the common-sense view. Are there expected changes in the general economy that will affect the forecast? Are there changes in industrial and private consumer behaviors? Will there be a shortage of essential complementary items? Continual review and updating in light of new data are basic to successful forecasting. Learning to live with forecast inaccuracy is an unavoidable requirement of most production systems and is accomplished by having a flexible production planning system and competent production managers.

6.1 DEMAND MANAGEMENT

Where does the demand for a firm's product or service come from, and what can a firm do about it?

Basically, the firm has two choices: sit back and simply respond to whatever demand there is, or try to control it. The first is a passive response to demand and the second, an active influence on demand. In some situations a firm simply accepts demand for its products or services as a given, without making any attempt to change it—for example, if a firm is running at full capacity or if trying to change demand is too expensive. In most cases, however, firms can take an active role in changing the demand for their existing products, through price cuts or price increases, managerial pressure on the sales force, incentives, campaigns, and so on. They can also affect demand on the workload of production facilities by a variety of internal actions, such as creating order backlogs or introducing countercyclical products.

A great deal of coordination is required to manage the demand on the firm's productive facilities since these demands originate from a variety of sources. For example, parts for repair of previously sold products originate from the product service department; new products are sold through the sales department; restocking standard items may be handled by the factory warehouse; and in-process inventories and partially completed subassemblies are handled by the manufacturing function. The challenge of *demand management* is to blend all these demands so that the productive system can be used efficiently and the products or services delivered on time.

6.2 TYPES OF FORECASTING

Forecasting can be classified into four basic types—*qualitative, time series analysis, causal relationships,* and *simulation.*

Qualitative techniques are subjective or judgmental and are based on estimates and opinions. **Time series analysis,** the focus of this chapter, is based on the idea that data relating to past demand can be used to predict future demand. Past data may include several components, such as trend, seasonal, or cyclical influences, and is described in the following section. Causal forecasting assumes that demand is related to some underlying factor or factors in the environment. Simulation models allow the forecaster to run through a range of assumptions about the condition of the forecast. Exhibit 6.12 in the conclusion of this chapter briefly describes a variety of the four basic types of forecasting models.

6.3 COMPONENTS OF DEMAND

In most cases, the observed demand for products or services can be broken down into six components: average demand for the period, a trend, seasonal influence, cyclical elements, random variation, and autocorrelation. Exhibit 6.2 illustrates a demand over a four-year period, showing the average, trend, seasonal components, and randomness around the smoothed demand curve.

EXHIBIT 6.2 **Historical Product Demand Consisting of a Growth Trend and Seasonal Demand**

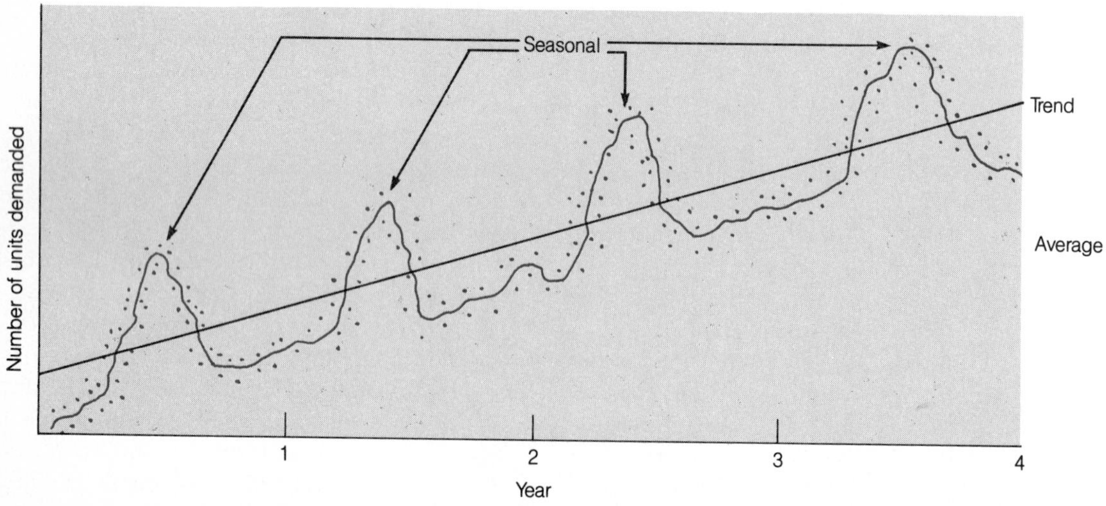

Cyclical factors are more difficult to determine since the time span may be unknown or the cause of the cycle may not be considered. Cyclical influence on demand may come from such occurrences as political elections, war, economic conditions, or sociological pressures.

Random variations are caused by chance events. Statistically, when all the known causes for demand (average, trend, seasonal, cyclical, and autocorrelative) are subtracted from the total demand, what remains is the unexplained portion of demand. If one is unable to identify the cause of this remainder, it is assumed to be purely random chance.

Autocorrelation denotes the persistence of occurrence. More specifically, the value expected at any point is highly correlated with its own past values. In waiting line theory, the length of a waiting line is highly autocorrelated. That is, if a line is relatively long at one time, then shortly after that time one would expect the line still to be long.

When the demand is random, the demand from one week to another may vary widely. Where high autocorrelation exists, the demand will not be expected to change very much from one week to the next.

6.4 CAUSAL RELATIONSHIPS

Although it is difficult to forecast the cyclical component, it is often possible to establish a mathematical relationship between demand, the dependent variable, and some *leading indicator,* the independent variable. If we can obtain the value for the leading indicator ahead of time, we may be able to forecast demand using this **causal relationship.** If cyclical is the most important component, this type of causal model may prove effective.

Example 6.1
The Carpet City Store in Carpenteria has kept records of its sales (in square yards) each year, along with the number of permits for new houses in its area.

Year	Number of Housing Start Permits	Sales (in sq. yds.)
1979	18	13,000
1980	15	12,000
1981	12	11,000
1982	10	10,000
1983	20	14,000
1984	28	16,000
1985	35	19,000
1986	30	17,000
1987	20	13,000

Carpet City's operations manager believes forecasting sales is possible if housing starts are known for that year. First, the data are plotted on Exhibit 6.3, with

x = Number of housing start permits
y = Sales of carpeting

Since the points appear to be in a straight line, the manager decides to fit a linear relationship between x and y: $y = a + bx$. Since the line intersects the y axis around 7,000 yards, we can estimate a (the y intercept) as 7,000. The manager interprets a as the demand for carpeting when no new houses are

EXHIBIT 6.3

Causal Relationship: Sales to Housing Starts

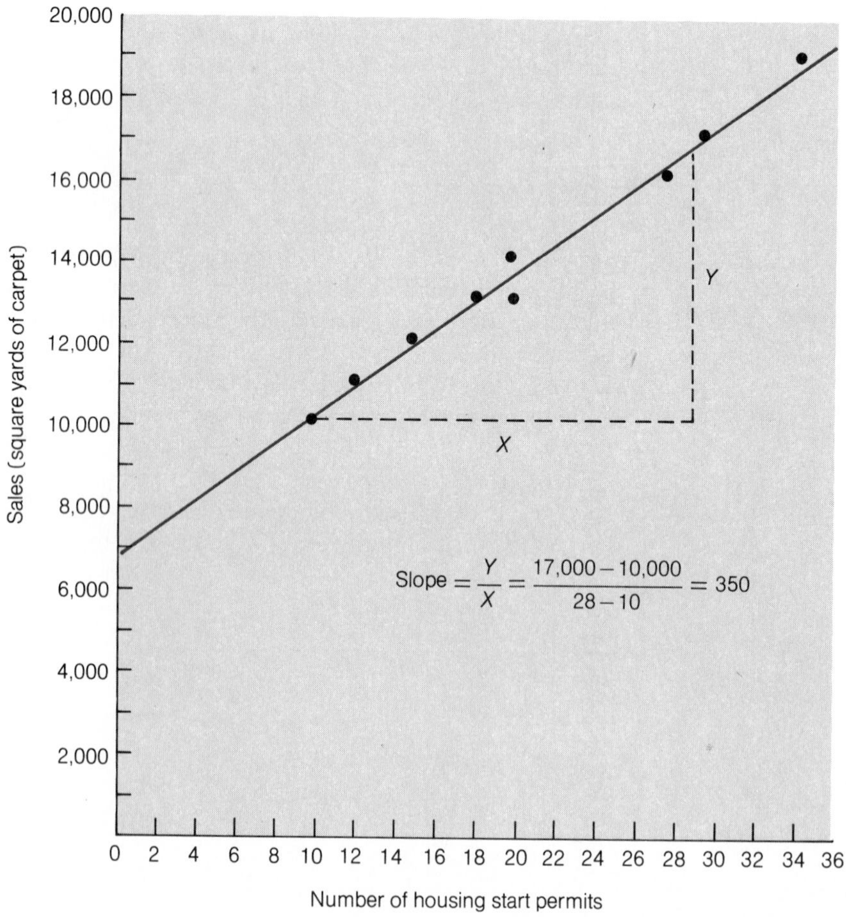

built, probably replacement for old carpeting. To estimate the slope, two points are selected close to the line, such as:

Year	x	y
1982	10	10,000
1986	30	17,000

From algebra the slope is calculated as:

$$b = \frac{y(86) - y(82)}{x(86) - x(82)} = \frac{17{,}000 - 10{,}000}{30 - 10} = \frac{7{,}000}{20} = 350$$

The manager interprets the slope as the average number of square yards of carpet sold for each new house built in the area. The forecasting equation is therefore:

$$y = 7{,}000 + 350x$$

Now suppose that there were 25 permits for houses to be built in 1988. The 1988 sales forecast would have been:

$$7{,}000 + 350(25) = 15{,}750 \text{ square yards}$$

6.5 TIME SERIES ANALYSIS

Time series forecasting models try to predict future occurrences based on past data. For example, weekly sales figures collected for six weeks may be used as a basis to forecast the seventh-week sales. Several familiar time series models are *moving average, exponential smoothing,* and *regression analysis.*

Past data, however, can contain a variety of elements (trend, seasonal, cyclical, random, autocorrelation). Thus, the managerial question is deciding how deeply to analyze the data. **Moving-average** techniques (simple, weighted, and exponential) use the data as observed. More complicated techniques (Box Jenkins, Fourier, Shiskin) try to improve the prediction by separating the data into components such as trends and cycles for analysis. (See Exhibit 6.12 for a brief description of the various forecasting techniques.)

Simple Moving Average

When demand for a product is neither growing nor declining rapidly, and if it does not have seasonal characteristics, a moving average can be useful in removing the random fluctuations for forecasting. Although moving averages are frequently "centered," it is more convenient to use past data to predict the following period directly. To illustrate, a centered five-month average of January, February, March, April, and May gives an average centered on

EXHIBIT 6.4

Forecast Demand Based on a Three- and a Nine-Week Simple Moving Average

Week	Demand	3 Week	9 Week	Week	Demand	3 Week	9 Week
1	800			16	1,700	2,200	1,811
2	1,400			17	1,800	2,000	1,800
3	1,000			18	2,200	1,833	1,811
4	1,500	1,067		19	1,900	1,900	1,911
5	1,500	1,300		20	2,400	1,967	1,933
6	1,300	1,333		21	2,400	2,167	2,011
7	1,800	1,433		22	2,600	2,233	2,111
8	1,700	1,533		23	2,000	2,467	2,144
9	1,300	1,600		24	2,500	2,333	2,111
10	1,700	1,600	1,367	25	2,600	2,367	2,167
11	1,700	1,567	1,467	26	2,200	2,367	2,267
12	1,500	1,567	1,500	27	2,200	2,433	2,311
13	2,300	1,633	1,556	28	2,500	2,333	2,311
14	2,300	1,833	1,644	29	2,400	2,300	2,378
15	2,000	2,033	1,733	30	2,100	2,367	2,378

EXHIBIT 6.5 **Moving Average Forecast of Three- and Nine-Week Periods versus Actual Demand**

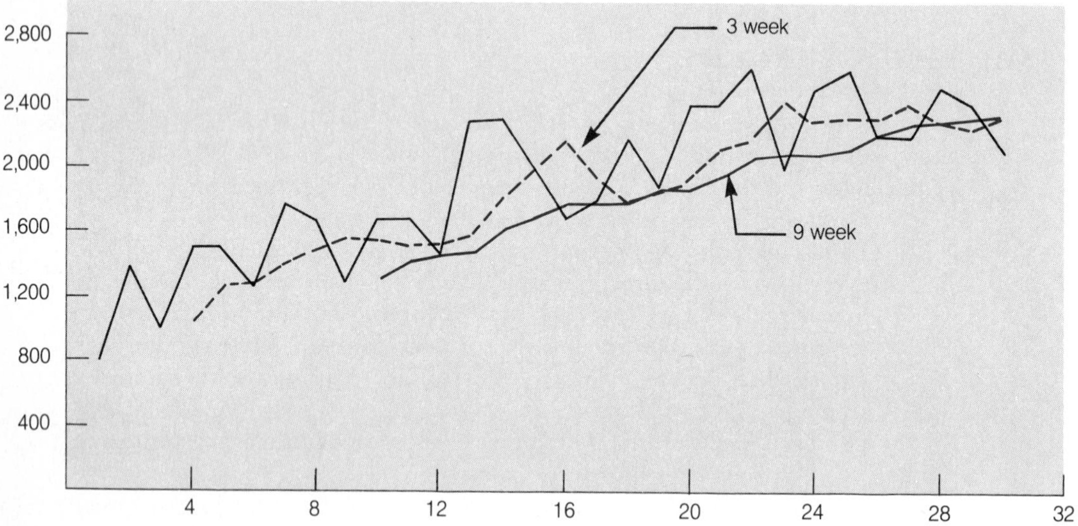

March. However, all five months of data must already exist. If our objective is to forecast for June, we must project our moving average—by some means—from March to June. If the average is not centered but is at the forward end, we can forecast more easily, though perhaps we will lose some accuracy. Thus if we want to forecast June with a five-month moving average, we can take the average of January, February, March, April, and May. When June passes, the forecast for July would be the average of February, March, April, May, and June. This is the way Exhibits 6.4 and 6.5 were computed.

Although it is important to try to select the best period for the moving average, there are several conflicting effects of different period lengths: the longer the moving-average period, the greater the random elements are smoothed (which may be desirable in many cases). However, if there is a trend in the data—either increasing or decreasing—the moving average has the adverse characteristic of lagging the trend. Therefore, while a shorter time span produces more oscillation, there is a closer "following" of the trend. Conversely, a longer time span gives a smoother response but lags the trend.

Exhibit 6.5, a plot of the data in Exhibit 6.4, illustrates the effects of various lengths of the period of a moving average. We see that the growth trend levels off at about the 23rd week. The three-week moving average responds better in following this change than the nine-week, although overall, the nine-week average is smoother.

The main disadvantage in calculating a moving average is that all individual elements must be carried as data since a new forecast period involves adding new data and dropping the earliest data. For a three- or six-period moving average, this is not too severe; however, plotting a 60-day moving average for the usage of each of 20,000 items in inventory would involve a significant amount of data.

Weighted Moving Average

Whereas the simple moving average gives equal weight to each component of the moving-average database, a weighted moving average allows any weights to be placed on each element, providing, of course, that the sum of all weights equals one. For example, a department store may find that in a four-month period the best forecast is derived by using 40 percent of the actual sales for the most recent month, 30 percent of two months ago, 20 percent of three months ago, and 10 percent of four months ago. If actual sales experience was as follows,

Month 1	Month 2	Month 3	Month 4	Month 5
100	90	105	95	?

the forecast for month 5 would be:

$$\begin{aligned} F_5 &= 0.40(95) + 0.30(105) + 0.20(90) + 0.10(100) \\ &= 38 + 31.5 + 18 + 10 \\ &= 97.5 \end{aligned}$$

Suppose sales for month 5 actually turned out to be 110; then the forecast for month 6 would be:

$$F_6 = 0.40(110) + 0.30(95) + 0.20(105) + 0.10(90)$$
$$= 44 + 28.5 + 21 + 9$$
$$= 102.5$$

The weighted moving average has a definite advantage over the simple moving average in being able to vary the effects of past data. However, it is more inconvenient and costly to use.

Exponential Smoothing

In the previous methods of forecasting (simple and weighted moving average), the major drawback is the need to continually carry a large amount of historical data. As each new piece of data is added in these methods, the oldest observation is dropped, and the new forecast is calculated. In many applications (perhaps in most), the most recent occurrences are more indicative of the future than those in the more distant past. If this premise is valid—that the importance of data diminishes as the past becomes more distant—then **exponential smoothing** may be the most logical and easiest method to use.

Exponential smoothing is the most used of all forecasting techniques. It is an integral part of virtually all computerized forecasting programs, and is widely used in ordering inventory in retail firms, wholesale companies, and service agencies.

The most comprehensive coverage of exponential smoothing is presented in a paper by Gardner.[1] Not only does he trace the history of the development of exponential smoothing from its development somewhere during the time of World War II, but he also critically comments on the merits of various models and challenges or discredits others based on his own work and the work of other writers.

The major reasons that exponential smoothing techniques have become so well accepted are:

1. Exponential models are surprisingly accurate.
2. Formulating an exponential model is relatively easy.
3. The user can understand how the model works.
4. There is very little computation required to use the model.
5. Computer storage requirements are small because of the limited use of historical data.
6. Tests for accuracy as to how well the model is performing are easy to compute.

In the exponential smoothing method, only three pieces of data are needed to forecast the future: the most recent forecast, the actual demand that oc-

[1] Everette S. Gardner, Jr., "Exponential Smoothing: The State of the Art," *Journal of Forecasting* 4, no. 1 (March 1985).

curred for that forecast period, and a **smoothing constant alpha** (α). This smoothing constant determines the amount of reaction to differences between forecasts and actual occurrences. The value for the constant is arbitrary and is determined both by the nature of the product and the manager's sense of what constitutes a good response rate. For example, if a firm produced a standard item with relatively stable demand, the reaction rate to differences between actual and forecast demand would tend to be small, perhaps just a few percentage points. However, if the firm were experiencing growth, it would be desirable to have a higher reaction rate, to give greater importance to recent growth experience. The more rapid the growth, the higher the reaction rate should be. Sometimes, users of the simple moving average will switch to exponential smoothing but would like to keep the forecasts about the same as the simple moving average. In this case, α is approximated by $2 \div (n + 1)$ where n was the number of time periods.

The equation for a single exponential smoothing forecast is simply

$$F_t = F_{t-1} + \alpha(A_{t-1} - F_{t-1})$$

where

F_t = The exponentially smoothed forecast for period t
F_{t-1} = The exponentially smoothed forecast made for the prior period
A_{t-1} = The actual demand in the prior period
α = The desired response rate, or smoothing constant

This equation states that the new forecast is equal to the old forecast plus a portion of the error (the difference between the previous forecast and what actually occurred).[2]

To demonstrate the method, assume that the long-run demand for the product under study is relatively stable and a smoothing constant (α) of 0.05 is considered appropriate. If the exponential method were used as a continuing policy, a forecast would have been made for last month.[3] Assume that last month's forecast (F_{t-1}) was 1,050 units. If 1,000 actually were demanded, rather than 1,050, the forecast for this month would be:

$$\begin{aligned} F_t &= F_{t-1} + \alpha(A_{t-1} - F_{t-1}) \\ &= 1{,}050 + 0.05(1{,}000 - 1{,}050) \\ &= 1{,}050 + 0.05(-50) \\ &= 1{,}047.5 \text{ units} \end{aligned}$$

Since the smoothing coefficient is small, the reaction of the new forecast to an "error" of 50 units is to decrease the next month's forecast by only 2½ units.

---

[2] Some writers prefer to call F_t a smoothed average.

[3] When exponential smoothing is first introduced, the initial forecast or starting point may be obtained by using a simple estimate or an average of preceding periods.

EXHIBIT 6.6 **Exponential Forecasts versus Actual Demands for Units of a Product over Time Showing the Forecast Lag**

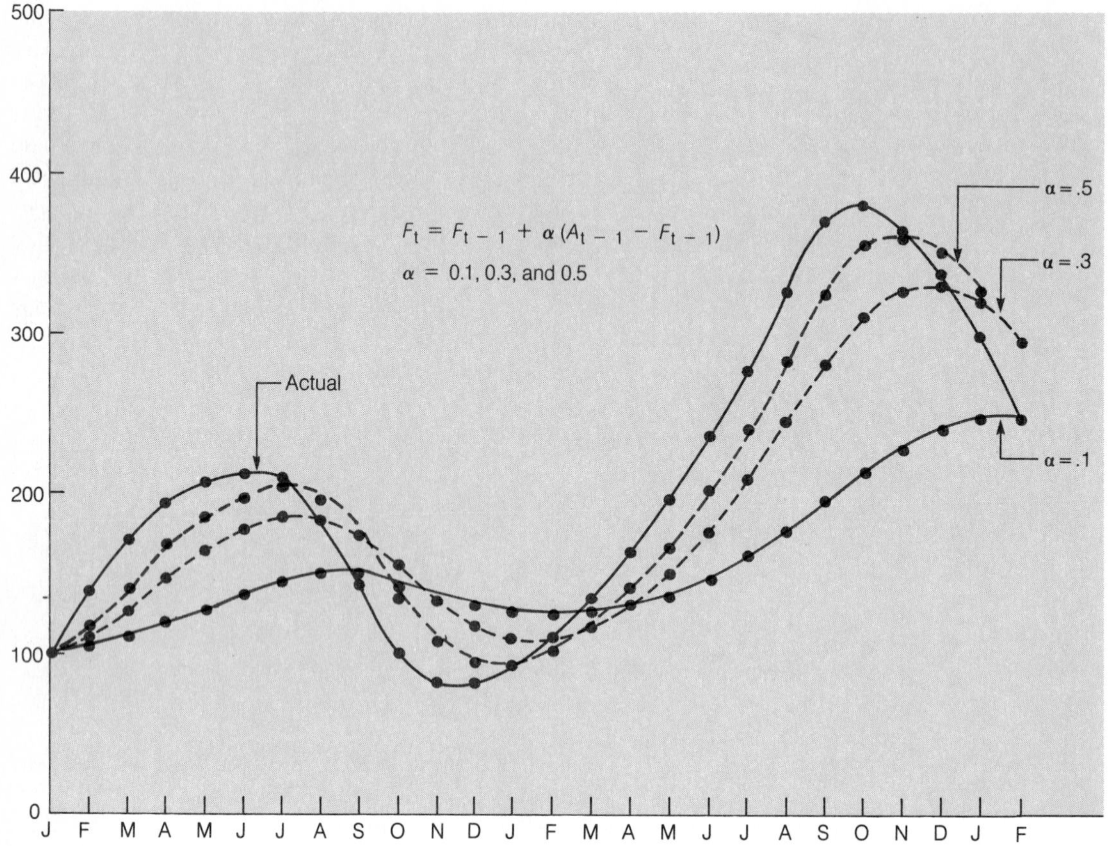

The reason this is called *exponential smoothing* is because each increment in the past is decreased by $(1 - \alpha)$, or

		Weighting at $\alpha = 0.05$
Most recent weighting	$= \alpha(1 - \alpha)^0$	0.0500
Data 1 time period older	$= \alpha(1 - \alpha)^1$	0.0475
Data 2 time periods older	$= \alpha(1 - \alpha)^2$	0.0451
Data 3 time periods older	$= \alpha(1 - \alpha)^3$	0.0429

As you can see, the exponents 0, 1, 2, 3 . . . and so on give it its name. Single exponential smoothing has the shortcoming of lagging changes in demand. Exhibit 6.6 shows actual data plotted as a smooth curve to show the lagging effects of the exponential forecasts. The forecast lags during an increase or decrease, but overshoots when a change in the direction occurs. Note that the higher the value of alpha, the more closely the forecast follows the actual. To help in closer tracking of actual demand, a trend factor may be added. What also will help is to adjust the value of alpha. This is termed *adaptive forecasting*. These techniques are available in many textbooks on forecasting.

The simple exponential smoothing model has many applications in OM in addition to inventory control. Berry, Mabert, and Marcus have shown that simple exponential smoothing can be valuable in scheduling services, such as bank tellers.[4] Their study showed that the causes of customer demand can be identified and used to improve forecasting (such as by banks located near large employers using known payday schedules). While this is often done intuitively, the study shows how such forecasting can be routinely used as an ongoing, continually updated planning tool.

Decomposition of a Time Series

A *time series* can be defined as chronologically ordered data that may contain one or more components of demand—trend, seasonal, cyclical, autocorrelation, and random. *Decomposition* of a time series means identifying and separating the time series data into these components. In practice, it is relatively easy to identify the trend (even without mathematical analysis, it is usually easy to plot and see the direction of movement) and the seasonal component (by comparing the same period year to year). It is considerably more difficult to identify the cycles (these may be many months or years long), autocorrelation, and random components (the forecaster usually calls random anything left over that cannot be identified as another component).

When demand contains both trend and seasonal effects at the same time, the question is how they relate to each other. In this description we examine two types of seasonal variation: *additive* and *multiplicative.*

Additive seasonal variation

Additive seasonal variation simply assumes that the seasonal amount is a constant no matter what the trend or average amount is.

Forecast, including trend and seasonal ($FITS$) = Trend + Seasonal

Exhibit 6.7A shows an example of increasing trend with constant seasonal amounts.

Multiplicative seasonal variation

In multiplicative seasonal variation, the trend is multiplied by the seasonal factors.

Forecast including trend and seasonal ($FITS$) = Trend × Seasonal factor

---

[4] William L. Berry, Vincent A. Mabert, and Myles Marcus, "Forecasting Teller Window Demand with Exponential Smoothing," *Journal of the Academy of Management* 22, no. 1 (March 1979), pp. 129–37.

EXHIBIT 6.7

Additive and Multiplicative Seasonal Variation Superimposed on Changing Trend

A. Additive seasonal

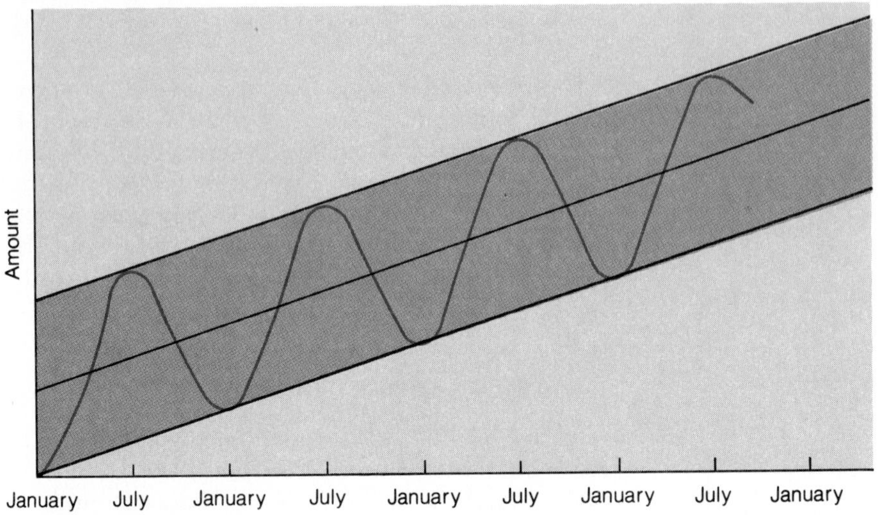

B. Multiplicative seasonal

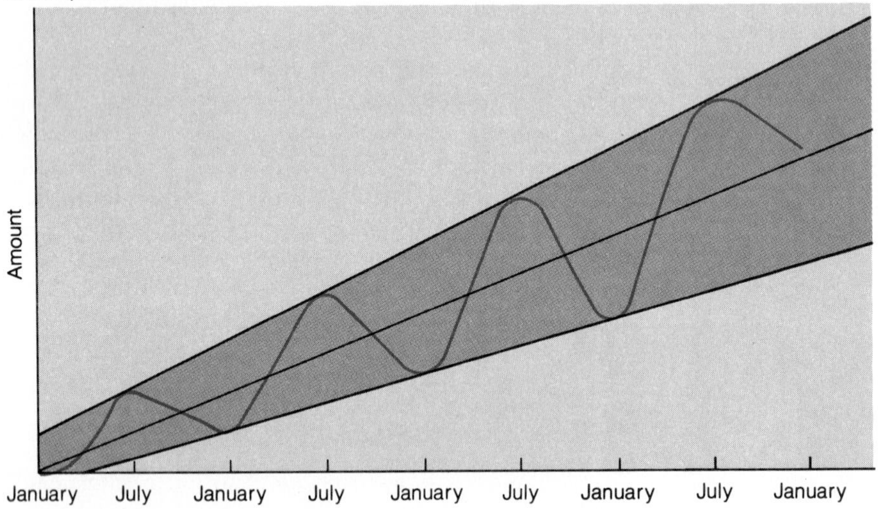

Exhibit 6.7B shows the seasonal variation increasing as the trend increases since its size depends on the trend.

The multiplicative seasonal variation is the more useful relationship and will be explained in more detail.

Seasonal Factor (or Index)

A **seasonal factor** is the amount of correction needed in a time series to adjust for the season of the year.

Example 6.2

Assume that a firm in past years sold an average 1,000 units of a particular product line each year. On the average, 200 units were sold in the spring, 350 in the summer, 300 in the fall, and 150 in the winter. The seasonal factor (or index) is the ratio of the amount sold during each season divided by the average for all seasons. In this example, the yearly amount divided equally over all seasons is 1,000 ÷ 4 = 250. The seasonal factors therefore are:

$$\begin{aligned} \text{Spring factor (index)} &= 200/250 = 0.80 \\ \text{Summer} &= 350/250 = 1.40 \\ \text{Fall} &= 300/250 = 1.20 \\ \text{Winter} &= 150/250 = 0.60 \end{aligned}$$

Using these factors, if we expected the demand for next year to be 1,100 units, we would forecast the demand to occur as:

$$\begin{aligned} &\text{Spring} && 1{,}100/4 \times 0.80 = 220 \\ &\text{Summer} && 1{,}100/4 \times 1.40 = 385 \\ &\text{Fall} && 1{,}100/4 \times 1.20 = 330 \\ &\text{Winter} && 1{,}100/4 \times 0.60 = 165 \end{aligned}$$

The seasonal factor may be periodically updated as new data are available. To illustrate the seasonal factor and the multiplicative seasonal variation, consider the following example:

Example 6.3—Forecast including trend and seasonal factors

Company A sells outdoor recreational equipment. Analyzing its past sales by quarters, the company sees a straight-line upward trend in sales of one of its product lines. The marketing department had calculated this trend to be of the form,

$$\text{Trend}_t = 1{,}000 + 75t$$

where t is the quarter of the year, with the first or base quarter January–March 1983. Thus, forecast sales for the four quarters of 1985 (quarters 9 through 12) are:

$$\begin{aligned} \text{Trend}_9 &= 1{,}000 + 75\ (9) = 1{,}675 \\ \text{Trend}_{10} &= 1{,}000 + 75(10) = 1{,}750 \\ \text{Trend}_{11} &= 1{,}000 + 75(11) = 1{,}825 \\ \text{Trend}_{12} &= 1{,}000 + 75(12) = 1{,}900 \end{aligned}$$

This product line does have a definite seasonal demand, however, and this is not shown in the trend. We must modify the trend equation to take this seasonal variation into account. Assume that we have analyzed past sales and found that the first quarter was only 30 percent of the average quarter, the second quarter was 50 percent of the average quarter, the third quarter was 170 percent of the average quarter, and the fourth quarter 50 percent of the average quarter. The seasonal pattern was thus:

S_1 = 0.3 January–March
S_2 = 1.5 April–June
S_3 = 1.7 July–September
S_4 = 0.5 October–December

The resulting forecasts including trend and seasonal (FITS) for the four quarters of 1985 are:

$$FITS_9 = 1{,}675 \times .3 = 502.5$$
$$FITS_{10} = 1{,}750 \times 1.5 = 2{,}625.0$$
$$FITS_{11} = 1{,}825 \times 1.7 = 3{,}102.5$$
$$FITS_{12} = 1{,}900 \times .5 = 950$$

Linear Regression Analysis

If we plot data points on a graph and try to eyeball a straight line through these points where we think it seems to fit best, we are using a linear trend logic. That is, we are presuming that the increase or decrease for the dependent variable follows a straight line. The examples in Section 6.4 and Exhibit 6.3 show a linear relationship. The term *linear regression* carries the simple fitting a step further and uses a simple mathematical technique to try to make a better fit than "eyeballing." Linear regression takes the differences between the actual data point and the point on the line and squares it. One main reason this number is squared is to get rid of the minus signs; if you subtract a point above the line from its corresponding point directly below the line you will have a negative number. If you subtract a point below the line from its corresponding point directly above on the line you will have a positive number. Unless you make all of these numbers of the same sign, when you add them up you might have a very small number because the negatives will cancel the positives. The illusion would be that you have a "good" fit of the line. Taking absolute values would solve the sign problem, but researchers believe that squaring the numbers (also changing the negatives to positives) gives a better line fit because it places more emphasis on the points more distant from the line. This "fitted" line is then used to read off other values or it may be projected into the future (if one of the axes is time). We will not go further into linear regression in this text.

6.6 FORECAST ERRORS

Demand for a product is generated through the interaction of a number of factors too complex to describe accurately in a model. Therefore, all forecasts will certainly contain some error. In discussing forecast errors, it is convenient to distinguish between *sources of error* and the *measurement of errors.*

Sources of Error

Errors can come from a variety of sources. One common source that many forecasters are unaware of is caused by projecting past trends into the future. For example, when we talk about statistical errors in regression analysis, we are referring to the deviations of observations from our regression line. It is common to attach a confidence band (i.e., statistical control limits, which were described in Chapter 5), to the regression line to reduce the unexplained error. However, when we then use this regression line as a forecasting device by projecting it into the future, the error may not be correctly defined by the projected confidence band. This is because the confidence interval is based on past data; it may or may not hold for projected data points and therefore cannot be used with the same confidence. In fact, experience has shown that the actual errors tend to be greater than those predicted from forecast models.

Errors can be classified as bias or random. *Bias errors* occur when a consistent "mistake" is made. Sources of bias are: failing to include the right variables; using the wrong relationships among variables; employing the wrong trend line; mistakenly shifting the seasonal demand from where it normally occurs; and the existence of some undetected secular trend.

Random errors can be defined as those that cannot be explained by the forecast model being used. There is a bit of irony in this statement, though, since, if one desires to minimize the error in explaining PAST data, a sophisticated model can be used, such as a Fourier series with a large number of terms. While this can reduce the forecasting model's error on the PAST data to almost zero, it may do no better in forecasting future demand than a simpler model with a higher error. The moral here is to beware of someone who tries to sell you a forecasting model that can fit, say, 99 percent of the past 50 years of data. It may be worthless in predicting next week, next month, or next year.

Measurement of Error

Several of the common terms used to describe the degree of error are *standard error, mean squared error* (or *variance*), and *mean absolute deviation.* In addition, tracking signals may be used to indicate the existence of any positive or negative bias in the forecast.

The **mean absolute deviation (MAD)** was in vogue in the past but subsequently was ignored in favor of standard deviation and standard error measures. In recent years, MAD has made a comeback because of its simplicity and usefulness in obtaining tracking signals. MAD is the average error in the forecasts, using absolute values. It is valuable because MAD, like the standard deviation, measures the dispersion of some observed value from some expected value.

MAD is computed using the differences between the actual demand and the forecast demand without regard to sign. It is equal to the sum of the absolute deviations divided by the number of data points, or, stated in equation form,

$$MAD = \frac{\sum_{t=1}^{n} \left| A_t - F_t \right|}{n}$$

where

t = Period number
A = Actual demand for the period
F = Forecast demand for the period
n = Total number of periods
$| \ |$ = A symbol used to indicate the absolute value disregarding positive and negative signs

When the errors that occur in the forecast are normally distributed (the usual case), the mean absolute deviation relates to the standard deviation as

$$1 \text{ standard deviation} = \sqrt{\frac{\pi}{2}} \times \text{MAD where } \pi = 3.1416, \text{ or approximately } 1.25 \times \text{MAD}$$

or conversely,

$$1 \text{ MAD} = 0.8 \text{ standard deviation}$$

The standard deviation is the larger measure. If the MAD of a set of points was found to be 60 units, then the standard deviation would be 75 units. And, in the usual statistical manner, if control limits were set at plus or minus 3 standard deviations (or ± 3.75 MADs), then 99.7 percent of the points would fall within these limits.

A **tracking signal** is a measurement that indicates whether the forecast average is keeping pace with any genuine upward or downward changes in demand. As used in forecasting, the tracking signal is the *number* of mean absolute deviations that the forecast value is above or below the actual occurrence. Exhibit 6.8 shows a normal distribution with a mean of zero and a MAD equal to one. Thus, if computing the tracking signal and finding it equal to minus 2, we can notice that the forecast model is providing forecasts that are quite a bit above the mean of the actual occurrences.

EXHIBIT 6.8

A Normal Distribution with a Mean = 0 and a MAD = 1

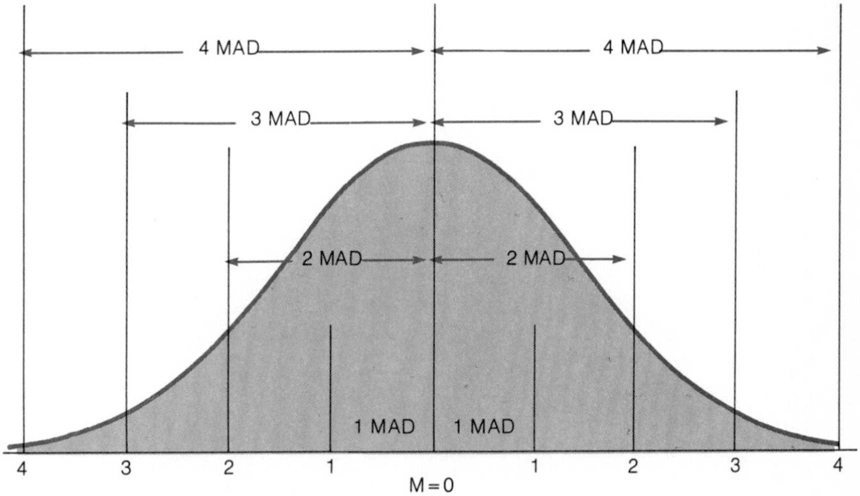

EXHIBIT 6.9

Computing the Mean Absolute Deviation (MAD), the Running Sum of Forecast Errors (RSFE), and the Tracking Signal from Forecast and Actual Data

Month	Demand Forecast	Actual	Deviation	(RSFE)	Abs Dev	Sum of Abs Dev	MAD*	$TS = \frac{RSFE\dagger}{MAD}$
1	1,000	950	−50	−50	50	50	50	−1
2	1,000	1,070	+70	+20	70	120	60	.30
3	1,000	1,100	+100	+120	100	220	73.3	1.64
4	1,000	960	−40	+80	40	260	65	1.2
5	1,000	1,090	+90	+170	90	350	70	2.4
6	1,000	1,050	+50	+220	50	400	66.7	3.3

*Mean absolute deviation (MAD) = 400 ÷ 6 = 66.7.

†Tracking signal = $\frac{RSFE}{MAD}$. For Month 6, TS = $\frac{RSFE}{MAD} = \frac{220}{66.7}$ = 3.3 MADs.

A tracking signal can be calculated using the arithmetic sum of forecast deviations divided by the mean absolute deviation. Exhibit 6.9 illustrates the procedure for computing MAD and the tracking signal for a six-month period where the forecast had been set at a constant 1,000 and the actual demands that occurred are as shown. In this example, the forecast, on the average, was off by 66.7 units and the tracking signal was equal to 3.3 mean absolute deviations.

EXHIBIT 6.10 **A Plot of the Tracking Signals Calculated in Exhibit 6.9**

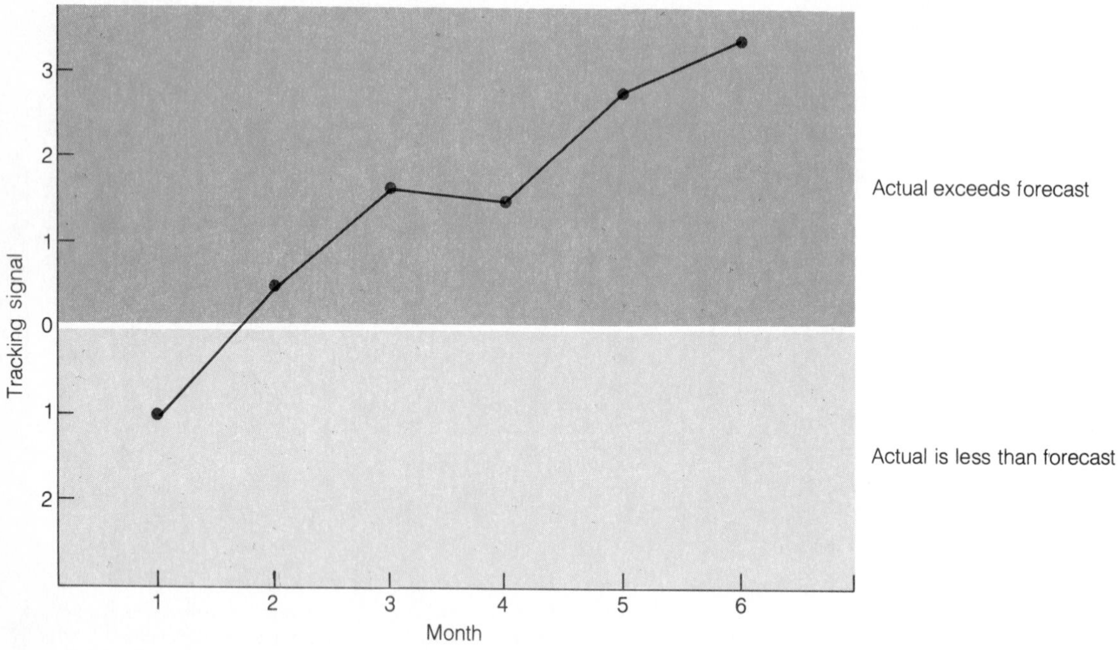

We can get a better feel for what the MAD and tracking signal mean by plotting the points on a graph. While not completely legitimate from a sample size standpoint, we plotted each month in Exhibit 6.10 to show the drifting of the tracking signal. Note that it drifted from minus 1 MAD to plus 3.3 MADs.

Statistically, what we have just done in plotting the tracking signal is not legitimate since the sample size is too small to allow a normal distribution of errors upon which the assumption is based. However, it does show the drifting of the tracking signal, meaning we are headed toward positive errors—such as on the right half of the normal distribution in Exhibit 6.8. At the sixth month (tracking signal 3.3) we would be between 3 and 4 MADs. As the number of data points grows, then the statistical requirements would be met.

Acceptable limits for the tracking signal depend on the size of the demand being forecast (high-volume or high-revenue items should be monitored frequently) and the amount of personnel time available (lower acceptable limits cause more forecasts to be out of limits and therefore require more time to investigate). Exhibit 6.11 shows the area within the control limits for a range of zero to four MADs.

EXHIBIT 6.11

The Percentages of Points Included within the Control Limits for a Range of 0 to 4 MADs

CONTROL LIMITS		
Number of MADs	Related Number of Standard Deviations	Percentage of Points Lying within Control Limits
±1	0.798	57.048
±2	1.596	88.946
±3	2.394	98.334
±4	3.192	99.856

In a perfect forecasting model the sum of the actual forecast errors would be zero; that is, the errors that result in overestimates should be offset by errors that are underestimates. The tracking signal would then also be zero, indicating an unbiased model, neither leading nor lagging the actual demands.

Often, MAD is used to forecast errors. It might then be desirable to make the MAD more sensitive to recent data. A useful technique to do this is to compute an exponentially smoothed MAD as a forecast for the next period's error range. The procedure is similar to single exponential smoothing covered earlier in this chapter. The value of the MAD forecast is to provide a range of error; in the case of inventory control, this is useful in setting safety stock levels.

$$MAD_t = \alpha \mid A_{t-1} - F_{t-1} \mid + (1 - \alpha)MAD_{t-1}$$

where

MAD_t = Forecast MAD for the tth period

α = Smoothing constant (normally in the range of 0.05 to 0.20)

A_{t-1} = Actual demand in the period t-1

F_{t-1} = Forecast demand for period t-1

6.7 COMPUTER PROGRAMS

Many commercial forecasting programs are available. Some exist as library routines within a mainframe computer system, some may be purchased separately from a vendor, and some are part of larger programs. Many programs are available for microcomputers. Most computer manufacturers produce their own, have teamed up with a software company, or have enticed software companies to write programs for their computers.

6.8 CONCLUSION

We cannot overemphasize the importance of forecasting. Forecasting should be done early in any analysis and on a continuing basis.

One of the authors had a consulting assignment with a small firm of approximately 100 employees. The task was a complete reorganization to prepare for significant growth. The logical first step is to make a forecast—even a simple one to take a quick look at past business, project this into the future, and modify this for industry growth, new products, and so on. The president of the company would give only his estimates to use and insisted they were valid. He continually resisted all questions about his forecast and kept insisting his numbers were correct. The author created the appropriate new organization around these assumptions: leasing a new building, new layouts, new personnel, scheduling programs, inventory requirements, and so on—an entire new system!

After the lease for the new building was signed, the president finally opened his treasured list of agents and proposed new channels of distribution to the author. Analyzing the data showed there was no possibility the forecast he had made was feasible. It was a case of extreme overconfidence. What happened when the author showed his forecasts to the president of the company on Friday? On Monday, the president essentially closed his plant except for a skeleton crew. He had accumulated such an oversupply of inventory that he could meet demand from stock for a very long time. There was also so much existing excess capacity that there was no need for the new facility. By the way, the president, shocked into reality, believed he no longer needed the consultant and terminated the contract!

Forecasting is fundamental to any planning effort. In the short run, a forecast is needed to predict the requirements for materials, products, services, or other resources in order to respond to changes in demand. Forecasts permit adjusting schedules and varying labor and materials. In the long run, forecasting is required as a basis for strategic changes, such as developing new markets, developing new products or services, and expanding or creating new facilities.

For long-term forecasts that lead to heavy financial commitments, great care should be taken to derive the forecast. Several approaches should be used. Exhibit 6.12 summarizes the common forecasting techniques. Causal methods such as regression analysis or multiple regression analysis are beneficial. These provide a basis for discussion. Economic factors, product trends, growth factors, and competition, as well as a myriad of other possible variables, will need to be considered and the forecast adjusted to reflect the influence of each.

Short- and intermediate-term forecasting, such as required for inventory control, and staffing and material scheduling, may be satisfied with simpler models, such as exponential smoothing with perhaps an adaptive feature or a

EXHIBIT 6.12 **Forecasting Techniques and Common Models**

I. Qualitative	Subjective; judgmental. Based on estimates and opinions.
Delphi method	Group of experts responds to questionnaire. A moderator compiles results and formulates new questionnaire again submitted to the group. Thus, there is a learning process for the group as they receive new information and there is no influence of group pressure or dominating individual.
Market research	Sets out to collect data in a variety of ways (surveys, interviews, etc.) to test hypotheses about the market. This is typically used to forecast long-range and new-product sales.
Panel consensus	Free open exchange at meetings. The idea is that discussion by the group will produce better forecasts than any one individual. Participants may be executives, salespeople, or customers.
Historical analogy	Ties what is being forecast to a similar item. Important in planning new products where a forecast may be derived by using the history of a similar product.
Grass roots	Derives a forecast by compiling input from those at the end of the hierarchy who deal with what is being forecast. For example, an overall sales forecast may be derived by combining inputs from each salesperson, who is closest to his or her own territory.
II. Time series analysis	Based on the idea that the history of occurrences over time can be used to predict the future.
Simple moving average	A time period containing a number of data points is averaged by dividing the sum of the point values by the number of points. Each, therefore, has equal influence.
Weighted moving average	Specific points may be weighted more or less than the others, as seen fit by experience.
Exponential smoothing	Recent data points are weighted more with weighting declining exponentially as data becomes older.
Regression analysis	Fits a straight line to past data generally relating the data value to time. Most common fitting technique is least squares.
Box Jenkins technique	Very complicated but apparently the most accurate statistical technique available. Relates a class of statistical models to data and fits the model to the time series by using Bayesian posterior distributions.
Shiskin time series	(Also called X-11). Developed by Julius Shiskin of the Census Bureau. An effective method to decompose a time series into seasonals, trends, and irregular. It needs at least three years of history. Very good in identifying turning points, for example, in company sales.
Trend projections	Fits a mathematical trend line to the data points and projects it into the future. Best known as least squares regression technique.
III. Causal	Tries to understand the system underlying and surrounding the item being forecast. For example, sales may be affected by advertising, quality, and competitors.
Regression analysis	Similar to least squares method in time series but may contain multiple variables. Basis is that forecast is caused by the occurrence of other events.
Econometric models	Attempts to describe some sector of the economy by a series of interdependent equations.
Input/output models	Focuses on sales of each industry to other firms and governments. Indicates the changes in sales that a producer industry might expect because of purchasing changes by another industry.
Leading indicators	Statistics that move in the same direction as the series being forecast but move before the series, such as an increase in the price of gasoline indicating a future drop in the sale of large cars.
IV. Simulation models	Dynamic models, usually computer based, that allow the forecaster to make assumptions about the internal variables and external environment in the model. Depending on the variables in the model, the forecaster may ask such questions as: What would happen to my forecast if price increased by 10 percent? What effect would a mild national recession have on my forecast?

seasonal index. In these applications, thousands of items are usually being forecast. The forecasting routine should therefore be simple and run quickly on a computer. The routines should also detect and respond rapidly to definite short-term changes in demand while at the same time ignoring the occasional spurious demands. Exponential smoothing, when monitored by management to control the value of alpha, is an effective technique.

In summary, forecasting is tough. The ideal philosophy is create the best forecast that you reasonably can and then hedge by maintaining flexibility in the system to account for the inevitable forecast error.

6.9 REVIEW AND DISCUSSION QUESTIONS

1. Give some very simple rules you might use to manage demand for a firm's product. (An example is "limited to stock on hand.")
2. What strategies are used by supermarkets, airlines, hospitals, banks, and cereal manufacturers to influence demand?
3. All forecasting methods using exponential smoothing, adaptive smoothing, and exponential smoothing including trend require starting values to get the equations going. How would you select the starting value for, say, F_{t-1}?
4. From the choice of simple moving average, weighted moving average, and exponential smoothing, which forecasting technique would you consider the most accurate? Why?
5. Give some examples that you can think of that have a multiplicative seasonal trend relationship.
6. Discuss the basic differences between the mean absolute deviation (MAD) and the standard deviation.
7 What implications do the existence of forecast errors have for the search for ultrasophisticated statistical forecasting models?

6.10 PROBLEMS

*1. Sunrise Baking Company markets doughnuts through a chain of food stores and has been experiencing over- and underproduction because of forecasting errors. The following data are their demands in dozens of doughnuts for the past four weeks. The bakery is closed Saturday, so Friday's production must satisfy both Saturday and Sunday demand.

---

* Problem 1 is solved in Appendix D.

	4 Weeks Ago	3 Weeks Ago	2 Weeks Ago	Last Week
Monday	2,200	2,400	2,300	2,400
Tuesday	2,000	2,100	2,200	2,200
Wednesday	2,300	2,400	2,300	2,500
Thursday	1,800	1,900	1,800	2,000
Friday	1,900	1,800	2,100	2,000
Saturday } Sunday }	2,800	2,700	3,000	2,900

Make a forecast for this week on the following basis:

a. Daily, using simple four-week moving average.

b. Daily, using a weighted average of 0.40, 0.30, 0.20, and 0.10 for the past four weeks.

c. Sunrise is also planning its purchases of ingredients for bread production. If bread demand had been forecast for last week at 22,000 loaves and only 21,000 loaves were actually demanded, what would Sunrise's forecast be for this week using exponential smoothing with $\alpha = 0.10$?

d. Supposing, with the forecast made in *(c)*, this week's demand actually turns out to be 22,500. What would the new forecast be for the next week?

2. The historical demand for a product is:

Month	Demand
January	12
February	11
March	15
April	12
May	16
June	15

a. Using a weighted moving average with weights of 0.60, 0.30, and 0.10, find the July forecast.

b. Using a simple three-month moving average, find the July forecast.

c. Using single exponential smoothing with $\alpha = 0.2$ and a June forecast = 13, find the July forecast. Make whatever assumptions you wish.

3. The following tabulations are actual sales of units for six months and a starting forecast in January.

	Actual	Forecast
January	100	80
February	94	
March	106	
April	80	
May	68	
June	94	

a. Calculate forecasts for the remaining five months using simple exponential smoothing with alpha = 0.2.

b. Calculate MAD for the forecasts.

4. Not all the items in your office supply store are evenly distributed as far as demand is concerned, so you decide to forecast demand to help you plan your stock. Past data for lined tablets for the month of August are as follows:

Week 1	300
Week 2	400
Week 3	600
Week 4	700

a. Using a three-week moving average, what would you forecast the next week to be?

b. Using exponential smoothing with alpha equal to 0.20, if the exponential forecast for week 3 was estimated as the average of the first two weeks [(300 + 400)/2 = 350)], what would you forecast week 5 to be?

5. Following are the actual tabulated demands for an item for a nine-month period, from January through September. Your supervisor wants to test two forecasting methods to see which method was better over this period.

	Actual
January	110
February	130
March	150
April	170
May	160
June	180
July	140
August	130
September	140

a. Forecast April through September using a three-month moving average.

b. Use simple exponential smoothing to estimate April through September.

c. Use MAD to decide which method produced the better forecast over the six-month period.

6. A particular forecasting model was used to forecast a six-month period. The forecasts and the actual demands that resulted are shown:

	Forecast	Actual
April	250	200
May	325	250
June	400	325
July	350	300
Aug	375	325
Sept	450	400

Find the tracking signal and state whether you think the model being used is giving acceptable answers.

7. Harlen Industries has a very simple forecasting model: take the actual demand for the same month last year and divide that by the number of fractional weeks in that month, producing the average weekly demand for that month. This weekly average is used as the weekly forecast this year.

   The following eight weeks shows the forecast (based on last year) and the demand that actually occurred.

Week	Forecast Demand	Actual Demand
1	140	137
2	140	133
3	140	150
4	140	160
5	140	180
6	150	170
7	150	185
8	150	205

   a. Compute the MAD of forecast errors.
   b. Using the RSFE, compute the tracking signal.
   c. Based on your answers to *(a)* and *(b)* what comments can you make about Harlen's method of forecasting?

8. The historical demand for a product is: January, 80; February, 100; March, 60; April, 80; and May, 90.
   a. Using a simple four-month moving average, what is the forecast for June? If June experienced a demand of 100, what would your forecast be for July?
   b. Using single exponential smoothing with $\alpha = 0.20$, if the forecast for January had been 70, compute what the exponentially smoothed forecast would have been for the remaining months through June.
   c. Using a weighted moving average with weights of 0.30, 0.25, 0.20, 0.15, and 0.10, what is June's forecast?

9. In this problem, you are to test the validity of your forecasting model. Following are the forecasts for a model you have been using and the actual demands that occurred.

Week	Forecast	Actual
1	800	900
2	850	1,000
3	950	1,050
4	950	900
5	1,000	900
6	975	1,100

   Use the method stated in the text to compute the MAD and the tracking signal and draw a conclusion as to whether the forecasting model you have been using is giving reasonable results.

10. Assume that your stock of sales merchandise is maintained based on the forecast demand. If the distributor's sales personnel call on the first day of each month, compute your forecast sales by each of the three methods requested here.

	Actual
June	140
July	180
August	170

a. Using a simple three-month moving average, what is the forecast for September?

b. Using a weighted moving average, what is the forecast for September with weights of .20, .30, and .50 for June, July, and August, respectively?

c. Using single exponential smoothing and assuming that the forecast for June had been 130, calculate the forecasts for September with a smoothing constant alpha of .30.

11. The historical demand for a product is:

Month	Demand
April	60
May	55
June	75
July	60
August	80
September	75

a. Using a simple four-month moving average, calculate a forecast for October.

b. Using single exponential smoothing with $\alpha = 0.2$ and a September forecast $= 65$, calculate a forecast for October.

12. A forecasting method you have been using to predict product demand is shown in the following table along with the actual demand that occurred.

Forecast	Actual
1,500	1,550
1,400	1,500
1,700	1,600
1,750	1,650
1,800	1,700

a. Compute the tracking signal using the mean absolute deviation and running sum of forecast errors.

b. Comment on whether you feel the forecasting method is giving good predictions.

13. Sales during the past six months have been as follows:

January	115
February	123
March	132
April	134
May	140
June	147

a. Using a simple three-month moving average, make forecasts for April through July. What is the main weakness of using a simple moving average with data that is patterned like this?

b. Using single exponential smoothing with alpha = 0.70, if the forecast for January had been 110, compute the exponentially smoothed forecasts for each month through July. Is this method more accurate for this data? Why or why not?

14. Actual demand for a product for the past three months was:

Three months ago	400 units
Two months ago	350 units
Last month	325 units

a. Using a simple three-month moving average, what would the forecast be for this month?

b. If 300 units actually occurred this month, what would your forecast be for next month?

c. Using simple exponential smoothing, what would your forecast be for this month if the exponentially smoothed forecast for three months ago was 450 units and the smoothing constant was 0.20?

15. After using your forecasting model for a period of six months, you decide to test it using MAD and a tracking signal. Following are the forecasted and actual demands for the six-month period:

Period	Forecast	Actual
May	450	500
June	500	550
July	550	400
August	600	500
September	650	675
October	700	600

a. Find the tracking signal.

b. Decide whether your forecasting routine is acceptable.

6.11 SELECTED BIBLIOGRAPHY

Abraham, B., and J. Ledolter. *Statistical Methods for Forecasting*. New York: John Wiley & Sons, 1983.

Armstrong, J. Scott. "Forecasting by Extrapolation: Conclusions from 25 Years of Research." *Interfaces* 14, no. 6 (November 1984), pp. 52–66.

Bails, Dale G., and Larry C. Peppers. *Business Fluctuations: Forecasting Techniques and Applications*. Englewood Cliffs, N.J.: Prentice-Hall, 1982.

Bowerman, B. L., and R. T. O'Connell. *Time Series Forecasting*. Boston: Duxbury, 1986.

Box, G. E. P., and G. M. Jenkins. *Time Series Analysis: Forecasting and Control*. 2nd ed. Oakland, Calif.: Holden-Day, 1987.

Cryer, J. *Time Series Analysis*. Boston: Duxbury, 1986.

Gardner, E. S. "Exponential Smoothing: The State of the Art." *Journal of Forecasting* 4, no. 1 (March 1985).

Hank, J. E., and A. Reitsch. *Business Forecasting*. 2nd ed. Boston: Allyn & Bacon, 1986.

Makridakis, Spyros; Steven C. Wheelwright; and Victor E. McGee. *Forecasting: Methods and Applications*. 2nd ed. New York: John Wiley & Sons, 1983.

———. "The Accuracy of Extrapolation (Time Series) Methods: Results of a Forecasting Competition." *Journal of Forecasting* 1 (1982), pp. 111–15.

Wheelwright, Steven, and Spyros Makridakis. *Forecasting Methods for Management*. 3rd ed. New York: John Wiley & Sons, 1980.

Chapter 7

Capacity Planning and Location

EPIGRAPH

We've included in our budget $23 million to expand our severe shortage of capacity.

(Is this really a shortage? How do you know? Can you prove it?)

CHAPTER OUTLINE

KEY TERMS

Capacity
Design Capacity
Maximum Capacity
Capacity Planning
Decision Trees

How much should a plant be able to produce? *Where should it be located?* These are questions of strategic importance that must be addressed when the company is starting out, when it expands, and when it contracts. Answering the "how much" question entails capacity planning, which is the focus of the first part of the chapter; answering the "where" question involves facility location analysis, the focus of the second part. In practice, however, the questions are very much linked together, as evidenced by the following two trends:

1. The growth of the network firm (sometimes called a *hollow corporation*), which uses the capacity of multiple decentralized plants or suppliers to provide all parts of its end products. It may then carry out final assembly and testing operations in its own central facility. In the extreme case (such as illustrated by the Insert on Lewis Galoob Toys), it may do little more than perform a distribution function.

INSERT Lewis Galoob Toys, Inc.

Lewis Galoob Toys, Inc. sells Golden Girl action figures and other trendy toys. A mere 115 employees run the entire operation. Independent inventors and entertainment companies dream up most of Galoob's products, while outside specialists do most of the design and engineering. Galoob farms out manufacturing and packaging to a dozen or so contractors in Hong Kong, and they, in turn, pass on the most labor-intensive work to factories in China. When the toys land in the United States, they are distributed by commissioned manufacturers' representatives. Galoob doesn't even collect its accounts. It sells its receivables to Commercial Credit Corp., a factoring company that also sets Galoob's credit policy.

Source: "And Now, the Post-Industrial Corporation," *Business Week,* March 3, 1986, p. 64.

2. The tendency for producers to locate close to their customers or their suppliers. This is the result of a host of factors including trade agreements, shipping costs, speed of delivery, and speed of new-product development. (See the Insert for a discussion of reasons why Taiwan executives want to produce in the United States.)

INSERT Taiwan's Desire to Produce in the United States

Taiwan executives cite a host of reasons for wanting to produce in the United States. Partly to avoid potential trade barriers, Multitech Industrial Co., Taiwan's largest computer maker, recently agreed to have Texas Instruments Inc. assemble up to 5,000 of Multitech's computers a month in Austin, Texas. Multitech president Stan Shih acknowledges that production costs, especially overhead, are higher in Texas, but says that the company will benefit by saving on shipping and by speeding up deliveries. Multitech also sees advantages in tapping U.S. research. In November the company acquired Counterpoint Computers Inc., a small Silicon Valley company that has developed a new minicomputer. The investment will help Multitech save two years in product development time.

Other Taiwan companies want to be close to their largest market and to supplies of raw materials. Formosa Plastics Corp., which already has 12 plants in the United States, is planning a $120 million expansion of its petrochemical facility in Baton Rouge, Louisiana. A Taiwan furniture maker is setting up a factory in Mississippi, and a food company wants to invest $5 million to expand its instant noodle factory in California.

Source: D. Jones Yang, "The States Are Vying for Those New Taiwan Dollars," *Business Week*, January 11, 1988, p. 56. Reprinted by permission.

The first part of this chapter focuses on capacity concepts, capacity planning, and how decision trees can be used to make capacity decisions. The second part discusses facility location in manufacturing and services and demonstrates two analytical techniques for making location decisions.

7.1 IMPORTANCE OF CAPACITY DECISIONS

The capacity of the production system defines the firm's competitive boundaries. Specifically, it sets the firm's response rate to the market, its cost structure, its work-force composition, its level of technology, its management and staff support requirements, and its general inventory strategy. If capacity is inadequate, a company may lose customers through slow service or by allowing competitors to enter the market. If capacity is excessive, a company may have to reduce its prices to stimulate demand, underutilize its work force, carry excess inventory, or seek additional, less profitable products to stay in business.

Definition of Capacity

Capacity is the rate of output that can be achieved from a process. This characteristic is measured in units of output per unit of time: an electronics plant can produce some number of computers per year, or a credit card company can process so many bills per hour. **Design capacity** is the amount that a firm would like to produce under normal circumstances and for which the system was designed. **Maximum capacity** is used to describe the maximum output that could be achieved when productive resources are used to their maximum. However, at this maximum level, utilization of resources may be inefficient (for example, increasing energy costs, the need for overtime, higher maintenance costs, etc.).

Factors Affecting Capacity

Capacity is affected by both external and internal factors. The external factors include government regulations (working hours, safety, pollution), union agreements, and supplier capabilities. The internal factors include product and service design, personnel and jobs (worker training, motivation, learning, job content, and methods), plant layout and process flow, equipment capabilities and maintenance, materials management and quality control systems, and management capabilities.

7.2 IMPORTANT CAPACITY CONCEPTS

Best Operating Level

The term *capacity* implies an attainable rate of output but says nothing about how long that rate can be sustained. Thus, if we say that a given plant has a capacity of X units, we don't know if this is its one-day peak or its six-month average. To avoid this problem, we use the concept of *best operating level:* the level of capacity for which the average unit cost is at a minimum. This is depicted in Exhibit 7.1. Note that as we move down the curve, we achieve economies of scale until we reach the best operating level, and we encounter diseconomies of scale as we exceed this point.

Economies of Scale

The basic notion is well known: as a plant gets larger and volume increases, the average cost per unit of output drops because each succeeding unit absorbs part of the fixed costs. This reduction in average unit cost continues until the plant

EXHIBIT 7.1 **Best Operating Level**

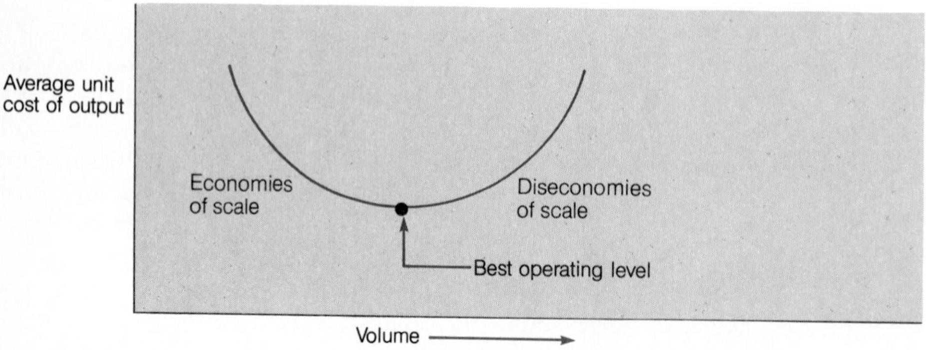

gets so big that coordination of material flows and staffing becomes so expensive that new sources of capacity must be found. This concept can be related to best operating levels by comparing the average unit cost of different sized plants. Exhibit 7.2 shows the best operating levels for 100, 200, and 300 unit (per year) plants. The average unit cost is shown as dropping from best operating level to best operating level as we move from 100 to 300 units. Diseconomies of scale would be evidenced if we had, say, a 400-unit plant where cost was higher than for the 300-unit plant. However, moving to the right along any of the three average cost curves would not be evidence of diseconomy of scale because the plant size has not increased. Rather, it would indicate that management has tried to get more from the plant than it can most efficiently provide.

In the past several years, we have begun to see that diseconomies of scale come much sooner than we once supposed. This recognition, along with technological capability to do more in a plant, has resulted in a shift toward small facilities. The steel industry, with its declining number of big, integrated plants and its corresponding shift toward minimills, is a well-known case in point.

Capacity Utilization Rate

The extent to which a firm uses its capacity is defined by its *capacity utilization rate,* which is calculated as follows:

Capacity used ÷ Design capacity

EXHIBIT 7.2 **Economies of Scale**

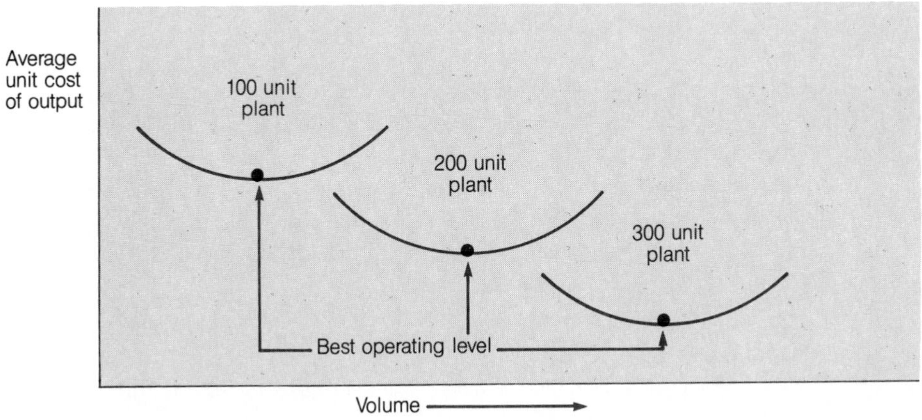

The capacity utilization rate is expressed as a percentage and requires that both the numerator and the denominator be measured in similar units and time periods (machine hours/day, barrels of oil/day, patients/day, dollar of output/month).

Capacity Cushions

A capacity cushion is an amount of capacity in excess of expected demand. For example, if the expected monthly demand on a facility is $1 million worth of products per month and the design capacity is $1.2 million per month, it has a 20 percent capacity cushion. A 20 percent capacity cushion equates to an 83 percent utilization rate (100% ÷ 120%).

When a firm's design capacity is less than the capacity required to meet its demand, it is said to have a *negative capacity cushion*. If, for example, a firm has a demand for $1.2 million of products per month but can produce only $1 million per month, it has a negative capacity cushion of 20 percent.

Capacity Focus

In 1974, Skinner introduced the concept of the focused factory, which holds that a production facility works best when it focuses on a fairly limited set of production objectives.[1] This means, for example, that a firm should not expect to excel in every aspect of manufacturing performance—cost, quality, flexibility, new-product introductions, reliability, short lead times, and low investment. Rather, it should select a limited set of tasks that contribute the most to corporate objectives. However, given the breakthroughs in manufacturing technology, there is an evolution in factory objectives toward trying to do everything well. How do we deal with these apparent contradictions? One way is to say that if the firm does not have the technology to master multiple objectives, then a narrow focus is the logical choice. Another way is to recognize the practical reality that not all firms are in industries that require them to use their full range of capabilities in order to compete.

The focus concept can also be operationalized through the mechanism of plants within plants—"PWPs," in Skinner's terms. A focused plant may have several PWPs, each of which may have separate suborganizations, equipment and process policies, work-force management policies, production control methods, and so forth for different products—even if they are made under the same roof. This, in effect, permits finding the best operating level for each component of the organization and thereby carries the focus concept down to the operating level.

---

[1] Wickham Skinner, "The Focused Factory," *Harvard Business Review* (May–June 1974), pp. 113–21.

Capacity Balance

In a perfectly balanced plant, the output of Stage 1 provides the exact input requirement for Stage 2, Stage 2's output provides the exact input requirement for Stage 3, and so on. In practice, however, achieving such a perfect design is difficult if not impossible. (See Chapter 17 for a challenge to the question of seeking a capacity balance.) One reason is that the best operating levels for each stage generally differ. For instance, Department 1 may operate most efficiently over a range of 90 to 110 units per month while Department 2, the next stage in the process, is most efficient at 75 to 85 units per month, and Department 3, the third stage, works best over a range of 150 to 200 units per month. Another reason is that variability in product demand and the processes themselves may lead to imbalance, at least over the short run.

There are various ways of dealing with imbalance (the pros and cons of which are discussed in detail in later chapters). One is to add capacity to those stages that are the bottlenecks. This can be done by temporary measures such as scheduling overtime, leasing equipment, or going outside the system and purchasing additional capacity through subcontracting. Another way is through the use of buffer inventories so that interdependence between two departments can be loosened. A third approach involves duplicating the facilities of one department upon which another is dependent.

Calculating Capacity Requirements

To find the amount of capacity required we need to first calculate standard hours. Then, to derive actual hours needed we must adjust for efficiencies of organization (E_o), workers (E_w), and equipment (E_m). We must also add times associated with batch and unit setup times.

The formulas for determining standard hours required, actual hours required, and the number of resource units required are:

Total productive standard hours required = Number of units × (Standard processing time per unit + Standard setup time per unit) + Number of batches × Setup time per batch

or

$$T = N_u(t_p + t_s) + nt_b$$

Actual hours required = Total number of standard hours required/Product of the efficiencies

or

$$A = T/(E_oE_wE_m)$$

The total number of units of resource (workers, machines, etc.) needed is simply the actual hours divided by the number of hours that the resource will be available during the time period. For example, if 8,000 additional worker hours were needed during the coming month of 21 working days, then at 8 hours per day we would need to add 8,000/(8 × 21) = 47.6 workers.

$$N_R = A \div H$$

where

N_R = Total number of resource units needed
A = Actual hours (from above)
H = Hours available during the time period

Example
A company has a demand for 200 units of a product next month. Standard operating time per unit is 8 hours and it takes 0.5 hours to set up each unit. The units will be processed in 10 batches, with 4 hours of recalibration time between each batch. Organizational efficiency is 95 percent, workers are operating at 100 percent efficiency, and the machines are operating at 90 percent efficiency. The plant will operate 22 days next month. How many machines are needed?

$$T = 200(8 + .5) + 4(10) = 1{,}740$$
$$A = 1{,}740/(.95 \times 1.0 \times .90) = 2{,}035.1$$
$$H = 22 \times 8 = 176$$
$$N_R = 2{,}035.1./176 = 11.56 \text{ machines}$$

where

T = Total standard hours needed
A = Total actual hours needed
H = Working hours in the month
N_R = Total number of machines needed

7.3 CAPACITY PLANNING

The objective of **capacity planning** is to specify the level of capacity that will meet market demands in a cost-efficient way. Capacity planning can be viewed in three time dimensions—long range, intermediate range, and short range. Various definitions exist, but long range can mean one to five years and short range a week to a month.

The capacity planning process is usually approached as a project involving several staff groups. Since the output of the plan invariably specifies physical facilities—plant and equipment—industrial engineering specialists play a major role in its development.

Hayes and Wheelwright propose the following eight-step planning process:[2]

1. Audit and evaluate existing capacity and facilities.
2. Forecast capacity/facilities requirements.
3. Define alternatives for meeting requirements.
4. Perform financial analyses of each alternative.
5. Assess key qualitative issues for each alternative.
6. Select the alternative to be pursued.
7. Implement the chosen alternative.
8. Audit and review actual results.

Expanding Capacity Cheaply

Often, available capacity is all around the firm. Sometimes it can be found easily, and other times it may take a bit more effort. Too often, managers assume that capacity expansion means building a new facility or making large investments to expand the existing one.

Barnett presents an excellent, concise format for managers to find ways to increase capacity cheaply.[3] In his article, he provides a questionnaire to help managers think about the problem and the steps to find and act on capacity expansion opportunities.

Two ways capacity can be increased cheaply are:

1. By finding the bottleneck operations and adding personnel or additional equipment there only.
2. By redesigning the product, using more reliable components, focusing production, and changing product and customer mixes.

Redesigning the product can increase the production volume by reducing setup times, run times, the type and equipment needed, and so on. More reliable components also reduce process failures, which may cause equipment downtime, and also result in less scrap and rework.

Focused production tries to make the best use of equipment by choosing the most efficient combination of product assignments, equipment, and personnel. Changing the product mix and the customer mix can take advantage of longer run lengths, reduced setup time, and so on. Choosing customers who will buy the firm's choice of products and avoiding customers whose demands tax the firm's system can greatly increase capacity and, of course, the resulting output quantity.

---

[2] Robert Hayes and Steven Wheelwright, *Restoring Our Competitive Edge: Competing through Manufacturing* (New York: John Wiley & Sons, 1984), p. 126.

[3] F. William Barnett, "Elastic Capacity and Skin-Tight Costs: Low Budget Production Improvements," *Sloan Management Review,* Spring 1990, pp. 65–71.

Capacity Planning Using Decision Trees

A handy way to lay out the steps of a problem is called a *decision tree*. The tree format helps not only in understanding the problem, but also in finding a solution. A decision tree is a schematic model of the sequence of steps in a problem and the conditions and consequences of each step.

Decision trees are composed of decision nodes with branches to and from them. By convention, squares represent decision points, and circles represent chance events. Branches from decision points show the choices available to the decision maker; branches from chance events show the probabilities for their occurrence.

In solving decision tree problems, we work from the end of the tree backward to the start of the tree. As we work back, we calculate the expected values at each step.

Once the calculations are made, we "prune" the tree by eliminating from each decision point all branches except for the one with the highest payoff. This process continues to the first decision problem, and the decision problem is thereby solved.

We will now demonstrate an application to capacity planning for CP's Video Rental Store.

The owner of CP's Video Rental Store is considering what to do with her business over the next five years. Sales growth over the last couple of years has been good, but sales could grow substantially if a major housing development is built in her area as proposed. CP sees three options, the first is to enlarge her current store, the second is to locate at a new site, and the third is to simply wait and do nothing. If nothing were done the first year and strong growth occurred, then the decision to expand would be reconsidered. Waiting longer than one year would allow competition to move in and make expansion no longer feasible. The decision to expand or move would take little time and therefore the store would not lose revenue.

The assumptions and conditions are:

1. Strong growth as a result of the increased population from the development has a 60 percent probability.
2. Strong growth with a new site would give annual returns of $220,000 per year. Weak growth with a new site would mean annual returns of $120,000.
3. Strong growth with an expansion would give annual returns of $200,000 per year. Weak growth with an expansion would mean annual returns of $110,0000.
4. At the existing store with no changes, there would be returns of $180,000 per year if there is strong growth, and $105,000 per year if growth is weak.
5. Expansion at the current site would cost $85,000.

EXHIBIT 7.3 **Decision Tree for CP's Video Rental Store**

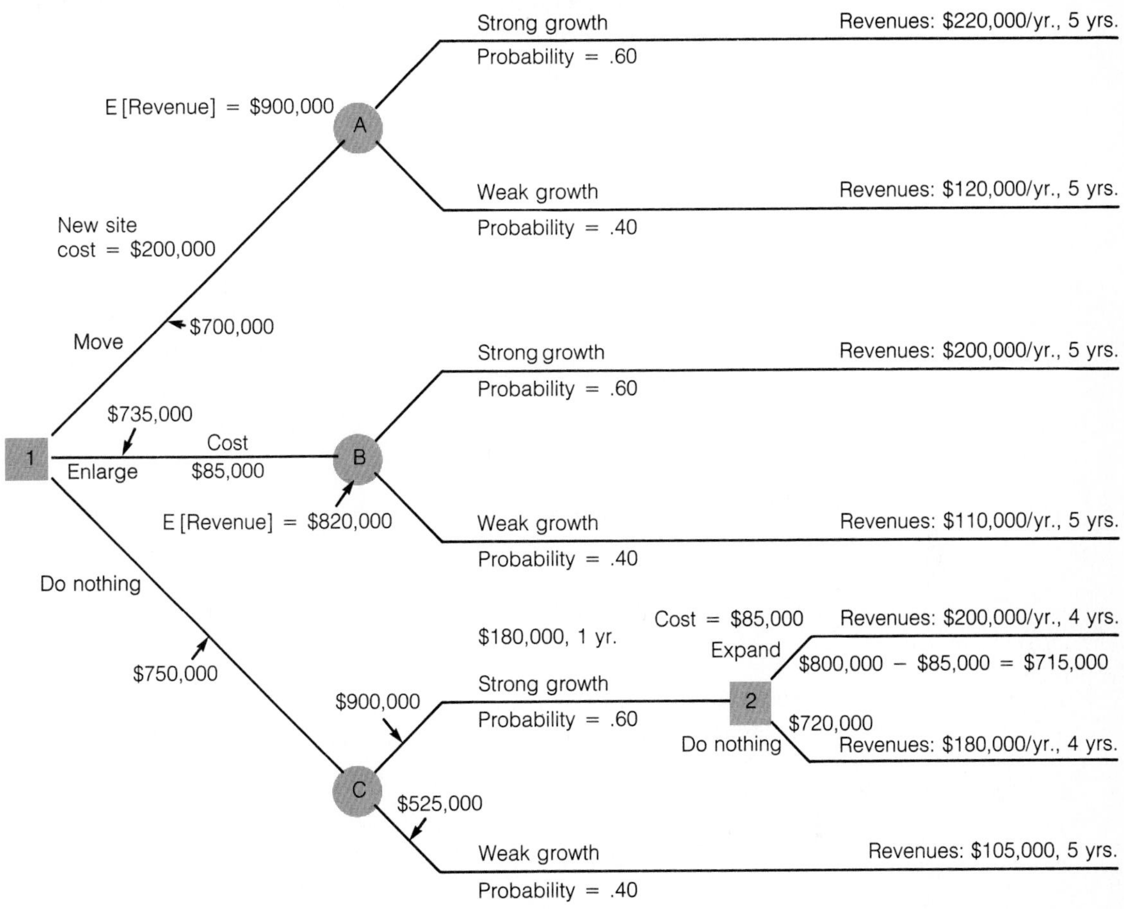

6. If growth is strong and the existing site is enlarged, the cost would still be $85,000.
7. The move to the new site would cost $200,000.
8. Operating costs for all options are equal.

Construct a decision tree and advise CP on the best action.

Exhibit 7.3 shows the decision tree for this problem. There are two decision points (square nodes), and three chance occurrences (round nodes). The value of the nodes and decision points are as follows:

Node A. Move to new location.

Return with strong growth	$220,000/year × 5 years =	$1,100,000
Return with weak growth	$120,000/year × 5 years =	$ 600,000

Expected return at A = ($1,100,000 × 0.6) + ($600,000 × 0.4)

Less new site costs	=	$900,000
		−$200,000
New site net return		$700,000

Node B. Enlarge the existing store.

Return with strong growth	$200,000/year × 5 years =	$1,000,000
Return with weak growth	$110,000/year × 5 years =	$ 550,000

Expected return at B = ($1,000,000 × 0.60) + ($550,000 × 0.40)

Less costs of expansion	=	$820,000
		− 85,000
Expansion net return		$735,000

Decision point 2. After one year, reconsider:

Enlarging existing store:

Return with strong growth	$200,000/year × 4 years =	$800,000
Less expansion costs		− 85,000
Net return		$715,000

Keeping existing store the same:

Return with strong growth $180,000/year × 4 years = $720,000

Decision point 2 shows the choice of $715,000 if the existing store is enlarged versus $720,000 if the existing store is kept the same. Therefore, we would "prune" the expansion branch because it is less.

Node C. Do nothing.

Strong growth in first year = $180,000 × 1 year	=	$180,000
Value of best decision of not to expand	=	720,000
		$900,000
Weak growth in first year	=	$105,000
Keep store the same next 4 years (4 × $105,000)	=	420,000
		$525,000

Expected return at Node C = (0.60 × $900,000) + (0.40 × $525,000)
= $750,000

The best choice is to do nothing with a value of $750,000, compared to $700,000 for the new site and $735,000 for the expansion.

In this example of a capacity decision analysis, the cost of capital or interest rates were not included to simplify the presentation.

7.4 FACILITY LOCATION

For manufacturers, the facility location problem is broadly categorized into factory location and warehouse location. Within this categorization, we may be interested in locating the firm's first factory or warehouse or locating a new factory or warehouse relative to existing facilities.

The general objective in choosing a location is to select that site or combination of sites that minimizes three classes of costs: regional costs, distribution costs, and raw material and supply cost. *Regional costs* are those associated with a given locale and include land, construction, labor, and state and local expenses. *Distribution costs* are those directly related to shipping supplies and products to customers and other branches of the distribution network. *Raw material and supply costs* refer to the availability and costs of production inputs including energy and water, as well as the lead time to acquire these inputs. Since the location of the initial factory is usually determined by the historical context of the firm, economic analysis of facility location has focused on the problem of adding warehouses or factories to the existing production-distribution system.

Plant Location Methods

When new plant locations are to be considered, the sequence of analysis follows the major decisions listed in Exhibit 7.4. That is, the company moves step by step from market region to ultimate site, using selected decision criteria to narrow the search.

The evaluation of alternative regions, subregions, and communities is commonly termed *macro analysis,* and the evaluation of specific sites in the selected community is termed *micro analysis.* Some of the techniques available to be used for macro analyses are linear programming, factor-rating systems, detailed cost analyses, and center of gravity.

After making lengthy and time-consuming analyses, the final results are quite simple to understand. It is interesting to note the major criteria used by Hewlett-Packard in selecting Boise, Idaho, as a new plant site were:

- Attractive place to live.
- Community that wants HP.
- Two hours by air to San Francisco.
- Freight rates.

EXHIBIT 7.4 **Plant Search: Company XYZ**

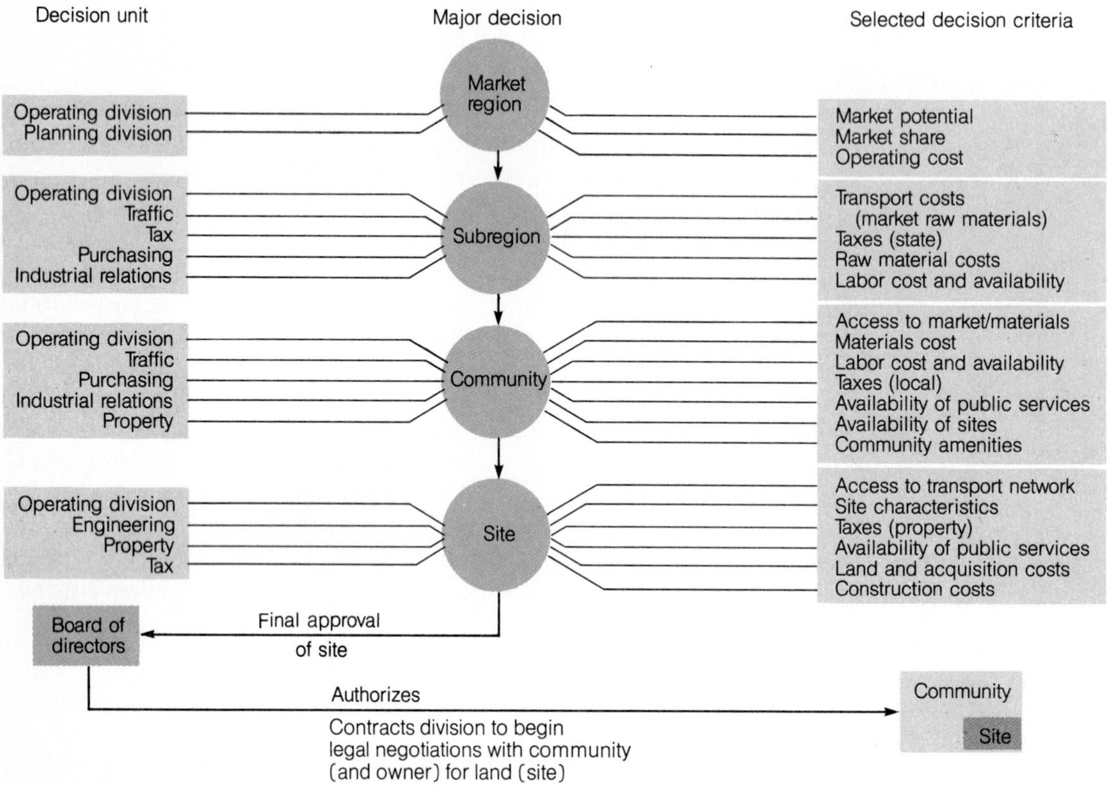

Source: Thomas M. Carroll and Robert D. Dean, "A Bayesian Approach to Plant-Location Decisions," *Decision Sciences* 11, no. 1 (January 1980), p. 87. *Decision Sciences* is published by the Decision Sciences Institute of Georgia State University.

- Graduate-level engineering.
- Labor base.

7.5 LOCATING SERVICE FACILITIES

In service organizations, the facility location decision is also major, but as a rule the choice of locale is based on nearness to the customer rather than on resource considerations. Because of the variety of service firms and the relatively low cost of establishing a service facility compared to one for manufacturing, new service facilities are far more common than new factories and warehouses. Indeed, there are few communities in which rapid population growth has not been paralleled by a concurrent rapid growth in retail outlets, restaurants, municipal services, and entertainment facilities.

Services typically have multiple sites in order to maintain close contact with the customer. The location decision is closely tied to the market selection decision. If the target market is college-age groups, locations in retirement communities, despite desirability in terms of cost, resource availability, etc., are not viable alternatives. Market needs also affect the number of sites to be built, the size, and the characteristics of the sites. Whereas manufacturing location decisions are often made by minimizing costs, many of the service location decision techniques maximize the profit potential of various sites.

Selecting Profitable Sites at La Quinta Motor Inns[4]

The previous section showed a procedure primarily used for locating manufacturing plants. Such a location decision involves major, long-term commitments and heavy investments to recover. There are also large transportation and other logistic costs because the plant's operating range in drawing resources and shipping goods may be thousands of miles. Smaller location decisions, such as locating service organizations that have as their market the immediate area, have different criteria.

Exhibit 7.5 shows the initial list of variables included in a study to assist in locating new La Quinta Motor Inns. Data were collected on 57 existing La Quinta Inns. Analysis of the data identified the variables that correlated with operating profit in 1983 and 1986 (see Exhibit 7.6). While this exhibit does give significant information, the intent of the study was to derive a relatively simple decision rule to determine profitability based on location.

A regression model was created from the variables that correlated with profitability in Exhibit 7.6. For the 57 La Quinta Motor Inns studied, the model that was developed was:

$$
\begin{aligned}
39.05 &- 5.41 \times \text{State population per inn (1,000)} \\
&+ 5.86 \times \text{Price of the inn} \\
&- 3.91 \times \text{Square root of the median income of the area (1,000)} \\
&+ 1.75 \times \text{College students within 4 miles.}
\end{aligned}
$$

The model shows that profitability is affected by market penetration, positively affected by price, negatively affected by higher incomes (the inns do better in lower median income area), and positively affected by colleges nearby.

La Quinta implemented the model on a Lotus spreadsheet and routinely uses the spreadsheet to screen potential real estate acquisitions. The founder

[4] Sheryl E. Kimes and James A. Fitzsimmons, "Selecting Profitable Hotel Sites at La Quinta Motor Inns," *Interfaces* 20 (March–April 1990), pp. 12–20.

EXHIBIT 7.5

Independent Variables Collected for the Initial Model Building Stage

Category	Name	Description
Competitive	INNRATE	Inn price
	PRICE	Room rate for the inn
	RATE	Average competitive room rate
	RMS1	Hotel rooms within 1 mile
	RMSTOTAL	Hotel rooms within 3 miles
	ROOMSINN	Inn rooms
Demand generators	CIVILIAN	Civilian personnel on base
	COLLEGE	College enrollment
	HOSP1	Hospital beds within 1 mile
	HOSPTOTL	Hospital beds within 4 miles
	HVYIND	Heavy industrial employment
	LGTIND	Light industrial acreage
	MALLS	Shopping mall square footage
	MILBLKD	Military base blocked
	MILITARY	Military personnel
	MILTOT	MILITARY + CIVILIAN
	OFCI	Office space within 1 mile
	OFCTOTAL	Office space within 4 miles
	OFCCBD	Office space in CBD
	PASSENGR	Airport passengers enplaned
	RETAIL	Scale ranking of retail activity
	TOURISTS	Annual tourists
	TRAFFIC	Traffic count
	VAN	Airport van
Demographic	EMPLYPCT	Unemployment percentage
	INCOME	Average family income
	POPULACE	Residential population
Market awareness	AGE	Years inn has been open
	NEAREST	Distance to nearest inn
	STATE	State population per inn
	URBAN	Urban population per inn
Physical	ACCESS	Accessibility
	ARTERY	Major traffic artery
	DISTCBD	Distance to downtown
	SIGNVIS	Sign visibility

Source: Reprinted by permission of Sheryl E. Kimes and James A. Fitzsimmons, "Selecting Profitable Hotel Sites at La Quinta Motor Inns," *Interfaces* 20 (March–April 1990). Copyright 1990 The Institute of Management Sciences, 290 Westminster Street, Providence, Rhode Island 02903 USA.

and president of La Quinta has accepted the model's validity and no longer feels obligated to personally select the sites.

This example shows that a specific model can be obtained from the requirements of service organizations and used to identify those features that are most important in making the right site selection.

EXHIBIT 7.6

A Summary of the Variables that Correlated with Operating Margin in 1983 and 1986

Variable	1983	1986
ACCESS	.20	
AGE	.29	.49
COLLEGE		.25
DISTCBD		−.22
EMPLYPCT	−.22	−.22
INCOME		−.23
MILTOT		.22
NEAREST	−.51	
OFCCBD	.30	
POPULACE	.30	.35
PRICE	.38	.58
RATE		.27
STATE	−.32	−.33
SIGNVIS	.25	
TRAFFIC	.32	
URBAN	−.22	−.26

Source: Reprinted by permission of Sheryl E. Kimes and James A. Fitzsimmons, "Selecting Profitable Hotel Sites at La Quinta Motor Inns," *Interfaces* 20 (March-April 1990). Copyright 1990 The Institute of Management Sciences, 290 Westminster Street, Providence, Rhode Island 02903 USA.

Locating Multiple Service Outlets—A Heuristic Method

A common problem encountered by service-providing organizations is deciding how many service outlets to establish within a geographical area, and where. The problem is complicated by the fact that there are usually many possible locations and several options in the absolute number of service centers. Thus, attempting to find a good solution, much less an optimal one, can be extremely time consuming, even for a relatively small problem. For example, there would be 243 possible solutions for a problem involving choosing among one, two, or three retail outlets to serve four geographically dispersed customer populations, even where there are only three possible locations for the outlets. To illustrate one approach to searching for feasible solutions to such problems, we apply to a sample problem a heuristic method based on one described by Ardalan.[5]

Example

Suppose that a medical consortium wishes to establish two clinics to provide medical care for people living in four communities in central Ohio. Assume that the sites under study are in each community and that the population of

[5] Alireza Ardalan, "An Efficient Heuristic for Service Facility Location," *Proceedings, Northeast AIDS,* 1984, pp. 181–82.

EXHIBIT 7.7

Distances, Population, and Relative Weights

From Community	MILES TO CLINIC A	B	C	D	Population of Community	Relative Weighting of Population
A	0	11	8	12	10,000	1.1
B	11	0	10	7	8,000	1.4
C	8	10	0	9	20,000	0.7
D	9.5	7	9	0	12,000	1.0

EXHIBIT 7.8

Weighted Population Distances

From Community	TO CLINIC A	B	C	D
A	0	121	88	132
B	123.2	0	112	78.4
C	112	140	0	126
D	114	84	108	0

each community is evenly distributed within the community's boundaries. Further, assume that the potential use of the clinics by members of the various communities has been determined and weighting factors reflecting the relative importance of serving members of the population of each community have been developed. (This information is given in Exhibit 7.7.) The objective of the problem: find the two clinics that can serve all communities at the lowest weighted travel-distance cost.

Procedure

Step 1. Construct a weighted population-distance table from initial data table, multiplying distance times weighting factor (Exhibit 7.8). For example, Community A to Clinic B is $11 \times 1.1 \times 10{,}000(.001) = 121$.

Step 2. Add the amounts in each column. Choose the community with the lowest cost and locate a facility there (Community C, in our example). (Recall that costs are expressed in weighted population-distance units.)

From Community	TO CLINIC LOCATED IN COMMUNITY A	B	C	D
A	0	121	88	132
B	123.2	0	112	78.4
C	112	140	0	126
D	114	84	108	0
	349.2	345	308	336.4

Step 3. For each row, compare the cost of each column entry to the communities already located. If the cost is less, do not change them. If the cost is greater, reduce the cost to the lowest of the communities already selected.

Step 4. If additional locations are desired, choose the community with the lowest cost from those not already selected (Community D in our example).

From Community	TO CLINIC LOCATED IN COMMUNITY A	B	C	D
A	0	88	88	88
B	112	0	112	78.4
C	0	0	0	0
D	108	84	108	0
	220	172	308	166.4

Step 5. Repeat step 3, reducing each row entry that exceeds the entry in the column just selected.

From Community	TO CLINIC LOCATED IN COMMUNITY A	B	D
A	0	88	88
B	78.4	0	78.4
C	0	0	0
D	0	0	0
	78.4	88	166.4

Continue repeating Steps 4 and 5 until the desired number of locations is selected. If we wished to compute the complete list, it would be as follows:

From Community	TO CLINIC LOCATED IN COMMUNITY A	B
A	0	88
B	78.4	0
C	0	0
D	0	0
	78.4	88

The problem has now been solved for all four possible locations. Choose C first, then D, then A, then B.

The logic in this procedure is as follows:

1. Selecting the least total cost column is obvious, since this column location represents the lowest travel cost of all communities traveling to that location.

2. Once a location is chosen, then no rational member of a community would travel to any other community that was more costly. In Step 2, for example, residents in Community A would certainly prefer going to a clinic located in Community C (88), which has already been decided on, than to B (121) or D (132). Therefore, the maximum number of weighted population-distance units that residents of A would be willing to pay is 88, and we can use this amount as our top limit. If a clinic is located in A, however, residents of A would patronize their own community clinic (at a cost of 0). Residents in Community B would prefer C (112) to A (123.2) but not to B (0) or D (78.4). Therefore, the cost 123.2 is reduced to 112, but 0 and 78.4 remain unchanged.
3. Once a community location is selected and the matrix costs adjusted, that community can be dropped from the matrix, since the column costs are no longer relevant.

7.6 CONCLUSION

Like so many topics in operations management, capacity planning and location decisions are becoming heavily affected by the information revolution and globalization of production. The emergence of the network firm has changed the way management views its available capacity, and the growth of international markets has altered its location strategies.

What this means for manufacturing operations is still unfolding, but it is already clear that the operations executives of many companies must catch a plane to see the multiple shop floors that constitute the capacity of their firm. In services, the emergence of factories in the field (such as one-hour eyeglass production and computer-aided custom shoe manufacture) suggests that service firm capacity decisions will focus more heavily on capital equipment. For both types of organizations, the name of the game is service: the ability to deliver customized products in short lead times at competitive prices. This translates into selecting flexible production capacity that can yield economies of scope.

7.7 REVIEW AND DISCUSSION QUESTIONS

1. Does it make sense to say that a particular plant is working at 110 percent of capacity?
2. List some practical limits to economies of scale; that is, when should a plant stop growing?
3. What are some capacity balance problems faced by the following organizations or facilities?
   a. An airline terminal.
   b. A university computing center.
   c. A clothing manufacturer.

4. What are the reasons behind the shift to minimills for steel production?
5. What are some major capacity considerations in a hospital? How do they differ from those of a factory?
6. Develop a list of five major reasons why a new electronics firm should move into your city or town.
7. How do facilities planning decisions differ for service facilities and manufacturing plants?
8. Management may choose to build up capacity in anticipation of demand or in response to developing demand. Cite the advantages and disadvantages of both approaches.
9. What do you think the primary capacity planning considerations were for foreign companies locating their facilities in the United States?

7.8 PROBLEMS

*1. Art Fern, owner of Tea Time Movies, Inc., is trying to decide whether to lease a movie theater at a site near the Ventura Freeway in Hollywood or build a new four-screen theater near a fork in the Slauson Freeway in Inglewood. The theater will be built on state-leased land that will be part of a new expanded intersection in 10 years. Thus, there is no salvage value at the termination of the 10-year period.

The initial lease will run for a period of two years. If the owner is satisfied at that time, he will extend the lease for an additional eight years. Art attaches a 50-50 probability to this renewal. If the lease is canceled, Art knows of another theater nearby that will be available for leasing, but the lease will be 30 percent more than the present site. Given this information and the information below, develop a decision tree to help Art choose between these sites. (Use a 10-year planning horizon.) Disregard the cost of capital.

Decision Variables	Hollywood Site	Probability	Inglewood Site	Probability
Cost to lease per year	$250,000			
Cost to build			$1,000,000	
Gross revenue per year				
High ticket sales	700,000	0.5	400,000	0.5
Medium ticket sales	500,000	0.3	300,000	0.3
Low ticket sales	300,000	0.2	200,000	0.2
Operating costs per year	200,000		200,000	

2. A drugstore chain plans to open four stores in a medium-size city. However, funds are limited, so only two can be opened this year.
   a. Given the following tableau showing the weighted population distance costs for each of the four areas and four store sites, select the two to be opened up first.

* Solution to Problem 1 is provided in Appendix D.

b. If additional funds become available, which store should be the third to open?

		Store 1	Store 2	Store 3	Store 4
Geographic Area	1	0	20	160	60
	2	80	0	40	80
	3	120	80	0	100
	4	80	100	60	0

3. There are four possible locations where a firm can locate an office within a particular city. Eventually, the firm would like to have an office in each location, but at the present time the firm's managers would like to open just one; however, they would like to know the sequence in which they should open all four offices. Following is a matrix that shows the costs for opening each office in each area. Determine the order in which they should be opened.

		Office A	Office B	Office C	Office D
Geographic Area	A	0	34	40	30
	B	24	0	36	54
	C	60	20	0	36
	D	50	40	60	0

4. A builder has located a piece of property that he would like to buy and eventually build on. What he does not yet know is exactly what he will build. The land is currently zoned for four homes per acre, but he is planning to request new zoning. What he builds depends on approval of zoning requests and your analysis of this problem to advise him. With his input and your help, the decision process has been reduced to the following costs, alternatives, and probabilities:

   Cost of land: $2 million.

   Probability of rezoning: .60.

   If the land is rezoned, there will be additional costs for new roads, lighting, etc., of $1 million.

   If the land is rezoned, then the contractor must decide whether to build a shopping center or build 1,500 apartments that the tentative plan shows would be possible. If he builds a shopping center, there is a 70 percent chance that he can sell the shopping center to a large department chain for $4 million over his construction cost which excludes the land, and there is a 30 percent chance that he may be able to sell it to an insurance company for $5 million over his construction cost (also excluding the land). If, instead of the shopping center, he decides to build the

1,500 apartments, he places probabilities on the profits as follows: There is a 60 percent chance that he can sell the apartments to a real estate investment corporation for $3,000 each over his construction cost and a 40 percent chance that he may be able to get only $2,000 each over his construction cost (both exclude his land cost).

If the land is not rezoned, then he will comply with the existing zoning restrictions and simply build 600 homes on which he expects to make $4,000 over his construction cost on each one (excluding his cost of land).

Draw a decision tree of the problem and determine the best solution and the expected net profit.

7.9 CASE: COMMUNITY HOSPITAL*

In 1983, Community Hospital, which had served the downtown area of a large West Coast city for over a quarter century, closed and then built a new hospital in a thinly populated area about 30 miles west of the city. The new hospital, also named Community Hospital, was located on a parcel of land owned by the original hospital for many years.

This new hospital, which opened October 1, 1983, is a four-story structure that includes all the latest innovations in health care technology. The first floor houses the emergency department; intensive care unit; operating room; radiology, laboratory, and therapy departments; pharmacy; and housekeeping and maintenance facilities and supplies, as well as other supportive operations. All administrative offices, such as the business office, medical records department, special services, and so forth, are located on the second floor, as are the cafeteria and food service facilities. The two upper floors contain patient rooms divided into surgical, medical, pediatric, and obstetric units.

Community Hospital has a total capacity of 177 beds assigned as follows:

Unit	Number of Beds
Surgical	45
Medical	65
Pediatrics	35
Obstetrics	20
Intensive care	12

For the first six months of the hospital's operation, things were rather chaotic for the administrator, Sam Jones. All his time was occupied with the multitude of activities that go along with starting a new facility, seeing that malfunctioning equipment is repaired, arranging for new staff to be hired and trained, establishing procedures and schedules, making necessary purchasing decisions, and attending endless conferences and meetings.

All during this period, Mr. Jones had been getting some rather disturbing reports from his controller, Bob Cash, regarding Community Hospital's financial situation.

* Based on *Hospital Cost Containment through Operations Management,* originally published by American Hospital Publishing, Inc., copyright 1980 (now out of print).

But he decided that these financial matters would simply have to wait until things had settled down.

Finally, in April, Mr. Jones asked Mr. Cash to prepare a comprehensive report on the hospital's financial position and to make a presentation to himself and his new assistant administrator, Tim Newman, who had recently received a degree in hospital administration.

In his report, Mr. Cash stated: "As you both know, we have been running at an operating cash deficit since we opened last October. We expected, of course, to be losing money at the start until we were able to establish ourselves in the community and draw in patients. We certainly were right. During our first month, we lost almost $221,000. Last month, in March, we lost $58,000.

"The reason, of course, is pretty straightforward. Our income is directly related to our patient load. On the other hand, our expenses are fixed and are running at about $235,000 a month for salaries and wages, $75,000 a month for supplies and equipment, and another $10,000 a month in interest charges. Our accumulated operating deficit for the six months we've been here totals $715,000, which we've covered with our bank line of credit. I suppose we can continue to borrow for another couple of months, but after that I don't know what we're going to do."

Mr. Jones replied, "As you said, Bob, we did expect to be losing money in the beginning, but I never expected the loss to go on for six months or to accumulate to almost three quarters of a million dollars. Well, at least last month was a lot better than the first month. Do you have any figures showing the month-to-month trend?"

Bob Cash laid the following worksheet on the table:

COMMUNITY HOSPITAL'S
Six-Month Operating Statement,
October 1983–March 1984
(in thousands of dollars)

	1983			1984			
	October	November	December	January	February	March	Total
Income	$ 101	$ 163	$ 199	$ 235	$ 245	$ 262	$ 1,205
Expenses (excluding interest)							
Salaries, wages	232	233	239	235	236	236	1,410
Supplies, others	80	73	74	75	73	75	450
Total	312	306	313	310	309	310	1,860
Interest	10	10	10	10	10	10	60
Operating loss	$(221)	$(153)	$(124)	$(85)	$(74)	$(58)	$(715)
Average daily census	42	68	83	98	102	109	
Occupancy	24%	38%	47%	55%	58%	62%	

QUESTIONS

1. Evaluate the situation at Community Hospital with respect to trends in daily census, occupancy rate, and income.
2. Has there been any change in revenue per patient-day over the six-month period (assuming a 30-day month)?
3. At what capacity level will the hospital achieve breakeven?
4. What questions might we raise about the constant level of salaries and supplies relative to past and future operations?

7.10 SELECTED BIBLIOGRAPHY

Buffa, Elwood, S. *Meeting the Competitive Challenge: Manufacturing Strategy for U.S. Companies.* Homewood, Ill.: Dow Jones-Irwin, 1984, chapter 4.

Carroll, Thomas M., and Robert D. Dean. "A Bayesian Approach to Plant Location Decisions." *Decision Sciences* 11, no. 1 (January 1980), p. 87.

Coyle, John J., and Edward J. Bardi. *The Management of Logistics.* 2nd ed. St. Paul: West Publishing, 1980, pp. 294–98.

Eppen, Gary D.; R. Kip Martin; and Linus Schrage. "A Scenario Approach to Capacity Planning." *Operations Research,* July–August 1989, pp. 517–28.

Francis, R. L., and J. A. White. *Facilities Layout and Location: An Analytical Approach.* Englewood Cliffs, N.J.: Prentice-Hall, 1987.

Graziano, Vincent J. "Production Capacity Planning—Long Term." *Production and Inventory Management* 15, no. 2 (Second Quarter 1974), pp. 66–80.

Kimes, Sheryl E., and James A. Fitzsimmons. "Selecting Profitable Hotel Sites at La Quinta Motor Inns." *Interfaces,* March–April 1990, pp. 12–20.

Skinner, Wickham. "The Focused Factory." *Harvard Business Review,* May–June 1974, pp. 113–21.

Tompkins, James A., and John A. White. *Facilities Planning.* New York: John Wiley & Sons, 1984.

Supplement

Linear Programming

EPIGRAPH

Unquestionably, linear optimization models are among the most commercially successful applications of operations research; in fact, there is considerable evidence that they rate highest in economic impact.

Harvey Wagner

SUPPLEMENT OUTLINE

KEY TERMS

Graphical Linear Programming
Objective Functions
Constraint Equations
Convex Polygon
Simplex Method
Slack Variables
Maximization and Minimization
Sensitivity Analysis
Shadow Prices
Integer Programming
Transportation Method
Assignment Method
Karmarkar's Algorithm

In many types of problems, the interactions and relationships of the various elements that make up the problem may be linear. For example, if one quart of fresh orange juice requires 20 oranges, then two quarts require 40 oranges, three quarts 60 oranges, and so on. The relationship is linear and we could state an equation as $X = 20A$ where X is the number of quarts of orange juice and A is the number of oranges.

We could have a number of linear relationships as part of a larger problem. For example, we might also have grapefruit that we can squeeze into juice at the rate of one quart of juice for each 8 grapefruit (or two quarts from 16 grapefruit, three quarts from 24 grapefruit, and so on). This equation is $Y = 8B$ where Y is the number of quarts of grapefruit juice and B is the number of grapefruit.

Also consider a third fruit drink that is an equal mixture of orange juice and grapefruit juice. That is, one quart of the mixed juice would take 10 oranges and 4 grapefruit, or $Z = 10A + 4B$, where Z is the number of quarts of orange/grapefruit juice. So far we have three simple linear equations. To make this a more realistic problem, we need a few more elements.

Suppose we can pick 1,000 oranges and 500 grapefruit each day. The demand for our juice is a daily maximum of 35 quarts of orange juice (X), 50 quarts of grapefruit juice (Y), and 40 quarts of the mixed orange/grapefruit juice (Z). To complete the problem we need to establish our objective. Say we want to maximize our revenue, and we are selling our orange juice for \$1.50 per quart, grapefruit juice for \$0.90 per quart, and the mixed orange/grapefruit juice for \$1.10 per quart. We can then state our problem as:

$X = 20A$	X = Quarts of orange juice
$Y = 8B$	Y = Quarts of grapefruit juice
$Z = 10A + 4B$	Z = Quarts of orange/grapefruit juice
$X \leq 35$	A = Number of oranges
$Y \leq 50$	B = Number of grapefruit
$Z \leq 40$	

There are 1,000 A available
There are 500 B available
Maximize $\$1.50X + \$0.90Y + \$1.10Z$

This problem is included as Problem 19 at the end of this supplement. However, if you look at this carefully, you can figure out the answer in a few minutes.

The four conditions for a linear programming problem are:

1. There must be limited resources (only so many oranges and grapefruit, for example).
2. There must be an objective (such as maximizing profit, minimizing cost, or maximizing revenue).

3. There must be linearity (twice as many oranges will give twice as much juice, etc.).
4. There must be homogeneity. That is, there are no differences in the products (all of the orange juice is the same, all of the grapefruit is the same, etc.).

One other condition must be known: divisibility. In normal linear programming, divisibility assumes that products and resources can be subdivided into fractions. If this subdivision is not possible (such as flying half an airplane or hiring one fourth of a person), then a modification of linear programming, called *integer programming,* can be used.

When a single objective is to be maximized (e.g., profit) or minimized (e.g., costs), we can use *linear programming*. When multiple objectives exist, *goal programming* is used. If a problem is best solved in stages or time frames, this is *dynamic programming*. Other restrictions on the nature of the problem may require that it be solved by other variations of the technique, such as *nonlinear programming* or *quadratic programming*.

S7.1 THE LINEAR PROGRAMMING MODEL

Stated formally, the linear programming problem entails an optimizing process in which nonnegative values for a set of decision variables $X_1, X_2 \ldots X_n$ are selected so as to maximize (or minimize) an objective function in the form

$$\text{Maximize (minimize) } Z = C_1X_1 + C_2X_2 + \ldots + C_nX_n$$

subject to resource constraints in the form

$$\begin{aligned} A_{11}X_1 + A_{12}X_2 + \ldots + A_{1n}X_n &\le B_1 \\ A_{21}X_1 + A_{22}X_2 + \ldots + A_{2n}X_n &\le B_2 \\ &\vdots \\ A_{m1}X_1 + A_{m2}X_2 + \ldots + A_{mn}X_n &\le B_m \end{aligned}$$

where C_j, A_{ij}, and B_i are given constants.

Depending upon the problem, the constraints may also be stated with equal-to signs (=) or greater-than-or-equal-to signs (≥).

To repeat from our supplement introduction, the conditions for linear programming are:

1. Resources must be limited.
2. There must be an objective function.
3. There must be linearity in the constraint equations and in the objective function.

4. Resources and products must be homogeneous.
5. For normal linear programming, variables must be divisible and non-negative.

S7.2 GRAPHICAL LINEAR PROGRAMMING

Though limited in application to problems involving two decision variables (or three variables for three-dimensional graphing), **graphical linear programming** provides a quick insight into the nature of linear programming and illustrates what takes place in the general simplex method described later.

We will describe the steps involved in the graphical method in the context of a sample problem, that of the Puck and Pawn Company, which manufactures hockey sticks and chess sets. Each hockey stick yields an incremental profit of \$2 and each chess set, \$4. A hockey stick requires four hours of processing at Machine center A and two hours at Machine center B. A chess set requires six hours at Machine center A, six hours at Machine center B, and one hour at Machine center C. Machine center A has a maximum of 120 hours of available capacity per day, Machine center B has 72 hours, and Machine center C has 10 hours.

If the company wishes to maximize profit, how many hockey sticks and chess sets should be produced per day?

1. Formulate the problem in mathematical terms. If H is the number of hockey sticks and C is the number of chess sets, to maximize profit the **objective function** may be stated as:

Maximize $Z = \$2H + \$4C$

The maximization will be subject to the following constraints:

(1) $4H + 6C \leq 120$ (Machine center A)
(2) $2H + 6C \leq 72$ (Machine center B)
(3) $1C \leq 10$ (Machine center C)
$H, C \geq 0$ (nonnegativity requirement)

2. Plot constraint equations. The **constraint equations** are easily plotted by letting one variable equal zero and solving for the axis intercept of the other. (The inequality portions of the restrictions are disregarded for this step.) For the Machine center A constraint equation, then, when $H = 0$, $C = 20$, and when $C = 0$, $H = 30$. For the Machine center B constraint equation, when $H = 0$, $C = 12$, and when $C = 0$, $H = 36$. For the Machine center C constraint equation, $C = 10$ for all values of H. These lines are graphed in Exhibit S7.1.

EXHIBIT S7.2

Initial Tableau of the Hockey Stick and Chess Set Problem

C_j	C_j Row	$2	$4	$0	$0	$0	
Column	Solution Mix	H	C	S_1	S_2	S_3	Quantity
$0	S_1	4	6	1	0	0	120
$0	S_2	2	6	0	1	0	72
$0	S_3	0	1	0	0	1	10 ←
	Z_j	$0	$0	$0	$0	$0	$0
	$C_j - Z_j$	$2	$4	$0	$0	$0	
			↑				

4. The amount of reduction in the variables in the solution that results from introducing one unit of each variable. This amount is termed the *substitution rate.*
5. The worth of an additional unit (e.g., hour) of resource capacity. This is referred to as a *shadow price.*

The first four features will be discussed in reference to the first tableau; the last one will be considered later.

The top row of Exhibit S7.2 contains the C_j's, or the contribution to total profit associated with the production of one unit of each alternative product. This row is a direct restatement of the coefficients of the variables in the objective function, and therefore remains the same for all subsequent tableaus. The first column, headed by C_j, merely lists, for convenience, the profit per unit of the variables included in the solution at any stage of the problem.

The variables chosen for the first tableau are listed under Solution Mix. As you can see, only slack variables are considered in the initial solution, and their profit coefficients are zero, which is indicated by the C_j column.

The constraint variables are listed to the right of Solution Mix, and under each one is the particular variable's coefficient in each constraint equation. That is, 4, 6, 1, 0, and 0 are the coefficients of the Machine center A constraint; 2, 6, 0, 1, and 0 for Machine center B; and 0, 1, 0, 0, and 1 for Machine center C.

Substitution rates can be ascertained from the numbers as well. For example, consider 4, 2, and 0, listed under H in the third column. For every unit of product H introduced into the solution, four units of S_1, two units of S_2, and zero units of S_3 must be withdrawn from the quantities available. The entries in the Quantity column refer to how many units of each resource are available in each machine center. In the initial tableau, this is a restatement of the right-hand side of each constraint equation. With the exception of the value in the quantity column, the Z_j values in the second row from the bottom refer to the amount of *gross* profit that is given up by introducing one unit of that variable into the solution. The subscript j refers to the specific variable being consid-

EXHIBIT S7.3 Calculations of Z_j and $C_j - Z_j$

C_j H	C_j C	C_j S_1	C_j S_2	C_j S_3	C_j Quantity
$\$0 \times 4 = 0$	$\$0 \times 6 = 0$	$\$0 \times 1 = 0$	$\$0 \times 0 = 0$	$\$0 \times 0 = 0$	$\$0 \times 120 = 0$
+	+	+	+	+	+
$\$0 \times 2 = 0$	$\$0 \times 6 = 0$	$\$0 \times 0 = 0$	$\$0 \times 1 = 0$	$\$0 \times 0 = 0$	$\$0 \times 72 = 0$
+	+	+	+	+	+
$\$0 \times 0 = 0$	$\$0 \times 1 = 0$	$\$0 \times 0 = 0$	$\$0 \times 0 = 0$	$\$0 \times 1 = 0$	$\$0 \times 10 = 0$
$Z_H = \$0$	$Z_C = \$0$	$Z_{S_1} = \$0$	$Z_{S_2} = \$0$	$Z_{S_3} = \$0$	$Z_Q = \$0$

$C_j - Z_j$ calculations:

$C_H - Z_H = \$2 - 0 = \$2$
$C_C - Z_C = \$4 - 0 = \$4$
$C_{S_1} - Z_{S_1} = \$0 - 0 = \$0$
$C_{S_2} - Z_{S_2} = \$0 - 0 = \$0$
$C_{S_3} - Z_{S_3} = \$0 - 0 = \$0$

ered. The Z_j value under the quantity column is the total profit for the solution. In the initial solution of a simplex problem, all values of Z_j will be zero because no real product is being produced (all machines are idle), and hence there is no gross profit to be lost if they are replaced.

The bottom row of the tableau contains the *net* profit per unit, obtained by introducing one unit of a given variable into the solution. This row is designated the $C_j - Z_j$ row. The procedure for calculating Z_j and each $C_j - Z_j$ is demonstrated in Exhibit S7.3.

The initial solution to the problem is read directly from Exhibit S7.2: the company will "produce" 120 units of S_1, 72 units of S_2, and 10 units of S_3. The total profit from this solution is $0. Thus, no capacity has yet been allocated and no real product produced.

Step 3: Determine which variable to bring into solution

An improved solution is possible if there is a positive value in the $C_j - Z_j$ row. Recall that this row provides the net profit obtained by adding one unit of its associated column variable in the solution. In this example, there are two positive values to choose from: $2, associated with *H*, and $4, associated with *C*. Since our objective is to maximize profit, the logical choice is to pick the variable with the largest payoff to enter the solution, so variable *C* will be introduced. The column associated with this variable is designated by the small arrow beneath column *C* in Exhibit S7.2. (It should be emphasized that only one variable at a time can be added in developing each improved solution.)

Step 4: Determine which variable to replace

Given that it is desirable to introduce *C* into the solution, the next question is to determine which variable it will replace. To make this determination, we

EXHIBIT S7.4

Calculation of New Row Values for Entering Variable

	C
	6
	6
S_3	0 ① 0 0 1 10 0 / 1 = 0, 1 / 1 = 1, 0 / 1 = 0, 0 / 1 = 0, 1 / 1 = 1, 10 / 1 = 10
	$4

divide each amount in the Quantity column by the amount in the comparable row of the C column and choose the variable associated with the smallest positive quotient as the one to be replaced:

For the S_1 row: 120/6 = 20
For the S_2 row: 72/6 = 12
For the S_3 row: 10/1 = 10

Since the smallest quotient is 10, S_3 will be replaced, and its row is identified by the small arrow to the right of the tableau in Exhibit S7.2. This is the maximum amount of C that can be brought into the solution; that is, production of more than 10 units of C would exceed the available capacity of Machine C. This can be verified mathematically by considering the constraint $C \leq 10$ and visually by examining the graphical representation of the problem in Exhibit S7.1. The graph also shows that the 20 and 12 are the C intercepts of the other two constraints, and if $C \leq 10$ were removed, the amount of C introduced could be increased by 2 units.

Step 5: Calculate new row values for entering variable

The introduction of C into the solution requires that the entire S_3 row be replaced. The values for C, the replacing row, are obtained by dividing each value presently in the S_3 row by the value in column C in the same row. This value is termed the *intersectional element* since it occurs at the intersection of a row and column. This intersectional relationship is abstracted from the rest of the tableau and the necessary divisions are shown in Exhibit S7.4.

Step 6: Revise remaining rows

The new third-row values (now associated with C) are 0, 1, 0, 0, 1, and 10, which in this case are identical to those of the old third row.

Introducing a new variable into the problem will affect the values of the remaining variables, and a second set of calculations must be performed to update the tableau. Specifically, we want to determine the effect of introducing C on the S_1 and S_2 rows. These calculations can be carried out by using what is termed the *pivot method* or by algebraic substitution. The pivot method is a more mechanical procedure and is generally used in practice, while algebraic substitution is more useful in explaining the logic of the updating process. The

EXHIBIT S7.5 **Pivot Method**

Old S_1 Row	−	(Intersectional Element of Old S_1 Row	×	Corresponding Element of New C Row)	=	Updated S_1 Row	Old S_2 Row	−	(Intersectional Element of Old S_2 Row	×	Corresponding Element of New C Row)	=	Updated S_2 Row
4	−	(6	×	0)	=	4	2	−	(6	×	0)	=	2
6	−	(6	×	1)	=	0	6	−	(6	×	1)	=	0
1	−	(6	×	0)	=	1	0	−	(6	×	0)	=	0
0	−	(6	×	0)	=	0	1	−	(6	×	0)	=	1
0	−	(6	×	1)	=	−6	0	−	(6	×	1)	=	−6
120	−	(6	×	10)	=	60	72	−	(6	×	10)	=	12

EXHIBIT S7.6

Algebraic Substitution

To find new values for S_1,

1. Reconstruct old S_1 row as a constraint with slack variables added (from first tableau):

$$4H + 6C + 1S_1 + 0S_2 + 0S_3 = 120$$

2. Write entering row as a constraint with slack variables added (these are the values computed in Exhibit S7.4):

$$0H + C + 0S_1 + 0S_2 + 1S_3 = 10$$

3. Rearrange entering row in terms of C, the entering variable:

$$10 - S_3$$

4. Substitute 10—S_3 for C in the first equation (the old S_1 row) and solve for each variable coefficient:

$$4H + 6(10 - S_3) + 1S_1 = 120$$
$$4H + 60 - 6S_3 + 1S_1 = 120$$
$$4H + 1S_1 - 6S_3 = 120 - 60$$
$$4H + 1S_1 - 6S_3 = 60$$

or

$$4H + 0C + 1S_1 + 0S_2 - 6S_3 = 60$$

procedure using the pivot method to arrive at new values for S_1 and S_2 is shown in Exhibit S7.5. (In essence, the method subtracts six times row 3 from both the S_1 and S_2 rows.)

Updating by algebraic substitution entails substituting the entire equation for the entering row into each of the remaining rows and solving for the revised values for each row's variable. The procedure, summarized in Exhibit S7.6, illustrates the fact that linear programming via the simplex method is essentially the solving of a number of simultaneous equations.

EXHIBIT S7.7

Second Tableau of the Hockey Stick and Chess Problem

C_j		\$2	\$4	\$0	\$0	\$0	
	Solution Mix	H	C	S_1	S_2	S_3	Quantity
\$0	S_1	4	0	1	0	−6	60
\$0	S_2	2	0	0	1	−6	12 ←
\$4	C	0	1	0	0	1	10
	Z_j	\$0	\$4	\$0	\$0	\$ 4	\$40
	$C_j - Z_j$	\$2 ↑	\$0	\$0	\$0	\$−4	

Isolating the variable coefficients yields the same values for the new S_1 row as did the pivot method: 4, 0, 1, 0, −6, 60.

The results of the computations carried out in Steps 3 through 6, along with the calculations of Z_j and $C_j - Z_j$ are shown in the revised tableau, Exhibit S7.7. In mathematical programming terminology, we have completed one *iteration* of the problem.

In evaluating this solution, we note two things: the profit is \$40, but, more important, further improvement is possible since there is a positive value in the $C_j - Z_j$ row.

Second iteration. The entering variable is H since it has the largest $C_j - Z_j$ amount (2). The replaced variable is S_2 since it has the smallest quotient when the Quantity column values are divided by their comparable amounts in the H column:

$$S_1 = 60/4 = 15,\ S_2 = 12/2 = 6,\ C_3 = 10/0 = \infty$$

Values of entering (H) row are

$$2/2 = 1,\ 0/2 = 0,\ 0/2 = 0,\ 1/2 = 1/2,\ -6/2 = -3,\ 12/2 = 6$$

Updated S_1 row from Exhibit S7.8: 0, 0, 1, −2, 6, 36.

Updated C row from Exhibit S7.8: 0, 1, 0, 0, 1, 10. Using the result from Exhibit S7.8, we obtain the third tableau: Exhibit S7.9.

Examination of the third tableau indicates that further improvement is possible by introducing the maximum amount of S_3 that is technically feasible. From the computation at the bottom of Exhibit S7.9, the maximum amount of S_3 that can be brought into the solution is six units because of the limited supply of S_1. Replacing S_1 by S_3 and performing the updating operations yields the tableau shown in Exhibit S7.10. Since the $C_j - Z_j$ row contains only negative numbers, no further improvement is possible, and an optimal solution ($H = 24$, $C = 4$) has been achieved in three iterations.

EXHIBIT S7.8

Updating S_1 and C rows

Old S_1 Row	–	(Intersectional Element of Old S_1 Row	×	Corresponding Element of New H Row)	=	New S_1 Row	Old C Row	–	(Intersectional Element of Old C Row	×	Corresponding Element of New H Row)	=	New C Row
4	–	(4	×	1)	=	0	0	–	(0	×	1)	=	0
0	–	(4	×	0)	=	0	1	–	(0	×	0)	=	1
1	–	(4	×	0)	=	1	0	–	(0	×	0)	=	0
0	–	(4	×	½)	=	−2	0	–	(0	×	½)	=	0
−6	–	(4	×	−3)	=	6	1	–	(0	×	−3)	=	1
60	–	(4	×	6)	=	36	10	–	(0	×	6)	=	10

EXHIBIT S7.9

Third Tableau of the Hockey Stick and Chess Set Problem

C_j	Solution Mix	$2	$4	$0	$0	$0	Quantity
		H	C	S_1	S_2	S_3	
$0	S_1	0	0	1	−2	6	36 ←
$2	H	1	0	0	½	−3	6
$4	C	0	1	0	0	1	10
	Z_j	$2	$4	$0	$ 1	$−2	$52
	$C_j - Z_j$	$0	$0	$0	$−1	$ 2	
						↑	

36/6 = 6
6/−3 = −2 (negative)*
10/1 = 10

* Since there are three constraint equations, there must be three variables with nonnegative values in the solution. Therefore a negative amount cannot be considered for introduction into the solution.

EXHIBIT S7.10

Fourth Tableau of the Hockey Stick and Chess Set Problem (Optimal solution)

C_j	Solution Mix	$2	$4	$0	$0	$0	Quantity
		H	C	S_1	S_2	S_3	
$0	S_3	0	0	⅙	−⅓	1	6
$2	H	1	0	½	−½	0	24
$4	C	0	1	−⅙	⅓	0	4
	Z_j	$2	$4	$ ⅓	$ ⅓	$0	$64
	$C_j - Z_j$	$0	$0	$−⅓	$−⅓	$0	

Summary of Steps in the Simplex Method: Maximization Problems

1. Formulate problem in terms of an objective function and a set of constraints.
2. Set up initial tableau with slack variables in the solution mix and calculate the Z_j and $C_j - Z_j$ rows.
3. Determine which variable to bring into solution (largest $C_j - Z_j$ value).
4. Determine which variable to replace (smallest positive ratio of quantity column to its comparable value in the column selected in Step 3).
5. Calculate new row values for entering variable and insert into new tableau (row to be replaced plus intersectional element).
6. Update remaining rows and enter into new tableau; compute new Z_j and $C_j - Z_j$ rows (old row minus intersectional element of old row times corresponding element in new row). If no positive $C_j - Z_j$ value is found, solution is optimal. If there is a positive value of $C_j - Z_j$, repeat Steps 3 to 6.

Minimization problems
Both **maximization and minimization** problems use identical procedures. When the objective is to minimize rather than maximize, however, a negative $C_j - Z_j$ value indicates potential improvement; therefore the variable associated with the largest negative $C_j - Z_j$ value would be brought into solution first. Also, additional variables must be brought in to set up such problems. Since minimization problems include greater-than-or-equal-to constraints, which must be treated differently from less-than-or-equal-to constraints, which typify maximization problems. (See the section dealing with greater-than-or-equal-to and equal-to constraints in the simplex method, later in this chapter.)

Search Path Followed by the Simplex Method

As mentioned earlier, the optimal solution to linear programming problems is obtained by finding the extreme corner point. The simplex procedure starts with an initial solution, searches for the most profitable direction to follow, and hops from point to point of intersecting lines (or planes in multidimensional space). The evaluation of a corner point takes one iteration, and when the furthermost point is reached (in the case of profit maximization problems as shown by the next point's decreasing profit), the solution is complete.

Consider the graph of the example problem shown in Exhibit S7.11, where the simplex method began at point *a* (profit = \$0). In the first iteration, 10 units of *C* were introduced at point *b* (profit = \$40). In the second iteration, 6 units of *H* were introduced at point *c* (profit = \$52). The third iteration left the problem at point *d* (profit = \$64), which is optimal. Note that the solution

EXHIBIT S7.11

Graph of Hockey Stick and Chess Set Problem Showing Successive Corner Evaluations

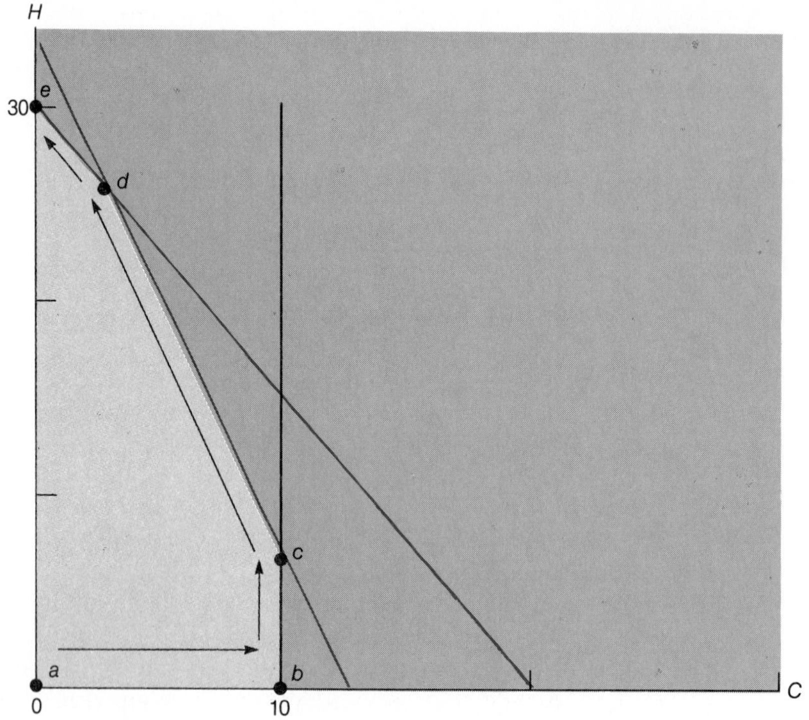

procedure did not calculate profit for all corners of this problem. It did, however, *look ahead*—by virtue of the $C_j - Z_j$ calculations—to see if further improvement was possible by moving to another point (point *e*), but no improvement was indicated by such a change. These two characteristics—evaluating corner points and looking ahead for improvements—are the essential features of the simplex method.

Another feature that is also characteristic of the basic simplex method is that it does not necessarily converge on the optimum point by the shortest route around the feasible area. Reference to the graph will show that if the solution procedure had proceeded along the path $a \longrightarrow e \longrightarrow d$, an optimum would have been reached in two iterations rather than three.

The reason why this route was not followed was that the profit per chess set was higher than for a hockey stick, and therefore, the simplex method indicated that *C*, rather than *H*, be introduced in the first iteration. This, in turn, set the pattern for subsequent iterations to points *c* and *d*. Note that since the solution space forms a convex polygon (as previously defined), profit cannot increase, decrease, and then again increase.

Shadow Prices, Ranging, and Sensitivity

By examining the final (optimal) simplex tableau, we can learn a great deal. In addition to showing the solution, the final tableau provides valuable information about the resources used, the range where the optimal decision remains unchanged, and the range where the coefficients in the objective function do not change the optimal solution. Specifically, it enables us to answer such questions as: Would you like to buy any more of a resource? If so, what price should you pay? How many units should you buy at that price? Similar questions can be answered about selling resources; even though a resource may be currently used in making products, at some price it is worthwhile to forgo production and sell it. These considerations are of interest since they lead to decisions that can increase profit or reduce cost. These profit increases or cost decreases are *in addition* to the optimal solution calculated in the final tableau objective function.

Other questions are of the sort: If we change the profit per unit (by changing the coefficient in the objective function) will this change the optimal solution? This is **sensitivity analysis,** and refers to how much the solution changes for a small change in the objective function or, conversely, for a small change in the solution, the change that occurs in the objective function.

Referring to Exhibit S7.10, the $C_j - Z_j$ values associated with the slack variables are termed **shadow prices,** *marginal values, incremental values,* or *break-even prices.* Note that the shadow prices for S_1 and S_2 were $\$1/3$ (or 33 cents) each, and the shadow price for S_3 was $0. Above each price, management would be willing to sell resources, and below each price, it would be willing to buy.

Let's look at the final simplex tableau in Exhibit S7.12. S_1 has a shadow price of $\$1/3$ per unit. If the price is less than $\$1/3$ then we would be willing to buy 24 units. (See Exhibit S7.12A.) The S_1 column shows that for every S_1 produced, $1/6$ of a chess set must be given up. Therefore, since 4 exist, giving up $1/6$ at a time means we can add 24 units.

If we sell S_1 (at a price greater than $\$1/3$) we would have to give up $1/6$ of an S_2 and $1/2$ of an H for each S_1 sold. Therefore, our limit would be the smallest of 36 or 48, which would limit our selling to just 36 units.

The same analysis of S_2 (not shown in the exhibit) would show that $18S_2$ could be purchased or $12S_2$ sold. There would be a total of 90 Machine B hours as the upper range (the original 72 plus the 18 purchased), and 60 as the lower range (the original 72 less 12 sold).

Dealing with greater-than-or-equal-to and equal-to constraints in the simplex

Greater-than-or-equal-to constraints ($\geq$) and equal-to constraints ($=$) must be handled somewhat differently from the less-than-or-equal-to constraints ($\leq$) in setting up and solving simplex problems.

EXHIBIT S7.12

Final Tableau for Hockey Stick and Chess Set Buy and Sell Questions

H	C	S_1	S_2	S_3	Quantity
0	0	⅙	− ⅓	1	6
1	0	½	− ½	0	24
0	1	− ⅙	⅓	0	4
		− ⅓	− ⅓		

A. For the S_1 decisions to buy if the price is less than $ ⅓.

S_1	Quantity	Limit
⅙	6	no limit
½	24	no limit
− ⅙	4	24 (4 divided by ⅙)

B. For the S_1 decisions to sell if the price is more than $ ⅓.

S_1	Quantity	Limit
⅙	6	36 (6 divided by ⅙)
½	24	48 (24 divided by ½)
− ⅙	4	no limit

Recall that with $\leq$ constraints, we added a slack variable to convert the inequality to an equality. For example, in converting the inequality $4H + 6C \leq 120$ to an equality, we added S_1, giving us $4H + 6C + S_1 = 120$. Now suppose that the sign was changed to a greater-than-or-equal-to sign, yielding $4H + 6C \geq 120$. Initially, we would surmise that subtracting a slack variable would convert this to an equality and it would be written as $4H + 6C - 1S_1 = 120$.

Unfortunately, this adjustment would lead to difficulties in the simplex method, because the initial simplex solution starts with fictitious variables and hence a negative value $(-1S_1)$ would be in the solution—a condition not permitted in linear programming. To overcome this problem, the simplex procedure requires that a different type of variable—an artificial variable—be added to each equal-to-or-greater-than equation. An artificial variable may be thought of as representing a fictitious product having a very high cost, which, though permitted in the initial solution to a simplex problem, would never appear in the final solution. Defining A as the artificial variable, the constraint given above would now appear as

$$4H + 6C - 1S_1 + 1A_1 = 120$$

And, assuming that we were minimizing cost rather than maximizing profit, the objective function would appear as

$$\$2H + \$4C + \$0S_1 + \$MA_1$$

where $\$M$ is assumed to be a very large cost, for example, a million or a billion dollars.[3] (Note also that S_1 is added to the objective function even though it is negative in the constraint equation.)

An artificial variable must also be included in constraints with equality signs. For example, if $4H + 6C = 120$, this must be changed to $4H + 6C + 1A_1 = 120$ to satisfy the simplex requirement that each constraint equation have a nonnegative variable in the initial solution. It would be reflected in the objective function, again as $\$MA_1$, but would have no slack variable accompanying it in the constraint equation.

Procedurally, where such constraints exist, the simplex method starts with artificial variables in the initial solution but otherwise treats them the same as it would real or slack variables.

Integer Programming

As we pointed out in the opening paragraphs of this chapter, linear programming assumes divisibility. Divisibility means that a variable can take on fractional values such as halves, quarters, eighths, or any fraction whatsoever.

Often, the solution to a problem must be in whole numbers—whole airplanes scheduled in airline routing, employees' times assigned in entirety to a project, products packaged in units only (tons, gross, barrels, etc.), capacity added or assigned in increments (buying another machine, adding another server in a restaurant, subcontracting a job lot). Requiring that the solution to a linear programming problem be in terms of whole numbers changes the problem to **integer programming.** If every variable must have an integer (nonfractional) value, the procedure is called *pure* integer programming. If some variables may be integers and some fractional, the procedure is called *mixed* integer programming.

S7.4 TRANSPORTATION METHOD

The **transportation method** is a simplified special case of the simplex method. It gets its name from its application to problems involving transporting products from several sources to several destinations.[4] The two common objectives of such problems are either (1) minimize the cost of shipping n units to m destinations or (2) maximize the profit of shipping n units to m destinations. There are three general steps in solving transportation problems, and we discuss each one in the context of a simple example.

---

[3] When a $\geq$ or $=$ constraint is encountered in a maximization problem, an artificial variable is assumed to have a large negative profit coefficient in the objective function to assure that it would not appear in the final solution.

[4] For other applications, see Exhibit S7.22.

EXHIBIT S7.13

Data for Chess Set Transportation Problem

Factory	Supply	Warehouse	Demand	SHIPPING COSTS PER CASE (IN DOLLARS) From	To E	To F	To G	To H
A	15	E	10	A	25	35	36	60
B	6	F	12	B	55	30	45	38
C	14	G	15	C	40	50	26	65
D	11	H	9	D	60	40	66	27

EXHIBIT S7.14

Transportation Matrix for Chess Set Problem

From \ To	E	F	G	H	Factory supply
A	25	35	36	60	15
B	55	30	45	38	6
C	40	50	26	65	14
D	60	40	66	27	11
Destination requirements	10	12	15	9	46 / 46

Suppose the Puck and Pawn Company has four factories supplying four warehouses and its management wants to determine the minimum-cost shipping schedule for its monthly output of chess sets. Factory supply, warehouse demands, and shipping costs per case of chess sets are as shown in Exhibit S7.13.

Step 1: Set Up Transportation Matrix

The transportation matrix for this example appears in Exhibit S7.14, where supply availability at each factory is shown in the far right-hand column and the warehouse demands are shown in the bottom row. The unit shipping costs are shown in the small boxes within the cells. It is important at this step to make sure that the total supply availabilities and total demand requirements are equal. In this case they are both the same, 46 units, but quite often there is an excess supply or demand. In such situations, in order for the transportation method to work, a dummy warehouse or factory must be added. Procedurally, this involves inserting an extra row (for an additional factory) or an extra column (for an additional warehouse). The amount of supply or demand required by the dummy will be equal to the difference between the row and column totals.

For example, the problem below might be restated to indicate a total demand of 36 cases, and therefore, a new column would be inserted with a demand of 10 cases to bring the total up to 46 cases. The cost figures in each cell of the dummy row would be set at zero, and therefore, any units "sent" there would not incur a transportation cost. Theoretically, this adjustment is equivalent to the simplex procedure of inserting a slack variable in a constraint inequality to convert it to an equation, and, as in the simplex, the cost of the dummy would be zero in the objective function.

Step 2: Make Initial Allocations

Initial allocation entails assigning numbers to cells to satisfy supply and demand constraints. There are several methods for carrying this out, but we describe only one, the northwest-corner method.

Northwest-corner method of allocation

The northwest-corner method, as the name implies, begins allocation by starting at the northwest corner of the matrix and assigning as much as possible to each cell in the first row.[5] The procedure is then repeated for the second row, third row, and so on, until all row and column requirements are met. Exhibit S7.15 shows a northwest-corner assignment. (Cell *A-E* was assigned first, *A-F* second, *B-F* third, and so forth.)

Inspection of Exhibit S7.15 indicates some high-cost cells were assigned and some low-cost cells bypassed by using the northwest-corner method. Indeed, this is to be expected since this method ignores costs in favor of following an easily programmable allocation algorithm.[6]

---

[5] Assign as many units as possible to each cell in order to meet the requirements of having no more than $m + n - 1$ filled cells, where m = number of rows and n = number of columns.

[6] Vogel's Approximation Method (VAM) does take account of costs. Its rules are: take the difference between the two lowest cost cells in all rows and columns, including dummies, and allocate as much as possible to the lowest cost cell in the row or column with the largest difference. The process is repeated until all cells are assigned. One study found that VAM yields an optimum solution in 80 percent of the sample problems tested. Our students have observed that the remaining 20 percent are found on examinations.

EXHIBIT S7.15

Northwest-Corner Assignment

From \ To	E	F	G	H	Factory supply
A	[25] 10	[35] 5	[36]	[60]	15
B	[55]	[30] 6	[45]	[38]	6
C	[40]	[50] 1	[26] 13	[65]	14
D	[60]	[40]	[66] 2	[27] 9	11
Destination requirements	10	12	15	9	46 / 46

Total cost = 10(\$25) + 5(\$35) + 6(\$30) + 1(\$50) + 13(\$26) + 2(\$66) + 9(\$27) = \$1,368

Step 3: Develop Optimal Solution

To develop an optimal solution in a transportation problem means evaluating each unused cell to determine whether a shift into it is advantageous from a total-cost standpoint. If it is, the shift is made, and the process is repeated. When all cells have been evaluated and appropriate shifts made, the problem is solved.

Stepping stone method of evaluation

One approach to making this evaluation is the stepping stone method. The term *stepping stone* appeared in early descriptions of the method, in which unused cells were referred to as "water" and used cells as "stones"—from the analogy of walking on a path of stones half submerged in water. We now apply the method to the northwest-corner solution to the sample problem, as shown in Exhibit S7.15.

Step a: Pick any empty cell.

Step b: Identify the closed path leading to the cell. A closed path consists of

EXHIBIT S7.16

Stepping Stone Method—Identification of Closed Paths

From \ To	E	F	G	H	Factory supply
A	[25] 10 (a)	[35] 5	[36] (b)	[60]	15
B	[55]	[30] 6	[45]	[38]	6
C	[40]	[50] 1	[26] 13	[65]	14
D	[60]	[40]	[66] 2	[27] 9	11
Destination requirements	10	12	15	9	46 \ 46

horizontal and vertical lines leading from an empty cell back to itself.[7] In the closed path there can only be one empty cell that we are examining. The 90-degree turns must therefore occur at those places that meet this requirement. Two closed paths are identified in Exhibit S7.16. Closed path *a* is required to evaluate empty cell *B-E;* closed path *b* is required to evaluate empty cell *A-H.*

Step c: Move one unit[8] into the empty cell from a filled cell at a corner of the closed path and modify the remaining filled cells at the other corners of the closed path to reflect this move. Modifying entails adding to and subtracting from filled cells in such a way that supply and demand constraints are not violated. This requires that one unit always be subtracted in a given row or column for each unit added to that row or column. Thus, the following additions and subtractions would be required for path *a.*

Add one unit to *B-E* (the empty cell).

Subtract one unit from *B-F.*

---

[7] If assignments have been made correctly, the matrix will have only one closed path for each empty cell.

[8] More than one unit could be used to test the desirability of a shift. However, since the problem is linear, if it is desirable to shift one unit, it is desirable to shift more than one, and vice versa.

Add one unit to *A-F*.

Subtract one unit from *A-E*.

And, for the longer path *b*,

Add one unit to *A-H* (the empty cell).

Subtract one unit form *D-H*.

Add one unit to *D-G*.

Subtract one unit from *C-G*.

Add one unit to *C-F*.

Subtract one unit from *A-F*.

Step d: Determine desirability of the move. This is easily done by (1) summing the cost values of the cell to which a unit has been added, (2) summing the cost values of the cells from which a unit has been subtracted, and (3) taking the difference between the two sums to determine if there is a cost reduction. If the cost is reduced by making the move, as many units as possible should be shifted out of the evaluated filled cells into the empty cell. If the cost is increased, no move should be made and the empty cell should be crossed out or otherwise marked to show that it has been evaluated. (A large plus sign is typically used to denote a cell that has been evaluated and found undesirable in cost-minimizing problems. A large minus sign is used for this purpose in profit-maximizing problems.) For cell *B-E*, the pluses and minuses are as follows.

+		−	
\$55	(*B-E*)	\$30	(*B-F*)
35	(*A-F*)	25	(*A-E*)
\$90		\$55	

For cell *A-H*:

+		−	
\$ 60	(*A-H*)	\$27	(*D-H*)
66	(*D-G*)	26	(*C-G*)
50	(*C-F*)	35	(*A-F*)
\$176		\$88	

Thus in both cases it is apparent that no move into either of the empty cells should be made.

Step e: Repeat steps *a* through *d* until all empty cells have been evaluated. To illustrate the mechanics of carrying out a move, consider cell *D-F* and the closed path leading to it, which is a short one: *C-F*, *C-G*, and *D-G*. The pluses and minuses are

+		−	
\$40	(*D-F*)	\$ 50	(*C-F*)
26	(*C-G*)	66	(*D-G*)
\$66		\$116	

Since there is a savings of $50 per unit from shipping via *D-F*, as many units as possible should be moved into this cell. In this case, however, the maximum amount that can be shifted is one unit—because the maximum amount added to any cell may not exceed the quantity found in the lowest-amount cell from which a subtraction is to be made. To do otherwise would violate the supply and demand constraints of the problem. Here we see that the limiting cell is *C-F*, since it contains only one unit.

The revised matrix, showing the effects of this move and the previous evaluations, is presented in Exhibit S7.17. Applying the stepping stone method to the remaining unfilled cells and making shifts where indicated yields an optimal solution.

In particular, the empty cell *A-G* in Exhibit S7.17 has closed path *D-G*, *D-F*, and *A-F*. The pluses and minuses are:

+		−	
36	(*A-G*)	35	(*A-F*)
40	(*D-F*)	66	(*D-G*)
76		101	

EXHIBIT S7.17

Revised Transportation Matrix

From \ To	*E*	*F*	*G*	*H*	Factory supply
A	[25] 10	[35] 5	[36]	[60] +	15
B	[55] +	[30] 6	[45]	[38]	6
C	[40]	[50] +	[26] 14	[65]	14
D	[60]	[40] 1	[66] 1	[27] 9	11
Destination requirements	10	12	15	9	46 \ 46

Total cost = 10($25) + 5($35) + 6($30) + 14($26) + 1($40) + 1($66) + 9($27) = $1,318

EXHIBIT S7.18

Optimal Solution to Transportation Problem

From \ To	E	F	G	H	Factory supply
A	25 10	35 5−1=4	36 0+1=1	60	15
B	55	30 6	45	38	6
C	40	50	26 14	65	14
D	60	40 1+1=2	66 1−1=0	27 9	11
Destination requirements	10	12	15	9	46

Total cost = 10($25) + 4($35) + 1($36) + 6($30) + 14($26) + 2($40) + 9($27) = $1,293

Since savings = 101 − 76 = $25, we shift 1 unit to *A-G*. Exhibit S7.18 shows the optimal matrix, with minimum transportation cost = $1,293.

To verify that we have the optimum, we should evaluate each empty cell to see if it is desirable to bring in that cell. If we did this, we would have a plus sign in each of these cells.

Degeneracy

Degeneracy exists in a transportation problem when the number of filled cells is less than the number of rows plus the number of columns minus one (i.e., $m + n - 1$). Degeneracy may be observed during the initial allocation when the first entry in a row or column satisfies *both* the row and column requirements. Degeneracy requires some adjustment in the matrix to evaluate the solution achieved. The form of this adjustment involves inserting some value in an empty cell so a closed path can be developed to evaluate other empty cells. This value may be thought of as an infinitely small amount, having no direct bearing on the cost of the solution.

Procedurally, the value (often denoted by the Greek letter theta, θ) is used in

EXHIBIT S7.19 **Degenerate Transportation Problem with Theta Added**

From \ To	W	X	Y	Factory supply
T	[8] 3	[6] 8	[4] θ	11
U	[9]	[8]	[0] 9	9
V	[5] 3	[3]	[10]	3
Destination requirements	6	8	9	23 \ 23

$m + n - 1 = 5$ filled cells

Actual allocation = 4 filled cells

exactly the same manner as a real number except that it may initially be placed in any empty cell, even though row and column requirements have been met by real numbers. A degenerate transportation problem showing an optimal minimum cost allocation is presented in Exhibit S7.19, where we can see that if θ were not assigned to the matrix, it would be impossible to evaluate several cells (including the one where it is added). Once a θ has been inserted into the solution, it will remain there until it is removed by subtraction or until a final solution is reached.

While the choice of where to put a θ is arbitrary, it saves time if it is placed where it may be used to evaluate as many cells as possible without being shifted. In this regard, verify for yourself that θ is optimally allocated in Exhibit S7.19.

Alternate optimal solutions

When the evaluation of an empty cell yields the same cost as the existing allocation, an alternate optimal solution exists.[9] In such cases, management has additional flexibility and can invoke nontransportation cost factors in deciding on a final shipping schedule. (A large zero is commonly placed in an empty cell that has been identified as an alternate optimal route.)

---

[9] Assuming that all other cells are optimally assigned.

S7.5 ASSIGNMENT METHOD

The **assignment method** is a special case of the transportation method of linear programming to apply to situations where there are *n* supply sources and *n* demand uses (e.g., five jobs on five machines) and the objective is to minimize or maximize some measure of effectiveness. Assignment problems are quite similar to transportation problems, but the fact that each allocation in an assignment problem simultaneously satisfies both a row and column requirement makes all such problems multidegenerate. This technique is convenient in applications such as in job shop scheduling to allocate people to jobs, jobs to machines, and so forth. The assignment method is appropriate in solving problems that have the following characteristics.

1. There are *n* "things" to be distributed to *n* "destinations."
2. Each "thing" must be assigned to one and only one "destination."
3. Only one criterion can be used—minimum cost, maximum profit, minimum completion time.

For example, suppose that a scheduler has five jobs that can be performed on any of five machines ($n = 5$) and that the cost of completing each job-machine combination is shown in Exhibit S7.20. The scheduler would like to devise a minimum-cost assignment. (There are 5!, or 120, possible assignments.) This problem may be solved by the assignment method, which consists of the following four steps.

1. Subtract the smallest number in each *row* from itself and all other numbers in that row. (There will then be at least one zero in each row.)
2. Subtract the smallest number in each *column* from all other numbers in that column.
3. Determine if the *minimum* number of lines required to cover each zero is equal to *n*. If so, an optimum solution has been found, since job machine assignments must be made at the zero entries and this test proves that this is possible. If the minimum number of lines required is less than *n,* go to Step 4.
4. Draw the least possible number of lines through all the zeros (these may be the same lines used in Step 3). Subtract the smallest number not covered by lines from itself and all other uncovered numbers and add it to the number at each intersection of lines. Repeat Step 3.

For the example problem, the steps listed in Exhibit S7.21 would be followed.

Note that even though there are two zeros in three rows and three columns, the solution shown in Exhibit S7.21 is the only one possible for this problem since Job III must be assigned to Machine C to meet the "assign to zero"

EXHIBIT S7.20

Assignment Matrix Showing Machine Processing Costs for Each Job

Job	MACHINE A	B	C	D	E
I	$5	$6	$4	$8	$3
II	6	4	9	8	5
III	4	3	2	5	4
IV	7	2	4	5	3
V	3	6	4	5	5

EXHIBIT S7.21 **Procedure to Solve an Assignment Matrix**

Step 1: Row Reduction—the smallest number is subtracted from each row.

Job	MACHINE A	B	C	D	E
I	2	3	1	5	0
II	2	0	5	4	1
III	2	1	0	3	2
IV	5	0	2	3	1
V	0	3	1	2	2

Step 2: Column reduction—the smallest number is subtracted from each column.

Job	MACHINE A	B	C	D	E
I	2	3	1	3	0
II	2	0	5	2	1
III	2	1	0	1	2
IV	5	0	2	1	1
V	0	3	1	0	2

Step 3: Apply line test—the number of lines to cover all zeros is 4; since 5 are required, go to step 4.

Job	MACHINE A	B	C	D	E
I	2	3	1	3	0
II	2	0	5	2	1
III	2	1	0	1	2
IV	5	0	2	1	1
V	0	3	1	0	2

Step 4: Subtract smallest uncovered number and add to intersection of lines—using lines drawn in step 3, smallest uncovered number is 1.

Job	MACHINE A	B	C	D	E
I	1	3	0	2	0
II	1	0	4	1	1
III	2	2	0	1	3
IV	4	0	1	0	1
V	0	4	1	0	3

Optimum solution—by "line test."

Job	MACHINE A	B	C	D	E
I	1	3	0	2	0
II	1	0	4	1	1
III	2	2	0	1	3
IV	4	0	1	0	1
V	0	4	1	0	3

Optimum assignments and their costs.

Job I to Machine E	$3
Job II to Machine B	$4
Job III to Machine C	$2
Job IV to Machine D	$5
Job V to Machine A	$3
Total cost	$17

requirement. Other problems may have more than one optimum solution, depending, of course, on the costs involved. The nonmathematical rationale of the assignment method is one of minimizing opportunity costs.[10] For example, if we decided to assign Job I to Machine A instead of to Machine E, we would be sacrificing the opportunity to save \$2 (\$5 − \$3). The assignment algorithm in effect performs such comparisons for the entire set of alternative assignments by means of row and column reduction, as described in Steps 1 and 2. It makes similar comparisons in Step 4. Obviously, if assignments are made to zero cells, no opportunity cost, with respect to the entire matrix, is incurred.

Typical Operations Management Applications of Linear Programming

Exhibit S7.22 summarizes some typical operations management applications of linear programming according to the particular technique by which the application is usually carried out.

While the simplex method can be applied to any of the situations presented in the table, it is generally more expedient to employ the transportation or the assignment method if the problem lends itself to these forms.

S7.6 KARMARKAR'S ALGORITHM FOR SOLVING LINEAR PROGRAMMING PROBLEMS

We have seen how the simplex algorithm can be used to solve linear programming problems, but many real-world linear programming problems are very large—their formulation would require 40,000 variables or more. Such large problems arise in many areas of business, including airline scheduling, oil refining, and the design of large telephone networks. Problems with 40,000 variables are not solvable on the computer using the simplex method because they would take too long. In 1984, Narendra Karmarkar of AT&T's Bell Laboratories proposed a faster algorithm for such large-scale problems. Its greater speed has made previously unsolvable problems solvable. Whereas the simplex method of linear programming moves to the optimal by way of

---

[10] The underlying rationale of the procedure of adding and subtracting the smallest cell values is as follows: Additional zeros are entered into the matrix by subtracting an amount equal to one of the cells from all cells. Negative numbers, which are not permissible, will occur in the matrix. In order to get rid of the negative numbers, an amount equal to the maximum negative number must be added to each element of the row or column in which it occurs. This results in adding this amount twice to any cell that lies at the intersection of a row and a column that were both changed. The net result is that the lined rows and columns revert to their original amounts, and the intersections increase by the amount subtracted from the uncovered cells. (The reader may wish to prove this by solving the example without using lines.)

EXHIBIT S7.22

Typical Operations Management Applications of Linear Programming*

Simplex*

Aggregate production planning: Finding the minimum-cost production schedule, including rate change costs, given constraints on size of work force and inventory levels.
Product planning: Finding the optimal product mix where several products have different costs and resource requirements (e.g., finding the optimal blend of constituents for gasolines, paints, human diets, animal feeds).
Product routing: Finding the optimal routing for a product that must be processed sequentially through several machine centers, with each machine in a center having its own cost and output characteristics.
Process control: Minimizing the amount of scrap material generated by cutting steel, leather, or fabric from a roll or sheet of stock material.
Inventory control: Finding the optimal combination of products to stock in a warehouse or store.

Transportation

Aggregate production planning: Finding the minimum-cost production schedule, taking into account inventory carrying costs, overtime costs, and subcontracting costs.
Distribution scheduling: Finding the optimal shipping schedule for distributing products between factories and warehouses or warehouses and retailers.
Plant location studies: Finding the optimal location of a new plant by evaluating shipping costs between alternative locations and supply and demand sources.
Materials handling: Finding the minimum cost routings of material handling devices (e.g., forklift trucks) between departments in a plant and of hauling materials from a supply yard to work sites by trucks, with each truck having different capacity and performance capabilities.

Assignment

Scheduling: Minimum cost assignment of trucks to pickup points and ships to berths.
Worker assignments: Minimum cost assignment of workers to machines and to jobs.

*The graphical method is not included since it may be applied in the same situations as simplex if the problem has fewer than three variables.

corner points at the outside boundary, Karmarkar starts inside the feasible area and proceeds toward the optimum by constructing a series of ovals.

Karmarkar's algorithm is difficult to understand because it requires understanding the "close enough ideas" of the ellipsoidal algorithm and the interior point search. It is difficult to explain what is going on since the simplest example requires multidimensional space. Finally, a computer is necessary to solve a problem of any size. A two-variable example in simplex requires a six-by-six matrix in Karmarkar's algorithm, and the numbers get worse with each iteration.[11] The procedure is quite complicated mathematically, but many researchers are currently working to improve on Karmarkar's method.

[11] Craig Tovey, "Teaching Karmarkar's Algorithm," *OR/MS Today* 15, no. 2 (April 1988), pp. 18–19.

S7.7 CONCLUSION

This supplement has dealt mainly with the mechanics of solution procedures for linear programming (LP) problems. It would be a rare instance when a linear programming problem would actually be solved by hand. There are too many computers around and too many LP software programs to justify spending time for manual solution. In order to use a computer program, it's necessary to be able to formulate the programming problem, with its constraints and objective function. This is the usual stumbling block in using linear programming methods. Then, given the computer output, one needs to understand what it means. We believe it is very helpful and necessary to take the time to solve some simple practice problems as we have done here.

S7.8 REVIEW AND DISCUSSION QUESTIONS

1. What structural requirements of a problem are needed in order to solve it by linear programming?
2. What type of information is provided in a solved simplex tableau?
3. What type of information is provided by shadow prices?
4. What are slack variables? Why are they necessary in the simplex method? When are they used in the transportation method?
5. It has been stated in this chapter that an optimal solution for a simplex problem always lies at a corner point. Under what conditions might an equally desirable solution be found anywhere along a constraint line?
6. What is a convex polygon? How is it identified?
7. How do you know if a transportation problem is degenerate? What must be done if a degenerate problem is to be tested for optimality?
8. Why is an assignment problem multidegenerate?
9. Why is Karmarkar's algorithm so important?

S7.9 PROBLEMS

*1. Two products, X and Y, both require processing time on Machines I and II. Machine I has 200 hours available, and Machine II has 400 hours available. Product X requires one hour on Machine I and four hours on Machine II. Product Y requires one hour on Machine I and one hour on Machine II. Each unit of product X yields \$10 profit and each unit of Y yields \$5 profit. These statements reduce to the following set of equations:

$$X + Y \leq 200$$
$$4X + Y \leq 400$$

Maximize $10X + 5Y$

---

* The complete solution to Problems 1 and 2 are in Appendix D.

Solve the problem graphically showing the optimal utilization of machine time.

*2. Solve Problem 1 using the simplex method.

3. Following is a set of linear equations. Solve *graphically* for the optimum point.

$$4A + 6B \geq 120$$
$$2A + 6B \geq 72$$
$$B \geq 10$$

Minimize $2A + 4B$

4. Solve the following problem using the graphical method of linear programming.

$$5X + 4Y \leq 40$$
$$3X + 2Y \geq 12$$
$$5X + 12Y \geq 60$$

Minimize $3X + Y$

5. Following is the partially completed simplex tableau of a linear programming product mix problem involving three products (X_1, X_2, and X_3) and three departments. All costs and profits are in dollars per unit. Department restrictions are expressed in hours.

C_j Row	2	5	3	0	0	0	
Solution Mix	X_1	X_2	X_3	S_1	S_2	S_3	Quantity
	0	0	2	−2	1	1	20
	1	0	−¼	½	−¼	0	100
	0	1	3/2	0	½	0	230
Z_j	2	5	7	1	2	0	
$(C_j - Z)$	0	0	−4	−1	−2	0	

a. What is the optimal product mix?

b. If a customer offers you a net $2 per hour, would you lease time in Department 3? How many hours would you lease?

6. The following equations define a linear programming problem. Solve the problem using the graphical method of linear programming.

$$16X + 10Y \leq 160$$
$$12X + 14Y \leq 168$$
$$Y \geq 2$$

Maximize $2X + 10Y$

Draw the graph, show the objective line, and point out the optimal answer.

7. A diet is being prepared for the University of Arizona dorms. The objective is to feed the students at the least possible cost, but the diet must have between 1,800 and 3,600 calories. No more than 1,400 calories can be starch, and no fewer than 400 can be protein. The varied diet is to be made of two foods, A and B. Food A

costs $0.75 per pound and contains 600 calories, 400 of which are protein and 200 starch. No more than two pounds of Food A can be used per resident. Food B costs $0.15 per pound and contains 900 calories, of which 700 are starch, 100 are protein, and 100 are fat.

a. Write out the equations representing the above information.

b. Solve the problem graphically for the amounts of each food that should be used.

8. Do problem 7 with the added constraint that not more than 150 calories shall be fat, and that the price of food has escalated to $1.75 per pound for Food A and $2.50 per pound for Food B.

9. Logan Manufacturing wants to mix two fuels (A and B) for its trucks to minimize cost. It needs no fewer than 3,000 gallons to run its trucks during the next month. It has a maximum fuel storage capacity of 4,000 gallons. There are 2,000 gallons of Fuel A and 4,000 gallons of Fuel B available. The mixed fuel must have an octane rating of no less than 80.

   When mixing fuels, the amount of fuel obtained is just equal to the sum of the amounts put in. The octane rating is the weighted average of the individual octanes, weighted in proportion to the respective volumes.

   The following is known: Fuel A has an octane of 90 and costs $1.20 per gallon; Fuel B has an octane of 75 and costs $0.90 per gallon.

   a. Write out the equations expressing the above information.

   b. Solve the problem graphically, giving the amount of each fuel to be used. State any assumptions necessary to solve the problem.

10. Shown here is a solved simplex tableau.

X	Y	Z	S_1	S_2	S_3	
0	5	0	−2	1	1	40
0	−3	1	3	−2	0	90
1	4	0	−4	3	0	60
0	−7	0	−2	−3	0	

a. What are the values of X, Y, Z, S_1, S_2, and S_3?

b.

Would you buy?	At what price?	How many?
S_1 S_2 S_3		

Would you sell?	At what price?	How many?
S_1 S_2 S_3		

11. The following tableau is the final optimal iteration in a simplex linear programming problem.

A	B	C	S_1	S_2	S_3	
−4	0	1	−3	4	0	400
2	0	0	1	−2	1	300
−3	1	0	−2	6	0	100
−2.00	0	0	−4.00	−6.00	0	

a. What are the values of A, B, C, S_1, S_2, and S_3?
b. Answer the following questions about S_1, S_2, and S_3.

Would you buy?	At what price?	How many?
S_1 S_2 S_3		

Would you sell?	At what price?	How many?
S_1 S_2 S_3		

12. Find the optimal solution for the following transportation-type linear programming problem.

Sources	Availability	Destinations	Required
A	200	D	300
B	300	E	125
C	150	F	140

Transportation costs

AD = $10	BD = $4	CD = $9
AE = $12	BE = $13	CE = $14
AF = $4	BF = $15	CF = $2

13. You are trying to create a budget to optimize the use of a portion of your disposable income. You have a maximum of $700 per month to be allocated to food, shelter, and entertainment. The amount spent on food and shelter combined must not exceed $500. The amount spent on shelter alone must not exceed $100. Entertainment cannot exceed $300 per month. Each dollar spent on food has a satisfaction value of 2, each dollar spent on shelter has a satisfaction value of 3, and each dollar spent on entertainment has a satisfaction value of 5.

Assuming a linear relationship, use the simplex method of linear programming to determine the optimal allocation of your funds.

14. A landscaping firm has asked you to help set up a method to schedule its jobs. You decide on the transportation method of linear programming, because you

understand that the company will be getting in a PC for the office and will be able to use this same format to get the optimum schedule when they get the computer and an LP program.

This information and data were supplied to you:

There are nine workers sent out on jobs. The normal work week is 40 hours, and overtime, if necessary, is limited to an additional 8 hours per week. The hourly rate is $15, which includes tools and overhead. If the work is not completed on time, there is an additional cost to the landscaping firm (by contract) of $5 per hour per week late. If the work is done early, there is an additional cost of $3 per hour per week because certain preparations have not been made that make the job more difficult.

Develop a transportation matrix showing your schedule for the next four weeks. Demands from customers (in hours) for the next four weeks are: 375, 400, 500, 400. Do not try to find the optimum, just develop a feasible (and reasonable) schedule.

15. Bindley Corporation has a one-year contract to supply motors for all washing machines produced by Rinso Ltd. Rinso manufactures the washers at four locations around the country: New York, Fort Worth, San Diego, and Minneapolis. Plans call for the following numbers of washing machines to be produced at each location.

New York	50,000
Ft. Worth	70,000
San Diego	60,000
Minneapolis	80,000

Bindley has three plants that are capable of producing the motors. The plants and production capacities are:

Boulder	100,000
Macon	100,000
Gary	150,000

Due to varying production and transportation costs, the profit Bindley earns on each 1,000 units depends on where it was produced and where it was shipped to. The following table gives the accounting department estimates of the profit per unit. (Shipment will be made in lots of 1,000.)

	SHIPPED TO			
Produced at	New York	Fort Worth	San Diego	Minneapolis
Boulder	7	11	8	13
Macon	20	17	12	10
Gary	8	18	13	16

Given profit *maximization* as a criterion, Bindley would like to determine how many motors should be produced at each plant and how many motors should be shipped from each plant to each destination.

a. Develop a transportation tableau for this problem.

b. Find the optimal solution.

16. Given the following transportation problem:

From \ To	A	B	C	D	Supply
1	$120	$100	$ 90	$150	360
2	100	80	20	100	250
3	90	50	130	80	300
Demand	260	400	250	300	

a. Find an initial solution by the northwest-corner method.
b. Solve the problem by the stepping stone method.

17. Minimize the following transportation problem.

From \ To	D	E	F	G	H	Supply
A	1	4	10	4	10	52
B	8	2	8	2	1	20
C	10	1	8	8	2	20
Demand	16	22	4	19	31	92 / 92

18. Maximize the following transportation problem.

From \ To	D	E	F	G	Supply
A	17	12	32	4	300
B	9	18	7	11	700
C	3	21	14	9	400
Demand	200	500	350	350	1400 / 1400

19. Solve for the optimal amounts of orange, grapefruit, and orange/grapefruit juices to maximize revenue in the problem given in the introduction to this Supplement on page 228.

S7.10 SELECTED BIBLIOGRAPHY

Barnes, Earl R. "A Variable of Karmarkar's Algorithm for Solving Linear Programming Problems." *Mathematical Programming* 36 (1986).

Bierman, H.; Charles Bonini; and W. Hausman. *Quantitative Analysis for Business Decisions*. 6th ed. Homewood, Ill.: Richard D. Irwin, 1981.

Eppen, G. D., and F. J. Gould. *Introductory Management Science*. 2nd ed. Englewood Cliffs, N.J.: Prentice-Hall, 1987.

Hooker, J. N. "Karmarkar's Linear Programming Algorithm." *Interfaces* 16, no. 4 (July–August 1986), pp. 75–90.

Karmarkar, N. "A New Polynomial Time Algorithm for Linear Programming." *Combinatorica* 4 (1984), pp. 373–95.

Luenberger, D. G. *Linear and Nonlinear Programming*. 2nd ed. Reading, Mass.: Addison-Wesley, 1985.

Murty, K. *Linear Programming*. 2nd ed. New York: John Wiley & Sons, 1983.

Rockett, A. M., and J. C. Stevenson. "Karmarkar's Algorithm." *Byte* (September 1987), pp. 146–60.

Thierauf, Robert J.; Robert C. Klenkamp; and Marcia L. Ruwe. *Management Science: A Model Formulation Approach with Computer Applications*. Columbus, Ohio: Charles E. Merrill, 1985.

Tovey, Craig. "Teaching Karmarkar's Algorithm." *OR/MS Today* 15, no. 2 (April 1988), pp. 18–19.

Winston, Wayne. *Operations Research*. Boston: Duxbury, 1987.

Chapter 8

Facility Layout

EPIGRAPH

Layout is where "the rubber meets the road" in every production system.

Anonymous

CHAPTER OUTLINE

KEY TERMS

Process Layout
Product Layout
Group Technology (GT) Layout
Just-in-Time Layout
Fixed-Position Layout
Cycle Time
Assembly Line Balancing
Precedence Relationship

While layout sounds like a dry topic, choosing how the system should be arranged to enhance the flow of a product or service can determine its success or failure. Over the years, banks, for example, have tried to divide customers into mortgage customers, savings deposit customers, commercial customers, checking account customers, and drive-through customers, among others. Universities are arranged as colleges; and within colleges, departments; and within departments, specializations. Both the bank and the university are examples of job-shop layout, which is based on the grouping of similar specializations. The customer moves through the system from one specialized area to other specialized areas as needed.

At the opposite extreme, consider a hospital (which is also basically arranged as a job shop of specializations) that occasionally has an emergency. In such emergencies, the patient remains in the same location and the required servers and equipment are brought from all over the hospital to meet the patient needs. This is called "fixed"-position layout, though the location and arrangement is temporary. Some hospitals try to create emergency or trauma rooms that are staffed by a mixture of personnel and equipment to meet special types of emergencies, such as burns, gunshot wounds, accidents, and so on. This combination of specializations to meet customer needs is "group technology" or "cellular" layout. We will discuss each of these in this chapter.

The layout decision determines where departments and workstations should be located for a smooth-flowing and efficient system. The inputs to the layout decision are:

1. Specification of objectives of the system in terms of output and flexibility.
2. Estimation of product or service demand on the system.
3. Processing requirements in terms of number of operations and amount of flow between departments and work centers.
4. Space availability within the facility itself.

All these inputs are, in fact, outputs of process selection and capacity planning, discussed in previous chapters. In our treatment of layout in this chapter, we examine how layouts are developed under various formats (or work-flow structures). Our emphasis will be on quantitative techniques used in locating departments within a facility and on workstation arrangements and balance in the important area of assembly lines. Before embarking on this discussion, however, it is useful to note some marks of a good layout listed in Exhibit 8.1.

8.1 BASIC LAYOUT FORMATS

The formats by which departments are arranged in a facility are defined by the general pattern of work flow, and are of three basic types: process layout, product layout, and fixed-position layout; and one hybrid type, group tech-

EXHIBIT 8.1

Marks of a Good Layout

Manufacturing and Back-Office Operations

1. Straight-line flow pattern (or adaptation).
2. Backtracking kept to a minimum.
3. Production time predictable.
4. Little interstage storage of materials.
5. Open plant floors so everyone can see what's going on.
6. Bottleneck operations under control.
7. Workstations close together.
8. Orderly handling and storage of materials.
9. No unnecessary rehandling of materials.
10. Easily adjustable to changing conditions.

Face-to-Face Services

1. Easily understood service flow pattern.
2. Adequate waiting facilities.
3. Easy communication with customers.
4. Customer surveillance easily maintained.
5. Clear exit and entry points with adequate checkout capabilities.
6. Departments and processes arranged so that customers see only what you want them to see.
7. Balance between waiting areas and service areas.
8. Minimum walking and material movement.
9. Lack of clutter.
10. High sales volume per square foot of facility.

nology or cellular layout. In this chapter we consider all but the fixed-position layout.

In a **process layout** (also called a *job-shop layout*), similar equipment or functions are grouped together, such as all lathes in one area and all stamping machines in another. A part being worked on then travels, according to the established sequence of operations, from area to area, where the proper machines are located for each operation. This type of layout is typical of hospitals, for example, where we find areas dedicated to particular types of medical care, such as maternity wards and intensive care units.

A **product layout** (also called a *flow-shop layout*) is one in which equipment or work processes are arranged according to the progressive steps by which the product is made. The path for each part is, in effect, a straight line. Production lines for automobiles, chemical plants, and cafeteria lines are all product layouts.

A **group technology (GT) layout** groups dissimilar machines into work centers (or cells) to work on products that have similar shapes and processing requirements. A GT layout is similar to process layout in that cells are designed to perform a specific set of processes, and it is similar to product layout in that the cells are dedicated to a limited range of products. (*Group technology* also refers to the parts classification and coding system that is used to specify machine types that go into a GT cell.)

A **Just-in-Time layout** is not really a layout type in the true sense, but rather a focus on the product or service flow through the system. The objective in a Just-in-Time system is to produce only enough items to satisfy what is immediately needed. This objective seems to be most successful when all of the required parts for producing that product or service are located together. In that way it is easier for workers to be aware of what is going on—for example, completing a process and then reaching back up the production sequence to get another item to work on. Therefore, a JIT layout arranges equipment, personnel, materials, and so on to enhance the flow of similar products requiring approximately the same processing. More on this in the JIT chapter.

In a **fixed-position layout** the product, by virtue of its bulk or weight, if it cannot be moved, or if it has some particular needs, remains at one location. The equipment is moved to the product or customer, rather than vice versa. Shipyards, construction sites, and hospital emergency rooms are examples of this format.

Many manufacturing facilities present a combination of layout types. For example, one floor may be laid out by process, another floor may be laid out by product. Still, other floors may contain areas arranged for JIT production. It is also common to find an entire plant arranged according to general product flow (fabrication, subassembly, and final assembly), coupled with process layout within fabrication and product layout within the assembly department. Likewise, group technology layout is frequently found within a department that itself is located according to a plantwide product-oriented layout.

8.2 PROCESS LAYOUT

The most common approach in developing a process layout is to arrange departments consisting of like processes in a way that optimizes their relative placement. In many installations, optimal placement often means placing departments with large amounts of interdepartment traffic adjacent to one another.

Consider the following example. Suppose that we want to arrange the eight departments of a toy factory to minimize the interdepartmental material handling cost. Initially, let us make the simplifying assumption that all departments have the same amount of space, say, 40 feet by 40 feet and that the building is 80 feet wide and 160 feet long (and thus compatible with the department dimensions). The first thing we would want to know is the nature of the flow between departments and the way the material is transported. If the company has another factory that makes similar products, information about flow patterns might be abstracted from the records. On the other hand, if this is a new product line, such information would have to come from routing sheets (see Chapter 3) or from estimates by knowledgeable personnel such as

EXHIBIT 8.2 **Interdepartmental Flow**

Flow between departments (number of moves)

	1	2	3	4	5	6	7	8
1		175	50	0	30	200	20	25
2			0	100	75	90	80	90
3				17	88	125	99	180
4					20	5	0	25
5						0	180	187
6							374	103
7								7
8								

Department	Activity
1	Shipping and receiving
2	Plastic molding and stamping
3	Metal forming
4	Sewing department
5	Small toy assembly
6	Large toy assembly
7	Painting
8	Mechanism assembly

process or industrial engineers. Of course these data, regardless of their source, will have to be modified to reflect the nature of future orders over the projected life at the proposed layout.

Let us assume that this information is available. We find that all material is transported in a standard-size crate by forklift truck, one crate to a truck (which constitutes one "load"). Now suppose that transportation costs are $1 to move a load between adjacent departments and $1 extra for each department in between. The expected loads between departments for the first year of operation are tabulated in Exhibit 8.2; the available plant space is depicted in Exhibit 8.3.

Given this information, our first step is to illustrate the interdepartmental flow by a model, such as Exhibit 8.4. This provides the basic layout pattern, which we will try to improve.

The second step is to determine the cost of this layout by multiplying the material handling cost by the number of loads moved between each department. Exhibit 8.5 presents this information, which is derived as follows. The annual material handling cost between Departments 1 and 2 is $175 ($1 × 175 moves), $60 between Departments 1 and 5 ($2 × 30 moves), $60 between

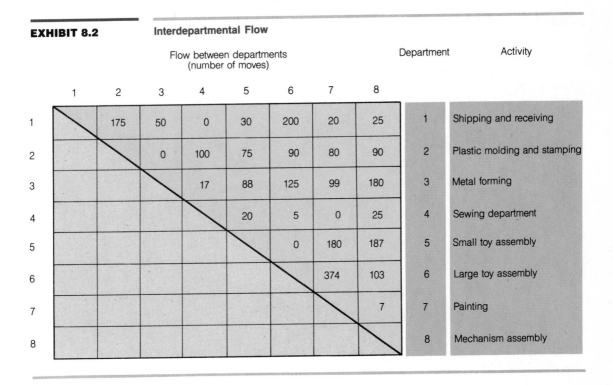

EXHIBIT 8.3

Building Dimensions and Departments

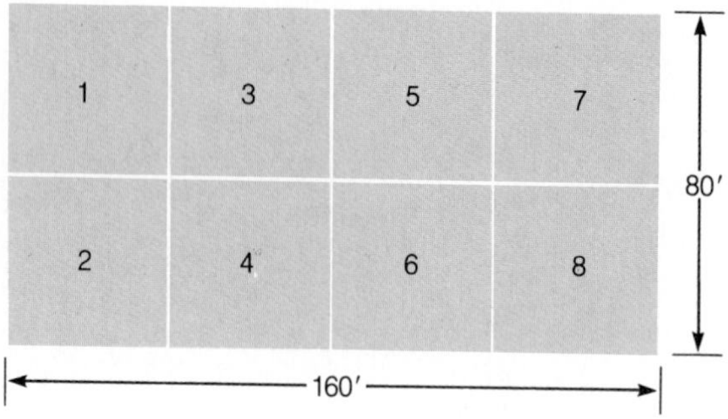

EXHIBIT 8.4

Interdepartmental Flow Graph with Number of Annual Movements

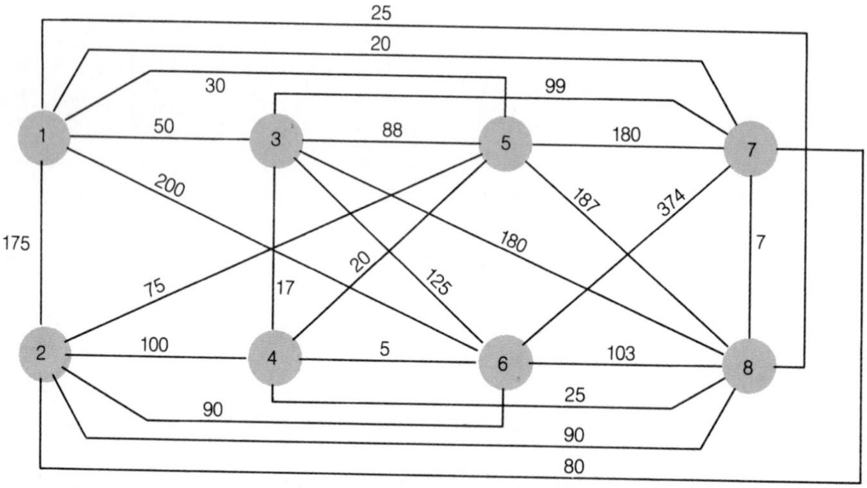

Departments 1 and 7 ($3 × 20 moves), and so forth. (The "distances" are taken from Exhibit 8.3 or 8.4, not Exhibit 8.2.)

The third step is a search for departmental changes that will reduce costs. On the basis of the graph and the cost matrix, it seems desirable to place Departments 1 and 6 closer together to reduce their high move-distance costs. However, this requires shifting several other departments, thereby affecting their move-distance costs and the total cost of the second solution. Exhibit 8.6 shows the revised layout resulting from relocating Department 6 and an

EXHIBIT 8.5

Cost Matrix—First Solution

$	1	2	3	4	5	6	7	8
1		175	50	0	60	400	60	75
2			0	100	150	180	240	270
3				17	88	125	198	360
4					20	5	0	50
5						0	180	187
6							374	103
7								7
8								

Total cost: $3,474

EXHIBIT 8.6

Revised Interdepartmental Flow Chart (Only interdepartmental flow with effect on cost is depicted)

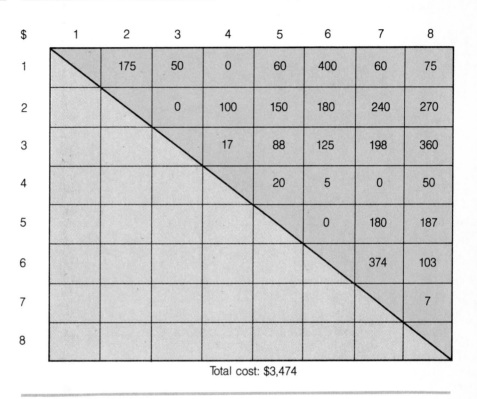

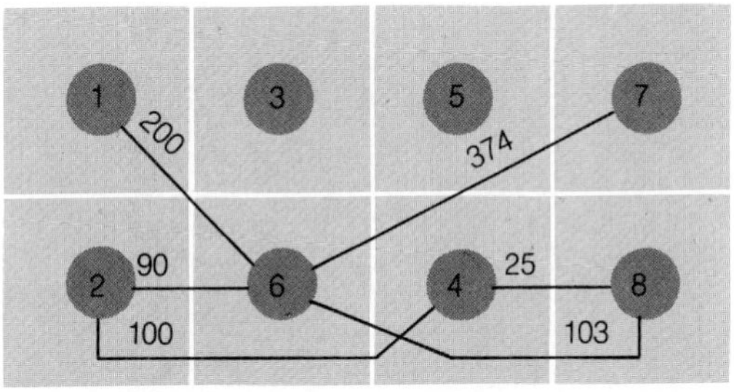

EXHIBIT 8.7 **Cost Matrix—Second Solution**

$	1	2	3	4	5	6	7	8	Net cost change
1		175	50	0	60	**200**	60	75	−$200
2			0	**200**	150	**90**	240	270	+ 10
3				17	88	125	198	360	
4					20	5	0	**25**	− 25
5						0	180	187	
6							**748**	**206**	+ $374, +$103
7								7	
8									
									+ $262 Total cost: $3,736

EXHIBIT 8.8

A Feasible Layout

Small toy assembly 5	Mechanism assembly 8	Shipping and receiving 1	Large toy assembly 6
Metal forming 3	Plastic molding and stamping 2	Sewing 4	Painting 7

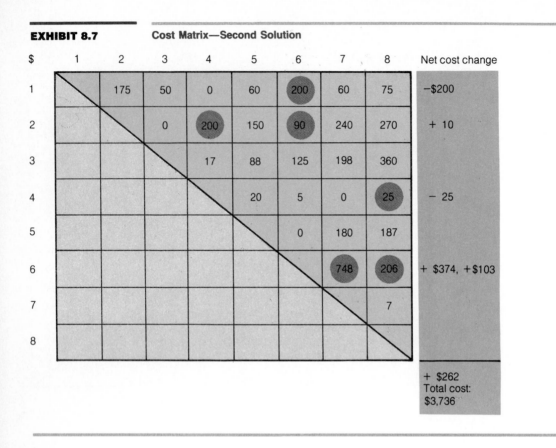

adjacent department (Department 4 is arbitrarily selected for this purpose). The revised cost matrix for the exchange, with the cost changes circled, is given in Exhibit 8.7. Note the total cost is $262 *greater* than in the initial solution. Clearly, doubling the distance between Departments 6 and 7 accounted for the major part of the cost increase. This points out the fact that, even in a small problem, it is rarely easy to decide the correct "obvious move" on the basis of casual inspection.

Thus far, we have shown only one exchange among a large number of potential exchanges; in fact, for an eight-department problem there are 8! (or 40,320) possible arrangements. Therefore, the procedure we have employed would have only a remote possibility of achieving an optimal combination in a "reasonable" number of tries. Nor does our problem stop here.

Suppose that we *do* arrive at a good cut-and-try solution solely on the basis of material handling cost, such as that shown in Exhibit 8.8 (whose total cost is $3,244). We would note, first of all, that our shipping and receiving department is near the center of the factory—an arrangement that probably would not be acceptable. The sewing department is next to the painting department, introducing the hazard that lint, thread, and cloth particles might drift onto painted items. Further, small-toy assembly and large-toy assembly are located at opposite ends of the plant, which would increase travel time for assemblers, who very likely would be needed in both departments at various times of the day, and for supervisors, who might otherwise supervise both departments simultaneously.

Systematic Layout Planning

In certain types of layout problems, numerical flow of items between departments either is impractical to obtain or does not reveal the qualitative factors that may be crucial to the placement decision. In these situations, the technique known as systematic layout planning (SLP) is commonly used.[1] It involves developing a relationship chart showing the degree of importance of having each department located adjacent to every other department. From this chart is developed an activity relationship diagram similar to the flow graph used for illustrating material handling between departments. The activity relationship diagram is then adjusted by trial and error until a satisficing adjacency pattern is obtained. This pattern, in turn, is modified department by department to meet building space limitations. Exhibit 8.9 illustrates the technique with a simple five-department problem involving laying out a floor of a department store.

---

[1] See Richard Muther and John D. Wheeler, "Simplified Systematic Layout Planning," *Factory* 120, nos. 8, 9, 10 (August, September, October 1962), pp. 68–77, 111–19, 101–13.

EXHIBIT 8.9 **Systematic Layout Planning for a Floor of a Department Store**

A. Relationship chart (based upon Tables B and C)

From	To 2	To 3	To 4	To 5	Area (sq. ft.)
1. Credit department	I 6	U —	A 4	U —	100
2. Toy department		U —	I 1	A 1,6	400
3. Wine department			U —	X 1	300
4. Camera department				X 1	100
5. Candy department					100

Letter ← Closeness rating
Number ← Reason for rating

B.

Code	Reason*
1	Type of customer
2	Ease of supervision
3	Common personnel
4	Contact necessary
5	Share same space
6	Psychology

*Others may be used.

C.

Value	Closeness	Line code*	Color code†
A	Absolutely necessary	(four lines)	Red
E	Especially important	(three lines)	Orange
I	Important	(two lines)	Green
O	Ordinary closeness OK	(one line)	Blue
U	Unimportant		None
X	Undesirable	(zigzag line)	Brown

* Used for example purposes only.
† Used in practice.

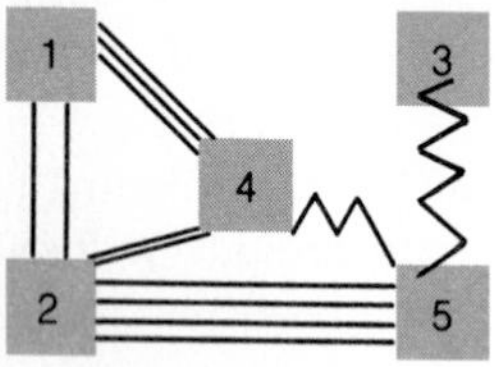

Initial relationship diagram (based upon Tables A and C)

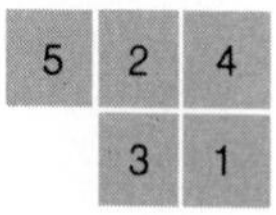

Initial layout based upon relationship diagram (ignoring space and building constraints)

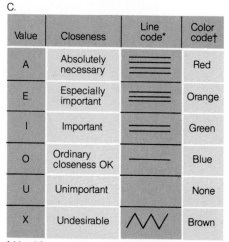

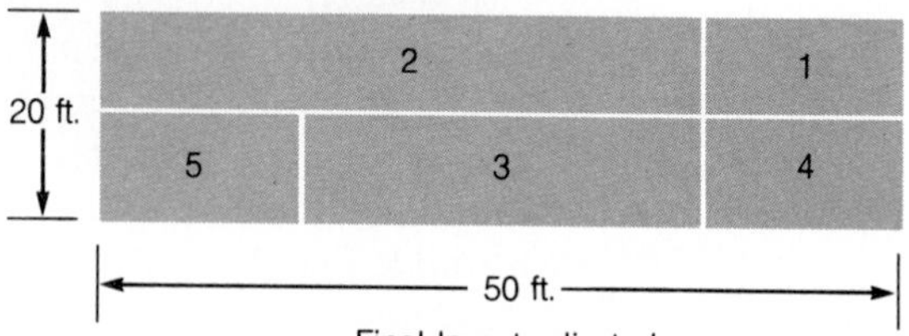

Final layout adjusted by square footage and building size

Computerized Layout Techniques—CRAFT

A number of computerized layout programs have been developed over the past 20 years to help devise good process layouts. Of these, the most widely applied is the Computerized Relative Allocation of Facilities Technique (CRAFT).[2]

The CRAFT method follows the same basic idea we developed in the layout of the toy factory, but with some significant operational differences. Like the toy factory example, it requires a load matrix and a distance matrix as initial inputs, but in addition requires a cost-per-unit distance traveled, say $.10 per foot moved. (Remember, we made the simplifying assumption that cost doubled when material had to jump one department, tripled when it had to jump two departments, and so forth.) With these inputs and an initial layout in the program, CRAFT then tries to improve the relative placement of the departments as measured by total material handling cost for the layout. (Material handling cost between departments = Number of loads × Rectilinear distance between department centroids × Cost-per-unit distance.) It makes improvements by exchanging pairs of departments in an iterative manner until no further cost reductions are possible. That is, the program calculates the effect on total cost of exchanging departments; if this yields a reduction the exchange is made, which constitutes an iteration.

CRAFT can handle up to 40 departments. While CRAFT does not guarantee an optimal solution, it usually does make significant improvements in layouts.

8.3 PRODUCT LAYOUT

The basic difference between product layout and process layout is the pattern of work flow. As we have seen in process layout, the pattern can be highly variable, since material for any given job may have to be routed to the same processing department several times during its production cycle. In product layout, equipment or departments are dedicated to a particular product line, duplicate equipment is employed to avoid backtracking, and a straight-line flow of material movement is achievable.

8.4 ASSEMBLY LINES

Assembly lines are a special case of product layout. In a general sense, the term *assembly line* refers to progressive assembly linked by some material handling device. The usual assumption is that some form of pacing is present and the

[2] For a discussion of CRAFT and other methods, see R. L. Francis and J. A. White, *Facility Layout and Location: An Analytical Approach* (Englewood Cliffs, N.J.: Prentice-Hall, 1987).

allowable processing time is equivalent for all workstations. Within this broad definition, there are important differences among line types. A few of these are: material handling devices (belt or roller conveyor, overhead crane); line configuration (U-shape, straight, branching); pacing (mechanical, human); product mix (one product or multiple products); workstation characteristics (workers may sit, stand, walk with the line, or ride the line); and length of the line (few or many workers).

The range of products partially or completely assembled on lines includes toys, appliances, autos, planes, guns, garden equipment, clothing, and a wide variety of electronic components. In fact, it is probably safe to say that virtually any product with multiple parts and produced in large volume uses assembly lines to some degree. Clearly, lines are an important technology, and to really understand their managerial requirements one must have some familiarity with how a line is balanced.

8.5 ASSEMBLY LINE BALANCING

The most common assembly line is a moving conveyor that passes a series of workstations in a uniform time interval called the **cycle time** (which is also the time between successive units coming off the end of the line). At each workstation, work is performed on a product either by adding parts or by completing assembly operations. The work performed at each station is made up of many bits of work, termed *tasks, elements,* or *work units.* Such tasks are described by motion-time analysis. Generally, they are groupings that cannot be subdivided on the assembly line without paying a penalty in extra motions.

The total work to be performed at a workstation is equal to the sum of the tasks assigned to that workstation. The **assembly line balancing** problem is one of assigning all tasks to a series of workstations so that each workstation has no more than can be done in the cycle time, and so that the unassigned (i.e., idle) time across all workstations is minimized. The problem is complicated by the relationships among tasks imposed by product design and process technologies. This is called the **precedence relationship,** which specifies the order in which the tasks must be performed in the assembly process.

Steps in Assembly Line Balancing

The steps in balancing an assembly line are straightforward:

1. Specify the sequential relationships among tasks using a precedence diagram. The diagram consists of circles and arrows. Circles represent individual tasks, arrows indicate the order of task performance.
2. Determine the required cycle time (C), using the following formula:

$$C = \frac{\text{Production time per day}}{\text{Output per day (in units)}}$$

3. Determine the theoretical minimum number of workstations (N_t) required to satisfy the cycle time constraint, using the following formula:

$$N_t = \frac{\text{Sum of task times } (T)}{\text{Cycle time } (C)}$$

4. Select a primary rule by which tasks are to be assigned to workstations, and a secondary rule to break ties.
5. Assign tasks, one at a time, to the first workstation until the sum of the task times is equal to the cycle time, or no other tasks are feasible because of time or sequence restrictions. Repeat the process for Workstation 2, Workstation 3, etc., until all tasks are assigned.
6. Evaluate the efficiency of the balance derived using the formula:

$$\text{Efficiency} = \frac{\text{Sum of task times } (T)}{\text{Actual number of workstations } (N_a) \times \text{Cycle time } (C)}$$

7. If efficiency is unsatisfactory, rebalance using a different decision rule.

Example Problem

The Model J Wagon is to be assembled on a conveyor belt. Five hundred wagons are required per day. Production time per day is 420 minutes, and the assembly steps and times for the wagon are given in Exhibit 8.10. Assignment: Find the balance that minimizes the number of workstations, subject to cycle time and precedence constraints.

EXHIBIT 8.10

Assembly Steps and Times for Model J Wagon

Task	Performance Time (in seconds)	Description	Tasks that Must Precede
A	45	Position rear axle support and hand fasten 4 screws to nuts	—
B	11	Insert rear axle	A
C	9	Tighten rear axle support screws to nuts	B
D	50	Position front axle assembly and hand fasten with 4 screws to nuts	—
E	15	Tighten front axle assembly screws	D
F	12	Position rear wheel #1 and fasten hub cab	C
G	12	Position rear wheel #2 and fasten hub cab	C
H	12	Position front wheel #1 and fasten hub cap	E
I	12	Position front wheel #2 and fasten hub cap	E
J	8	Position wagon handle shaft on front axle assembly and hand fasten bolt and nut	F, G, H, I
K	9	Tighten bolt and nut	J
	195		

1. Draw precedence diagram. Exhibit 8.11 illustrates the sequential relationships identified in Exhibit 8.10. (The length of the arrows has no meaning.)
2. Cycle time determination. Here we have to convert to seconds since our task times are in seconds.

$$C = \frac{\text{Production time per day}}{\text{Output per day}} = \frac{60 \text{ sec.} \times 420 \text{ min.}}{500 \text{ wagons}} = \frac{25{,}200}{500} = 50.4$$

3. Theoretical minimum number of workstations required (the actual number may be greater):

$$N_t = \frac{T}{C} = \frac{195 \text{ seconds}}{50.4 \text{ seconds}} = 3.86$$

4. Select assignment rules. Research has demonstrated that some rules are better than others for certain problem structures. In general, the strategy is to use a rule that assigns tasks that either have many followers or are of long duration since they effectively limit the balance achievable. In this case we will use as our primary rule:
   a. Assign tasks in order of the largest number of following tasks.
   Our secondary rule, to be invoked where ties exist from our primary rule, is:

EXHIBIT 8.11

Precedence Graph for Model J Wagon

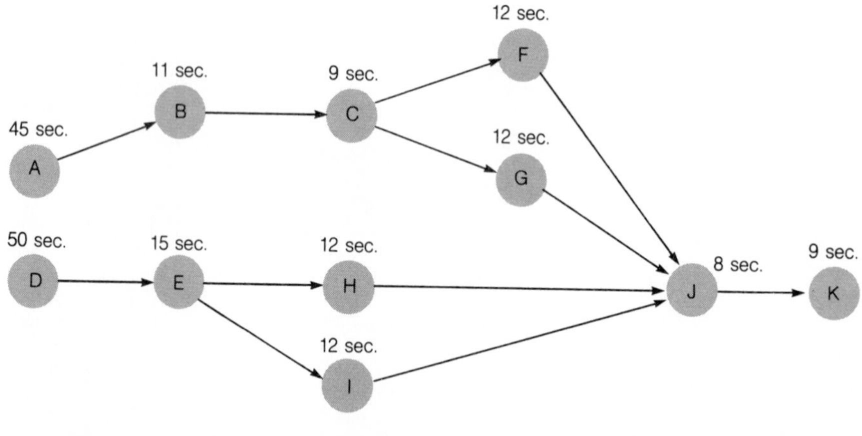

b. Assign tasks in order of longest operating time.

Task	Number of Following Tasks
A	6
B or D	5
C or E	4
F, G, H, or I	2
J	1
K	0

5. Make task assignments to form Workstation 1, Workstation 2, and so forth, until all tasks are assigned. The actual assignment is given in Exhibit 8.12A and is shown graphically in Exhibit 8.12B.
6. Do the efficiency calculation. This is shown in Exhibit 8.12C.
7. Evaluate solution. An efficiency of 77 percent indicates an imbalance or idle time of 23 percent (1.0 − .77) across the entire line. From Exhibit 8.12A we can see that there are 57 total seconds of idle time, and the "choice" job is at Workstation 5.

Is a better balance possible? In this case, yes. Try balancing the line with rule *b* and breaking ties with rule *a*. (This will give you a feasible four-station balance.)

EXHIBIT 8.12

A. Balance Made According to Largest Number of Following Tasks Rule

	Task	Task Time (in seconds)	Remaining Unassigned Time (in seconds)	Feasible Remaining Tasks	Task with Most Followers	Task with Longest Operation Time
Station 1	A	45	5.4 idle	None		
Station 2	D	50	0.4 idle	None		
Station 3	B	11	39.4	C, E	C, E	E
	E	15	24.4	C, H, I	C	
	C	9	15.4	F, G, H, I	F, G, H, I	F, G, H, I
	F*	12	3.4 idle	None		
Station 4	G	12	38.4	H, I	H, I	H, I
	H*	12	26.4	I		
	I	12	14.4	J		
	J	8	6.4 idle	None		
Station 5	K	9	41.4 idle	None		

* Denotes task arbitrarily selected where there is a tie between longest operation times.

EXHIBIT 8.12
(concluded)

B. Precedence Graph for Model J Wagon

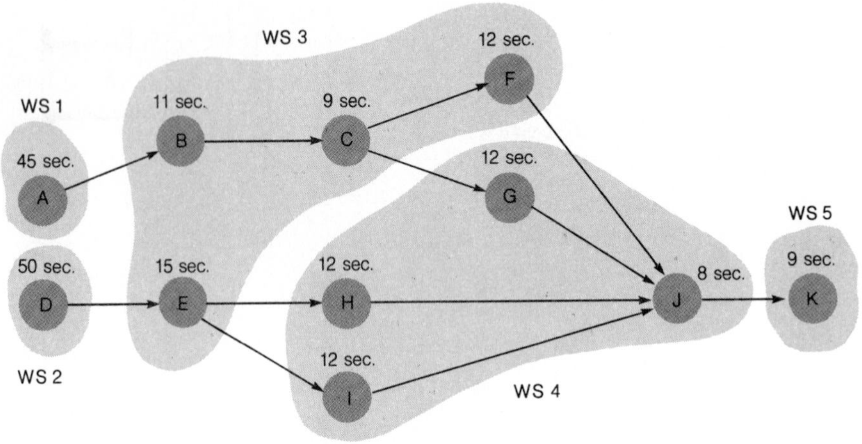

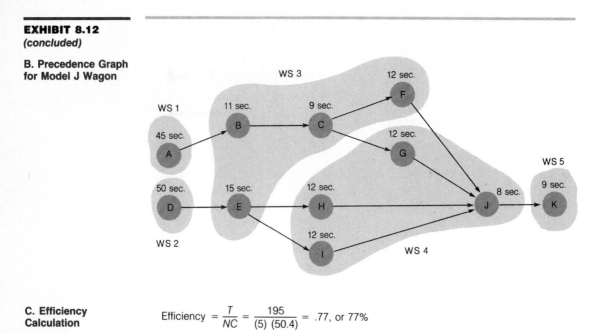

C. Efficiency Calculation

$$\text{Efficiency} = \frac{T}{NC} = \frac{195}{(5)\ (50.4)} = .77, \text{ or } 77\%$$

Flexible Line Layouts

As we saw in the preceding example, assembly line balances frequently result in unequal workstation times. Flexible line layouts such as shown in Exhibit 8.13 are a common way of dealing with this problem. In our toy company example, a U-shaped line with work sharing (see bottom of the figure) could help resolve the imbalance.

8.6 GROUP TECHNOLOGY (CELLULAR) LAYOUT

Intuitively, one might hypothesize that there are some advantages to grouping products and processes together under some conditions. But what conditions? Group products of the same shape? Same size? Those that use the same material? Those with the same environmental requirements, such as clean rooms? And so on. Currently, many studies are trying to establish logical rules for grouping products and processes together and to find efficient ways to search through production records to make these groupings. Appropriate records consist of the product designs, the routing sheets, all of the equipment and machines on hand and their capacities, processing requirements, and so on.

EXHIBIT 8.13

Flexible Line Layouts

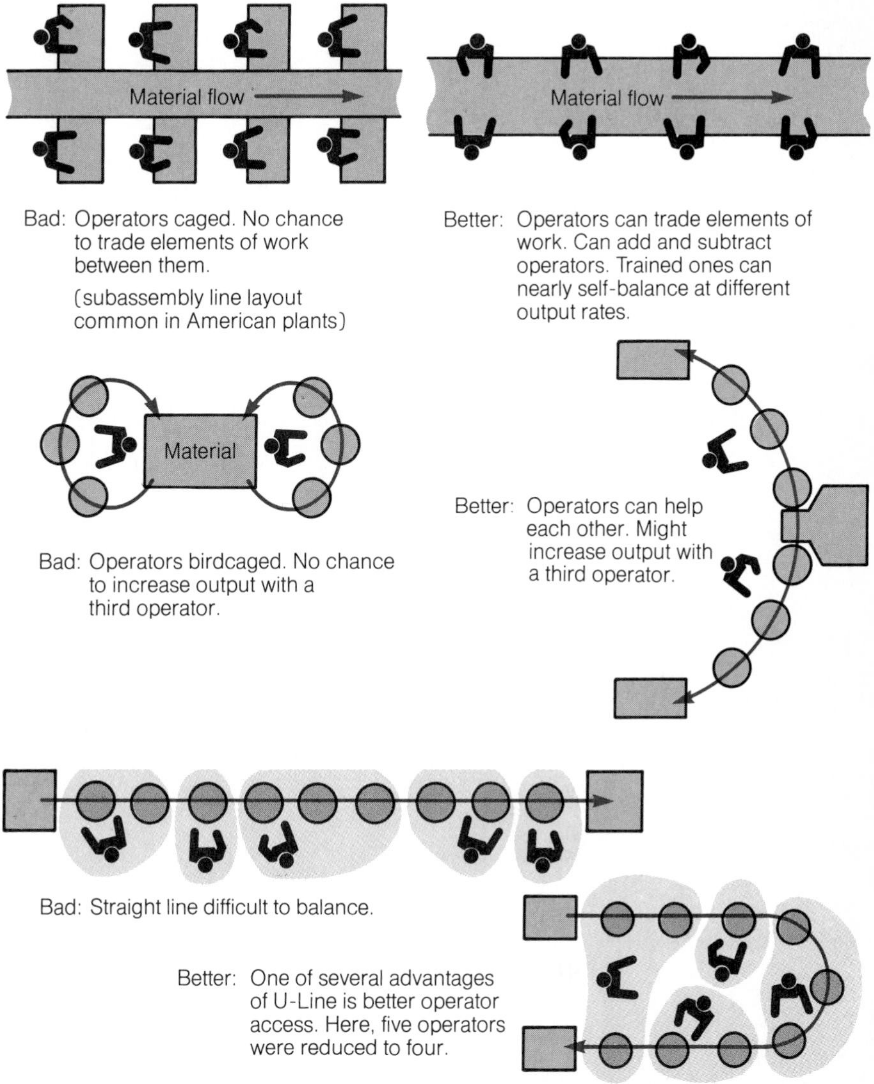

Material flow
Material flow
Bad: Operators caged. No chance to trade elements of work between them.
(subassembly line layout common in American plants)
Better: Operators can trade elements of work. Can add and subtract operators. Trained ones can nearly self-balance at different output rates.
Material
Bad: Operators birdcaged. No chance to increase output with a third operator.
Better: Operators can help each other. Might increase output with a third operator.
Bad: Straight line difficult to balance.
Better: One of several advantages of U-Line is better operator access. Here, five operators were reduced to four.

Source: Robert W. Hall, *Attaining Manufacturing Excellence* (Homewood, Ill.: Dow Jones-Irwin, 1987), p. 125.

One approach in manufacturing simply starts with a matrix of items to be processed and machines that do the processing. Exhibit 8.14A shows items a through o and their processing requirements on machines 1 through 12. Note that there doesn't seem to be much order. By reordering the rows and

EXHIBIT 8.14A

Product Items a through o and Their Designated Processing Requirements on Machines 1 through 12

Machines

Items	1	2	3	4	5	6	7	8	9	10	11	12
a	x		x				x				x	
b				x						x		
c		x										x
d	x						x		x			
e			x		x							
f			x		x							x
g										x		
h									x			x
i							x				x	
j		x							x			
k		x			x			x				
l	x										x	
m		x				x				x		x
n				x		x						
o			x					x				

EXHIBIT 8.14B

Cellular Grouping for Product Items a through o and Their Designated Processing Requirements on Machines 1 through 12.

Machines

Items	12	9	2	11	7	1	10	6	4	3	8	5
c	x		x									
h	x	x				x						
j		x	x									
a				x	x	x				x		
l				x		x						
d		x			x	x						
i				x	x							x
b							x		x			
m	x		x				x	x				
g							x					
n								x	x			
e										x		x
o										x	x	
k			x								x	x
f	x									x		x

columns, we come up with Exhibit 8.14B. This exhibit indicates that five cells can be used as follows:

Cell	Products	Machines within Cell
1	c, h, j	12, 9, 2
2	a, l, d, i	11, 7, 1
3	b, m, g, n	10, 6, 4
4	e, o, k, f	3, 8, 5
5	h, a, d, i, m, k, f	12, 9, 2, 1, 3, 5

Cell 5, as you notice, is a catchall cell. What doesn't fit into existing cells can be routed to a general purpose cell that contains a variety of machines.

Our original assumption in creating this layout was based on items requiring the same machines. In a larger system, we could be more restrictive in our cell design by first screening items based on similar sizes, shapes, materials, and so forth as we mentioned earlier.

Group technology (GT) layouts are now widely used in metal fabricating, computer chip manufacture, and assembly work. The overall objective is to gain the benefits of product layout in job-shop kind of production. These benefits include:

1. Better human relations. Cells consist of a few workers who form a small work team; a team turns out complete units of work.
2. Improved operator expertise. Workers see only a limited number of different parts in a finite production cycle, so repetition means quick learning.
3. Less in-process inventory and material handling. A cell combines several production stages, so fewer parts travel through the shop.
4. Faster production setup. Fewer jobs mean reduced tooling and hence faster tooling changes.

Developing a GT Layout

Three steps are involved to shift from a process layout to a GT cellular layout for manufactured products.

1. Group parts into families that follow a common sequence of steps. This step requires developing and maintaining a computerized parts classification and coding system. This is often a major expense with such systems, although many companies have developed short-cut procedures for identifying parts families.
2. Identify dominant flow patterns of parts families as a basis for location or relocation of processes.

3. Physically group machines and processes into cells. Often there will be parts that cannot be associated with a family and specialized machinery that cannot be placed in any one cell because of its general use. These unattached parts and machinery are placed in a "remainder cell."

8.7 CONCLUSION

The big question affecting layout decisions in manufacturing is: How flexible should the layout be to deal with changes in product demand and product mix? Some have argued that the best strategy is to have movable equipment that can be shifted easily from place to place to reduce material flow time for near-term contracts. However, while this is appealing in general, the limitations of existing buildings and firmly anchored equipment, and the general plant disruption that is created make this a very costly strategy.

A major trend in layout is to envision the plant as an assembly line, whether it is physically so or not. One way to think of this in a more concrete fashion is to view departments as workstations whose work load is balanced in the same general way as workstations on a line. The Just-in-Time methods and some of the newer computer scheduling approaches implicitly follow this conceptualization.

In service systems, particularly franchises, the study of layout has become extremely important since the selected layout may become replicated at hundreds or even thousands of facilities. Indeed, a layout error in a fast-food chain will have a more immediate, and generally a more far-reaching, effect on profits than a layout error in a factory.

8.8 REVIEW AND DISCUSSION QUESTIONS

1. What kind of layout is used in a physical fitness center?
2. What is the objective of assembly line balancing? How would you deal with the situation where one worker, although trying hard, is 20 percent slower than the other ten people on a line?
3. How do you determine the idle-time percentage from a given assembly line balance?
4. What information of particular importance do routes sheets and process charts (discussed in Chapter 3) provide to the layout planner?
5. What is the "ranked positional weight technique"?
6. In what respects is facility layout a marketing problem in services? Give an example of a service system layout designed to maximize the amount of time the customer is in the system.

8.9 PROBLEMS

*1. A university advising office has four rooms, each dedicated to specific problems: petitions (Room A), schedule advising (Room B), grade complaints (Room C), and student counseling (Room D). The office is 80 feet long and 20 feet wide. Each room is 20 feet by 20 feet. The present location of rooms is A, B, C, D; that is, a straight line. The load summary shows the number of contacts that each advisor in a room has with other advisors in the other rooms. Assume that all advisors are equal in this value.

Load summary: $AB = 10$, $AC = 20$, $AD = 30$,
$BC = 15$, $BD = 10$, $CD = 20$.

a. Evaluate this layout according to one of the methods in the chapter.

b. Improve the layout by exchanging functions within rooms. Show your amount of improvement using the same method as in *(a)*.

*2. The following tasks must be performed on an assembly line in the sequence and times specified.

Task	Task Time (seconds)	Tasks That Must Precede
A	50	—
B	40	—
C	20	A
D	45	C
E	20	C
F	25	D
G	10	E
H	35	B, F, G

a. Draw the schematic diagram.

b. What is the theoretical minimum number of stations required to meet a forecasted demand of 400 units per eight-hour day?

c. Use the longest operating time rule and balance the line in the minimum number of stations to produce 400 units per day.

3. Given the following data on the task precedence relationships for an assembled product and assuming the tasks cannot be split, what is the theoretical minimum cycle time? Assume a cycle time of seven minutes.

Task	Performance Time in Minutes	Tasks That Must Precede
A	3	
B	6	A
C	7	A
D	5	A
E	2	A
F	4	B, C
G	5	C
H	5	D, E, F, G

* Solutions to Problems 1 and 2 are given in Appendix D.

a. Determine the minimum number of workstations needed to achieve this cycle time using the "ranked positional weight" rule.
b. Determine the minimum number of stations needed to meet a cycle time of 10 minutes according to the "largest number of following tasks" rule.
c. Compute the efficiency of the balances achieved.

4. The Dorton University president has asked the OM department to assign eight biology professors (A, B, C, D, E, F, G, and H) to eight offices (numbered 1 to 8 in the diagram) in the new Biology building.

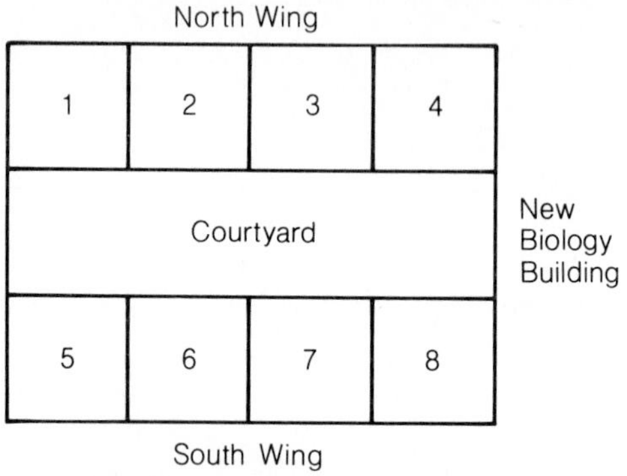

The following distances and two-way flows are given:

DISTANCES BETWEEN OFFICES (FEET)

	1	2	3	4	5	6	7	8
1	—	10	20	30	15	18	25	34
2		—	10	20	18	15	18	25
3			—	10	25	18	15	18
4				—	34	25	18	15
5					—	10	20	30
6						—	10	20
7							—	10
8								—

TWO-WAY FLOWS (UNITS PER PERIOD)

	A	B	C	D	E	F	G	H
A	—	2	0	0	5	0	0	0
B		—	0	0	0	3	0	2
C			—	0	0	0	0	3
D				—	4	0	0	0
E					—	1	0	0
F						—	1	0
G							—	4
H								—

a. If there are no restrictions (constraints) on the assignment of professors to offices, how many alternative assignments are there to evaluate?
b. The Biology department has sent the following information and requests to the OM department:

Offices 1, 4, 5, and 8 are the only offices with windows.
A must be assigned Office 1.
D and E, the Biology department co-chairpeople, must have windows.
H must be directly across the courtyard from D.
A, G, and H must be in the same wing.
F must *not* be next to D or G or directly across from G.

Find the optimal assignment of professors to offices that meets all the requests of the Biology department and minimizes total material handling cost. You may use the path flow list as a computational aid.

Path	Flow	Path	Flow	Path	Flow	Path	Flow	Path	Flow
A–B	2	B–C	0	C–D	0	D–E	4	E–F	1
A–C	0	B–D	0	C–E	0	D–F	0	E–G	0
A–D	0	B–E	0	C–F	0	D–G	0	E–H	0
A–E	5	B–F	3	C–G	0	D–H	0	F–G	1
A–F	0	B–G	0	C–H	3			F–H	0
A–G	0	B–H	2					G–H	4
A–H	0								

8.10 SELECTED BIBLIOGRAPHY

Apple, James M., and Leon F McGinnis "Innovations in Facilities and Materials Handling Systems: an Introduction." *Industrial Engineering*, March 1987, pp. 33–38.

Francis, R. L., and J. A. White. *Facility Layout and Location: An Analytical Approach.* Englewood Cliffs, N.J.: Prentice-Hall, 1987.

Gowan, Norm. "Radar Manufacturer Improves Productivity with Computerized Assembly Planning System." *Industrial Engineering*, July 1989, pp. 30–32.

Green, Timothy J., and Randall P. Sadowski. "A Review of Cellular Manufacturing Assumptions, Advantages and Design Techniques." *Journal of Operations Management* 4, no. 2 (February 1984), pp. 85–97.

Hyer, Nancy Lea. "The Potential of Group Technology for U.S. Manufacturing." *Journal of Operations Management* 4, no. 3 (May 1984), pp. 183–202.

Mayo, William, and Russell Horne. "Considerations for Developing Standards in Long Cycle Assembly." *Industrial Engineering*, March 1990, pp. 38–43.

Mondon, Yasuhiro. *Toyota Production System, Practical Approach to Production Management.* Atlanta, Ga.: Industrial Engineering and Management Press, 1983.

Supplement

Simulation

EPIGRAPH

This is only a test. . . . This is only a test. . . .

SUPPLEMENT OUTLINE

KEY TERMS

Computer Models
Monte Carlo Simulation
Probability Distribution
Random Number Table
Run Length or Run Time

In Arizona, Biosphere II is being built to learn about our Earth.[1] Eight humans will be placed in a completely enclosed glass structure 85 feet high and 539 feet long that covers 3 acres. Inside are a lake, streams, and species of plants and fish. The self-contained system will have its own atmosphere, food production, and so on. During the two-year study there will be no entry or exit from the sphere.

The purpose of Biosphere II is to simulate the Earth to learn more about it and how we, as humans, exist within it. The ultimate goal is to understand and be able to create structures that will allow humans to live on the Moon, Mars, and beyond. This is a complete physical simulation, since everything does exist but on a miniature scale.

An automobile manufacturer wants to study the effects of a head-on collision on the occupants of its newly designed car. Naturally, the manufacturer uses dummies with attached sensors that are monitored. The dummies are placed in a real car and the car is crashed, head-on, into a wall. This is an example of a mixed simulation model; a real car is crashed, but the dummies are a physical representation simulating humans.

At the far end of the spectrum, away from reality, is complete computer simulation. An interesting computer simulation is the work of Jaron Lanier of VPL Research in Redwood, California.[2] The term *virtual* reality is used to describe the system because it exists only within a computer. VPL supplies virtual-reality clothing wired into a computer. An example of the capability of this system is a person wanting to ski. The skier wears a ski outfit connected to the computer. A helmet projects the user into the ski slope environment, giving the impression of reality. As the wearer moves, the visual world moves as if it were really happening.

In a medical school or hospital, a surgeon could practice a procedure by performing an operation as if it were real. Wearing the helmet, the surgeon sees his patient. As he moves his hands, he sees himself performing the operation.

While the range of use for this system is intriguing, the cost is high; a system currently sells for about $200,000.

The choice of the degree of reality depends on what is expected to be learned, as well as on the cost and time involved. Before opening a new department store, employees may spend two or three days in a simulation. "Pretend" customers (store employees) spend play money in the various departments. Sale are rung up and goods are wrapped the same way as would be expected in the real situation. This simulation gives store management the opportunity to test the organization and layout of the store itself as well as to train employees, most of whom are new.

---

[1] Earth has been designated as Biosphere I.

[2] Gurney Williams III, "Experiencing Eternity," *Longevity*, June 1990, pp. 52–58.

EXHIBIT S8.1

Functional Areas for Simulation in Companies

Functional Area	Percent
Production	59
Corporate planning	53
Engineering	46
Finance	41
Research and development	37
Marketing	24
Data processing	16
Personnel	10

For a business firm, simulating reality on a computer by reducing all of the elements to mathematical and symbolic relationships has almost unlimited application. In a simple case, a firm may simulate demands for its products by using past history and thereby develop a demand forecast that can then be used for planning purposes. In a far more encompassing simulation, a firm can simulate its entire operations over some period of years to test certain decisions of product choice, marketing strategies, equipment purchases, and so on.

Computer-based simulation has had very rapid growth for two reasons: one, the phenomenal growth in computer storage capability and speed; two, the development of simulation languages.

In operations management, simulation is used to determine production schedules and material needs; to analyze waiting line systems, inventory levels, and maintenance procedures; to do capacity planning, resource requirements planning, and process planning; and the list goes on. Often, when a mathematical technique fails, we turn to simulation to save us. A survey of non-academic members of the Institute of Management Science showed that 89 percent of their firms use simulation.[3] Exhibit S8.1 shows the functional areas where it is applied. Note that production heads the list, with 59 percent. Another interesting finding of the study is that 54 percent of the respondents said that simulation models are created within the functional areas themselves.

While simulation is one of the easiest techniques to understand, it is also one of the most misunderstood and misused. Some claim it is the ultimate technique to understand problems and systems; others say it is too expensive and too time consuming to be useful for most applications. In this supplement we will define simulation, present a simple example of the simulation methodology, discuss simulation languages, and comment on various aspects of the techniques.

[3] David P. Christy and Hugh J. Watson, "The Application of Simulation: A Survey of Industry Practice," *Interfaces* 13, no. 5 (October 1983), pp. 47–52.

S8.1 DEFINITION OF SIMULATION

The dictionary definitions are:

> *Simulation:* the imitative representation of the functioning of one system or process by means of the functioning of another (a computer simulation of an industrial process); examination of a problem often not subject to direct experimentation by means of a simulation device.
>
> *Simulator:* one that simulates; esp. a device that enables the operator to reproduce or represent under test conditions phenomena likely to occur in actual performance.[4]

These definitions are somewhat incomplete. Perhaps the best way to define and understand simulation is to consider it as two parts: First, there must be a *model* of whatever is to be simulated. There are several classifications of models but the usual types are: physical (e.g., airplane model), analog (e.g., a scale where the deflection of a spring or beam represents weight), schematic (e.g., electrical circuit diagrams, organization charts), and symbolic (e.g., computer code or mathematical models representing a bank teller or a machine). In computer simulation we are primarily interested in symbolic models that we can use to represent a real system on a computer. We will describe symbolic models later and show several examples, but the main point we wish to make here is that a model is created to represent *something,* and that the model is *static*—that is, it shows only a point in time and does not move.

The second part of simulation is to *pass the model through time.* Simulation gives the model "life." In pilot training, for example, a trainee sits in a replica of a cockpit complete with instruments and controls (a *model* of a real airplane). This is a *physical* model of the system. The trainee then sees a variety of situations as the model is given life and is passed through time. Instruments change values and the trainee is expected to respond. Those responses are fed into a computer, which then creates new values to which the trainee must again respond. In the flight training simulator, these values are usually fed into an *analog* system as well, where the new values create electrical signals to cause physical movement. In this way, the trainee experiences the approach of a crosswind, a stall, or a tailspin. Thus the simulation is a series of actions of the model with reactions of the environment on the model.

Simulation is said to run some number of iterations or some amount of time. A model of a teller in the bank can be simulated to wait on 100 customers (i.e., 100 iterations). The trainee in the cockpit (model) can experience the same sensations as those in real flight; i.e., a half hour of simulator time equals a half hour of an actual flight. Or time can be compressed so that the trainee, during that half hour, can be fed all the situations that could be expected during a nine-hour transoceanic flight. This is much like the automobile manufacturer that tests the opening and closing of a car door. Whereas a car

[4] *Webster's New Collegiate Dictionary,* 9th ed. (Springfield, Mass.: Merriam-Webster, 1983).

owner may open and close a car door an average of six times a day, the manufacturer can test years of usage in a short period of time by opening and closing the car door every five seconds. The basic difference is that the flight simulator is a computer-based program and the automobile manufacturer actually uses a mechanical arm to open and close the car door.

While the term *simulation* can have various meanings depending on its application, in business it generally refers to using a computer to perform experiments on a model of a real system. These experiments may be undertaken before the real system is operational, to aid in its design, to see how the system might react to changes in its operating rules, or to evaluate the system's response to changes in its structure. Simulation is particularly appropriate to situations in which the size or complexity of the problem makes the use of optimizing techniques difficult or impossible. Thus, job shops, which are characterized by complex queuing problems, have been studied extensively via simulation, as have certain types of inventory, layout, and maintenance problems (to name but a few). Simulation can also be used in conjunction with traditional statistical and management science techniques.

In addition, simulation is useful in training managers and workers in how the real system operates, in demonstrating the effects of changes in system variables, in real-time control, and in developing new theories about mathematical or organizational relationships. See Exhibit S8.2 for more examples.

It is commonly suggested by simulation instructors that the best way to learn about simulation is to simulate. Therefore, we will turn to a simple simulation problem and develop the topic as we go along.

A Simulation Example: Al's Fish Market

Al, the owner of a small fish market, wishes to evaluate his daily ordering policy for codfish. His current rule is *order the amount demanded the previous day,* but he thinks it is time to consider another rule. Al purchases codfish at $0.20 a pound and sells it for $0.60 a pound. The fish are ordered at the end of each day and are received the following morning. Any fish not sold during the day are thrown away.

From past experience, Al has determined that his demand for codfish has ranged between 30 and 80 pounds per day. He has also kept a record of the relative frequency of demand amounts:

Average Demand per Day	Relative Frequency
35 pounds	1/10
45	3/10
55	2/10
65	3/10
75	1/10

EXHIBIT S8.2

Applications of Simulation Methods

- Aircraft maintenance scheduling
- Airport design
- Air traffic control queuing
- Ambulance location and dispatching
- Assembly line scheduling
- Bank teller scheduling
- Bus (city) scheduling
- Circuit design
- Clerical processing system design
- Communication system design
  - Computer time sharing
  - Telephone traffic routing
  - Message system
  - Mobile communications
- Computer memory-fabrication test-facility design
- Consumer behavior prediction
  - Brand selection
  - Promotion decisions
  - Advertising allocation
  - Court system resource allocation
- Distribution system design
  - Warehouse location
  - Mail (post office)
  - Soft drink bottling
  - Bank courier
  - Intrahospital material flow
- Enterprise models
  - Steel production
  - Hospital
  - Shipping line
  - Railroad operations
  - School district
- Equipment scheduling
  - Aircraft
- Facility layout
  - Pharmaceutical center
- Financial forecasting
  - Insurance
  - Schools
  - Computer leasing
- Grain terminal operation
- Harbor design
- Industry models
  - Textiles
  - Petroleum (financial aspects)
- Information system design
- Insurance staffing decisions
- Intergroup communication (sociological studies)
- Inventory reorder rule design
  - Aerospace
  - Manufacturing
  - Military logistics
  - Hospitals
- Job shop scheduling
  - Aircraft parts
  - Metals forming
  - Work-in-process control
  - Shipyard
- Library operations design
- Maintenance scheduling
  - Airlines
  - Glass furnaces
  - Steel furnaces
  - Computer field service
- National manpower adjustment system
- Natural resource (mine) scheduling
  - Iron ore
  - Strip mining
- Numerically controlled production facility design
- Parking facility design
- Personnel scheduling
  - Inspection department
  - Spacecraft trips
- Petrochemical process design
  - Solvent recovery
- Police response system design
- Political voting prediction
- Rail freight car dispatching
- Railroad traffic scheduling
- Steel mill scheduling
- Taxi dispatching
- Traffic light timing
- Truck dispatching and loading
- University financial and operational forecasting
- Urban traffic system design
- Water resources development

After some deliberation, Al settles on the following ordering rule, which he would like to compare with his current rule: *Each day order the amount of fish that was demanded in the past* (that is, the expected value based on past daily demands), which in this case is

$$(35 \times 1/10) + (45 \times 3/10) + (55 \times 2/10) + (65 \times 3/10) + (75 \times 1/10) = 55 \text{ pounds}$$

Analysis. We will designate Al's current ordering rule as Rule 1 and the alternative as Rule 2. These rules can be stated mathematically, as follows.

Rule 1: $Q_n = D_{n-1}$
Rule 2: $Q_n = 55$

where

Q_n = Amount ordered on day n
D_{n-1} = Amount demanded the previous day

These ordering rules can be compared in terms of Al's daily profits, which can be stated as follows.

$$P_n = (S_n \times p) - (Q_n \times c)$$

where

P_n = Profit on day n
S_n = Amount sold on day n
p = Selling price per pound
Q_n = Amount ordered on day n (as defined above)
c = Cost per pound

To prepare the problem for simulation, we must develop some method of generating demand each day so we can compare the two decision rules. One way to do this is to treat demand generation as a game of roulette, with the slots in the roulette wheel associated with specific levels of demand. The term **Monte Carlo simulation,** taken from the name of the famous European gambling casino, is applied to simulation problems in which a chance process is used to generate occurrences in the system. For example, if the wheel has 100 slots, we might apportion them so that 10 represent a demand for 35 pounds, 30 represent a demand for 45 pounds, 20 represent a demand for 55 pounds, and so forth. Proceeding this way and using the relative frequencies listed previously, each turn of the wheel could simulate one day of demand for Al's fish.

While a roulette wheel has a certain appeal, a more efficient way of generating demand is to use a **probability distribution** and a **random number table.** This entails converting the relative frequency values to probabilities. Then, specific numbers are attached to each probability value to reflect the proportion of numbers from 00 to 99 that corresponds to each probability entry.[5] For example, 00 to 09 represent 10 percent of the numbers from 00 to 99, 10 to 39 represent 30 percent of the numbers, 40 to 59 represent 20 percent

[5] A cumulative probability distribution is sometimes developed to help assure that each random number is associated with only one level of demand. It is our experience, however, that this step, as well as graphing such a distribution, is not necessary in understanding or performing a simulation.

EXHIBIT S8.3

Demand Frequency Represented by Random Numbers

Demand per Day	Relative Frequency	Probability	Random Number Interval
35	1/10	0.10	00–09
45	3/10	0.30	10–39
55	2/10	0.20	40–59
65	3/10	0.30	60–89
75	1/10	0.10	90–99

of the numbers, and so on. The probabilities and their associated random numbers (arranged in intervals) are given in Exhibit S8.3.

With this information and a random number table (Exhibit S8.4), we are ready to carry out a hand simulation to determine the relative desirability of Rules 1 and 2. If the initial demand for day zero is arbitrarily set at the average demand level of 55 pounds and a 20-day period is selected, each rule would be tested as follows:

1. Draw a random number from Exhibit S8.4. (The starting point on the table is immaterial, but a consistent, unvaried pattern should be followed in drawing random numbers. For example, take the first two digits in each entry in row 1, then row 2, row 3, and so forth.
2. Find the random number interval associated with the random number.
3. Read the daily demand (D_n) corresponding to the random number interval.
4. Calculate the amount sold (S_n). If $D_n \geq Q_n$, then $S_n = Q_n$; if $D_n < Q_n$, $S_n = D_n$.
5. Calculate daily profit $[P_n = (S_n \times p) - (Q_n \times c)]$.
6. Repeat Steps 1 to 5 until 20 days have been simulated.

The results of this procedure, along with the random numbers (*RN*) used, are summarized in Exhibit S8.5. We will compare these results with those achieved by a computer simulation of the problem later in the supplement. We will now show the computer simulation model.

S8.2 COMPUTERIZATION OF THE FISH MARKET EXAMPLE

A computer program is often the easiest way to study a problem because more operations and more repetitions can be included. Further, values, such as costs, profits, order points, and so on, can be changed to test the effects on the output. In Al's case, the computer program simulated 2,000 days of operation compared to the hand simulation of 20 days.

EXHIBIT S8.4

Uniformly Distributed Random Numbers

06433	80674	24520	18222	10610	05794	37515	48619	02866
39208	47829	72648	37414	75755	01717	29899	78817	03500
89884	59051	67533	08123	17730	95862	08034	19473	03071
61512	32155	51906	61662	64130	16688	37275	51262	11569
99653	47635	12506	88535	36553	23757	34209	55803	96275
95913	11045	13772	76638	48423	25018	99041	77529	81360
55804	44004	13122	44115	01691	50541	00147	77685	58788
35334	82410	91601	40617	72876	33967	73830	15405	96554
59729	88646	76487	11622	96297	24160	09903	14041	22917
57383	89317	63677	70119	94739	25875	38829	68377	43918
30574	06039	07967	32422	76791	39725	53711	93385	13421
81307	13314	83580	79974	45929	85113	72208	09858	52104
02410	96385	79007	54039	21410	86980	91772	93307	34116
18969	87444	52233	62319	08598	09066	95288	04794	01534
87803	80514	66800	62297	80198	19347	73234	86265	49096
68397	10538	15438	62311	72844	60203	46412	05943	79232
28520	54247	58729	10854	99058	18260	38765	90038	94200
44285	09452	15867	70418	57012	72122	36634	97283	95943
80299	22510	33517	23309	57040	29285	07870	21913	72958
84842	05748	90894	61658	15001	94055	36308	41161	37341

EXHIBIT S8.5

Hand Simulation of Al's Fish Market

			RULE 1			RULE 2		
Day	*RN*	D_n	Q_n	S_n	P_n	Q_n	S_n	P_n
0	—	55	—	—	—	—	—	—
1	06	35	55	35	$ 10	55	35	$ 10
2	39	45	35	35	14	"	45	16
3	89	65	45	45	18	"	55	22
4	61	65	65	65	26	"	55	22
5	99	75	65	65	26	"	55	22
6	95	75	75	75	30	"	55	22
7	55	55	75	55	18	"	55	22
8	35	45	55	45	16	"	45	16
9	59	55	55	55	22	"	55	22
10	57	55	45	45	18	"	55	22
11	30	45	55	45	16	"	45	16
12	81	65	45	45	18	"	55	22
13	02	35	65	35	8	"	35	10
14	18	45	35	35	14	"	45	16
15	87	65	45	45	18	"	55	22
16	68	65	65	65	26	"	55	22
17	28	45	65	45	14	"	45	16
18	44	55	45	45	18	"	55	22
19	80	65	55	55	22	"	55	22
20	84	65	65	65	26	"	55	22
Total		1,120	1,110	1,000	$378	1,100	1,010	$386
Daily average		56	55.5	50.00	$ 18.90	55	50.5	$ 19.3

EXHIBIT S8.6

Simulation Flowchart for Fish Market Problem

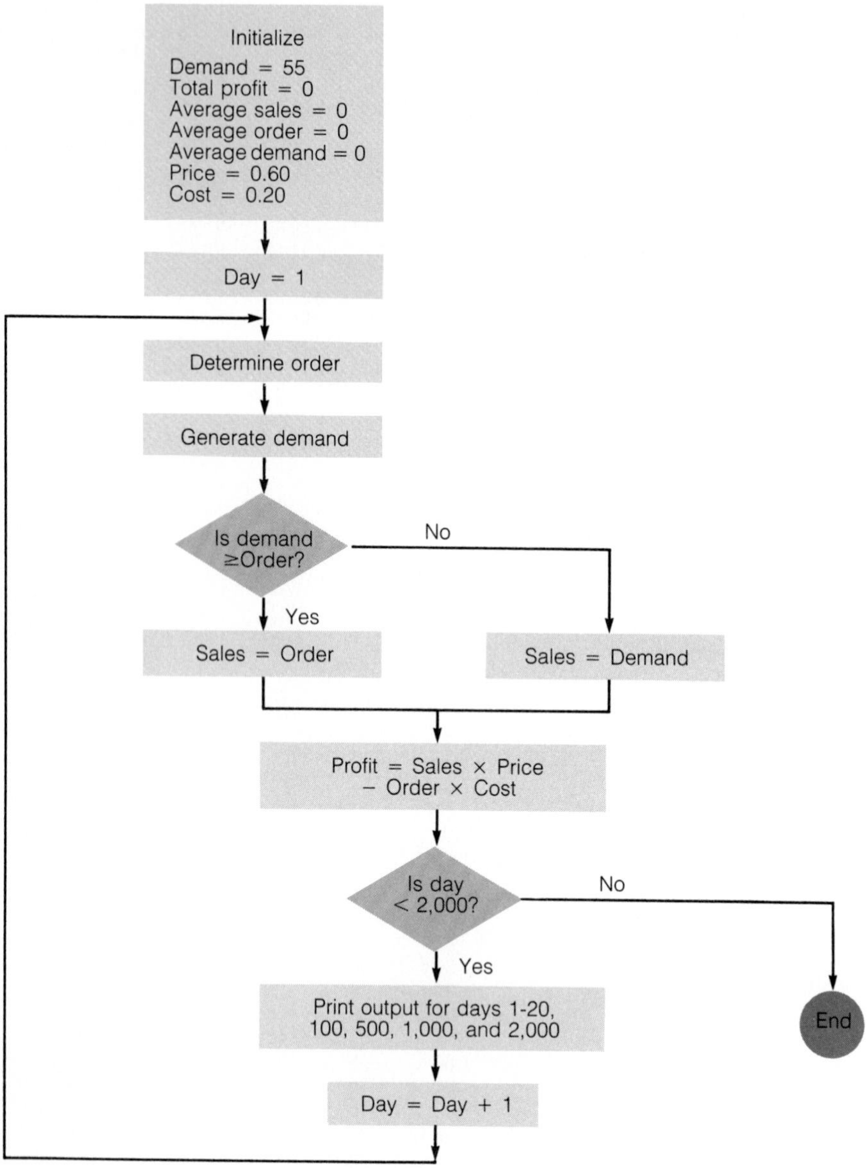

EXHIBIT S8.7 **FORTRAN Program for Simulation of Al's Fish Market**

```
100   PROGRAM FISHMKT (INPUT,OUTPUT)
250   DEMAND=55
260   TPROFIT=0.
265   ADD=0.
270   AOO=0.
275   ASS=0.
300   DO 100 I=1,2000
400   IDAY=I
450   ORDER=55
500   X=RANF(0)*100.
600   IF (X.GE.0.AND.X.LT.10) DEMAND=35
700   IF (X.GE.10.AND.X.LT.40) DEMAND=45
800   IF (X.GE.40.AND.X.LT.60) DEMAND=55
900   IF (X.GE.60.AND.X.LT.90) DEMAND=65
1000  IF (X.GE.90.AND.X.LT.100) DEMAND=75
1050  SALES=DEMAND
1100  IF (DEMAND.GT.ORDER) SALES = ORDER
1200  COST=.20
1300  PRICE=.60
1400  PROFIT=SALES*PRICE-ORDER*COST
1500  TPROFIT=TPROFIT+PROFIT
1550  DAY=IDAY
1560  ADD=ADD+DEMAND
1565  AD=ADD/DAY
1570  AOO=AOO+ORDER
1575  AO=AOO/DAY
1580  ASS=ASS+SALES
1585  AS=ASS/DAY
1600  AVPROF=TPROFIT/DAY
1700  IF(IDAY.GE.1.AND.IDAY.LE.20.OR.IDAY.EQ.100.OR.IDAY.EQ.500)GO TO 99
1800  IF(IDAY.EQ.1000.OR.IDAY.EQ.2000) GO TO 99
1850  GO TO 100
1900  99  PRINT 999,IDAY,DEMAND,AD,ORDER,AO,SALES,AS,PROFIT,AVPROF
2000  999  FORMAT (I5,8F8.2)
2100  100  CONTINUE
2150  PRINT 37,ADD,AOO,ASS,TPROFIT
2175  37 FORMAT(F15.2)
2200  STOP
2300  END
```

A flowchart was drawn to represent Al's Fish Market (Exhibit S8.6). The flowchart was then coded in FORTRAN and is shown in Exhibit S8.7. Exhibits S8.8 and S8.9 show the computer output, which compares the effects of Rule 1 (order the same amount of fish for tomorrow as was sold today), and Rule 2 (order 55 pounds of fish every day).

After simulating 2,000 days of operation, Rule 2 was better at $19.02, compared to $18.05 for Rule 1. The hand simulation performed in the previous section found Rule 2 at $19.30 and Rule 1 at $18.90. The hand simulation

EXHIBIT S8.8 **Simulation of Fish Market—Rule 1 Output**

```
READY.
450 ORDER=DEMAND
RUN
```

Day	Demand	Cumulative Average Demand	Order for Day	Cumulative Average Order	Sales for Day	Cumulative Average Sales	Profit for Day	Cumulative Average Profit
1	35.00	35.00	55.00	55.00	35.00	35.00	10.00	10.00
2	45.00	40.00	35.00	45.00	35.00	35.00	14.00	12.00
3	75.00	51.67	45.00	45.00	45.00	38.33	18.00	14.00
4	45.00	50.00	75.00	52.50	45.00	40.00	12.00	13.50
5	65.00	53.00	45.00	51.00	45.00	41.00	18.00	14.40
6	65.00	55.00	65.00	53.33	65.00	45.00	26.00	16.33
7	65.00	56.43	65.00	55.00	65.00	47.86	26.00	17.71
8	55.00	56.25	65.00	56.25	55.00	48.75	20.00	18.00
9	75.00	58.33	55.00	56.11	55.00	49.44	22.00	18.44
10	55.00	58.00	75.00	58.00	55.00	50.00	18.00	18.40
11	55.00	57.73	55.00	57.73	55.00	50.45	22.00	18.73
12	65.00	58.33	55.00	57.50	55.00	50.83	22.00	19.00
13	45.00	57.31	65.00	58.08	45.00	50.38	14.00	18.62
14	65.00	57.86	45.00	57.14	45.00	50.00	18.00	18.57
15	45.00	57.00	65.00	57.67	45.00	49.67	14.00	18.27
16	45.00	56.25	45.00	56.88	45.00	49.38	18.00	18.25
17	45.00	55.59	45.00	56.18	45.00	49.12	18.00	18.24
18	65.00	56.11	45.00	55.56	45.00	48.89	18.00	18.22
19	65.00	56.58	65.00	56.05	65.00	49.74	26.00	18.63
20	35.00	55.50	65.00	56.50	35.00	49.00	8.00	18.10
100	65.00	55.30	35.00	55.20	35.00	48.20	14.00	17.88
500	75.00	55.24	75.00	55.20	75.00	48.40	30.00	18.00
1000	45.00	55.22	45.00	55.23	45.00	48.52	18.00	18.07
2000	65.00	55.17	35.00	55.16	35.00	48.46	14.00	18.05

Total demand 110340.00   Total sales 96930.00
Total order 110330.00   Total profit 36092.00

contained some error because it covered only 20 days. The results were not bad, though, considering that the computer simulated 100 times as many days (2,000 days versus 20 days).

Looking at the totals for the computer simulation, it is interesting to note that for the 2,000 days Rule 2 yielded $1,944 greater profit than Rule 1, yet the amount of fish ordered was 330 pounds less under Rule 1. This finding would tend to make Rule 2 even more attractive if the problem were enriched to include such factors as inventory holding costs and the opportunity cost of funds. Similarly, we note that Rule 2 resulted in 3,130 more orders being filled (compared to Rule 1), which would enhance the desirability of Rule 1 if a stockout penalty were included in the problem.

EXHIBIT S8.9 **Simulation of Fish Market—Rule 2 Output**

```
450 ORDER=55
RUN.
```

Day	Demand	Cumulative Average Demand	Order for Day	Cumulative Average Order	Sales for Day	Cumulative Average Sales	Profit for Day	Cumulative Average Profit
1	35.00	35.00	55.00	55.00	35.00	35.00	10.00	10.00
2	45.00	40.00	55.00	55.00	45.00	40.00	16.00	13.00
3	75.00	51.67	55.00	55.00	55.00	45.00	22.00	16.00
4	45.00	50.00	55.00	55.00	45.00	45.00	16.00	16.00
5	65.00	53.00	55.00	55.00	55.00	47.00	22.00	17.20
6	65.00	55.00	55.00	55.00	55.00	48.33	22.00	18.00
7	65.00	56.43	55.00	55.00	55.00	49.29	22.00	18.57
8	55.00	56.25	55.00	55.00	55.00	50.00	22.00	19.00
9	75.00	58.33	55.00	55.00	55.00	50.56	22.00	19.33
10	55.00	58.00	55.00	55.00	55.00	51.00	22.00	19.60
11	55.00	57.73	55.00	55.00	55.00	51.36	22.00	19.82
12	65.00	58.33	55.00	55.00	55.00	51.67	22.00	20.00
13	45.00	57.31	55.00	55.00	45.00	51.15	16.00	19.69
14	65.00	57.86	55.00	55.00	55.00	51.43	22.00	19.86
15	45.00	57.00	55.00	55.00	45.00	51.00	16.00	19.60
16	45.00	56.25	55.00	55.00	45.00	50.63	16.00	19.38
17	45.00	55.59	55.00	55.00	45.00	50.29	16.00	19.18
18	65.00	56.11	55.00	55.00	55.00	50.56	22.00	19.33
19	65.00	56.58	55.00	55.00	55.00	50.79	22.00	19.47
20	35.00	55.50	55.00	55.00	35.00	50.00	10.00	19.00
100	65.00	55.30	55.00	55.00	55.00	50.00	22.00	19.00
500	75.00	55.24	55.00	55.00	55.00	50.02	22.00	19.01
1000	45.00	55.22	55.00	55.00	45.00	50.05	16.00	19.03
2000	65.00	55.17	55.00	55.00	55.00	50.03	22.00	19.02

Total demand	110340.00	Total sales	100060.00
Total ordered	110000.00	Total profit	38036.00

S8.3 SIMULATION PROGRAMS AND LANGUAGES

Simulation programs can be classified as *continuous* or *discrete*. Continuous models are based on mathematical equations and therefore are continuous, with values for all points in time. In contrast, discrete simulation occurs only at specific points. For example, customers arriving at a bank teller's window would be discrete simulation. The simulation jumps from point to point; the arrival of a customer, the start of a service, the ending of service, the arrival of the next customer, and so on. Discrete simulation can also be triggered to run by units of time (daily, hourly, minute by minute). This is called *event simulation*; points in-between either have no interest or cannot be computed because of the lack of some sort of mathematical relationships to link the succeeding events. Operations management applications almost exclusively use discrete (event) simulation.

Simulation software also can be categorized as general purpose and special purpose. General-purpose software is really language that allow programmers to build their own models. Examples are SLAM II, SIMSCRIPT II.5, SIMAN, GPSS/H, GPSS/PC, PCMODEL, and RESQ. Special-purpose software is really simulation programs specially built to simulate specific applications, such as MAP/1, and SIMFACTORY. In a specialized simulation for manufacturing, for example, provisions in the model allow for specifying the number of work centers, their description, arrival rates, processing time, batch sizes, quantities of work in process, available resources including labor, sequences, and so on. Additionally, the program may allow the observer to watch the animated operation and see the quantities and flows throughout the system as the simulation is running. Data is collected, analyzed, and presented in a form most suitable for that type of application.

There are many software simulation programs available to use on computers, from micros to mainframes. How, then, does one choose a program from a long list?

The first step is to understand the different types of simulation. Then it becomes a matter of reviewing programs on the market to try to obtain a "fit" to the specific needs. Even if a program does exist, however, sometimes it's still easier to create a special purpose one. It may be better suited and less troublesome to use.

Desirable Features of Simulation Software

Simulation software takes a while to learn to use. Once a specific software is learned, the tendency is to stay with it for a long time. Therefore, care should be taken when making the choice.

Simulation software

1. Should be capable of being used interactively as well as allowing complete runs.
2. Should be user friendly, easy to understand.
3. Should allow modules to be built and then connected. In this way models can be worked on separately without affecting the rest of the system.
4. Should allow users to write and incorporate their own routines, since it is impossible for the simulation program to provide for all needs.
5. Should have building blocks that contain built-in commands (such as statistical analysis or decision rules of where to go next).
6. Should have macro capability, such as the ability to develop machining cells.

7. Should have material-handling capability. In manufacturing, such a large portion of operations involves the movement of material that the program should have the ability to model trucks, cranes, conveyers, etc.
8. Should output standard statistics such as cycle times, utilizations, wait times, etc.
9. Should allow a variety of data analysis alternatives for both input and output data.
10. Should have animation capabilities to display graphically the product flow through the system.
11. Should permit interactive debugging of the model so the user can trace flows through the model and more easily find errors.[6]

S8.4 ADVANTAGES AND DISADVANTAGES OF SIMULATION

The following is not intended as a comprehensive list of reasons why one should elect or not elect to use simulation as a technique. Rather, it states some of the main points usually raised.

Advantages

1. Developing the model of a system often leads to a better understanding of the real system.
2. Time can be compressed in simulation; years of experience in the real system can be compressed into seconds or minutes.
3. Simulation does not disrupt ongoing activities of the real system.
4. Simulation is far more general than mathematical models and can be used where conditions are not suitable for standard mathematical analysis.
5. Simulation can be used as a "game" for training experience.
6. Simulation provides a more realistic replication of a system than mathematical analysis.
7. Simulation can be used to analyze transient conditions whereas mathematical techniques usually cannot.

[6] S. Wali Haider and Jerry Banks, "Simulation Software Products for Analyzing Manufacturing Systems," *Industrial Engineering* 18, no. 7 (July 1986), pp. 98–103.

8. Many standard "packaged" models, covering a wide range of topics, are available commercially.
9. Simulation answers "what if" questions.

Disadvantages

1. While a great deal of time and effort may be spent to develop a model for simulation, there is no guarantee that the model will, in fact, provide good answers.
2. The output of a simulation model cannot be "proved." Simulation involves numerous repetitions of sequences that are based on randomly generated occurrences. An apparently stable system can, with the right combination of events—however unlikely—explode. There is no way to prove that a model's performance is completely reliable.
3. Depending on the system to be simulated, building a simulation model can take anywhere from an hour to 100 worker years. Complicated systems can be very costly and take a long time.
4. Simulation may be less accurate than mathematical analysis, since it is randomly based. If a given system can be represented by a mathematical model, it may be better to use than simulation.
5. A significant amount of computer time may be needed to run complex models.
6. The technique of simulation, while making progress, still lacks a standardized approach. Therefore, models of the same system built by different individuals may differ widely.

S8.5 CONCLUSION

We could make the statement that anything that can be done mathematically can be done with simulation. However, simulation is not always the best choice. Mathematical analysis, when appropriate to a specific problem, is usually faster and less expensive. Also, it is usually provable as far as the technique is concerned, and the only real question is whether the system is adequately represented by the mathematical model.

Simulation, however, has nothing fixed; there are no boundaries to building a model or making assumptions about the system. Thus, the area of application has no limit. Users are not required to possess particular constraints, specific distribution frequencies, or a limited numbers of variables. Expanding computer power and memory have pushed out the limits of what can be simulated. Further, the continued development of simulation languages and programs promises to make the entire process of creating simulation models very much easier.

S8.6 REVIEW AND DISCUSSION QUESTIONS

1. Why is it that simulation is often referred to as "a technique of last resort"?
2. Give an example of a third rule that Al (of Al's Fish Market) could use in his inventory ordering.
3. Do you have to use a computer to get good information from a simulation? Explain.
4. What is the importance of run length in simulation? Is a run of 100 observations twice as valid as a run of 50? Explain.

S8.7 PROBLEMS

*1. To use an old statistical-type example for simulation, if an urn contains 100 balls, of which 10 percent are green balls, 40 percent are red balls, and 50 percent are spotted balls, develop a simulation model of the process of drawing balls at random from the urn. Each time a ball is drawn and its color noted, it is replaced. For your random numbers, use those shown below as you desire.

Simulate drawing 10 balls from the urn. Show which numbers you have used.

26768	83125
42613	55503
95457	47019
95276	84828
66954	08021
17457	36458
03704	05752
56970	05752

*2. A rural clinic receives a delivery of fresh plasma once each week from a central blood bank. Supply varies according to demand from other clinics and hospitals in the region but ranges between four and nine pints of the most widely used blood type, type O. The number of patients per week requiring this blood varies from zero to four, and each patient may need from one to four pints. Given the following delivery quantities, patient distribution, and demand per patient, what will be the number of pints in excess or short for a six-week period? Use Monte Carlo simulation to derive your answer. Consider that plasma is storable and there is currently none on hand.

* Solutions to Problems 1 and 2 are in Appendix D.

DELIVERY QUANTITIES		PATIENT DISTRIBUTION		DEMAND PER PATIENT	
Pints per Week	Frequency	Patients per Week Requiring Blood	Frequency	Pints	Frequency
4	0.15	0	0.25	1	0.40
5	0.20	1	0.25	2	0.30
6	0.25	2	0.30	3	0.20
7	0.15	3	0.15	4	0.10
8	0.15	4	0.05		
9	0.10				

3. CLASSROOM SIMULATION: FISH FORWARDERS

This is a competitive exercise designed to test players' skills at setting inventory ordering rules over a 10-week planning horizon. Maximum profit at the end determines the winner.

Fish Forwarders supplies fresh shrimp to a variety of customers in the New Orleans area. It places orders for cases of shrimp from fleet representatives at the beginning of each week to meet a demand from its customers at the middle of the week. The shrimp are subsequently delivered to Fish Forwarders and then, at the end of the week, to its customers.

Both the supply of shrimp and the demand for shrimp are uncertain. The supply may vary as much as ±10 percent from the amount ordered, and by contract, Fish Forwarders must purchase this supply. The probability associated with this variation is: −10 percent, 30 percent of the time; 0 percent, 50 percent of the time, and +10 percent, 20 percent of the time. The weekly demand for shrimp is normally distributed with a mean of 800 cases and a standard deviation of 100 cases.

A case of shrimp costs Fish Forwarders $30 and sells for $50. Any shrimp not sold at the end of the week are sold to a cat-food company at $4 per case. Fish Forwarders may, if it chooses, order the shrimp flash-frozen by the supplier at dockside, but this raises the cost of a case by $4 and, hence, costs Fish Forwarders $34 per case. Flash-freezing enables Fish Forwarders to maintain an inventory of shrimp, but it costs $2 per case per week to store the shrimp at a local icehouse. The customers are indifferent to whether they get regular or flash-frozen shrimp. Fish Forwarders figures that its shortage cost is equal to its markup; that is, each case demanded but not available costs the company $50 − $30 or $20.

Procedure for play. The game requires that each week a decision be made as to how many cases to order of regular shrimp and flash-frozen shrimp. The number ordered may be any amount. The instructor will play the role of referee and supply the random numbers. The steps in playing the game are as follows.

a. Decide on the order amount of regular shrimp or flash-frozen shrimp and enter the figures in column 3 of the worksheet (see Exhibit S8.10). Assume that there is no opening inventory of flash-frozen shrimp.

b. Determine the amount that arrives and enter it at Orders received. To accomplish this, the referee will draw a random number from a uniform random number table (such as that in Exhibit S8.4) and find its associated

EXHIBIT S8.10 **Simulation Worksheet**

(1) Week	(2) Flash-frozen inventory	(3) Orders placed: Regular	Orders placed: Flash-frozen	(4) Orders received: Regular	Orders received: Flash-frozen	(5) Available (regular and flash-frozen)	(6) Demand (800 + 100Z)	(7) Sales (minimum of demand or available)	(8) Excess: Regular	Excess: Flash	(9) Shortages
1											
2											
3											
4											
5											
6											
7		MARDI GRAS				*					
8											
9											
10											
Total											

*Flash-frozen only.

level of variation from following random number intervals: 00 to 29 = −10 percent, 30 to 79 = 0 percent, and 80 to 99 = +10 percent. If the random number is, say, 13, the amount of variation will be −10 percent. Thus, if you decide to order 1,000 regular cases of shrimp and 100 flash-frozen cases, the amount you would actually receive would be 1,000 − 0.10(1,000), or 900 regular cases, and 100 − 0.10(100), or 90 flash-frozen cases. (Note that the amount of variation is the same for both regular and flash-frozen shrimp.) These amounts are then entered in column 4.

c. Add the amount of flash-frozen shrimp in inventory (if any) to the quantity of regular and flash-frozen shrimp just received and enter this amount in column 5. This would be 990, using the figures provided above.

d. Determine the demand for shrimp. To accomplish this, the referee draws a random normal deviate value from Appendix B and enters it into the equation at the top of column 6. Thus, if the deviate value is −1.76, demand for the week will be 800 + 100(−1.76), or 624.

e. Determine the amount sold. This will be the lesser of the amount demanded (column 6) and the amount available (column 5). Thus, if a player has received 990 and demand is 624, the quantity entered will be 624 (with 990 − 624, or 366 left over).

EXHIBIT S8.11

Profit from Fish Forwarders' Operations

Revenue from sales ($50 × Col. 7)	$______	
Revenue from salvage ($4 × Col. 8 reg.)	$______	
Total revenue		$______
Cost of regular purchases ($30 × Col. 4 reg.)	$______	
Cost of flash-frozen purchases ($34 × Col. 4 flash)	$______	
Cost of holding flash-frozen shrimp ($2 × Col. 8 flash)	$______	
Cost of shortages ($20 × Col. 9)	$______	
Total cost	$______	
Profit	$______	

f. Determine the excess. The amount of excess is simply that quantity remaining after demand for a given week is filled. Always assume that regular shrimp are sold before the flash-frozen. Thus, if we use the 366 figure obtained in *(e)*, the excess would include all the original 90 cases of flash-frozen shrimp.

g. Determine shortages. This is simply the amount of unsatisfied demand each period, and it occurs only when demand is greater than sales. (Since all customers use the shrimp within the week in which they are delivered, back orders are not relevant.) The amount of shortages (in cases of shrimp) is entered in column 9.

Profit determination. Exhibit S8.11 is provided for determining the profit achieved at the end of play. The values to be entered in the table are obtained by summing the relevant columns of Exhibit S8.10 and making the calculations.

Assignment. Simulate operations for a total of 10 weeks. It is suggested that a 10-minute break be taken at the end of Week 5 and the players attempt to evaluate how they may improve their performance. They might also wish to plan an ordering strategy for the week of Mardi Gras, when no shrimp will be supplied.

4. The manager of a small post office is concerned that her growing township is overloading the one-window service being offered. She decides to obtain sample data concerning 100 individuals who arrive for service. The data are summarized below.

Time between Arrivals (minutes)	Frequency
1	8
2	35
3	34
4	17
5	6
	100

Service Time (minutes)	Frequency
1.0	12
1.5	21
2.0	36
2.5	19
3.0	7
3.5	5
	100

Using the following random number sequence, simulate six arrivals; estimate the average customer waiting time and the average teller idle time.
RN: 08, 74, 24, 34, 45, 86, 31, 32, 45, 21, 10, 67, 60, 17, 60, 87, 74, 96

5. A bank of machines in a manufacturing shop breaks down according to the following interarrival-time distribution. The time it takes one repairperson to complete the repair of a machine is given in the service-time distribution:

Interarrival Time (hours)	*P*(*X*)	RN
.5	.30	0–29
1.0	.22	30–51
1.5	.16	52–67
2.0	.10	68–77
3.0	.14	78–91
4.0	.08	92–99
	1.00	

Service Time (hours)	*P*(*X*)	RN
.5	.25	0–24
1.0	.20	25–44
2.0	.25	45–69
3.0	.15	70–84
4.0	.10	85–94
5.0	.05	95–99
	1.00	

Simulate the breakdown of five machines. Calculate the average machine downtime using two repairpersons and the following random number sequence (both repairpersons cannot work on the same machine):
RN: 30, 81, 02, 91, 51, 08, 28, 44, 86, 84, 29, 08, 37, 34, 99

6. A professional football coach has six running backs on his squad. He wants to evaluate how injuries might affect his stock of running backs. A minor injury causes a player to be removed from the game and miss only the next game. A major injury puts the player out of action for the rest of the season. The probability of a major injury in a game is 0.05. There is at most one major injury per game. The probability distribution of minor injuries per game is:

Number of Injuries	Probability
0	.2
1	.5
2	.22
3	.05
4	.025
5	.005
	1.000

Injuries seem to happen in a completely random manner, with no discernible pattern over the season. A season is 10 games.

Using the following random numbers, simulate the fluctuations in the coach's stock of running backs over the season. Assume that he hires no additional running backs during the season.
RN: 044, 392, 898, 615, 986, 959, 558, 353, 577, 866, 305, 813, 024, 189, 878, 023, 285, 442, 862, 848, 060, 131, 963, 874, 805, 105, 452

7. Jethro's service station has one gasoline pump. Because everyone in Kornfield County drives big cars, there is room at the station for only three cars, including the car at the pump. Cars arriving when there are already three cars at the station

drive on to another station. Use the following probability distributions to simulate the arrival of four cars to Jethro's station.

Interarrival Time (minutes)	$P(X)$	RN
10	.40	0–39
20	.35	40–74
30	.20	75–94
40	.05	95–99

Service Time (minutes)	$P(X)$	RN
5	.45	0–44
10	.30	45–74
15	.20	75–94
20	.05	95–99

Calculate the average time cars spend at the station using the following random number sequence:
RN: 99, 00, 73, 09, 38, 53, 72, 91

S8.8 SELECTED BIBLIOGRAPHY

Bulgren, William G. *Discrete System Simulation*. Englewood Cliffs, N.J.: Prentice-Hall, 1982.

Haider, S. Wali, and Jerry Banks. "Simulation Software Products for Analyzing Manufacturing Systems." *Industrial Engineering* 18, no. 7 (July 1986), pp. 98–103.

Law, Averill M. "Computer Simulation of Manufacturing Systems: Part I." *Industrial Engineering* 18, no. 5, (May 1986), pp. 46–63.

Law, Averill M., and W. David Kelton. *Simulation Modeling and Analysis*. 2nd ed. New York: McGraw-Hill, 1990.

Payne, James A. *Introduction to Simulation*. New York: McGraw-Hill, 1982.

Solomon, Susan L. *Simulation of Waiting Lines*. Englewood Cliffs, N.J.: Prentice-Hall, 1983.

Watson, Hugh J. *Computer Simulation in Business*. New York: John Wiley & Sons, 1981.

Woolsey, G. "Whatever Happened to Simple Simulation? A Question and Answer." *Interfaces* 9, no. 4 (August 1979), pp. 9–11.

Chapter 9

Job Design and Work Measurement

EPIGRAPH

Strange things happen at the best plants. Workers complain about machines being idle for too long and then fix them on their own to reduce the downtime. A plant manager smiles approvingly when he encounters the head of the janitorial crew dictating a letter to the manager's own secretary. The fanciest conference rooms are sometimes found not in the administration building, but inside the plant for workers to use when meeting with foremen.

Gene Bylinsky, "America's Best Managed Factories," *Fortune*, May 28, 1984, p. 16.

CHAPTER OUTLINE

KEY TERMS

Job Design

Specialization of Labor

Sociotechnical Systems

Time Standard

Financial Incentive Plans

In order to produce a product or service, three basic questions must be answered: What does the job consist of? What rate of output can we expect from a worker performing that job? How should we pay workers. One more question that we must answer relates to whether we should emphasize output per worker as individuals or output from a number of workers working as a group.

The quote that opens this chapter captures the flavor of how many of our better-run companies are now relating to their work force, and how the work force is relating to them. In the first part of this chapter we touch on some of the job-design concepts that are giving rise to and support these relationships. In the remainder of the chapter we discuss the technical concepts required to standardize and measure work and compensate the work force.

9.1 JOB DESIGN

Perhaps the most challenging (and perplexing) design activity encountered by the productive system is the development of the jobs that each worker and work group are to perform. This is so for at least three reasons:

1. There is often an inherent conflict between the needs and goals of the worker and work group, and the requirements of the production process.
2. The unique nature of each individual results in a wide range of attitudinal, physiological, and productivity responses in performing any given task.
3. The character of the work force and the work itself are changing, which lays open to question the traditional models of worker behavior and the efficacy of standard approaches to work development.

In this section, we explore these and other issues in job design and present some guidelines for carrying out the job-design function. We will begin by noting some trends in job design:

1. Quality control as part of the worker's job.
2. Cross training workers to perform multiskilled jobs.
3. Worker participation in job design.
4. Proliferation of worker teams with more autonomy in decision making.
5. Substitution of robots for people in dull, hazardous jobs.
6. Much less of a distinction between women's work and men's work.
7. Most important of all, organizational commitment to providing meaningful and rewarding jobs for all employees. (See Exhibit 9.1.)

EXHIBIT 9.1

People-Related Objectives of Hewlett-Packard

1. **Belief in our people**
   - Confidence in, and respect for, our people as opposed to depending upon extensive rules, procedures, etc.
   - Depend upon people to do their job right (individual freedom) without constant directives.
   - Opportunity for meaningful participation (job dignity).
2. **Emphasis on working together and sharing rewards (teamwork and partnership)**
   - Share responsibilities; help each other; learn from each other; chance to make mistakes.
   - Recognition based on contribution to results—sense of achievement and self-esteem.
   - Profit sharing; stock purchase plan; retirement program; etc., aimed at employees and company sharing in each other's successes.
   - Company financial management emphasis on protecting employee's job security.
3. **A superior working environment which other companies seek but few achieve**
   - Informality—open, honest communications; no artificial distinctions between employees (first-name basis); management by walking around; and open-door communication policy.
   - Develop and promote from within—lifetime training, education, career counseling to help employees get maximum opportunity to grow and develop with the company.
   - Decentralization—emphasis on keeping work groups as small as possible for maximum employee identification with our businesses and customers.
   - Management-by-objectives (MBO)—provides a sound basis for measuring performance by employees as well as managers and is objective, not political.

Job Design Defined

Job design may be defined as the function of specifying the work activities of an individual or group in an organizational setting. Its objective is to develop work assignments that meet the requirements of the organization and the technology and that satisfy the personal and individual requirements of the jobholder. The term *job* (in the context of nonsupervisory work) and the activities subsumed under it are defined here.

1. *Micromotion:* the smallest work activities, involving such elementary movements as reaching, grasping, positioning, or releasing an object.
2. *Element:* an aggregation of two or more micromotions, usually thought of as a more or less complete entity, such as picking up, transporting, and positioning an item.
3. *Task:* an aggregation of two or more elements into a complete activity, such as wiring a circuit board, sweeping a floor, or cutting a tree.
4. *Job:* the set of all tasks that must be performed by a given worker. A job may consist of several tasks, such as typing, filing, and taking dictation (in secretarial work), or it may consist of a single task, such as attaching a wheel to a car (as in automobile assembly).

EXHIBIT 9.2 **Factors in Job Design**

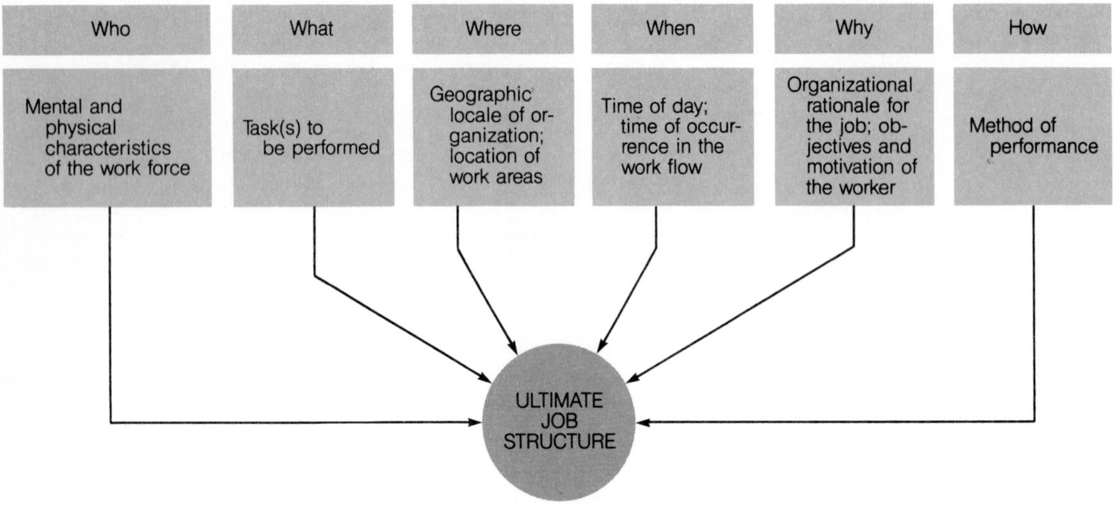

Job design is a complex function because of the variety of factors that enter into arriving at the ultimate job structure. Decisions must be made about who is to perform the job, where it is to be performed, and how. And, as we can see in Exhibit 9.2, each of these factors may have additional considerations.

9.2 BEHAVIORAL CONSIDERATIONS IN JOB DESIGN

Degree of Labor Specialization

Specialization of labor is the two-edged sword of job design. On one hand, specialization has made possible high-speed, low-cost production, and, from a materialistic standpoint, has greatly enhanced our standard of living. On the other hand, it is well known that extreme specialization, such as that encountered in mass-production industries, often has serious adverse effects on the worker, which in turn are passed on to the production system. In essence, the problem is to determine how much specialization is enough: at what point do the disadvantages outweigh the advantages? (See Exhibit 9.3.)

Recent research suggests that the disadvantages dominate the advantages much more commonly than was thought in the past. However, simply stating that, for purely humanitarian reasons, specialization should be avoided is risky. The reason, of course, is that people differ in what they want from their work and what they are willing to put into it. Some workers prefer not to make decisions about their work, some like to daydream on the job, and

EXHIBIT 9.3

Advantages and Disadvantages of Specialization of Labor

Advantages of specialization

To management

1. Rapid training of the work force
2. Ease in recruiting new workers
3. High output due to simple and repetitive work
4. Low wages due to ease of substitutability of labor
5. Close control over work flow and workloads

To labor

1. Little or no education required to obtain work
2. Ease in learning job

Disadvantages of specialization

To management

1. Difficulty in controlling quality since no one person has responsibility for entire product
2. "Hidden" costs of worker dissatisfaction, arising from
   a. turnover
   b. absenteeism
   c. tardiness
   d. grievances
   e. intentional disruption of production process

To labor

1. Boredom stemming from repetitive nature of work
2. Little gratification from work itself because of small contribution to each item
3. Little or no control over the work pace, leading to frustration and fatigue (in assembly-line-type situations)
4. Little opportunity to progress to a better job since significant learning is rarely possible on fractionated work
5. Little opportunity to show initiative through developing better methods or tools
6. Local muscular fatigue caused by use of the same muscles in performing the task
7. Little opportunity for communication with fellow workers because of layout of the work area

others are simply not capable of performing more complex work. Still, there is a good deal of worker frustration with the way many jobs are structured, leading reasearchers and thoughtful businesspeople to try different approaches to job design. Two popular contemporary approaches are job enrichment and sociotechnical systems. The philosophical objective underlying these approaches is to improve the quality of work life of the employee, and so they are often applied as central features of what is termed a quality of work life (QWL) program.

Working as Individuals versus Working as Part of a Group[1]

The Japanese have demonstrated the importance of the group as the principal work unit, rather than the individual. When part of a group, employees will

[1] David Halpern, Stephen Osofsky, and Myron I. Peskin, "Taylorism Revisited and Revised for the 1990s," *Industrial Management,* January–February 1989, pp. 20–23.

identify with the group, have greater job satisfaction, and, through interaction within the group, will also improve their jobs and performances. Higher quality is one of the biggest benefits observed.

From a management control standpoint, it is easier to work with groups rather than individuals. Work can be scheduled in larger pieces to the group; the group usually develops its own standards of performance; and training of new workers is easily handled by the group.

Incentive payment systems wherein individuals share in the performance of the group also have some advantages. Rather than the competitive nature of individual incentives, the group-based incentive system encourages workers to cooperate with one another.

Job Enrichment

Job enlargement generally entails making adjustments to a specialized job to make it more interesting to the jobholder. A job is said to be enlarged *horizontally* if the worker performs a greater number or variety of tasks, and it is said to be enlarged *vertically* if the worker is involved in planning, organizing, and inspecting his or her own work. Horizontal job enlargement is intended to counteract oversimplification and to permit the worker to perform a "whole unit of work." Vertical enlargement (traditionally termed *job enrichment*) attempts to broaden the workers' influence in the transformation process by giving them certain managerial powers over their own activities. Today, common practice is to apply both horizontal and vertical enlargement to a given job and refer to the total approach as *job enrichment*.

Sociotechnical Systems

Consistent with the job-enrichment philosophy but focusing more on the interaction between technology and the work group is the **sociotechnical systems** approach. It attempts to develop jobs that adjust the needs of the production process technology to the needs of the worker and work group. The term was developed from studies of weaving mills in India and coal mines in England in the early 1950s. In these studies, it was discovered that work groups could effectively handle many production problems better than management if they were permitted to make their own decisions on scheduling, work allocation among members, bonus sharing, and so forth. This was particularly true when there were variations in the production process requiring quick reactions by the group or when the work of one shift overlapped with the work of other shifts.

Since these pioneering studies, the sociotechnical approach has been applied in many countries, though often under the heading of "autonomous work groups" or "Japanese-style work groups."

One of the major philosophical points underlying these studies is that the individual or the work group requires a logically integrated pattern of work activities that incorporates the following job design principles:

Task variety. An attempt must be made to provide an optimal variety of tasks within each job. Too much variety can be inefficient for training and frustrating for the employee. Too little can lead to boredom and fatigue. The optimal level is one that allows the employee to take a rest from a high level of attention or effort while working on another task or, conversely, to stretch after periods of routine activity.

Skill variety. Research suggests that employees derive satisfaction from using a number of different kinds of levels of skill.

Feedback. There should be some means for informing employees quickly when they have achieved their targets. Fast feedback aids the learning process. Ideally, employees should have some responsibility for setting their own standards of quantity and quality.

Task identity. Sets of tasks should be separated from other sets of tasks by some clear boundary. Whenever possible, a group or individual employee should have responsibility for a set of tasks that is clearly defined, visible, and meaningful. In this way, work is seen as important by the group or individual undertaking it, and others understand and respect its significance.

Task autonomy. Employees should be able to exercise some control over their work. Areas of discretion and decision making should be available to them.[2]

Examples of Sociotechnical Systems in Three Countries

Holland: Phillips N.V.

The truck chassis assembly groups have real decision-making power. Production groups of 5 to 12 workers with related job duties decide among themselves how they will do their jobs, within the quality and production standards defined by higher management; they can rotate job assignments—do a smaller or larger part of the overall task. At the same time, the jobs of all members of the production groups were enlarged, making them jointly responsible for simple service and maintenance activities, housekeeping, and quality control in their work area, duties formerly performed by staff personnel.[3]

United States: Travelers Insurance Company

The objective was to enrich the keypunching job itself, starting with a training program for the supervisors. At the time of the initial implementation, work

---

[2] This summary is taken from Enid Mumford and Mary Weir, *Computer Systems in Work Design—the ETHICS Method* (New York: Halstead, 1979), p. 42.

[3] William F. Dawling, "Farewell to the Blue-Collar Blues," *Organizational Dynamics*, Autumn 1973.

output was deemed inadequate, the error rate was excessive, and absenteeism too high. The keypunch job lacked skill variety, task identity, task significance, and autonomy. The changes introduced were:

1. *Natural units of work.* The random batch assignment of work was replaced by assigning to each operator continuing responsibility for certain accounts—either particular departments or particular recurring jobs.
2. *Task combination.* Some planning and control functions were combined with the central task of keypunching.
3. *Client relationships.* Each operator was given several channels of direct contact with clients. The operators, not their assignment clerks, now inspect their documents for correctness and legibility. When problems arise, the operator, not the supervisor, takes them up with the client.
4. *Feedback.* In addition to feedback from client contact . . . the computer department now returns incorrect cards to the operator who punched them, and the operators correct their own errors. . . . Each operator receives weekly a computer printout of her errors and productivity that is sent to her directly, rather than given to her supervisor.
5. *Vertical loading.* Operators now have the authority to correct obvious coding errors on their own. Operators may set their own schedules and plan their daily work. Some competent operators have been given the option of not verifying their work.

The results of the study: A reduction in keypunch operators needed, reduction in absenteeism, improved job attitudes, and less need for controls. Actual first-year savings totaled over $64,000. Potential annual savings from potential expanded application was given as $92,000.[4]

An American Motors Company study team observed Japanese workers at five automobile manufacturers and noted these characteristics of Japanese production style:[5]

- The work force is dedicated. The workers believe they are better, and consequently they strive to demonstrate their capabilities and loyalty to the company. They have tremendous pride.
- The pace of work varies between 110 and 140 percent. Employees help each other.
- Workers do not eat or smoke on the job. There is almost no talking on the line.

[4] John Miner, *Theories of Organizational Behavior* (Hinsdale, Ill.: Dryden Press, 1980), pp. 256–57.

[5] Reprinted from Irwin Otis, "Observations on the Japanese Automotive Industry: A Lesson for American Managers," *Industrial Management,* May–June 1987, p. 8. Copyright Institute of Industrial Engineers, 25 Technology Park/Atlanta, Norcross, Georgia 30092.

- Worker support includes low absenteeism (1–2 percent), high morale, and strong support of management plans for further automation.
- Worker recognition is evident in the plants. Pictures of employees, with listing of their skills, are posted on numerous department bulletin boards.
- All plants visited operated on a mass relief plan (two 10-minute break periods) for which employees are not paid.
- Time-card racks were installed in each department, accessible to work areas, rather than at an entrance to the plant, thus avoiding long lines for checking in and checking out.
- In addition to Ping-Pong tables and basketball courts, skip ropes were provided for employees to use at their leisure.
- Not only is the plant clean, every worker is clean. Each plant was orderly—there was a place for everything and everything was in its place. Little or no cardboard was visible in the plants.
- Most of the plants had only a few work classifications—one for direct labor and two or three for indirect labor.
- Employees, including production management, change shifts weekly. Also, the company rotates a portion of the work force to different jobs every six months, with no interference from the union.
- The goal of job rotation is practiced. There are no job jurisdiction problems in the Japanese automotive industry.
- Techniques of statistical quality control are taught to all workers. Job training is actually on-the-job training, and is offered on a one-to-one basis.
- Technical training and education are provided, either through off-the-job, on-site training, or through basic education.
- Quality is an obsession with Japanese workers. They perform their jobs while thinking of ways to upgrade it. Workers are authorized to stop the line any time they deem it necessary in order to maintain quality.
- A system of colored lights, bells, or music is used by employees to alert supervisors when there is a problem on the line that requires assistance. If there is no response, the employee is empowered to stop the line. The essence of this concept is to build the job correctly on the line, not in the garage. At Mitsubishi, where this practice was not followed, there were numerous vehicles in the garage area in need of repair.
- Departments are distinguished by color-coded hard hats (skilled trades, quality control, etc.). Color-coded rings around hard hats identify foremen, group leaders, etc.
- There is a broad range of indirect participation in management through the union in the form of union-management joint consultation councils. These councils meet once every three months, or when necessary, to

promote understanding and to exchange views and information on all matters directly or indirectly concerning the workers.

- As a whole, computer applications were limited. Many manual applications were noted.
- Rather than stopwatch studies, Work Factor Systems of Elemental Motion Times (developed by WOFAC division of Science Management Corp. of New Jersey) was used for developing work assignments.
- People can work wonders when they:
  - are treated like intelligent human beings.
  - are never placed in a position where their dignity is compromised.
  - are always treated with respect.
  - are allowed to be involved in the pursuit of the company's goals.
  - are well trained for their jobs.
  - have a clear and common goal.
  - feel secure and confident.
  - are allowed to make a significant contribution to the organization.
  - are assured of sharing some of the gains of a successful enterprise.
- This great team spirit—everyone pulling together for the good of the organization, everyone dedicated and committed to achieving the company's goals—is the most important key to success and an absolute necessity for producing products of perfect quality.

INSERT Sanyo Electric Company's Experiences in the U.S.

Today, Japanese-owned factories are commonplace in America, and their success is presumed. But as Japanese plants and ventures in the U.S. multiply—tripling since 1981—one thing is becoming clear: Some of the problems that have bedeviled domestic manufacturers can vex newly arrived Japanese companies, too.

Sanyo took charge of a Warwick Electronics Inc. plant in 1977. Employment had been skidding, and the television sets being made for Sears, Roebuck & Co. were suffering both from Japanese competition and from their own quality problems.

Here came Sanyo, pouring in capital and engineering talent. It rehired hundreds of cast-off workers. It set high quality standards, yet embraced the local union and sponsored outings for employees and townspeople.

For a while, things were great. Production jumped fifteen-fold. Sanyo heaped praise on the teamwork and spirit of its workers, and the born-again plant came to symbolize the superiority of Japanese management.

The miracle was a mirage. Initial productivity and sales gains were real enough but mostly reflected use of high-grade Japanese-made components that were easy to assemble and reduced rejects.

The plant location is in a half-black, half-white community of 13,803, situated 90 miles east of Little Rock. Its first integrated high school prom made headlines just last month. The arrival of a clutch of Japanese executives—and some alien management concepts—was a shock.

Sanyo initially wanted to import quality circles, calisthenics, and company uniforms, but it backed off. Tanemichi Sohma, a retired Sanyo vice president, recalls, "The union would have just thought we were trying to brainwash them." Sanyo tried consensus management with an operating committee of three Americans and three Japanese. But only one Sanyo executive spoke fluent English, so every meeting required an interpreter.

Tensions exploded in 1985, with the second strike in six years. Sanyo, fearing an industry shakeout, was on a tough tack. It demanded medical-insurance cuts, seniority-system changes, and the right to shift workers from job to job. The strike left the Japanese bitter and disillusioned. "How could we survive if the workers wouldn't help us?" asks Mr. Sohma. "With the union, no matter what we do, it was not enough for them. It got to be so difficult, the attitude was to heck with them."

Only 350 employees work at the plant now; more than 2,000 used to. It will roll up something like a $28 million loss this fiscal year, on top of $40 million in losses over the past three years. In March 1988 a microwave oven production line was shut down, and only two of the nine television lines now operate.

Source: Excerpted from J. Ernest Beazley, "In Spite of Mystique, Japanese Plants in U.S. Find Problems Abound," *The Wall Street Journal*, June 22, 1988. Reprinted with permission.

9.3 METHODS, MEASUREMENT, AND PAYMENT

In this section, our focus narrows to the specifics of job performance. In particular, we wish to consider:

1. How the work should be accomplished (work methods).
2. How performance may be evaluated (work measurement).
3. How workers should be compensated (wage payment plans).

The first two constitute the basis for setting work standards, which in turn are the basis for capacity and production-planning decisions.

Work Methods

In our development of the productive system, we have defined the tasks that must be done by workers. But how should they be done? The responsibility for developing work methods in large firms is typically assigned either to a staff department designated *methods analysis* or to an industrial engineering department. In small firms, this activity is often performed by consulting firms that specialize in work methods design.

The principal approach to the study of work methods is the construction of charts, such as operations charts, worker-machine charts, simo (simultaneous motion) charts, and activity charts, in conjunction with time study or standard

EXHIBIT 9.4

Work Methods Design Aids

Activity	Objective of Study	Study Techniques
Overall productive system	Eliminate or combine steps; shorten transport distance; identify delays	Flow diagram, process chart
Worker at fixed workplace	Simplify method; minimize motions	Operations charts, simo charts; apply principles of motion economy
Worker interacts with equipment	Minimize idle time; find number of combination of machines to balance cost of worker and machine idle time	Activity chart, worker-machine charts
Worker interacts with other workers	Maximize productivity; minimize interference	Activity charts, gang process charts

time data. The choice of which charting method to use depends on the activity level of the task; that is, whether the focus is on (1) the overall productive system, (2) the worker at a fixed workplace, (3) a worker interacting with equipment, or (4) a worker interacting with other workers (see Exhibit 9.4). (Several of these charting techniques were introduced in Chapter 3, where they were used to aid process selection.)

Overall productive system

The objective in studying the overall productive system is to identify delays, transport distances, processes, and processing time requirements, in order to simplify the entire operation. The underlying philosophy is to eliminate any step in the process that does not add value to the product. The approach is to flow chart the process and then ask the following questions:

What is done? Must it be done? What would happen if it were not done?

Where is the task done? Must it be done at that location or could it be done somewhere else?

When is the task performed? Is it critical that it be done then or is there flexibility in time and sequence? Could it be done in combination with some other step in the process?

How is the task done? Why is it done this way? Is there another way?

Who does the task? Can someone else do it? Should the worker be of a higher or lower skill level?

These thought-provoking questions usually help to eliminate much unnecessary work, as well as to simplify the remaining work, by combining a number of processing steps and changing the order of performance.

Use of the process chart is valuable in studying an overall system, though care must be taken to follow the same item throughout the process. The

EXHIBIT 9.5

Flow Diagram and Process Chart of an Office Procedure—Present Method*

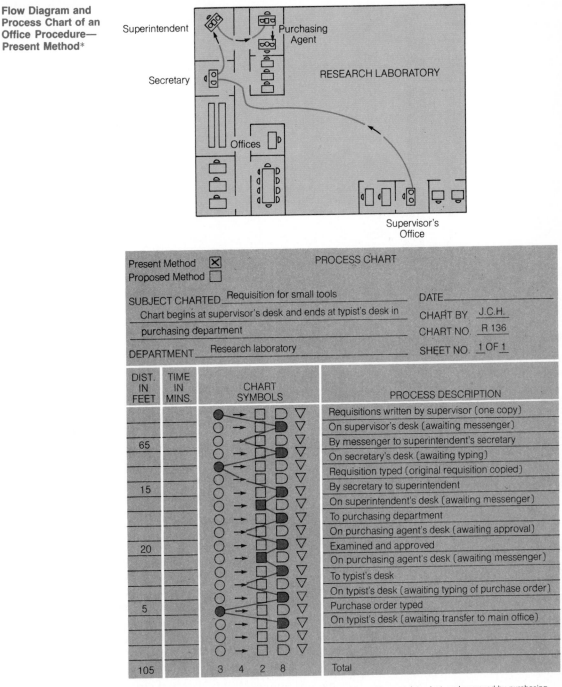

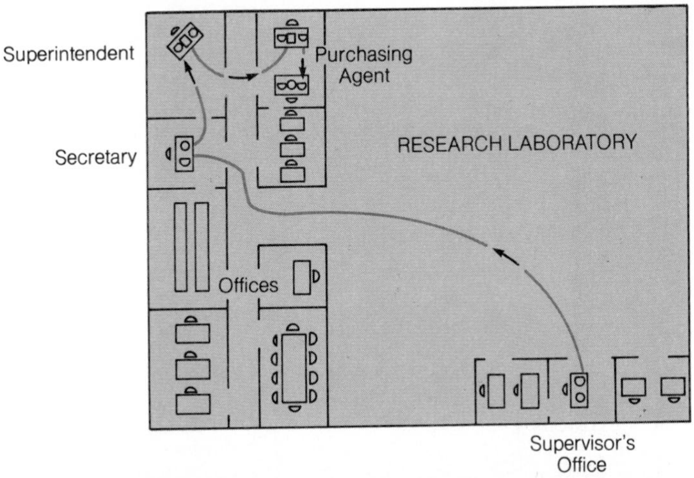

PROCESS CHART

Present Method [X]
Proposed Method [ ]

SUBJECT CHARTED Requisition for small tools

Chart begins at supervisor's desk and ends at typist's desk in purchasing department

DEPARTMENT Research laboratory

DATE ______

CHART BY J.C.H.

CHART NO. R 136

SHEET NO. 1 OF 1

DIST. IN FEET	TIME IN MINS.	CHART SYMBOLS	PROCESS DESCRIPTION
			Requisitions written by supervisor (one copy)
			On supervisor's desk (awaiting messenger)
65			By messenger to superintendent's secretary
			On secretary's desk (awaiting typing)
			Requisition typed (original requisition copied)
15			By secretary to superintendent
			On superintendent's desk (awaiting messenger)
			To purchasing department
			On purchasing agent's desk (awaiting approval)
20			Examined and approved
			On purchasing agent's desk (awaiting messenger)
			To typist's desk
			On typist's desk (awaiting typing of purchase order)
5			Purchase order typed
			On typist's desk (awaiting transfer to main office)
105		3 4 2 8	Total

* Requisition is written by supervisor, typed by secretary, approved by superintendent, and approved by purchasing agent; then a purchase order is prepared by a stenographer.

Source: Ralph M. Barnes, *Motion and Time Study* (New York: Wiley & Sons, 1968), pp. 76–79.

EXHIBIT 9.6

Common Notation in Process Charting

●	Operation. Something is actually being done. This may be work on a product, some support activity or anything that is directly productive in nature.
➡	Transportation. The subject of the study (product, service, or person) moves from one location to another.
■	Inspection. The subject is observed for quality and correctness.
◗	Delay. The subject of the study must wait before starting the next step in the process.
▼	Storage. The subject is stored, such as finished products in inventory or completed papers in a file. Frequently, a distinction is made between temporary storage and permanent storage by inserting a T or P in the triangle.

subject may be a product being manufactured, a service being created, or a person performing a sequence of activities. An example of a process chart (and flow diagram) for a clerical operation is shown in Exhibit 9.5. Common notation in process charting is given in Exhibit 9.6.

Worker at a fixed workplace

Many jobs require the worker to remain at a specified workstation. When the nature of the work is primarily manual (such as sorting, inspecting, making entries, or assembly operations), the focus of work design is on simplifying the work method and making the required operator motions as few and as easy as possible.

There are two basic ways to determine the best method when a method analyst studies a single worker performing an essentially manual task. The first is to search among the workers and find the one who performs the job best. That person's method is then accepted as the standard, and others are trained to perform it in the same way. This was basically F. W. Taylor's approach, though after determining the best method, he searched for "first-class men" to perform according to the method. (A "first-class man" possessed the natural ability to do much more productive work in a particular task than the average. Men who were not "first class" were transferred to other jobs.) The second way is to observe the performance of a number of workers, analyze in detail each step of their work, and pick out the superior features of each worker's performance. This results in a composite method that combines the best elements of the group studied. This was the procedure used by Frank Gilbreth, the "father of motion study," to determine the "one best way" to perform a work task.

Taylor observed actual performance to find the best method; Frank Gilbreth and his wife Lillian relied on movie film. Through "micromotion analysis"—observing the filmed work performance frame by frame—the Gilbreths studied work very closely and defined its basic elements, which were termed

EXHIBIT 9.7

Principles of Motion Economy

Using the human body the way it works best

1. The work should be arranged to provide a natural rhythm that can become automatic.
2. The symmetrical nature of the body should be considered:
   a. The motions of the arms should be simultaneous, beginning and completing their motions at the same time.
   b. Motions of the arms should be opposite and symmetrical.
3. The human body is an ultimate machine and its full capabilities should be employed:
   a. Neither hand should ever be idle.
   b. Work should be distributed to other parts of the body in line with their ability.
   c. The safe design limits of the body should be observed.
   d. The human should be employed at its highest use.
4. The arms and hands as weights are subject to the physical laws, and energy should be conserved:
   a. Momentum should work for the person and not against him or her.
   b. The smooth, continuous arc of the ballistic is more efficient.
   c. The distance of movements should be minimized.
   d. Tasks should be turned over to machines.
5. The tasks should be simplified:
   a. Eye contacts should be few and grouped together.
   b. Unnecessary actions, delays, and idle time should be eliminated.
   c. The degree of required precision and control should be reduced.
   d. The number of individual motions should be minimized along with the number of muscle groups involved.

Arranging the workplace to assist performance

1. There should be a definite place for all tools and materials.
2. Tools, materials, and controls should be located close to the point of use.
3. Tools, materials, and controls should be located to permit the best sequence and path of motions.
4. Mechanical devices can multiply human abilities.
5. Mechanical systems should be fitted to human use.

Using mechanical devices to reduce human effort

1. Vises and clamps can hold the work precisely where needed.
2. Guides can assist in positioning the work without close operator attention.
3. Controls and foot-operated devices can relieve the hands of work.
4. Mechanical devices can multiply human abilities.
5. Mechanical systems should be fitted to human use.

Source: Frank C. Barnes, "Principles of Motion Economy: Revisited, Reviewed, and Restored," *Proceedings of the Southern Management Association Annual Meeting*, Atlanta, 1983, p. 298.

therbligs ("Gilbreth" spelled backward, with the *t* and *h* transposed). Their study led to the rules or principles of motion economy listed in Exhibit 9.7.

Worker interaction with equipment

When a person and equipment operate together to perform the productive process, interest focuses on the efficient use of the person's time and equipment time. When the working time of the operator is less than the equipment run time, a worker-machine chart is a useful device in analysis. If the operator can operate several pieces of equipment, the problem is to find the most

EXHIBIT 9.8

Worker-Machine Chart for a Gourmet Coffee Store

	PERSON				MACHINE	
	Customer	Time in sec.	Clerk	Time in sec.	Coffee grinder	Time in sec.
1.	Ask grocer for 1 pound of coffee (brand and grind)	5	Listen to order	5	Idle	5
2.	Wait	15	Get coffee and put in machine, set grind and start grinder	15	Idle	15
3.	Wait	21	Idle while machine grinds	21	Grind coffee	21
4.	Wait	12	Stop grinder, place coffee in package and close it	12	Idle	12
5.	Receive coffee from grocer, pay grocer, and receive change	17	Give coffee to customer, wait for customer to pay for coffee, receive money, and make change	17	Idle	17

Time in seconds: 0, 10, 20, 30, 40, 50, 60, 70

Summary

	Customer	Clerk	Coffee grinder
Idle time	48 sec.	21 sec.	49 sec.
Working time	22	49	21
Total cycle time	70	70	70
Utilization in percent	Customer utilization = $\frac{22}{70} = 31\%$	Clerk utilization = $\frac{49}{70} = 70\%$	Machine utilization = $\frac{21}{70} = 30\%$

The customer, the clerk, and the coffee grinder (machine) are involved in this operation. It required 1 minute and 10 seconds for the customer to purchase a pound of coffee in this particular store. During this time the customer spent 22 seconds, or 31 percent of the time, giving the clerk his order, receiving the ground coffee, and paying the clerk for it. He was idle during the remaining 69 percent of the time. The clerk worked 49 seconds, or 70 percent of the time, and was idle 21 seconds, or 30 percent of the time. The coffee grinder was in operation 21 seconds, or 30 percent of the time, and was idle 70 percent of the time.

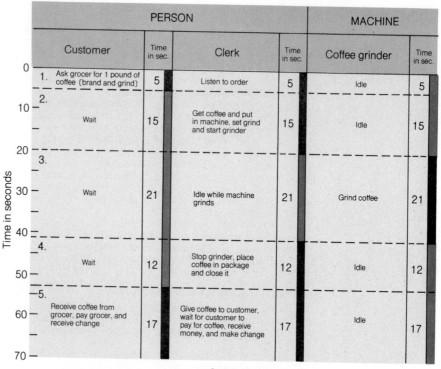

economical combination of operator and equipment: when the combined cost of the idle time of a particular combination of equipment and the idle time for the worker is at a minimum.

Worker-machine charts are always drawn to scale, the scale being time as measured by length. Exhibit 9.8 gives an example of a worker-machine chart in a service setting. The question here is, Whose "use" is most important?

Workers interacting with other workers

A great amount of our productive output in manufacturing and service industries is performed by teams. The degree of interaction may be as simple as one operator handing a part to another, or as complex as a cardiovascular surgical team of doctors, nurses, anesthesiologist, operator of an artificial heart machine, X-ray technician, standby blood donors, and pathologist (and perhaps a minister to pray a little).

An activity chart is useful in plotting the activities of several individuals on a time scale similar to that of the worker-machine chart. A process chart can trace the interaction of a number of workers with machines of a specified operating cycle, to find the best combination of workers and machines. An activity chart is also valuable in developing a standardized procedure for a specific task. Exhibit 9.9, for example, shows an activity chart for a hospital's emergency routine in performing a tracheotomy (opening a patient's throat surgically to allow him or her to breathe), where detailed activity analysis is of major importance and any delay could be fatal.

Work Measurement

"*When you can measure it, you know something about it.*"—Lord Kelvin.

The efficient operation of any firm is predicated on some knowledge of how long it takes to make a product or perform a service. We can then begin to estimate costs, quote prices, determine budgets, evaluate performance, and develop employee incentive payment programs. Without performance time,

- Costs could not be estimated, and therefore, prices could not be quoted.
- Budgets could not be made.
- Evaluation of performance would not be possible since there would be no basis for comparison.
- Incentive plans and merit increases become unpredictable.

There are four accepted ways to derive the time required in the performance of a human task:

1. Time study (stopwatch and micromotion analysis).
2. Elemental standard time data.
3. Predetermined motion-time data.
4. Work sampling.

EXHIBIT 9.9 **Activity Chart of Emergency Tracheotomy**

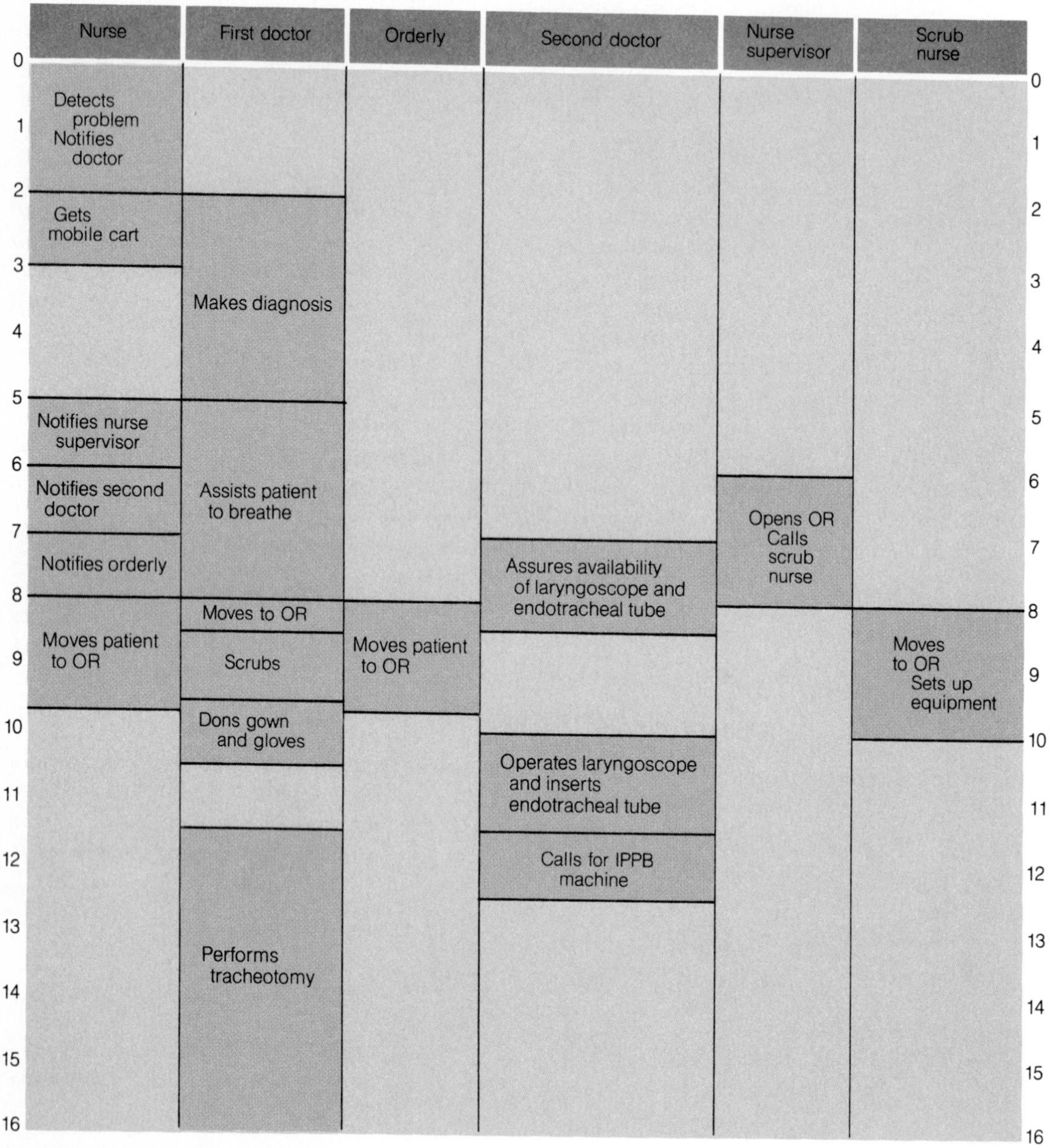

Source: Data taken from Harold E. Smalley and John Freeman, *Hospital Industrial Engineering* (New York: Reinhold, 1966), p. 409.

EXHIBIT 9.10

Types of Work Measurement Applied to Differing Tasks

Type of Work	Major Methods of Determining Task Time
Very short interval, highly repetitive	Film analysis
Short interval, repetitive	Stopwatch time study: predetermined motion-time data
Task in conjunction with machinery or other fixed-processing-time equipment	Elemental data
Infrequent work or work of a long cycle time	Work sampling

Each method has some advantages over the others and has particular areas of application. Exhibit 9.10 lists these methods and relates them to a general class of jobs.

Time study

Time study was formalized by Frederick W. Taylor in 1881. Since Taylor's time, volumes have been written on time study, and the technique is undoubtedly the most widely used of the quantitatively based methods of work measurement.

A time study is generally made with a stopwatch, although in some instances film analysis or a timed recording device may be used. Procedurally, the job or task to be studied is separated into measurable parts or elements, and each element is timed individually. After a number of repetitions, the collected times are averaged. (The standard deviation may be computed to give a measure of variance in the performance times.) The averaged times for each element are added, and the result is the performance time for the operator. However, to make this operator's time usable for all workers, a measure of speed or *performance rating* must be included to "normalize" the job. The application of a rating factor gives what is called *normal time*. For example, if an operator performs a task in 2 minutes and the time study analyst estimates him or her to be performing about 20 percent faster than normal, the normal time would be computed as 2 minutes + 0.20(2 minutes), or 2.4 minutes. In equation form,

$$\text{Normal time} = \text{Observed performance time per unit} \times \text{Performance rating}$$

In the above example, denoting normal time by NT,

$$NT = 2(1.2) = 2.4 \text{ minutes}$$

When an operator is observed for a period of time, the number of units produced during this time, along with the performance rating, gives the normal time as

$$NT = \frac{\text{Time worked}}{\text{Number of units produced}} \times \text{Performance rating}$$

Standard time is derived by adding to normal time allowances for personal needs (washroom and coffee breaks, and so forth), unavoidable work delays (equipment breakdown, lack of materials, and so forth), and worker fatigue (physical or mental).

$$\text{Standard time} = \text{Normal time} + (\text{Allowances} \times \text{Normal time})$$

or

$$ST = NT(1 + \text{Allowances})$$

Using the data from our normal time example above, if the allowances for personal needs, delays, and fatigue total 15 percent, then

$$ST = 2.4(1 + 0.15) = 2.76 \text{ minutes}$$

In an eight-hour day, the worker would produce 174 units. The day would consist of 408 minutes working and 72 minutes not working.

Before a time study is made, the task is broken down into elements or parts. Some general rules for this breakdown are:

1. Define each work element short in duration but long enough so each can be timed with a stopwatch and the time can be written down.
2. If the operator works with equipment that runs separately—the operator performs a task and the equipment runs independently—separate the actions of the operator and of the equipment into different elements.
3. Define any delays by the operator or equipment into separate elements.

Exhibit 9.11 shows a time study of 10 cycles of a four-element job. For each element, there is a space for the watch reading in 100ths of a minute (R) and each element subtracted time (T). The value for T is obtained after the time-study observations are completed, since in this case the watch is read continuously.[6] PR denotes the performance rating and $\bar{T}$ the average time for each element. The standard time, calculated according to equation (1), is given at the bottom of the time study sheet.

How many observations are enough? Time study is really a sampling process, that is, we take relatively few observations as being representative of many subsequent cycles to be performed by the worker. Based on a great deal of analysis and experience, Niebel's table shown in Exhibit 9.12 indicates that "enough" is a function of cycle length and number of repetitions of the job over a one-year planning period.

Elemental standard-time data

Elemental standard-time data is obtained from previous time studies, and is codified in tables in a handbook or computer data bank. Such data are used to

[6] Not surprisingly, this is called the *continuous method* of timing. When the watch is reset after each element is recorded, it is called the *snapback method*.

EXHIBIT 9.11

Time-Study Observation Sheet

Time Study Observation Sheet			
Identification of operation	*Assemble 24" × 36" chart blanks*		Date *10/9*
Began timing: *9:26* Ended timing: *9:32*	Operator *109*	Approval *BGR*	Observer *LDT*

	Element description and breakpoint		Cycles 1 (*0.00*)	2	3	4	5	6	7	8	9	10	Summary ΣT	$\bar{T}$	PR	NT
1	*Fold over end (grasp stapler)*	T	.07	.07	.05	.07	.09	.06	.05	.08	.08	.06	.68	.07	.90	.06
		R	.07	.61	.14	.67	.24	.78	.33	.88	.47	.09				
2	*Staple five times (drop stapler)*	T	.16	.14	.14	.15	.16	.16	.14	.17	.14	.15	1.51	.15	1.05	.16
		R	.23	.75	.28	.82	.40	.94	.47	.05	.61	.24				
3	*Bend and insert wire (drop pliers)*	T	.22	.25	.22	.25	.23	.23	.21	.26	.25	.24	2.36	.24	1.00	.24
		R	.45	.00	.50	.07	.63	.17	.68	.31	.86	.48				
4	*Dispose of finished chart (touch next sheet)*	T	.09	.09	.10	.08	.09	.11	.12	.08	.17	.08	1.01	.10	.90	.09
		R	.54	.09	.60	.15	.72	.28	.80	.39	.03	.56				
5		T														*0.55 normal minute for cycle*
		R														
6		T														
10		T														
		R														

Normal cycle time *0.55* + Allowance *(0.55 × 0.143) or 0.08* = Std. time *0.63 min./pc.*

Source: E. V. Krick, *Methods Engineering* (New York: John Wiley & Sons, 1962), p. 246.

develop time standards for new jobs or to make time adjustments to reflect changes in existing jobs. They are more correctly viewed as *normal-time data,* since tabled values have been modified by an average performance rating, and allowances must be added to obtain a standard time.

Calculating a **time standard** for a new job using elemental standard-time data tables entails breaking down the new job into its basic elements; matching these elements to the time for similar elements in the table; adjusting element times for special characteristics of the new job (in metal cutting, for instance, this is often done by a formula that modifies the time required as a function of

EXHIBIT 9.12

Guide to Number of Cycles to Be Observed in a Time Study

When Time per Cycle Is More than	MINIMUM NUMBER OF CYCLES OF STUDY (ACTIVITY) Over 10,000 per Year	1,000–10,000	Under 1,000
8 hours	2	1	1
3	3	2	1
2	4	2	1
1	5	3	2
48 minutes	6	3	2
30	8	4	3
20	10	5	4
12	12	6	5
8	15	8	6
5	20	10	8
3	25	12	10
2	30	15	12
1	40	20	15
.7	50	25	20
.5	60	30	25
.3	80	40	30
.2	100	50	40
.1	120	60	50
Under .1	140	80	60

Source: Benjamin W. Niebel, *Motion and Time Study*, 7th ed. (Homewood, Ill.: Richard D. Irwin, Inc., 1982), p. 337.

the type of metal, size of the cutting tool, depth of the cut, and so forth); and adding element times together.

The obvious benefit of elemental standard data is cost savings: it eliminates the need for a new time study for each new job. This saves staff time and avoids disruption of the work force.

Predetermined motion-time data systems

Predetermined motion-time data systems (PMTS) also use existing tabled data to artificially create a time standard. These systems differ from elemental standard data systems in several respects. First, they provide times for basic motions rather than job-specific work elements. Second, they are generic to a wide range of manual work; elemental standard data is company or industry specific. Finally, since they typically require the use of many basic motions to describe even a short-duration job, they require far more analyst time to develop a standard. For this reason, the systems discussed below are being simplified as much as possible to facilitate their use, and new, faster versions with computer support are being marketed.

The three predetermined motion-time data systems that are most often used are *methods time measurement* (MTM), *basic motion time study* (BMT), and *work factor*. Each was developed in the laboratory, and all are proprietary. MTM

EXHIBIT 9.13

MTM Predetermined Motion-Time Data for the Hand and Arm Movement "Reach" (1 TMU = .0006 minutes)

REACH—R

Distance Moved Inches	Time TMU				Hand in motion		CASE AND DESCRIPTION
	A	B	C or D	E	A	B	
¾ or less	2.0	2.0	2.0	2.0	1.6	1.6	A Reach to object in fixed location, or to object in other hand or on which other hand rests.
1	2.5	2.5	3.6	2.4	2.3	2.3	
2	4.0	4.0	5.9	3.8	3.5	2.7	
3	5.3	5.3	7.3	5.3	4.5	3.6	
4	6.1	6.4	8.4	6.8	4.9	4.3	B Reach to single object in location which may vary slightly from cycle to cycle.
5	6.5	7.8	9.4	7.4	5.3	5.0	
6	7.0	8.6	10.1	8.0	5.7	5.7	
7	7.4	9.3	10.8	8.7	6.1	6.5	
8	7.9	10.1	11.5	9.3	6.5	7.2	C Reach to object jumbled with other objects in a group so that search and select occur.
9	8.3	10.8	12.2	9.9	6.9	7.9	
10	8.7	11.5	12.9	10.5	7.3	8.6	
12	9.6	12.9	14.2	11.8	8.1	10.1	
14	10.5	14.4	15.6	13.0	8.9	11.5	D Reach to a very small object or where accurate grasp is required.
16	11.4	15.8	17.0	14.2	9.7	12.9	
18	12.3	17.2	18.4	15.5	10.5	14.4	
20	13.1	18.6	19.8	16.7	11.3	15.8	
22	14.0	20.1	21.2	18.0	12.1	17.3	
24	14.9	21.5	22.5	19.2	12.9	18.8	E Reach to indefinite location to get hand in position for body balance or next motion or out of way.
26	15.8	22.9	23.9	20.4	13.7	20.2	
28	16.7	24.4	25.3	21.7	14.5	21.7	
30	17.5	25.8	26.7	22.9	15.3	23.2	

Source: Copyright by the MTM Association for Standards and Research. Reprinted with permission from the MTM Association, 9–10 Saddle River Road, Fair Lawn, New Jersey 07410.

even has its own journal, user certification program, and an association of MTM organizations (the International MTM Directorate).

Exhibit 9.13 presents a sample MTM table. This table describes the movement designated as Reach, stipulating the different times allowed for varying conditions. (Other standard movement categories in the basic version of the system, MTM-1, are Grasp, Move, Position, and Release.) Note that times are measured in *time measurement units* (TMUs) of .0006 minutes. To derive an MTM standard time for a job, you would list all the movements that go into it, find the appropriate TMU value for each, sum the times, and add allowances.

PMTS have been used successfully for more than 40 years. Among their advantages are:

1. They enable development of standards before the job is done.
2. They have been tested extensively in the laboratory and the field.
3. They include performance rating in the times given in the tables, so the user need not calculate them.
4. They can be used to audit time studies for accuracy.
5. They are accepted as part of many union contracts.

Work sampling

As the name suggests, work sampling involves observing a portion or sample of the work activity. Then, based on the findings in this sample, some statements can be made about the activity. For example, if we were to observe a fire department rescue squad 100 random times during the day and found it was involved in a rescue mission for 30 of the 100 times (en route, on site, or returning from a call), we would estimate that the rescue squad spends 30 percent of its time directly on rescue mission calls. (The time it takes to make an observation depends on what is being observed. Many times only a glance is needed to determine the activity, and the majority of studies require only several seconds' observation.)

Observing an activity even 100 times may not, however, provide the accuracy desired in the estimate. To refine this estimate, three main issues must be decided (these points will be discussed later in this section, along with an example):

1. What level of statistical confidence is desired in the results?
2. How many observations are necessary?
3. Precisely when should the observations be made?

The three primary applications for work sampling are:

1. *Ratio delay:* to determine the activity-time percentage for personnel or equipment. For example, management may be interested in the amount of time a machine is running or idle.
2. *Performance measurement:* to develop a performance index for workers. When the amount of work time is related to the quantity of output, a measure of performance is developed. This is useful for periodic performance evaluation.
3. *Time standards:* to obtain the standard time for a task. When work sampling is used for this purpose, however, the observer must be experienced since he or she must attach a performance rating to the observations.

The number of observations required in a work sampling study can be fairly large, ranging from several hundred to several thousand, depending on the activity and the desired degree of accuracy. Although the number can be computed from formulas, the easiest way is to refer to a table such as Exhibit 9.14, which gives the number of observations needed for a 95 percent confi-

EXHIBIT 9.14 **Determining Number of Observations Required for a Given Absolute Error at Various Values of *p*, with 95 Percent Confidence Level**

Percentage of Total Time Occupied by Activity or Delay, *p*	ABSOLUTE ERROR					
	±1.0%	±1.5%	±2.0%	±2.5%	±3.0%	±3.5%
1 or 99	396	176	99	63	44	32
2 or 98	784	348	196	125	87	64
3 or 97	1,164	517	291	186	129	95
4 or 96	1,536	683	384	246	171	125
5 or 95	1,900	844	475	304	211	155
6 or 94	2,256	1003	564	361	251	184
7 or 93	2,604	1157	651	417	289	213
8 or 92	2,944	1308	736	471	327	240
9 or 91	3,276	1456	819	524	364	267
10 or 90	3,600	1600	900	576	400	294
11 or 89	3,916	1740	979	627	435	320
12 or 88	4,224	1877	1056	676	469	344
13 or 87	4,524	2011	1131	724	503	369
14 or 86	4,816	2140	1204	771	535	393
15 or 85	5,100	2267	1275	816	567	416
16 or 84	5,376	2389	1344	860	597	439
17 or 83	5,644	2508	1411	903	627	461
18 or 82	5,904	2624	1476	945	656	482
19 or 81	6,156	2736	1539	985	684	502
20 or 80	6,400	2844	1600	1024	711	522
21 or 79	6,636	2949	1659	1062	737	542
22 or 78	6,864	3050	1716	1098	763	560
23 or 77	7,084	3148	1771	1133	787	578
24 or 76	7,296	3243	1824	1167	811	596
25 or 75	7,500	3333	1875	1200	833	612
26 or 74	7,696	3420	1924	1231	855	628
27 or 73	7,884	3504	1971	1261	876	644
28 or 72	8,064	3584	2016	1290	896	658
29 or 71	8,236	3660	2059	1318	915	672
30 or 70	8,400	3733	2100	1344	933	686
31 or 69	8,556	3803	2139	1369	951	698
32 or 68	8,704	3868	2176	1393	967	710
33 or 67	8,844	3931	2211	1415	983	722
34 or 66	8,976	3989	2244	1436	997	733
35 or 65	9,100	4044	2275	1456	1011	743
36 or 64	9,216	4096	2304	1475	1024	753
37 or 63	9,324	4144	2331	1492	1036	761
38 or 62	9,424	4188	2356	1508	1047	769
39 or 61	9,516	4229	2379	1523	1057	777
40 or 60	9,600	4266	2400	1536	1067	784
41 or 59	9,676	4300	2419	1548	1075	790
42 or 58	9,744	4330	2436	1559	1083	795
43 or 57	9,804	4357	2451	1569	1089	800
44 or 56	9,856	4380	2464	1577	1095	804
45 or 55	9,900	4400	2475	1584	1099	808
46 or 54	9,936	4416	2484	1590	1104	811
47 or 53	9,964	4428	2491	1594	1107	813
48 or 52	9,984	4437	2496	1597	1109	815
49 or 51	9,996	4442	2499	1599	1110	816
50	10,000	4444	2500	1600	1111	816

Note: Number of observations is obtained from the formula $E = Z\sqrt{\frac{p(1-p)}{N}}$; the required sample ($N$) is $N = \frac{Z^2 p(1-p)}{E^2}$

where E = Absolute error

p = Percentage occurrence of activity or delay being measured

N = Number of random observations (sample size)

Z = Number of standard deviations to give desired confidence level (e.g., for 90 percent confidence, $Z = 1.65$; 95 percent, $Z = 1.96$; 99 percent, $Z = 2.23$). In this table $Z = 2$.

dence level in terms of absolute error. Absolute error is the actual range of the observations. For example, if a clerk is idle 10 percent of the time and the designer of the study is satisfied with a 2.5 percent range (meaning that the true percentage lies within 7.5 and 12.5 percent), the number of observations required for the work sampling study is 576. A 2 percent error (or an interval of 8 to 12 percent) would require 900 observations.

The steps involved in making a work sampling study are:

1. Identify the specific activity or activities that are the main purpose for the study. For example, to determine the percentage of time equipment is working, idle, or under repair.
2. Estimate the proportion of time of the activity of interest to the total time (e.g., that the equipment is working 80 percent of the time). These estimates can be made from the analyst's knowledge, past data, reliable guesses from others, or a pilot work-sampling study.
3. State the desired accuracy in the study results.
4. Determine the specific times when each observation is to be made.
5. At two or three intervals during the study period, recompute the required sample size by using the data collected thus far. Adjust the number of observations if appropriate.

The number of observations to be taken in a work sampling study is usually divided equally over the study period. Thus, if 500 observations are to be made over a 10-day period, the observations are usually scheduled at 500/10, or 50 per day. Each day's observations are then assigned a specific time by using a random number table.

Work sampling applied to nursing. There has been a long-standing argument that a large amount of nurses' hospital time is spent on nonnursing activities. This, the argument goes, creates an apparent shortage of well-trained nursing personnel, a significant waste of talent, a corresponding loss of efficiency, and increased hospital costs, since nurses' wages are the highest single cost in the operation of a hospital. Further, pressure is growing for hospitals and hospital administrators to contain costs. With that in mind, let us use work sampling to test the hypothesis that a large portion of nurses' time is spent on nonnursing duties.

Assume at the outset that we have made a list of all the activities that are part of nursing and will make our observations in only two categories: nursing and nonnursing activities.[7] Assume that we (or the nursing supervisor) estimate that nurses spend 60 percent of their time in nursing activities. Assume that we would like to be 95 percent confident that the findings of our study will be within the absolute error range of plus or minus 3 percent; that is, that if our

[7] Actually, there is much debate on what constitutes nursing activity. For instance, is talking to a patient a nursing duty?

EXHIBIT 9.15

Assignment of Numbers to Corresponding Minutes

Time	Assigned Numbers
7:00– 7:59 A.M.	100–159
8:00– 8:59 A.M.	200–259
9:00– 9:59 A.M.	300–359
10:00–10:59 A.M.	400–459
11:00–11:59 A.M.	500–559
12:00–12:59 P.M.	600–659
1:00– 1:59 P.M.	700–759
2:00– 2:59 P.M.	800–859

study shows nurses spend 60 percent of their time on nursing duties, we are 95 percent confident that the true percentage lies between 57 and 63 percent. From Exhibit 9.14, we find that 1,067 observations are required for 60 percent activity time and ±3 percent error. If our study is to take place over 10 days, we will start with 107 observations per day.

To determine when each day's observations are to be made, we assign specific numbers to each minute and a random number table to set up a schedule. If the study extends over an eight-hour shift, we can assign numbers to correspond to each consecutive minute.[8] The list in Exhibit 9.15 shows the assignment of numbers to corresponding minutes. For simplicity, since each number corresponds to one minute, a three-number scheme is used, with the second and third number corresponding to the minute of the hour. A number of other schemes would also be appropriate.[9]

If we refer to a random number table and list three-digit numbers, we can assign each number to a time. The random numbers shown in Exhibit 9.16 demonstrate the procedure.

This procedure is followed to generate 107 observation times, and the times are rearranged chronologically for ease in planning. Rearranging the times determined in Exhibit 9.16 gives the total observations per day shown in Exhibit 9.17.

To be perfectly random in this study, we should also "randomize" the nurse we observe each time (the use of various nurses minimizes the effect of bias). In the study, our first observation is made at 7:13 A.M. for Nurse X. We walk into Nurse X's area and check a nursing or a nonnursing activity. Each observation need be only long enough to determine the class of activity—in most cases only a glance. At 8:04 A.M. we observe Nurse Y. We

[8] For this study, it is likely that the night shift (11:00 P.M. to 7:00 A.M.) would be run separately, since the nature of nighttime nursing duties is considerably different from daytime duties.

[9] If a number of studies are planned, a computer program may be used to generate a randomized schedule for the observation times.

EXHIBIT 9.16

Determination of Observation Times

Random Number	Corresponding Time from the Preceding List
669	Nonexistent
831	2:31 P.M.
555	11:55 A.M.
470	Nonexistent
113	7:13 A.M.
080	Nonexistent
520	11:20 A.M.
204	8:04 A.M.
732	1:32 P.M.
420	10:20 A.M.

EXHIBIT 9.17

Observation Schedule

Observation	Scheduled Time	Nursing Activity (✓)	Nonnursing Activity (✓)
1	7:13 A.M.		
2	8:04 A.M.		
3	10:20 A.M.		
4	11:20 A.M.		
5	11:55 A.M.		
6	1:32 P.M.		
7	2:31 P.M.		

continue in this way to the end of the day and the 107 observations. At the end of the second day (and 214 observations), we decide to check for the adequacy of our sample size.

Let's say we made 150 observations of nurses working and 64 of them not working, which gives 70.1 percent working. From Exhibit 9.14, this corresponds to 933 observations. Since we have already taken 214 observations, we need take only 719 over the next eight days, or 90 per day. We should make another similar check or two as the study progresses to make any more adjustments needed.

How do we interpret the results of the nursing study? Suppose we found that 66 percent of the time was in nursing activities. Another 12 to 15 percent is reasonable for coffee breaks and personal needs. This leaves approximately 20 percent unexplained by these two categories and warrants further investigation.

Setting time standards using work sampling. As mentioned earlier, work sampling can also be used to set time standards. To do this, the analyst must

EXHIBIT 9.18

Deriving a Time Standard Using Work Sampling

Information	Source of Data	Data for One Day
Total time expended by operator (working time and idle time)	Time cards	480 min.
Number of parts produced	Inspection Department	420 pieces
Working time in percent	Work sampling	85%
Idle time in percent	Work sampling	15%
Average performance index	Work sampling	110%
Total allowances	Company time-study manual	15%

$$\text{Standard time per piece} = \frac{\begin{pmatrix}\text{Total time}\\ \text{in minutes}\end{pmatrix} \times \begin{pmatrix}\text{Working time}\\ \text{proportion}\end{pmatrix} \times \begin{pmatrix}\text{Performance}\\ \text{rating}\end{pmatrix}}{\text{Total number of pieces produced}} \times (1 + \text{Allowances})$$

$$= \left(\frac{480 \times 0.85 \times 1.10}{420}\right) \times 1.15 = 1.23 \text{ minutes}$$

Source: R. M. Barnes, *Working Sampling,* 2nd ed. (New York: John Wiley & Sons, 1966), p. 81.

record the subject's performance rate (or index) along with working observations. The data required and the formula for calculating standard time are given in Exhibit 9.18.

Work sampling compared to time study. Work sampling offers several advantages:

1. Several work sampling studies may be conducted simultaneously by one observer.
2. The observer need not be a trained analyst unless the purpose of the study is to determine a time standard.
3. No timing devices are required.
4. Work of a long cycle time may be studied with fewer observer hours.
5. The duration of the study is longer, so that the effects of short-period variations are minimized.
6. The study may be temporarily delayed at any time with little effect.
7. Since work sampling needs only instantaneous observations (made over a longer period), the operator has less chance to influence the findings by changing his or her work method.

When the cycle time is short, time study rather than work sampling is more appropriate.

Financial Incentive Plans

The third piece of the job design equation is the paycheck. In this section we briefly review common methods for setting financial incentives.

Basic compensation systems. The main forms of basic compensation are hourly pay, straight salary, piece rate, and commissions. The first two are based on time spent on the job, with individual performance rewarded by an increase in the base rate. Piece-rate plans reward on the basis of direct daily output (a worker is paid $5 a unit and if he produces 10 units per day, he earns $50). Sometimes, a guaranteed base is included in a piece-rate plan; a worker would receive this base amount regardless of output, plus his piece-rate bonus. (For example, the worker's hourly base pay is $4, so this coupled with $50 piece-rate earnings would give him $82 for an eight-hour day.) Commissions may be thought of as sales-based piece rates, and are calculated in the same general way.

There are two broad categories of incentive plans: Individual or small group incentive plans; and organizationwide plans.

Individual or small group incentive plans. Individual and work-group plans traditionally have rewarded performance by using output (often defined by piece rates) and quality measures. Quality is accounted for by a quality adjustment factor, say percent of rework.[10] (For example: Incentive pay = Total output × [1 − Percent deduction for rework].) In recent years skill development has also been rewarded. Sometimes called *pay for knowledge,* this means a worker is compensated for learning new tasks. This is particularly important in job shops using group technology, and in banking, where supervisors' jobs require knowledge of new types of financial instruments and selling approaches.

Organizationwide plans. Profit sharing and gain sharing are the major types of organizationwide plans.

Profit sharing is simply distributing a percentage of corporate profits across the work force. In the United States, at least one third of all organizations have profit sharing. In Japan, most of the major companies give profit-based bonuses twice a year to all employees. Such bonuses may go as high as 50 percent of salaries in good years, to nothing in bad years.

Gain sharing also involves giving organizationwide bonuses, but differs from profit sharing in two important respects. First, it typically measures controllable costs or units of output, not profits, in calculating a bonus. Second, gain sharing is always combined with a participative approach to management. The original and best-known gainsharing plan is the Scanlon Plan (discussed below); others are Improshare and the Rucker Plan. In addition, many companies have their own custom-designed gain-sharing plans.

Scanlon Plan. In the late 1930s, the Lapointe Machine and Tool Company was on the verge of bankruptcy, but through the efforts of union president

---

[10] For a complete discussion of incentive plans including quality measures, see S. Globerson and R. Parsons, "Multi-factor Incentive Systems: Current Practices," *Operations Management Review* 3, no. 2, Winter 1985.

Joseph Scanlon and company management, a plan was devised to save the company by reducing labor costs. In essence, this plan started with "normal" labor cost within the firm. Workers as a group were rewarded for any reductions in labor cost below this base cost. The plan's success depended on committees of workers throughout the firm whose purpose was to search out areas for cost saving and to devise ways of improvement. There were many improvements, and the plan did, in fact, save the company.

Gain-sharing plans are now used by over a thousand firms in the United States and Europe, and are growing in popularity. One recent survey in the United States indicated that about 13 percent of all firms have them, and that over 70 percent were started after 1982.[11] Though originally established in small companies such as Lapointe, Lincoln Electric, and Herman Miller, gain sharing is now being installed by large firms such as TRW, General Electric, Motorola, and Firestone. These companies apply gain sharing to organizational units; Motorola, for example, has virtually all its plant employees covered by gain sharing. These plans are increasing because "they are more than just pay incentive plans; they are a participative approach to management and are often used as a way to install participative management.[12]

9.4 CONCLUSION

Automation of blue-collar factory work has become a fact of life in contemporary industry. But what about white-collar jobs in manufacturing? We will conclude this chapter with some provocative comments on this subject by Hal Mather, a leading production management consultant.[13]

> The . . . factory of the future has been 10 years in the future the past 30 years. It is coming true this time. The impact on people will be severe. No one's job will be left untouched. This is especially true for the white-collar worker.
>
> What skills will these people need? They will need to be multispecialists, able to view manufacturing as an interrelated process, not as a set of discrete activities or functions. Design engineers will have to become expert in process technology or be constrained by artificial intelligence routines so the design fits the factory's capabilities. Process plans and optimum factory schedules will be created automatically from the designer's inputs.
>
> Industrial engineers, manufacturing engineers, production and inventory control people and maybe accounting will merge into one position called *manufacturing technologist* or some such name. These people will need varied skills, such as statistics, mathematics, and data processing. Simulation and optimization will be routine tools of this new breed. This change all adds up to extensive training, but

---

[11] C. O'Dell, *People, Performance, and Pay* (Houston: American Productivity Center, 1987).

[12] E. E. Lawler III, "Paying for Organizational Performance," Report G 87–1 (92) Center for Effective Organizations, University of Southern California, 1987.

[13] Hal Mather, "Industrial Automation's Impact on the White Collar Worker," *Production and Inventory Management Review,* December 1987, p. 50.

not in one speciality, such as production and inventory control, but in far broader and more technical areas.

The people in the driver's seat tomorrow will be data processing, engineering of all disciplines, and mathematicians. Their jobs will be to support the only three important things for a manufacturer—design, production, and sales.

9.5 REVIEW AND DISCUSSION QUESTIONS

1. What does the chapter opening quotation imply to you about good management? Is there a loser in such free-wheeling plants?
2. A management consultant, Roy Walters, occasionally publishes a list of the "Ten Worst Jobs." On one such list, he included the followng (in no special order): highway toll collector, car watcher in a tunnel, pool typist, copy-machine operator, bogus-type setter (i.e., type that is not to be used), computer-tape librarian, housewife (not to be confused with mother), and automatic-elevator operator.
   a. With reference to the sociotechnical systems discussion, what characteristics of good job design are absent from each of these jobs?
   b. Do you have any job you might suggest for inclusion in Walters' list? What makes this job undesirable?
3. Why might the job enrichment and sociotechnical approaches to job design be looked at with skepticism by practicing managers and industrial engineers?
4. Comment on the statement, "Heavy manual work is really such a small component of modern American industry that further study of it is not really necessary."
5. Is there an inconsistency when a company requires precise time standards and encourages job enlargement?
6. Match the following techniques to their most appropriate application:

MTM	Purchase of a second washing machine
SIMO chart	Tracing your steps in getting a parking permit
Man-machine chart	Faculty office hours kept
Process chart	Development of a new keyboard for typewriter
Work sampling	Planning the assembly process for a new electronic device

7. You have timed your friend, Lefty, assembling widgets. His time averages 12 minutes for the two cycles you timed. He was working very hard, and you believe that none of the nine other operators doing the same job would beat his time. Are you ready to put this time forth as the standard for making an order of 5,000 widgets? If not, what else should yo do?
8. Comment on the following:
   a. "Work measurement is old hat. We have automated our office, and now we run every bill through our computer (after our 25 clerks have typed the data into our computer database)."
   b. "It's best that our workers don't know that they are being time studied. That way, they can't complain about us getting in the way when we set time standards."

c. "Once we get everybody on an incentive plan, then we will start our work measurement program."

d. "Rhythm is fine for singing and dancing, but it has no place on the shop floor."

9. The American Motors study team observed that the Japanese used techniques such as job rotation, making line workers responsible for quality control, minimal work classifications, and indirect employee participation in management. What gains could be made with this approach, contrasted with the job specialization approach? If this approach is applied in a specialized job environment, what changes would be necessary?

10. Organizationwide financial incentive plans cover all the workers. Some units or individuals may have contributed more to corporate profits than others. Does this detract from the effectiveness of the incentive plan system? How would your incentive scheme for a small software development firm compare to an established automobile manufacturing firm?

11. The conclusion of this chapter predicts that future manufacturing white-collar jobs will be less specialized. What do you see as the advantages and disadvantages of this projected shift away from job specialization?

9.6 PROBLEMS

*1. Felix Unger is a very organized person and wants to plan his day perfectly. To do this, he has his friend Oscar time him on his daily activities. Following are the results of Oscar timing Felix on polishing two pairs of black shoes using the snapback method of timing. What is the standard time for polishing two pair? (Assume a 5 percent allowance factor for Felix to get Oscar an ashtray for his cigar. Account for noncyclically recurring elements by dividing their observed times by the total number of cycles observed.)

	OBSERVED TIMES							
Element	1	2	3	4	ΣT	T	Performance Rating	NT
Get shoeshine kit	0.50						125%	
Polish shoes	0.94	0.85	0.80	0.81			110	
Put away kit				0.75			80	

*2. A total of 15 observations have been taken on a head baker for a school district. The numercial breakdown of her activities is:

Make Ready	Do	Clean Up	Idle
2	6	3	4

* Problems 1 and 2 are completely solved in Appendix D.

Based on this information, how many work sampling observations will be required to determine how much of the baker's time is spent in "doing"? Assume a 5 percent desired absolute accuracy and 95 percent confidence level.

3. As time-study analyst, you have observed that a worker has produced 40 parts in a one-hour period. From your experience you rate the worker as performing slightly faster than 100 percent—so you estimate performance as 110 percent. The company allows 15 percent for fatigue and delay.
   a. What is the normal time?
   b. What is the standard time?
   c. If a worker produces 300 units per day and has a base rate of $6 per hour, what would the day's wages be for this worker if payment was on a 100 percent wage incentive payment plan?
4. A time study was made of an existing job to develop new time standards. A worker was observed for a period of 45 minutes. During that period, 30 units were produced. The analyst rated the worker as performing at a 90 percent performance rate. Allowances in the firm for rest and personal time are 12 percent.
   a. What is the normal time for the task?
   b. What is the standard time for the task?
   c. If the worker produced 300 units in an eight-hour day, what would the day's pay be if the basic rate was $6 per hour and the premium payment system paid on a 100 percent basis?
5. A time-study analyst has obtained the following performance times by observing a worker over 15 operating cycles:

Performance Number	Time (seconds)
1	15
2	12
3	16
4	11
5	13
6	14
7	16
8	12
9	14
10	18
11	13
12	15
13	16
14	15
15	11

The worker was rated as performing at 115 percent. Allowances for personal time and fatigue in the company are 10 percent. The base rate for the worker is $5 per hour and the company operates on a 100 percent premium plan.
   a. What is the normal time?
   b. What is the standard time?

c. If the worker produced 2,500 in a day, what would the gross pay for the day be if the premium rate was 100 percent?

6. A work-sampling study is to be conducted over the next 30 consecutive days of an activity in the city fire department. Washing trucks, which is the subject of the study, is to be observed, and it is estimated that this occurs 10 percent of the time. A 3.5 percent accuracy with 95 percent confidence is acceptable. State specifically when observations should be made on one day. Use a 10-hour day from 8:00 A.M. to 6:00 P.M.

7. Suppose you want to set a time standard for the baker making her specialty, square donuts. A work-sampling study of her on "donut day" yielded the following results.

Time spent (working and idle)	320 minutes
Number of donuts produced	5,000
Working time	280 minutes
Performance rating	125%
Allowances	10%

What is the standard time per donut?

8. In an attempt to increase productivity and reduce costs, Rho Sigma Corporation is planning to install an incentive pay plan in its manufacturing plant.

In developing standards for one operation, time-study analysts observed a worker for a 30-minute period. During that time the worker completed 42 parts. The analysts rated the worker as producing at 130 percent. The base wage rate of the worker is $5 per hour. The firm has established 15 percent as a fatigue and personal time allowance.

a. What is the normal time for the task?
b. What is the standard time for the task?
c. If the worker produced 500 units during an eight-hour day, what wages would the worker have earned?

9. Since new regulations will greatly change the products and services offered by savings and loan associations, time studies must be performed on tellers and other personnel to determine the number and types of personnel that will be needed and incentive wage payment plans that might be installed.

As an example of the studies that the various tasks will undergo, consider the following problem and come up with the appropriate answers:

A hypothetical case was set up in which the teller (to be retitled later to *account adviser*) was required to examine a customer's portfolio and determine whether it was more beneficial for the customer to consolidate various CDs into a single issue currently offered, or to leave the portfolio unaltered. A time study was made of the teller, with the following findings:

Time of study	90 minutes
Number of portfolios examined	10 portfolios
Performance rating	130 percent
Rest for personal time	15 percent
Teller's proposed new pay rate	$12 per hour

a. What is the normal time for the teller to do a portfolio analysis for the CDs?
b. What is the standard time for the analysis?
c. If the S&L decides to pay the new tellers on a 100 percent premium payment plan, how much would a teller earn for a day in which he or she analyzed 50 customer portfolios?

10. A work-sampling study was made of an order clerk in order to estimate the percentage of the total week that she spent on each activity (results listed below). In addition to classifying the order clerk's activity, the observer rated her performance level whenever a sampling observation found her doing one of the productive activities. Since all order forms carried consecutive preprinted numbers, it was an easy matter to determine how many orders the order clerk wrote.

    Assume that such a check revealed that the order clerk under study wrote 583 orders during the week of the sampling study. Further assume that on the basis of the sampling study, it is determined that the averages of the performance ratings made of her working pace for the four productive activities are those given here. The company policy is to give a personal allowance of 10 percent of the normal time for all office work. From the results of the sampling study, the assumptions just given, and the fact that the order clerk worked a total of 40 hours during the week covered by the sampling study, determine the standard time (minutes per order) for the order-writing operation.

Activity	Actual Percentage of Week	Average Performance Rating (normal = 100%)
Order writing	52.5%	80%
Filing	12.5%	90%
Walking	15.0%	75%
Receiving instructions	9.6%	100%
Idle	10.4%	
	100.0%	

9.7 SELECTED BIBLIOGRAPHY

Barnes, Ralph M. *Motion and Time Study: Design and Measurement of Work.* 8th ed. New York: John Wiley & Sons, 1980.

Carlisle, Brian. "Job Design Implications for Operations Managers." *International Journal of Operations and Production Management* 3, no. 3 (1983), pp. 40–48.

Davis, L. E., and J. C. Taylor. *Design of Jobs.* 2nd ed. Santa Monica, Calif.: Goodyear Publishing, 1979.

Halpern, David; Stephen Osofsky; and Myron Peskin. "Taylorism Revised and Revisited for the 1990's." *Industrial Management,* January–February 1989, pp. 20–24.

Kirkman, Frank. "Who Cares About Job Design? Some Reflections on Its Present and Future." *International Journal of Operations and Production Management* 2, no. 1 (1981), pp. 3–13.

Konz, Stephan. *Work Design: Industrial Ergonomics*. 2nd ed. New York: John Wiley & Sons, 1983.

McCormick, E. J. *Human Factors in Engineering and Design*. 4th ed. New York: McGraw-Hill, 1976.

Niebel, Benjamin W. *Motion and Time Study*. 7th ed. Homewood, Ill.: Richard D. Irwin, 1982.

Niles, John L. "To Increase Productivity, Audit the Old Incentive Plan." *Industrial Engineering* (January 1980), pp. 20–23.

Chapter 10

Project Planning and Control

EPIGRAPH

Ninety-Ninety Rule of Project Schedules: the first 90 percent of the task takes 90 percent of the time, the last 10 percent takes the other 90 percent.

CHAPTER OUTLINE

KEY TERMS

Project

Program

Milestones

Work Breakdown Structure

Matrix Organizational Structure

PERT

CPM

Gantt Chart

Early Start/Late Start Schedules

Time-Cost Models

Project management plans, directs, and controls resources to achieve some end goal. Project management breaks up the total project into smaller activities and tasks and assures that the sequence is performed. The technique is very appropriate in managing today's rapidly changing business environment.

We seem to be on an exponential curve as to the pace in which technology, products, and markets are changing. Changes are occurring more and more rapidly virtually throughout all phases of production: from technology as the basis of design and manufacturing, through methods of operation and control of production, to delivery to the marketplace. Whereas two or three decades ago a product may have had a life cycle of several years, today's products in many areas (particularly in electronics) may have an existence of only several months.

If firms are to survive in such an environment where forecasting is very difficult and the time span from product design to full production just a matter of months, they must focus on the management of change. We believe that project management offers the best available technique to plan, operate, and control operations.

Project management techniques are also very appropriate for exactly the opposite type of environment: one where product lead time may be long. The

The Gary Larson cartoon from THE FAR SIDE is reprinted by permission of Chronicle Features, San Francisco, CA.

key factor in this case is that where frequency of production is low, each item produced tends to be a separate project. Examples are shipbuilding, airplane manufacture, and production of large turbines and generators.

What distinguishes project management from other techniques is that it is goal oriented. It focuses on achieving an objective, which can be almost anything that can be defined within the project management criteria—constructing a house, opening a new facility, controlling research and development effort, managing a campaign (whether it is someone running for a public office or raising funds), or introducing a new product.

There are two main thrusts in project management: one heavily emphasizes the organization and the behavior of *people,* and the other focuses on technology of the *method* (computing start and completion times, critical paths, etc.). In this chapter we lean far more toward describing the techniques of project management and leave the balance to a course on management and organizational behavior. We describe the work breakdown structure, review basic forms of traditional functional management, and contrast this to project management and matrix organization. Most of the chapter concentrates on project scheduling techniques, primarily CPM and PERT.

10.1 DEFINITION OF PROJECT MANAGEMENT

A project is simply a statement or proposal of something to be done. In a broader sense, a **project** could be defined as a series of related jobs usually directed toward some major output and requiring a significant period of time to perform. *Project management* can be defined as planning, directing, and controlling resources (people, equipment, material) to meet the technical, cost, and time constraints of the project.

While projects are often thought to be one-time occurrences, the fact is that many projects can be repeated or transferred to other settings or products. The result will be another project output. Spirer states that even though fast-food outlets go through the same acquisition, approval process, and completion of the food outlet, it is still best to consider these as projects.[1]

A project starts out as a *statement of work* (SOW). The SOW may be a written description of the objectives to be achieved, with a brief statement of the work to be done and a proposed schedule specifying the start and completion dates. It could also contain performance measures in terms of budget and completion steps (milestones) and the written reports to be supplied.

If the proposed work is a large endeavor, it is often referred to as a **program,** although the terms *project* and *program* are often used interchangeably. A program is the highest order of complexity, may take some years to complete, and may be made up of interrelated projects completed by many

[1] Herbert F. Spirer, "The Basic Principles of Project Management," *Operations Management Review* 1, no. 1 (Fall 1982), pp. 8–10, 49–52.

organizations. As examples, the development of a missile system would be best termed a *program*. The introduction of a new statewide medical health care system is a program.

As implied above a project is similar to a program, but is less complex and of shorter duration. A program may be to build a missile system; a project may be to develop the guidance control portion. In a health care system one project is to develop a bid proposal system for health care providers.

A *task* is a further subdivision of a project. It is usually not longer than several months in duration, and is performed by one group or organization.

A *subtask* may be used if needed, to further subdivide the project into more meaningful pieces.

A *work package* is a group of activities combined to be assignable to a single organizational unit. It still falls into the format of all project management—that the package provides a description of what is to be done, when it is to be started and completed, the budget, measures of performance, and specific events to be reached at points in time (called **milestones**). Typical milestones might be the completion of the design, the production of a prototype, the completed testing of the prototype, and the approval of a pilot run.

Work Breakdown Structure

The **work breakdown structure** (WBDS) is the heart of project management. This subdivision of the objective into smaller and smaller pieces clearly defines the system and contributes to its understanding and success. Conventional use shows the work breakdown structure decreasing in size from top to bottom and shows this level by indentation to the right, as follows:

```
Level
  1        Program
  2            Project
  3                Task
  4                    Subtask
  5                        Work Package
```

Exhibit 10.1 shows the work breakdown structure for a project. Note the ease in identifying activities through the level numbers. For example, telescope design (the third item down) is identified as 1.1.1 (the first item in level 1, the first item in level 2, and the first item in level 3). Data recording (the 13th item down) is 1.2.4.

The keys to a good work breakdown structure are:

- Allow the elements to be worked on independently.
- Make them manageable in size.
- Give authority to carry out the program.

EXHIBIT 10.1

Work Breakdown Structure, Large Optical Scanner Design

Level 1	2	3	4	5	
X					Optical simulator design
	X				Optical design
		X			Telescope design/fab
		X			Telescope/simulator optical interface
		X			Simulator zoom system design
		X			Ancillary simulator optical component specification
	X				System performance analysis
		X			Overall system firmware and software control
			X		Logic flow diagram generation and analysis
			X		Basic control algorithm design
		X			Far beam analyzer
		X			System inter- and intra-alignment method design
		X			Data recording and reduction requirements
	X				System integration
	X				Cost analysis
		X			Cost/system schedule analysis
		X			Cost/system performance analysis
	X				Management
		X			System design/engineering management
		X			Program management
	X				Long lead item procurement
		X			Large optics
		X			Target components
		X			Detectors

- Monitor and measure the program.
- Provide the required resources.

10.2 MATRIX ORGANIZATIONAL FORM

A **matrix organizational structure** retains some of the efficiencies of the functional grouping, while giving the project manager some input and control. Exhibit 10.2 shows a matrix organization; the responsibilities for functional performance are shown vertically, the responsibility for getting projects done is shown horizontally, and the various project managers use the services of the functional departments. If a project is large, the project manager may take personnel on temporary loan from the functional areas to work directly for him or her. If full-time help is not needed, then the project manager competes with other jobs in that department's schedule, as well as with other project managers to get work done within each functional area. Here is an area that truly requires the skills of a good project manager—the ability to get the work done while maintaining a good relationship with functional managers.

EXHIBIT 10.2 **Matrix Organization**

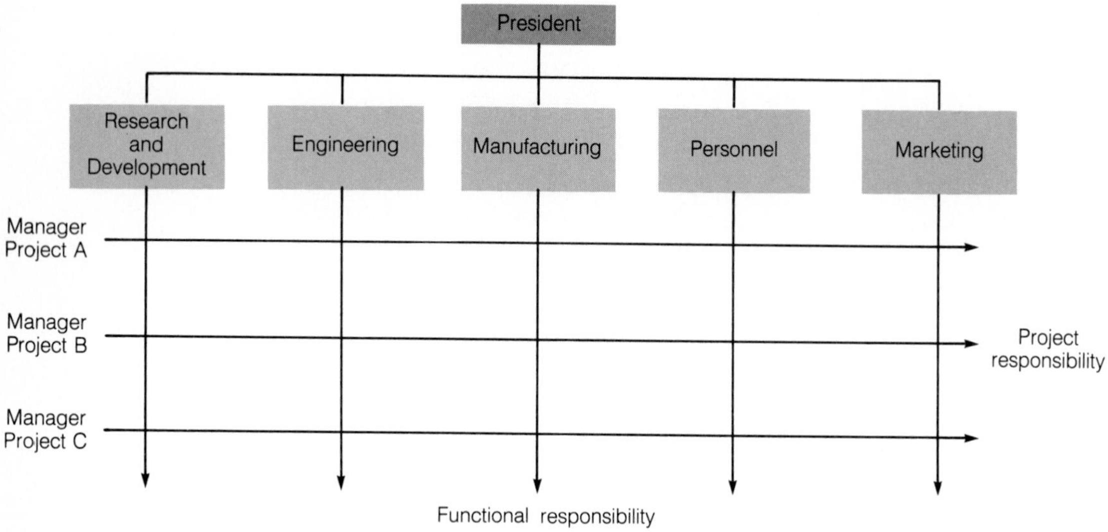

While matrix organization has its advantages, some writers have criticized its workability. Peters and Waterman describe it as a hopelessly complicated structure.[2] Sinclair also dislikes the matrix structure, claiming that if authority and responsibility are adequately delegated and accepted, the traditional organization would be the better choice.[3] His reason is that the project manager may be manager of several projects, as well as a person in a functional job working on several project teams as well.

Project

When a program is very large, it may be able to be organized along the traditional functional lines to take advantage of efficiency and control. This is especially true when people are working full time on the project over a long term. The project itself is the output, with the project manager at the top of a traditional hierarchy. Exhibit 10.3 shows a program with three projects, each with its own functional departmentation. While there may be loss in use of the

[2] T. J. Peters and R. H. Waterman, Jr., *In Search of Excellence* (New York: Harper & Row, 1982).

[3] John M. Sinclair, "Is the Matrix Really Necessary?" *Project Management Journal* 15, no. 1 (March 1984), pp. 49–52.

EXHIBIT 10.3 **Organization by Project**

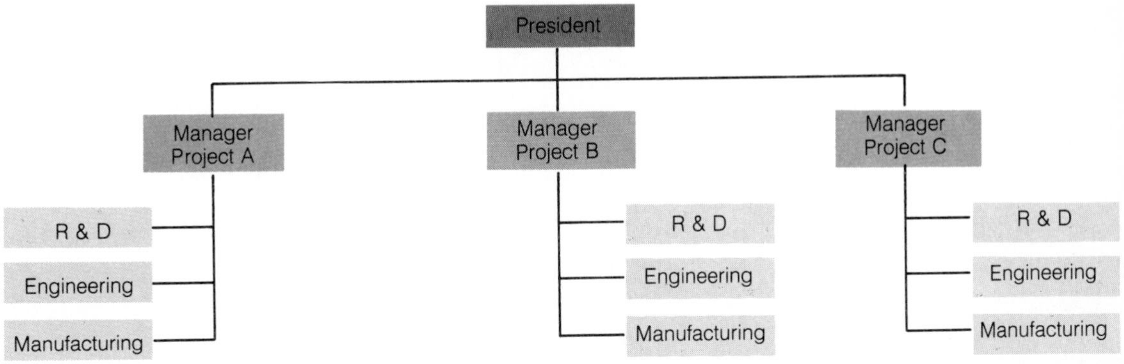

functional areas within each project because of duplication, the advantage of focus and control may well justify the structure.

10.3 CRITICAL PATH SCHEDULING

Critical path scheduling refers to a set of graphic techniques used in planning and controlling projects. In any given project, there are three factors of concern: time, cost, and resource availability. Critical path techniques have been developed to deal with each of these, individually and in combination. The remainder of this chapter focuses on time-based models, time-cost models, and limited-resource models.

PERT *(program evaluation and review technique)* and **CPM** *(critical path method),* the two best-known techniques, were both developed in the late 1950s. PERT was developed under the sponsorship of the U.S. Navy Special Projects Office in 1958 as a management tool for scheduling and controlling the Polaris missile project. CPM was developed in 1957 by J. E. Kelly of Remington-Rand and M. R. Walker of Du Pont to aid in scheduling maintenance shutdowns of chemical processing plants. A number of variants have since been devised, which, though little different in basic concept, have raised the invention of acronyms almost to an art form. Exhibit 10.4 shows the origin of network techniques and the directions they are growing.[4]

Critical path scheduling techniques display a project in graphic form and relate its component tasks in a way that focuses attention on those crucial to

[4] Jerome D. Wiest, "Gene Splicing PERT and CPM: The Engineering of Project Network Models," *Conference Proceedings of the Institute of Industrial Engineers,* 1982, pp. 225–28.

EXHIBIT 10.4 **PERT/CPM Family**

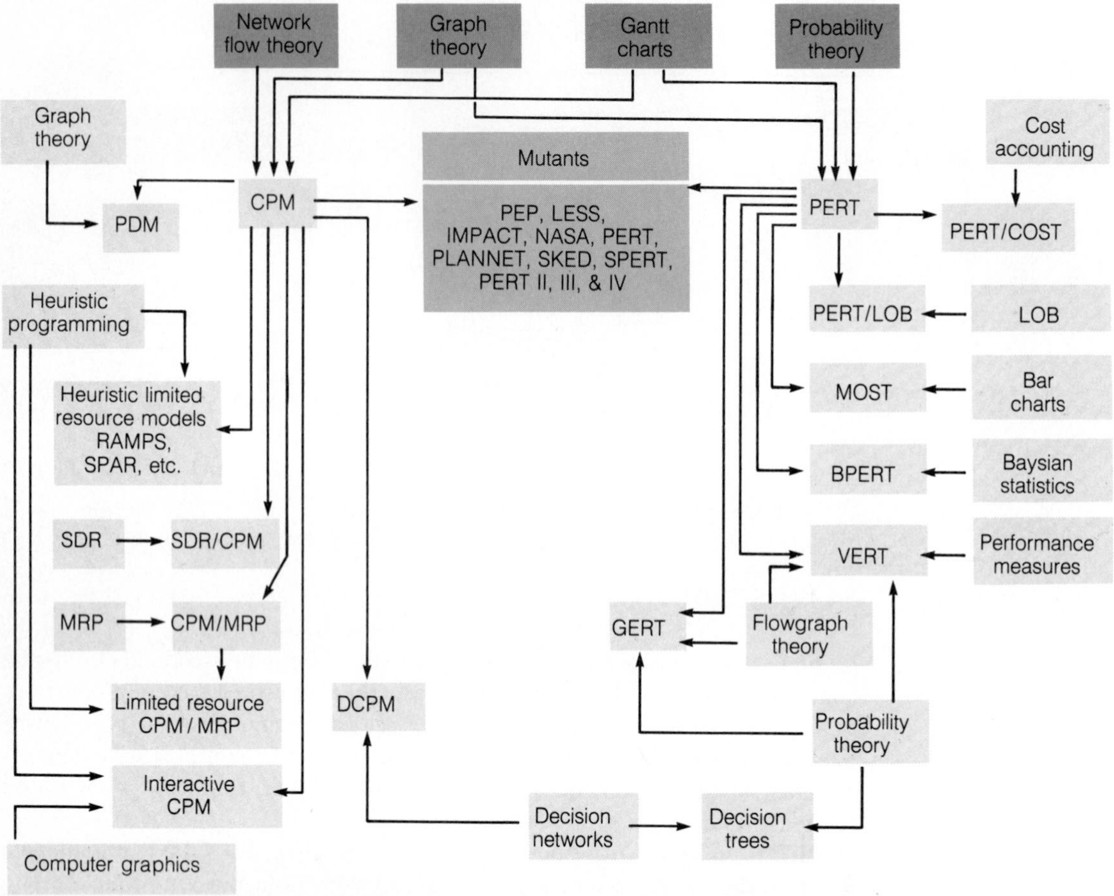

Source: Reprinted from Jerome D. Wiest, "Gene Splicing PERT and CPM: The Engineering of Project Network Models," *Conference Proceedings of the Institute of Industrial Engineers*, 1982, p. 226. Copyright Institute of Industrial Engineers, 25 Technology Park/Atlanta, Norcross, GA.

the project's completion. For critical path scheduling techniques to be most applicable, a project must have the following characteristics:

1. It must have well-defined jobs or tasks whose completion marks the end of the project.
2. The jobs or tasks are independent; they may be started, stopped, and conducted separately within a given sequence.
3. The jobs or tasks are ordered; they must follow each other in a given sequence.

Construction, aerospace, and shipbuilding industries commonly meet these criteria, and critical path techniques find wide application within them. We previously noted also, that the applications of project management and critical path techniques are becoming much more common within firms in rapidly changing industries.

10.4 TIME-ORIENTED TECHNIQUES

The basic forms of PERT and CPM focus on finding the longest time-consuming path through a network of tasks as a basis for planning and controlling a project. As you will see, there are some differences in the way the networks of the two techniques are structured and in their terminologies. However, the basic difference lies in the fact that PERT permits explicit treatment of probability in its time estimates whereas CPM does not. This distinction reflects PERT's origin in scheduling advanced development projects that are characterized by uncertainty and CPM's origin in the scheduling of the fairly routine activity of plant maintenance.

In a sense, both techniques owe their development to their widely used predecessor, the **Gantt chart.** While the Gantt chart is able to relate activities to time in a usable fashion for very small projects, the interrelationship of activities, when displayed in this form, becomes extremely difficult to visualize and to work with for projects greater than 25 or 30 activities. Moreover, the Gantt chart provides no direct procedure for ascertaining the critical path, which, despite its theoretical shortcomings, is of great practical value.

PERT

The following steps are required in developing and solving a PERT network.

1. *Identify each activity to be done in the project.* Assuming that the PERT analyst has an understanding of the technical aspects of the program, the output from this step is simply a listing of activities. While it is important that all activities required to complete the project are included, care should be taken to ensure that they are presented at a constant level of detail. For example, in building a house, an activity such as "nail down front step" would not be shown on the same PERT chart as "lay foundation." In network terminology, they are at different *levels* of *indenture,* and such a mixture of major and minor activities would be inappropriate.

2. *Determine the sequence of activities and construct a network reflecting the precedence relationships.* This is a valuable step, even if a complete PERT analysis is not performed, since it forces the analyst to consider the interrelationships of activities and present them in visual form. PERT networking follows a structure of *activity on arrow, event on node;* that is, arrows denote activities and nodes denote events. Activities consume time and resources, and

EXHIBIT 10.5

PERT Network Showing Activities and Events

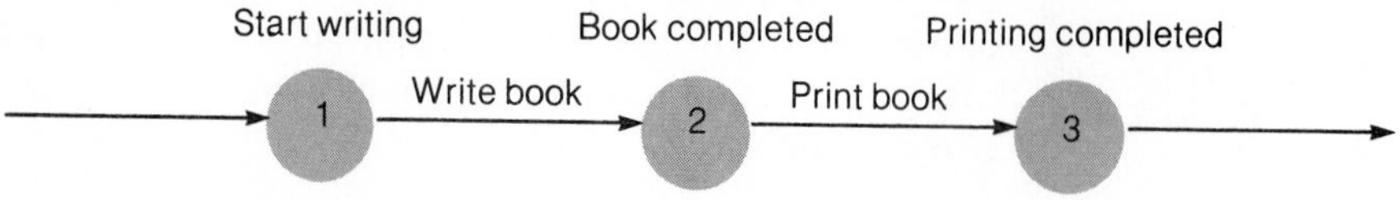

events mark their start or completion. Thus, "write book" would be an activity and "book completed" would be an event.

In the network segment illustrated in Exhibit 10.5, we have specified three events and two activities, although each event node signifies two events: the end of one event and the beginning of another. That is, Event 2 marks not only the completion of the book but the start of printing the book. Event 3 signifies the completion of printing, and perhaps the start of the distribution, and so on.

When constructing a network, take care to ensure that the activities and events are in the proper order and that the logic of their relationships is maintained. For example, it would be illogical to have a situation where Event A precedes Event B, B precedes C, and C precedes A. Also, in many projects, problems arise in showing the precise form of dependencies, and the networking device termed a *dummy activity* must be employed. Dummy activities consume no resources and are typically depicted as thin arrows. A summary of some of the situations in which dummies are used is provided in Exhibit 10.6.

3. *Ascertain time estimates for each activity.* The PERT algorithm requires that three estimates be obtained for each activity.

a = Optimistic time: the minimum reasonable period of time in which the activity can be completed. (There is only a small probability, typically assumed to be 1 percent, that the activity can be completed in a shorter period of time.)

m = Most likely time: the best guess of the time required. (This would be the only time estimate submitted if one is using CPM.) Since m would be the time thought most likely to appear, it is also the mode of the beta distribution discussed in Step 4.

b = Pessimistic time: the maximum reasonable period of time the activity would take to be completed. (There is only a small probability, typically assumed to be 1 percent, that it would take longer.)

Typically, this information is gathered from those people who are to perform the activity.

4. *Calculate the expected time (ET) for each activity.* The formula for this calculation is as follows:

$$ET = \frac{a + 4m + b}{6}$$

EXHIBIT 10.6 **The Use of Dummy Activities in Network Construction**

1. Partial dependence

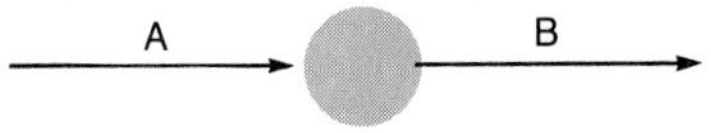

Implies A must be completely finished before B can start.

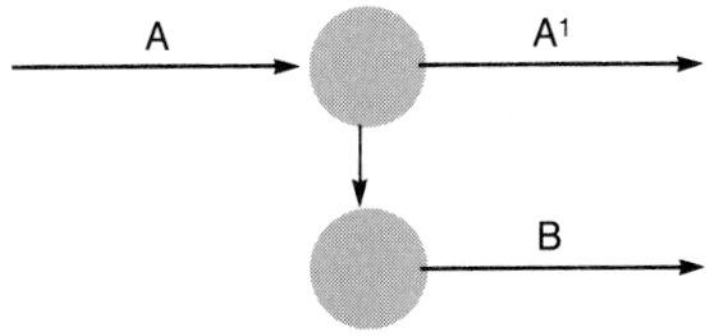

Indicates that B can start when A is partially completed.

2. Clarify precedence relationships

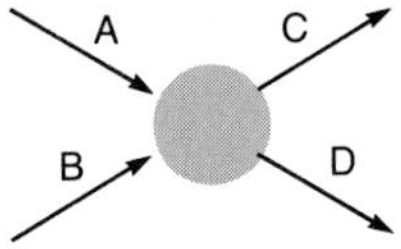

Implies that C and D are dependent on A and B.

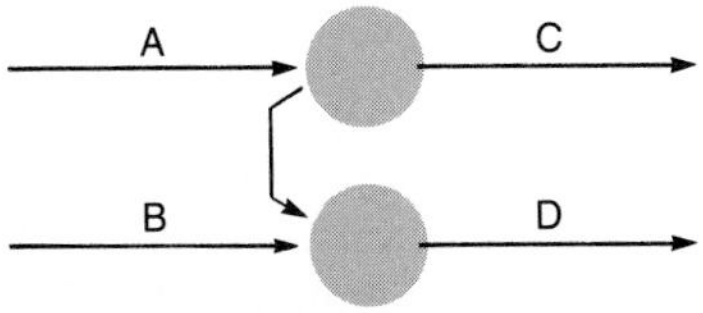

Indicates that D depends on A and B; C depends only on A.

3. Existence of competing resource requirements

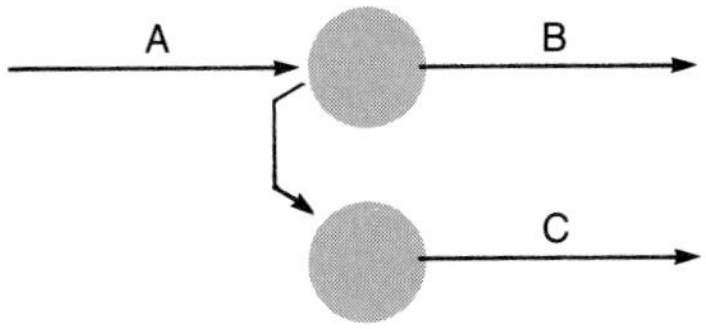

Indicates that C cannot start (in this case) until equipment becomes available from A.

4. Clarify event numbers for computer use

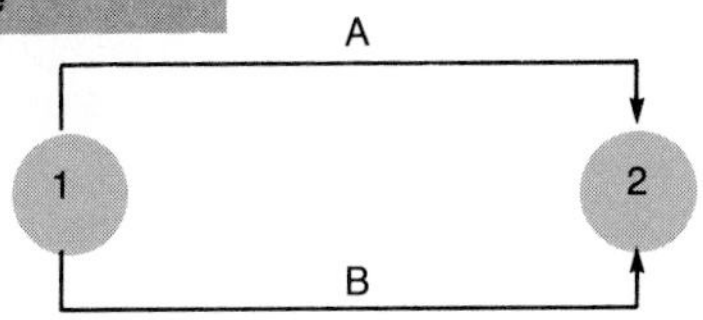

Conceptually correct but two activities have identical event numbers.

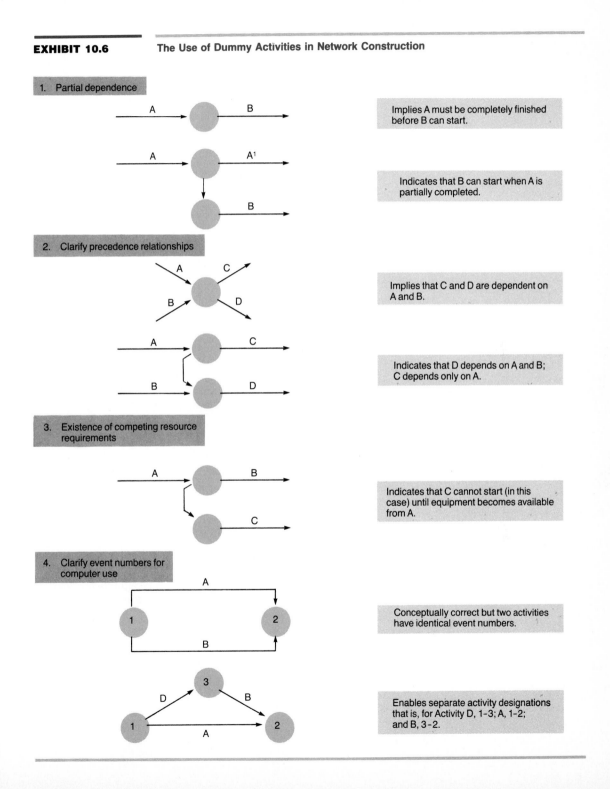

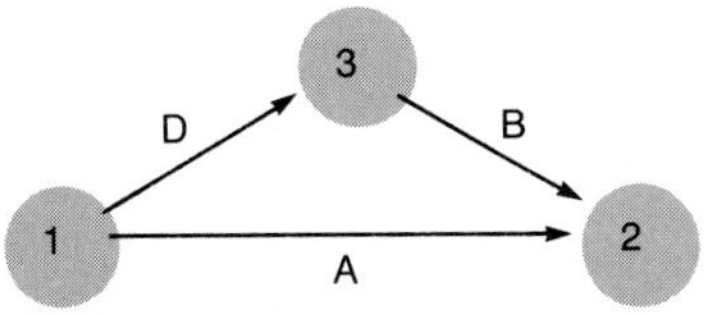

Enables separate activity designations that is, for Activity D, 1-3; A, 1-2; and B, 3-2.

EXHIBIT 10.7 **Typical Beta Curves**

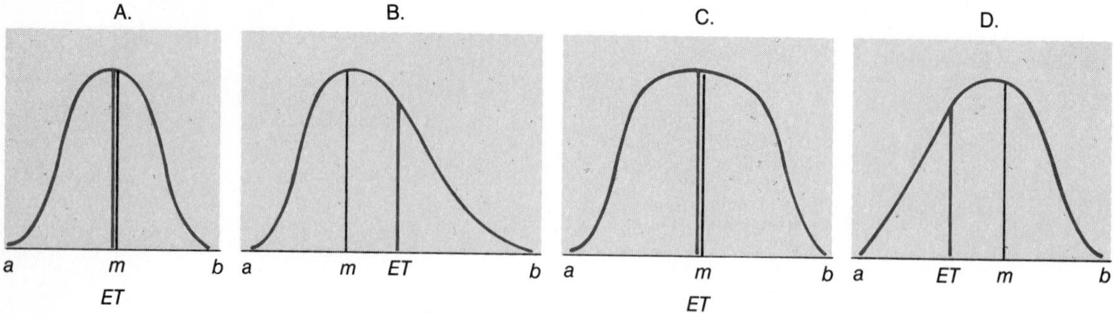

Curve A indicates very little uncertainty about the activity time, and since it is symmetrical, the expected time (*ET*) and the most likely or modal time (*m*) fall along the same point.

Curve B indicates a high probability of finishing the activity early, but if something goes wrong, the activity time could be greatly extended.

Curve C is almost a rectangular distribution, which suggests that the estimator sees the probability of finishing the activity early or late as equally likely, and $m \cong ET$.

Curve D indicates that there is a small chance of finishing the activity early, but it is more probable that it will take an extended period of time.

This is based on the beta statistical distribution and weights the most likely time (m) four times more than either the optimistic time (a) or the pessimistic time (b). The beta distribution was selected by the PERT research team because it is extremely flexible; it can take on the variety of forms that typically arise, it has finite end points, which limit the possible activity times to the area between a and b (see Exhibit 10.9), and, in the simplified version used in PERT, it permits straightforward computation of the activity mean and standard deviation. Four "typical" beta curves are illustrated in Exhibit 10.7.

5. *Calculate the variances* (σ^2) *of the activity times.* Specifically, this is the variance, σ^2, associated with each ET, and is computed as follows:

$$\sigma^2 = \left(\frac{b - a}{6}\right)^2$$

As you can see, the variance is the square of one sixth the difference between the two extreme time estimates, and of course, the greater this difference, the larger the variance.

6. *Determine the critical path.* The critical path is the longest sequence of connected activities through the network and is defined as the path with zero slack time. *Slack time* (Ts), in turn, is calculated for each event; it is the difference between the earliest and the latest expected completion time for an event. Slack may be thought of as the amount of time the start of a given event may be delayed without delaying the completion of the project.

7. *Determine the probability of completing the project on a given date.* A unique feature of PERT is that it enables the analyst to assess the effect of uncertainty on project completion time. The mechanics of deriving this probability are as follows:

a. Sum the variance values associated with each activity on the critical path.

b. Substitute this figure, along with the project due date and the project expected completion time, into the Z transformation formula. This formula is:

$$Z = \frac{D - T_E}{\sqrt{\Sigma\sigma_{cp}^2}}$$

where

D = Due date for project
T_E = Earliest expected completion time for last activity
$\Sigma\sigma_{cp}^2$ = Sum of the variances along critical path

c. Calculate the value of Z, which is the number of standard deviations the project due date is from the expected completion time.

d. Using the value for Z, find the probability of meeting the project due date (using a table of normal probabilities). The *earliest expected completion time* for an event is found by starting at the beginning of the network and summing the expected times for each event preceding the event of interest. If two or more arrows converge on an event node, use the largest computed figure. The *latest expected completion time* (T_L) for an event is found by starting at the end of the network and working toward the beginning, subtracting the expected completion time for each event from the value of the T_L for each successor event. To begin the process requires the establishment of some T_L for the last event. This value is typically set equal to T_E for that event, or to the desired project completion time (D). If two or more arrows converge on an event node, take the smallest computed figure as the T_L value.

A PERT example problem

Many firms that have tried to enter the lap-size and briefcase computer market have failed. Your firm believes that there is a big demand in this market, but existing products have not been designed correctly. The intended computer will be small enough to carry inside a jacket pocket if need be. The ideal size will be no larger than 4 inches × 9½ inches × 1 inch with a standard typewriter keyboard. It should weigh no more than 15 ounces, have a 4 to 8 line × 80 character LCD display, have a micro disk drive, and a micro printer. It should be aimed toward word processing use but have plug-in ROMs for an assortment of languages and programs. This should appeal to traveling businesspeople, but it could have a much wider market. If it can be priced to sell retail in the \$175–\$200 range, it should appeal to anyone who uses a typewriter. A big market is also expected to be students. College students could use this to create reports; college, high school, and elementary schoolchildren could take notes during class and during library research.

The project, then, is to design, develop, and produce a prototype of this small computer. In the rapidly changing computer industry, it is crucial to hit the market with a product of this sort in not much more than one year, preferably less. Therefore, the project team has been allowed approximately eight months (35 weeks) to produce the prototype.

The first charge of the project team is to develop a PERT chart and estimate the likelihood of completing the prototype computer within the 35 weeks. Let's follow the steps in the development of the PERT chart.

1. *Activity identification.* The project team decides that the following activities are the major components of the project: design of the computer, prototype construction, prototype testing, methods specification (summarized in a report), evaluation studies of automatic assembly equipment, an assembly equipment study report, and a final report summarizing all aspects of the design, equipment, and methods.

2. *Activity sequencing and network construction.* On the basis of discussion with his staff, the project manager develops the precedence table and sequence network shown in Exhibit 10.8. Note that he must add a dummy timeline to permit unique activity designations for writing the equipment report and methods report. In this example, the table reflects this adjustment, even though it is presumed to be identified before the network was developed. In practice, the manager would be unlikely to recognize the need for dummy activities before at least a rough network is drawn.

3 and 4. Establish time estimates and calculate activity time variances. Once the team decides on the activities to be performed, the project manager asks the appropriate personnel to estimate the optimistic, most likely, and pessimistic times for those activities under their control. The next step would be to calculate ET and σ^2 for each activity and list it in a form such as that shown in Exhibit 10.9.

5. *Determine critical path.* Exhibit 10.10 is a "working" PERT chart, in that it is in the form an analyst would use to arrive at the critical path and expected completion time for the project. Each T_E is found first by summing from event 0 forward; each T_L is found next by setting T_L and T_E equal to 38 and subtracting, moving backward through the network. Slack times are calculated below the chart. Examining the slack values, we see that events 0, 1, 2, 3, 5, and 6 are critical and that part of the network shows two critical paths, since the event associated with parallel activities 1–3 and 1–2, 2–3 each has zero slack.

6. *Probability of completion.* Since there are two critical paths in the network, a decision must be made as to which variances to use in arriving at the probability of completion. A conservative approach dictates that the path with the largest total variance be used since this would focus management's atten-

EXHIBIT 10.8

Precedence Relationships for Computer Project

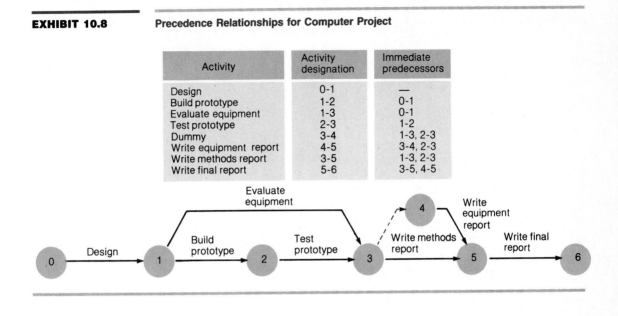

Activity	Activity designation	Immediate predecessors
Design	0-1	—
Build prototype	1-2	0-1
Evaluate equipment	1-3	0-1
Test prototype	2-3	1-2
Dummy	3-4	1-3, 2-3
Write equipment report	4-5	3-4, 2-3
Write methods report	3-5	1-3, 2-3
Write final report	5-6	3-5, 4-5

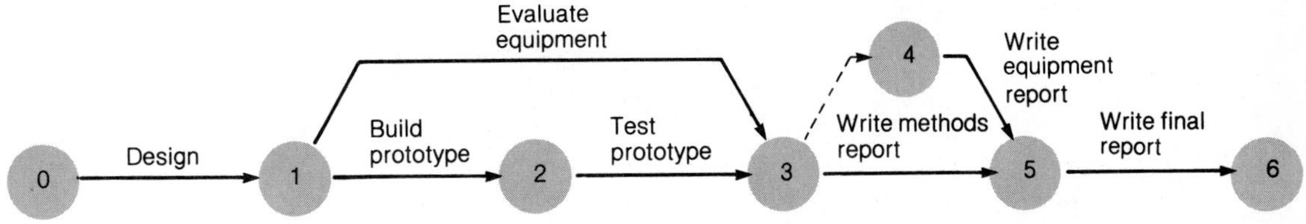

EXHIBIT 10.9

Activity Expected Times and Variances

Activity	Activity Designation	TIME ESTIMATES *a*	*m*	*b*	Expected Times (*ET*) $\frac{a + 4m + b}{6}$	Activity Variances (σ^2) $\left(\frac{b - a}{6}\right)^2$
Design	0–1	10	22	28	21	9
Build prototype	1–2	4	4	10	5	1
Evaluate equipment	1–3	4	6	14	7	2 7/9
Test prototype	2–3	1	2	3	2	1/9
Dummy	3–4	—	—	—	—	—
Write report	4–5	1	5	9	5	1 7/9
Write methods report	3–5	7	8	9	8	1/9
Write final report	5–6	2	2	2	2	0

tion on the activities most likely to exhibit broad variations. On this basis, the variances associated with activities 0–1, 1–3, 3–5, and 5–6 would be used to find the probability of completion. Thus $\Sigma\sigma_{cp}^2 = 9 + 2\frac{7}{9} + \frac{1}{9} + 0 = 11.89$. The due date ($D$) was given as 35 weeks and the earliest expected completed time (T_E for the last event) was found to be 38. Substituting into the Z equation and solving, we obtain

$$Z = \frac{D - T_E}{\sqrt{\Sigma\sigma_{cp}^2}} = \frac{35 - 38}{\sqrt{11.89}} = -0.87$$

EXHIBIT 10.10 Identification of Critical Path

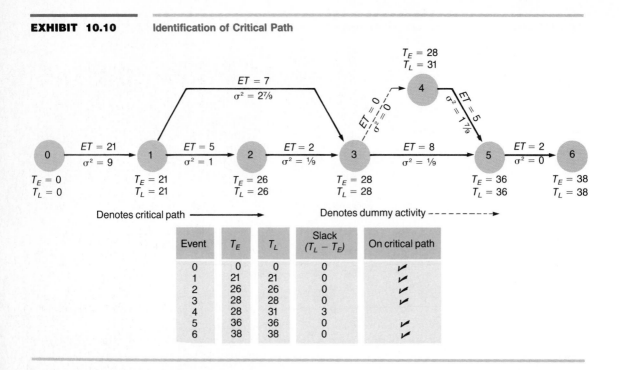

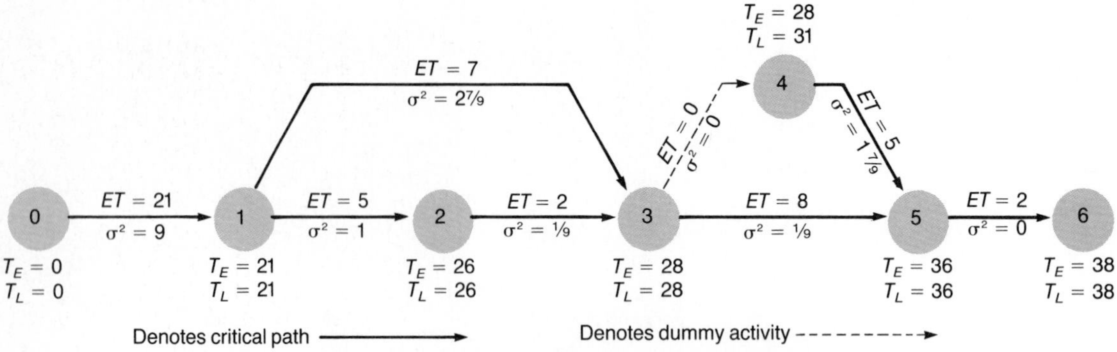

Event	T_E	T_L	Slack ($T_L - T_E$)	On critical path
0	0	0	0	✓
1	21	21	0	✓
2	26	26	0	✓
3	28	28	0	✓
4	28	31	3	
5	36	36	0	✓
6	38	38	0	✓

Appendix C, in the back of this book, is an abbreviated table showing only the positive half of the normal distribution. To convert this to the left or negative half, we need to subtract the numbers from 0.50. From Appendix C, the Z value of -0.87 (which we obtained above) gives an area value of 0.3078 for a positive 0.87. Therefore, the value for -0.87 is $0.50 - 0.3078$ or 0.1922. This means the project manager has only about a 19 percent chance of completing the project on time.

CPM

The major distinction between CPM and PERT is the use of statistics in the latter. Otherwise, despite some differences in network construction and terminology, approaches are similar.

The following steps are required in developing and solving a CPM network.

1. *Identify each activity to be done in the project.* In CPM, the term *job* is often used to refer to the task being performed, rather than separating activities and events as in PERT. However, since current practice seems to be to treat the terms as synonymous, we will refer to the CPM tasks to be done as *activities*.

2. *Determine the sequence of activities and construct a network reflecting precedence relationships.* CPM is activity oriented, with arrows denoting precedence only. A typical segment using the book-writing example from PERT (Step 2) would show the activity above the node rather than on the arrow. To restate, nodes in CPM represent activities in the PERT sense, not events.

3. *Ascertain time estimates for each activity.* This is the "best guess" time or can be thought of as equivalent to expected time, which is derived statistically in PERT (Step 4). While the CPM procedure has no provision for statistical estimation of this value, the individual who provides the estimate may use a simple statistical model in arriving at a figure. For example, he or she may feel that two times are equally likely and therefore take the average as an estimate.

4. *Determine the critical path.* As in PERT, this is the path with zero slack. To arrive at slack time requires the calculation of four time values for each activity:

Early start time (ES), the earliest possible time that the activity can begin.

Early finish time (EF), the early start time plus the time needed to complete the activity.

Late start time (LS), the latest time an activity can begin without delaying the project.

Late finish time (LF), the latest time an activity can end without delaying the project.

The procedure for arriving at these values and for determining slack and the critical path can best be explained by reference to the simple network shown (Exhibit 10.13). The letters denote the activities and the numbers the activity times.

a. Find ES time. Take 0 as the start of the project and set this equal to ES for Activity A. To find ES for B, we add the duration of A (which is 2) to 0 and obtain 2. Likewise, ES for C would be 0 + 2, or 2. To find ES for D, we take the larger ES and duration time for the preceding activities: since B = 2 + 5 = 7 and C = 2 + 4 = 6, ES for D = 7. These values are entered on the diagram (Exhibit 10.11, Step a). The largest value is selected since activity D cannot begin until the longest time-consuming activity preceding it is completed.

b. Find EF times. The EF for A is its ES time, 0, plus its duration of 2. B's EF is its ES of 2 plus its duration of 5, or 7. C's is 2 + 4, or 6, and D's is 7 + 3, or 10 (Exhibit 10.11, step b). In practice, one computes ES and EF together while proceeding through the network. Since ES plus activity time equals EF, the EF becomes the ES of the following event, and so forth.

c. Find late start and late finish times. While the procedure for making these calculations can be presented in mathematical form, the concept is much easier to explain and understand if it is presented in an intuitive way. The basic approach is to start at the end of the project with some desired or assumed completion time. Working back toward the beginning, one activity at a time,

EXHIBIT 10.11 **Steps to Develop and Solve a CPM Network**

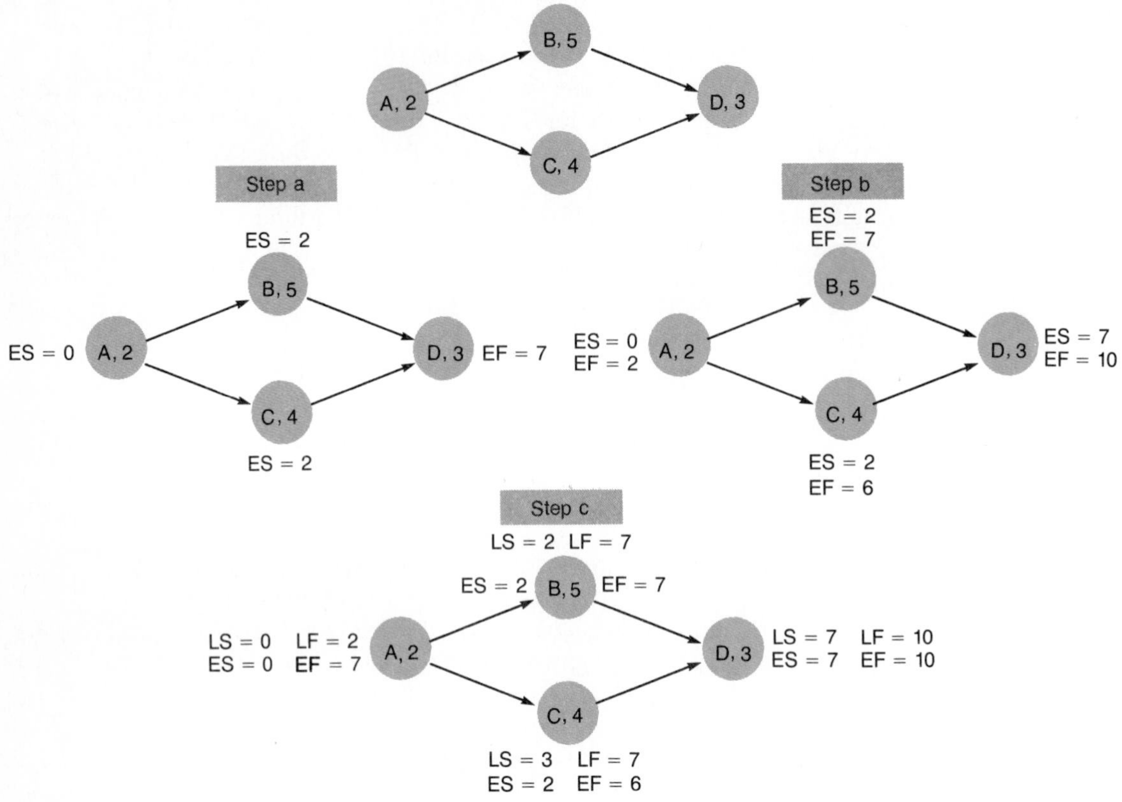

we determine how long the starting of this activity may be delayed without affecting the start of the one that follows it.

In reference to the sample network, let us assume that the late finish time for the project is equal to the early finish time for activity D, that is, 10. If this is the case, the latest possible starting time for D will be 10 − 3, or 7. The latest time C can finish without delaying the LS of D is 7, which means that C's LS is 7 − 4, or 3. The latest time B can finish without delaying the LS of D is also 7, which means that B's LS is 7 − 5, or 2. Since A precedes two activities, the choice of LS and LF values depends upon which of those activities must be started first. Clearly, B determines the LF for A since its LS is 2, whereas C can be delayed one day without extending the project. Finally, since A must be finished by Day 2, it cannot start any later than Day 0, and hence, its LS is 0. These LS and LF values are entered in the network (Exhibit 10.11, Step c).

d. Determine slack time for each activity. Slack for each activity is defined as either LS − ES or LF − EF. In this example, only activity C has slack (1 day); therefore the critical path is A, B, D.

Early start and late start schedules

An **early start schedule** is one which lists all of the activities by their early start times. For activities not on the critical path, there will be slack time between the activity completion and the start of the next activity which succeeds it. The early start schedule completes the project and all of its activities as soon as possible.

A **late start schedule** lists the activities to start as late as possible without delaying the completion date of the project. One of the motivations for using a late start schedule is that savings will be realized by postponing purchases of materials, the use of labor, and other costs until necessary.

Applying CPM to the computer design project

For the sake of brevity, we have summarized the results of the various steps of the CPM procedure in the form shown in Exhibit 10.12. Note that the CPM network appears greatly different from the PERT network even though the activities and the critical path(s) are the same. Also note that no dummy arrows are required for this problem. (In general, CPM uses fewer dummies than PERT because an activity is designated only by a node rather than by an arrow connecting two events.)

Standardized Networks

When projects are repeated (another building built, another golf course designed) logic seems to imply that some part of the experience on the last project should be reusable. Gray et al. suggest the use of standardized networks.[5] Often project managers have been reluctant to use network techniques because of the high cost to analyze project components, determine resource levels, develop networks, and collect data. The clearest case for standard networks would be the contractor who uses the same activity network in a high-rise apartment, office, or hotel because each floor is typically similar. How about a home builder who builds standard models?

[5] Clifford F. Gray, Bruce Woodworth, and Sean Shanahan, "Standardized Networks: An Extension for Further Reducing Input Requirements," *Project Management Quarterly* 13, no. 3 (September 1982), pp. 32–34.

EXHIBIT 10.12 **CPM Network for Computer Design Project**

	CPM activity designations and time estimates			
Activity	Designation	Immediate predecessors	Time in weeks	(ET values of PERT used for comparison)
Design	A	—	21	
Build prototype	B	A	5	
Evaluate equipment	C	A	7	
Test prototype	D	B	2	
Write equipment report	E	C, D	5	
Write methods report	F	C, D	8	
Writer final report	G	E, F	2	

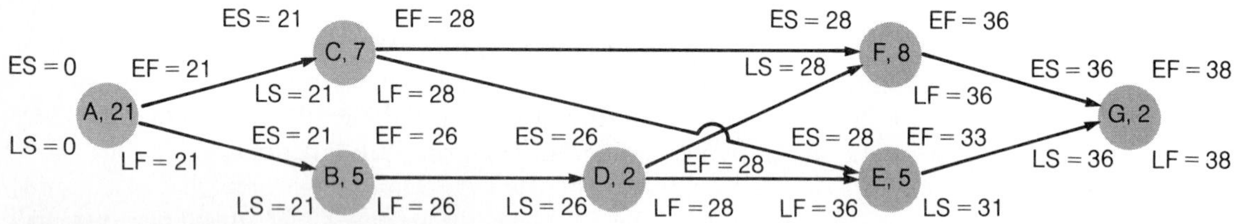

Slack calculations and critical path determinations			
Activity	LS – ES	Slack	On critical path
A	0-0	0	✓
B	21-21	0	✓
C	21-21	0	✓
D	26-26	0	✓
E	31-28	3	
F	28-28	0	✓
G	36-36	0	✓

The advantages of standardized networks are:

1. Preparation effort for the network is greatly reduced.
2. Data are more reliable since they resulted from a prior application.
3. The entire project planning process can be performed by lower-level personnel.
4. Planning time is greatly reduced.
5. Through close replication of the same or similar projects, communication and coordination are greatly improved.

10.5 TIME-COST MODELS

In practice, project managers are as much concerned with the cost to complete a project as with the time to complete the project. For this reason, **time-cost models** have been devised. These models—extensions of PERT and CPM—attempt to develop a minimum-cost schedule for an entire project and to control budgetary expenditures during the project. The basic assumption in minimum-cost scheduling is that there is a relationship between activity completion time and the cost of a project. On one hand, it costs money to expedite an activity; on the other, it costs money to sustain (or lengthen) the project.

The approaches that focus on minimum-cost scheduling typically use CPM networks, and those that focus on budgetary control generally fall under the heading PERT-cost.

10.6 COMPUTER PROGRAMS FOR PROJECT SCHEDULING

Many project scheduling programs are available for microcomputers as well as mainframe computers. O'Neal presents data on software produced by 55 companies, organized by price, which ranges from under $100 to $46,000.[6] A program can be purchased, such as Microsoft's Project 4.0, which retails for $495. This program will run on a PC and has a capacity of 1,000 tasks and 250 resources. For $2,500, the Primavera Project Planner 3.0 program will also run on a PC and has a capacity of 10,000 tasks with unlimited resources. Naturally, faster PCs with more memory and larger computers will be able to use more of the software program's capacities and capabilities and run in less time.

10.7 CONCLUSION

Although much of this chapter has dealt with networking techniques used in project management, effective project management involves much more than simply setting up a CPM or PERT schedule. It requires, in addition, clearly identified project responsibilities, a simple and timely progress reporting system, and good people-management practices.

Projects seem to fail for one of two reasons.[7] The first is improper focus. The project manager needs to focus on the project goal and not let the PERT or CPM network divert the focus to the nodes (activities) instead. The second

---

[6] Kim O'Neal, "Project Management Computer Software Buyer's Guide," *Industrial Engineering* 19, no. 1 (January 1987).

[7] Michael William Hughes, "Why Projects Fail: The Effects of Ignoring the Obvious," *Industrial Engineering* 18, no. 4 (April 1986), pp. 14–18.

source of trouble is failure to revise initial estimates. Estimates, often crude, are used at the beginning of the project. As new data are acquired, the estimates must be upgraded and a new schedule created.

10.8 REVIEW AND DISCUSSION QUESTIONS

1. Define project management.
2. Describe or define work breakdown structure, program, project, task, subtask, and work package.
3. Discuss a matrix organization. How does it differ from a traditional organization hierarchy?
4. What characteristics must a project have in order for critical path scheduling to be applicable? What types of projects have been subjected to critical path analysis?
5. How does a PERT network differ from a CPM network?
6. Why was the beta distribution chosen by PERT developers to represent activity-time variation?
7. "Project control should always focus on the critical path." Comment.
8. Why would subcontractors for a government project want their activities on the critical path? Under what conditions would they try to avoid being on the critical path?

10.9 PROBLEMS

*1. A project has been defined to contain the following list of activities, along with their required times for completion.

Activity	Time (days)	Immediate Predecessors
A	1	—
B	4	A
C	3	A
D	7	A
E	6	B
F	2	C, D
G	7	E, F
H	9	D
I	4	G, H

a. Draw the critical path diagram.
b. Show the early start and early finish times.
c. Show the critical path.
d. What would happen if Activity F was revised to take four days instead of two?

* Complete solutions for Problems 1 and 2 are in Appendix D.

*2. Following is a PERT network. The three time estimates for the activities are shown in weeks.

a. What is the earliest the project can be completed?
b. What is the critical path?
c. What is the standard deviation of the critical path?
d. What is the probability that the project will be completed in 20 weeks?

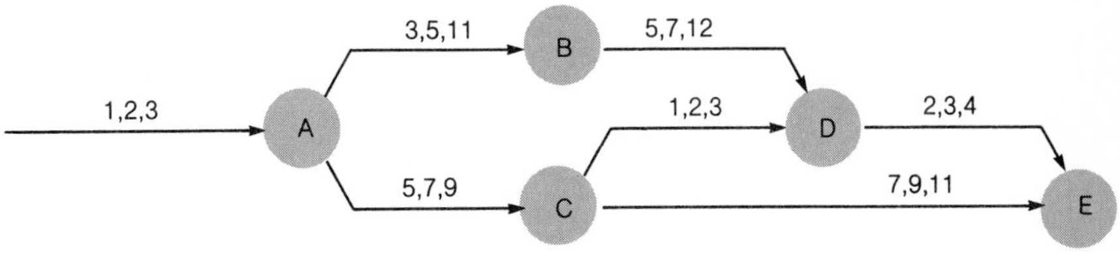

3. The following activities are part of a project to be scheduled using CPM.

Activity	Immediate Predecessor	Time (weeks)
A	—	6
B	A	3
C	A	7
D	C	2
E	B, D	4
F	D	3
G	E, F	7

a. Draw the network.
b. What is the critical path?
c. How many weeks will it take to complete the project?
d. How much slack does activity B have?

4. A manufacturing concern has received a special order for a number of units of a special product that consists of two component parts, X and Y. The product is a nonstandard item that the firm has never produced before, and scheduling personnel have decided that the application of CPM is warranted. A team of manufacturing engineers has prepared the following table:

Activity	Description	Immediate Predecessors	Expected Time (days)
A	Plan production	—	5
B	Procure materials for Part X	A	14
C	Manufacture Part X	B	9
D	Procure materials for Part Y	A	15
E	Manufacture Part Y	D	10
F	Assemble Parts X and Y	C, E	4
G	Inspect assemblies	F	2
H	Completed	G	0

a. Construct a graphical representation of the CPM network.
b. Identify the critical path.

c. What is the length of time to complete the project?
d. Which activities have slack, and how much?

5. Given the following PERT network:

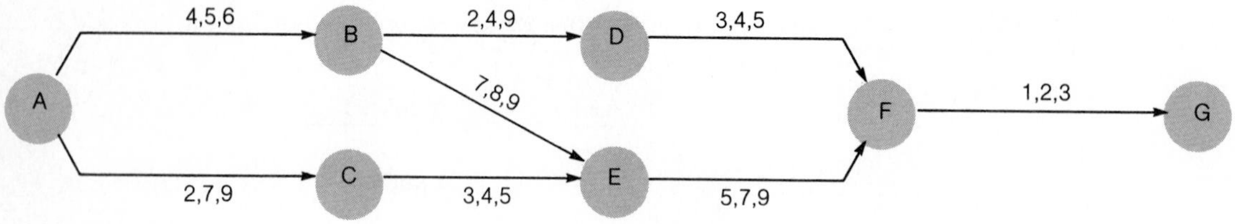

a. Find the critical path.
b. What is the standard deviation of the critical path?

6. Following is a CPM network with activity times in weeks.

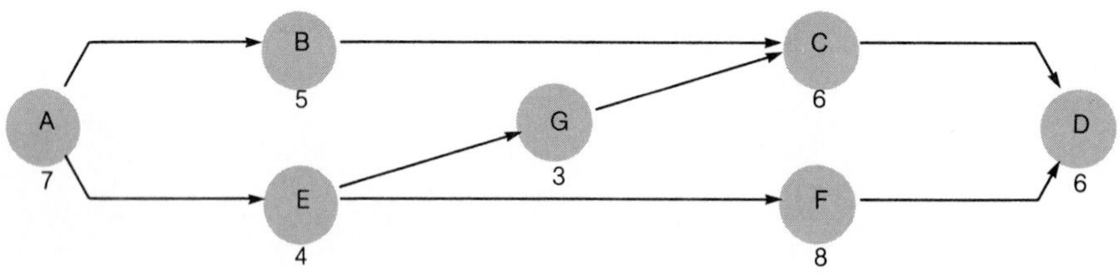

a. Determine the critical path.
b. How many weeks will the project take to complete?
c. Supposing F could be shortened by two weeks and B by one week. What effect would this have on the completion date?

7. The following represents a plan for a project in PERT terms.

Job No.	Predecessor Job(s)	*a*	*m*	*b*
1	—	2	3	4
2	1	1	2	3
3	1	4	5	12
4	1	3	4	11
5	2	1	3	5
6	3	1	2	3
7	4	1	8	9
8	5, 6	2	4	6
9	8	2	4	12
10	7	3	4	5
11	9, 10	5	7	8

a. Construct the appropriate network diagram.
b. Indicate the critical path.

c. What is the expected completion time for the project?
d. What is the probability that the project will take more than 30 days to complete?

8. The home office billing department of a chain of department stores prepares monthly inventory reports for use by the stores' purchasing agents. Given the information below, use the critical path method to determine
a. How long the total process will take.
b. Which jobs can be delayed without delaying the early start of any subsequent activity.

	Job and Description	Immediate Predecessors	Time (hours)
a	Start	—	0
b	Get computer printouts of customer purchases	a	10
c	Get stock records for the month	a	20
d	Reconcile purchase printouts and stock records	b, c	30
e	Total stock records by department	b, c	20
f	Determine reorder quantities for coming period	e	40
g	Prepare stock reports for purchasing agents	d, f	20
h	Finish	g	0

9. The PERT network and activity statistics for a construction project are shown below. Note that the expected time and variance have already been computed from the usual estimates. The time unit is weeks.
a. Identify the activities on the critical path.
b. Identify the activities with slack, and show how much.
c. What is the expected time to complete the project?
d. What is the probability of completing the project in 30 weeks?

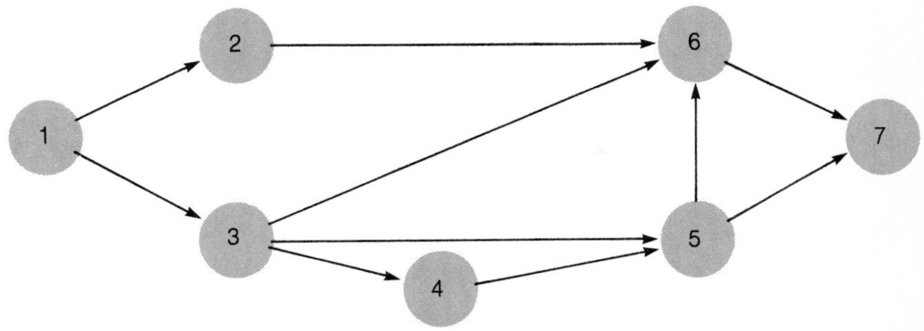

Activity	*ET*	σ^2
1–2	9	0.12
1–3	7	0.25
2–6	12	1.00
3–4	5	0.00
3–5	10	0.25
3–6	15	2.25
4–5	4	0.25
5–6	6	0.25
5–7	10	0.50
6–7	6	0.25

10. A CPM network is given here, with best estimates of the *normal time* listed for the activities.
    a. Identify the critical path.
    b. What is the length of time to complete the project?
    c. Which activities have slack, and how much?

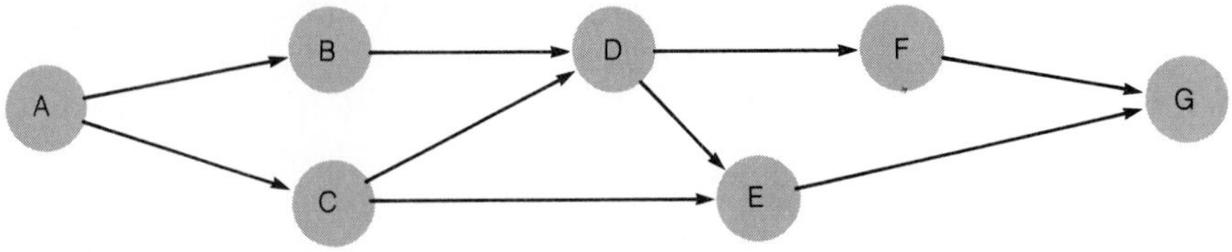

Activity	Time (weeks)
A	7
B	2
C	4
D	5
E	2
F	4
G	5

11. Following is a PERT network with the three time estimates shown in weeks.

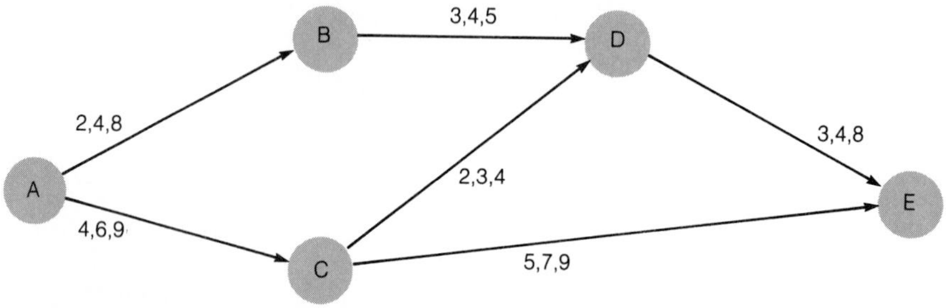

a. Find the earliest that the project can be completed if it is started at time zero.
b. Find the standard deviation of the critical path.
c. What is the probability that the project will be completed in 14 weeks?

10.10 SELECTED BIBLIOGRAPHY

Cleland, David I., and William R. King. *Project Management Handbook.* New York: Van Nostrand Reinhold, 1983.

Dane, C. W.; C. F. Gray; and B. M. Woodworth. "Factors Affecting the Successful Application of PERT/CPM Systems in Governmental Organizations." *Interfaces* 9, no. 5. (November 1979), pp. 94–98.

Goodman, Louis J., and Ralph N. Love. *Project Planning and Management: An Integrated Approach*. New York: Pergamon Press, 1980.

Hughes, Michael William. "Why Projects Fail: The Effects of Ignoring the Obvious." *Industrial Engineering* 18, no. 4 (April 1986), pp. 14–18.

Kerzner, Harold, and Hans Thamhain. *Project Management for Small and Medium Size Business*. New York: Van Nostrand Reinhold, 1984.

Kerzner, Harold. *Project/Matrix Management Policy and Strategy*. New York: Van Nostrand Reinhold, 1984.

———. *Project Management for Executives*. New York: Van Nostrand Reinhold, 1984.

O'Neal, Kim. "Project Management Computer Software Buyer's Guide." *Industrial Engineering* 19, no. 1 (January 1987).

Peterson, P. "Project Control Systems." *Datamation,* June 1979, pp. 147–63.

Smith-Daniels, Dwight E., and Viki L. Smith-Daniels. "Optimal Project Scheduling with Materials Ordering." *IIE Transactions* 19, no. 2 (June 1987), pp. 122–29.

Wiest, Jerome D., and Ferdinand K. Levy. *A Management Guide to PERT/CPM*. Englewood Cliffs, N.J.: Prentice-Hall, 1977.

Supplement

Learning Curves

EPIGRAPH

If at first you don't succeed, try and try again.

SUPPLEMENT OUTLINE

KEY TERMS

Learning Curve

Exponential Curve

Learning Percentages

Industry Learning Curves

Progress Curves

Common sense implies that the more we do something, the better we will become at doing it. We obviously can cite some exceptions to this premise: physically, repetition may cause muscle strain; mentally, repetition may cause monotony and boredom. But generally, the more we do something, the more we learn from doing it, and the more efficient we become.

One of the authors of this text made a mistake years ago in establishing time standards for some new tasks in a service industry. The time study was performed in the usual manner, which used experienced workers, industrial engineered performance methods, the appropriate rating system, and so on. These time standards were then adopted and incorporated into the firm's incentive payment system. What was unanticipated was the tremendous amount of learning that the service workers experienced and incorporated into the performance of their jobs. Service personnel changed the methods, sequences, equipment, and even the interaction with other service personnel. The outcome was that the firm was committed to pay very high bonuses for almost a year until the employees voluntarily agreed to accept new standards.

Learning goes on constantly. The rate of learning depends on many things, such as prior experience, how bad one is to begin with (the worse one is at the start, the greater the percentage increases one can show as performance improvement), the motivation to improve, the degree of control one has over the performance of the job, and so on.

All firms should include the effects of learning on performance. Corporations use learning curves in forecasting demand, in product development, in product pricing, in establishing corporate strategy for domestic and international competition, in quality control, in establishing product performance times and costs in bidding, in planning capacities, as well as in many other areas.

In this supplement we will present what is called the *simple learning curve model*. This is a simple exponential curve that is very useful and fits many applications in the real world. We will follow this with discussion on the duration of learning, management's use of learning curves, and the range of application of learning curves.

S10.1 PREDICTING STARTUP PROGRESS: LEARNING CURVES

A **learning curve** (or experience curve), in its basic form and applied to production, is simply a line displaying the relationship between unit production time and the number of consecutive units of production. Learning curves may be viewed as "internal forecasts" of production output and, as such, are particularly useful in developing bids for new projects.

Learning curves can be applied to individuals or organizations. Individual learning is improvement that results when people repeat a process and gain skill or efficiency from their own experience. That is, "practice makes perfect." Organizational learning results from practice as well but also comes from changes in administration, equipment, and product design. In organizational settings, we expect to see both kinds of learning occurring simultaneously and often describe the combined effect with a single learning curve.

Learning curve theory is based on three assumptions:

1. The amount of time required to complete a given task or unit of a product will be less each time the task is undertaken.
2. The unit time will decrease at a decreasing rate.
3. The reduction in time will follow a predictable pattern.

Each of these assumptions was found to hold true in the airframe industry, where learning curves were first applied. Specifically, it was observed that, as output doubled, there was a 20 percent reduction in direct production worker-hours per unit between doubled units. Thus, if it took 100,000 hours for Plane 1, it would take 80,000 hours for Plane 2, 64,000 hours for Plane 4, and so forth. Since the 20 percent reduction meant that, say, Unit 4 took only 80 percent of the production time required for Unit 2, the line connecting the coordinates of output and time was referred to as an "80 percent learning curve." (By convention, the percentage learning rate is used to denote any given exponential learning curve.)

A learning curve may be developed from an arithmetic tabulation, by logarithms or by some other curve-fitting method, depending on the amount and form of the available data.

There are two ways to think of the improved performance that comes with learning curves; that is time per unit (as in Exhibit S10.1A) or as units of output per time period (as in S10.1B and C). *Time per unit* shows the decrease in time required for each successive unit. *Cumulative average time* shows the cumulative average performance times as the total number of units increases. Time per unit and cumulative average times are also called *progress curves* or *product learning,* and are useful for complex products or products with a longer cycle time. *Units of output per time period* is also called *industry learning* and is generally applied to high-volume production (short cycle time).

Note in Exhibit S10.1A that the cumulative average curve does not decrease as fast as the time per unit because the time is being averaged. For example, if the time for Units 1, 2, 3, and 4 were 100, 80, 70, and 64, they would be plotted that way on the time per unit graph, but would be plotted as 100, 90, 83.3, and 78.5 on the cumulative average time graph.

There are, of course, many ways to analyze past data in order to fit a useful trend line, but in this supplement we will focus on two techniques of learning curves: (1) a simple **exponential curve** and (2) time-constant learning. The simple exponential curve will be viewed first as an arithmetic procedure and then by a logarithmic analysis.

EXHIBIT S10.1

Learning Curves Plotted as Times and Numbers of Units

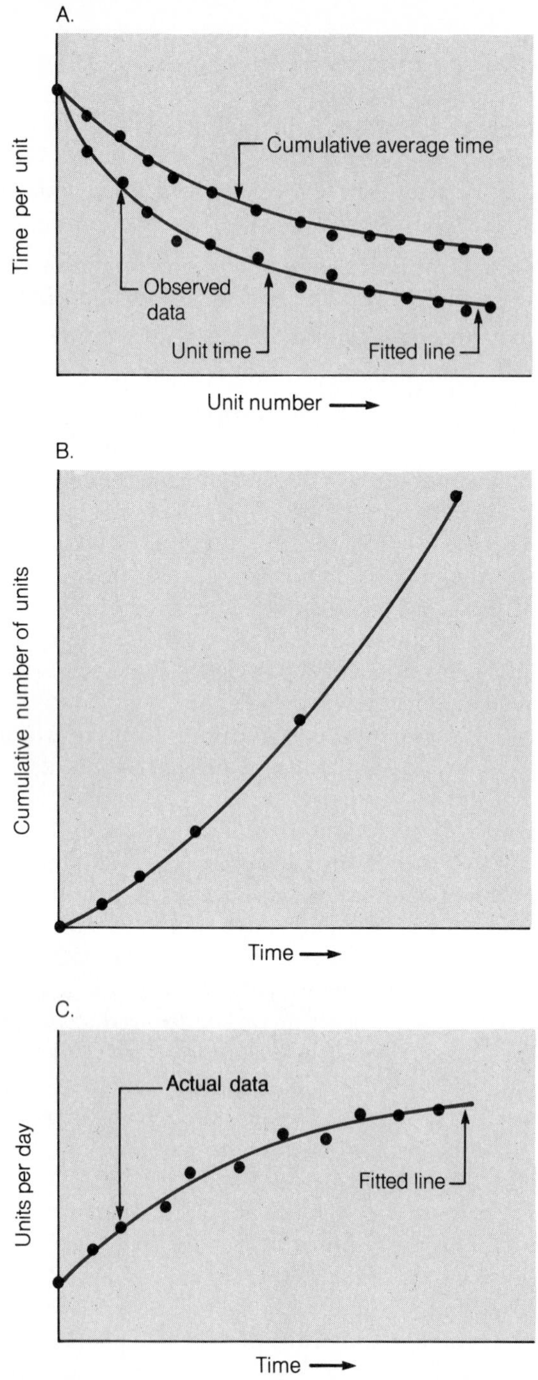

S10.2 SIMPLE EXPONENTIAL CURVE

Arithmetical Tabulation

In an arithmetical tabulation approach, the number of units produced (proposed or actual) is listed and the corresponding labor hours for each doubled unit level are calculated by multiplying the unit's direct labor hours by the selected learning percentage. Thus, if we are developing an 80 percent learning curve, we would arrive at the figures listed in column 2 of Exhibit S10.2. Since it is often desirable for planning purposes to know the cumulative direct labor hours, column 4, which lists this information, is also provided. The calculation of these figures is straightforward; for example, for Unit 4, cumulative average direct labor hours would be found by dividing cumulative direct labor hours by 4, yielding the figure given in column 4.

Exhibit S10.3 shows three curves with different learning rates: 90 percent, 80 percent, and 70 percent. Note that if the cost of the 1st unit was $100, the 30th unit would cost $59.63 at the 90 percent rate and $17.37 at the 70 percent rate. Differences in learning rates can have dramatic effects.

In practice, learning curves are plotted on log-log paper, with the results that the unit curves become linear throughout their entire range and the cumulative curve becomes linear after the first few units.

Logarithmic Analysis

The normal form of the learning curve equation is[1]:

$$Y_x = Kx^n \qquad (1)$$

EXHIBIT S10.2

Unit, Cumulative, and Cumulative Average Direct Labor Worker-Hours Required for an 80 Percent Learning Curve

(1) Unit Number	(2) Unit Direct Labor Hours	(3) Cumulative Direct Labor Hours	(4) Cumulative Average Direct Labor Hours
1	100,000	100,000	100,000
2	80,000	180,000	90,000
4	64,000	314,210	78,553
8	51,200	534,591	66,824
16	40,960	892,014	55,751
32	32,768	1,467,862	45,871
64	26,214	2,392,453	37,382
128	20,972	3,874,395	30,269
256	16,777	6,247,318	24,404

[1] This equation says that the number of direct labor hours required for any given unit is reduced exponentially as more units are produced.

EXHIBIT S10.3 Arithmetic Plot of 70, 80, and 90 Percent Learning Curves

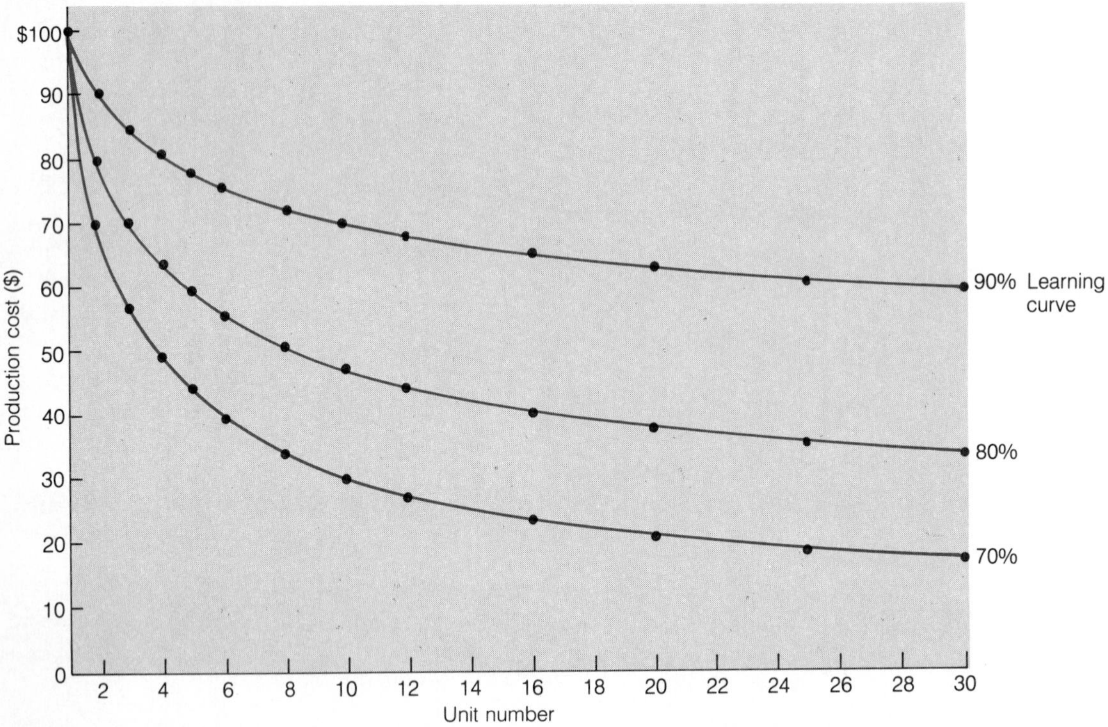

where

x = Unit number

Y_x = Number of direct labor hours required to produce the xth unit

K = Number of direct labor hours required to produce the first unit

n = Log b/log 2 where b = Learning percentage

Thus to find the labor-hour requirement for the eighth unit in our example (Exhibit S10.2), we would substitute as follows:

$$Y_8 = (100{,}000)\,(8)^n$$

This may be solved by using logarithms:

$$\begin{aligned} Y_8 &= 100{,}000\,(8)^{\log 0.8/\log 2} \\ &= 100{,}000(8)^{-0.322} \\ &= \frac{100{,}000}{(8)^{0.322}} \end{aligned}$$

$$= \frac{100{,}000}{1.9535}$$

$$= 51{,}200$$

Therefore, it would take 51,200 hours to make the eighth unit.

Learning Curve Tables

When the learning percentage is known, Exhibits S10.4 and S10.5 can be easily used to calculate estimated labor hours for a specific unit or for cumulative groups of units. We need only multiply the initial unit labor hour figure by appropriate tabled value.

To illustrate, suppose we want to double check the figures in Exhibit S10.2 for unit and cumulative labor hours for Unit 16. From Exhibit S10.4, the improvement factor for Unit 16 at 80 percent is .4096. This multiplied by 100,000 (the hours for Unit 1) gives 40,960, the same as in Exhibit S10.5. From Exhibit S10.5, the improvement factor for cumulative hours for the first 16 units is 8.920. When multiplied by 100,000, this gives 892,000, which is reasonably close to the exact value of 892,014 shown on Exhibit S10.2.

A more involved example of the application of a learning curve to a production problem is given in the Insert.

INSERT Sample Learning Curve Problem

Captain Nemo, owner of the Suboptimum Underwater Boat Company (SUB), is puzzled. He has a contract for 11 boats and has completed 4 of them. He has observed that his production manager, young Mr. Overick, has been reassigning more and more people to torpedo assembly after the construction of the first four boats. The first boat, for example, required 225 workers, each working a 40-hour week, while 45 fewer workers were required for the second boat. Overick has told them that "this is just the beginning" and that he will complete the last boat in the current contract with only 100 workers!

Overick is banking on the learning curve, but has he gone overboard?

Answer: Since the second boat required 180 workers and using a simple exponential curve, then the learning percentage is 80% (180 ÷ 225). To find out how many workers are required for the 11th boat, we look up unit 11 for an 80% improvement ratio in Exhibit S10.4 and multiply this value by the number required for the first sub. By interpolating between unit 10 and unit 12 we find the improvement ratio equal to 0.4629. This yields 104.15 workers (.4629 interpolated from table × 225). Thus, Overick's assertion can't be substantiated.

SUB has produced the first unit of a new line of minisubs at a cost of $500,000—$200,000 for materials and $300,000 for labor. It has agreed to accept a 10 percent profit, based on cost, and it is willing to contract on the basis of a 70 percent learning curve. What will be the contract price for three minisubs?

EXHIBIT S10.4

Improvement Curves: Table of Unit Values

	IMPROVEMENT RATIOS							
Unit	60%	65%	70%	75%	80%	85%	90%	95%
1	1.0000	1.0000	1.0000	1.0000	1.0000	1.0000	1.0000	1.0000
2	.6000	.6500	.7000	.7500	.8000	.8500	.9000	.9500
3	.4450	.5052	.5682	.6338	.7021	.7729	.8462	.9219
4	.3600	.4225	.4900	.5625	.6400	.7225	.8100	.9025
5	.3054	.3678	.4368	.5127	.5956	.6857	.7830	.8877
6	.2670	.3284	.3977	.4754	.5617	.6570	.7616	.8758
7	.2383	.2984	.3674	.4459	.5345	.6337	.7439	.8659
8	.2160	.2746	.3430	.4219	.5120	.6141	.7290	.8574
9	.1980	.2552	.3228	.4017	.4930	.5974	.7161	.8499
10	.1832	.2391	.3058	.3846	.4765	.5828	.7047	.8433
12	.1602	.2135	.2784	.3565	.4493	.5584	.6854	.8320
14	.1430	.1940	.2572	.3344	.4276	.5386	.6696	.8226
16	.1296	.1785	.2401	.3164	.4096	.5220	.6561	.8145
18	.1188	.1659	.2260	.3013	.3944	.5078	.6445	.8074
20	.1099	.1554	.2141	.2884	.3812	.4954	.6342	.8012
22	.1025	.1465	.2038	.2772	.3697	.4844	.6251	.7955
24	.0961	.1387	.1949	.2674	.3595	.4747	.6169	.7904
25	.0933	.1353	.1908	.2629	.3548	.4701	.6131	.7880
30	.0815	.1208	.1737	.2437	.3346	.4505	.5963	.7775
35	.0728	.1097	.1605	.2286	.3184	.4345	.5825	.7687
40	.0660	.1010	.1498	.2163	.3050	.4211	.5708	.7611
45	.0605	.0939	.1410	.2060	.2936	.4096	.5607	.7545
50	.0560	.0879	.1336	.1972	.2838	.3996	.5518	.7486
60	.0489	.0785	.1216	.1828	.2676	.3829	.5367	.7386
70	.0437	.0713	.1123	.1715	.2547	.3693	.5243	.7302
80	.0396	.0657	.1049	.1622	.2440	.3579	.5137	.7231
90	.0363	.0610	.0987	.1545	.2349	.3482	.5046	.7168
100	.0336	.0572	.0935	.1479	.2271	.3397	.4966	.7112
120	.0294	.0510	.0851	.1371	.2141	.3255	.4830	.7017
140	.0262	.0464	.0786	.1287	.2038	.3139	.4718	.6937
160	.0237	.0427	.0734	.1217	.1952	.3042	.4623	.6869
180	.0218	.0397	.0691	.1159	.1879	.2959	.4541	.6809
200	.0201	.0371	.0655	.1109	.1816	.2887	.4469	.6757
250	.0171	.0323	.0584	.1011	.1691	.2740	.4320	.6646
300	.0149	.0289	.0531	.0937	.1594	.2625	.4202	.6557
350	.0133	.0262	.0491	.0879	.1517	.2532	.4105	.6482
400	.0121	.0241	.0458	.0832	.1453	.2454	.4022	.6419
450	.0111	.0224	.0431	.0792	.1399	.2387	.3951	.6363
500	.0103	.0210	.0408	.0758	.1352	.2329	.3888	.6314
600	.0090	.0188	.0372	.0703	.1275	.2232	.3782	.6229
700	.0080	.0171	.0344	.0659	.1214	.2152	.3694	.6158
800	.0073	.0157	.0321	.0624	.1163	.2086	.3620	.6098
900	.0067	.0146	.0302	.0594	.1119	.2029	.3556	.6045
1,000	.0062	.0137	.0286	.0569	.1082	.1980	.3499	.5998
1,200	.0054	.0122	.0260	.0527	.1020	.1897	.3404	.5918
1,400	.0048	.0111	.0240	.0495	.0971	.1830	.3325	.5850
1,600	.0044	.0102	.0225	.0468	.0930	.1773	.3258	.5793
1,800	.0040	.0095	.0211	.0446	.0895	.1725	.3200	.5743
2,000	.0037	.0089	.0200	.0427	.0866	.1683	.3149	.5698
2,500	.0031	.0077	.0178	.0389	.0806	.1597	.3044	.5605
3,000	.0027	.0069	.0162	.0360	.0760	.1530	.2961	.5530

Source: R. C. Meier, *Cases in Production and Operations Management* (New York: McGraw-Hill), pp. 310–14.

EXHIBIT S10.5

Improvement Curves: Table of Cumulative Values

IMPROVEMENT RATIOS

Unit	60%	65%	70%	75%	80%	85%	90%	95%
1	1.000	1.000	1.000	1.000	1.000	1.000	1.000	1.000
2	1.600	1.650	1.700	1.750	1.800	1.850	1.900	1.950
3	2.045	2.155	2.268	2.384	2.502	2.623	2.746	2.872
4	2.405	2.578	2.758	2.946	3.142	3.345	3.556	3.774
5	2.710	2.946	3.195	3.459	3.738	4.031	4.339	4.662
6	2.977	3.274	3.593	3.934	4.299	4.688	5.101	5.538
7	3.216	3.572	3.960	4.380	4.834	5.322	5.845	6.404
8	3.432	3.847	4.303	4.802	5.346	5.936	6.574	7.261
9	3.630	4.102	4.626	5.204	5.839	6.533	7.290	8.111
10	3.813	4.341	4.931	5.589	6.315	7.116	7.994	8.955
12	4.144	4.780	5.501	6.315	7.227	8.244	9.374	10.62
14	4.438	5.177	6.026	6.994	8.092	9.331	10.72	12.27
16	4.704	5.541	6.514	7.635	8.920	10.38	12.04	13.91
18	4.946	5.879	6.972	8.245	9.716	11.41	13.33	15.52
20	5.171	6.195	7.407	8.828	10.48	12.40	14.61	17.13
22	5.379	6.492	7.819	9.388	11.23	13.38	15.86	18.72
24	5.574	6.773	8.213	9.928	11.95	14.33	17.10	20.31
25	5.668	6.909	8.404	10.19	12.31	14.80	17.71	21.10
30	6.097	7.540	9.305	11.45	14.02	17.09	20.73	25.00
35	6.478	8.109	10.13	12.72	15.64	19.29	23.67	28.86
40	6.821	8.631	10.90	13.72	17.19	21.43	26.54	32.68
45	7.134	9.114	11.62	14.77	18.68	23.50	29.37	36.47
50	7.422	9.565	12.31	15.78	20.12	25.51	32.14	40.22
60	7.941	10.39	13.57	17.67	22.87	29.41	37.57	47.65
70	8.401	11.13	14.74	19.43	25.47	33.17	42.87	54.99
80	8.814	11.82	15.82	21.09	27.96	36.80	48.05	62.25
90	9.191	12.45	16.83	22.67	30.35	40.32	53.14	69.45
100	9.539	13.03	17.79	24.18	32.65	43.75	58.14	76.59
120	10.16	14.11	19.57	27.02	37.05	50.39	67.93	90.71
140	10.72	15.08	21.20	29.67	41.22	56.78	77.46	104.7
160	11.21	15.97	22.72	32.17	45.20	62.95	86.80	118.5
180	11.67	16.79	24.14	34.54	49.03	68.95	95.96	132.1
200	12.09	17.55	25.48	36.80	52.72	74.79	105.0	145.7
250	13.01	19.28	28.56	42.08	61.47	88.83	126.9	179.2
300	13.81	20.81	31.34	46.94	69.66	102.2	148.2	212.2
350	14.51	22.18	33.89	51.48	77.43	115.1	169.0	244.8
400	15.14	23.44	36.26	55.75	84.85	127.6	189.3	277.0
450	15.72	24.60	38.48	59.80	91.97	139.7	209.2	309.0
500	16.26	25.68	40.58	63.68	98.85	151.5	228.8	340.6
600	17.21	27.67	44.47	70.97	112.0	174.2	267.1	403.3
700	18.06	29.45	48.04	77.77	124.4	196.1	304.5	465.3
800	18.82	31.09	51.36	84.18	136.3	217.3	341.0	526.5
900	19.51	32.60	54.46	90.26	147.7	237.9	376.9	587.2
1,000	20.15	34.01	57.40	96.07	158.7	257.9	412.2	647.4
1,200	21.30	36.59	62.85	107.0	179.7	296.6	481.2	766.6
1,400	22.32	38.92	67.85	117.2	199.6	333.9	548.4	884.2
1,600	23.23	41.04	72.49	126.8	218.6	369.9	614.2	1001.
1,800	24.06	43.00	76.85	135.9	236.8	404.9	678.8	1116.
2,000	24.83	44.84	80.96	144.7	254.4	438.9	742.3	1230.
2,500	26.53	48.97	90.39	165.0	296.1	520.8	897.0	1513.
3,000	27.99	52.62	98.90	183.7	335.2	598.9	1047.	1791.

Cost of first sub		$ 500,000
Cost of second sub		
Materials	$200,000	
Labor: $300,000 × .70	210,000	410,000
Cost of third sub		
Materials	200,000	
Labor: $300,000 × .5682	170,460	370,460
Total cost		1,280,460
Markup: $1,280,460 × .10		128,046
Selling price		$1,408,506

If the operation is interrupted, then some relearning must occur. How far to go back up the learning curve can be estimated in some cases; we will discuss this later in the chapter.

Estimating the Learning Percentage

If production has been underway for some time, then the learning percentage is easily obtained from production records. Generally speaking, the longer the production history, the more accurate the estimate will be. Since a variety of other problems can occur during the early stages of production, most companies do not begin to collect data for learning curve analysis until some units have been completed.

Statistical analysis and graphical analysis should also be used. For example, in an exponential learning curve to find out how well the curve fits past data, it can be converted to a straight-line logarithmic (data plotted on log-log graph paper).

If production has not started, estimating the learning percentage becomes enlightened guesswork. In these cases the analyst has these options:

1. Assume that the learning percentage will be the same as it has been for previous applications within the same industry.
2. Assume that it will be the same as it has been for the same or similar products.
3. Analyze the similarities and differences between the proposed startup and previous startups and develop a revised learning percentage that appears best to fit the situation.

In selecting the option, the decision turns on how closely the startup under consideration approximates previous startups in the same industry or with the same or similar products. In any case, while a number of industries have used learning curves extensively, acceptance of the industry norm (such as the 80 percent figure for the airframe industry) is risky. An analysis of the company's own data should be undertaken even though it may ultimately lead to the industry improvement percentage.

There are two reasons for disparities between a firm's learning rate and that of its industry. First, there are the inevitable differences in operating characteristics between any two firms, stemming from the equipment, methods, product design, plant organization, and so forth. Second, procedural differences are manifested in the development of the learning percentage itself, such as whether the industry rate is based on a single product or on a product line, and the manner in which the data were aggregated.

How Long Does Learning Go On?

Does output stabilize, or is there continual improvement? Some areas can be shown to improve continually even over decades—radios, computers, and other electronic devices; and, if we allow for the effects of inflation, also automobiles, washing machines, refrigerators, and most other manufactured goods. If the learning curve has been valid for several hundreds or thousands of units, it will probably be valid for several hundreds or thousands more.[2] On the other hand, highly automated systems may have a near zero learning curve since, after installation, they quickly reach a constant volume.

Managerial Considerations in Using the Learning Curve

Management should be aware of the following factors in using the learning curve.

1. *Individual learning and incentives.* A study by Globerson indicates that subjects performing a manual task under controlled conditions showed significant improvement only when an incentive was applied.[3] This is consistent with findings from an earlier study by Gershoni (as well as others) in which the learning curve leveled off quickly in cases where incentives were absent.[4] The implication of these findings is clear: if you want to enhance worker learning, there must be adequate incentives. (Note, however, that the concept of incentives may be broadened to include any of the positive or negative administrative options available to managers.)

2. *Learning on new jobs versus old jobs.* The newer the job, the greater will be the improvement in labor hours and cost. Conversely, when production has been underway for a long time, improvement will be less discernible. For example, for an 80 percent exponential learning curve situation, the improvement between the first and second units will be 20 percent. However, if the

[2] Robert Irving, "A Convenient Method for Computing the Learning Curve," *Industrial Engineering* 14, no. 5 (May 1982), pp. 52–54.

[3] Shlomo Globerson, "The Influence of Job-Related Variables on the Predictability Power of Three Learning Curve Models," *AIIE Transactions* 12, no. 1 (March 1980), pp. 64–89.

[4] Haim Gershoni, "Motivation and Micro-Method When Learning Manual Tasks," *Work Study and Management Services* 15, no. 9 (September 1971), pp. 585–95.

product has been manufactured for 50 years, it will take another 50 years to reduce labor hours by 20 percent.

3. *Improvement comes from working smarter, not harder.* While incentives must be included to motivate the individual worker, most improvement in output comes from better methods and effective support systems rather than simply increased worker effort.

4. *Built-in production bias from suggesting any learning rate.* If a manager expects an 80 percent improvement factor, he or she may treat this percentage as a goal rather than as an unbiased measure of actual learning. In short, it may be a self-fulfilling prophecy. This, however, is not necessarily undesirable. What is wrong with setting a target improvement factor and then attempting to control production to achieve it?

5. *Preproduction versus postproduction adjustments.* The amount of learning shown by the learning curve depends both on the initial unit(s) of output and on the learning percentage. If there is much preproduction planning, experimentation, and adjustment, the early units will be produced more rapidly than if improvements are made after the first few units—other things being equal. In the first case, therefore, the apparent learning will be less than in the second case, even though subsequent "actual" learning may be the same in each instance.

6. *Changes in indirect labor and supervision.* Learning curves represent direct labor output, but if the mix of indirect labor and supervision changes, it is likely that the productivity of direct labor will be altered. We would expect, for example, that more supervisors, repairpersons, and material handlers would speed up production, whereas a reduction in their numbers would slow it down.

7. *Changes in technology, methods, and organization structure.* Obviously, significant adjustments in any of these factors will affect the production rate and, hence, the learning curve. Likewise, preventive maintenance programs, zero-defect programs, and other schemes designed to improve efficiency or product quality generally would have some impact on the learning phenomenon.

8. *Contract phaseout.* Though not relevant to all contract situations, note that the learning curve may begin to turn upward as a contract nears completion. This may result from transferring trained workers to other projects, nonreplacement of worn tooling, and reduced attention to efficiency on the part of management.

Range of application

While the learning curve is most commonly thought to be appropriate for primarily manual work, such as assembly, it is generally applicable to any situation in which deliberate efforts are made to improve a productive process. In airframe manufacturing, the 80 percent learning factor is derived not only from increasing experience by direct labor but also from various staff and service groups that contributed improvements in methods, tooling, material handling, and so forth. Thus, the general improvement phenomenon depicted by learning curves really reflects the results of the constellation of all of the activities performed by organization personnel whose function is to enhance production. The terms *improvement curve, experience curve, manufacturing progress function, progress acceleration curve,* and *performance curve* are alternative designations used to emphasize the fact that the learning curve describes more than worker learning. This point is underscored when we note that learning curves have been successfully applied in a number of industries that exhibit highly dissimilar production processes, such as petroleum, construction, textiles, candymaking, and metalworking.

Necessity for maintaining a file of learning curves

Learning curves will differ among applications because of differences in workers, machines, materials, tools, operations, and so forth. Therefore, a learning curve file should be developed and continually updated. In this way management can monitor the experience curves and more effectively track performances, assessing whether it is "good" or "bad." Also, if a file of curves is maintained, analysis of the curves could discover causal relationships that might suggest changes in design or procedures. Also, such files would enable the creation of estimated learning curves for applications not yet performed, from knowledge contained in other learning curves.

Learning curves and corporate strategy. No discussion of learning curves is complete without commenting on their wide use by major firms in developing corporate strategy.

Learning curves reflect the cost-volume relationship that exists for a company's product line. This means that a firm has at its disposal a tool to predict its manufacturing costs and, hence, to set cost-based sales prices. For setting corporate strategy then, a firm with a good understanding of its own learning curve might choose the following approach for a new product: Price the product low to establish its market share and then sustain this share by continuing to reduce its price to reflect the cost reduction gained from experience. Alternatively, a firm facing an existing market may use the learning curve idea to see if it is logical to enter with a similar product. This company may examine its own facilities management and worker skills and conclude that it can take advantage of the learning it has achieved from similar products and be competitive sooner (e.g., at a lower volume).

Entering an existing market requires recognition of competitors' learning curves as well. Assume that an existing firm entered the market two years ago, producing 1,000 units per year with an 80 percent learning curve and an initial product cost of $100. If a new firm decides to enter the market now, the existing firm already has its price down to $8.66 for that 2,000th unit. In order to compete, the new firm either must have a faster learning rate or must start at a much lower initial cost. In fact, successful newcomers that enter existing product markets often do so using a high degree of mechanization or even complete automation.

Learning curves used in contracts. Contracts, such as those that specify the delivery of items in several spaced batches and those that specify bidding for followup on contracts, must be especially careful in considering learning rates. Interruption in production of the product leads to "forgetting." That is, while learning curves imply that learning is a continual process, interruptions create the need to re-learn. In effect, this means that restarting the production process also means starting back somewhat on the learning curve. It takes some time to recover to that point wherein the previous learning curve was interrupted. One other point is also important—often materials, equipment, and personnel may also change over the sequence of intermittent batch deliveries of several contracts in sequence. This can cause new learning rates as well as the "forgetting" factor.

S10.3 CONCLUSION

Learning curves are of great value to the operations manager. They provide a practical yet powerful tool to estimate production costs, lead times, and the likelihood of successfully entering existing product markets. Keep in mind, though, that new technology may well have a significant impact on the applicability of learning curves. Computer software programs for finance, marketing, production, and inventory control allow us to improve the points at which we start our operations. Automated processes tend to be relatively constant over time, and equipment that has computer control greatly reduces setup times and begins production at close to the long-term rate. In many cases, learning rates have flattened. This means that there is less learning—or that we are starting somewhere down the learning curve from our unautomated days. This could create a tendency to overestimate the amount of learning.

S10.4 REVIEW AND DISCUSSION QUESTIONS

1. How might the following business specialists use learning curves: accountants, marketers, financial analysts, personnel managers, and computer programmers?
2. As a manager, which learning percentage would you prefer (other things being equal), 110 percent or 60 percent? Explain.
3. Discuss the influence of the learning curve forgetting factor on a company's contract bidding.
4. What difference does it make if a customer wants a 10,000-unit order produced and delivered all at one time or in 2,500-unit batches over a period of time?

S10.5 PROBLEMS

*1. After completing a total of 10 minisubs, SUB (see the Insert) receives an order for two subs from a Loch Ness Monster search team. Given the fact that a 70 percent learning curve prevailed for the previous order, what price should SUB quote the search team, assuming that it wishes to make the same percentage profit as before?

2. A time standard was set as .20 hours per unit after observing 50 cycles. If the task has a 90 percent learning curve, what would be the average time per unit after 100, 200, and 400 cycles? What percent of standard would be expected at each number if the worker performed at 100 percent capacity?

3. You have just received 10 units of a special subassembly from an electronics manufacturer at a price of $250 per unit. A new order has also just come in for your company's product that uses these subassemblies, and you wish to purchase 40 more to be shipped in lots of 10 units each. (The subassemblies are bulky, and you need only 10 a month to fill your new order.)
   a. Assuming a 70 percent learning curve by your supplier on a similar product last year, how much should you pay for each lot? What would be your justification for your bid to the supplier? (Hint: Treat each lot of 10 as your basis for pricing.)
   b. Suppose you are the supplier and can produce 20 units now but cannot start production on the second 20 units for two months. Discuss price levels for the second batch.

4. United Research Associates (URA) had received a contract to produce two units of a new cruise missile guidance control. The first unit took 4,000 hours to complete and cost $30,000 in materials and equipment usage. The second took 3,200 hours and cost $21,000 in materials and equipment usage. Labor cost is charged at $18 per hour.

   The prime contractor has now approached URA and asked to submit a bid for the cost of producing *another* 20 guidance controls. Disregarding any additional time required for re-learning:
   a. What will the last unit cost to build?
   b. What will be the average time for the 20 missile guidance controls?
   c. What will the average cost be per guidance control for the 20 in the contract?

5. United Assembly Products (UAP) has a personnel screening process for job applicants that tests each applicant's ability to perform at the department's long-term average rate. UAP has asked you to modify the test by incorporating learning theory. From the company's data, you discovered that if people can perform a given task in 30 minutes or less on the 20th unit, they achieve the group long-run average. Obviously, all job applicants cannot be subjected to 20 performances of such a task, so you are to determine whether they will likely achieve the desired rate based only on two performances.
   a. Suppose a person took 100 minutes on the first unit and 80 minutes on the second. Should this person be hired?

* Answers for Problems 1 and 6 are contained in Appendix D.

b. What approximate learning rate would you establish for hiring (i.e., what rate must the job applicant show for his or her two performances in order to be hired)?

*6. A job applicant is being tested for an assembly line position. Management feels that steady-state times have been approximately reached after 1,000 performances. Regular assembly line workers are expected to perform the task within four minutes.

a. If the job applicant performed the first test operation in 10 minutes and the second one in 9 minutes, should this applicant be hired?

b. What is the expected time that the job applicant would be expected to finish the 10th unit?

7. A potentially large customer has promised to subcontract assembly work to you if you can perform the operations at an average time of less than 20 hours each. The contract is for 1,000 units.

You run a test and do the first one in 50 hours and the second one in 40 hours.

a. How long would you expect it to take to do the third one?

b. Would you take the contract? Explain.

S10.6 SELECTED BIBLIOGRAPHY

Camm, Jeffrey D. "A Note on Learning Curve Parameters." *Decision Sciences* 16, no. 3 (Summer 1985), pp. 325–27.

Globerson, Shlomo. "The Influence of Job-Related Variables on the Predictability Power of Three Learning Curve Models." *AIIE Transactions* 12, no. 1 (March 1980), pp. 64–69.

Irving, Robert. "A Convenient Method for Computing the Learning Curve." *Industrial Engineering* 14, no. 5 (May 1982), pp. 52–54.

Kopsco, David P., and William C. Nemitz. "Learning Curves and Lot Sizing for Independent and Dependent Demand." *Journal of Operations Management* 4, no. 1 (November 1983), pp. 73–83.

Smunt, Timothy L. "A Comparison of Learning Curve Analysis and Moving Average Ratio Analysis for Detailed Operational Planning." *Decision Sciences* 17, no. 4 (Fall 1986), pp. 475–95.

Towill, D. R. "The Use of Learning Curve Models for Prediction of Batch Production Performance." *International Journal of Operations and Production Management* 5, no. 2 (1985), pp. 13–24.

Yelle, Louie E. "The Learning Curves: Historical Review and Comprehensive Survey." *Decision Sciences* 10, no. 2 (April 1979), pp. 302–28.

Chapter 11

Aggregate Planning

EPIGRAPH

"Harry, I just got the forecast. Can you rough out a plan to make 20,000 toy robots for next year?"

CHAPTER OUTLINE

KEY TERMS

Long-, Medium-, and Short-Range Planning
Aggregate Production Planning
Master Production Schedule
Rough-Cut Capacity Planning
Capacity Requirements Planning
Final Assembly Scheduling
Input/Output Planning and Control
Production Activity Control
Purchase Planning and Control
Production Rate
Work-Force Level
Inventory on hand
Production Planning Strategies
Pure Strategy
Mixed Strategy

Suppose you are thinking about throwing a big party. The first questions you would have might be:

How many people should be invited?
How much space is needed?
How much food?
How much drink?
How much help?
How much money?
What sort of entertainment?

This is "aggregate" planning. Your initial interest is in the broad aspects of the problem. Once you have defined the limits or at least set acceptable ranges for each of the categories raised in the questions, then you can get down to the nitty-gritty of specifying exactly who to invite, what food to serve, what help to hire, and so on.

In planning, you could have created an interim stage of decisions between the aggregate and detailed plans. For example, the population from which you would send invitations could consist of colleagues, friends, neighbors, and relatives. You might then decide on some ratio or specific number from each category. Similarly with food, the total aggregate amount of food might be subdivided into hot and cold food, Italian, Mexican, and traditional American. Then, specific selections from each could be made.

In manufacturing, a parallel example to the party preparation would be, at the aggregate level, asking such questions as:

How much demand do we have?
How much total output (in terms of dollars or standard units of output) should we produce?
How many people do we need?
How much capacity is needed?
How much money do we need?
How much inventory should we have?

After we answer each of these questions by defining acceptable limits for each category, we can then be more specific, such as in dividing demand and production into product groups and then into specific products. The total number of personnel required can be subdivided into categories such as finance people, accounting people, personnel people, manufacturing people, and so on. Further subdivision in manufacturing might be: production scheduling people and machinists. Production scheduling people could be again subdivided into master schedulers, MRP personnel, expediters, customer liaison personnel. Machinists could be specified as lathe operators, NC machine operators, setup men, and so on.

Planning is simply a process of dis-aggregation, starting from some initial broad level and then dividing the plan into smaller and smaller more clearly defined pieces. The result is a detailed plan that specifies exactly what should be done.

This chapter deals with the highest level in planning, the aggregate plan. In our planning for a party, the aggregate plan is to answer the first set of broad questions—How many people, etc.

Any business organization—public or private, manufacturing, services, or agriculture—must start with a plan. Aggregate planning translates annual and quarterly business plans into broad categories. In manufacturing and services, aggregate plans specify product lines rather than specific products in the line; and general numbers of workers needed, rather than by each skill.

In this chapter, we touch on level scheduling (which is basic to the Japanese Just-in-Time system) and on quantitative techniques for aggregate planning. In later chapters, we discuss how the aggregate plan becomes converted into short-term schedules for the work center.

11.1 OVERVIEW OF MANUFACTURING PLANNING ACTIVITIES

The firm must plan its manufacturing activities at a variety of levels and operate these as a system. Exhibit 11.1 presents an overall view of planning and shows how aggregate production planning relates to other activities of a manufacturing firm. The time dimension is also shown as long, medium, and short range.

Long-range planning is generally done annually, focusing on a horizon greater than one year. **Medium-range planning** usually covers the period from 6 to 18 months, with time increments that are monthly or sometimes quarterly. **Short-range planning** covers the period from one day to several weeks, with the time increment usually weekly. Because heavier operations management is involved in medium- and short-range planning, planning activities in these two time frames will be discussed in greater detail than long-range planning activities.

Long-Range Planning

Long-range planning begins with a statement of organizational objectives and goals for the next two to ten years. *Corporate strategic planning* articulates how these objectives and goals are to be achieved in light of the company's capabilities and its economic and political environment as projected by its *business forecasting*. Elements of the strategic plan include product-line delineation, quality and pricing levels, and market penetration goals. *Product and market planning* translates these into individual market and product-line objectives, and includes a long-range production plan (basically a forecast of items

EXHIBIT 11.1

Overview of Manufacturing Planning Activities

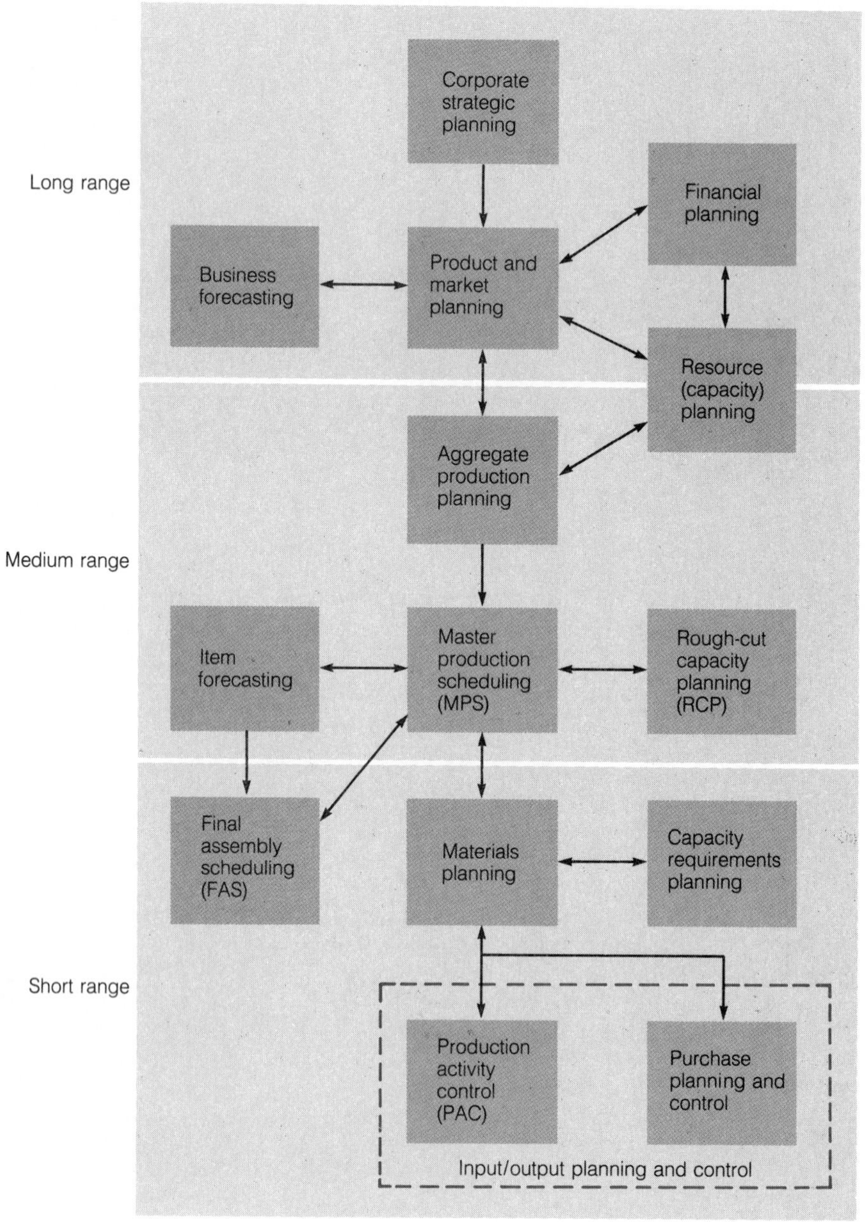

to be manufactured for two years or more into the future). *Financial planning* analyzes the financial feasibility of these objectives relative to capital requirements and return on investment goals. *Resource planning* identifies the facilities, equipment, and personnel needed to accomplish the long-range production plan, and thus is frequently referred to as *long-run capacity planning*.

Medium-Range Planning

Aggregate production planning

This system specifies output requirements by major product groups either in labor hours required or in units of production for monthly periods up to 18 months into the future. Its main inputs are the product and market plans and the resource plan. **Aggregate production planning** seeks to find that combination of monthly work force levels and inventory levels that minimizes total production-related costs over the planning period.

Item forecasting

This provides an estimate of specific products (and replacement parts), which, when integrated with the aggregate production plan, becomes the output requirement for the master production schedule. The process of monitoring and integrating this information is termed *demand management* (as discussed in Chapter 6).

Master production scheduling (MPS)

The MPS generates the amounts and dates for the manufacture of specific end products. The **master production schedule** is usually fixed over the short run (six to eight weeks). Beyond six to eight weeks, various changes can be made, with essentially complete revisions possible after six months (see Chapter 13).

Rough-cut capacity planning

This reviews the MPS to make sure that there are no obvious capacity constraints that would require changing the schedule. **Rough-cut capacity planning** includes verifying that production and warehouse facilities, equipment, and labor are available and that key vendors have allocated sufficient capacity to provide materials when needed.

Short-Range Planning

Materials planning

Also known as *material requirements planning* (MRP), this system takes the end product requirements from the MPS and breaks them down into their component parts and subassemblies. The materials plan specifies when production and purchase orders must be placed for each part and subassembly in order to complete the products on schedule (see Chapter 13).

Capacity requirements planning

Capacity requirements planning (CRP) should really be referred to as capacity requirements *scheduling,* since it provides a detailed schedule of when each operation is to be run on each work center and how long it will take to process. The information it uses comes from planned and open orders from the materials plan. The CRP itself helps to validate the rough cut capacity plan.

Final assembly scheduling

Final assembly scheduling provides the operations required to put the product in its final form. It is here that customized or final features of the product are scheduled. For example, a printer manufacturer would typically specify from various options a control panel configuration at this scheduling stage.

Input/output planning and control

Input/output planning and control refers to a variety of reports and procedures focusing on schedule demands and capacity constraints deriving from the materials plan. (See Chapter 14.)

Production activity control

Production activity control (PAC) is a relatively new term used to describe scheduling and shop-floor control activities.

Purchase planning and control

Purchase planning and control deals with the acquisition and control of purchased items, again as specified by the materials plan. Input/output planning and control are necessary to make sure that purchasing not only is obtaining materials in time to meet the schedule, but is aware of those orders that, for various reasons, call for rescheduling purchases.

In summary, all the planning approaches attempt to balance capacity required with capacity available, and then schedule and control production in light of changes in the capacity balance. A good planning system is complete without being overwhelming, and has the confidence of its users up and down the organization structure.

11.2 HIERARCHICAL PRODUCTION PLANNING

So far we have looked at manufacturing planning activities within a framework of *long range, medium range, and short range*. If we were to overlay the organization chart of a firm onto Exhibit 11.1, we would note that higher levels within the organization deal with long-range and lower levels with

EXHIBIT 11.2

Hierarchical Planning Process

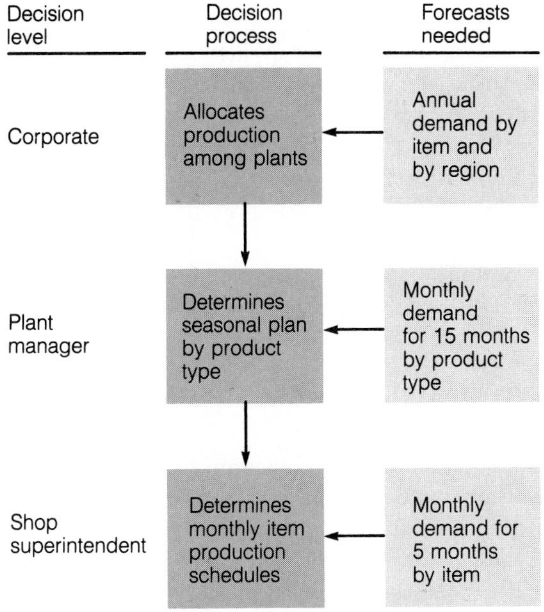

Source: Harlan C. Meal, "Putting Production Decisions Where They Belong," *Harvard Business Review* 62, no. 2 (March–April 1984), p. 101.

short-range planning. In a more formal way, Meal uses the term *hierarchical production planning* (HPP) to tailor the planning structure to the organization.[1] As noted in Exhibit 11.2, higher levels of management would use aggregate data for top-level decisions and shop-floor decisions would be made using detailed data. In the extreme case HPP logically states that top management should not become involved in determining the production lot size at a machine center. By the same token, the production line supervisor should not become involved in planning new product lines.

Meal cites as an example a tire manufacturer with several plants. With a *conventional* approach, each plant would tend to build a stock of tires it was confident of selling. An unsatisfactory consequence was that slow-moving items were produced in small quantities during peak season when capacity was scarce.

By centralizing the decision, top managers expected that they would be able to somehow decide which plants would produce which tires in what quan-

[1] Harlan C. Meal, "Putting Production Decisions Where They Belong," *Harvard Business Review* 62, no. 2 (March–April 1984), pp. 102–11.

tities. This became impossible; not only were the number of detailed variables much too large to review, but it took the decision-making power away from plant management where it rightly belonged.

The hierarchical procedure divided the decision making, with top management allocating tire production among the plants on an annual basis. Plant management in each of the plants would decide on seasonal effects, buildup of inventory, hiring, etc. Shop management would perform the detailed scheduling of individual items. Shop supervisors, knowing the proportion of time they needed to spend on each product group, could then fill up available capacity.

An advantage of hierarchical planning is that each successive level has a smaller database and a simpler structure.

11.3 AGGREGATE PRODUCTION PLANNING

Again, aggregate production planning is concerned with setting production rates by product group or other broad categories for the intermediate term (6 to 18 months). Note again from our first exhibit that the aggregate plan precedes the master schedule. *The main purpose of the aggregate plan is to specify the optimal combination of production rate, the work-force level, and inventory on hand.* **Production rate** refers to the number of units completed per unit of time (such as per hour or per day). **Work-force level** is the number of workers needed for production. **Inventory on hand** is the balance of unused inventory carried over from the previous period.

A formal statement of the aggregate planning problem is: Given the demand forecast for each period in the planning horizon, determine the production level, inventory level, and work-force level for each period to minimize the relevant costs over the planning horizon.[2]

The form of the aggregate plan varies from company to company. In some firms, it is a formalized report containing planning objectives and the planning premises upon which it is based. In other companies, particularly smaller ones, "it may take shape in verbal directives or writings on the back of matchbook covers."[3]

The process by which the plan itself is derived also varies. One common approach is to derive it from the corporate annual plan, as was shown in Exhibit 11.1. A typical corporate plan contains a section on manufacturing that specifies how many units in each major product line need to be produced over

---

[2] J. M. Mellichamp and R. M. Love, "Production Switching Heuristics for the Aggregate Planning Problem," *Management Science* 24, no. 12 (1978), p. 1242.

[3] M. Nelson, "I Read the Book: The Master Scheduler Did It" (21st Annual American Production and Inventory Control Society Conference proceedings, 1978), p. 666.

the next 12 months to meet the sales forecast. The planner takes this information and attempts to determine how to best meet these requirements in terms of available resources. Alternatively, some organizations combine output requirements into equivalent units and use this as the basis for aggregate planning. For example, a division of General Motors may be asked to produce a certain number of cars of all types at a particular facility. The production planner would then take the average labor hours required for all models as a basis for the overall aggregate plan. Refinements to this plan, specifically model types to be produced, would be reflected in shorter-term production plans.

Another approach is to develop the aggregate plan by simulating various master production schedules and calculating corresponding capacity requirements to see if adequate labor and equipment exist at each work center. If capacity is inadequate, additional requirements for overtime, subcontracting, extra workers, and so forth are specified for each product line and combined into a rough-cut plan. This plan is then modified by cut-and-try or mathematical methods to derive a final and, one hopes, lower-cost plan.

Production Planning Environment

Exhibit 11.3 illustrates the internal and external factors that constitute the production planning environment. In general, the external environment is outside the production planner's direct control. In some firms, demand for the product can be managed, as noted in Chapter 6, but even so, the production planner must live with the sales projections and orders promised by the marketing function. This leaves the internal factors as the variables that can be manipulated in deriving a production plan.

The internal factors themselves differ in terms of their controllability. Current physical capacity (plant and equipment) is usually pretty nearly fixed in the short run; union agreements often constrain what can be done in terms of changing the work force; physical capacity cannot always be increased; and top management may set limits on the amount of money that can be tied up in inventories. Still, there is always some flexibility in managing these factors, and production planners can implement one or a combination of the **production planning strategies** discussed here.

Production planning strategies

There are essentially four alternatives that deal with the work force, work time, inventory, and backlogs.

1. Vary the work force size by hiring and laying off employees as demand fluctuates.
2. Maintain a stable work force, but vary the output rate by varying the number of hours worked through variable work weeks or overtime.

EXHIBIT 11.3 Required Inputs to the Production Planning System

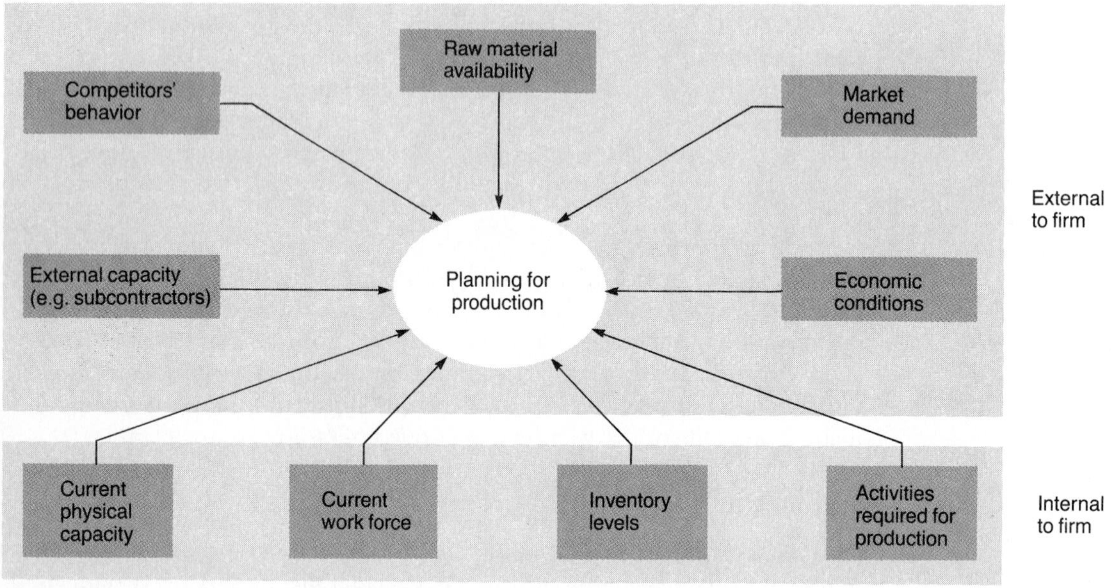

3. Maintain a stable work force and constant output rate, but absorb demand fluctuations by allowing inventory to vary.
4. Allow backlogs (delivery lead times) to increase during periods of increased demand and decrease during periods of decreased demand.

When just one of these variables is used to absorb demand fluctuations, it is termed a **pure strategy;** when one or more are used in combination, that is a **mixed strategy.** As you might suspect, mixed strategies are more widely applied in industry.

Relevant Costs

There are four basic costs relevant to aggregate production planning. These relate to the production cost itself, as well as the cost to hold inventory and to have unfilled orders. More specifically, these are:

1. Basic production costs. These are the fixed and variable costs incurred in producing a given product type in a given time period. Included are

direct and indirect labor costs and regular as well as overtime compensation.

2. Costs associated with changes in the production rate. Typical costs in this category are those involved in hiring, training, and laying off personnel.
3. Inventory holding costs. A major component is the cost of capital tied up in inventory. Other components are storing, insurance, taxes, spoilage, and obsolescence.
4. Backlogging costs. Usually these are very hard to measure and include costs of expediting, loss of customer goodwill, and loss of sales revenues resulting from backlogging.

11.4 AGGREGATE PLANNING TECHNIQUES

Companies still use simple "cut-and-try" charting and graphic methods in developing their aggregate plans. A cut-and-try approach involves costing out various production planning alternatives and selecting the one with the lowest cost. In addition, there are more sophisticated approaches, including linear programming, the Linear Decision Rule, and various heuristic methods. Of these, only linear programming has seen broad application and we will discuss it later.

A Cut-and-Try Example: The C&A Company

A firm with pronounced seasonal variation will normally plan production for a full year in order to capture the extremes in demand during the busiest and slowest months. However, it is possible to illustrate the general principles involved with a shorter horizon. Suppose we wish to set up a production plan for the C&A Company for the next six months. We are given the following information:

Month	Demand Forecast	Number of Working Days
January	1,800	22
February	1,500	19
March	1,100	21
April	900	21
May	1,100	22
June	1,600	20
	8,000 units	125 days

Costs	
Materials	$100/unit
Inventory holding cost	$1.50/unit-month
Marginal cost of stockout	$5/unit/month
Marginal cost of subcontracting	$20/unit ($120 subcontracting cost less $100 material savings)
Hiring and training cost	$200/worker
Layoff cost	$250/worker
Labor hours required	5/unit
Straight time cost (first 8 hours each day)	$4/hour
Overtime cost (time and a half)	$6/hour

Inventory	
Beginning inventory	400 units

Note that in solving this problem we can exclude the material costs. We could have included this $100 cost in all our calculations, but if we assume that a $100 cost is common to each demanded unit, then we need only to concern ourselves with the marginal costs. Since the subcontracting cost is $120, our true cost for subcontracting is just $20, since we save the materials.

Note also that many costs are expressed in a different form than typically found in the accounting records of a firm. Therefore, do not expect to obtain all these costs directly from such records, but indirectly from management personnel, who can help interpret the data.

Inventory at the beginning of the first period is 400 units. Because the demand forecast is imperfect, the C&A Company has determined that a *safety stock*, or buffer inventory, should be established to reduce the likelihood of stockouts. For this example, assume the safety stock should be one-quarter of the demand forecast (Chapter 12 will cover this topic in more depth).

Before investigating alternative production plans, it is often quite useful to convert demand forecasts into *production requirements*, which take into account the safety stock estimates. In Exhibit 11.4, note that these requirements implicitly assume that the safety stock is never actually used, so that the ending inventory each month equals the safety stock for that month. For example, the January safety stock of 450 (25 percent of January demand of 1,800) becomes the inventory at the end of January. The production requirement for January is demand plus safety stock minus beginning inventory (1,800 + 450 − 400 = 1,850).

Now we must formulate alternative production plans for the C&A Company. We will investigate four different plans with the objective of finding the one with the lowest total cost.

Plan 1. Produce to exact monthly production requirements using a regular eight-hour day by varying work force size.[4]

[4] This is often termed a *chase* strategy (no relation to one of the authors of this text).

EXHIBIT 11.4

Aggregate Production Planning Requirements

Month	(1) Beginning Inventory	(2) Demand Forecast	(3) = .25 × (2) Safety Stock	(4) = (2) + (3) − (1) Production Requirement	(5) = (1) + (4) − (2) Ending Inventory
January	400	1,800	450	1,850	450
February	450	1,500	375	1,425	375
March	375	1,100	275	1,000	275
April	275	900	225	850	225
May	225	1,100	275	1,150	275
June	275	1,600	400	1,725	400
				8,000	

Plan 2. Produce to meet expected average demand over the next six months by maintaining a constant work force. This constant number of workers is calculated by *averaging* the demand forecast over the horizon. Take the total production requirements for all six months and determine how many workers would be needed if each month's requirements were the same [(8,000 units × 5 hours per unit) ÷ (125 days × 8 hours per day) = 40 workers]. Inventory is allowed to accumulate, with shortages filled from next month's production by back ordering.

Plan 3. Produce to meet the minimum expected demand (April) using a constant work force on regular time. Subcontract to meet additional output requirements. The number of workers is calculated by locating the minimum monthly production requirement and determining how many workers would be needed for that month [(850 units × 6 months × 5 hours per unit) ÷ (125 days × 8 hours per day) = 25 workers] and subcontracting any monthly difference between requirements and production.

Plan 4. Produce to meet expected demand for all but the first two months using a constant work force on regular time. Use overtime to meet additional output requirements. The number of workers is more difficult to compute for this plan, but the goal is to finish June with an ending inventory as close as possible to the June safety stock. By trial and error it can be shown that constant work force of 38 workers is the closest approximation.

The next step is to calculate the cost of each plan. This requires a series of simple calculations, which are shown in Exhibit 11.5. Note that the headings in each column are different for each plan since each is a different problem requiring its own data and calculations.

The final step is to tabulate and graph each plan and make a comparison of their costs. From Exhibit 11.6, we can see that making use of subcontracting resulted in the lowest cost (Plan 3). Exhibit 11.7 shows the effects of the four plans. This is a cumulative graph illustrating the expected results on the total production requirement.

EXHIBIT 11.5 **Costs of Four Production Plans**

PRODUCTION PLAN 1: EXACT PRODUCTION; VARY WORK FORCE

Month	(1) = (4) in Exhibit 11.4 Production Requirement	(2) = (1) × 5 Hr/Unit Production Hours Required	(3) Working Days per Month	(4) = (3) × 8 Hr/Day Hours per Month per Worker	(5) = (2) ÷ (4) Workers Required	(6) New Workers Hired	(7) = (6) × $200 Hiring Cost	(8) Workers Laid Off	(9) = (8) × $250 Layoff Cost	(10) = (2) × $4 Straight-Time Cost
Jan.	1,850	9,250	22	176	53	0*	—	—	—	$ 37,000
Feb.	1,425	7,125	19	152	47	0	0	6	$1,500	28,500
Mar.	1,000	5,000	21	168	30	0	0	17	4,250	20,000
Apr.	850	4,250	21	168	25	0	0	5	1,250	17,000
May	1,150	5,750	22	176	33	8	$1,600	0	0	23,000
June	1,725	8,625	20	160	54	21	4,200	0	0	34,500
							$5,800		$7,000	$160,000

* Assuming opening work force equal to first month's requirement of 53 workers.

PRODUCTION PLAN 2: CONSTANT WORK FORCE; VARY INVENTORY AND STOCKOUT

Month	(1) Beginning Inventory	(2) Working Days per Month	(3) = (2) × 8 Hr/Day × 40 Workers* Production Hours Available	(4) = (3) ÷ 5 Hr/Unit Actual Production	(5) = (2) in Exhibit 11.4 Demand Forecast	(6) = (1) + (4) − (5) Ending Inventory	(7) Units Short	(8) = (7) × $5 Shortage Cost	(9) = (3) in Exhibit 11.4 Safety Stock	(10) = (6) − (9) Units Excess	(11) = (10) × $1.50 Inventory Cost	(12) = (3) × $4 Straight-Time Cost
Jan.	400	22	7,040	1,408	1,800	8	0	0	450	0	0	$ 28,160
Feb.	8	19	6,080	1,216	1,500	−276	276	$1,380	375	0	0	$ 24,320
Mar.	−276	21	6,720	1,344	1,100	−32	32	160	275	0	0	$ 26,880
Apr.	−32	21	6,720	1,344	900	412	0	0	225	187	$281	$ 26,880
May	412	22	7,040	1,408	1,100	720	0	0	275	445	667	$ 28,160
June	720	20	6,400	1,280	1,600	400	0	0	400	0	0	$ 25,600
		125						$1,540			$948	$160,000

* (Sum of Col. (4) in Exhibit 11.4 × 5 hr/unit) ÷ (Sum of Col. (2) × 8 hr/day) = (8,000 × 5) ÷ (125 × 8) = 40.

PRODUCTION PLAN 3: CONSTANT LOW WORK FORCE; SUBCONTRACT

Month	(1) = (4) in Exhibit 11.4 Production Requirement	(2) Working Days per Month	(3) = (2) × 8 Hr/Day × 25 Workers* Production Hours Available	(4) = (3) ÷ 5 Hr/Unit Actual Production	(5) = (1) − (4) Units Subcontracted	(6) = (5) × $20 Subcontracting Cost	(7) = (3) × $4 Straight-Time Cost
Jan.	1,850	22	4,400	880	970	$19,400	$ 17,600
Feb.	1,425	19	3,800	760	665	13,300	15,200
Mar.	1,000	21	4,200	840	160	3,200	16,800
Apr.	850	21	4,200	840	10	200	16,800
May	1,150	22	4,400	880	270	5,400	17,600
June	1,725	20	4,000	800	925	18,500	16,000
						$60,000	$100,000

* Minimum production requirement. For example, (Col (1) for April × 6 months × 5 hr/unit) ÷ (Sum of Col (2) × 8 hr/day) = (850 × 6 × 5) ÷ (125 × 8) = 25 workers.

PRODUCTION PLAN 4: CONSTANT WORK FORCE; OVERTIME

Month	(1) Beginning Inventory	(2) Working Days per Month	(3) = (2) × 8 Hr/Day × 38 Workers Production Hours Available	(4) = (3) ÷ 5 Hr/Unit Regular Shift Production	(5) = (2) in Exhibit 11.4 Demand Forecast	(6) = (1) + (4) − (5) Units Available before Overtime	(7) From (6) Units Overtime	(8) = (7) × 5 Hr/Unit × $6/Hr Overtime Cost	(9) = (3) in Exhibit 11.4 Safety Stock	(10) = (6) − (9) Units Excess	(11) = (10) × $1.50 Inventory Cost	(12) = (3) × $4 Straight-Time Cost
Jan.	400	22	6,688	1,338	1,800	−62	62	$ 1,860	450	0	0	$ 26,752
Feb.	0	19	5,776	1,155	1,500	−345	345	10,350	375	0	0	23,104
Mar.	0	21	6,384	1,277	1,100	177	0	0	275	0	0	25,536
Apr.	177	21	6,384	1,277	900	554	0	0	225	329	$ 493	25,536
May	554	22	6,688	1,338	1,100	792	0	0	275	517	776	26,752
June	792	20	6,080	1,216	1,600	408	0	0	400	8	12	24,320
								$12,210			$1281	$152,000

EXHIBIT 11.6

Comparison of Four Plans

Cost	Plan 1: Exact Production; Vary Work Force	Plan 2: Constant Work Force; Vary Inventory and Stockout	Plan 3: Constant Low Work Force; Subcontract	Plan 4: Constant Work Force; Overtime
Hiring	$ 5,800	$ 0	$ 0	$ 0
Layoff	7,000	0	0	0
Excess inventory	0	948	0	1,281
Shortage	0	1,540	0	0
Subcontract	0	0	60,000	0
Overtime	0	0	0	12,210
Straight time	160,000	160,000	100,000	152,000
	$172,800	$162,488	$160,000	$165,491

Note that we have made one other assumption in this example: the plan can start with any number of workers with no hiring or layoff cost. This usually is the case since an aggregate plan draws on existing personnel, and we can start the plan that way. However, in an actual application, the availability of existing personnel transferable from other areas of the firm will change the assumptions in this example.

Each of these four plans focused on one particular cost, and the first three were simple pure strategies. Obviously, there are many other feasible plans, some of which would use a combination of work-force changes, overtime, and some subcontracting. The problem set at the end of this chapter includes examples of such mixed strategies. In practice, the final plan chosen would come from searching a variety of alternatives and future projections beyond the six-month planning horizon we have used.

Keep in mind that the cut-and-try approach does not guarantee that we will find the minimum-cost solution. However, recent advances in computer hardware and software have elevated this kind of "what-if" analysis to a fine art. Spreadsheet programs, such as Lotus or SuperCalc, can perform cut-and-try cost estimates in seconds on a microcomputer. More sophisticated programs can generate much better solutions without the user having to intercede, as in the cut-and-try method.

Aggregate Planning Applied to Services: Tucson Parks and Recreation Department

Charting and graphic techniques are also very useful for aggregate planning in service applications. The following example shows how a city's parks and recreation department could use the alternatives of full-time employees, part-time employees, and subcontracting to meet its commitment to provide a service to the city.

EXHIBIT 11.7

Four Plans for Satisfying a Production Requirement over the Number of Production Days Available

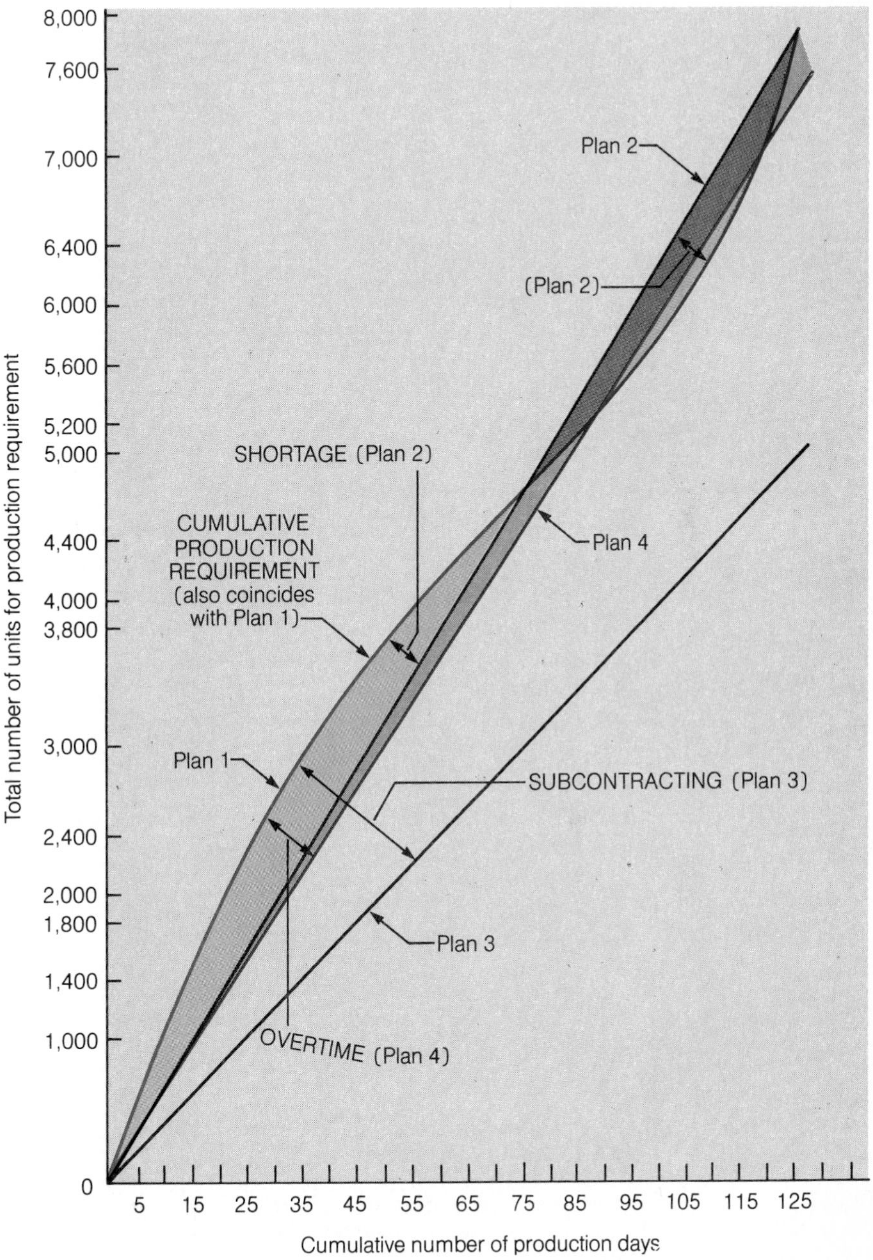

Tucson Parks and Recreation Department has an operation and maintenance budget of $9,760,000. The department is responsible for developing and maintaining open space, all public recreational programs, adult sports leagues, golf courses, tennis courts, pools, and so forth. There are 336 full-time-equivalent employees (FTEs). Of these, 216 are full-time permanent personnel who provide the administration and year-round maintenance to all areas. The remaining 120 year-long FTE positions are all part time; about three-quarters of them are used during the summer and the remaining quarter in the fall, winter, and spring seasons. The three-fourths (or 90 FTE positions) show up as approximately 800 part-time summer jobs: lifeguards, baseball umpires, and instructors in summer programs for children. Eight hundred part-time jobs came from 90 FTEs because many last only for a month or two while the FTEs are year-long FTEs.

Currently, the only parks and recreation work subcontracted amounts to less than $100,000. This is for the golf and tennis pros and for grounds maintenance at the libraries and veterans cemetery.

Because of the nature of city employment, the probable bad public image, and civil service rules, the option to hire and fire full-time help daily or weekly to meet seasonal demand is pretty much out of the question. However, temporary part-time help is authorized and traditional. Also, it is virtually impossible to have regular (non part-time) staff for all the summer jobs. During the summer months, the approximately 800 part-time employees are staffing the many programs that occur simultaneously, prohibiting level scheduling over a normal 40-hour week. Also, a wider variety of skills is required than can be expected from full-time employees (e.g., umpires, coaches, lifeguards, teachers of ceramics, guitar, karate, belly dancing, and yoga).

There are three options open to the department in its aggregate planning.

1. The present method, which is to maintain a medium-level full-time staff and schedule work during off seasons (such as rebuilding baseball fields during the winter months) and to use part-time help during peak demands.
2. Maintain a lower level of staff over the year and subcontract all additional work presently done by full-time staff (still using part-time help).
3. Maintain an administrative staff only and subcontract all work, including part-time help. (This would entail contracts to landscaping firms, pool-maintenance companies, and to newly created private firms to employ and supply part-time help.)

The common unit of measure of work across all areas is full-time equivalent jobs or employees (or FTEs). For example, assume in the same week that 30 lifeguards worked 20 hours each, 40 instructors worked 15 hours each, and 35 baseball umpires worked 10 hours each. This is equivalent to $(30 \times 20) +$

(40 × 15) + (35 × 10) = 1,550 ÷ 40 = 38.75 FTE positions for that week. Although a considerable amount of workload can be shifted to off season, most of the work must be done when required.

Full-time employees consist of three groups: (1) the skeleton group of key department personnel coordinating with the city, setting policy, determining budgets, measuring performance, and so forth; (2) the administrative group of supervisory and office personnel who are responsible for or whose jobs are directly linked to the direct-labor workers; and (3) the direct-labor work force of 116 full-time positions. These workers physically maintain the department's areas of responsibility, such as cleaning up, mowing golf greens and ballfields, trimming trees, and watering grass.

Cost information needed to determine the best alternative strategy is:

Full-time direct-labor employees	
Average wage rate	$4.45 per hour
Fringe benefits	17% of wage rate
Administrative costs	20% of wage rate
Part-time employees	
Average wage rate	$4.03 per hour
Fringe benefits	11% of wage rate
Administrative costs	25% of wage rate
Subcontracting all full-time jobs	$1.6 million
Subcontracting all part-time jobs	$1.85 million

June and July are the peak demand seasons in Tucson. Exhibits 11.8 and 11.9 show the high requirements for June and July personnel. The part-time help reaches 575 full-time-equivalent positions (although in actual numbers, this is approximately 800 different employees). After a low fall and winter staffing level, the demand shown as "full-time direct" reaches 130 in March when grounds are reseeded and fertilized and then increases to a high of 325 in July. The present method levels this uneven demand over the year to an average of 116 full-time year-round employees by early scheduling of work. As previously mentioned, no attempt is made to hire and lay off full-time workers to meet this uneven demand.

Exhibit 11.10 shows the cost calculations for all three alternatives. Exhibit 11.11 compares the total costs for each alternative.

From this analysis, it appears that the department is already using the lowest-cost alternative (Alternative 1).

Level Scheduling

In this chapter we have looked at four primary strategies for production planning: vary work-force size to meet demand, work overtime and undertime, vary inventory through excess and shortages, and subcontract.

Our worthy competitors, the Japanese, take a different approach. They concentrate on keeping a *level production schedule*. A level schedule focuses on

EXHIBIT 11.8 Actual Demand Requirement for Full-Time Direct Employees and Full-Time-Equivalent (FTE) Part-Time Employees

	January	February	March	April	May	June	July	August	September	October	November	December	Total
Days	22	20	21	22	21	20	21	21	21	23	18	22	252
Full-time employees	66	28	130	90	195	290	325	92	45	32	29	60	
Full-time days*	1,452	560	2,730	1,980	4,095	5,800	6,825	1,932	945	736	522	1,320	28,897
Full-time-equivalent part-time employees	41	75	72	68	72	302	576	72	0	68	84	27	
FTE days	902	1,500	1,512	1,496	1,512	6,040	12,096	1,512	0	1,564	1,512	594	30,240

Note: Some work weeks are staggered to include weekdays, but this does not affect the number of work days per employee.
* Full-time days derived by multiplying the number of days in each month by the number of workers.

EXHIBIT 11.9 **Monthly Requirement for Full-Time Direct-Labor Employees (other than key personnel) and Full-Time-Equivalent Part-Time Employees**

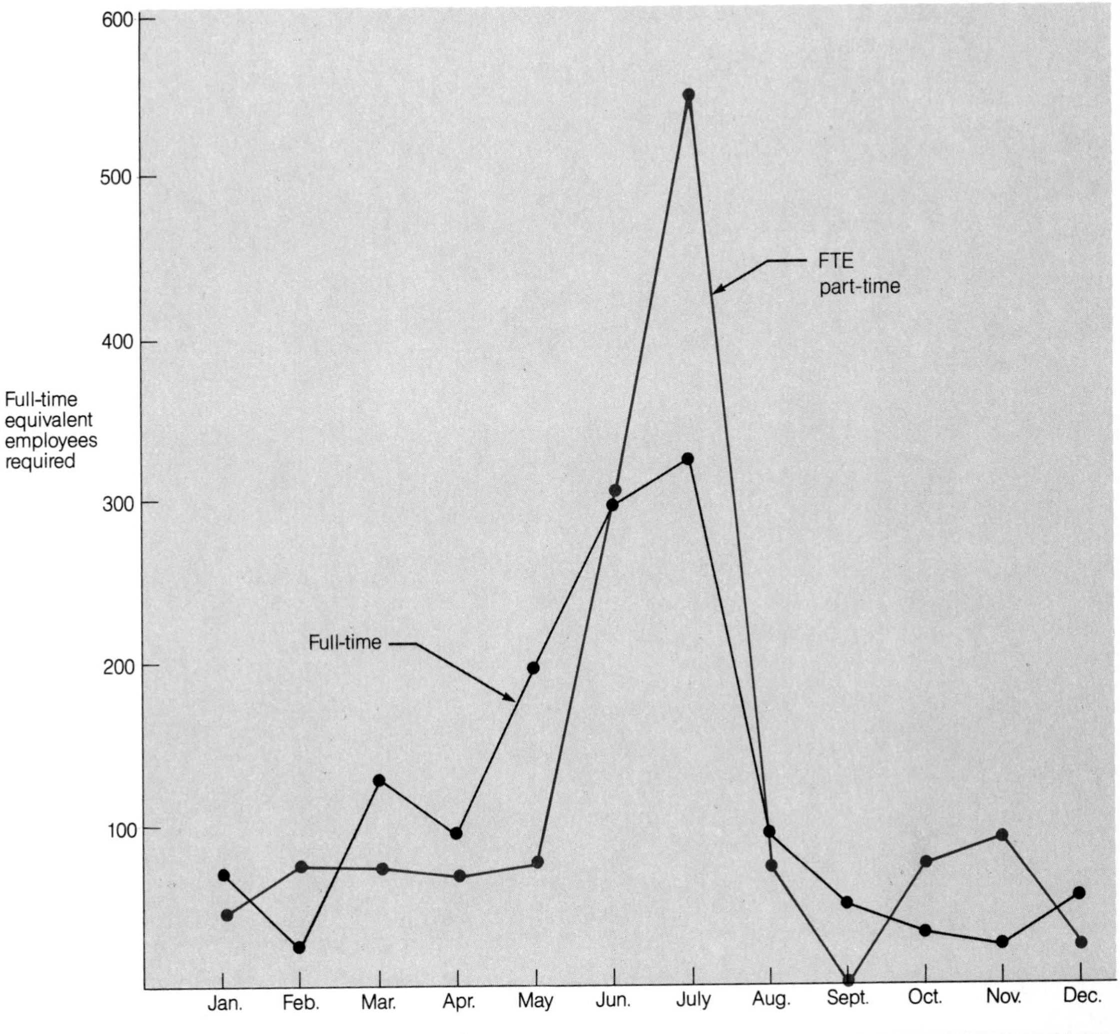

holding production constant over a period of time. It is something of a combination of the strategies we have mentioned here: for that period it keeps the work force constant and inventory low, and depends on demand to pull products through. Level production has a number of advantages:

1. The entire system can be planned to minimize inventory and work in process.

EXHIBIT 11.10 **Three Possible Plans for the Parks and Recreation Department**

Alternative 1: Maintain 116 full-time regular direct workers. Schedule work during off seasons to level work load throughout the year. Continue to use 120 full-time-equivalent (FTE) part-time employees to meet high demand periods.

Costs	Days per Year (Exhibit 11.8)	Hours (employees × days × 8 hours)	Wages (full-time, \$4.45; part-time, \$4.03)	Fringe Benefits (full-time, 17%; part-time, 11%)	Administrative Cost (full-time, 20%; part-time, 25%)
116 full-time regular employees	252	233,856	\$1,040,659	\$176,912	\$208,132
120 part-time employees	252	241,920	974,938	107,243	243,735
Total cost = \$2,751,619			\$2,015,597	\$284,155	\$451,867

Alternative 2: Maintain 50 full-time regular direct workers and the present 120 FTE part-time employees. Subcontract jobs releasing 66 full-time regular employees. Subcontract cost, \$1,100,000.

Cost	Days per Year (Exhibit 11.8)	Hours (employees × days × 8 hours)	Wages (full-time, \$4.45; part-time, \$4.03)	Fringe Benefits (full-time 17%; part-time, 11%)	Administrative Cost (full-time, 20%; part-time, 25%)	Subcontract Cost
50 full-time employees	252	100,800	\$ 448,560	\$ 76,255	\$ 89,712	\$1,100,000
120 FTE part-time employees subcontracting cost	252	241,920	974,938	107,243	243,735	
Total cost = \$3,040,443			\$1,423,498	\$183,498	\$333,447	\$1,100,000

Alternative 3: Subcontract all jobs previously performed by 116 full-time regular employees. Subcontract cost \$1,600,000. Subcontract all jobs previously performed by 120 full-time-equivalent part-time employees. Subcontract cost \$1,850,000.

Cost	Subcontract Cost
0 Full-time employees	
0 Part-time employees	
Subcontract full-time jobs	\$1,600,000
Subcontract part-time jobs	1,850,000
Total cost	\$3,450,000

EXHIBIT 11.11 Comparison of Costs for All Three Alternatives

	Alternative 1: 116 Full-Time Direct Labor Employees, 120 Full-Time Equivalent Part-Time Employees	Alternative 2: 50 Full-Time Direct Labor Employees, 120 Full-Time Equivalent Part-Time Employees, Subcontracting	Alternative 3: Subcontracting Jobs Formerly Performed by 116 Direct Labor Full-Time Employees and 120 FTE Part-Time Employees
Wages	$2,015,597	$1,423,498	—
Fringe benefits	284,155	183,498	—
Administrative costs	451,867	333,447	—
Subcontracting, full-time jobs		1,100,000	$1,600,000
Subcontracting, part-time jobs			1,850,000
Total	$2,751,619	$3,040,443	$3,450,000

2. Product modifications are up-to-date because of the low amount of work in process.
3. There is a smooth flow throughout the production system.
4. Purchased items from vendors can be delivered when needed, and, in fact, often directly to the production line.

Toyota, for example, creates a yearly production plan that shows the total number of cars to be made and sold. The aggregate production plan creates the system requirements to produce this total number with a level schedule. The secret to success in the Japanese level schedule is *production smoothing*. The aggregate plan is translated into monthly and daily schedules that *sequence* products through the production system. The procedure is essentially this: Two months in advance, the car types and quantities needed are established. This is converted to a detailed plan one month ahead. These quantities are given to subcontractors and vendors so that they can plan on meeting Toyota's needs. The monthly needs of various car types are then translated into daily schedules. For example, if 8,000 units of car type A are needed in one month, along with 6,000 type B, 4,000 type C, and 2,000 type D, then this would be translated to a daily outut of 400, 300, 200, and 100, respectively. Further, this would be sequenced as four units of A, three of B, two of C, and one of D each 9.6 minutes of a two-shift day (960 minutes).

Each worker operates a number of machines, producing a sequence of products.

In order to use this level scheduling technique:

1. Production should be repetitive (assembly-line format).
2. The system must contain excess capacity.
3. Output of the system must be fixed for a period of time (preferably a month).

4. There must be a smooth relationship among purchasing, marketing, and production.
5. The cost of carrying inventory must be high.
6. Equipment costs must be low.
7. Work force must be multiskilled.

We will have more to say about level scheduling in Chapter 16 on Just-in-Time production systems.

Mathematical Techniques

Linear programming

Linear programming (LP) is appropriate to aggregate planning if the cost and variable relationships are linear and demand can be treated as deterministic. For the general case, the simplex method can be used. For the special case where hiring and firing are not considerations, the more easily formulated transportation method can be applied.

The application of an LP transportation matrix to aggregate planning is illustrated by the solved problem in Exhibit 11.12. This formulation is termed a *period model* since it relates production demand to production capacity by periods. In this case, there are four subperiods with demand forecast as 800 units in each. The total capacity available is 3,950 or an excess capacity of 750 (3,950 − 3,200). However, the bottom row of the matrix indicates a desire for 500 units in inventory at the end of the planning period, so unused capacity is reduced to 250. The left-hand side of the matrix indicates the means by which production is made available over the planning period: that is, beginning inventory and regular and overtime work during each period. The shaded area indicates that production cannot be backlogged. That is, you can't produce in, say, Period 3 to meet demand in Period 2 (this is feasible if the situation allows back orders). Finally, the costs in each cell are incremented by a holding cost of $5 for each period. Thus, if one produces on regular time in Period 1 to satisfy demand for Period 4, there will be a $15 holding cost. Overtime is of course more expensive to start with, but holding costs in this example are not affected by whether production is on regular time or overtime. The solution shown is an optimal one. The same allocation and evaluation methods (e.g., the stepping stone method) applied to the transportation problems shown in Supplement to Chapter 7 can be applied to the period model.

The transportation matrix is remarkably versatile and can incorporate a variety of aggregate planning factors as described in Exhibit 11.13.

Observations on linear programming and mathematical techniques

Linear programming is appropriate when the cost and variable relationships are linear or can be cut into approximately linear segments. Regarding current

EXHIBIT 11.12 **Aggregate Planning by the Transportation Method of Linear Programming**

Production periods (sources)		Sales periods 1	2	3	4	Ending inventory	Unused capacity	Total capacity
Beginning inventory		[0] 50	[5]	[10]	[15]	[20]	[0]	50
1	Regular time	[50] 700	[55]	[60]	[65]	[70]	[0]	700
	Overtime	[75] 50	[80]	[85]	[90]	[95] 50	[0] 250	350
2	Regular time	X	[50] 700	[55]	[60]	[65]	[0]	700
	Overtime	X	[75] 100	[80]	[85]	[90] 150	[0]	250
3	Regular time	X	X	[50] 700	[55]	[60]	[0]	700
	Overtime	X	X	[75] 100	[80]	[85] 150	[0]	250
4	Regular time	X	X	X	[50] 700	[55]	[0]	700
	Overtime	X	X	X	[75] 100	[80] 150	[0]	250
Total requirements		800	800	800	800	500	250	3,950

application of several aggregate planning techniques in industry (see Exhibit 11.14), only linear programming has seen wide usage. Commenting on this issue, Peterson and Silver suggest that the answer lies in the decision-making style of management.[5] The basic issue, in their view, is management's attitude toward models in general. Those companies where modeling is a way of life are likely to try the more sophisticated methods; in those where it is not, one would suspect that graphic and charting approaches would be used. Somewhere in the middle ground lie companies that have substantial experience in data processing and use the computer primarily for detailed scheduling. In these types of firms, we would expect to see experimentation with alternative cut-and-try plans in developing master schedules.

[5] R. Peterson and E. A. Silver, *Decision Systems for Inventory Management and Production Planning* (New York: John Wiley & Sons, 1979), p. 662.

EXHIBIT 11.13

Additional Factors That Can Be Included in the Transportation Method for Aggregate Planning

1. **Multiproduct Production.** When more than one product shares common facilities, additional columns are included corresponding to each product. For each month, the number of columns will be equal to the number of products, and the cost entry in each cell will be equal to the cost for the corresponding product.
2. **Backlogging.** The backlog time and the cost of backlogging can be included by treating the shaded assignments in Exhibit 11.12 as feasible. If a product demanded in period 1 is delivered in period 2, this is equivalent to meeting period 1's demand with production in period 2. For, say, a $10 unit cost associated with such a backlog, the cost entry in the cell corresponding to period 2 regular time row and period 1 column will be $60 ($10 plus the $50 cost of regular-time production in period 2).
3. **Lost Sales.** When stockouts are allowed and a part of the demand is not met, the firm incurs opportunity cost equal to the lost revenue. This can be included in the matrix by adding a "lost-sales" row for each period. The cost entry in the cell will be equal to lost revenue per unit.
4. **Perishability.** When perishability does not permit the sale of a product after it has been in stock for a certain period, the corresponding cells in the matrix are treated as infeasible. If the product in Exhibit 11.12 cannot be sold after it has been in stock for two periods, the cells occupying the intersection of period 1 rows and columns beyond period 3 will be infeasible.
5. **Subcontracting.** This can be included by adding a "subcontracting" row for each period. Cost values in each cell would be the unit cost to subcontract plus any inventory holding cost (incremented in the same fashion as regular time and overtime costs).
6. **Learning Effects.** Learning effects result in increased capacity and lower cost per unit. These changes are incorporated by making corresponding adjustments in capacity (total amount available from source) column and cost entry in the cells.

Source: K. Singhal, "A Generalized Model for Production Scheduling by Transportation Method of LP," *Industrial Management* 19, no. 5 (September-October 1977), pp. 1-6.

EXHIBIT 11.14 **Summary Data on Aggregate Planning Methods**

Methods	Assumptions	Technique
1. Graphic and charting	None	Tests alternative plans through trial and error. Nonoptimal, but simple to develop and easy to understand.
2. Simulation of master schedule	Existence of a computer-based production system	Tests aggregate plans developed by other methods.
3. Linear programming—transportation method	Linearity, constant work force	Useful for the special case where hiring and firing costs are not a consideration. Gives optimal solution.
4. Linear programming—simplex method	Linearity	Can handle any number of variables but often difficult to formulate. Gives optimal solution.
5. Linear decision rules*	Quadratic cost functions	Uses mathematically derived coefficients to specify production rates and work-force levels in a series of equations.
6. Management coefficients†	Managers are basically good decision makers	Uses statistical analysis of past decisions to make future decisions. Applies, therefore, to just one group of managers; nonoptimal.
7. Search decision rules‡	Any type of cost structure	Uses pattern search procedure to find minimum points on total cost curves. Complicated to develop, nonoptimal.

* Charles C. Holt et al., *Planning Production, Inventories, and Work Force* (Englewood Cliffs, N.J.: Prentice-Hall, 1960).
† Edward H. Bowman and Robert B. Fetter, *Analysis for Production and Operations Management,* 3rd ed. (Homewood, Ill.: Richard D. Irwin, 1957).
‡ William H. Taubert, "A Search Decision Rule for the Aggregate Scheduling Problem," *Management Science,* February 1978, pp. B343-59.

11.5 CONCLUSION

It is important to remember that aggregate planning translates the corporate strategic plan into broad categories of work-force size, inventory quantity, and production levels. It does not do detailed planning. It is also useful to point out some practical considerations in aggregate planning.

First, demand variations are a fact of life, so the planning system must include sufficient flexibility to cope with such variations. Flexibility can be achieved by developing alternative sources of supply, cross training workers to handle a wide variety of orders, and engaging in more frequent replanning during high demand periods.

Second, decision rules for production planning should be adhered to once they have been selected. However, they should be carefully analyzed prior to implementation by such checks as simulation of historical data to see what really would have happened if they had been in operation in the past.

11.6 REVIEW AND DISCUSSION QUESTIONS

1. What are the basic controllable variables of a production planning problem? What are the four major costs?
2. Distinguish between pure and mixed strategies in production planning.
3. Define level scheduling. How does it differ from the pure strategies in production planning?
4. Compare the best plans in the C&A Company and the Tucson Parks and Recreation Department. What do they have in common?
5. Under what conditions would you have to use the general simplex method rather than the period model in aggregate planning?
6. How does forecast accuracy relate, in general, to the practical application of the aggregate planning models discussed in the chapter?
7. In what way does the time horizon chosen for an aggregate plan determine whether or not it is the best plan for the firm?

11.7 PROBLEMS

*1. Jason Enterprises (JE) is producing video telephones for the home market. Quality is not quite as good as it could be at this point, but selling price is low and Jason has the opportunity to study market response while spending more time in additional R&D work.

At this stage, however, JE needs to develop an aggregate production plan for the six months from January through June. As you can guess, you have been commissioned to create the plan.

* Solution to Problem 1 given in Appendix D.

The following information is available to help you:

	January	February	March	April	May	June
Demand data						
Beginning inventory	200					
Forecast demand	500	600	650	800	900	800
Cost data						
Holding cost		$10/unit/month				
Stockout cost		$20/unit/month				
Subcontracting cost/unit		$100				
Hiring cost/worker		$50				
Layoff cost/worker		$100				
Labor cost/hour—straight time		$12.50				
Labor cost/hour—overtime		$18.75				
Production data						
Labor hours/unit	4					
Workdays/month	22					
Current work force	10					

What is the cost of each of the following production strategies?

a. Exact production; vary work force (assuming a starting work force of 10).

b. Constant work force; vary inventory and stockout only (assuming a starting work force of 10).

c. Constant work force of 10; vary overtime only.

2. For Problem 1, devise the least costly plan you can. You may choose your starting work force level.

3. Assume that Alan Industries has purchased Jason Enterprises and has instituted Japanese-style management in which workers are guaranteed a job for life (with no layoffs). Based on the data in Problem 1 (and additional information provided here), develop a production plan using the transportation method of linear programming. To keep things simple, plan for the first three months only and convert costs from hours to units in your model. Additional information: overtime is limited to 11 units per month per worker and up to 5 units per month may be subcontracted at a cost of $100 per unit.

4. Develop a production plan and calculate the annual cost for a firm whose demand forecast is: fall = 10,000; winter = 8,000; spring = 7,000; summer = 12,000. Inventory at the beginning of fall is 500 units. At the beginning of fall you currently have 30 workers, but you plan to hire temporary workers at the beginning of summer and lay them off at the end of summer. In addition, you have negotiated with the union an option to use the regular work force on overtime during winter or spring if overtime is necessary to prevent stockouts at the end of those quarters. Overtime is *not* available during the fall. Relevant costs are: hiring = $100 for each temp; layoff = $200 for each worker laid off; inventory holding = $5 per unit-quarter; back order = $10 per unit; straight time = $5 per hour; overtime = $8 per hour. Assume that the productivity is two worker hours per unit, with 8 hours per day and 60 days per season.

5. Plan production for a four-month period: February through May. For February and March, you should produce to exact demand forecast. For April and May, you should use overtime and inventory with a stable work force; *stable* means that

the number of workers needed for March will be held constant through May. However, government constraints put a maximum of 5,000 hours of overtime labor per month in April and May (zero overtime in February and March). If demand exceeds supply, then back orders will occur. There are 100 workers on January 1. You are given the following demand forecast: February = 80,000; March = 64,000; April = 100,000; May = 40,000. Productivity is four units per worker hour, 8 hours per day, 20 days per month. Assume zero inventory on February 1. Costs are: hiring = \$50 per new worker; layoff = \$70 per worker laid off; inventory holding = \$10 per unit-month; straight-time labor = \$10 per hour; overtime = \$15 per hour; back order = \$20 per unit. Find the total cost of this plan.

6. Plan production for the next year. The demand forecast is: spring = 20,000; summer = 10,000; fall = 15,000; winter = 18,000. At the beginning of spring you have 70 workers and 1,000 units in inventory. The union contract specifies that you may lay off workers only once a year, at the beginning of summer. Also, you may hire new workers only at the end of summer to begin regular work in the fall. The number of workers laid off at the beginning of summer and the number hired at the end of summer should result in planned production levels for summer and fall that equal the demand forecasts for summer and fall respectively. If demand exceeds supply, use overtime in spring only, which means that back orders could occur in winter. You are given these costs: hiring = \$100 per new worker; layoff = \$200 per worker laid off; holding = \$20 per unit-quarter; back-order cost = \$8 per unit; straight-time labor = \$10 per hour; overtime = \$15 per hour. Productivity is two worker hours per unit, 8 hours per day, 50 days per quarter. Find the total cost.

7. DAT, Inc. needs to develop an aggregate plan for its product line. Relevant data are:

Production time	1 hour per unit
Average labor cost	\$10 per hour
Work week	5 days, 8 hours each day
Days per month	Assume 20 work days per month
Beginning inventory	500 units
Safety stock	One half month
Shortage cost	\$20 per unit per month
Carry cost	\$5 per unit per month

The forecast for January to December 1988 is:

January	February	March	April	May	June	July	August	September	October	November	December
2,500	3,000	4,000	3,500	3,500	3,000	3,000	4,000	4,000	4,000	3,000	3,000

Management prefers to keep a constant work force and production level, absorbing variations in demand through inventory excesses and shortages. Demand not met is carried over to the following month.

Develop an aggregate plan that will meet the demand and other conditions of the problem. Do not try to find the optimum; just find a good solution and state the procedure you might use to test for a better solution. Make any necessary assumptions.

8. Old Pueblo Engineering Contractors creates six-month "rolling" schedules, which are recomputed monthly. For competitive reasons (they would need to divulge proprietary design criteria, methods, etc.), Old Pueblo does not subcontract. Therefore, its only options to meet customer requirements are (1) work on regular time; (2) work on overtime, which is limited to 30 percent of regular time; (3) do customers' work early, which would cost an additional $5 per hour per month; (4) perform customers' work late, which would cost an additional $10 per hour per month penalty, as provided by their contract.

   Old Pueblo has 25 engineers on its staff at an hourly rate of $30. Customers' requirements for the six months from January to June are:

January	February	March	April	May	June
5,000	4,000	6,000	6,000	5,000	4,000

   Develop an aggregate plan using the transportation method of linear programming. Assume 20 working days in each month.

9. Alan Industries is expanding its product line to include new models: Model A, Model B, and Model C. These are to be produced on the same productive equipment and the objective is to meet the demands for the three products using overtime where necessary. The demand forecast for the next four months, in required hours, is:

Product	April	May	June	July
Model A	800	600	800	1,200
Model B	600	700	900	1,100
Model C	700	500	700	850

   Because the products deteriorate rapidly, there is a high loss in quality and, consequently, a high carryover cost into subsequent periods. Each hour's production carried into future months costs $3 per productive hour of Model A, $4 for Model B, and $5 for Model C.

   Production can take place either during regular working hours or during overtime. Regular time is paid at $4 when working on Model A, $5 for Model B, and $6 for Model C. Overtime premium is 50 percent.

   The available production capacity for regular time and overtime is:

	April	May	June	July
Regular time	1,500	1,300	1,800	1,700
Overtime	700	650	900	850

   a. Set the problem up in matrix form and show appropriate costs.
   b. Show a feasible solution.

10. Shoney Video Concepts produces a line of video disc players to be linked to personal computers for video games. Video discs have much faster access time than tape. With such a computer/video link, the game becomes a very realistic experience. In a simple driving game where the joystick "steers" the vehicle, for example, rather than seeing computer graphics on the screen, the player is

actually viewing a segment of a video disc shot from a real moving vehicle. Depending on the action of the player (hitting a guard rail, for example) the disc moves virtually instantaneously to that segment and the player becomes part of an actual accident of real vehicles (staged, of course).

Shoney is trying to determine a production plan for the next 12 months. The main criterion for this plan is that the employment level is to be held constant over the period. Shoney is continuing in its R&D efforts to develop new applications and prefers not to cause any adverse feeling with the local work force. For the same reasons, all employees should put in full work weeks, even if this is not the lowest-cost alternative. The forecast for the next 12 months is:

Month	Forecast Demand	Month	Forecast Demand
January	600	July	200
February	800	August	200
March	900	September	300
April	600	October	700
May	400	November	800
June	300	December	900

Manufacturing cost is $200 per set, equally divided between materials and labor. Inventory storage costs are $5 per month. A shortage of sets results in lost sales and is estimated to cost an overall $20 per unit short.

The inventory on hand at the beginning of the planning period is 200 units. Ten labor hours are required per TV set. The work day is eight hours.

Develop an aggregate production schedule for the year using a constant work force. For simplicity, assume 22 working days each month except July, when the plant closes down for three weeks' vacation (leaving seven working days). Make any assumptions you need.

11. Develop a production schedule to produce the exact production requirements by varying the work force size for the following problem. Use the example in the chapter as a guide (Plan 1).

The monthly forecast for Product X for January, February, and March is 1,000, 1,500, and 1,200, respectively. Safety stock policy recommends that one half of the forecast for that month be defined as safety stock. There are 22 working days in January, 19 in February, and 21 in March. Beginning inventory is 500 units.

Following are additional data: Manufacturing cost is $200 per unit, storage costs are $3 per unit per month, standard pay rate is $6 per hour, overtime rate is $9 per hour, cost of stockout is $10 per unit per month, marginal cost of subcontracting is $10 per unit, hiring and training cost is $200 per worker, layoff costs are $300 per worker, and production worker hours required per unit are 10. Make whatever assumptions necessary.

11.8 SELECTED BIBLIOGRAPHY

Buffa, Elwood S., and Jeffrey G. Miller. *Production-Inventory Systems: Planning and Control*. 3rd ed. Homewood, Ill.: Richard D. Irwin, 1979.

Fisk, J. C., and J. P. Seagle. "Integration of Aggregate Planning with Resource Requirements Planning." *Production and Inventory Management,* Third Quarter 1978, p. 87.

McLeavy, D., and S. Narasimhan. *Production Planning and Inventory Control.* Boston: Allyn & Bacon, 1985.

Monden, Yasuhiro. *Toyota Production System.* Atlanta, Ga.: Industrial Engineering and Management Press, 1983.

Plossl, G. W. *Production and Inventory Control: Principles and Techniques.* 2nd ed. Englewood Cliffs, N.J.: Prentice-Hall, 1985.

Silver, E. A., and R. Peterson. *Decision Systems for Inventory Management and Production Planning.* 2nd ed. New York: John Wiley & Sons, 1985.

Vollman, T. E.; W. L. Berry; and D. C. Whybark. *Manufacturing Planning and Control Systems.* 2nd ed. Homewood, Ill.: Richard D. Irwin, 1988.

Wight, Oliver W. *Production and Inventory Management in the Computer Age.* Boston: Cahners Publishing, 1974.

Chapter 12

Inventory Systems for Independent Demand

EPIGRAPH

When the bottle gets down to four, that's the time to buy some more.

Alka-Seltzer jingle from the 1950s.

"Honey, I'm all out of shampoo."

CHAPTER OUTLINE

KEY TERMS

Raw Materials, Finished Goods, Work-in-Process Inventory

Independent and Dependent Demand

Fixed-Order Quantity Model

Fixed-Time Period Model

Service Level

Safety Stock

ABC Analysis

Inventory Accuracy

Cycle Counting

Inventory is a way of life for all of us. It's not necessary to be a manufacturer or in a service industry to realize the importance of inventory. We may be short on eggs in our refrigerator or a manufacturer may be short of steel in his stockpile. We all need to plan for inventory by assessing the consequences of shortages and evaluating the costs of carrying the extra stock.

The president of Iraq, Saddam Hussein, opened an old wound for all of us recently. He reminded us of our dependence on foreign oil. During the early 1970s, OPEC (Organization of Petroleum Exporting Countries) was formed to control the world price and production of oil. This cartel raised prices and cut supplies, creating such far-felt effects as inflation, sector recessions, high interest rates, a complete shake-up of American automobile manufacturers, and perhaps the beginning of Japanese automobile inroads into the American market.

Government leaders in Washington talked of our goal of becoming energy independent by developing high mileage cars, increasing domestic oil production, encouraging research into alternative energy sources, and stockpiling oil as strategic petroleum reserves, or SPR.

Memories are short, and the concern for the various programs waned. Automobile manufacturers were given extensions on meeting miles-per-gallon target goals. The public no longer seemed interested in alcohol-enhanced fuels. Coal was again perceived as "dirty," and groups amassed against nuclear power generation. We seem to be back to where we started. While our strategic petroleum reserves provide only a 90-day supply, our dependence on foreign oil is higher than ever. In 1973, when OPEC was formed, the United States imported 34 percent of its oil. Now, after supposedly having learned our lesson the hard way, we now import over 50 percent of our oil.

In all fairness to the oil producing countries, we need to realize that in the early 1970s they were an oligopsony, or a relatively few suppliers. The large oil companies that were drilling, extracting, piping, and shipping the oil were an oligopoly, or few buyers. The Arab states believed the oil companies were not paying a fair price for the oil, and this prompted formation of OPEC (the oligopsony) to raise the price.

What we have in this world oil example is not unlike what we have in our ordinary manufacturing and service industries. Because there are few countries producing oil, they have the ability to control its price and output. The United States has a similar position in foodstuffs and certainly could control, for example, the world price of wheat.

In manufacturing, there are usually only a few suppliers for parts and components that a manufacturer needs. The same is usually true for services; there are only a few sources for lumber, windows, roofing, and so on for a building contractor. There are very few sources for drugs for a pharmacy, hospital, or physician. If there were many and reliable sources for the things we need, inventory would not be necessary and we could discard this chapter.

However, a manufacturer can't run down to the corner store to buy some new circuit boards when supplies run low. There might be a three-month wait between ordering and receiving circuit boards.

Inventory is probably the most discussed topic in manufacturing today. Historically, manufacturers have avoided shortage problems by having large amounts of inventory of everything. Now, however, because of the costs of having inventory and the additional time inventory adds to the production time, the name of the game is to reduce inventory quantities at all levels: in raw materials and purchased parts through direct delivery by the vendor (often directly to the production line); in work in process by techniques such as Just-in-Time production or scheduling with small batch sizes; and finally, in finished goods through a close matching of output to market requirements, and shipments to those markets as soon as possible. There is a spreading effort to reduce all inventory inspired by new measurements and performance evaluation based not on the percentage of resource utilization, but rather on inventory turns and product quality.

We are in a transition stage in our view of inventory. Do we discard the classical models, which have been taught and used for many years, because some researchers and practitioners tell us we should not use these models any longer, or should we present them because there are still useful applications for them? In writing this chapter we settled on a compromise: we are including some models, omitting others, and (we hope) simplifying and clarifying other issues. While classical inventory models are being abandoned in planning the manufacturing process, they still appear to be appropriate in many areas in the service industries and the thousands of companies engaged in product and parts distribution.

12.1 DEFINITION OF INVENTORY

Inventory is the stock of any item or resource used in an organization. An *inventory system* is the set of policies and controls that monitors levels of inventory and determines what levels should be maintained, when stock should be replenished, and how large orders should be.

In its complete scope, inventory includes inputs such as human, financial, energy, equipment, and **raw materials;** outputs such as parts, components, and **finished goods;** and interim stages of the process, such as partially finished goods or **work in process.** The choice of which items to include in inventory depends on the organization. A manufacturing operation can have an inventory of personnel, machines, and working capital, as well as raw materials and finished goods. An airline can have an inventory of seats; a modern drugstore, an inventory of medicines, batteries, and toys; and an engineering firm, an inventory of engineering talent.

By convention, manufacturing inventory generally refers to materials entities that contribute to or become part of a firm's product output. Manufacturing inventory is typically classified into segments:

Raw materials.
Finished products.
Component parts.
Supplies.
Work in process.

In services, inventory generally refers to the tangible goods to be sold and the supplies necessary to administer the service.

The basic purpose of inventory analysis in manufacturing and stockkeeping services is to specify (1) when items should be ordered and (2) how large the order should be. Recent trends in industry have modified the simple questions of "when" and "how many." Many firms are tending to enter into longer-term relationships with vendors to supply their needs for perhaps the entire year. This changes the "when" and "how many to order" to "when" and "how many to deliver."

12.2 PURPOSES OF INVENTORY

In goods production, a stock of inventory is kept to satisfy the following needs:

1. *To maintain independence of operations.* A supply of materials at a work center allows that center flexibility in operations. For example, since there are costs for making each new production setup, this inventory allows management to reduce the number of setups.

Workplaces on an assembly line usually are not independent because raw materials and products to work on are fed at the line speed. There may be none or only a few extra products to work on in the event the worker performs either faster or slower than line speed, or if the workstation upstream slows down output. The unit completed at a workstation passes to the next person.

2. *To meet variation in product demand.* If the demand for the product is known precisely, it may be possible (though not necessarily economical) to produce the product to exactly meet the demand. Usually, however, demand is not completely known, and a safety or buffer stock must be maintained to absorb variation.

3. *To allow flexibility in production scheduling.* A stock of inventory relieves the pressure on the production system to get the goods out. This causes longer lead times, which permit production planning for smoother flow and lower-cost operation through larger lot-size production. High setup costs, for exam-

ple, favor the production of a larger number of units once the setup has been made.

4. To provide a safeguard for variation in raw material delivery time. When material is ordered from a vendor, delays can occur for a variety of reasons: a normal variation in shipping time, a shortage of material at the vendor's plant, causing backlogs, an unexpected strike at the vendor's plant or at one of the shipping companies, a lost order, or a shipment of incorrect or defective material.

5. To take advantage of economic purchase-order size. Obviously, there are costs to place an order: labor, phone calls, typing, postage, etc. Therefore, the larger the size of each order, the fewer the number of orders that need be written. Also, the nonlinearity of shipping costs favors larger orders: the larger the shipment, the lower the per-unit cost.

12.3 INVENTORY COSTS

In making any decision that will affect inventory size, the following costs must be considered.

1. Holding (or carrying) costs. This broad category includes the costs for storage facilities, handling, insurance, pilferage, breakage, obsolescence, depreciation, taxes, and the opportunity cost of capital. Obviously, high holding costs tend to favor low inventory levels and frequent replenishment.

2. Setup (or production change) costs. To make each different product involves obtaining the necessary materials, arranging specific equipment setups, filling out the required papers, appropriately charging time and materials, and moving out the previous stock of material. In addition, other costs may be involved in hiring, training, or layoff of workers, and in idle time or overtime.

If there were no costs or loss of time in changing from one product to another, many small lots would be produced. This would reduce inventory levels, with a resulting savings in cost. However, changeover costs usually exist, and one of the challenges today is to try to reduce these setup costs to permit smaller lot sizes.

3. Ordering costs. These costs refer to the managerial and clerical costs to prepare the purchase or production order. Common terminology subdivides these into two categories: (1) header cost, which is the cost of identifying and issuing an order to a single vendor and (2) line cost, which is the cost for computing each separate item ordered from the same vendor. Thus, ordering three items from a vendor entails one header cost and three line costs.

4. Shortage costs. When the stock of an item is depleted, an order for that item must either wait until the stock is replenished or be canceled. There is a trade-off between carrying stock to satisfy demand and the costs resulting from stockout. This balance is sometimes difficult to obtain, since it may not be possible to estimate lost profits, the effects of lost customers, or lateness penalties. Frequently, the assumed shortage cost is little more than a guess, although it is usually possible to specify a range of such costs.

Establishing the correct quantity to order from vendors or the size of lots submitted to the firm's productive facilities involves a search for the minimum total cost resulting from the combined effects of three individual costs: holding costs, setup or ordering costs, and shortage costs.

12.4 INDEPENDENT VERSUS DEPENDENT DEMAND

Briefly, the distinction between **independent and dependent demand** is this: In independent demand, the demand for various items is unrelated to each other and therefore needed quantities of each must be determined separately. In dependent demand, the need for any one item is a direct result of the need for some other item, usually a higher-level item of which it is part.

In concept, dependent demand is a relatively straightforward computational problem. Needed quantities of a dependent-demand item are simply computed, based on the number needed in each higher-level item where it is used. For example, if an automobile company plans on producing 500 automobiles per day, then obviously it will need 2,000 wheels and tires (plus spares). The number of wheels and tires needed is *dependent* on the production levels and not derived separately. The demand for automobiles, on the other hand, is *independent*—it comes from many sources external to the automobile firm and is not a part of other products and so is unrelated to the demand for other products.

To determine the quantities of independent items that must be produced, firms usually turn to their sales and market research departments. They use a variety of techniques, including customer surveys, forecasting techniques, and economic and sociological trends. Because independent demand is uncertain, extra units must be carried in inventory. This chapter presents models to determine how many extra units should be carried to provide a specified *service level* (percentage of independent demand) that the firm would like to satisfy.

12.5 INVENTORY SYSTEMS

An inventory system provides the organizational structure and the operating policies for maintaining and controlling goods to be stocked. The system is responsible for ordering and receipt of goods: timing the order placement and keeping track of what has been ordered, how much, and from whom. The system must also provide follow-up to provide answers to such questions as: Has the vendor received the order? Has it been shipped? Are the dates correct? Are the procedures established for reordering or returning undesirable merchandise?

Classifying Models by Fixed-Order Quantity or Fixed-Time Period

There are two general types of inventory systems: **fixed-order quantity models** (also called the *economic order quantity*, or EOQ) and **fixed-time period models** (also referred to variously as the *periodic* system, the *periodic review* system, and the *fixed-order interval* system).

The basic distinction is that fixed-order quantity models are "event triggered" and fixed-time period models are "time triggered." That is, a fixed-order quantity model initiates an order when the "event" of reaching a specified reorder level occurs. This event may take place at any time, depending on the demand for the items considered. In contrast, the fixed-time period model is limited to placing orders at the end of a predetermined time period; only the passage of time "triggers" the model.

To use the fixed-order quantity model, which places an order when the remaining inventory drops to a predetermined order point, *R,* the inventory remaining must be continually monitored. Thus, the fixed-order quantity model is a *perpetual* system, which requires that every time a withdrawal from inventory or an addition to inventory is made, records must be updated to assure that the reorder point has or has not been reached. The review period for the fixed-time period model is only at the review period. No counting takes place in the interim (although some firms have created variations of systems that combine features of both).

Some additional differences that tend to influence the choice of systems (see Exhibit 12.1):

- The fixed-time period model has a larger average inventory since it must protect against stockout during the review period, *T;* the fixed-quantity model has no review period.

EXHIBIT 12.1

Fixed-Order Quantity and Fixed-Time Period Differences

Feature	Fixed-Order Quantity Model	Fixed-Time Period Model
Order quantity	*Q*—constant (the same amount ordered each time)	*Q*—variable (varies each time order is placed)
When to place order	*R*—when quantity on hand drops to the reorder level	*T*—when the review period arrives
Record keeping	Each time a withdrawal or addition is made	Counted only at review period
Size of inventory	Less than fixed time-period model	Larger than fixed order-quantity model
Time to maintain	Higher, since perpetual recordkeeping	
Type of items	Higher-priced, critical, or important items	

EXHIBIT 12.2 **Comparison of Fixed-Order Quantity and Fixed-Time Period Reordering Inventory Systems**

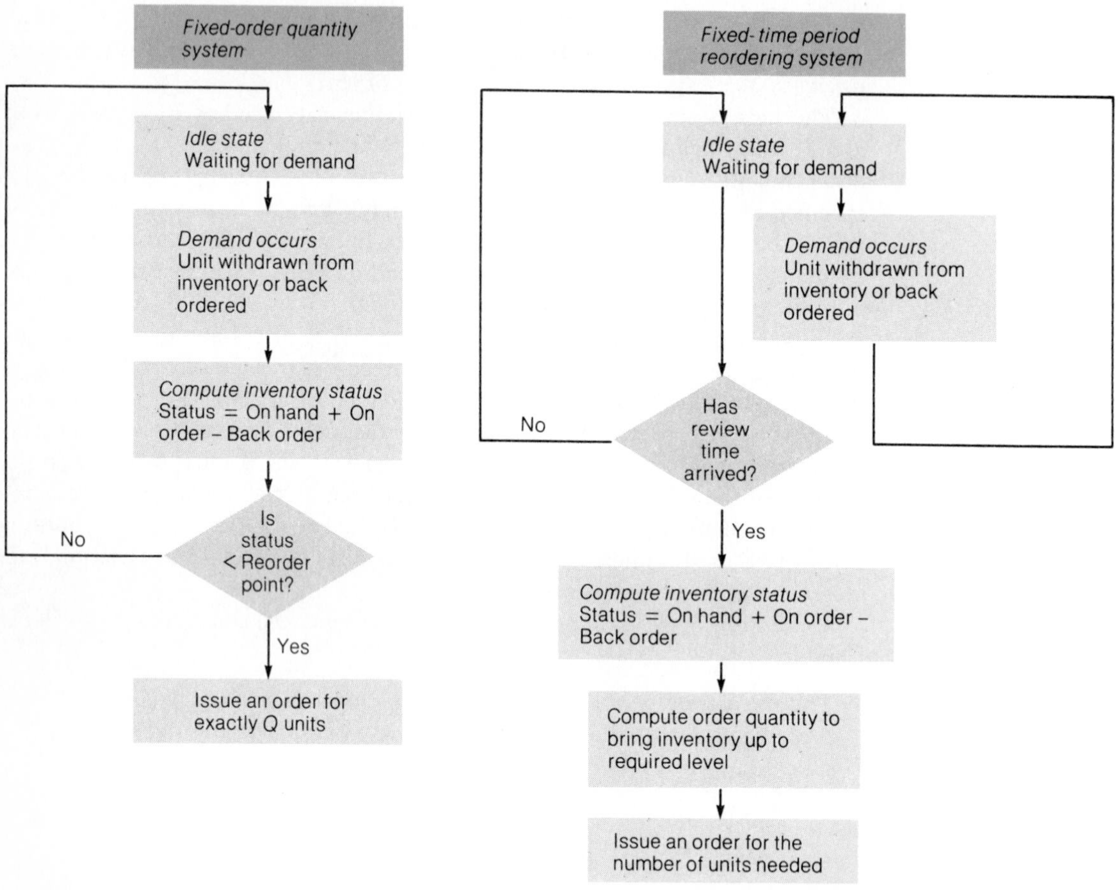

- The fixed-order quantity model favors more expensive items since average inventory is lower.
- The fixed-order quantity model is more appropriate for important items such as critical repair parts since there is closer monitoring and therefore quicker response to potential stockout.
- The fixed-order quantity model requires more time to maintain since every addition or withdrawal is logged.

Exhibit 12.2 depicts what occurs when each of the two models is put into use and becomes an operating system. As we can see, the fixed-order quantity system focuses on order quantities and reorder points. Procedurally, each time a unit is taken out of stock, the withdrawal is logged and the amount remaining in inventory is immediately compared to the reorder point. If it has dropped to this point, an order for Q items is placed. If it has not, the system remains in an idle state until the next withdrawal.

In the fixed-time period system, a decision to place an order is made after the stock has been counted or "reviewed." Whether an order is actually placed depends on the inventory status at that time.

12.6 BASIC MODEL TYPES

Basic Sawtooth Model

The simplest models in this category occur when all aspects of the situation are known with certainty. If the annual demand for a product is 1,000 units, it is precisely 1,000—not 1,000 plus or minus 10 percent. The same is true for setup costs and holding costs. Although the assumption of complete certainty is rarely valid, it provides a good starting point for our coverage of inventory models.

Fixed-order quantity models

Fixed-order quantity models attempt to determine the specific point, R, at which an order will be placed and the size of that order, Q. The order point, R, is always a specified number of units actually in inventory. The solution to a fixed-order quantity model may stipulate something like this: When the number of units of inventory on hand drops to 36, place an order for 57 more units.

Exhibit 12.3 and the discussion about deriving the optimal order quantity are based on the following characteristics of the model:

- Demand for the product is constant and uniform throughout the period.
- Lead time (time from ordering to receipt) is constant.
- Price per unit of product is constant.
- Inventory holding cost is based on average inventory.
- Ordering or setup costs are constant.
- All demands for the product will be satisfied (no back orders are allowed).

The "sawtooth effect" relating Q and R in Exhibit 12.3 shows that when inventory drops to point R, a reorder is placed. This order is received at the end of time period L, which does not vary in this model.

In constructing any inventory model, the first step is to develop a functional relationship between the variables of interest and the measure of effectiveness.

EXHIBIT 12.3 **Basic Fixed-Order Quantity Model**

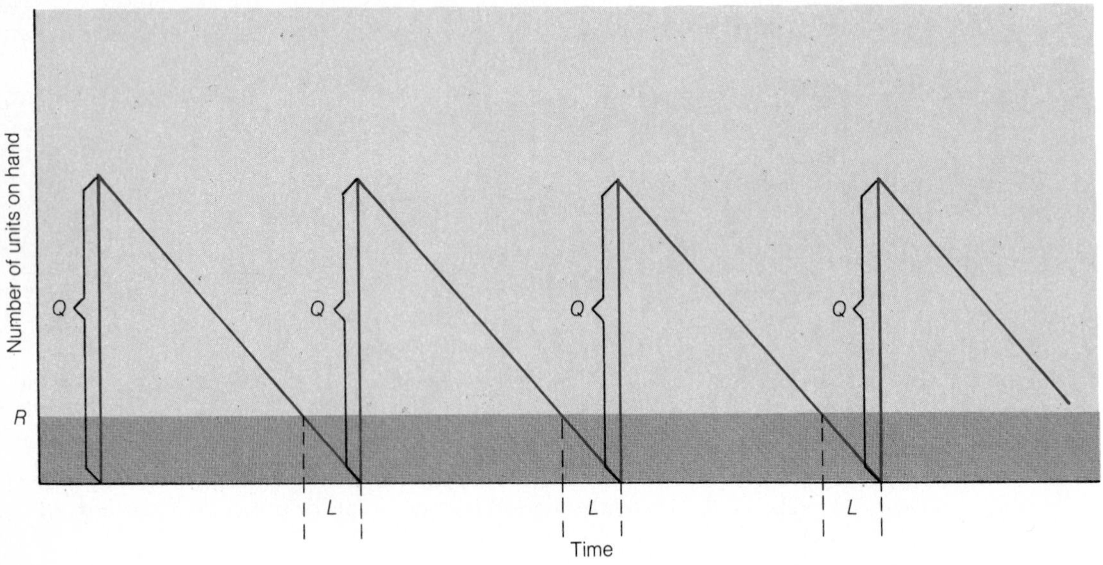

In this case, since we are concerned with cost, the following equation would pertain.

$$\text{Total annual cost} = \text{Annual purchase cost} + \text{Annual ordering cost} + \text{Annual holding cost}$$

or

$$TC = DC + \frac{D}{Q}S + \frac{Q}{2}H \qquad (1)$$

where

TC = Total annual cost
D = Demand (annual)
C = Cost per unit
Q = Quantity to be ordered (the optimum amount is termed the *economic order quantity*—EOQ, or Q_{opt})
S = Setup cost or cost of placing an order
R = Reorder point

EXHIBIT 12.4 **Annual Product Costs, Based on Size of the Order**

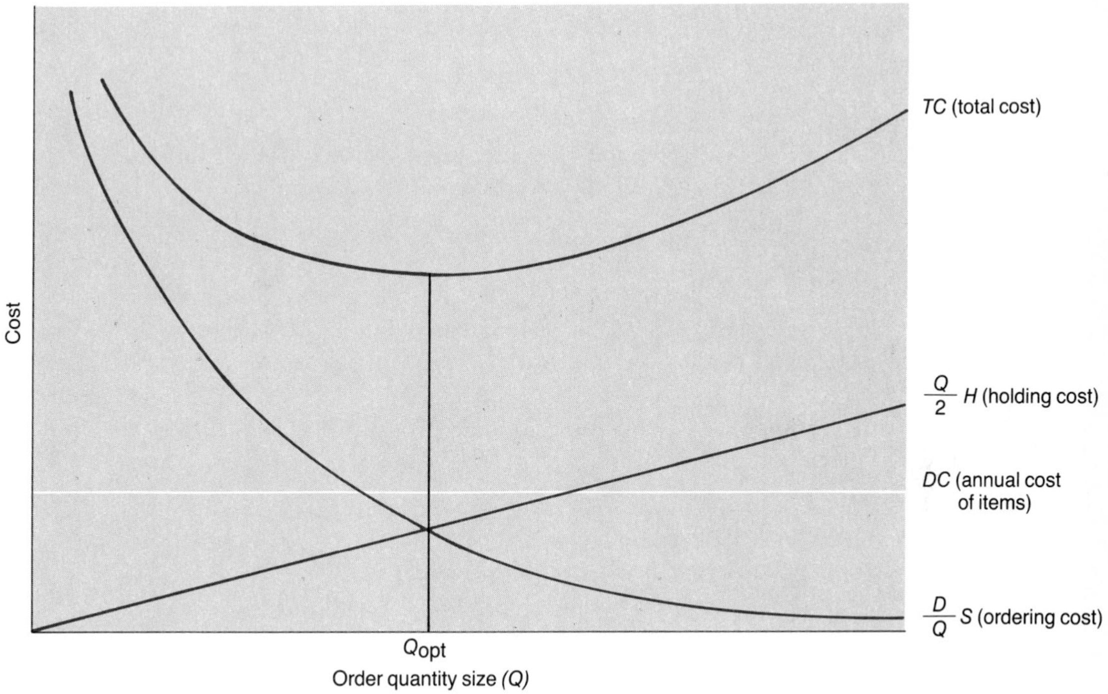

L = Lead time

H = Annual holding and storage cost per unit of average inventory. (Often, holding cost is taken as a percent of the cost of the item, such as $H = iC$ where i is the percent carrying cost.)

On the right-hand side of the equation, DC is the annual purchase cost for the units, $(D/Q)S$ is the annual ordering cost (the actual number of orders placed, D/Q, times the cost of each order, S), and $(Q/2)H$ is the annual holding cost (the average inventory, $Q/2$, times the cost per unit for holding and storage, H). These cost relationships are shown graphically in Exhibit 12.4.

The second step in model development is to find that order quantity, Q, for which total cost is a minimum. In Exhibit 12.4, total cost is minimum at the point where the slope of the curve is zero. Using calculus, the appropriate procedure involves taking the derivative of total cost with respect to Q and setting this equal to zero. For the basic model considered here, the calculations would be as follows.

$$TC = DC + \frac{D}{Q}S + \frac{Q}{2}H$$

$$\frac{dTC}{dQ} = 0 + \left(\frac{-DS}{Q^2}\right) + \frac{H}{2} = 0$$

$$Q_{opt} = \sqrt{\frac{2DS}{H}} \tag{2}$$

Since this simple model assumes constant demand and lead time, no safety stock is necessary, and the reorder point, R, is simply

$$R = \bar{d}\,L \tag{3}$$

where

$\bar{d}$ = average daily demand [constant]
L = lead time in days [constant]

Example 12.1. Find the economic order quantity and the reorder point, given the following data:

Annual demand (D)	= 1,000 units
Average daily demand ($\bar{d}$)	= 1,000/365
Ordering cost (S)	= \$5 per order
Holding cost (H)	= \$1.25 per unit per year
Lead time (L)	= 5 days
Cost per unit (C)	= \$12.50

The optimal order quantity is

$$Q_{opt} = \sqrt{\frac{2DS}{H}} = \sqrt{\frac{2(1{,}000)5}{1.25}} = \sqrt{8{,}000} = 89.4 \text{ units}$$

The reorder point is

$$R = \bar{d}L = \frac{1{,}000}{365}(5) = 13.7 \text{ units}$$

Rounding to the nearest unit, the inventory policy is as follows: When the number of units in inventory drops to 14, place an order for 89 more.

The total annual cost will be

$$TC = DC + \frac{D}{Q}S + \frac{Q}{2}H$$

$$= 1{,}000(12.50) + \frac{1{,}000}{89}(5) + \frac{89}{2}(1.25)$$

$$= \$12{,}611.81$$

Note that in this example, the purchase cost of the units was not required to determine the order quantity and the reorder point.

Establishing Safety Stocks Using Service Levels

Service level refers to the number of units that can be supplied from stock currently on hand. For example, if the annual demand for an item is 1,000 units, a 95 percent service level means that 950 can be supplied immediately from stock and 50 units will be short. (This concept assumes that orders are small and randomly distributed—one or several at a time; this model would not apply, for example, where the entire annual demand might be sold to a dozen customers.)

Safety stock can be defined as inventory that is carried to assure that the desired service level is met. Safety stock is usually thought to be some quantity *in addition* to the expected demand during the period to be protected. However, it is interesting to note that this safety stock can be negative; that is, computing the reorder point based on the expected demand can provide a *higher* service level than desired, so what is needed is to *subtract* units to create some shortages. See Example 12.3 on pages 450–51 for such a case.

The discussion in this section on service levels is based on a statistical concept known as Expected z, or $E(z)$. $E(z)$ is the expected number of units short during each lead time. This entire discussion assumes, as previously stated, that demands (withdrawals from the inventory stock) are in very small quantities—in comparison to the total stock—and are normally distributed.

To compute service level, we need to know *how many* units are short. For example, assume that the average weekly demand for an item is 100 units with a standard deviation of 10 units. If we stock 110 units, how many will we expect to be short? To do this we need to summarize the probability that 111 is demanded (1 short), the probability that 112 is demanded (2 short), plus the probability that 113 is demanded (3 short), and so on. This summary would give us the number of units we would expect to be short by stocking 110 units.

While the concept is simple, the equations are impractical to solve by hand. Fortunately, Brown has provided tables of expected values that we have included as Exhibit 12.5.[1]

We'll carry the explanations further within the context of our two basic model types: the fixed-order quantity and fixed-time period. We'll also discuss the important questions to be answered, such as: How do we control our inventory to provide a customer service level of 95 percent?

Fixed-Order Quantity Model with Specified Service Level

A fixed-order quantity system perpetually monitors the inventory level and places a new order when stock reaches some level, R. The danger of stockout in this model occurs only during the lead time, between the time an order is

---

[1] Robert G. Brown, *Decision Rules for Inventory Management* (New York: Holt, Rinehart & Winston, 1967).

EXHIBIT 12.5

Expected Number Out of Stock versus the Standard Deviation (This table is normalized to a mean of zero and a standard deviation of 1)

$E(z)$	z	$E(z)$	z
4.500	−4.50	0.399	0.00
4.400	−4.40	0.351	0.10
4.300	−4.30	0.307	0.20
4.200	−4.20	0.267	0.30
4.100	−4.10	0.230	0.40
4.000	−4.00	0.198	0.50
3.900	−3.90	0.169	0.60
3.800	−3.80	0.143	0.70
3.700	−3.70	0.120	0.80
3.600	−3.60	0.100	0.90
3.500	−3.50	0.083	1.00
3.400	−3.40	0.069	1.10
3.300	−3.30	0.056	1.20
3.200	−3.20	0.046	1.30
3.100	−3.10	0.037	1.40
3.000	−3.00	0.029	1.50
2.901	−2.90	0.023	1.60
2.801	−2.80	0.018	1.70
2.701	−2.70	0.014	1.80
2.601	−2.60	0.011	1.90
2.502	−2.50	0.008	2.00
2.403	−2.40	0.006	2.10
2.303	−2.30	0.005	2.20
2.205	−2.20	0.004	2.30
2.106	−2.10	0.003	2.40
2.008	−2.00	0.002	2.50
1.911	−1.90	0.001	2.60
1.814	−1.80	0.001	2.70
1.718	−1.70	0.001	2.80
1.623	−1.60	0.001	2.90
1.529	−1.50	0.000	3.00
1.437	−1.40	0.000	3.10
1.346	−1.30	0.000	3.20
1.256	−1.20	0.000	3.30
1.169	−1.10	0.000	3.40
1.083	−1.00	0.000	3.50
1.000	−0.90	0.000	3.60
0.920	−0.80	0.000	3.70
0.843	−0.70	0.000	3.80
0.769	−0.60	0.000	3.90
0.698	−0.50	0.000	4.00
0.630	−0.40	0.000	4.10
0.567	−0.30	0.000	4.20
0.507	−0.20	0.000	4.30
0.451	−0.10	0.000	4.40
0.399	0.00	0.000	4.50

z = Number of standard deviations of safety stock
$E(z)$ = Expected number of units short

Source: Revised from Robert G. Brown, *Decision Rules for Inventory Management* (New York: Holt, Rinehart & Winston, 1967), pp. 95–103.

EXHIBIT 12.6 **Fixed-Order Quantity Model**

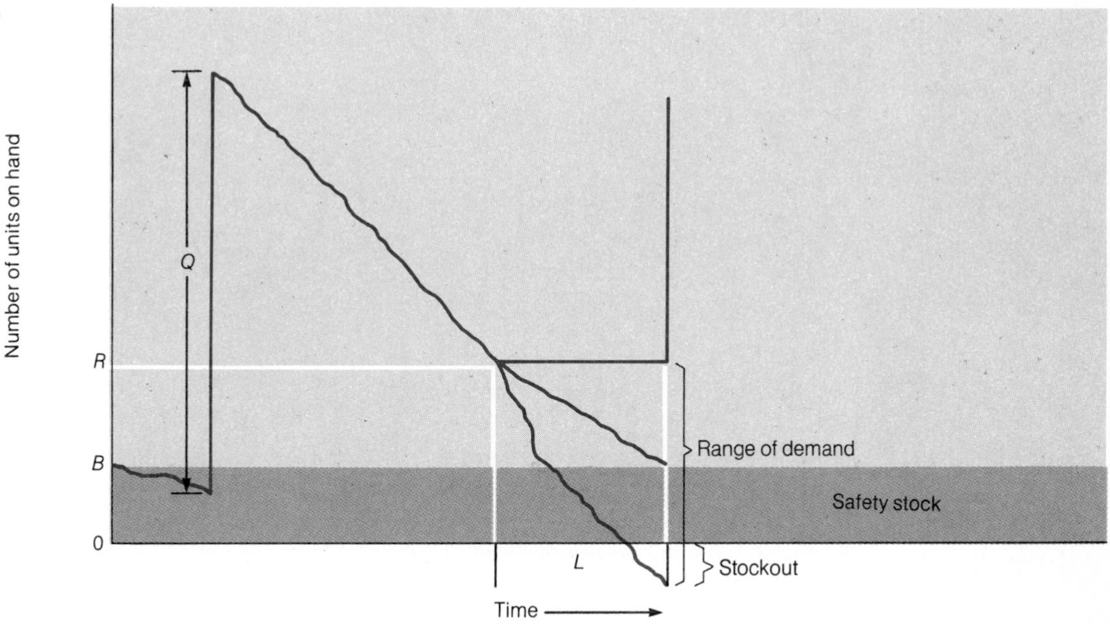

placed and the time it is received. As shown in Exhibit 12.6, an order is placed when the inventory level drops to the reorder point, R. During this lead time (L), a range of demands is possible. This range is determined either from an analysis of past demand data or from an estimate (if past data are not available).

The amount of safety stock depends on the service level desired, as previously discussed. The quantity to be ordered, Q, is calculated in the usual way considering the demand, shortage cost, ordering cost, holding cost, and so forth. A fixed-order quantity model can be used to compute Q such as the simple Q_{opt} model previously discussed. The reorder point is then set to cover the expected demand during the lead time plus a safety stock determined by the desired service level. Thus, *the key difference between a fixed-order quantity model under certainty in demand and uncertainty in demand is not in computing the order quantity (both will be the same) but in computing the reorder point, which includes safety stock.*

The reorder point is

$$R = \bar{d}L + z\sigma_L \tag{4}$$

where

R = Reorder point in units

$\bar{d}$ = Average daily demand
L = Lead time in days (time between placing an order and receiving the items)
z = Number of standard deviations for a specified service level
σ_L = Standard deviation of usage during lead time

The term $z\sigma_L$ is the amount of safety stock. Note that if safety stock is positive, the effect is to place a reorder sooner. That is, R without safety stock is simply the average demand during the lead time. If lead time usage was expected to be 20, for example, and safety stock was computed to be 5 units, then the order would be placed sooner, when 25 units remained. The greater the safety stock, the sooner the order is placed.

Computing $\bar{d}$, σ_L and z. Demand during the lead time to receive a replenishment order is really an estimate or forecast of what is expected. It may be a single number (for example if the lead time is a month, then the demand may be taken as the previous year's demand divided by 12), or it may be a summation of expected demands over the lead time (such as the sum of daily demands over a 30-day lead time). For the daily demand situation, d can be a forecasted demand using one of the models in Chapter 6 on forecasting. For example, if a 30-day period was used to calculate $\bar{d}$, then

$$\bar{d} = \frac{\sum_{i=1}^{30} d_i}{30} \tag{5}$$

The error in using $\bar{d}$ to forecast the future is measured by the standard deviation of errors, which is

$$\sigma_d = \frac{\sqrt{\sum_{i=1}^{30} (d - \bar{d})^2}}{30} \tag{6}$$

Since σ_d refers to one day, if lead time extends over several days we can use the statistical premise that the standard deviation of a series of independent occurrences is equal to the square root of the sum of the variances. That is, in general,

$$\sigma_s = \sqrt{\sigma_1{}^2 + \sigma_2{}^2 + \ldots \sigma_i{}^2} \tag{7}$$

For example, suppose we computed the standard deviation of demand to be 10 units per day. If our lead time to get an order is five days, the standard deviation for the five-day period, since each day can be considered independent, would be

$$\sigma_L = \sqrt{(10)^2 + (10)^2 + (10)^2 + (10)^2 + (10)^2} = 22.36$$

Next we need to compute z. We do this by computing $E(z)$, the number of units short that meets our desired service level, and then looking this up in Exhibit 12.5 for the appropriate z.

Suppose we wanted a service level of P (for example, P might be 95 percent). In the course of a year we would be short $(1 - P)\ D$ units, or $0.5D$, where D is the annual demand. If we ordered Q units each time, then we would be placing D/Q orders per year. Exhibit 12.5 is based on $\sigma_L = 1$. Therefore, any $E(z)$ that we read from the table needs to be multiplied by σ_L if it is other than 1. The number of units short per order, therefore, is $E(z)\sigma_L$. For the year, the number of units short is $E(z)\sigma_L D/Q$. Stated again, we have,

$$\text{Percentage short} \times \text{Annual demand} = \text{Number short per order} \times \text{Number of orders per year}$$

$$(1 - P) \times D = E(z)\sigma_L \times \frac{D}{Q}$$

which simplifies to

$$E(z) = \frac{(1 - P)Q}{\sigma_L} \tag{8}$$

where

P = Service level desired (such as satisfying 95 percent of demand from items in stock)
$(1 - P)$ = Unsatisfied demand
D = Annual demand
σ_L = Standard deviation of demand during lead time
Q = Economic order quantity calculated in the usual way (such as $Q = \sqrt{2DS/H}$)
$E(z)$ = Expected number of units short from a normalized table where the mean = 0 and σ = 1

We will now compare two examples. The difference between them is that in the first, the variation in demand is stated in terms of standard deviation over the entire lead time, and in the second, it is stated in terms of standard deviation per day (or other unit of time).

Example 12.2. Consider an economic order quantity case where annual demand D = 1,000 units, economic order quantity Q = 200 units, the desired service level P = .95, the standard deviation of demand during lead time σ_L = 50 units, and lead time L = 15 days. Determine the reorder point.

In our example, $\bar{d}$ = 4 (1,000 over a 250-workday year), and lead time is 15 days. Therefore, from the equation

$$R = \bar{d}L + z\sigma_L \qquad (9)$$
$$= 4(15) + z(50)$$

In order to find z, we use the equation for $E(z)$ and look this value up in the table. Our problem data gave us $Q = 200$, service level $P = .95$ and standard deviation of demand during lead time = 50. Therefore,

$$E(z) = \frac{(1 - P)Q}{\sigma_L} = \frac{(1 - .95)200}{50} = .2$$

From Exhibit 12.5, and through interpolation at $E(z) = .2$, we find $z = .49$. Completing the solution for R above, we find

$$R = 4(15) + z(50) = 60 + .49(50) = 84.5 \text{ units}$$

This says when the stock on hand gets down to 85 units, order 200 more.

Just to satisfy our skepticism, we can calculate the number served per year to see if it really is 95 percent. $E(z)$ is the expected number short on each order based on a standard deviation of 1. The number short on each order for our problem is $E(z)\sigma_L = .2(50) = 10$. Since there are five orders per year (1,000/200), this results in 50 units short. This verifies our achievement of a 95 percent service level, since 950 out of 1,000 demand were filled from stock.

Example 12.3. The daily demand for a certain product is normally distributed with a mean of 60 and a standard deviation of 7. The source of supply is reliable and maintains a constant lead time of six days. If the cost of placing the order is \$10 and annual holding costs are \$0.50 per unit, find the order quantity and reorder point to satisfy 95 percent of the customers. There are no stockout costs, and unfilled orders are filled as soon as the order arrives. Assume sales occur over the entire year.

In this problem we need to calculate the order quantity Q, as well as the reorder point R.

$\bar{d} = 60$

$\sigma_d = 7$

$D = 60(365)$

$S = \$10$

$H = \$0.50$

$L = 6$

The optimal order quantity is

$$Q_{\text{opt}} = \sqrt{\frac{2DS}{H}} = \sqrt{\frac{2(60)365(10)}{0.50}} = \sqrt{876,000} = 936 \text{ units}$$

To compute the reorder point, we need to calculate the amount of product used during the lead time and add this to the safety stock.

The standard deviation of demand during the lead time of six days is calculated from the variance of the individual days. Since each day's demand is independent[2]

$$\sigma_L = \sqrt{\sum_{i=1}^{L} \sigma_{d_i}^2} = \sqrt{6(7)^2} = 17.2$$

Next we need to know how many standard deviations are needed for a specified service level. From equation (8)

$$E(z) = \frac{(1 - P)Q}{\sigma_L}$$

Therefore

$$E(z) = \frac{936(1 - .95)}{17.2} = 2.721$$

From Exhibit 12.5, interpolating at $E(z) = 2.721$, $z = -2.72$. The reorder point from equation (9) is

$$\begin{aligned} R &= \bar{d}L + z\sigma_L \\ &= 60(6) + -2.72(17.2) \\ &= 313.2 \text{ units} \end{aligned}$$

To summarize the policy derived in this example, an order for 936 units is placed whenever the number of units remaining in inventory drops to 313.

Note that in this case the safety stock ($z\sigma_L$) turns out to be negative. This means that if we had ordered the average demand of 360 units during the lead time (60 × 6), we would have had a higher service level than we wanted. In order to get down to 95 percent service, we need to create more shortages by ordering less. We can verify our service level in this example by noting that we would place 23.4 orders per year [60(365)/936]. Each period would experience 46.8 units out of stock (2.72 × 17.2). Thus we would be out of stock 1,095 units per year (46.8 × 23.4). Service level, therefore, is 0.95 as we intended [(21,900 − 1,095)/21,900].

As shown in these two examples, this technique of determining safety stock levels is relatively simple and straightforward. It allows us to control inventory to meet our desired service levels.

Fixed-Time Period Model with Service Level

In a fixed-time period system, inventory is counted only at particular times, such as every week or every month. Counting inventory and placing orders on

[2] As previously discussed the standard deviation of a sum of independent variables is equal to the square root of the sum of the variances.

a periodic basis is desirable in situations such as when vendors make routine visits to customers and take orders for their complete line of products, or when buyers want to combine orders to save transportation costs. Other firms operate on a fixed time period to facilitate planning their inventory count; for example, Distributor X calls every two weeks and employees know that all Distributor X's product must be counted.

Fixed-time period models generate order quantities that vary from period to period, depending on the usage rates. These generally require a higher level of safety stock than a fixed-order quantity system. The fixed-order quantity system assumes continual counting of inventory on hand, with an order immediately placed when the reorder point is reached. In contrast, the standard fixed-time period models assume that inventory is counted only at the time specified for review. It is possible that some large demand will draw the stock down to zero right after an order is placed. This condition could go unnoticed until the next review period. Then the new order, when placed, still takes time to arrive. Thus, it is possible to be out of stock throughout the entire review period, T, and the order lead time, L. Safety stock, therefore, must provide protection against stockouts during the review period itself, as well as during the lead time from order placement to order receipt.

In a fixed-time period system, reorders are placed at the time of review (T), and the safety stock that must be reordered is

$$\text{Safety stock} = z\sigma_{T+L}$$

Exhibit 12.7 shows a fixed-time period system with a review cycle of T and a constant lead time L. In this case, demand is randomly distributed about a mean $\bar{d}$. The quantity to order, q, is

$$\begin{matrix} \text{Order quantity} & = & \text{Average demand over the vulnerable period} & + & \text{Safety stock} & - & \text{Inventory currently on hand (plus on order, if any)} \\ q & = & \bar{d}(T+L) & + & z\sigma_{T+L} & - & I \end{matrix} \quad (10)$$

where

q = Quantity to be ordered
T = The number of days between reviews
L = Lead time in days (time between placing an order and receiving it)
$\bar{d}$ = Forecasted average daily demand
z = Number of standard deviations for a specified service level
σ_{T+L} = Standard deviation of demand over the review and lead time
I = Current inventory level (includes items on order)

Note: The demand, lead time, review period, and so forth can be any time units such as days, weeks, or years, so long as it is consistent throughout the equation.

EXHIBIT 12.7 **Fixed-Time Period Inventory Model**

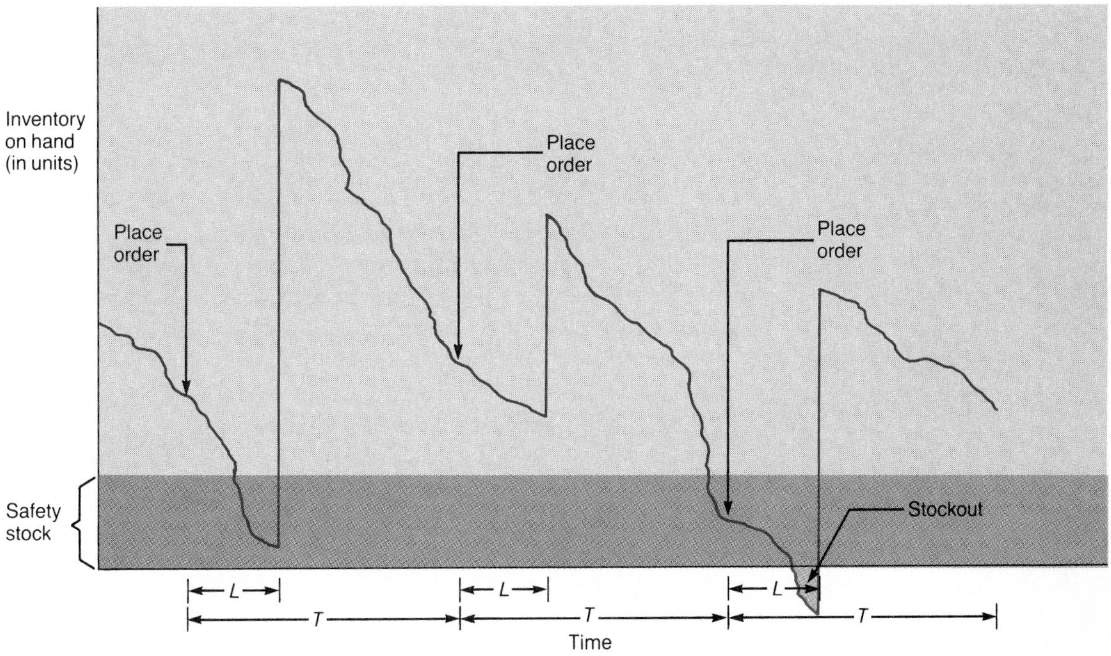

Constant review period T and lead time L; inventory is counted and orders are calculated and placed at the beginning of T; order is received at the end of the lead time L.

In this model, demand ($\bar{d}$) can be forecast and revised each review period, if desired, or the yearly average may be used if appropriate.

The value of z can be obtained by solving the following equation for $E(z)$ and reading the corresponding z value from Exhibit 12.5.

$$E(z) = \frac{\bar{d}T(1 - P)}{\sigma_{T+L}} \tag{11}$$

where

$E(z)$ = Expected number units short from a formalized table where the mean = 0 and σ = 1

P = Service level desired

$\bar{d}T$ = Demand during the review period where $\bar{d}$ is daily demand and T is the number of days

σ_{T+L} = Standard deviation over the review period and lead time

Example 12.4. Daily demand for a product is 10 units with a standard deviation of 3 units. The review period is 30 days, and lead time is 14 days. Management has set a policy of satisfying 98 percent of demand from items in stock. At the beginning of this review period, there are 150 units in inventory. How many units should be ordered?

The quantity to order is

$$\begin{aligned} q &= \bar{d}(T + L) + z\sigma_{T+L} - I \\ &= 10(30 + 14) + z\sigma_{T+L} - 150 \end{aligned}$$

Before we can complete the solution, we need to find σ_{T+L} and z. To find σ_{T+L}, we use the notion, as before, that the standard deviation of a sequence of independent random variables is equal to the square root of the sum of the variances. Therefore, the standard deviation during the period $T + L$ is the square root of the sum of the variances for each day, or

$$\sigma_{T+L} = \sqrt{\sum_{i=1}^{T+L} \sigma_{d_i}^2} \qquad (12)$$

Since each day is independent and σ_d is constant,

$$\sigma_{T+L} = \sqrt{(T + L)\,\sigma_d^2} = \sqrt{(30 + 14)(3)^2} = 19.90$$

Now in order to find z, we first need to find $E(z)$ and look this value up in the table. In this case, demand during the review period is $\bar{d}T$. Therefore,

$$E(z) = \frac{\bar{d}T(1 - P)}{\sigma_{T+L}} = \frac{10(30)(1 - .98)}{19.90} = 0.30151$$

From Exhibit 12.5 at $E(z) = 0.30151$, by interpolation $z = .21$.

The quantity to order, then, is

$$\begin{aligned} q &= \bar{d}(T + L) + z\sigma_{T+L} - I \\ &= 10(30 + 14) + .21(19.90) - 150 \\ &= 294 \text{ units} \end{aligned}$$

To satisfy 98 percent of the demand for units, order 294 at this review period.

12.7 A MAJOR PROBLEM: DETERMINING REALISTIC COSTS

Most inventory models will give optimal solutions so long as conditions of the system meet the constraints of the model. While this is easy to state, it is difficult to meet. Obtaining actual order, setup, carrying, and shortage costs is difficult—sometimes impossible. Part of the problem occurs because accounting data are usually averages, whereas we need the marginal cost. Exhibit 12.8 compares the assumed smoothly ascending cost to the more realistic actual cost. For example, a buyer is a salaried person. The marginal cost for the

EXHIBIT 12.8

Cost to Place Orders versus the Number of Orders Placed: Linear Assumption and Normal Reality

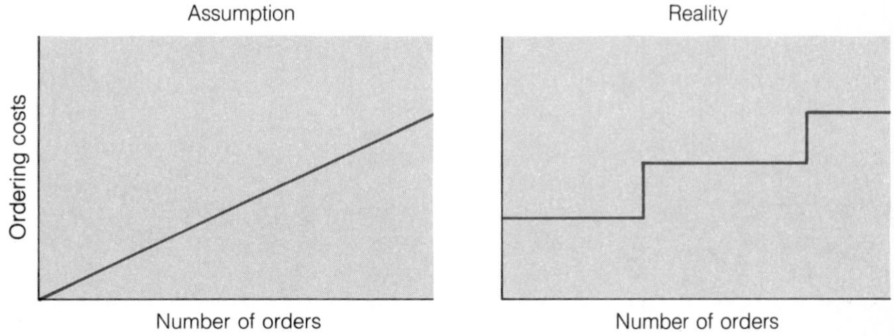

buyer's labor to place additional orders up to a full workload is zero. When another buyer is hired, it is a step function. (In theory, the marginal cost of the order that caused hiring the new buyer is the cost for the additional buyer.)

The same problem occurs in determining carrying costs. Warehouse cost, for example, may be close to zero if empty storage areas are still available. Also, most companies can only estimate true carrying costs, since they include obsolescence (a guess, at best), cost of capital (depends on internal money available, alternate investment opportunities, and sources of new capital), and insurance costs (which may range from zero if current insurance premiums cover more than the assets on hand, to the cost of a new policy).

We can take two approaches to deal with this data inaccuracy. First, we can analyze the effects of error. That is, we can do a sensitivity analysis of our inventory model to errors in ordering, setup, and carrying costs and the effect on total annual cost. Second, we can conduct our inventory analysis in terms of inventory investment and workload, rather than in terms of order costs and carrying costs.

Errors in Costs

Inventory models generally involve quadratic equations. Therefore, even significant errors often have less effect than one might expect. The point here is that a high degree of accuracy is not necessary to receive the major part of the potential benefit. These comments are not meant to suggest you should reduce emphasis on computing order quantities but rather to recognize where inventory costs come from and where emphasis must be placed to reduce costs significantly.

Exhibit 12.9 shows the computed order quantity for an item with an annual demand of 1,000 units, unit cost of \$25, an inventory carrying cost of 25 percent of the cost (or \$6.25), and various setup costs. The model used for the computation was the simple sawtooth model without safety stock. Note the

EXHIBIT 12.9 Cost Effects of Changing Setup Cost *S*

(1) *D*	(2) Setup Cost *S*	(3) *C*	(4) *i*	(5) $\frac{H}{i \times C}$	(6) *Q*	(7) $D/Q \times S$	(8) $Q/2 \times H$	(9) Total Variable (7 + 8)	(10) Total Annual Cost	(11) Change in Variable Cost	(12) Change in Total Cost
1,000	5	25	.25	6.25	40.00	125.00	125.00	250.00	25,250	−.29	−.0041
1,000	6	25	.25	6.25	43.82	136.93	136.93	273.86	25,274	−.23	−.0031
1,000	7	25	.25	6.25	47.33	147.90	147.90	295.00	25,296	−.16	−.0023
1,000	8	25	.25	6.25	50.60	158.11	158.11	316.22	25,316	−.11	−.0015
1,000	9	25	.25	6.25	53.67	167.71	167.71	335.41	25,335	−.05	−.0007
1,000	10	25	.25	6.25	56.57	176.78	176.78	353.55	25,354	.00	.0000
1,000	12	25	.25	6.25	61.97	193.65	193.65	387.30	25,387	.10	.0013
1,000	14	25	.25	6.25	66.93	209.17	209.17	418.33	25,418	.18	.0026
1,000	16	25	.25	6.25	71.55	223.61	223.61	447.21	25,447	.26	.0037
1,000	18	25	.25	6.25	75.89	237.17	237.17	474.34	25,474	.34	.0048
1,000	20	25	.25	6.25	80.00	250.00	250.00	500.00	25,500	.41	.0058

effects on variable and total cost. If we assume that the true setup cost was \$10, then the optimal order quantity is 56.57 units. If a setup cost of \$5 is used instead (half as much), the variable cost would be computed 29 percent low. If a setup cost of \$20 (twice as much) is used, the variable cost would be computed as 41 percent higher. (The total variable cost at S = \$10 is \$353.55; at S = \$5, total variable cost is \$250; at S = \$20, total variable cost is \$500.) The total range of error in using S—from half as much to double the true value—made a total annual difference of \$250. The total cost, however, varies less than 1 percent—ranging from 0.4 percent low to 0.6 percent high. Clearly, then, if a company seeks to make significant reductions in total cost of inventory, it must cut setup times to 5–10 percent of current times or reduce the existing level of inventory through major lead-time reductions. How this is done is discussed in Chapter 16.

All inventory systems are plagued by two major problems: maintaining adequate control over each inventory item and ensuring that accurate records of stock on hand are kept. In this section, we will present **ABC analysis**—an inventory system offering a control technique and inventory cycle counting that can improve record accuracy.

ABC Inventory Planning

Maintaining inventory through counting, placing orders, receiving stock, and so on takes personnel time and costs money. When there are limits on these resources, the logical move is to try to use what resources you have to control inventory in the best way. In other words, focus on the most important items in inventory.

EXHIBIT 12.10

Annual Usage of Inventory by Value

Item Number	Annual Dollar Usage	Percent of Total Value
22	95,000	40.8
68	75,000	32.1
27	25,000	10.7
03	15,000	6.4
82	13,000	5.6
54	7,500	3.2
36	1,500	0.6
19	800	0.3
23	425	0.2
41	225	0.1
	233,450	100.0

In the 18th century, Villefredo Pareto, in a study of the distribution of wealth in Milan, found that 20 percent of the people controlled 80 percent of the wealth. This logic of the few having the greatest importance and the many having little importance has been broadened to include many situations and is termed the *Pareto Principle*. This is true in our everyday lives (most of the decisions we make are relatively unimportant but a few shape our future) and is certainly true in inventory systems (where a few items account for the bulk of our investment).

Any inventory system must specify when an order is to be placed for an item and how many units to order. In most situations involving inventory control, there are so many items involved, it is not practical to model and give thorough treatment to each item. To get around this problem, the ABC classification scheme divides inventory items into three groupings: high dollar volume (A), moderate dollar volume (B), and low dollar volume (C). Dollar volume is a measure of importance; an item low in cost but high in volume can be more important than a high-cost item with low volume.

ABC classification

If the annual usage of items in inventory is listed according to dollar volume, generally the list will show that a small number of items account for a large dollar volume and that a large number of items account for a small dollar volume. Exhibit 12.10 illustrates the relationship.

The ABC approach divides this list into three groupings by value: A items constitute roughly the top 15 percent of the items, B items the next 35 percent, and C items the last 50 percent. From observation, it appears that the list in Exhibit 12.10 may be meaningfully grouped with A including 20 percent (2 of the 10), B including 30 percent, and C including 50 percent. These points show clear delineations between sections. The result of this segmentation is shown in Exhibit 12.11 and is plotted in Exhibit 12.12.

EXHIBIT 12.11

ABC Grouping of Inventory Items

Classification	Item Number	Annual Dollar Usage	Percent of Total
A	22, 68	170,000	72.9
B	27, 03, 82	53,000	22.7
C	54, 36, 19, 23, 41	10,450	4.4
		233,450	100.0

EXHIBIT 12.12

ABC Inventory Classification (Inventory value for each group versus the group's portion of the total list)

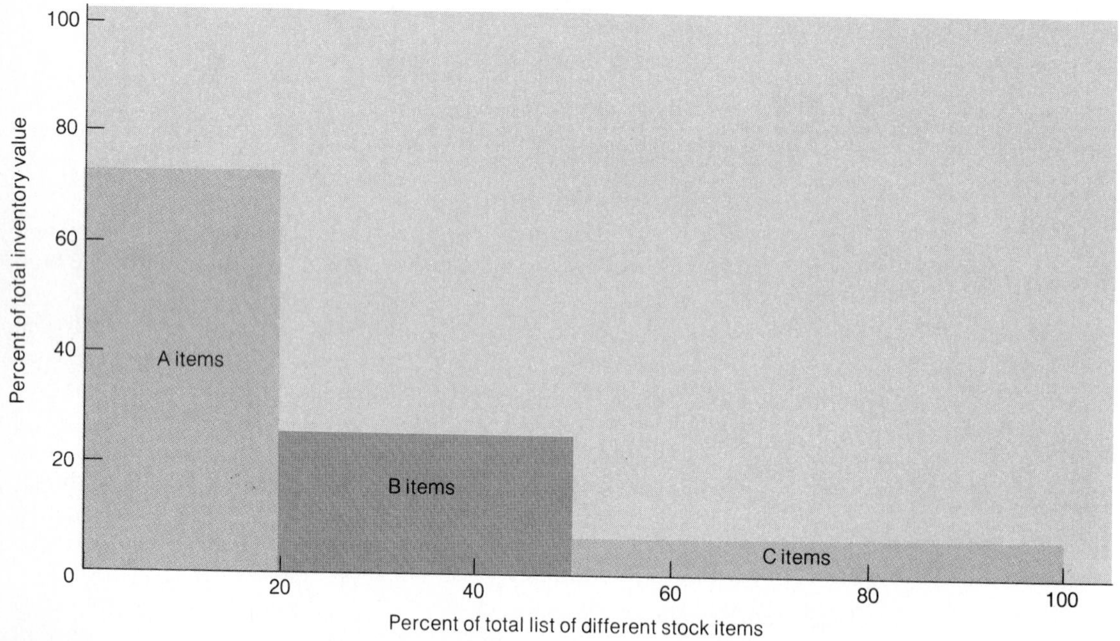

Segmentation may not always occur so neatly. The objective, though, is to try to separate the important from the unimportant. Where the lines actually break will depend on the particular inventory under question and on how much personnel time is available (with more time a firm could define larger A or B categories).

The purpose of classifying items into groups is to establish the appropriate degree of control over each item. On a periodic basis, for example, Class A items may be more clearly controlled with weekly ordering, B items may be ordered biweekly, and C items may be ordered monthly or bimonthly. Note that the unit cost of items is not related to their classification. An A item may have a high dollar volume through a combination of either low cost and high usage or high cost and low usage. Similarly, C items may have a low dollar volume either because of low demand or low cost. In an automobile service station, gasoline would be an A item with daily tabulation; tires, batteries, oil, grease, and transmission fluid may be B items and ordered every two to four weeks; and C items would consist of valve stems, windshield wiper blades, radiator caps, hoses, fan belts, oil and gas additives, car wax, and so forth. C items may be ordered every two or three months or even be allowed to run out before reordering since the penalty for stockout is not serious.

Sometimes, an item may be critical to a system if its absence creates a sizable loss. In this case, regardless of the item's classification, sufficiently large stocks should be kept on hand to prevent runout. One way to ensure closer control is to designate this item an A or a B, forcing it into the category even if its dollar volume does not warrant such inclusion.

Inventory Accuracy and Cycle Counting

Inventory records usually differ from the actual physical count and **inventory accuracy** refers to how well the two agree. The question is, How much error is acceptable? If the record shows a balance of 683 of Part X and an actual count shows 652, is this within reason? Suppose the actual count shows 750, an excess of 67 over the record; is this any better?

Every production system must have agreement, within some specified range, between what the record says is in inventory and what actually is in inventory. There are many reasons records and inventory may not agree. For example, an open stockroom area allows items to be removed for both legitimate and unauthorized purposes. The legitimate removal may have been done in a hurry and simply not recorded. Sometimes parts are misplaced, turning up months later. Parts are often stored in several locations, but records may be lost or the location recorded incorrectly. Sometimes stock replenishment orders are recorded as received, when in fact they never were. Occasionally, a group of parts are recorded as removed from inventory, but the customer order is cancelled and the parts are replaced in inventory without canceling the record. To keep the production system flowing smoothly without parts shortages and efficiently without excess balances, it is important that records are accurate.

How can a firm keep accurate, up-to-date records? The first general rule is to keep the storeroom locked. If only storeroom personnel have access, and one of their measures of performance when it comes time for personnel evaluation and merit increases is record accuracy, there is a strong motivation to comply. Every location of inventory storage, whether in a locked storeroom or on the production floor, should have a recordkeeping mechanism. A second way is to convey the importance of accurate records to all personnel and depend on them to assist in this effort. (What this all boils down to is: Put a fence around the storage area that goes all the way to the ceiling so that workers can't climb over to get parts; put a lock on the gate and give one person the key. Nobody, but nobody, can pull parts without the transaction authorized and recorded.)

Another way to ensure accuracy is to count inventory frequently and match this against records. A widely used method is called **cycle counting.**

Cycle counting is a physical inventory-taking technique in which inventory is counted on a periodic basis rather than once or twice a year. The key to effective cycle counting and, therefore, to accurate records lies in deciding which items are to be counted, when, and by whom.

Since virtually all inventory systems these days are computerized, the computer can be programmed to produce a cycle count notice in the following cases:

1. When the record shows a low or zero balance on hand. (Obviously it is easier to count fewer items.)
2. When the record shows a positive balance but a backorder was written (indicating a discrepancy).
3. After some specified level of activity.
4. To signal a review based on the importance of the item (as in the ABC system above) such as in the following example.

Annual Dollar Usage	Review Period
$10,000 or more	30 days or less
$3,000–$10,000	45 days or less
$250–$3,000	90 days or less
Less than $250	180 days or less

Obviously, the easiest time for stock to be counted is when there is no activity in the stockroom or on the production floor. This means on the weekends or during the second or third shift, when the facility is less busy. If this is not possible, then more careful logging and separation of items are required to do an inventory count while production is going on and transactions are occurring.

The counting cycle depends on the available personnel. Some firms schedule regular stockroom personnel to do the counting during the lull times of the regular working day. Other companies contract out to private firms who come in and count inventory. Still other firms use full-time cycle counters who do nothing but count inventory and resolve differences with the records. While this last method sounds expensive, many firms believe that it is actually less costly than the usual hectic annual inventory count generally performed during the two- or three-week annual vacation shutdown.

The question of how much error is tolerable between physical inventory and records has been much debated. While some firms strive for 100 percent accuracy, others accept 1, 2, or 3 percent error. The accuracy level recommended by the American Production and Inventory Control Society (APICS) is: ± 0.2 percent for A items, ± 1 percent for B items, and ± 5 percent for C items. Regardless of the specific accuracy decided upon, the important point is that the level be dependable so that safety stocks may be provided as a cushion. Accuracy is important for a smooth production process so that customer orders can be processed as scheduled and not held up because of the unavailability of parts.

Inventory Control in Services

To demonstrate how inventory control is conducted in service organizations, we have selected two areas to describe: a department store and an automobile service agency.

Department store inventory policy

The common term used to identify an inventory item in a department store is stock-keeping unit or SKU. The SKU identifies each item, its manufacturer, and its cost. The number of SKUs becomes large even for small departments. For example, if towels carried in a domestic items department are obtained from three manufacturers in three quality levels, three sizes (hand towel, face towel, and bath towel), and four colors, there are 108 different items ($3 \times 3 \times 3 \times 4$). Even if towels are sold only in sets of three pieces (hand towel, face towel, and bath towel), the number of SKUs needed to identify the towel sets is $3 \times 3 \times 1 \times 4$, or 36. Depending on the store, a housewares department may carry 3,000 to 4,000 SKUs, and a linen and domestic items department may carry 5,000 to 6,000.

Obviously, such large numbers mean that individual economic order quantities cannot be calculated for each item by hand. How, then, does a department keep tab on its stock and place orders for replenishment? We will answer this question in the context of an example dealing with a housewares department.

Housewares department. Generally, housewares are divided into staple and promotional items. Within these major divisions, further classifications are used, such as cookware and tableware. Also, items are frequently classified by price, as $5 items, $4, $3, and so forth.

The housewares department usually purchases from a distributor rather than directly from a manufacturer. The use of a distributor, who handles products from many manufacturers, has the advantage of fewer orders and faster shipping time (shorter lead time). Further, the distributor's sales personnel may visit the housewares department weekly and count all the items they supply to this department. Then, in line with the replenishment level that has been established by the buyer, the distributor's salesperson will place orders for the buyer. This saves the department time in counting inventory and placing orders. The typical lead time for receipt of stock from a housewares distributor is two or three days. The safety stock, therefore, is quite low, and the buyer establishes the replenishment level so as to supply only enough items for the two- to three-day lead time, plus expected demand during the period until the distributor's salesperson's next visit.

It is interesting to note that a formal method of estimating stockout and establishing safety-stock levels is usually not followed because the number of items is too great. Instead, the total value of items in the department is monitored. Thus, replenishment levels are set by dollar allocation.

Through planning, each department has an established monthly value for inventory. By tabulating inventory balance, monthly sales, and items on order, an "open-to-buy" figure is determined ("open-to-buy" is the unspent portion of the budget). This dollar amount is the sum available to the buyer for the following month. When an increase in demand is expected (Christmas, Mother's Day, and so forth), the allocation of funds to the department is increased, resulting in a larger open-to-buy position. Then the replenishment levels are raised in line with the class of goods, responding to the demand increase, thereby creating a higher stock of goods on hand.

In practice, the open-to-buy funds are largely spent during the first days of the month. However, the buyer tries to reserve some funds for special purchases or to restock fast-moving items. Promotional items in housewares are controlled individually (or by class) by the buyer.

Maintaining an auto replacement-parts inventory

A firm in the automobile service business purchases most of its parts supplies from a small number of distributors. Franchised new-car dealers purchase the great bulk of their supplies from the automobile manufacturer. A dealer's demand for auto parts originates primarily from the general public and other departments of the agency, such as the service department or body shop. The problem, in this case, is to determine the order quantities for the several thousand items carried.

A franchised automobile agency of medium size may carry a parts inventory valued in the area of $500,000. Because of the nature of this industry, alternate uses of funds are plentiful, and therefore, opportunity costs are high. For example, dealers may lease cars, carry their own contracts, stock a larger new-car inventory, or open sidelines such as tire shops, trailer sales, or recreational vehicle sales—all with potentially high returns. This creates pressure to try to carry a low inventory level of parts and supplies while still meeting an acceptable service level.

While many dealers still perform their inventory ordering by hand, there is a definite trend in the industry to use computers. For both manual and computerized systems, an ABC classification works well. Expensive and high-turnover supplies are counted and ordered frequently; low-cost items are ordered in large quantities at infrequent intervals. A common drawback of frequent order placement is the extensive amount of time needed to physically put the items on the shelves and log them in. (However, this restocking procedure does not greatly add to an auto agency's cost, since parts department personnel generally do this during slow periods.)

A great variety of computerized systems is currently in use. One program gives a choice of using either a simple weighted average or exponential smoothing to forecast the next period's demand. In a monthly reordering system, for example, the items to be ordered are counted and the number on hand is entered into the computer. By subtracting the number on hand from the previous month's inventory and adding the orders received during the month, the usage rate is determined. Some programs use exponential smoothing forecasts while others use a weighted-average method. For the weighted-average method the computer progam stores the usage rate for, say, four previous months. Then, with the application of a set of weighting factors, a forecast is made in the same manner as described in Chapter 6. This works as follows. Suppose usage of a part during January, February, March, and April was 17, 19, 11, and 23, respectively, and the set of corresponding weights was 0.10, 0.20, 0.30, and 0.40. Thus, the forecast for May is 0.10(17) + 0.20(19) + 0.30(11) + 0.40(23), or 18 units. If safety stock were included and equal to one-month demand, then 36 units would be ordered (one-month demand plus one-month safety stock) less whatever is on hand at the time of order placement. The simple two-month rule allows for forecasted usage during the lead time plus the review period, with the balance providing the safety stock.

The computer output provides a useful reference file, identifying the item, cost, order size, and number of units on hand. The output itself constitutes the purchase order and is sent to the distributor or factory supply house. The simplicity in this is attractive since, once the forecast weighting is selected, all that must be done is to input the number of units of each item on hand. Thus, negligible computation is involved, and very little preparation is needed to send the order out.

12.8 CONCLUSION

This chapter introduced the two main classes of demand: independent demand referring to the external demand for a firm's end product, and dependent demand, usually referring—within the firm—to the demand for items created because of the demand for more complex items of which they are a part. Most industries have items in both classes. In manufacturing, for example, independent demand is common for finished products, service and repair parts, and operating supplies; and dependent demand is common for those parts and materials needed to produce the end product. In wholesale and retail sales of consumer goods, most demand is independent—each item is an end item, with the customer doing no further assembly or fabrication.

Independent demand, the focus of this chapter, is based on statistics. In the fixed-order quantity and fixed-time period models, the influence of service level was shown on safety stock and reorder point determinations. Two special-purpose models—price break and single-period—were also presented.

To distinguish among item categories for analysis and control, the ABC method was offered. The importance of inventory accuracy was also noted, and cycle counting was described. Finally, brief descriptions of inventory procedures in a department store and an auto parts shop were given to illustrate some of the simpler ways nonmanufacturing firms carry out their inventory control function.

It is important to recognize that firms have very large investments in inventory, and the cost to carry this inventory runs from 25 to 35 percent of the inventory's worth annually. The goal for firms today is to increase the inventory turns by reducing inventory levels at all points in the process.

Booz, Allen & Hamilton Inc. estimated that in the early 1980s it cost General Motors well over $3 billion per year to carry its $9 billion inventory. During that time, Chrysler reduced its inventory by $750 million, thereby saving $250 million a year in carrying costs.[3]

12.9 REVIEW AND DISCUSSION QUESTIONS

1. Distinguish between dependent and independent demand in a McDonald's, in an integrated manufacturer of personal copiers, and in a pharmaceutical supply house.
2. Distinguish between in-process inventory, safety stock inventory, and seasonal inventory.
3. Discuss the nature of the costs that affect inventory size.
4. Under what conditions would a plant manager elect to use a fixed-order quantity model as opposed to a fixed-time period model? What are the disadvantages of using a fixed-time period ordering system?
5. Define the term *service level* as used in this text. How does it differ from the concept of probability of stockout?
6. What two basic questions must be answered by an inventory-control decision rule?
7. Discuss the assumptions that are inherent in production setup cost, ordering cost, and carrying costs. How valid are they?
8. "The nice thing about inventory models is that you can pull one off the shelf and apply it so long as your cost estimates are accurate." Comment.

[3] John Koten, *The Wall Street Journal*, April 7, 1982, p. 29.

9. What type of inventory system do you use in the following situations?
   a. Supplying your kitchen with fresh food.
   b. Obtaining a daily newspaper.
   c. Buying gasoline for your car.
   To which of these items do you impute the highest stockout cost?
10. Why is it desirable to classify items into groups, as the ABC classification does?
11. What kind of policy or procedure would you recommend to improve the inventory operation in a department store? What advantages and disadvantages does your system have vis-à-vis the department store inventory operation described in this chapter?

12.10 PROBLEMS

*1. Items purchased from a vendor cost $20 each, and the forecast for next year's demand is 1,000 units. If it costs $5 every time an order is placed for more units and the storage cost is $4 per unit per year, what quantity should be ordered each time?
   a. What is the total ordering cost for a year?
   b. What is the total storage cost for a year?

*2. Daily demand for a product is 120 units, with a standard deviation of 30 units. The review period is 14 days and the lead time is 7 days. At the time of review there are 130 units in stock. If 99 percent of all demand is to be satisfied from items in stock, how many units should be ordered?

3. Electronic Memos, Inc., (EMI) produces pocket-size microcassette recorders for business and professional people, for recording notes and for transcribing. These recorders are sold through retailers nationally.

   EMI would like to provide its retailers with guidelines to help them determine what size orders they should place, what safety stocks to carry, the reorder points, and so forth. EMI has just hired you to develop a set of charts that would be distributed to its retailers and would be useful to them during their reordering periods.

   Because technology in the entire electronics area is changing so rapidly (recorders included), EMI is recommending that its dealers review their inventory on hand and place orders monthly.

   During an interview for a job with EMI, the recruiter has explained this reordering situation to you and has asked you to demonstrate that you are qualified to take on this task as your first assignment with the company. You happen to have a copy of your operations management text with you and he is allowing you to use the equations and tables.

   The tables will be for a wide variety of possibilities. The problem you are to solve has the following features:

   Demand for the coming 30-day month is 40 units.

   Standard deviation of daily demand is 4 units.

* Problems 1 and 2 are completely solved in Appendix D.

The firm will be open every day.

It takes 10 calendar days to receive an order.

The firm would like to satisfy 95 percent of the customers.

There are currently 30 units in stock.

How many units should be ordered?

4. Dunstreet's Department Store would like to develop an inventory ordering policy to satisfy 95 percent of its customers' demands for products directly from inventory stock on hand. To illustrate your recommended procedure, use as an example the ordering policy for white percale sheets.

   Demand for white percale sheets is 5,000 per year. The store is open 365 days per year. Every two weeks (14 days) an inventory count is made and a new order is placed. It takes 10 days for the sheets to be delivered. Standard deviation of demand for the sheets is 5 per day. There are currently 150 sheets on hand.

   How many sheets should you order?

5. The annual demand for a product is 15,600 units. The weekly demand is 300 units with a standard deviation of 90 units. The cost to place an order is $31.20, and the time from ordering to receipt is four weeks. The annual inventory carrying cost is $0.10 per unit. Find the reorder point necessary to provide a 99 percent service level.

   Suppose the production manager is ordered to reduce the safety stock of this item by 50 percent. If he does so, what will the new service level be?

6. Daily demand for a product is 100 units, with a standard deviation of 25 units. The review period is 10 days and the lead time is 6 days. At the time of review there are 50 units in stock. If 98 percent of all demand is to be satisfied from items in stock, how many units should be ordered?

7. Item X is a standard item stocked in a company's inventory of component parts. Each year, the firm, on a random basis, uses about 2,000 of Item X, which costs $25 each. Storage costs, which include insurance and cost of capital, amount to $5 per unit of average inventory. Every time an order is placed for more Item X, it costs $10.

   a. Whenever Item X is ordered, what should the order size be?

   b. What is the annual cost for ordering Item X?

   c. What is the annual cost for storing Item X?

8. The annual demand for a product is 13,000 units; the weekly demand is 250 units with a standard deviation of 40 units. The cost of placing an order is $100, and the time from ordering to receipt is four weeks. The annual inventory carrying cost is $0.65 per unit. In order to provide a 99 percent service level, what must the reorder point be?

   Suppose the production manager is told to reduce the safety stock of this item by 10 units. If this is done, what will the new service level be?

9. In the past, Taylor Industries has used a fixed-time inventory system that involved taking a complete inventory count of all items each month. However, increasing labor costs are forcing Taylor Industries to examine alternate ways to reduce the amount of labor involved in inventory stockrooms, yet without increasing other costs, such as shortage costs.

Following is a random sample of 20 of Taylor's items.

Item Number	Annual Usage	Item Number	Annual Usage
1	$ 1,500	11	$13,000
2	12,000	12	600
3	2,200	13	42,000
4	50,000	14	9,900
5	9,600	15	1,200
6	750	16	10,200
7	2,000	17	4,000
8	11,000	18	61,000
9	800	19	3,500
10	15,000	20	2,900

a. What would you recommend Taylor do to cut back its labor cost? (Illustrate using an ABC plan.)

b. Item 15 is critical to continued operations. How would you recommend it be classified?

10. Gentle Ben's Bar and Restaurant uses 5,000 quart bottles of an imported wine each year. The effervescent wine costs $3 per bottle and is served in whole bottles only since it loses its bubbles quickly. Ben figures that it costs $10 each time an order is placed, and holding costs are 20 percent of the purchase price. It takes three weeks for an order to arrive. Weekly demand is 100 bottles (closed two weeks per year) with a standard deviation of 30 bottles.

    Ben would like to use an inventory system that minimizes inventory cost and will satisfy 95 percent of his customers who order this wine.

    a. What is the economic order quantity for Ben to order?

    b. At what inventory level should he place an order?

    c. How many bottles of wine will be short during each order cycle?

11. Retailers Warehouse is an independent supplier of household items to department stores. RW attempts to stock enough items to satisfy 98 percent of the requests from its customers.

    A stainless steel knife set is one of the items stocked by RW. Demand is 2,400 sets per year, relatively stable over the entire year. Whenever new stock is ordered, a buyer must ensure that numbers are correct for stock on hand and phone in a new order. The total cost involved to place an order is about $5. RW figures that to hold inventory in stock and to pay for interest on borrowed capital, insurance, etc., adds up to about $4 holding cost per unit per year.

    Analysis of the past data shows that the standard deviation of demand from retailers is about four units per day for a 365-day year. Lead time to get the order once placed is seven days.

    a. What is the economic order quantity?

    b. What is the reorder point?

12. Daily demand for a product is 60 units with a standard deviation of 10 units. The review period is 10 days, and the lead time is 2 days. At the time of review there are 100 units in stock. If 98 percent of all demand is to be satisfied from items in stock, how many units should be ordered?

13. University Drug Pharmaceuticals orders its antibiotics every two weeks (14 days) when a salesperson visits from one of the pharmaceutical companies. Tetracycline is one of its most prescribed antibiotics, with an average daily demand of 2,000 capsules. The standard deviation of daily demand was derived from examining prescriptions filled over the past three months and was found to be 800 capsules. It takes five days for the order to arrive. University Drug would like to satisfy 99 percent of the prescriptions. The salesperson just arrived, and there are currently 25,000 capsules in stock.

    How many capsules should be ordered?

14. Alpha Products, Inc. is having a problem trying to control inventory. There is insufficient time to devote to all its items equally. Following is a sample of some items stocked, along with the annual usage of each item expressed in dollar volume.

Item	Annual Dollar Usage	Item	Annual Dollar Usage
a	$ 7,000	k	$80,000
b	1,000	l	400
c	14,000	m	1,100
d	2,000	n	30,000
e	24,000	o	1,900
f	68,000	p	800
g	17,000	q	90,000
h	900	r	12,000
i	1,700	s	3,000
j	2,300	t	32,000

    Can you suggest a system for allocating control time? Specify where each item from the list would be placed.

15. After graduation you decide to go into a partnership in an office supply store. The store has existed for a number of years and, walking through the store and stockrooms, you find a great discrepancy in service levels. Some spaces and bins for items are completely empty; others have supplies covered with dust and have obviously been there a long time. You decide to take on the project of establishing consistent levels of inventory to meet customer demands. Most of your supplies are purchased from just a few distributors, and these distributors call on your store once every two weeks.

    You choose, as your first item for study, computer printer paper. You examine the sales records and purchase orders and find that demand for the past 12 months was 5,000 boxes. Using your calculator you sample some days' demands and estimate that the standard deviation of daily demand is 10 boxes. You also searched out these figures:

    Cost per box of paper: $11.
    Desired service level: 98 percent.
    Store is open every day.
    Salesperson visits every 2 weeks.
    Delivery time following visit: 3 days.

Using your procedure, how many boxes of paper would be ordered if, on the day the salesperson calls, there are 60 boxes on hand?

16. A distributor of large appliances needs to determine the order quantities and reorder points for the various products it carries. The following data refers to a specific refrigerator in its product line:

Cost to place an order	\$30
Holding cost	20 percent of product cost per year
Cost of refrigerator	\$300 each
Annual demand	500 refrigerators
Standard deviation during lead time	10 refrigerators
Lead time	7 days

Consider an even daily demand and a 365-day year.

a. What is the economic order quantity?

b. If the distributor wants to satisfy 97 percent of its demand, what reorder point, *R*, should be used?

17. It is your responsibility, as the new head of the automotive section of Nichols Department Store, to assure that reorder quantities for the various items have been correctly established. You decide to test one of the items and choose Michelin tires, XW size 185 × 14 BSW.

A perpetual inventory system has been used so you examine this as well as other records and come up with the following data:

Cost per tire	\$35 each
Holding cost	20 percent of tire cost per year
Demand	1,000 per year
Ordering cost	\$20 per order
Standard deviation of daily demand	3 tires
Delivery lead time	4 days

Since customers will generally not wait for tires but will go elsewhere, you decide on a service level of 98 percent.

a. Determine the order quantity.

b. Determine the reorder point.

18. UA Hamburger Hamlet places an order for its high-volume items daily (hamburger patties, buns, milk, etc.) UAHH counts its current inventory on hand once per day and phones in its order for delivery 24 hours later.

Your problem here is to determine the number of hamburgers UAHH should order for the following conditions:

Average daily demand	600
Standard deviation of demand	100
Desired service level	99%

On the particular day for this problem, inventory count shows 800 hamburgers on hand. How many hamburgers should be ordered?

19. DAT, Inc. produces digital audio tapes to be used in the consumer audio division. DAT doesn't have sufficient personnel in its inventory supply section to closely control each item stocked, so others asked you to determine an ABC classification. The following shows a sample from the inventory records:

Item	Average Monthly Demand	Price per Unit
1	700	$ 6.00
2	200	4.00
3	2,000	12.00
4	1,100	20.00
5	4,000	21.00
6	100	10.00
7	3,000	2.00
8	2,500	1.00
9	500	10.00
10	1,000	2.00

Develop an ABC classification for these 10 items.

12.11 SELECTED BIBLIOGRAPHY

Backes, Robert W. "Cycle Counting—A Better Way for Achieving Accurate Inventory Records." *Production and Inventory Management* 21, no. 2 (Second Quarter 1980), pp. 36–44.

Bagchi, Uttarayan; Jack Hayya; and J. Keith Ord. "Modeling Demand during Lead Time." *Decision Sciences* 15, no. 2 (Spring 1984), pp. 157–76.

Brown, Robert G. *Materials Management Systems*. New York: John Wiley & Sons, 1977.

International Business Machines Corporation. *Basic Principles of Wholesale IMPACT*. Publication E20-8105-1.

———. *Introduction to IBM Wholesale IMPACT*. Publication E20-0278-0.

———. *Inventory Control*. Publication 520-14491.

———. *Wholesale IMPACT—Advanced Principles and Implementations Manual*. Publication E20-0174-0.

Plossl, George W., and W. Evert Welch. *The Role of Top Management in the Control of Inventory*. Reston, Va.: Reston Publishing, 1979.

Vollmann, T. E.; W. L. Berry; and D. C. Whybark. *Manufacturing Planning and Control Systems*. 2nd ed. Homewood, Ill.: Richard D. Irwin, 1988.

Wight, Oliver W. *Production and Inventory Management in the Computer Age*. Boston: Cahners Books, 1974.

Chapter 13

Inventory Systems for Dependent Demand: Material Requirements Planning

EPIGRAPH

To make Grandma's Chocolate Cake, take 1 cup shortening, 2 cups sugar, 1 teaspoon salt, 1 teaspoon vanilla, 2 eggs, 2¼ cups flour, 1 cup buttermilk, ½ cup cocoa, 2 teaspoons soda, and 1 cup hot water. . . .

CHAPTER OUTLINE

KEY TERMS

Material Requirements Planning (MRP)
Master Production Schedule (MPS)
Bill of Materials (BOM)
Inventory Records Files
Net Change Systems
Closed-Loop MRP
Manufacturing Resource Planning (MRP II)
Micro-MRP

In the previous chapter on independent inventory demand, we assumed that demand for items in inventory were unrelated to one another—that is, the demand for one item would not instigate demand for another item. In this chapter, the premise is that many items are related. The demand for one item may cause the demand for another, which, in turn, may cause the demand for a third, and so on. Such is the case in manufacturing or services where the demand for a product or service triggers the demands for all of the items needed to deliver that product or service. To manufacture a chair, we would need wood, upholstery, cotton, springs, stain, varnish, wheels if necessary, and so on. To replace the brakes on a car, the mechanic needs brake shoes or disks, perhaps new springs, brake fluid, and so on. Because the demand for one item results in the chain reaction for demands for other items, this type of inventory control is called *dependent* demand inventory.

When we talk about dependent demand inventory control, we generally mean more than just computing order quantities of all of the various raw materials, components, and parts that go into making the parent item. We are usually referring to major methods for tracking what is going on and controlling the process. The major methods include *Just-in-Time* systems, which are covered in Chapter 15, *Synchronous Production,* which is covered in Chapter 17, and *Material Requirements Planning,* which will be covered in this chapter. Each method tries to control the production process and the inventory levels required to sustain that production. A Just-in-Time system uses the philosophy that nothing extra should be made until it is needed. JIT works by using a "pull" logic. Visualize for a moment that a product involves 10 steps, with step 10 providing the finishing operations. When step 10 finishes the item, the worker reaches back to step 9 to get another one to finish. This gives the step 9 worker the right to reach back to step 8 to get another item to process. The step 8 worker than reaches back to step 7 and so on. The simple logic is that as items are pulled away from a workstation, the worker reaches back for another one. If items are not pulled away from a workstation, then the worker cannot work on any new items and the workstation remains idle. The purpose of JIT is to drop inventory levels to a low level and to prevent any unneeded buildup.

Synchronous production, whose logic is derived from optimized production technology (OPT), has as one of its main focuses that the output capacity of a production system is controlled by the processes that have the least capacity. A machine working continually with work to be processed still waiting would be called a *bottleneck*. Machines that have significant excess capacity are called *nonbottlenecks*. The objective is to control the flow and inventory levels in the system to always make sure the bottleneck does not stop working, since its output is directly related to the output of the system. For the nonbottlenecks, the objective is to permit as little inventory as possible with the result that the flow of goods through the system is rapid, while the total inventory in the system is small.

Material requirements planning, the subject of this chapter, has the most stringent and complete control over the entire process. It starts with the demand for a product and then, using the bill of materials that shows how the product is made, multiplies item for item down through the entire chain. This gives the number of each item needed to produce that number of product. Further, it not only tabulates the number of items, but it also considers the time it takes to make each item in the chain. The final result is a schedule that shows the number of each item needed in the sequence and the time in which it must be produced. One very important recent development seems to be occurring in industry; that is, a combination of systems. Companies may use MRP to create the detail scheduling and JIT for local control or synchronous production to focus on bottlenecks. More on this later. At this point, let's proceed with a simple example of one product that is made from five other items. Then we'll more fully develop the topic and study a more involved example.

13.1 A SIMPLE MRP EXAMPLE

Based on incoming orders, forecasts, and capacities, management creates a **master production schedule (MPS).** This is simply a list of end products that are needed to satisfy demands in specific time periods. Manufacturing firms generally use weeks as their time period. This master production schedule is the input to the material requirements planning system (MRP).

The manufacturing process is controlled by the release of an order for an item to the appropriate production area. This paperwork (or computer display) authorizes the appropriate inventory, personnel, machines, and so on to be used to perform the operations that will transform the item through to the next stage toward the production of the end item. The release of this work order to the production system is generally termed *order release*. After the work has been completed, the process step is called *order receipt*. Note a fine point here that will appear later in the chapter. An order release or order receipt is an actual occurrence. However, an MRP system displays future releases and receipts. Therefore, an MRP schedule showing future time periods shows *planned order release and planned order receipts*. When what was planned actually happens, it is the actual order release and order receipt.

This example will show how quantities are calculated, how the lead times (required processing time for that operation) are introduced, and how the order releases and order receipts are established.

Suppose that we are to produce a product called T, which is made of two parts U and three parts V. Part U, in turn, is made of one part W and two parts X. Part V is made of two parts W and two parts Y. Exhibit 13.1 shows the product structure tree of product T. By simple computation, then, we can calculate that if 100 units of T are required, then we will need:

EXHIBIT 13.1

Product Structure Tree for Product T

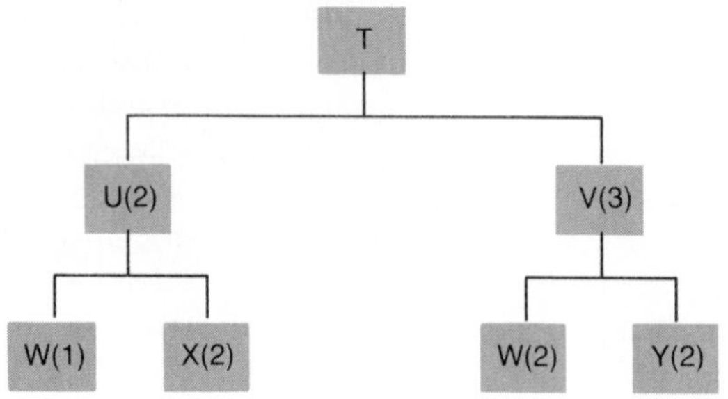

EXHIBIT 13.2

Material Requirements Plan for Completing 100 Units of Product T in Period 7

		Week 1	2	3	4	5	6	7	
T	Order receipt							100	T Lead time = 1 week
	Order release						100		
U	Order receipt						200		U Lead time = 2 weeks
	Order release				200				
V	Order receipt						300		V Lead time = 2 weeks
	Order release				300				
W	Order receipt				800				W Lead time = 3 weeks
	Order release	800							
X	Order receipt				400				X Lead time = 1 week
	Order release			400					
Y	Order receipt				600				Y Lead time = 1 week
	Order release			600					

$$
\begin{array}{lrlrl}
\text{Part U:} & 2 \times \text{number of Ts} = & & 2 \times 100 & = 200 \\
\text{Part V:} & 3 \times \text{number of Ts} = & & 3 \times 100 & = 300 \\
\text{Part W:} & \left\{ \begin{array}{r} 1 \times \text{number of Us} = \\ +2 \times \text{number of Vs} = \end{array} \right. & & \left\{ \begin{array}{r} 1 \times 200 \\ +2 \times 300 \end{array} \right\} & = 800 \\
\text{Part X:} & 2 \times \text{number of Us} = & & 2 \times 200 & = 400 \\
\text{Part Y:} & 2 \times \text{number of Vs} = & & 2 \times 300 & = 600
\end{array}
$$

Now, consider the time needed to obtain these items, either to produce the part internally or to obtain it from an outside vendor. Assume, now, that T takes one week to make; U, 2 weeks; V, 2 weeks; W, 3 weeks; X, 1 week; and Y, 1 week. If we know when Product T is required, we can create a time schedule chart specifying when all materials must be ordered and received to meet the demand for T. Exhibit 13.2 shows which items are needed and when. We have thus created a material requirements plan based on the demand for Product T and the knowledge of how T is made and the time needed to obtain each part.

From this simple illustration, it is apparent that developing a material requirements plan manually for thousands or even hundreds of items would be impractical—a great deal of computation is needed, and a tremendous amount of data must be available about the inventory status (number of units on hand, on order, and so forth) and about the product structure (how the product is made and how many units of each material are required). Because of this, we are compelled to use a computer, and hence, our emphasis from here on in this chapter is to discuss the files that are needed for a computer program and the general makeup of the system. However, the basic logic of the program is essentially the same as that for our simple example.

13.2 MATERIAL REQUIREMENTS PLANNING (MRP) SYSTEMS

Based on a master schedule derived from a production plan, a material requirements planning (MRP) system creates schedules identifying the specific parts and materials required to produce end items, the exact numbers needed, and the dates when orders for these materials should be released and be received or completed within the production cycle. Today's MRP systems use a computer program to carry out these operations. Most firms have used computerized inventory systems for years, but they were independent of the scheduling system; MRP links them together.

Material requirements planning is not new in concept. Logic dictates that the Romans probably used it in their construction projects, the Venetians in their shipbuilding, and the Chinese in building the Great Wall. Building contractors have always been forced into planning for material to be delivered when needed and not before, because of space limitations. What is new is the larger scale and the more rapid changes that can be made by the use of computers. Now firms that produce many products involving thousands of parts and materials can take advantage of MRP.

Purposes, Objectives, and Philosophy of MRP

The main purposes of a basic MRP system are to control inventory levels, assign operating priorities for items, and plan capacity to load the production system. These may be briefly expanded as follows:

Inventory
Order the right part.
Order in the right quantity.
Order at the right time.

Priorities
Order with the right due date.
Keep the due date valid.

Capacity
Plan for a complete load.
Plan an accurate load.
Plan for an adequate time to view future load.

The *theme* of MRP is "getting the right materials to the right place at the right time."

The *objectives* of inventory management under an MRP system are to improve customer service, minimize inventory investment, and maximize production operating efficiency.

The *philosophy* of material requirements planning is that materials should be expedited (hurried) when their lack would delay the overall production schedule and de-expedited (delayed) when the schedule falls behind and postpones their need. Traditionally, and perhaps still typically, when an order is behind schedule, significant effort will be spent trying to get it back on schedule. However, the opposite is not always true; when an order, for whatever reason, has its completion date delayed, the appropriate adjustments are not made in the schedule. This results in a one-sided effort—later orders are hurried, but early orders are not rescheduled for later. Aside from perhaps using scarce capacity, it is preferable not to have raw materials and work in process before the actual need since inventories tie up finances, clutter up stockrooms, prohibit design changes, and prevent the cancellation or delay of orders.

Benefits of an MRP System

Manufacturing companies with over $10 million in annual sales likely have a computerized MRP system. A computerized system is necessary because of the sheer volume of materials, supplies, and components that are part of expanding product lines, and the speed that firms need to react to constant changes in the system. In past years, when firms switched from existing manual or computerized systems to an MRP system, they realized many benefits as:

Increased sales.
Reduced sales price.
Reduced inventory.
Better customer service.
Better response to market demands.

Ability to change the master schedule.

Reduced setup and tear-down costs.

Reduced idle time.

In addition, the MRP system:

Gives advance notice so managers can see the planned schedule before actual release orders.

Tells when to de-expedite as well as expedite.

Delays or cancels orders.

Changes order quantities.

Advances or delays order due dates.

Aids capacity planning.

During their conversions to an MRP system, many firms claimed as much as a 40 percent reduction in inventory investment.

13.3 MATERIAL REQUIREMENTS PLANNING SYSTEM STRUCTURE

The material requirements planning portion of manufacturing activities most closely interacts with the master schedule, bill of materials file, inventory records file, and the output reports. Exhibit 13.3 shows a portion of Exhibit 11.1 with several additions. Note that capacity is not considered in this exhibit, nor are there any feedback loops to higher levels. We will discuss these elements later in this chapter under MRP II and capacity requirements planning.

Each facet of Exhibit 13.3 will be explained in more detail in the following sections, but essentially the MRP system works as follows: Orders for products are used to create a master production schedule, which states the number of items to be produced during specific time periods. A bill of materials file identifies the specific materials that are used to make each item and the correct quantities of each. The inventory records file contains data such as the number of units on hand and on order. These three sources—master production schedule, bill of materials file, and inventory records file—become the data sources for the material requirements program, which expands the production schedule into a detailed order scheduling plan for the entire production sequence.

Demand for Products

Product demand for end items stems primarily from two main sources. The first is known customers who have placed specific orders, such as those generated by sales personnel, or from interdepartment transactions. These orders usually carry promised delivery dates. There is no forecasting involved

EXHIBIT 13.3

Overall View of the Inputs to a Standard Material Requirements Planning Program and the Reports Generated by the Program

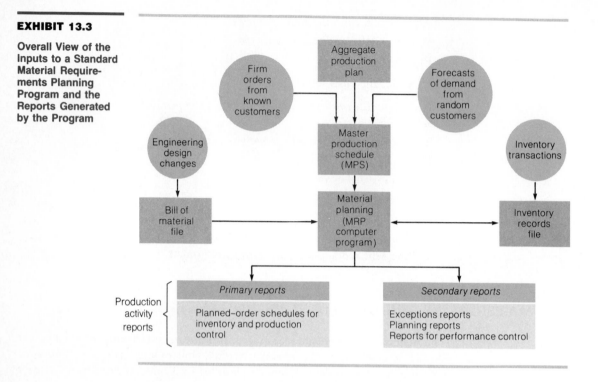

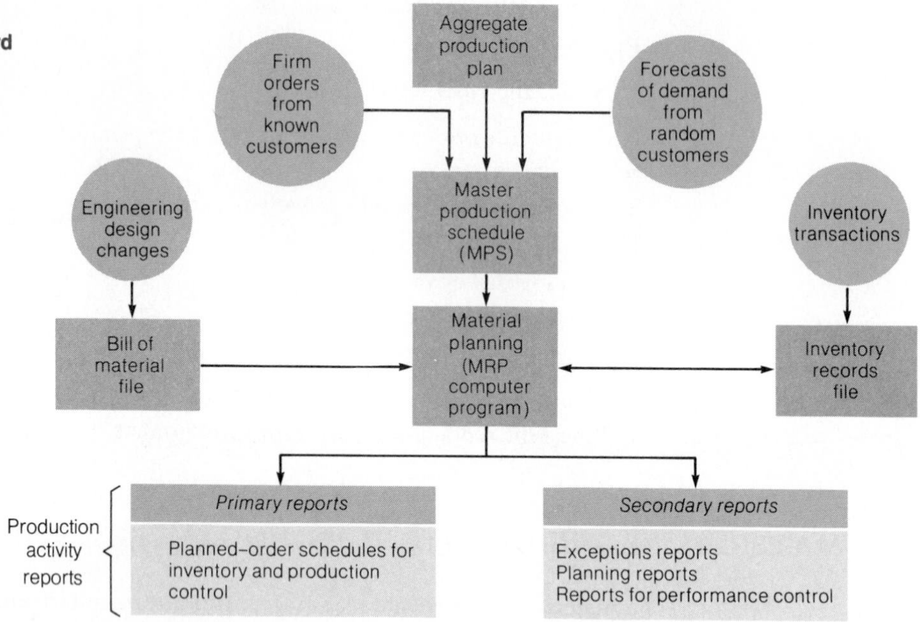

in these orders—simply add them up. The second source is forecast demand. These are the normal independent-demand orders, and the forecasting models presented in Chapter 6 can be used to predict the quantities.

The demand from the known customers and the forecast demand are combined and become the input for the master production schedule.

Demand for repair parts and supplies

In addition to the demand for end products, customers also order specific parts and components either as spares, or for service and repair. These demands for items less complex than the end product are not usually part of the master production schedule; instead, they are fed directly into the material requirements planning program at the appropriate levels. That is, they are added in as a gross requirement for that part or component.

Master Production Schedule

As discussed in Chapter 11, the aggregate production plan specifies product needs in broad terms, such as product groups. The master production schedule takes this to the next step by specifying each item to be produced in terms of quantity and time period to be completed. Generally, the master schedule deals

EXHIBIT 13.4

The Environment of the Master Scheduler

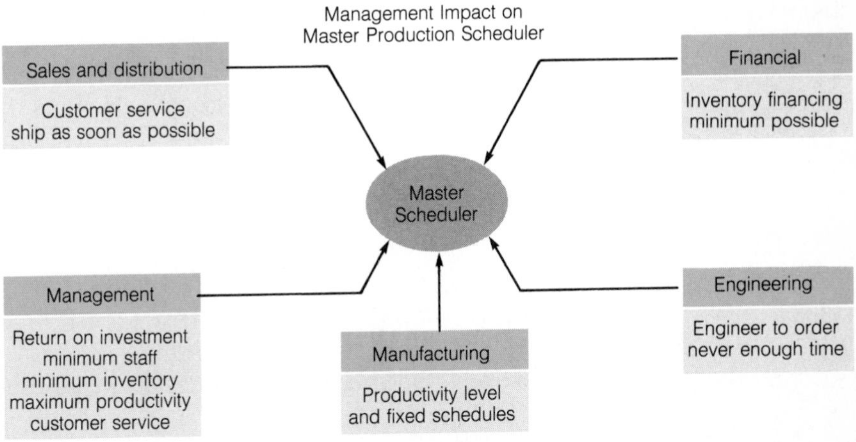

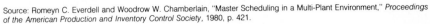

Source: Romeyn C. Everdell and Woodrow W. Chamberlain, "Master Scheduling in a Multi-Plant Environment," *Proceedings of the American Production and Inventory Control Society*, 1980, p. 421.

with end items. If the end item is quite large or quite expensive, however, the master schedule may schedule major subassemblies or components instead.

All production systems have limited capacity and limited resources. This presents a challenging job for the master scheduler. Exhibit 13.4 shows the environment in which the master scheduler works. While the aggregate plan provides the general range of operation, the master scheduler must specify exactly what is to be produced. These decisions are made while responding to pressures from various functional areas.

To determine an acceptable feasible schedule to be released to the shop, trial master production schedules are run through the MRP program. The resulting planned order releases (the detailed production schedules) are checked to make sure that resources are available and the completion times are reasonable. What appears to be a feasible master schedule may turn out to require excessive resources once the product explosion has taken place and materials, parts, and components from lower levels are determined. If this does happen (the usual case), the master production schedule is then modified with these limitations and the MRP program is run again.

To ensure good master scheduling, the master schedul*er* (the human being) must:

Include all demands from product sales, warehouse replenishment, spares, and interplant requirements.

Never lose sight of the aggregate plan.

Be involved with customer order promising.

EXHIBIT 13.5

Master Production Schedule for Products X, Y, and Z

	Week									
	1	2	3	4	5	6	7	8	9	10
Product X	200			400		200	100			900
Product Y		100	100		150		100		300	
Product Z			100			200		200		100

Be visible to all levels of management.

Objectively trade off manufacturing, marketing, and engineering conflicts.

Identify and communicate all problems.

We will now show a simple master schedule (Exhibit 13.5) for three products X, Y, and Z in weekly time periods. The master production schedule is exploded into the required parts, materials, and components. The **bill of materials (BOM)** file contains the complete product description, listing not only the materials, parts, and components, but also the sequence in which the product is created. This BOM file is one of the three main inputs to the MRP program (the other two are the master schedule and the inventory records file).

Bill of Materials File

The BOM file is often called the *product structure file* or *product tree* since it shows how a product is put together. It contains the information to identify each item and the quantity used per unit of the item of which it is a part. To illustrate this, consider Product A shown in Exhibit 13.6. Product A is made of two units of Part B and three units of Part C. Part B, in turn, is made of one unit of Part D and four units of Part C. Part B, in turn, is made of one unit of Part D and four units of Part E. Part C is made of two units of Part F, five units of Part G, and four units of Part H.

In the past, bill of materials files have often listed parts as an "indented" file. This clearly identifies each item and the manner in which it is assembled, since each indentation signifies the components of the item. A comparison of the indented parts in Exhibit 13.7 with the item structure in Exhibit 13.6 shows the ease of relating the two displays. From a computer standpoint, however, storing items in indented parts lists is very inefficient. In order to compute the amount of each item needed at the lower levels, each item would need to be expanded ("exploded") and summed. A more efficient procedure is to store parts data in a single-level explosion. That is, each item and component is listed showing only its parent and the number of units that are needed per unit

EXHIBIT 13.6

Product Structure Tree for Product A

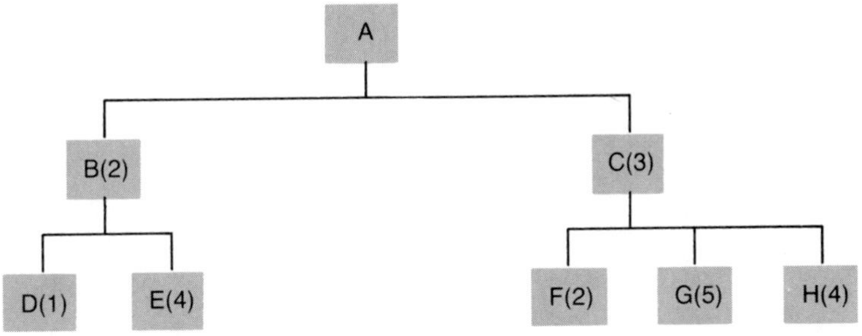

EXHIBIT 13.7

Parts List Shown Both in an Indented Format and in a Single-Level List

Indented Parts List			Single-Level Parts List	
A			A	
	B(2)			B(2)
		D(1)		C(3)
		E(4)	B	
	C(3)			D(1)
		F (2)		E(4)
		G(5)	C	
		H(4)		F (2)
				G(5)
				H(4)

of its parent. Exhibit 13.7 shows both the single-level parts list and the indented parts for Product A. This avoids duplication because it includes each assembly only once.

A data element (called a *pointer* or *locator*) is also contained in each file to identify the parent of each part and allow a retracing upward through the process.

A *modular* bill of materials is the term for a buildable item that can be produced and stocked as a subassembly. It is also a standard item with no options within the module. Many end items that are large and expensive are better scheduled and controlled as modules (or subassemblies). It is particularly advantageous to schedule subassembly modules when the same subassemblies appear in different end items. For example, a manufacturer of cranes can combine booms, transmissions, and engines in a variety of ways to meet a customer's needs. Using a modular bill of materials simplifies the scheduling and control and also makes it easier to forecast the use of different modules. Another benefit in using modular bills is that if the same item is used

EXHIBIT 13.8 Product L Hierarchy in (A) Expanded to the Lowest Level of Each Item in (B)

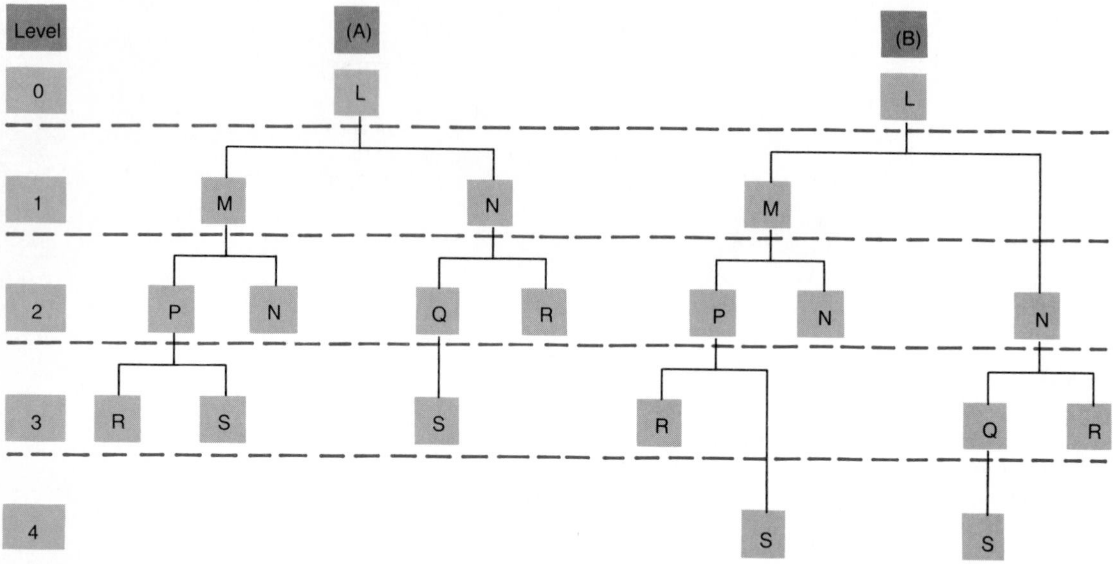

in a number of products, then the total inventory investment can be minimized.

A *planning* bill of materials includes options with fractional options. (A planning bill can specify, for example, 0.3 of a part. What that means is that 30 percent of the units produced will contain that part and 70 percent will not.)

Low-level coding

If all identical parts occur at the same level for each end product, then the total number of parts and materials needed for a product can be computed easily. Consider Product L shown in Exhibit 13.8A. Notice that Item N, for example, occurs both as an input to L and as an input to M. Item N therefore needs to be lowered to level 2 (part B) to bring all Ns to the same level. If all identical items are placed at the same level, it then becomes a simple matter for the computer to scan across each level and summarize the number of units of each item required.

Inventory Records File

The **inventory records file** under a computerized system can be quite lengthy. Each item in inventory is carried as a separate file and the range of

EXHIBIT 13.9

The Inventory Status Record for an Item in Inventory

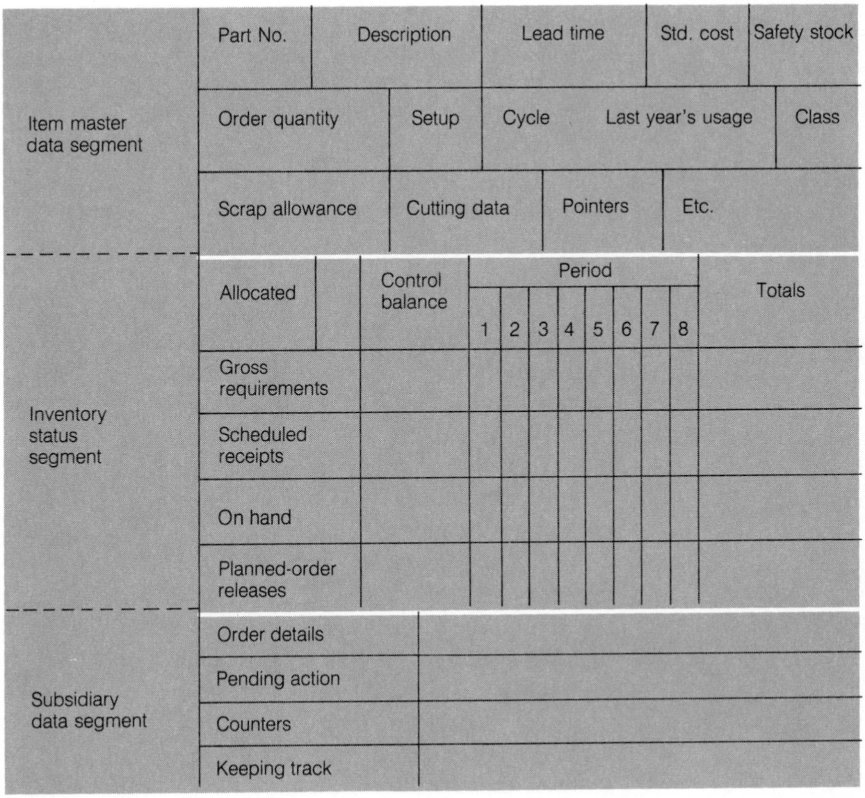
Item master data segment
Part No.
Description
Lead time
Std. cost
Safety stock
Order quantity
Setup
Cycle
Last year's usage
Class
Scrap allowance
Cutting data
Pointers
Etc.
Inventory status segment
Allocated
Control balance
Period
1 2 3 4 5 6 7 8
Totals
Gross requirements
Scheduled receipts
On hand
Planned-order releases
Subsidiary data segment
Order details
Pending action
Counters
Keeping track

Source: Joseph Orlicky, *Materials Requirements Planning* (New York: McGraw-Hill, 1975), p. 182.

details carried about an item is almost limitless. Though Exhibit 13.9 is from the earlier versions of the MRP, it shows the variety of information that is contained in the inventory records files. The MRP program accesses the *status* segment of the file according to specific time periods (called *time buckets* in MRP slang). These files are accessed as needed during the program run.

The MRP program performs its analysis from the top of the product structure downward, exploding requirements level by level. There are times, however, when it is desirable to identify the parent item that caused the material requirement. The MRP program allows the creation of a *peg record* file either separately or as part of the inventory record file. Pegging requirements allows us to retrace a material requirement upward in the product structure through each level, identifying each parent item that created the demand.

Inventory transactions file
The inventory status file is kept up to date by posting inventory transactions as they occur. These changes occur because of stock receipts and disbursements, scrap losses, wrong parts, canceled orders, and so forth.

MRP Computer Program

The material requirements planning program operates on the inventory file, the master schedule, and the bill of materials file. It works in this way: A list of end items needed by time periods (as in the discussion of master scheduling in this chapter) is specified by the master schedule. A description of the materials and parts needed to make each item is specified in the bill of materials file. The number of units of each item and material currently on hand and on order are contained in the inventory file. The MRP program "works" on the inventory file (which is segmented into time periods) while continually referring to the bill of materials file to compute the quantities of each item needed. The number of units of each item required is then corrected for on-hand amounts, and the net requirement is "offset" (set back in time) to allow for the lead time needed to obtain the material.

If the MRP program being used does not consider capacity constraints, the master scheduler must do some capacity balancing by hand. Through an iterative process, the master scheduler feeds a tentative master schedule into the MRP system (along with other items requiring the same resources) and the output is examined for production feasibility. The master schedule is adjusted to try to correct any imbalances, and the program is executed again. This process is repeated until the output is acceptable. Although it would seem to be a simple matter to have the computer simulate some schedules that consider resource limitations, in reality it is a very large and very time-consuming problem for the computer. Another generation or two of computers may provide the data storage and access speed to handle the problem using MRP.

To further complicate the problem today, there is not simply one master scheduler; there are a number of them. Often firms will divide the scheduling work among the schedulers by assigning one master scheduler for each major product line. The result of this is competition: each master scheduler competes for limited resources for his or her own product line. As a group, however, they are trying to balance resource usage and due dates for the production system as a whole.

Output Reports

Since the MRP program has access to the bill of materials file, the master production schedule, and the inventory records file, outputs can take on an almost unlimited range of format and content. These reports are usually classified as *primary* and *secondary* reports. (With the expansion of MRP into MRP II, which we discuss later, many additional reports are available.)

Primary reports

Primary reports are the main or "normal" reports used for inventory and production control. These reports consist of:

1. *Planned orders* to be released at a future time.
2. *Order release notices* to execute the planned orders.
3. *Changes in due dates* of open orders due to rescheduling.
4. *Cancellations or suspensions* of open orders due to cancellation or suspension of orders on the master production schedule.
5. *Inventory status data.*

Secondary reports

Additional reports, which are optional under the MRP system, fall into the following main categories:

1. *Planning reports* to be used, for example, in forecasting inventory and specifying requirements over some future time horizon.
2. *Performance reports* for purposes of pointing out inactive items and determining the agreement between actual and programmed item lead times and between actual and programmed quantity usage and costs.
3. *Exceptions reports* that point out serious discrepancies, such as errors, out-of-range situations, late or overdue orders, excessive scrap, or nonexistent parts.

Net Change Systems

Ordinarily an MRP system is initiated from a master schedule every week or two. This results in the complete explosion of items and the generation of the normal and exception reports. Some MRP programs, however, offer the option of generating intermediate schedules, called *net change* schedules. Net change systems are "activity" driven. Only if a transaction is processed against a particular item, would that item be reviewed in a **net change system.** However, net change systems can be modified to respond only to unplanned or exception occurrences. Rather than being buried in paperwork output from an MRP system (which is easy to do) management may elect not to have the expected occurrences reported, but only deviations that should be noted. For example, if orders are received on time there need be no report. On the other hand, if the quantity delivered differs significantly from the order, this item is included in the net change report. Other reasons to include an item in a net change run might be to note a lost shipment, scrap losses, lead time changes, or a counting error in inventory. Based on these changes, new reports are generated.

13.4 AN EXAMPLE USING MRP

Ampere, Inc., produces a line of electric meters installed in residential buildings by electric utility companies to measure power consumption. Meters used on single-family homes are of two basic types for different voltage and amperage ranges. In addition to complete meters, some parts and subassemblies are sold separately for repair or for changeovers to a different voltage or power load. The problem for the MRP system, then, is to determine a production schedule that would identify each item, the period it is needed, and the appropriate quantities. This schedule is then checked for feasibility, and the schedule is modified if necessary.

Forecasting Demand

Demand for the meters and components originates from two sources: regular customers that place firm orders, and unidentified customers that make the normal random demands for these items. The random requirements were forecast using one of the usual classical techniques such as in Chapter 6 and past demand data. Exhibit 13.10 shows the requirement for Meters A and B, Subassembly D, and Part E for a six-month period.

Developing a Master Production Schedule

For the meter and component requirements specified in Exhibit 13.10, assume that the quantities to satisfy the known demands are to be delivered according to customers' delivery schedules throughout the month, but that the items to satisfy random demands must be available during the first week of the month.

EXHIBIT 13.10

Future Requirements for Meters A and B, Subassembly D, and Part E Stemming from Specific Customer Orders and from Random Sources

	METER A		METER B		SUBASSEMBLY D		PART E	
Month	Known	Random	Known	Random	Known	Random	Known	Random
3	1,000	250	400	60	200	70	300	80
4	600	250	300	60	180	70	350	80
5	300	250	500	60	250	70	300	80
6	700	250	400	60	200	70	250	80
7	600	250	300	60	150	70	200	80
8	700	250	700	60	160	70	200	80

Our schedule will assume that *all* items are to be available the first week of the month. This assumption trial is reasonable since management prefers to produce meters in one single lot each month rather than a number of lots throughout the month.

Exhibit 13.11 shows the trial master schedule that we will use under these conditions, with demands for months 3 and 4 shown as the first week of the month, or as weeks 9 and 13. For brevity, we will work only with these two demand periods. The schedule we develop should be examined for resource availability, capacity availability, etc., and then revised and run again. We will stop at the end of this one schedule, however.

Bill of Materials (Product Structure) File

The product structure for Meters A and B is shown in Exhibit 13.12 in the typical way using low-level coding, in which each item is placed at the lowest level at which it appears in the structure hierarchy. Meters A and B consist of two subassemblies, C and D, and two parts, E and F. Quantities in parentheses indicate the number of units required per unit of the parent item.

Exhibit 13.13 shows an indented parts list for the structure of Meters A and B. As mentioned earlier in the chapter, the BOM file carries all items without indentation for computational ease, but the indented printout clearly shows the manner of product assembly.

Inventory Records (Item Master) File

The inventory records file would be similar to the one that was shown in Exhibit 13.9. The differences, as we saw earlier in this chapter, are that the inventory records file also contains much additional data, such as vendor identity, cost, and lead times. For this example, the pertinent data contained in the inventory records file are the on-hand inventory at the start of the program

EXHIBIT 13.11

A Master Schedule to Satisfy Demand Requirements as Specified in Exhibit 13.10

	Week								
	9	10	11	12	13	14	15	16	17
Meter A	1,250				850				550
Meter B	460				360				560
Subassembly D	270				250				320
Part E	380				430				380

EXHIBIT 13.12

Product Structure for Meters A and B

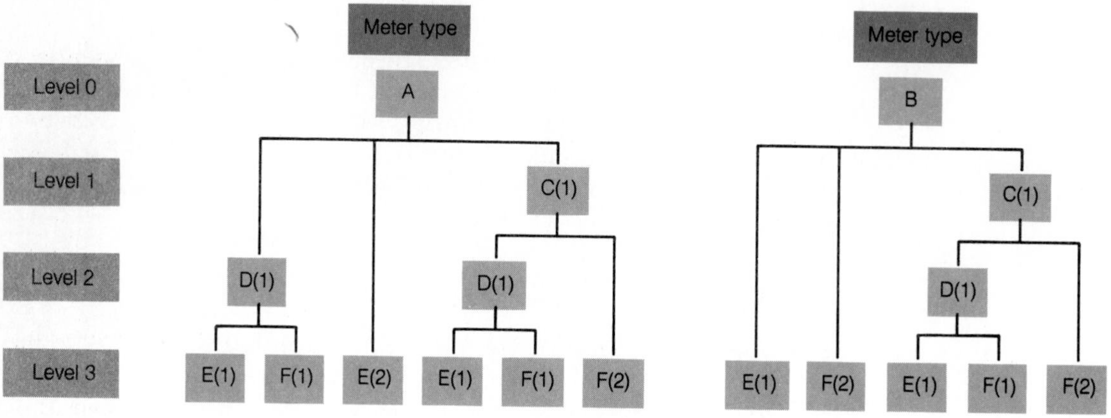

Exhibit shows the subassemblies and parts that make up the meters and shows the numbers of units required per unit of parent in parentheses.

EXHIBIT 13.13

Indented Parts List for Meter A and Meter B, with the Required Number of Items per Unit of Parent Listed in Parentheses

METER A

- A
  - D(1)
    - E(1)
    - F(1)
  - E(2)
  - C(1)
    - D(1)
      - E(1)
      - F(1)
    - F(2)

METER B

- B
  - E(1)
  - F(2)
  - C(1)
    - D(1)
      - E(1)
      - F(1)
    - F(2)

EXHIBIT 13.14

Number of Units on Hand and Lead Time Data that Would Appear on the Inventory Record File

Item	On-hand Inventory	Lead Time (weeks)
A	50	2
B	60	2
C	40	1
D	30	1
E	30	1
F	40	1

run and the lead times. These data are taken from the inventory records file and shown in Exhibit 13.14.

Running the MRP Program

The correct conditions are now set to run the MRP computer program—end-item requirements have been established through the master production schedule, the status of inventory and the order lead times are contained in the inventory item master file, and the bill of materials file contains the product structure data. The MRP program now explodes the item requirements according to the BOM file, level by level, in conjunction with the inventory records file. A release date for the net requirements order is offset to an earlier time period to account for the lead time. Orders for parts and subassemblies are added through the inventory file, bypassing the master production schedule, which, ordinarily, does not schedule at a low enough level to include spares and repair parts.

Exhibit 13.15 shows the planned order release dates for this particular run. The program logic can best be understood by following the analysis below. (We will confine our analysis to the problem of meeting the gross requirements for 1,250 units of Meter A, 460 units of Meter B, 270 units of Subassembly D and 380 units of Part E, all in week 9.)

The 50 units of A on hand result in a net requirement of 1,200 units of A. To receive Meter A in week 9, the order must be placed in week 7 to account for the two-week lead time. The same procedure follows for Item B, resulting in a planned 400-unit order released in period 7.

The rationale for these steps is that for an item to be released for processing, all its components must be available. The planned order release date for the parent item therefore becomes the same gross requirement period for the subitems.

Referring to Exhibit 13.12, level 1, one unit of C is required for each A and each B. Therefore, the gross requirements for C in week 7 are 1,600 units (1,200 for A and 400 for B). Taking into account the 40 units on hand and the one-week lead time, 1,560 units of C must be ordered in week 6.

Level 2 of Exhibit 13.12 shows that one unit of D is required for each A and each C. The 1,200 units of D required for A are gross requirements in week 7, and the 1,560 units of D for item C are the gross requirements for week 6. Using the on-hand inventory first and the one-week lead time results in the planned order releases for 1,530 units in week 5 and 1,200 units in week 6.

Level 3 contains Items E and F. Because E and F are each used in several places, Exhibit 13.16 is presented to identify more clearly the parent item, the number of units required for each parent item, and the week in which it is required. Two units of Item E are used in each Item A. The 1,200-unit planned order release for A in period 7 becomes the gross requirement for 2,400 units of E in the same period. One unit of E is used in each B, so the planned order release for 400 units of B in period 7 becomes the gross requirement for 400

EXHIBIT 13.15 **Material Requirements Planning Schedule for Meters A and B, Subassemblies C and D, and Parts E and F**

Item		Week 4	5	6	7	8	9	10	11	12	13
A	Gross requirements						1,250				850
	On hand 50						50				
	Net requirements						1,200				
(LT = 2)	Planned-order receipt						1,200				
	Planned-order release				1,200						
B	Gross requirements						460				360
	On hand 60						60				
	Net requirements						400				
(LT = 2)	Planned-order receipt						400				
	Planned-order release				400						
C	Gross requirements				400 / 1,200						
	On hand 40				40						
	Net requirements				1,560						
(LT = 1)	Planned-order receipt				1,560						
	Planned-order release			1,560							
D	Gross requirements			1,560	1,200		270				250
	On hand 30			30	0		0				
	Net requirements			1,530	1,200		270				
(LT = 1)	Planned-order receipt			1,530	1,200		270				
	Planned-order release		1,530	1,200		270					
E	Gross requirements		1,530	1,200	2,400 / 400	270	380				430
	On hand 30		30	0	0	0	0				
	Net requirements		1,500	1,200	2,800	270	380				
(LT = 1)	Planned-order receipt		1,500	1,200	2,800	270	380				
	Planned-order release	1,500	1,200	2,800	270	380					
F	Gross requirements		1,530	3,120 / 1,200	800	270					
	On hand 40		40	0	0	0					
	Net requirements		1,490	4,320	800	270					
(LT = 1)	Planned-order receipt		1,490	4,320	800	270					
	Planned-order release	1,490	4,320	800	270						

units of E in week 7. Item E is also used in Item D at the rate of one per unit. The 1,530-unit planned order release for D in period 5 becomes the gross requirement for 1,530 units of E in period 5 and a 1,500-unit planned order release in period 4 after accounting for the 30 units on hand and the one-week lead time. The 1,200-unit planned order release for D in period 6 results in

EXHIBIT 13.16

The Identification of the Parent of Items C, D, E, and F and Item Gross Requirements Stated by Specific Weeks

Item	Parent	Number of Units per Parent	Resultant Gross Requirement	Gross Requirement Week
C	A	1	1,200	7
C	B	1	400	7
D	A	1	1,200	7
D	C	1	1,560	6
E	A	2	2,400	7
E	B	1	400	7
E	D	1	1,530	5
E	D	1	1,200	6
F	B	2	800	7
F	C	2	3,120	6
F	D	1	1,200	6
F	D	1	1,530	5

gross requirements for 1,200 units of E in week 6 and a planned order release for 1,200 units in week 5.

Item F is used in B, C, and D. The planned order releases for B, C, and D become the gross requirements for F for the same week, except that the planned order release for 400 units of B and 1,560 of C become gross requirements for 800 and 3,120 units of F, since the usage rate is two per unit.

The independent order for 270 units of subassembly D in week 9 is handled as an input to D's gross requirements for that week. This is then exploded into the derived requirements for 270 units of E and F. The 380-unit requirement for part E to meet an independent repair part demand is fed directly into the gross requirements for Part E.

The independent demands for week 13 have not been expanded as yet.

The bottom line of each item in Exhibit 13.15 is taken as a proposed load on the productive system. The final production schedule is developed manually or with the firm's computerized production package. If the schedule is infeasible or the loading unacceptable, the master production schedule is revised and the MRP package is run again with the new master schedule.

Where MRP Can Be Used

MRP is being used in a variety of industries, all with a job-shop environment (meaning that a number of products are made in batches using the same productive equipment). The list in Exhibit 13.17 includes process industries, but note that the processes mentioned are confined to job runs that alternate output product and do not include continuous processes such as petroleum or steel.

As you can see in the exhibit, MRP is most valuable to companies involved in assembly operations and least valuable to those in fabrication.

EXHIBIT 13.17

Industry Applications and Expected Benefits*

Industry Type	Examples	Expected Benefits
Assemble-to-stock	Combines multiple component parts into a finished product, which is then stocked in inventory to satisfy customer demand. Examples: Watches, tools, appliances.	High
Fabricate-to-stock	Items are manufactured by machine rather than assembled from parts. These are standard stock items carried in anticipation of customer demand. Examples: Piston rings, electrical switches.	Low
Assemble-to-order	A final assembly is made from standard options which the customer chooses. Examples: Trucks, generators, motors.	High
Fabricate-to-order	Items manufactured by machine to customer order. These are generally industrial orders. Examples: Bearings, gears, fasteners.	Low
Manufacture-to-order	Items fabricated or assembled completely to customer specification. Examples: Turbine generators, heavy machine tools.	High
Process	Industries, such as foundries, rubber and plastics, specialty paper, chemicals, paint, drug, food processors.	Medium

**IBM Manufacturing Implementation Guide*, SH 30-0211-0, 1 (July 1977), pp. 3-6.

One more point to note: MRP does not work well in companies that have a low annual number of units produced. Especially for companies producing complex expensive products requiring advanced research and design, experience has shown that lead times tend to be too long and too uncertain, and the product configuration too complex for MRP to handle. Such companies need the control features that network scheduling techniques offer and would be better off using project scheduling (covered previously in Chapter 10).

13.5 MRP IN SERVICES

Applications of MRP in services are rare—not because the technique is not applicable but because the growth in MRP has been limited to inventoriable items. As more powerful MRP systems are developed, they will be able to control the full range of resources from materials, facilities, equipment, and labor as well. Such a system will be able to control inventoriable items as well as nonrenewable items (such as labor) that cannot be carried over to subsequent periods if they are not consumed in the specific period as planned.

It appears quite certain that an MRP approach would be a very valuable asset in the production of services. If we simply consider the producing resources as inventory (equipment, space, personnel), the method becomes valid. Consider, for example a hospital operating room planning an open-heart surgery. The master schedule can establish a time for the surgery (or surgeries, if several are scheduled). The BOM could specify all required equipment and personnel—MDs, nurses, anesthesiologist, operating room, heart/lung machine, defibrillator, and so forth. The inventory status file would show the availability of the resources and commit them to the project. The MRP program could then produce a schedule showing when various parts of the operation are to be started, expected completion times, required materials, and so forth. Checking this schedule would allow "capacity planning" in answering such questions as: "Are all the materials and personnel available?" and "Does the system produce a feasible schedule?"

We believe that it is inevitable that MRP type systems will be used in service applications in the future.

13.6 CAPACITY REQUIREMENTS PLANNING

In the sections of this chapter that concerned the master production schedule and running the MRP program, we mentioned that production capacity is usually some finite amount and obviously has limits. We also cited the interaction between the scheduler and rerunning the MRP program to obtain feasible schedules in light of this limited capacity. In this section we will explicitly point out how capacity is computed and what the usual procedure is to cope with capacity constraints.

Computing Work Center Load

The place to start in computing capacity requirements is right from the routing sheets for the jobs scheduled to be processed. Exhibit 3.13 in Chapter 3 shows the routing sheet for a plug assembly. Note that the routing sheet specifies where a job is to be sent, the particular operations involved, and the standard setup time and run time per piece. These are the types of figures used to compute the total work at each work center.

While the routing sheet is a "job view," since it follows a particular job around the productive facility, a work center file is the view seen from a work center. The routing sheets for each job send them to appropriate work centers for some sort of processing. Each work center is generally a functionally defined center so that jobs routed to it require the same type of work, and on the same equipment. From the work center view, if there is adequate capacity, the problem is one of priorities: which job to do first. (We discuss priority scheduling rules in Chapter 14.) If there is insufficient capacity, however, rather than a local issue at the work center, the problem must be resolved by the master scheduler.

Exhibit 13.18 shows a work center that has various jobs assigned to it. Note that the capacity per week was computed at the bottom of the exhibit as 161.5

EXHIBIT 13.18

Workload for Work Center A

Day	Job #	Number of Units	Setup Time	Run Time per Unit	Total Job Time	Total for Week
10	145	100	3.5	.23	26.5	
	167	160	2.4	.26	44.0	
	158	70	1.2	.13	10.3	
	193	300	6.0	.17	57.0	137.8
11	132	80	5.0	.36	33.8	
	126	150	3.0	.22	36.0	
	180	180	2.5	.30	56.5	
	178	120	4.0	.50	64.0	190.3
12	147	90	3.0	.18	19.2	
	156	200	3.5	.14	31.5	
	198	250	1.5	.16	41.5	
	172	100	2.0	.12	14.0	
	139	120	2.2	.17	22.6	128.8

Computing Work Center Capacity

The available capacity in standard hours is 161.5 hours per five-day week, calculated as: (2 machines) (2 shifts) (10 hours/shift) (85% machine utilization) (95% efficiency).

EXHIBIT 13.19

Scheduled Workload for Work Center A

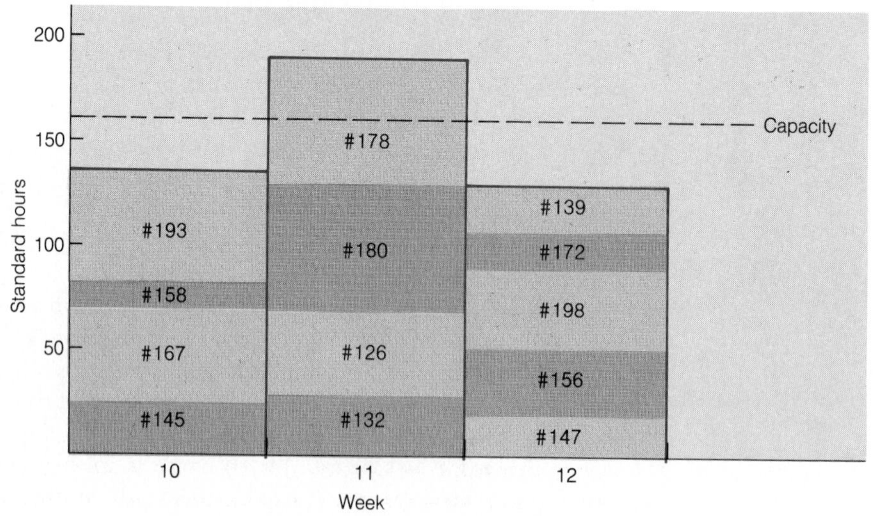

hours. The jobs scheduled for the three weeks result in two weeks planned under work center capacity, and one week over capacity.

Exhibit 13.19 shows a loading representation of Work center A for the three weeks. The scheduled work exceeds capacity for week 2. There are several options available:

1. Work overtime.
2. Select an alternate work center that could perform the task.
3. Subcontract to an outside shop.
4. Try to schedule part of the work of day 2 earlier into day 1, and delay part of the work into day 3.
5. Renegotiate the due date and reschedule.

An MRP program with a capacity requirements planning module allows rescheduling to try to level capacity (option 4 on our list above). Two techniques used are backward scheduling and forward scheduling. The objective of the master scheduler is to try to spread the load in Exhibit 13.19 more evenly to remain within the available capacity.

13.7 MANUFACTURING RESOURCE PLANNING (MRP II)

In our earlier discussions of MRP in this chapter, we limited ourselves in two respects: First, we concentrated on the *material* requirements that resulted from an explosion of the master schedule, and we discussed lot sizing and safety stocks. We did not include the needs for all the other types of resources, such as staffing, facilities, or tools. Second, while we discussed *capacity requirements planning,* we did this somewhat externally to the MRP system. In this section we will discuss closed-loop MRP and the logic of more advanced versions of MRP that include a wider range of resources and outputs.

Closed-Loop MRP

When the material requirements planning (MRP) system has information feedback from its module outputs, this is termed **closed-loop MRP.** The American Production and Inventory Control Society defines closed-loop MRP as:

> A system built around material requirements planning and also including the additional planning functions of Production Planning, Master Production Scheduling, and Capacity Requirements Planning. Further, once the planning phase is complete and the plans have been accepted as realistic and attainable, the execution functions come into play. These include shop floor control functions of Input-Output measurement, detailed Scheduling and Dispatching, plus Anticipated Delay Reports

EXHIBIT 13.20 **A Closed-Loop MRP System Showing Feedback**

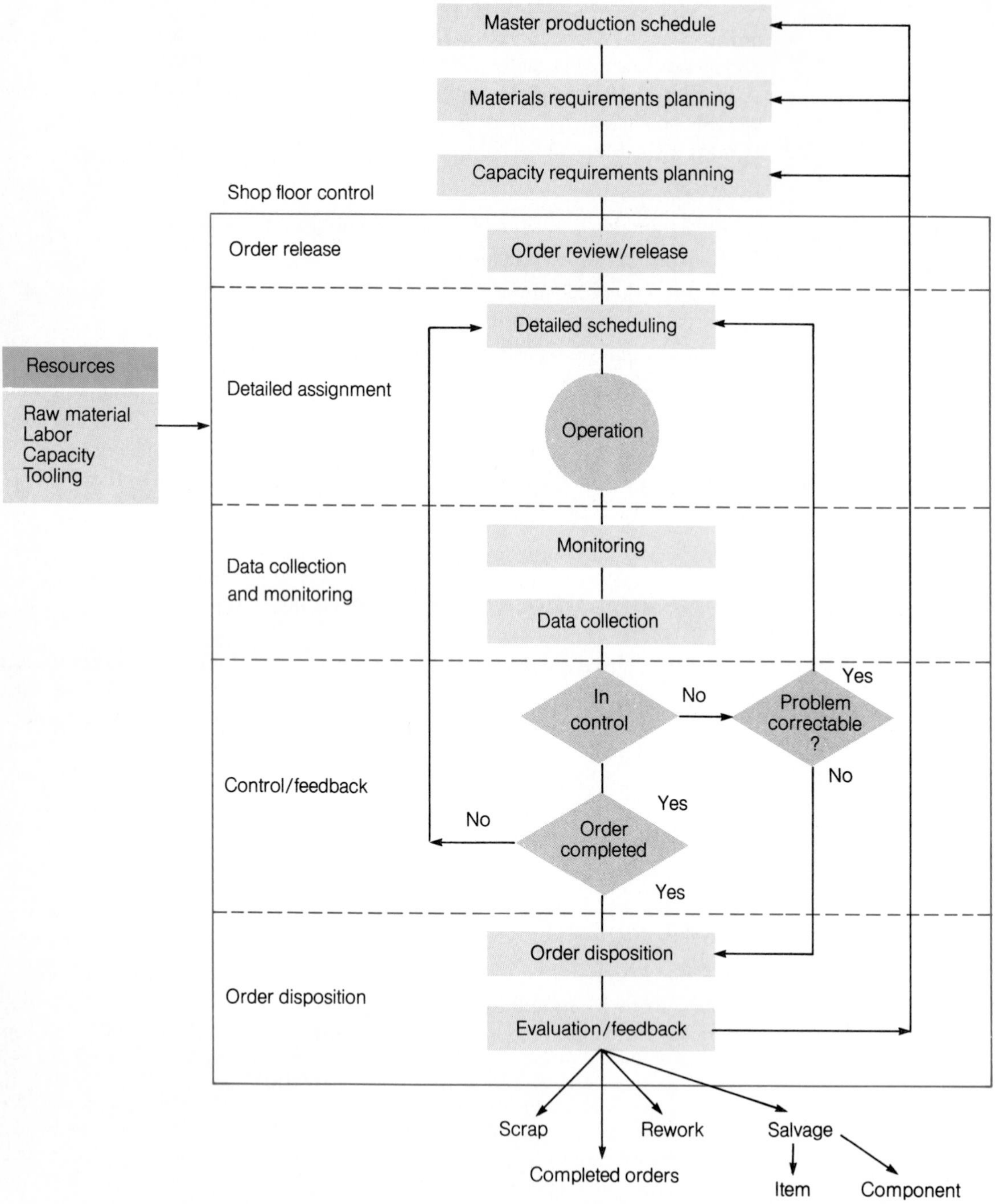

Source: S. Melnyk, P. L. Carter, D. M. Dilts, and D. M. Lyth, *Shop Floor Control* (Homewood, Ill.: Dow Jones-Irwin, 1985), p. 40.

from both the shop and vendors, Purchasing Follow-Up and Control, etc. The term "closed-loop" implies that not only is each of these elements included in the overall system but also that there is feedback from the execution functions so that the planning can be kept valid at all times.[1]

Exhibit 13.20 shows an MRP system with capacity feedback built in. The computer program sums up the needs created by an explosion of product requirements in the master schedule. If adequate capacity does not exist at work centers, feedback causes a revision of the master schedule and a rerun of the MRP program.

MRP II

An expansion of the materials requirements planning to include other portions of the productive system was natural and to be expected. One of the first to be included was the purchasing function. At the same time there was a more detailed inclusion of the production system itself—on the shop floor, in dispatching, and in the detailed scheduling control. MRP had already included work center capacity limitations, so it was obvious the name *material requirements planning* no longer was adequate to describe the expanded system. Someone (probably Ollie Wight) introduced the name **manufacturing resource planning (MRP II)** to reflect the idea that more and more of the firm was becoming involved in the program. To quote Wight,

> The fundamental manufacturing equation is:
> What are we going to make?
> What does it take to make it?
> What do we have?
> What do we have to get?[2]

The initial intent for MRP II was to plan and monitor all the resources of a manufacturing firm—manufacturing, marketing, finance, and engineering—through a closed-loop system generating financial figures. The second important intent of the MRP II concept was that it simulate the manufacturing system. It is generally conceived now as being a total, companywide system with everyone (buyers, marketing staff, production, accounting) working with the same game plan, using the same numbers, and capable of simulation to plan and test strategies.

We will look more closely at two MRP systems—MAPICS, from IBM, and MAX, from Micro-MRP, Inc. For information about additional MRP II

---

[1] *APICS Dictionary* (Falls Church, Va.: American Production and Inventory Control Society, 1984), p. 4.

[2] Oliver Wight, *The Executive's Guide to Successful MRP II* (Williston, Vt.: Oliver Wight Limited Publications, 1982), pp. 6, 17.

systems, consult Smolik for the following programs described in various levels of detail:[3]

Ask Computer Systems' MANMAN.
Burroughs Corp.'s Production Control System (PCS) III.
Hewlett-Packard's Factory Management System (FMS).
IBM's COPICS.
Martin Marietta Data Systems's MAS II.
Arthur Anderson & Co.'s MAC-PAC.
National Cash Register's Manufacturing Flow Concept.

Cost of an MRP II System

Several software companies regularly advertise MRP systems in manufacturing-oriented journals, as well as in widely read publications such as *The Wall Street Journal*. Prices go as low as $500 and as high as $300,000, since MRP II systems can vary widely in the modules and capabilities included.

Costs for the computer hardware also have a wide range. An MRP program for a very small company can be run on a microcomputer with hard disk drives. However, most MRP II systems are run on minicomputers or mainframes because of the very large data storage requirements and the number of program modules involved. Lease costs may range from $30,000 to $500,000 per year; however, technology is changing rapidly, with a consequent drop in cost. In terms of additional personnel needed, the experiences of many companies seem to indicate that the overall net change in personnel is close to zero. What seems to happen is simply the switching of people from existing areas into the MRP system roles.

The typical MRP II system takes about 18 months to install. However, this can vary widely depending on the size of the application, the condition of the existing databases and how much they may have to be revised, the quality of the bills of materials, routing sheets, and inventory records, and the amount of training that is required. Another factor is whether the firm has been using an MRP system and is switching to an MRP II system. The entire range of time can vary from several months to three years.

Payback for an MRP installation can be quite short. When larger companies first installed MRP systems several years ago, they realized an average annual return on investment of about 300 percent.[4]

When we think of MRP II, we tend to think of large computer programs with applications confined to business "giants." In fact, however, MRP II is economically feasible for manufacturing companies with annual sales of under

---

[3] Donald P. Smolik, *Material Requirements of Manufacturing* (New York: Van Nostrand Reinhold, 1983), pp. 302–42.

[4] Wight, *Executive's Guide,* pp. 34–35.

$1 million. Also, much of the current software is user friendly and easy to operate.

Prices and quality of software vary widely, and not necessarily in a direct relationship. Customer service is another very important factor. This is a "buyer beware" market, and care should be taken in choosing a program because it is a long-term commitment.

Micro-MRP

High capacity quick access hard disk drives have opened the way for microcomputers to be used for MRP by smaller companies and for departments or divisions of larger companies. The most widely used of the MRP programs for microcomputers is "MAX," a product of Micro-MRP Inc.[5]

Exhibit 13.21 shows the positioning and applications of the various modules of MAX. We will present some of the specifications, costs, and equipment requirements in order to gain a perspective of the application areas and then briefly describe some of the modules.

Number of MAX applications. Marketed since 1983. Currently there are 1,500 installations. MAX is the leader in microcomputer MRP (the next closest competitor has 300 installations).

Size of using company or division. Sales in the $0.5 to $20 million range.

Hardware. IBM PC/AT/XT or compatible with 640K of RAM, 20 megabyte hard disk, clock card, and 132-column printer. A 60-meg disk can store about 10,000 part numbers.

Cost of MAX software program. An average of $7,500 for a small to medium-size manufacturer with all the manufacturing and accounting modules, but specific requirements could result in a wide range of costs as low as $495 and as high as $25,000 for a multi-user package.

Software. MAX consists of nine basic modules and a utility module:

1. Bill of materials.
2. Interface.
3. Inventory control.
4. Master Production Scheduling (MPS).
5. Material requirements planning.
6. Purchasing control.

---

[5] From information provided by Micro-MRP, Inc., Century Plaza I, Foster City, California, 94404, and Datapro Research Corp., Delran, New Jersey.

EXHIBIT 13.21 Micro-MRP Company's MAX Programs

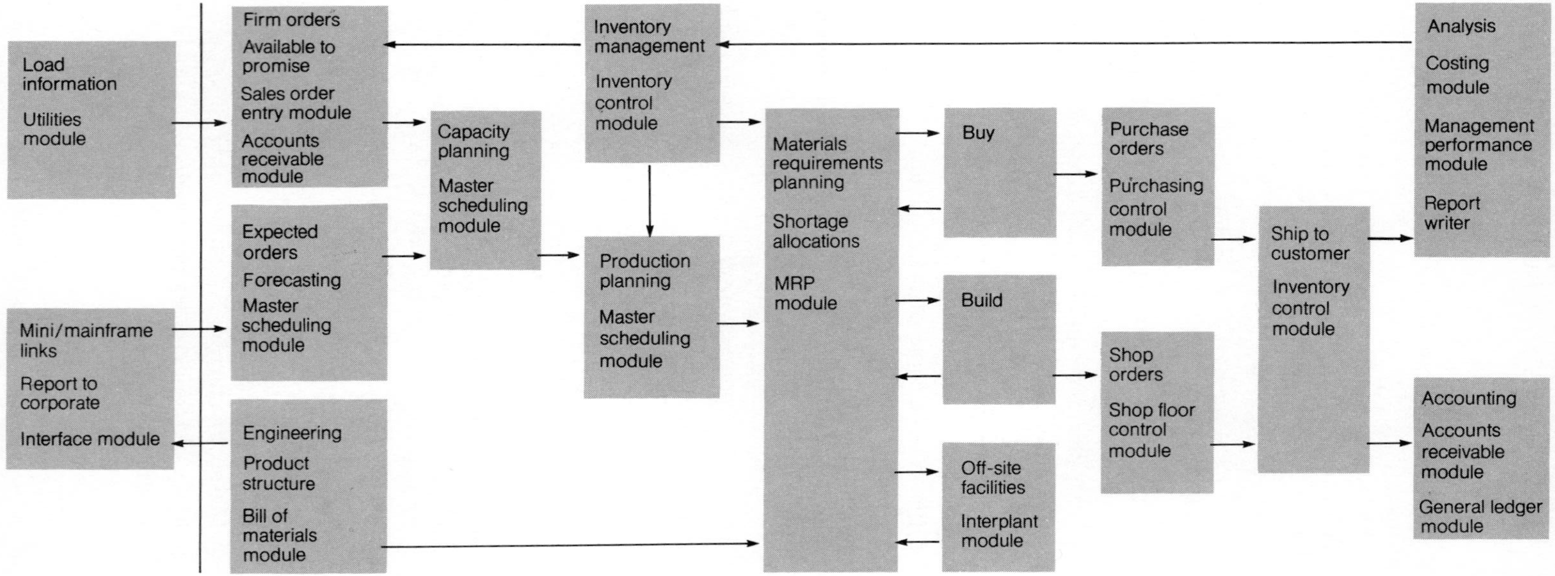

7. Shop floor control.
8. Cost performance.
9. Management performance.

A brief description of several modules follows:

Master Production Scheduling Module—accepts customer orders and forecasts. Computes what's available-to-promise. There is also an order entry/invoicing module as part of the accounting package.

Purchasing Control Module—issues purchase orders, tracks costs and deliveries, maintains vendor history, and examines cash requirements.

Shop Floor Control Module—prepares job packets, tracks the progress of orders through the shop, communicates MRP decisions to the shop floor, tracks WIP, and analyzes shortages.

Cost Performance Module—tracks cost variances between planned and actual costs. Also generates general ledger detail information and work-in-process analysis reports.

Management Performance Module—generates reports such as surplus inventory analysis, inventory cost by location and class, purchase order activity, vendor performance analysis, costed materials requirements, work order activity, production schedule analysis, posted transaction activity, part shortage analysis.

Solomon III Accounting Module—Max uses the Solomon III integrated accounting package, which consists of 15 interactive modules including Accounts Payable, Accounts Receivable, General Ledger, Order Entry/Invoicing, Payroll, Job Costing, Sales Analysis, and other overlapping modules.

13.8 MISCELLANEOUS MRP ISSUES

Problems in Installing and Using MRP Systems

MRP is very well developed technically, and implementation of an MRP system should be pretty straightforward. Yet there are many problems with the MRP systems and many "failures" in trying to install them. Why do such problems and outright failures occur with a "proven" system?

The answer partially lies with organizational and behavioral factors. Three major causes have been identified: the lack of top management commitment, the failure to recognize that MRP is only a software tool that needs to be used correctly, and the integration of MRP and JIT.

Part of the blame for the lack of top management's commitment may be MRP's image. It sounds like a manufacturing system rather than a business plan. However, an MRP system is used to plan resources and develop schedules. And a well-functioning schedule can use the firm's assets effectively with the result of increased profits. MRP should be presented to top management as a planning tool with specific reference to profit results. Intensive executive education is needed, emphasizing the importance of MRP as a closed-loop, integrated, strategic planning tool.

The second cause of the problem concerns the MRP proponents that overdid themselves in selling the concept. MRP was presented and perceived as a complete and stand-alone system to run a firm, rather than part of the total system. The third issue is how MRP can be made to function with JIT as we shall discuss in Chapter 16. JIT and MRP can live together but there are few rules as to how they should be integrated. The system consists of the functional areas of engineering, marketing, personnel, manufacturing, etc., and techniques and concepts such as quality circles, CAD/CAM and robotics. MRP needs to be *part* of the system, not *the* system.

In many meetings we have attended, both professional and industrial, we have heard similar installation and operational problems. It seems to distill down to the fact that the MRP essentially runs the firm with the main objective simply to meet the schedule. People become subservient to the MRP system. Even such simple decisions as determining a run-lot size cannot be made outside the system.

As it stands right now, MRP is a "formal system" that requires strict adherence to function properly. Often supervisors and workers develop an "informal system" for getting the job done. MRP advocates would say this informal system arises because the existing formal system was inadequate to deal with real inventory scheduling problems. In any event, it appears that employees at all levels must change—from the company president to the lowest-level employee. While MRP currently does work in many installations, it should be thoroughly understood as to its good features and its shortcomings.

Safety Stock

Ordinarily adding a safety stock to required quantities is not advised in an MRP system that is based on derived demand. There is some feeling, however, that when the availability of parts could suffer from a long and inflexible lead time or is subject to strikes or cancellation, a safety stock offers protection against production delays. A safety stock is sometimes intentionally created by overplanning. One of the main arguments against using safety stock is that the MRP system considers it a fixed quantity, and the safety stock will never actually be used.

Ordering and Production Lot Sizes

Using lot sizes for convenience in production runs or in economic order quantities is practical only for lower-level items (basic parts or raw materials).

The difficulty in using a lot size at a higher level is that the discrepancy between actual demand and the lot size becomes exaggerated for the subitems. Consider the following illustration:

Item A is made of one unit of B, which is made of one unit of C, and the lot sizes of A, B, and C are 100, 150, and 200, respectively. If there are no units currently in inventory, then a demand for 75 units of A will cause 200 units of C to be ordered, and the 25-unit excess in A leads to a 125-unit excess of C.

A			Lot size of A = 100
	B(1)		Lot size of B = 150
		C(1)	Lot size of C = 200

The higher the product-structure level of lot sizing, the greater the potential exaggeration of demand at low levels.

Several lot-sizing approaches have been used. The lot-for-lot method (L4L), probably the most common, orders the exact amount determined in the net requirements. Thus, it has no standard lot size. The least total cost (LTC) method balances the cost of ordering with the holding cost for an order size that satisfies the MRP scheduled net requirements. The least unit cost (LUC) method selects the order quantity size that offers the minimum cost per unit. Both LTC and LUC will be discussed shortly.

The period order quantity (POQ) computes the number of orders that occur within a year using the simple economic order quantity model. If a firm plans its MRP on a weekly basis, then the number of units to order is equal to the amount needed for the average duration. For example, if $D/Q = 10$ orders per year, then $52/10 = 5$ weeks' worth. Purchasers could add up the amount needed for the next five weeks and place that order.

Least total cost and least unit cost methods of lot sizing

The least total cost method (LTC) is a dynamic lot-sizing technique that calculates the order quantity by comparing the carrying cost and the setup (or ordering) costs for various lot sizes and then selects the lot in which these are most nearly equal.

The least unit cost method (LUC) is a dynamic lot-sizing technique that adds ordering cost and inventory carrying cost for each trial lot size and divides by the number of units in the lot size, picking the lot size with the lowest unit cost. Both methods are similar, and we will illustrate them using the same data.

The top portion of Exhibit 13.22 shows the bottom line of an MRP schedule—the net requirements. Consider the following costs:

Cost per item = \$1.

Cost to set up or to place an order = \$6.

Inventory carrying cost = 2 percent per period.

EXHIBIT 13.22 **Computing the Least Total Cost and the Least Unit Cost Run Size for an MRP Schedule**

Period	1	2	3	4	5	6	7	.....
Net requirements	50	60	70	70	80	75		

(1) Order (or run) Quantity to Include Requirement for Period(s)	(2) Quantity to Be Ordered	(3) Ordering or Setup Cost	(4) Item Cost	(5) Carrying Cost*	(6) Total Cost (3) + (5)	(7) Unit Cost Col(6)/Col(2)
1	50	$6.00	$1.00	$ 0.00	$ 6.00	$0.12
1–2	110	6.00	1.00	1.20	7.20	.065
1–3	180	6.00	1.00	4.00	10.00	.056
1–4	250	6.00	1.00	8.20	14.20	.057
1–5	330	6.00	1.00	14.60	20.60	.062

* Note: Column (5) was calculated as follows:
Period 1: 50 × .02 × $1 × 0 period = $0.00
Periods 1–2: 50 × .02 × $1 × 0 periods + 60 × .02 × $1 × 1 period = $1.20
Periods 1–3: 50(.02)1(0) + 60(.02)1(1) + 70(.02)1(2) = $4.00
Periods 1–4: 50(.02)1(0) + 60(.02)1(1) + 70(.02)1(2) + 70(.02)1(3) = $8.20
Periods 1–5: 50(.02)1(0) + 60(.02)1(1) + 70(.02)1(2) + 70(.02)1(3) + 80(.02)1(4) = $14.60

Which lot size to choose

Using the least total cost method, we would choose to order 180 units, because the ordering cost of $6.00 is closer to the $4.00 carrying cost of 180 units rather than the $8.20 carrying cost of 250 units. (Not by much, but it is closer.)

With the least unit cost method we would choose the same order quantity of 180 units, because the average cost per unit is lowest at that point (.056 in column 7 of Exhibit 13.22).

The advantage of the least unit cost method is that it is a more complete analysis and would take into account ordering or setup costs that might change as the order size increases. If the ordering or setup costs remain constant, then the lowest total cost method is more attractive because it is simpler and easier to compute; yet it would be just as accurate under that restriction.

13.9 INSTALLING AN MRP SYSTEM

The average time for a company to effectively install an MRP system seems to range from 18 to 24 months—not for the software, but because so much other preparation and training must take place. At the cost of being somewhat redundant, we will repeat some cautions about installing an MRP system.

Preparation Steps

Bill of materials. The BOM lists all the materials required to create a product in a hierarchical form, which is usually the way in which a product is produced. The BOM is extremely important in an MRP system since it is the main driver of the system. Inaccuracies really cannot be tolerated. Without an MRP or some such computer system, BOM accuracy is not critical and firms can live with some errors. A first step before installing an MRP system is to go through the BOM for all products and ensure that they are correct.

Routing sheets and processing times. Similar to the BOM above, many firms have not needed to be specific about which machine or process should be used, since adjustments could always be made on the shop floor. The same for processing; with the usual longer times in the shop (as opposed to MRP installations) there were opportunities to make up discrepancies (in spite of the fact that the data for accounting purposes would be in error).

Inventory stock. Most firms have errors in their inventory records. Oftentimes it is because no one wants to take the time needed to count and verify records and physical stock. Another reason is that often inventory stock is old or obsolete and bringing records up to date may mean that much inventory that is carried on company books as assets may have to be declared as scrap. Few managers are willing to bite the bullet and do this. Reducing inventory flows directly to the bottom line and quickly catches the attention of top management. However, installing an MRP system means that errors must be removed and inventory carried must be of usable quality.

Procedures. In addition to the actual records mentioned above, procedures must be installed to keep these records up to date. Examples are adding stock to inventory when received from vendors, and making appropriate changes when issuing stock to production. Also, ways of handling changes to the bill of materials, routing, or processing times need to be decided.

Training. Everyone—from top management through to purchasing staff, supervisors, and the workers on the shop floor—must be trained in effective use of an MRP system—how to read its reports, what leeways are allowable in quantity or schedule variations, and what results can be expected. People, by nature, are reluctant to change. Throughout MRP's history of almost two decades, we have blamed people whenever poor performance occurred in their MRP system (lack of understanding, lack of top management support, lack of adequate discipline, etc.). While this is now recognized as a problem caused in large part by the MRP itself (noted elsewhere in this chapter), nevertheless without support of all involved, MRP would be doomed to failure.

A full-blown MRP II system encompassing all phases of the firm is a major undertaking requiring years to implement. IBM's MAPICS II system, for instance, includes all phases of a firm's operation; the nineteen modules cover everything from engineering, production, accounting, and finance with little left out. Needless to say, once on such a system, a firm is committed. Getting off one and onto another could take years.

13.10 CONCLUSION

In less than two decades, MRP has grown from simple applications to determine time schedules for material needs, to comprehensive MRP II systems tying together all major functions of the organization. The next stage in its application is to integrate it with CIM technology and with JIT.

13.11 REVIEW AND DISCUSSION QUESTIONS

1. Since material requirements planning appears so reasonable, discuss reasons why it did not become popular until recently.
2. Discuss the meaning of MRP terms such as *planned order release* and *order receipts*.
3. What is the role of safety stock in an MRP system?
4. How does MRP relate to CIM? (See Chapter 3.)
5. Contrast the significance of the term *lead time* in the traditional EOQ context and in an MRP system.
6. Discuss the importance of the master production schedule in an MRP system.
7. "MRP just prepares shopping lists—it doesn't do the shopping or cook the dinner." Comment.
8. What are the sources of demand in an MRP system? Are these dependent or independent, and how are they used as inputs of the system?
9. State the types of data that would be carried in the bill of materials file and the inventory record file.
10. How does MRP II differ from MRP?
11. What is the range of costs to install an MRP system?

13.12 PROBLEMS

*1. Product X is made of two units of Y and three of Z. Y is made of one unit of A and two units of B. Z is made of two units of A and four units of C.

Lead time for X is one week; Y, two weeks; Z, three weeks; A, two weeks; B, one week; and C, three weeks.

a. Draw the product structure tree.

b. If 100 units of X are needed in week 10, develop a planning schedule showing when each item should be ordered and in what quantity.

*2. Product M is made of two units of N and three of P. N is made of two units of R and four units of S. R is made of one unit of S and three units of T. P is made of two units of T and four units of U.

a. Show the product structure tree.

b. If 100 M are required, how many units of each component are needed?

c. Show both a single-level bill of materials and an indented bill of materials.

3. In the following MRP planning scheduling for Item J, indicate the correct net requirements, planned order receipts, and planned order releases to meet the gross requirements. Lead time is one week.

	Week Number					
Item J	0	1	2	3	4	5
Gross requirements			75		50	70
On hand 40						
Net requirements						
Planned order receipt						
Planned order releases						

4. Repeat Problem 1 except that current on-hand inventories are 20 X, 40 Y, 30 Z, 50 A, 100 B, and 900 C.

5. Assume that Product Z is made of two units of A and four units of B. A is made of three units of C and four of D. D is made of two units of E.

The lead time for purchase or fabrication of each unit is: final assembly Z takes two weeks, A, B, C, and D take one week each, and E takes three weeks.

Fifty units are required in period 10. (Assume that there is currently no inventory on hand of any of these items.)

a. Draw a product structure tree.

b. Develop an MRP planning schedule showing gross and net requirements, order release and order receipt dates.

---

* Problems 1 and 2 are solved in Appendix D.

6. *Note:* For Problems 6 through 9, in order to simplify data handling to include the receipt of orders that have actually been placed in previous periods, a six-level scheme can be used. (There are a number of different techniques used in practice, but the important issue is to keep track of what is on hand, what is expected to arrive, what is needed, and what size orders should be placed.) One way to calculate the numbers is as follows:

	Week								
Gross requirements									
Scheduled receipts									
On hand from prior period									
Net requirements									
Planned order receipt									
Planned order release									

One unit of A is made of three units of B, one unit of C, and two units of D. B is composed of two units of E and one unit of D. C is made of one unit of B and two units of E. E is made of one unit of F.

Items B, C, E, and F have one-week lead times; A and D have lead times of two weeks.

Assume that lot-for-lot (L4L) lot sizing is used for items A, B, and F; lots of size 50, 50, and 200 are used for items C, D, and E, respectively. Items C, E, and F have on-hand (beginning) inventories of 10, 50, and 150, respectively; all other items have zero beginning inventory. We are scheduled to receive 10 units of A in week 5, 50 units of E in week 4, and also 50 units of F in week 4. There are no other scheduled receipts. If 30 units of A are required in week 8, use the low-level-coded product structure tree to find the necessary planned order releases for all components.

7. One unit of A is made of two units of B, three units of C, and two units of D. B is composed of one unit of E and two units of F. C is made of two units of F and one unit of D. E is made of two units of D. Items A, C, D, and F have one-week lead times; B and E have lead times of two weeks. Lot-for-lot (L4L) lot sizing is used for Items A, B, C, and D; lots of size 50 and 180 are used for items E and F, respectively. Item C has an on-hand (beginning) inventory of 15; D has an on-hand inventory of 50; all other items have zero beginning inventory. We are scheduled to receive 20 units of Item E in week 4; there are no other scheduled receipts.

Construct simple and low-level-coded product structure trees and indented and summarized bills of material.

If 20 units of A are required in week 8, use the low-level-coded product structure tree to find the necessary planned order releases for all components. (See note in Problem 6.)

8. One unit of A is made of one unit of B and one unit of C. B is made of four units of C and one unit of E and F. C is made of two units of D and one unit of E. E is made of three units of F. Item C has a lead time of one week; items A, B, E, and F have two-week lead times; and item D has a lead time of three weeks. Lot-for-lot lot sizing is used for items A, D, and E; lots of size 50, 100, and 50 are used for Items B, C, and F, respectively. Items A, C, D, and E have on-hand (beginning) inventories of 20, 50, 100, and 10, respectively; all other items have zero beginning inventory. We are scheduled to receive 10 units of A in week 5, 100 units of C in week 6, and 100 units of D in week 4; there are no other scheduled receipts. If 50 units of A are required in week 10, use the low-level-coded product structure tree to find the necessary planned order releases for all components. (See note in Problem 6.)

9. The MRP gross requirements for item A are shown here for the next 10 weeks. Lead time for A is three weeks and setup cost is $10 per setup. There is a carrying cost of $0.01 per unit per week. Beginning inventory is 90 units.

	WEEK									
	1	2	3	4	5	6	7	8	9	10
Gross requirements	30	50	10	20	70	80	20	60	200	50

Use the least total cost or the least unit cost lot-sizing method to determine when and for what quantity the first order should be released.

10. Product A consists of two units of subassembly B, three units of C, and one unit of D. B is composed of four units of E and three units of F. C is made of two units of H and three units of D. H is made of five units of E and two units of G.
   a. Construct a simple product structure tree.
   b. Construct a product structure tree using low-level coding.
   c. Construct an indented bill of materials.
   d. In order to produce 100 units of A, determine the numbers of units of B, C, D, E, F, G, and H required.

11. The MRP gross requirements for Item X are shown here for the next 10 weeks. Lead time for A is two weeks, and setup cost is $9 per setup. There is a carrying cost of $0.02 per unit per week. Beginning inventory is 70 units.

	WEEK									
	1	2	3	4	5	6	7	8	9	10
Gross requirements	20	10	15	45	10	30	100	20	40	150

Use the least total cost or the least unit cost lot-sizing method to determine when and for what quantity the first order should be released.

12. Audio Products, Inc., produces two AM/FM cassette players for automobiles. Both radio/cassette units are identical, but the mounting hardware and finish trim differ. The standard model fits intermediate and full-size cars, and the sports model fits small sports cars.

Audio Products handles the production in the following way. The chassis (radio/cassette unit) is assembled in Mexico and has a manufacturing lead time of two weeks. The mounting hardware is purchased from a sheet steel company and has a three-week lead time. The finish trim is purchased from a Taiwan electronics company with offices in Los Angeles as prepackaged units consisting of knobs and various trim pieces. Trim packages have a two-week lead time. Final assembly time may be disregarded, since adding the trim package and mounting are performed by the customer.

Audio Products supplies wholesalers and retailers, who place specific orders for both models up to eight weeks in advance. These orders, together with enough additional units to satisfy the small number of individual sales, are summarized in the following demand schedule:

	Week 1	2	3	4	5	6	7	8
Standard model				300				400
Sports model					200			100

There are currently 50 radio/cassette units on hand but no trim packages or mounting hardware.

Prepare a material requirements plan to meet the demand schedule exactly. Specify the gross and net requirements, on-hand amounts, and the planned order release and receipt periods for the cassette/radio chassis, the standard trim and sports car model trim, and the standard mounting hardware and the sports car mounting hardware.

13. Brown and Brown Electronics manufactures a line of digital audio tape players. While there are differences among the various products, there are a number of common parts within each player. The product structure, showing the number of each item required, lead times, and the current inventory on hand for the parts and components, follows:

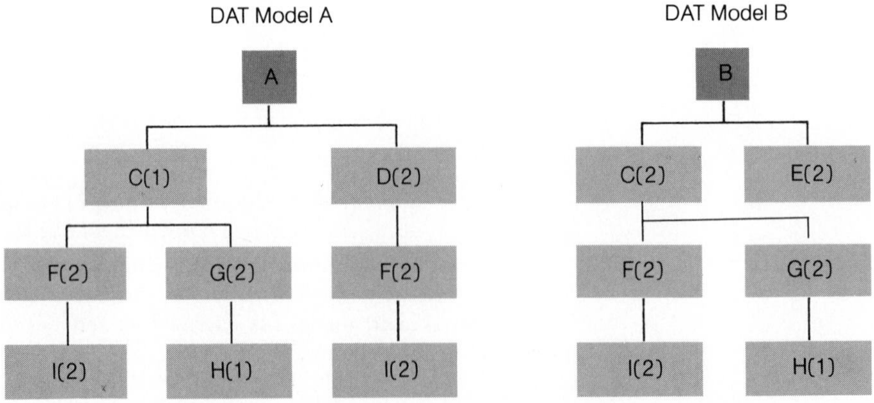

	Number Currently in Stock	Lead Time (weeks)
DAT Model A	30	1
DAT Model B	50	2
Subassembly C	75	1
Subassembly D	80	2
Subassembly E	100	1
Part F	150	1
Part G	40	1
Raw material H	200	2
Raw material I	300	2

Brown and Brown created a forecast that it plans to use as its master production schedule, producing exactly to schedule. Part of the MPS shows a demand for 700 units of Model A and 1,200 units of Model B in week 10.

Develop an MRP schedule to meet that demand.

13.13 CASE: NICHOLS COMPANY

This particular December day seemed bleak to Joe Williams, president of Nichols Company (NCO). He sat in his office watching the dying embers of his fireplace, hoping to clear his mind. Suddenly there came a tapping by someone gently rapping, rapping at his office door. "Another headache," he muttered, "tapping at my office door. Only that and nothing more."

The intruder was Barney Thompson, director of marketing. "A major account has just canceled a large purchase of A units because we are back ordered on tubing. This can't continue. My sales force is out beating the bushes for customers and our production manager can't provide the product."

For the past several months, operations at NCO have been unsteady. Inventory levels have been too high, while at the same time there have been stockouts. This resulted in many late deliveries, complaints, and cancellations. To compound the problem, overtime was excessive.

HISTORY

Nichols Company was started by Joe Williams and Peter Schaap, both with MBAs from the University of Arizona. Much has happened since Joe and Peter formed the company. Peter has left the company and is working in real estate development in Queensland, Australia. Under the direction of Joe, NCO has diversified to include a number of other products.

NCO currently has 355 full-time employees directly involved in manufacturing the three primary products, A, B, and C. Final assembly takes place in a converted warehouse adjacent to NCO's main plant.

THE MEETING

Joe called a meeting the next day to get input on the problems facing NCO and to lay the groundwork for some solutions. Attending the meeting, besides himself and

Barney Thompson, were Phil Bright of production and inventory control, Trevor Hansen of purchasing, and Steve Clark of accounting.

The meeting lasted all morning. Participation was vocal and intense.

Bright said, "The forecasts that marketing sends us are always way off. We are constantly having to expedite one product or another to meet current demand. This runs up our overtime."

Thompson said, "Production tries to run too lean. We need a larger inventory of finished goods. If I had the merchandise, my salespeople could sell 20 percent more product."

Clark said, "No way! Our inventory is already uncomfortably high. We can't afford the holding costs, not to mention how fast technology changes around here causing even more inventory, much of it obsolete."

Bright said, "The only way I can meet our stringent cost requirement is to buy in volume."

At the end of the meeting, Joe had lots of input but no specific plan. What do you think he should do? (There are specific questions at the end of the case.)

Exhibits 13.23 through 13.26 show the relevant data for the case.

EXHIBIT 13.23

Bills of Materials for Products A, B, and C

Product A	Product B	Product C
.A	.B	.C
.D(4)	.F (2)	.G(2)
.I(3)	.G(3)	.I(2)
.E(1)	.I(2)	.H(1)
.F(4)		

EXHIBIT 13.24

Work Center Routings for Products and Components

Item	Work Center Number	Standard Time (hours per unit)
Product A	1	0.20
	4	0.10
Product B	2	0.30
	4	0.08
Product C	3	0.10
	4	0.05
Component D	1	0.15
	4	0.10
Component E	2	0.15
	4	0.05
Component F	2	0.15
	3	0.20
Component G	1	0.30
	2	0.10
Component H	1	0.05
	3	0.10

QUESTIONS

Use Lotus (or another spreadsheet if you prefer) to solve the Nichols case.

Simplifying assumption: In order to get the program started, some time is needed at the beginning since MRP backloads the system. For simplicity, assume that the forecasts (and therefore demands) are zero for periods 1 through 3. Also assume that the

EXHIBIT 13.25

Inventory Levels and Lead Times for Each Item on the Bill of Materials at the Beginning of Week 1

Product/Component	On Hand (units)	Lead Time (weeks)
Product A	100	1
Product B	200	1
Product C	175	1
Component D	200	1
Component E	195	1
Component F	120	1
Component G	200	1
Component H	200	1
I (Raw material)	300	1

EXHIBIT 13.26

Forecasted Demand for Weeks 4–27

Week	Product A	Product B	Product C
1			
2			
3			
4	1500	2200	1200
5	1700	2100	1400
6	1150	1900	1000
7	1100	1800	1500
8	1000	1800	1400
9	1100	1600	1100
10	1400	1600	1800
11	1400	1700	1700
12	1700	1700	1300
13	1700	1700	1700
14	1800	1700	1700
15	1900	1900	1500
16	2200	2300	2300
17	2000	2300	2300
18	1700	2100	2000
19	1600	1900	1700
20	1400	1800	1800
21	1100	1800	2200
22	1000	1900	1900
23	1400	1700	2400
24	1400	1700	2400
25	1500	1700	2600
26	1600	1800	2400
27	1500	1900	2500

starting inventory specified in Exhibit 13.25 is available from week 1. For the master production schedule, use only the end items A, B, and C.

To modify production quantities, adjust only the products A, B, and C. Do not adjust the quantities of D, E, F, G, H, and I. These should be linked so that changes in A, B, and C will automatically adjust them.

1. Disregarding machine-center limitations, develop an MRP schedule and also capacity profiles for the four machine centers.
2. Work center capacities and costs are specified below. Repeat (1) above, but create a *feasible* schedule (within the capacities of the machine centers) and compute the relevant costs. Do this by adjusting the MPS only. Try to minimize the total cost of operation for the 27 weeks.

	Capacity	Cost
Work Center 1	6000 hours available	$20 per hour
Work Center 2	4500 hours available	$25 per hour
Work Center 3	2400 hours available	$35 per hour
Work Center 4	1200 hours available	$65 per hour

Inventory carrying cost	
End items A, B, and C	$2.00 per unit
Components D, E, F, G, and H	$1.50 per unit
Raw material I	$1.00 per unit
Back-order cost	
End items A, B, and C	$20 per unit
Components D, E, F, G, and H	$14 per unit
Raw material I	$ 8 per unit

3. Supposing end items had to be ordered in lots which are in multiples of 100 units, components in multiples of 500 units, and raw materials in multiples of 1,000 units. How would this change your schedule?

13.14 SELECTED BIBLIOGRAPHY

Bockerstette, Joseph A. "Misconceptions Abound Concerning Just-in-Time Operating Philosophy." *Industrial Engineering,* September 1988, pp. 54–58.

Bose, Gerald J., and Ashok Rao. "Implementing JIT with MRP Creates Hybrid Manufacturing Environment." *Industrial Engineering,* September 1988, pp. 49–54.

Funk, Paul. "Throughput Planning Instead of Capacity Planning Is the Next Logical Step for MRP." *Industrial Engineering,* January 1989, pp. 40–44.

Journal of American Institute of Decision Science. (Articles appear discussing MRP and MRP II from a more analytical basis, examining topics such as lot sizing, safety stocks, and multiechelon inventory.)

Journal of American Production and Inventory Control Society. (Numerous articles on MRP and MRP II appear. Most of these cite the difficulties and experiences of practitioners.)

Penelesky, Richard J.; William L. Berry; and Urban Wemmerlov. "Open Order Due Date Maintenance in MRP Systems." *Management Science,* May 1989, pp. 571–84.

Proceedings of APICS and DSI. (Many papers on all aspects of MRP and MRP II are usually presented at the annual society meetings and reprinted in the proceedings.)

Tallon, William J. "A Comparative Analysis of Master Production Scheduling Techniques for Assemble to Order Products." *Decision Sciences,* Summer 1989, pp. 492–507.

Vollmann, Thomas E.; William L. Berry; and D. Clay Whybark. *Manufacturing Planning and Control Systems*. Homewood, Ill.: Richard D. Irwin, 1988.

Chapter 14

Operations Planning and Control—Job Shops

EPIGRAPH

"Hey Chief—I finished my part of this job, who gets it next?"

Universities are arranged as job shops:

The Business School shop,
The Engineering shop,
The Fine Arts shop,
and so on . . .

CHAPTER OUTLINE

KEY TERMS

Job Shop
Flow Shop
Dispatching of Orders
Expediting
Machine-Limited and Labor-Limited Systems
Priority Rules
Critical Ratio Rule
Runout Time Method
Shop-Floor Control
Input/Output (I/O) Control
n/m Job Shop Problem (*n* jobs, *m* machines)

YOU WANT IT WHEN ?!

Thanks to Professor Bob Parsons, Management Science Department, Northeastern University, Boston, MA.

Despite what the cartoon says, attitudes that belittle scheduling and delivery due dates are no laughing matter.

In previous chapters we have addressed scheduling issues in repetitive manufacturing environments (assembly line balancing)[1] and in project environments (project scheduling). In this chapter we will focus on scheduling job shops—the most difficult of scheduling environments—and then touch on some personnel scheduling issues in service systems.

14.1 JOB SHOP DEFINED

While a brief definition of the term *job shop* was given in an earlier chapter, an expanded definition will be helpful at this point: A **job shop** is a functional organization whose departments or work centers are organized around particular types of equipment or operations, such as drilling, forging, spinning, or assembly. Products flow through departments in batches corresponding to individual orders—either stock orders or individual customer orders.[2]

Job shops are often contrasted with flow shops, being considered as two distinctly different types of production environments.[3] The scheduling liter-

[1] Scheduling in repetitive manufacturing will also be discussed in Chapter 16.

[2] *APICS Dictionary* (Falls Church, Va.: American Production and Inventory Control Society, 1984), p. 15.

[3] For an excellent summary of these differences, see Sam G. Taylor, Samuel M. Seward, and Steven F. Bolander, "Why the Process Industries Are Different," *Production and Inventory Management,* 4th Quarter 1981, pp. 9–24.

ature, however, treats the flow shop as an extreme case of the general job-shop organization defined here, and we follow that convention in this chapter. Specifically in a **flow shop** all jobs follow the same processing sequence.

Job shops tend to be cumbersome and have been relatively resistant to change. Part of the reason many job shops have been able to stay this way is that foreign competition has not been as fierce for them. Volumes are lower, product mix varies, work tends to be highly specialized, and rescheduling of orders is common. The Insert shows one firm that has taken an aggressive step to change its performance.

INSERT What's Wrong with Job Shops

The HDS Division of Schlumberger builds electromechanical sensors (logging tools) that collect and process geological data for oil and gas exploration. The division operates under all the demands facing the classic job shop. Its Houston factory turns out 200 different products with 30,000 line items in inventory. Engineering changes—sometimes major changes—are an inescapable fact of life. Logging tools must be customized to reflect the kind of drilling they are used for, the underground formations they operate in, and other geological, climatic, and performance factors. Monthly output of each product ranges from 1 to 20 units; prices range from $5,000 to $15,000. Monthly sales volume has ranged from $15 million to less than $1 million, a reflection of the cyclical nature of the oil and gas business.

The manufacturing process is long and complex and draws on a wide range of labor skills. Fabrication of housings and mechanical parts takes place in a sheet-metal shop and machine shop of aerospace-grade sophistication. The Houston complex also does hand assembly of printed circuit boards (composed largely of purchased components), which are wave soldered and tested as a subassembly. Final assembly involves wiring, soldering, mechanical assembly, and system test, all largely performed on work benches or holding fixtures.

In the summer of 1985, HDS was struggling. Operations were costly, chaotic, and falling short of acceptable standards. Customers were dissatisfied. About 15 percent of the logging tools failed on final acceptance test. Most products were built to schedules established far in advance, but on-time delivery was no better than 70 percent. The average lead times exceeded 12 months.

Senior management was also dissatisfied. Cost of sales was unacceptably high (as exemplified by the nearly two-to-one ratio of overhead to direct labor), and the plant was bulging with inventories. WIP alone averaged five months of output.

Most job shop managers will instantly recognize these troubled conditions; the situation at HDS has been the rule for job shops, not the exception. In our experience, on-time delivery for master-scheduled items seldom exceeds 75 percent and can be as low as 20 percent. Lead times have grown insidiously over the past decade, and most job shops cannot respond effectively to swings in the business cycle. Backlogs (and lead times) shrink during recessions but soar during periods of robust economic growth—a phenomenon that managers explain away with the slogan, "Backlogs always grow in expansionary periods."

HAPPY ENDING

HDS revised its shop and defect rates fell sharply (from 20 percent to 2 percent in the machine shop, for example); on-time delivery approached and has remained around 100 percent. Within two years, the division halved its ratio of overhead personnel to direct labor and halved its break-even point. Meanwhile, total inventory declined by 60 percent and WIP turns quadrupled.

These dramatic results did not require large-capital expenditures. The management team initially cut the capital budget by 50 percent; annual spending has since run at less than half of depreciation. Those results did not require sophisticated computer applications. In fact, we turned off our shop floor computer, adopted a manual floor-control approach, and canceled a $400,000 automation project. Nor did our success require significant changes in personnel. The turnaround at HDS was achieved largely by the managers and workers already in place.

Source: Reprinted by permission of Harvard Business Review. An excerpt from "Time to Reform Job Shop Manufacturing," by James E. Ashton and Frank X. Cook, Jr. (March/April 1989).

14.2 SCHEDULING AND CONTROL IN THE JOB SHOP

A schedule is a timetable for performing activities, using resources, or allocating facilities. The purpose of operations scheduling in the job shop is to disaggregate the master production schedule into time-phased weekly, daily, or hourly activities—in other words, to specify in precise terms the planned workload on the productive system in the very short run. Operations control entails monitoring job-order progress and, where necessary, expediting orders or adjusting system capacity to make sure that the master schedule is met.

In designing a scheduling and control system, provision must be made for efficient performance of the following functions:

1. Allocating orders, equipment, and personnel to work centers or other specified locations. Essentially, this is short-run capacity planning.
2. Determining the *sequence* of order performance; that is, establishing job priorities.
3. Initiating performance of the scheduled work. This is commonly termed the **dispatching of orders.**
4. Shop-floor control (or production activity control) involving:
   a. Reviewing the status and controlling the progress of orders as they are being worked on.
   b. **Expediting** late and critical orders.[4]
5. Revising the schedule in light of changes in order status.

---

[4] Despite the fact that expediting is frowned upon by production control specialists, it is nevertheless a reality of life. In fact, a very typical entry-level job in production control is that of expediter or "stock-chaser." In some companies, a good expediter—one who can negotiate a critical job through the system or can scrounge up materials nobody thought were available—is a prized possession.

EXHIBIT 14.1

Typical Scheduling Process

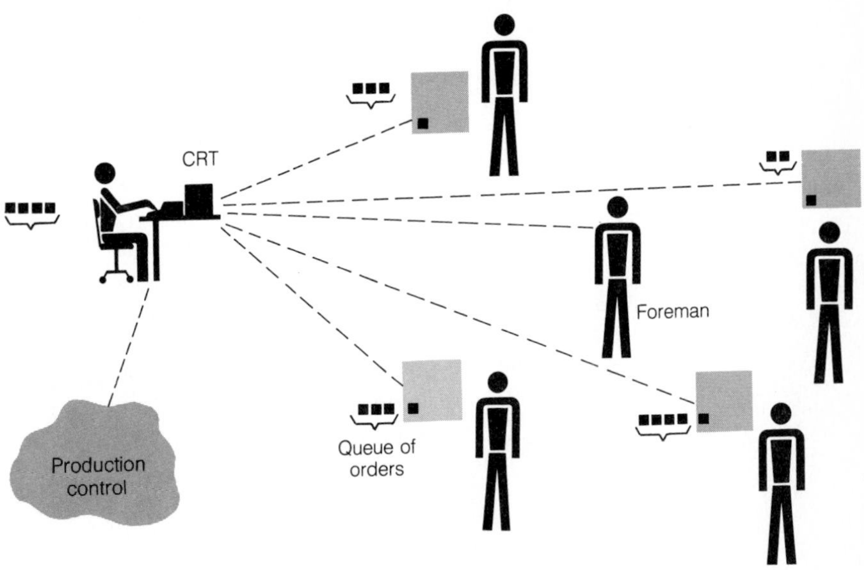

A simple shop-scheduling process is shown in Exhibit 14.1. Here the job dispatcher (in this case, a production control person assigned to this department) at the start of the day selects and sequences available jobs to be run at individual workstations. The dispatcher's decisions would be based on the operations and routing requirements of each job, status of existing jobs on the machines, the queue of work before each machine, job priorities, material availability, anticipated job orders to be released later in the day, and worker and machine capabilities. To help organize the schedule, the dispatcher would draw on shop-floor information from the previous day and external information provided by central production control, process engineering, and so on. The dispatcher would also confer with the supervisor of the department about the feasibility of the schedule, especially work-force considerations and potential bottlenecks.

14.3 ELEMENTS OF THE JOB-SHOP SCHEDULING PROBLEM

The classic approach to job-shop scheduling focuses on the following six elements, with a great deal of research invested in evaluating which priority rules are best at satisfying various performance criteria.

1. Job arrival patterns.
2. Number and variety of machines in the shop.

3. Ratio of workers to machines in the shop.
4. Flow pattern of jobs through the shop.
5. Priority rules for allocating jobs to machines.
6. Schedule evaluation criteria.

Job Arrival Patterns

Jobs can arrive at the scheduler's desk either in a batch or over a time interval according to some statistical distribution. The first arrival pattern is termed *static,* the second *dynamic.* Static arrival does not mean that orders are placed by customers at the same moment, only that they are subject to being scheduled at one time. Such a situation occurs when a production control clerk makes out a schedule, say, once a week and does not dispatch any jobs until all the previous week's incoming orders are on hand. In a dynamic arrival, jobs are dispatched as they arrive, and the overall schedule is updated to reflect their effect on the production facility.

Number and Variety of Machines in the Shop

The number of machines in the shop obviously affects the scheduling process. If there is but one machine, or if a group of machines can be treated as one, the scheduling problem is greatly simplified. On the other hand, as the number and variety of machines increase, the more complex the scheduling problem is likely to become.

Ratio of Workers to Machines in the Shop

If there are more workers than machines or an equal number of workers and machines, the shop is referred to as a **machine-limited system.** If there are more machines than workers, it is referred to as a **labor-limited system.** The machine-limited system has received a far greater amount of study, although recent investigations suggest that labor-limited systems are more pervasive in practice. In studying labor-limited systems, the primary areas of concern are the utilization of the worker on several machines and determination of the best way to allocate workers to machines.

Flow Patterns of Jobs through the Shop

The pattern of flow through the shop ranges from what is termed a *flow shop* (noted earlier), where all the jobs follow the same path from one machine to the next, to a *randomly routed job shop,* where there is no similar pattern of movement of jobs from one machine to the next. (Exhibit 14.2 approximates the latter situation.) Most shops fall somewhere in between. The extent to

EXHIBIT 14.2

Work Flow Patterns for a Hypothetical Job Shop

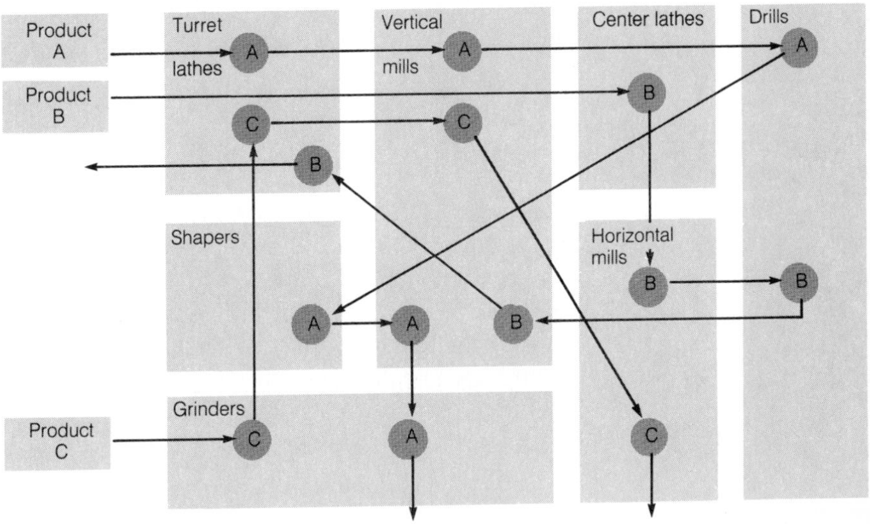

Note: First work center for each product is termed the *gateway* work center.

which a shop is a flow shop or a randomly routed job shop can be determined by noting the statistical probability of a job's moving from one machine to the next. Frequently such probabilities are expressed in a transitional probability matrix derived from historical data on the percentage of jobs in Machine center I going next to Machine center J, Machine center K, etc. A pure flow shop would show a probability of 1.0 for a job going from I to J; 1.0 from J to K, 1.0 from K to L, and so on. A pure random job shop would show equal probabilities of a job going from I to J, K, or L. Likewise, if a job were in L, the pure job-shop case would show it had an equal probability of going back to either J or K. (Clearly, the pure random job shop is an unlikely configuration in the real world.)

Priority Rules for Allocating Jobs to Machines

A **priority rule** is a rule for selecting which job is started first on some machine or work center. Priority rules can be very simple, requiring only that jobs be sequenced according to one piece of data, such as processing time, due date, or order of arrival. Other rules, though equally simple, may require several pieces of information, typically to derive an index number such as in the "least slack" rule and the **critical ratio rule** (both defined later). Still others, such as Johnson's rule (discussed later), apply to job scheduling on a sequence of machines and require a computational procedure to specify the order of performance. Ten of the more common rules are:[5]

1. FCFS—first-come, first-served; orders are run in the order they arrive in the department.
2. SOT—shortest operation time; orders are run in the inverse order to the time required to process them in the department. This is identical to SPT—shortest processing time.
3. Due date—earliest due date first; run the job with the earliest due date first. DDate—when referring to the entire job; OPNDD—when referring to the next operation.
4. Start date—due date minus normal lead time. (Run the job with the earliest due date first.)
5. STR—slack time remaining; this is calculated as the difference between the time remaining before the due date minus the processing time remaining. Orders with the shortest STR are run first.
6. STR/OP—Slack time remaining per operation; orders with shortest STR/OP are run first. Calculated as follows:

$$\text{STR/OP} = \frac{\begin{matrix}\text{Time remaining} \\ \text{before due date}\end{matrix} - \begin{matrix}\text{Remaining} \\ \text{processing time}\end{matrix}}{\text{Number of remaining operations}}$$

7. CR—critical ratio; this is calculated as the difference between the due date and the current date divided by the work remaining. Orders with the smallest CR are run first.
8. QR—queue ratio; this is calculated as the slack time remaining in the schedule divided by the planned remaining queue time. Orders with the smallest QR are run first.
9. LCFS—last-come, first-served; this rule occurs frequently by default. As orders arrive they are placed on the top of the stack and the operator usually picks up the order on top to run first.
10. Random order—whim; the supervisors or the operators usually select whichever job they feel like running.

Schedule Evaluation Criteria

The following constitute standard measures of schedule performance and are used to evaluate priority rules:

1. Meeting due dates of customers or downstream operations.
2. Minimizing flow time (the time a job spends in the shop).

---

[5] List modified from Donald W. Fogarty and Thomas R. Hoffmann, *Production and Inventory Management* (Cincinnati: South-Western Publishing, 1983), p. 392.

3. Minimizing work in process.
4. Minimizing idle time of machines and workers.

14.4 PRIORITY RULES AND TECHNIQUES

Scheduling *n* Jobs on One Machine

Let's look at how 2 of the 10 priority rules compared in a static scheduling situation involving four jobs on one machine. (In scheduling terminology, this class of problems is referred to as an "*n* job—one-machine problem," or simply $n/1$. The theoretical difficulty of this type of problem increases as more machines are considered rather than by the number of jobs that must be processed; therefore, the only restriction on n is that it be a specified, finite number. The rules to be tested are FCFS and SOT; the evaluation criterion will be minimum flow time. The data are as follows:

Job (in order of arrival)	Processing Time (days)
A	7
B	6
C	5
D	8

		Flow Time/Job	
FCFS Schedule:			
A	7 days	0 + 7 = 7	
B	6	7 + 6 = 13	
C	5	13 + 5 = 18	
D	8	18 + 8 = 26	
Total flow time		64	Mean flow time = 64/4 = 16 days
SOT Schedule:			
C	5 days	0 + 5 = 5	
B	6	5 + 6 = 11	
A	7	11 + 7 = 18	
D	8	18 + 8 = 26	
Total flow time		60	Mean flow time = 60/4 = 15 days

Obviously, here SOT is the better of the two rules, but is this always the case? The answer is yes. Moreover, it can be shown mathematically that the SOT rule yields an optimum solution for the $n/1$ case in terms of such other evaluation criteria as mean waiting time and mean completion time. In fact, so powerful is this simple rule that it has been termed "the most important concept in the entire subject of sequencing."[6]

[6] R. W. Conway, William L. Maxwell, and Louis W. Miller, *Theory of Scheduling* (Reading, Mass.: Addison-Wesley Publishing, 1967), p. 26. A classic book on the subject.

Runout method of scheduling n jobs on one machine

The **runout time method** can be used to determine production runs for a group of items that share the same production facilities or resources. Runout time is that period of time for which previously scheduled production, plus inventory on hand, will satisfy demands for an item. The basic objective of this method is to balance the utilization of production capacity—for example, machine hours—so that the runout time for all items is the same. Production efforts are thereby balanced across the group of items rather than concentrated on a few items (while other items are neglected). Examples are running parts through a testing machine, sewing a unique line of dresses by a seamstress, and sequencing textbook binding through a binding machine.

This procedure is illustrated in Exhibit 14.3 for six items, where 96.5 machine hours are available to be scheduled during a week. The aggregate runout time (3.72 weeks) is then used in column 7 to determine the inventories needed at the end of the week if each item is to have a runout time of 3.72

EXHIBIT 14.3

Runout Time Calculations

Item	(1) Production Time (machine hours per unit)	(2) Inventory on Hand (units)	(3) Inventory on Hand (machine hours) (1) × (2)	(4) Forecast Weekly Usage (units)	(5) Forecast Weekly Usage (machine hours) (1) × (4)
A	0.2	125	25.00	60	12.00
B	0.08	250	20.00	85	6.80
C	0.5	75	37.50	30	15.00
D	0.09	300	27.00	96	8.64
E	0.15	239	35.85	78	11.70
F	0.7	98	68.60	42	29.40
Aggregate totals			213.95		83.54

$$\text{Aggregate runout time} = \frac{\text{Inventory on hand in machine hours (col. 3)} + \text{Available machine hours}}{\text{Forecast weekly usage (col. 5)}}$$

$$= \frac{213.95 + 96.5}{83.54} = 3.72 \text{ weeks}$$

Item	(6) Runout Time (computed above)	(7) Total Items Required (units) (4) × (6)	(8) Schedule (total items less beginning inventory) (7) − (2)	(9) Production Schedule (machine hours) (1) × (8)
A	3.72	223	98	19.6
B	3.72	316	66	5.3
C	3.72	112	37	18.5
D	3.72	357	57	5.1
E	3.72	290	51	7.7
F	3.72	156	58	40.6
				96.8

weeks. Column 9 shows units that must be scheduled for production in order to meet these inventory requirements. (Note that additional calculations would have to be made if there were an established production lot size for each item.)

Scheduling *n* Jobs on Two Machines

The next step up in complexity of job-shop types is the $n/2$ flow-shop case, where two or more jobs must be processed on two machines in a common sequence. As in the $n/1$ case, there is an approach that leads to an optimal solution according to certain criteria. This approach, termed Johnson's rule or method (after its developer), consists of the following steps:

1. List the operation time for each job on both machines.
2. Select the shortest operation time.
3. If the shortest time is for the first machine, do the job first; if it is for the second machine, do the job last.
4. Repeat steps 2 and 3 for each remaining job until the schedule is complete.

We can illustrate this procedure by scheduling four jobs through two machines.

Step 1: List operation times.

Job	Operation Time on Machine 1	Operation Time on Machine 2
A	3	2
B	6	8
C	5	6
D	7	4

Steps 2 and 3: Select shortest operation time and assign. Job A is shortest on Machine 2 and is assigned first and performed last. (Job A is no longer available to be scheduled.)

Step 4: Repeat Steps 2 and 3. Job D is second shortest on Machine 2 and is assigned second and performed second to last. Job C is third shortest on Machine 2 and second shortest on Machine 1 and is assigned third and performed first. Job B is fourth shortest on Machine 2 and third shortest on Machine 1 and is assigned fourth and performed second.

In summary, the solution sequence is C → B → D → A, and the flow time is 25 days, which is a minimum. Also minimized are total idle time and mean idle time. The final schedule appears in Exhibit 14.4.

Johnson's method has been extended to yield an optimal solution for the $n/3$ case. When flow-shop scheduling problems larger than $n/3$ arise (and they generally do), analytical solution procedures leading to optimality are not available. The reason for this is that even though the jobs may arrive in static

EXHIBIT 14.4

Optimal Schedule of Jobs Using Johnson's Rule

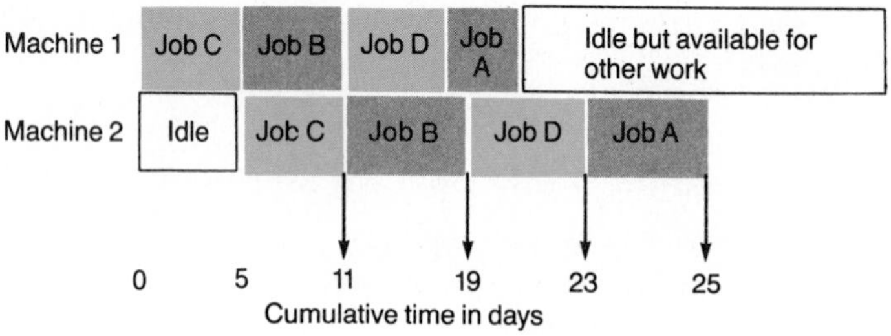

fashion at the first machine, the scheduling problem becomes dynamic, and series of waiting lines start to form in front of machines downstream.

Scheduling *n* Jobs on *m* Machines—Complex Job Shops

Complex job shops are characterized by multiple machine centers processing a variety of different jobs arriving at the machine centers in an intermittent fashion throughout the day. If there are *n* jobs to be processed on *m* machines and all jobs are processed on all machines, then there are $(n!)^m$ alternative schedules for this job set. Because of the large number of schedules that exist for even small job shops, Monte Carlo simulation (see Supplement to Chapter 8) is the only practical way to determine the relative merits of different priority rules in such situations. As in the *n* job—one machine case, the 10 priority rules (and more) have been compared relative to their performance on the evaluation criteria mentioned above.

By way of example, Kanet and Hayya focused on due date-oriented priority rules to see which one was best. Their simulation of a complex job shop led to the finding that total job competition rules of "DDATE, STR, and CR were outperformed by their 'operation' counterparts OPNDD, STR/OP, and OPCR" for all seven of the performance criteria used.[7]

Which priority rule should be used? We believe that the needs of most manufacturers will be reasonably satisfied by a relatively simple priority scheme that embodies the following principles:

1. It should be dynamic, that is, computed frequently during the course of a job to reflect changing conditions.
2. It should be based in one way or another on slack (the difference between the work remaining to be done on a job and the time remaining to do it in). This embodies the due-date features suggested by Kanet and Hayya.

---

[7] John K. Kanet and Jack C. Hayya, "Priority Dispatching with Operation Due Dates in a Job Shop," *Journal of Operations Management* 2, no. 3 (May 1982), p. 170.

EXHIBIT 14.5

Shop-Floor Control

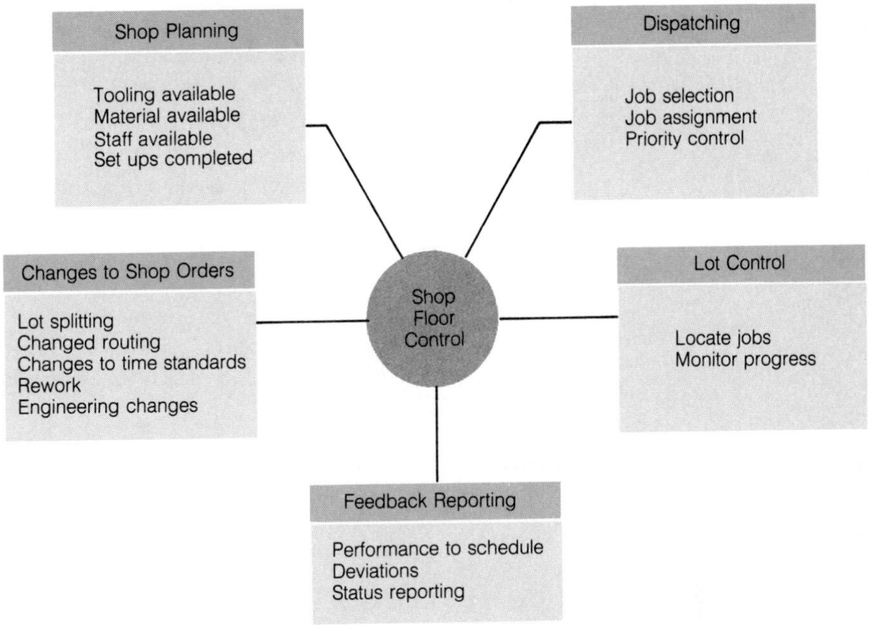

Source: "Shop Floor Control—Closing the Loop," *Inventory Management Newsletter* (Stone Mountain, Ga.: Center for Inventory Management), August 1982.

14.5 SHOP-FLOOR CONTROL

Scheduling job priorities is just one aspect of **shop-floor control** (now often called *production activity control*). The *APICS Dictionary* defines *shop-floor control system* as:

> A system for utilizing data from the shop floor as well as data processing files to maintain and communicate status information on shop orders and work centers. The major functions of shop-floor control are:
>
> 1. Assigning priority of each shop order.
> 2. Maintaining work-in-process quantity information.
> 3. Conveying shop-order status information to the office.
> 4. Providing actual output data for capacity control purposes.
> 5. Providing quantity by location by shop order for WIP inventory and accounting purposes.
> 6. Providing measurement of efficiency, utilization, and productivity of manpower and machines.

Exhibit 14.5 illustrates some more of the details.

Tools of Shop-Floor Control

The basic tools of shop-floor control are:

1. The *daily dispatch list,* which tells the supervisor what jobs are to be run, their priority, and how long each will take. (See Exhibit 14.6A.)
2. Various *status and exception reports,* including
   a. The anticipated delay report, made out by the shop planner once or twice a week and reviewed by the chief shop planner to see if there are any serious delays that could affect the master schedule. (See Exhibit 14.6B.)
   b. Scrap reports.
   c. Rework reports.
   d. Performance summary reports, giving the number and percentage of orders completed on schedule, lateness of unfilled orders, volume of output, etc.
   e. Shortage list.
3. An *input/output control report,* which is used by the supervisor to monitor the workload-capacity relationship for each workstation. (See Exhibit 14.6C.)

Input/Output Control

Input/Output (I/O) control is a major feature of a manufacturing planning and control system. Its major precept is that the planned work input to a work center should never exceed the planned work output. When the input exceeds the output, backlogs build up at the work center, which in turn increases the lead-time estimates for jobs upstream. Moreover, when jobs pile up at the work center, congestion occurs, processing becomes inefficient, and the flow of work to downstream work centers becomes sporadic. (The water flow analogy to shop capacity control in Exhibit 14.7 illustrates the general phenomenon.) Exhibit 14.6C shows an I/O report for a downstream work center. Looking first at the lower or output half of the report, we see that output is far below plan. It would seem that a serious capacity problem exists for this work center. However, looking at the input part of the plan, it becomes apparent that the serious capacity problem exists at an upstream work center feeding this work center. The control process would entail finding the cause of upstream problems and adjusting capacity and inputs accordingly. The basic solution is "simple": either increase capacity at the bottleneck station, or reduce the input to it. (Input reduction at bottleneck work centers, incidentally, is usually the first step recommended by production control consultants when job shops get into trouble.)

Data Integrity

Shop-floor control systems in many modern plants are now computerized, with job status information entered directly into a CRT terminal as the job

EXHIBIT 14.6

Some Basic Tools of Shop-Floor Control

A. Dispatch list

Work center 1501 – Day 205

Start date	Job #	Description	Run time
201	15131	Shaft	11.4
203	15143	Stud	20.6
205	15145	Spindle	4.3
205	15712	Spindle	8.6
207	15340	Metering rod	6.5
208	15312	Shaft	4.6

B. Anticipated delay report

Dept. 24 April 8

Part #	Sched. date	New date	Cause of delay	Action
17125	4/10	4/15	Fixture broke	Toolroom will return on 4/15
13044	4/11	5/1	Out for plating—plater on strike	New lot started
17653	4/11	4/14	New part-holes don't align	Engineering laying out new jig

C. Input/output control report (B)

Work center 0162

Week ending	505	512	519	526
Planned input	210	210	210	210
Actual input	110	150	140	130
Cumulative deviation	–100	–160	–230	–310
Planned output	210	210	210	210
Actual output	140	120	160	120
Cumulative deviation	–70	–160	–210	–300

(All figures in standard hours)

enters and leaves a work center. Some plants have gone heavily into bar coding and optical scanners to speed up the reporting process and to cut down on data-entry errors.[8] As you might guess, the key problems in shop-floor control are data inaccuracy and lack of timeliness. When these occur, data fed

[8] Some companies also use "smartshelves"—inventory bins with weight sensors beneath each shelf. When an item is removed from inventory a signal is sent to a central computer, which notes the time, date, quantity, and location of the transaction.

back to the overall planning system are wrong and incorrect production decisions are made. Typical results are excess inventory or stockout problems or both, missed due dates, and inaccuracies in job costing.

Of course, maintaining data integrity requires that a sound data-gathering system be in place, but more important it requires adherence to the system by everybody interacting with it. Most firms recognize this, but maintaining what is variously referred to as *shop discipline, data integrity,* or *data responsibility* is not always easy. And despite periodic drives to publicize the importance of careful shop-floor reporting, creating data-integrity task forces, inaccuracies can still creep into the system in many ways: A line worker drops a part under the workbench and pulls a replacement from stock without recording either transaction. An inventory clerk makes an error in a cycle count. A manufac-

EXHIBIT 14.7

Shop Capacity Control Load Flow

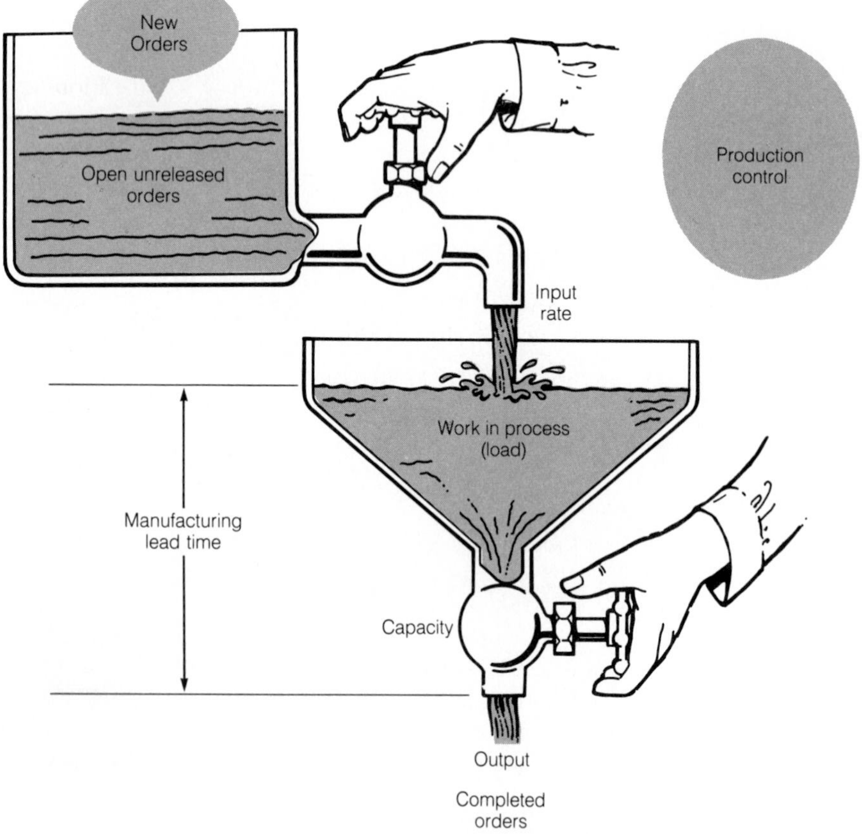

Source: American Production and Inventory Control Society, "Training Aid—Shop Floor Control," undated.

turing engineer fails to note a change in the routing of a part. A department supervisor decides to work jobs in a different order than specified in the dispatch list.

14.6 EXAMPLE OF A TOTAL SYSTEM: H.P.'S PRODUCTION MANAGEMENT/3000

The Hewlett-Packard *Production Management/3000* system (summarized in Exhibit 14.8) reflects and integrates many of the ideas we have been discussing thus far. Although the exhibit expresses them in somewhat different terminology, the system uses two scheduling concepts discussed in Chapter 13:

1. *Infinite loading of work centers.* That is, the scheduling routine assumes that infinite production capacity is available at all times. Each work order is scheduled independently and requirements in excess of available capacity are then identified by the capacity requirements planning (CRP) module. Modifications to the plan are then made in light of capacity constraints indicated by the CRP process. (This is in contrast to *finite loading* approaches, where no work centers are initially loaded beyond their capacity.)

2. *Backward and forward scheduling.* Once a job's processing sequence and lead time have been established, the scheduling program permits determining ideal start dates in either of two ways: *backward scheduling* from a user-supplied order due date, or *forward scheduling* from a user-supplied order start date. The

EXHIBIT 14.8

Hewlett-Packard Production Planning and Control System

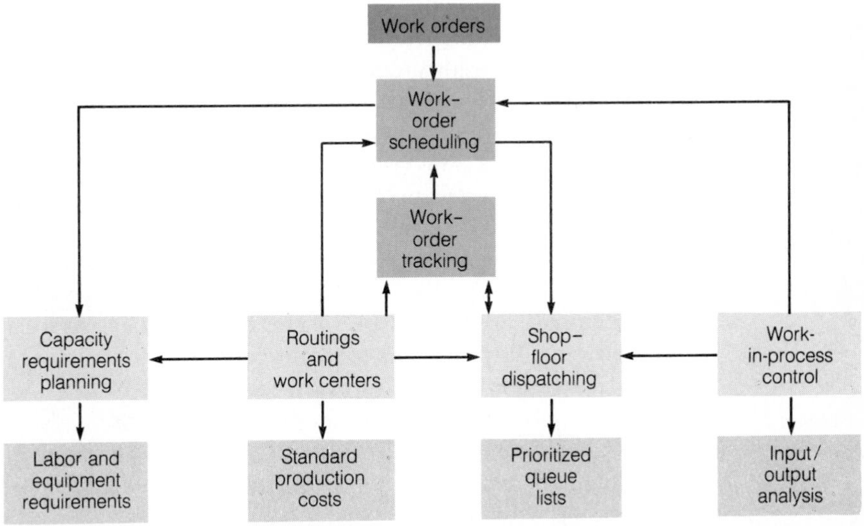

Source: HP Manufacturing Systems, *Production Management/3000*, 1981, p. 71.

dates are established by calculating actual elapsed time required to perform any production sequence and by examining the shop calendar for each work center to determine the number of working hours scheduled for any given date and shift. Backward scheduling is desirable because it delays investment in inventories; forward scheduling is desirable because it provides a greater likelihood of meeting the due date. (In general, companies use both of these to balance work flow and capacity.)

14.7 PERSONNEL SCHEDULING IN SERVICES

The scheduling problem in most service organizations revolves around setting staffing levels and scheduling the workweek. This is in contrast to manufacturing, where the focus of operations scheduling is on materials. In this section we will present brief examples of how personnel scheduling is done in banking and nursing and provide a simple technique for scheduling days off, which can be used in a variety of settings.

Setting Staffing Levels in Banks

This example illustrates how central clearinghouses and back-office operations of large bank branches establish a staffing plan. Basically, management wants to derive a staffing plan that (1) requires the least number of workers to accomplish the daily workload and (2) minimizes the variance between actual output and planned output.

In structuring the problem, bank management defines inputs (checks, statements, investment documents, and so forth) as *products,* which are routed through different processes or *functions* (receiving, sorting, encoding, and so forth).

To solve the problem, a monthly demand forecast is made by product for each function. This is converted to labor hours required per function, which in turn is converted to workers required per function. These figures are then tabled, summed, and adjusted by an absence and vacation factor to give planned hours. Then they are divided by the number of hours in the workday to yield the number of workers required. This yields the daily staff hours required. (See Exhibit 14.9.) This becomes the basis for a departmental staffing plan that lists the workers required, workers available, variance, and managerial action in light of variance. (See Exhibit 14.10.)

In addition to their use in day-to-day planning, the hours required and the staffing plan provide information for scheduling individual workers, controlling operations, comparing capacity utilization with other branches, and starting up new branches.

EXHIBIT 14.9 **Daily Staff Hours Required**

		FUNCTION								
		RECEIVE		PREPROCESS		MICROFILM		VERIFY		TOTALS
Product	Daily Volume	P/H	H_{std}	P/H	H_{std}	P/H	H_{std}	P/H	H_{std}	H_{std}
Checks	2,000	1,000	2.0	600	3.3	240	8.3	640	3.1	16.7
Statements	1,000	—	—	600	1.7	250	4.0	150	6.7	12.4
Notes	200	30	6.7	15	13.3		—			20.0
Investments	400	100	4.0	50	8.0	200	2.0	150	2.7	16.7
Collections	500	300	1.7			300	1.7	60	8.4	11.8
			—		—		—		—	—
Total hours required			14.4		26.3		16.0		20.9	77.6
Times 1.25 (absences and vacations)			18.0		32.9		20.0		26.1	
			—		—		—		—	
Divided by 8 hours equals staff required			2.3		4.1		2.5		3.3	

Note: P/H indicates production rate per hour; H_{std} indicates required hours.

EXHIBIT 14.10

Staffing Plan

Function	Staff Required	Staff Available	Variance (±)	Management Actions
Receive	2.3	2.0	−0.3	Use overtime
Pre-process	4.1	4.0	−0.1	Use overtime
Microfilm	2.5	3.0	+0.5	Use excess to verify
Verify	3.3	3.0	−0.3	Get 0.3 from micro-film.

Nurse Staffing and Scheduling

Abernathy, Baloff, and Hershey state, "The key element of effective nurse staffing is a well-conceived procedure for achieving an overall balance between the size of the nursing staff and the expected patient demand."[9] Their procedure, termed *aggregate budgeting,* is predicated on a variety of interrelated activities and has a short-term schedule as a primary output. A number of severe practical problems confront hospitals in deriving an effective yet low-cost aggregate budget. These difficulties, along with possible remedies, are listed in Exhibit 14.11.

[9] W. Abernathy, N. Baloff, and J. Hershey, "The Nurse Staffing Problem: Issues and Prospects," *Sloan Management Review* 13, no. 1 (Fall 1971), pp. 87–109.

EXHIBIT 14.11

General Problems in Nurse Scheduling

Problem	Possible Solution
Accuracy of patient load forecast	Forecast frequently and rebudget monthly. Closely monitor seasonal demands, communicable diseases, and current occupancy.
Forecasting nurse availability	Develop work standards for nurses for each level of possible demand (requires systematic data collection and analysis).
Complexity and time to rebudget	Use available computer programs.
Flexibility in scheduling	Use variable staffing: Set regular staff levels slightly above minimum and absorb variation with broadskilled float nurses, part-time nurses, and overtime.

Though most hospitals still use cut-and-try methods in schedule development, management scientists have applied optimizing techniques to the problem with some success. For example, a linear programming model has been developed.[10] It assumes a known, short-run (three to four days) demand for nursing care and develops a staffing pattern that:

1. Specifies the number of nurses of each skill class to be assigned among the wards and nursing shifts.
2. Satisfies total nursing personnel capacity constraints.
3. Allows for limited substitution of tasks among nurses.
4. Minimizes the cost of nursing care shortage for the scheduling period.

Scheduling Consecutive Days Off

A practical problem encountered in many organizations is setting schedules so that employees can have two consecutive days off. The importance of the problem stems from the fact that the Fair Labor Standards Act requires overtime for any work hours (by hourly workers) in excess of 40 hours per week. Obviously, if two consecutive days off can't be scheduled each week for each employee, the likelihood of unnecessary overtime is quite high. In addition, most people probably prefer two consecutive days off per week. Below is an heuristic procedure modified from Browne and Tibrewala to deal with this problem.[11]

[10] D. Warner and J. Prawda, "A Mathematical Programming Model for Scheduling Nursing Personnel in a Hospital," *Management Science* 19, no. 4 (December 1972), pp. 411–22.

[11] James J. Browne and Rajen K. Tibrewala, "Manpower Scheduling," *Industrial Engineering* 7, no. 8 (August 1975), pp. 22–23.

Objective. Find the schedule that minimizes the number of five-day workers with two consecutive days off, subject to the demands of the daily staffing schedule.

Procedure. Starting with the total number of workers required for each day of the week, create a schedule by adding one worker at a time. This is a two-step procedure:

Step 1. Circle the lowest pair of consecutive days off. The lowest pair is the one where the highest number in the pair is equal to or lower than the highest number in any other pair. This ensures that the days with the highest requirements are covered by staff. (Monday and Sunday may be chosen even though they are at opposite ends of the array of days.) In case of ties choose the days-off pair with the lowest requirement on an adjacent day. This day may be before or after the pair. If a tie still remains, choose the first of the available tied pairs. (Do not bother using further tie-breaking rules, such as second lowest adjacent days.)

Step 2. Subtract 1 from each of the remaining five days (i.e., the days not circled). This indicates that one less worker is required on these days, since the first worker has just been assigned to them.

The two steps are repeated for the second worker, the third worker, and so forth, until no more workers are required to satisfy the schedule.

Example.

	M	Tu	W	Th	F	S	Su
Requirement	4	3	4	2	3	1	2
Worker 1	4	3	4	2	3	(1	2)
Worker 2	3	2	3	1	(2	1)	2
Worker 3	2	1	2	0	2	(1	1)
Worker 4	1	(0	1)	0	1	1	1
Worker 5	0	0	1	0	0	0	0

This solution consists of 5 workers covering 19 worker days, although slightly different assignments may be equally satisfactory.

The schedule is Worker 1 assigned S–Su off, Worker 2 F–S off, Worker 3 S–Su off, Worker 4 Tu–W off, and Worker 5 works only on Wednesday, since there are no further requirements for the other days.

14.8 CONCLUSION

The objective of this chapter has been to provide some insight into the nature of operations planning and control, with emphasis on job-shop environments.

Job-shop scheduling, like most other aspects of OM, has become computer dependent and, of equal importance, is now seen as being inseparable from the total manufacturing planning and control systems of which it is a part.

14.9 REVIEW AND DISCUSSION QUESTIONS

1. Distinguish between a job shop and a flow shop.
2. What is meant by a schedule evaluation criterion?
3. What practical considerations are deterrents to using SOT rule?
4. What priority rule do you use in scheduling your study time for midterm examinations? If you have five exams to study for, how many alternative schedules exist?
5. Data integrity is a big deal in industry. Why?
6. In the United States, we make certain assumptions about the customer-service priority rules used in banks, restaurants, and retail stores. If you have the opportunity, ask a foreigner what rules are used in his or her country. To what factors might you attribute the differences, if any?
7. What job characteristics would lead you to schedule jobs according to "longest processing time first"?
8. In what way is the scheduling problem in the home office of a bank different from that of a branch?

14.10 PROBLEMS

*1. Mr. Regan has just run across the runout method of scheduling and wonders whether he could apply this technique to allocating expense money among his three children. He would like to occasionally divide a lump sum among his children so that when added to what they currently have, it will cover each of their expenses for the same period of time. Mr. Regan's son is a freshman in high school and uses $1.95 per day ($0.50 each way bus fare plus $0.95 for lunch). His daughter is in junior high and uses $1.65 per day (bus fare $0.50 each way plus $0.65 for lunch). His youngest son is in elementary school and uses $0.55 per day (there is a free school bus). Following is the current expense money held by each child along with the scheduled expenses just mentioned.

	Expense Money in Hand	Daily Expenses
Eldest son	$3.20	$1.95
Daughter	2.40	1.65
Youngest son	1.80	0.55

* Solutions to Problems 1 and 2 are given in Appendix D.

Mr. Regan would like to divide $20 among his children so that each would have the same number of days of expense money. Use the runout method to find the appropriate allocation.

*2. Joe's Auto Seat Cover and Paint Shop is bidding on a contract to do all the custom work for Smiling Ed's used car dealership. One of the main requirements in obtaining this contract is rapid delivery time, since Ed—for reasons we shall not go into here—wants the cars facelifted and back on his lot in a hurry. Ed has said that if Joe can refit and repaint five cars that Ed has just received (from an unnamed source) in 24 hours or less, the contract will be his. Following is the time (in hours) required in the refitting shop and the paint shop for each of the five cars. Assuming that cars go through the refitting operations before they are repainted, can Joe meet the time requirements and get the contract?

Car	Refitting Time (hours)	Repainting Time (hours)
A	6	3
B	0	4
C	5	2
D	8	6
E	2	1

3. Joe has three cars that must be overhauled by his ace mechanic, Jim. Given the following data about the cars, use Conway's "Rule 4" (least slack per remaining operation) to determine Jim's scheduling priority for each.

Car	Customer Pick-Up Time (hours hence)	Remaining Overhaul Time (hours)	Remaining Operations
A	10	4	Painting
B	17	5	Wheel alignment, painting
C	15	1	Chrome plating, painting, seat repair

4. There are seven jobs that must be processed in two operations: A and B. All seven jobs must go through A and B in that sequence—A first, then B. Determine the optimal order in which the jobs should be sequenced through the process using these times:

Job	Time Required in Process A	Time Required in Process B
1	9	6
2	8	5
3	7	7
4	6	3
5	1	2
6	2	6
7	4	7

5. Joe has the opportunity to do a big repair job for a local motorcycle club. (Their cycles were accidentally run over by a garbage truck.) The compensation for the job is good, but it is very important that the total repair time for the five cycles to be fixed be less than 40 hours. (The leader of the club has stated that he would be very distressed if the cycles were not available for a planned rally.) Joe knows from experience that repairs of this type often entail several trips between processes for a given cycle, so estimates of time are difficult to provide. Still, Joe has historical data about the probability that a job will start in each process, processing time in each process, and transitional probabilities between each pair of processes. (The data are tabulated here.)

Process	Probability of Job Starting in Process	PROCESSING TIME PROBABILITY (HOURS)			PROBABILITY OF GOING FROM PROCESS TO OTHER PROCESSES OR COMPLETION (OUT)			
		1	2	3	Frame	Engine Work	Painting	Out
Frame repair	0.5	0.2	0.4	0.4	—	0.4	0.4	0.2
Engine work	0.3	0.6	0.1	0.3	0.3	—	0.4	0.3
Painting	0.2	0.3	0.3	0.4	0.1	0.1	—	0.8

Given this information, use simulation to determine the repair times for each cycle and display your results on a Gantt chart showing an FCFS schedule. (Assume that only one cycle can be worked on at a time in each process.) Based on your simulation, what do you recommend Joe do next?

6. Tabulated below is a list of jobs, with their estimated times required, in a critical department.

Job	Required Time (days)	Days to Delivery Promise	Slack
A	8	12	4
B	3	9	6
C	7	8	1
D	1	11	10
E	10	−10	—
F	6	10	4
G	5	−8	—
H	4	6	2

a. Use the shortest operation time rule to schedule these jobs:

What is the schedule?

What is the mean flow time?

What property does the mean flow time have?

b. The boss doesn't like the schedule in *(a)*. Jobs E and G must be done first, for obvious reasons. Reschedule and do the best you can while scheduling Jobs E and G first and second, respectively.

What is the new schedule?

What is the new mean flow time?

7. John Adams is a shop supervisor for Foley and Burnham, Inc., in the component insertion area. F&B runs a fairly loose shop schedule, leaving it pretty much up to the lower managers to determine the within-week schedule for production. Since John produces standard items for stock, and since setup times are minimal, he normally tries to use up his production resources in a way that provides equal time coverages for all products.

   Assume that John has four machine centers working eight hours per day, five days per week, for a total of 160 production hours available per week. John needs to plan how he will allocate his 160 total available hours over the five printed circuit board configurations for next week. Your task is to help him. (Use the runout method.)

Item	Production Time per Unit (minutes)	Inventory on Hand (units)	Forecasted Usage for Next Week (units)
PC1	4	900	600
PC2	1	1100	700
PC3	3	800	1200
PC4	5	500	300
PC5	8	125	75

8. A manufacturing facility has five jobs to be scheduled into production. The following table gives the processing times plus the necessary wait times and other necessary delays for each of the jobs.

   Assume that today is April 3 and the jobs are due on the dates shown:

Job	Days of Actual Processing Time Required	Days of Necessary Delay Time	Total Time Required	Date Job Due
1	2	12	14	April 30
2	5	8	13	April 21
3	9	15	24	April 28
4	7	9	16	April 29
5	4	22	28	April 27

   Determine *two* schedules, stating the order in which the jobs are to be done. Use the critical ratio priority rule for one. You may use any other rule for the second schedule as long as you state what it is.

9. An accounting firm, Debits 'R Us, would like to keep its auditing staff to a maximum of four people yet satisfy the staffing needs and the policy of two days off per week. Given the following requirements, is this possible?

   Requirements (Monday through Sunday): 4, 3, 3, 2, 2, 4, 4.

10. Jobs A, B, C, D, and E must go through Processes I and II in that sequence (i.e., Process I first, then Process II).

    Use Johnson's rule to determine the optimal sequence to schedule the jobs to minimize the total required time.

Job	Required Processing Time on A	Required Processing Time on B
A	4	5
B	16	14
C	8	7
D	12	11
E	3	9

11. For a variety of reasons, our friend Joe now finds himself in charge of what might be called a *captive machine shop* in a government-operated establishment. The machine shop fabricates and paints metal products, including license plates, road signs, window screens, and door frames, and Joe's major responsibility is to balance the utilization of the equipment across all four products in such a way that demand for each product is satisfied. Given the following data, how might he schedule the four products to achieve this objective for the next week? What would his schedule look like?

Item	Inventory	Production Time per Unit	Forecast Weekly Usage
Window screens	200	0.1 hour	100
Door frames	100	0.06	50
Road signs	70	0.3	60
License plates	150	0.7	125

Available machine hours = 90/week

12. A textile manufacturer is planning his next week's production and wants to use the runout method of scheduling. Part of his logic for using the runout method in this case is that he is running the same design on towels, washcloths, sheets, and pillowcases. He would therefore like to carry the same period amounts in the event the design is changed.

Following are the existing quantities on hand, the production times of each, and the forecast demands. There are 120 hours of capacity available on the mill in three shifts. (The same machine is used to make all the items, so the problem is to determine which will be made, how many, and how much machine time to allocate to each.)

Item	Number of Units on Hand	Production Time for Each in Hours	Forecast Demand per Week
Washcloths	500	0.1	300
Towels	200	0.15	400
Sheets	150	0.20	200
Pillowcases	300	0.15	200

13. Joe has now been released from his government job. Based on his excellent performance, he was able to land a job as production scheduler in a brand-new custom refinishing auto service shop located near the border. Techniques have improved in the several years he was out of circulation, so processing times are

considerably faster. This system is capable of handling 10 cars per day. The sequence now is: customizing first, followed by repainting.

Car	Customizing Time (hours)	Painting (hours)
1	3.0	1.2
2	2.0	0.9
3	2.5	1.3
4	0.7	0.5
5	1.6	1.7
6	2.1	0.8
7	3.2	1.4
8	0.6	1.8
9	1.1	1.5
10	1.8	0.7

In what sequence should Joe schedule the cars?

14.11 CASE: McCALL DIESEL MOTOR WORKS (NEED FOR A COMPLETE SYSTEM OF PRODUCTION CONTROL)

The McCall Diesel Motor Works has been a pioneer in the manufacture of a particular type of internal combustion engine. The plant is located on tidewater in the state of New Jersey, because the company originally built engines for the marine field, chiefly fishing boats and pleasure craft. Subsequently, its activities were extended to the stationary type of engines, used primarily for the production of power in small communities, in manufacturing plants, or on farms.

During the earlier years of the company's operation, its engines were largely special-order jobs. Even at the present time about 60 percent of the output is made to order. There has been in recent years, however, a trend toward standardization of component parts and reduction in the variety of engines produced. The Engineering Department has followed the principle of simplification and standardization in the case of minor parts, such as studs, bolts, and springs, giving a degree of interchangeability of these components among the various sizes and types of engines. Sizes of marine engines have been standardized to some extent, although customer requirements still necessitate some designs. In the small engines for agricultural use there has been a genuine effort to concentrate sales on a standard line of engines of three sizes—20 HP, 40 HP, and 60 HP.

The company has always been advanced in its engineering development and design. The production phase, on the other hand, has not been progressive. The heritage of job-shop operation persists, and despite the definite trend toward standardization, manufacture continues largely on a made-to-order basis. The increasing popularity of diesel engines has brought many new producing companies into the field, with a consequent tightening of the competitive situation.

High manufacturing costs and poor service have been reflected in the loss of orders. Customer complaints, together with pressure from the Sales Department, prompted management to call in a consulting engineer to make a survey of the Manufacturing Department and recommend a plan of action.

The report of the engineer showed the following:

1. Manufacturing methods, while still largely of the job-shop character, are in the main good, and no wholesale change should be made. As production is still 60 percent special, a complete shift to line manufacture or departmentalization by product is not feasible.

2. Machinery and equipment are for the most part general purpose, in line with manufacturing requirements. Some machine tools are approaching obsolescence, and for certain operations high-production, single-purpose machines would be advisable. Extensive replacement of machine tools is not a pressing need, but an increased use of jigs and fixtures should be undertaken immediately. There are many bottlenecks existing in the plant, but contrary to your belief, as well as that of your foreman and other shop executives, there is no serious lack of productive equipment. The trouble lies in the improper utilization of the machine time available.

3. Production control is the major element of operating weakness, and improvement is imperative. The lack of proper control over production shows up in many ways:

(a) High in-process inventory, as indicated by piles of partially completed parts over the entire manufacturing floor areas.

(b) Absence of any record concerning the whereabouts of orders in the process from their initiation to delivery at assembly.

(c) Inordinate number of rush orders, particularly in assembly but also in parts manufacture.

(d) Too many parts chasers who force orders through the shops by pressure methods.

(e) Piecemeal manufacture—a lot of 20 parts usually is broken up into four or five lots before it is finished. Not infrequently the last sublot remains on the shop floor for months and, in a number of instances, is "lost" as far as records are concerned. Subsequent orders for the same part are issued and new lots pass through to completion while the remains of the old lot lie in partially fabricated condition.

(f) Excessive setup costs resulting from the piecemeal methods mentioned in *(e),* as well as failure to use proper lot sizes, even when lots are not broken up during manufacture.

(g) Failure of all necessary component parts to reach assembly at approximately the same time. The floor of the assembly department is cluttered with piles of parts awaiting receipt of one or more components before engines can be assembled.

(h) Lack of definite sequence of manufacturing operations for a given part. Responsibility for the exact way by which a part is to be made rests entirely on the various department foremen; these men are able machinists, but, burdened with detail, their memories cannot be relied upon to ensure that parts will always be manufactured in the best, or even the same, sequence of operations. Moreover, they have the responsibility for determining the department to which a lot of parts should be sent when it has been completed in their department.

(i) In the case of certain small standard parts, shop orders have been issued as many as six or eight times in a single month.

(j) Information is lacking from which to estimate, with any degree of close approximation, the overall manufacturing time for an engine. The result is failure to meet delivery promises or high production cost due to rush or overtime work.

(k) Parts in process or in stores, and destined for imminent assembly, are frequently taken by the Service Department to supply an emergency repair order. The question here is not the academic determination or priority between the customer whose boat

may be lying idle because of a broken part and the customer who has not yet received his engine; the question is why there should be any habitual difficulty in rendering adequate repair service and at the same time meeting delivery promises.

(l) Virtually all basic manufacturing data resides in the heads of the superintendent, departmental foreman, assistant foremen, and setup men.

(m) Delivery dates are set by the Sales Department and generally are dates that customers arbitrarily stipulate.

(n) The general superintendent shows little enthusiasm for the idea of a system of production control; in fact he is opposed to such an installation. He is of the opinion that reasonably satisfactory results are now being obtained by placing responsibility on the foremen and maintaining contact between them and the parts chasers, who in turn are held responsible for meeting delivery promises. He believes that no system can be substituted for the foremen's knowledge of the ability of the workers. He feels that operation of a production-control system requires time studies of all jobs. Time study, he points out, is difficult because of the many operations involved, the high degree of special work, the probable resistance of the workers, and the cost. He further protests that emergencies and rush orders would upset any rigid scheduling of work through the plant. Finally, he is convinced that any system of production control involves an excessive amount of clerical detail to which the foremen, who are practical shop men, object.

The state of affairs the consultant found had, he realized, two main causes:

1. The strong influence of the original job-shop character of manufacture and the very slow evolution to large-scale operation.
2. The fact that the top management of the company was essentially sales minded.

His recommendations, therefore, had to be a simple, straightforward program that would provide adequate control over production and could be instituted gradually and logically.

QUESTIONS

1. Outline the essential features of a production-control system for this company, giving sufficient detail to make clear how the system will function.
2. Indicate what part of your procedure should be centralized and what part decentralized, i.e., what functions should be handled by a central production-control office and what functions should be carried out in the various production and assembly departments.
3. What data must be compiled before your system can become fully effective?
4. Enumerate the benefits the company will derive when your production-control system is in operation.
5. Set forth in proper order the steps that should be taken and the departments that should be involved in the determination of delivery promises to customers.
6. What arguments would you advance in answer to the general superintendent's objections, as presented in paragraph *(n)* of the consultant's report?
7. Generally speaking, what is the foremen's place in the scheme of things when a fully developed production-control system is in operation and when a Production Control Department has been established?

14.12 SELECTED BIBLIOGRAPHY

Baker, K. R. "The Effects of Input Control in a Simple Scheduling Model." *Journal of Operations Management* 4, no. 2 (February 1984), pp. 99–112.

Berry, W. L.; R. Penlesky; and T. E. Vollmann. "Critical Ratio Scheduling: Dynamic Due-Date Procedures under Demand Uncertainty." *IIE Transactions* 16, no. 1 (March 1984), pp. 81–89.

Conway, R. W.; William L. Maxwell; and Louis W. Miller. *Theory of Scheduling.* Reading, Mass.: Addison-Wesley Publishing, 1967.

Johnson, S. M. "Optimal Two Stage and Three Stage Production Schedules with Setup Times Included." *Naval Logistics Quarterly* 1, no. 1 (March 1954), pp. 61–68.

Sandman, W. E., with J. P. Hayes. *How to Win Productivity in Manufacturing.* Dresher, Pa.: Yellow Book of Pennsylvania, 1980.

Chapter 15

Just-in-Time Production in Manufacturing and Services

EPIGRAPH

I need it now! Not yesterday, and not tomorrow!

Delivery within 30 minutes or the pizza's free.

Domino's Pizza

CHAPTER OUTLINE

KEY TERMS

Eliminate Waste

Respect for People

Focused Factory Networks

Kanban Pull System

Total Quality Control

JIT Themes

Focused Improvement Groups

A Just-in-Time (JIT) system follows the logic that nothing is made until it is needed. This is not entirely true because some small amounts of inventory are allowed in the productive system to provide some evenness of flow and some protection against delays. But those amounts may keep a machine or service worker occupied for only minutes or hours—certainly not the days, weeks, or even months worth of inventory in front of a workstation that has been common in past years. JIT is being introduced widely into manufacturing firms throughout the United States and is being promoted heavily by the American Production Inventory Control Society (APICS), a 63,000-member organization. JIT can offer many benefits when installed correctly and in the right applications. It cannot be installed anywhere at random, but it does have a wide area of application. It is currently being considered by virtually every major manufacturing organization. It is almost impossible to attend a professional conference or pick up a journal on production without encountering several presentations on JIT. In this text, we have sometimes referred to JIT and Japanese management interchangeably. This is because JIT was created in Japan at the Toyota automobile plant. It has since been used in almost all manufacturing and even some service industries.

In the largest sense, JIT can be viewed as a philosophy of management that encompasses all aspects of a firm's productive activities—human relations, vendor relations, technology, materials management, and so on. We can refer to this as "Big JIT." "Little JIT" focuses on production control methods—specifically Just-in-Time deliveries and inventory management.

The first part of this chapter presents an edited paper written by Kenneth A. Wantuck describing the Japanese approach to productivity.[1] This paper is a superb overview of the techniques and philosophy of the major developers and users of the JIT approach, the Japanese. The second part of the chapter develops some of these issues in more detail and presents an approach to JIT implementation. The third part of the chapter examines the application of JIT to services.

15.1 THE JAPANESE APPROACH TO PRODUCTIVITY

The increasing penetration of the Japanese "manufacturing machine" in selected American markets has received widespread coverage in the media. The impact on our automotive industry has been of sufficient magnitude to make it a national issue. It is prudent for us to examine what the Japanese are doing in the area of productivity, to isolate the significant factors in their approach, and to determine which things we might emulate to our advantage.

Everyone is aware of the inroads the Japanese have made in U.S. markets. Many product areas, such as televisions, video recorders, cameras, watches,

---

[1] Kenneth A. Wantuck, "The Japanese Approach to Productivity," Southfield, Mich.: Bendix Corporation.

EXHIBIT 15.1

1977 Hertz Repair Study

Model	Repairs per 100 Vehicles
Ford	326
Chevrolet	425
Pinto	306
Toyota	55

motorcycles, and even shipbuilding, have become dominated by Japanese companies. Of particular concern today are machine tools and automotive products, but an impact is also being felt in the aerospace-electronics field. In all areas, we know that not only do the Japanese compete with us at competitive prices but the level of quality they have been demonstrating in recent years has been phenomenal.

For example, consider the famous study done by the Hertz Corporation in 1977. The objective was to determine which cars in its fleet had the lowest number of repairs for the first 12,000 miles of operation, the warranty period. Ford, Chevrolet, and Pinto automobiles produced similar results: three to four repairs per vehicle. On the other hand, Toyota repairs were significantly lower, only one eighth as great. In this case, as shown in Exhibit 15.1, Japanese quality was better by almost an order of magnitude.

And the Japanese have been able to accomplish this with much lower investments. Exhibit 15.2 shows inventory turnovers for 15 Japanese and U.S. industries. Note that the exhibit is a ratio; the right side is Japan's inventory turnover divided by the United States' inventory turnover. Note, for example, that Japan's auto and truck inventory turnover rate is more than double that of the United States (113 percent). The left side of the exhibit shows the United States' inventory turnover divided by Japan's inventory turnover. This left side only pertains to the last two items—forest products and construction machinery—to show that the United States has a slightly higher turnover rate than Japan (2 percent and 7 percent, respectively). In all but two industries, the Japanese "turns" are higher.

U.S. Application

Many people believe these accomplishments are attributable to cultural differences. They envision the Japanese dedicating their lives to their companies and working long hours for substandard wages, which would be unthinkable in America. The evidence, however, is contrary to these distorted notions. Consider the following. In 1977, a Japanese company named Matsushita purchased a television plant in Chicago from a U.S. company. In the purchase contract, Matsushita agreed that all the hourly personnel would be retained. Two years later, they still had essentially the same 1,000 hourly employees and

EXHIBIT 15.2

Comparative U.S. and Japanese Inventory Turnover Rates for 15 Industries

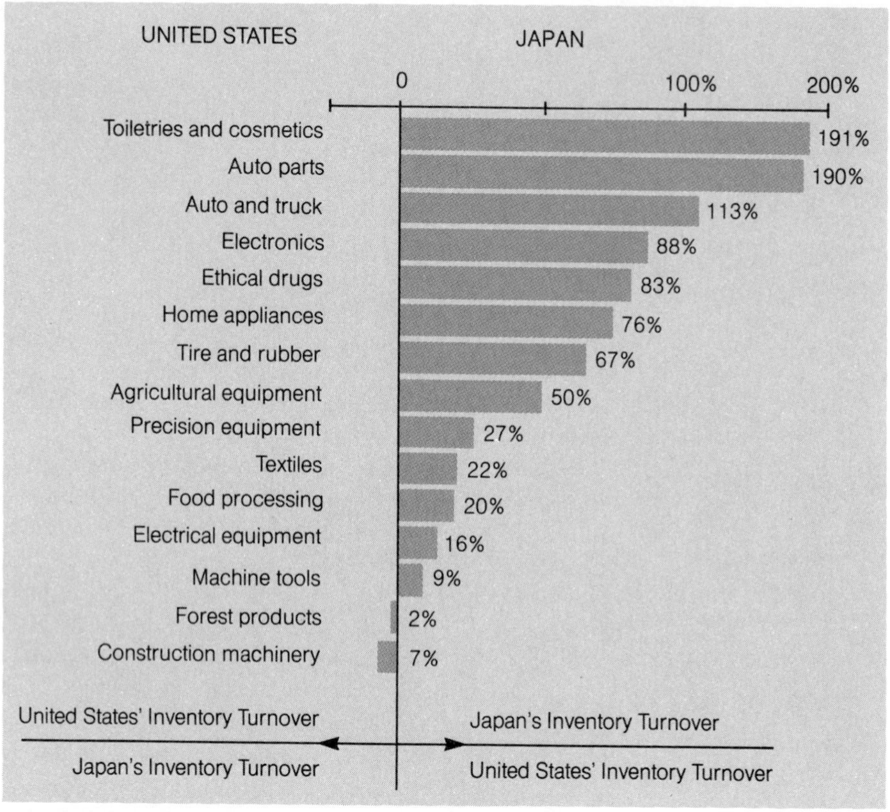

Source: Booz, Allen & Hamilton Survey of 1,500 Companies, 1981.

EXHIBIT 15.3

Quasar Plant Productivity

	Under Motorola	Under Matsushita*
Direct labor employees	1,000	1,000†
Indirect employees	600	300
Total employees	1,600	1,300
Daily production	1,000	2,000
Assembly repairs	130%	6%
Annual warranty cost ($ millions)	$16	$2

* 2 years later.
† Same people.

had managed to reduce the indirect staff by 50 percent (see Exhibit 15.3). Yet, during that period, daily production had doubled. The quality, as measured by the number of repairs done in-house, improved more than 20-fold. Outside quality indicators also improved. Where the U.S. company (Motorola) had spent an average amount of $16 million a year on warranty costs, Matsushita expenditures were $2 million. (That's for twice as many TV sets, so it's really a 16 to 1 ratio.) These are big differences, achieved in the United States with American workers. The issue is, How do the Japanese do this and what can we learn from them?

Isolating the Elements

First, it's important to understand that the Japanese, as a nation, have had one fundamental economic goal since 1945: full employment through industrialization. The strategy employed to achieve it called for obtaining market dominance in very select product areas. They very carefully chose those industries in which they believed they could become dominant and concentrated on them, rather than diluting their efforts over a broad spectrum.

The tactics of the Japanese were threefold: (1) They imported their technology. (The entire Japanese semiconductor industry was built around a $25,000 purchase from Texas Instruments for the rights to the basic semiconductor process.) Instead of reinventing the wheel, they avoided major R&D expenditures, with the attendant risks, then negotiated license agreements to make the successful, workable new products. (2) They concentrated their ingenuity on the factory to achieve high productivity and low unit cost. The best engineering talent available was directed to the shop floor, instead of the product design department. (3) Finally, they embarked on a drive to improve product quality and reliability to the highest possible levels, to give their customers product reliability that competitors were not able to supply.

Implementation of these tactics was governed by two fundamental concepts (most of us agree with these things in principle, but the difference is the degree to which the Japanese practice them):

1. They are firm believers that in every way, shape, and form you must **eliminate waste.**
2. They practice a great **respect for people.**

Elimination of waste

When the Japanese talk about waste, the definition given by F. Cho, from the Toyota Motor Company, probably states it as well as anything. He calls it "anything other than the *minimum* amount of equipment, materials, parts, and workers (working time) which are *absolutely essential* to production." That means no surplus, no safety stock. That means nothing is banked. If you can't use it now you don't make it now because it's waste. There are seven basic elements under this concept:

1. Focused factory networks.
2. Group technology.
3. Jidoka—quality at the source.
4. Just-in-Time production.
5. Uniform plant loading.
6. Kanban production control system.
7. Minimized setup times.

Focused factory networks. The first element is **focused factory networks.** Instead of building a large manufacturing facility that does everything (highly vertically integrated) the Japanese build small plants that are specialized. There are several reasons for doing this. First, it's very difficult to manage a large installation; the bigger it gets, the more bureaucratic it gets. Their management style does not lend itself to this kind of environment.

When a plant is specifically designed to do a specific thing, it can be constructed and operated more economically than its universal counterpart. It's comparable to buying a special machine tool to do a critical job instead of trying to adapt a universal tool. Fewer than 750 plants in Japan have as many as 1,000 employees. The bulk of them, some 60,000 plants, have between 30 and 1,000 workers and over 180,000 have fewer than 30 employees. When we talk about the Japanese approach to productivity and the impressive things they're doing, we're talking primarily about the middle group, where most of their model manufacturing plants fit.

Two illustrative examples have been cited by the Ford Motor Company. The Escort automobile needed a transaxle, which was going to require a $300 million expansion at the Ford plant in Batavia, Ohio. Ford asked the Japanese for an equivalent quotation and Toyo-Kogyo offered to construct a brand-new plant with the same rate of output at a competitive unit price for $100 million, a one-third ratio. A second example relates to Ford's Valencia engine plant, which produces two engines per employee per day, and requires 900,000 square feet of floor space. An almost identical engine is produced by the Toyota Motor Company in Japan, where they make nine engines per employee per day in a plant that has only 300,000 square feet of space. The issue is not only productivity per person but also a much lower capital investment in order to achieve this manufacturing capability.

Group technology. Inside the plant the Japanese employ a technique called *group technology*. Incidentally, group technology is nothing new to America; it was invented here, like so many of the techniques the Japanese successfully employ, but it hasn't been practiced very much in the United States. A simplified diagram of the technique is shown in Exhibit 15.4. The lower portion shows the way we operate our plants today. Most companies process a job and send it from department to department because that's the way our plants are organized (saw department, grinders, lathes). Each machine in those

EXHIBIT 15.4

Group Technology versus Departmental Specialty

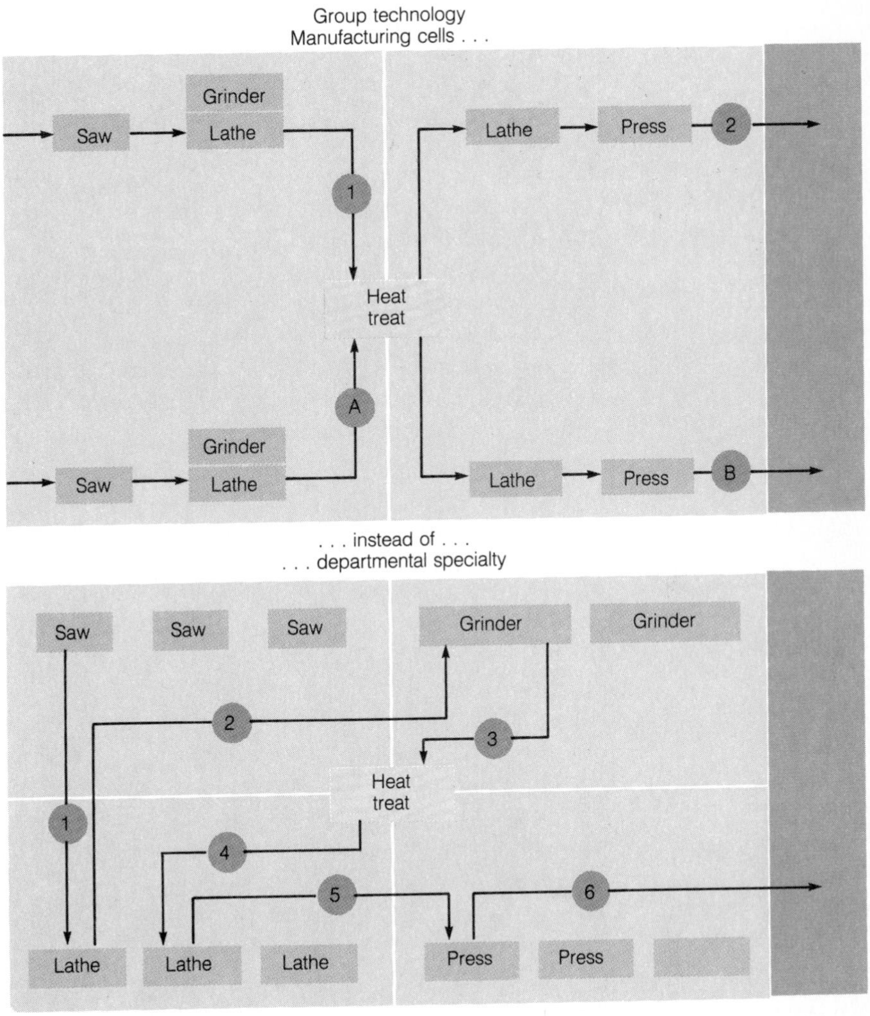

departments is usually staffed by a worker who specializes in that function. Getting a job through a shop can be a long and complicated process because there's a lot of waiting time and moving time involved (usually between 90 percent and 95 percent of the total processing time).

The Japanese, on the other hand, consider all the operations required to make a part and try to group those machines together. The upper part of Exhibit 15.4 shows clusters of dissimilar machines that are designed to be a work center for a given part or family of parts. One operator runs all three machines shown in the upper left-hand corner, which increases the utility of the individual operator and eliminates the move and queue time between operations in a given cluster. Thus, not only does productivity go up, but work-in-process inventory comes down dramatically.

To achieve this, people have to be flexible; to be flexible, people must identify with their company and have a high degree of job security.

Jidoka—quality at the source. When management demonstrates a high degree of confidence in people, it is possible to implement a quality concept that the Japanese call *Jidoka*. The word means "Stop everything when something goes wrong." It can be thought of as controlling quality at the source. Instead of using inspectors to find the problems that somebody else may have created, the worker in a Japanese factory becomes his or her own inspector. This concept was developed by Taiichi Ohno, who was vice president of manufacturing for Toyota Motor Company, in the early 1950s.

Ohno was convinced that one of the big problems faced by Toyota was bringing quality levels up to the necessary standards to penetrate the world automotive market. He felt that there was too much looking over each other's shoulders; he wanted every individual to be responsible personally for the quality of the product or component that he or she produced.

Ohno determined that the best thing to do was to give each person only one part to work on at a time so that under no circumstances would he or she be able to bury problems by working on alternate parts. Jidoka push buttons were installed on the assembly lines. If anything went wrong—if a worker found a defective part, if he or she could not keep up with production, if production was going too fast according to the pace that was set for the day, or if he or she found a safety hazard—that worker was obligated to push the button. When the button was pushed, a light flashed, a bell rang, and the entire assembly line came to a grinding halt. People descended on the spot where the light was flashing. It was something like a volunteer fire department: people were coming from the industrial engineering department, from management, from everywhere to respond to that particular alarm, and they fixed the problem on the spot. Meanwhile, the workers polished their machines, swept the floor, or did whatever else they could to keep busy, but the line didn't move until the problem was fixed.

Jidoka also encompasses automated inspection, sometimes called *autonomation*. Just like automation and robotics, the Japanese believe that if inspection can be done by a machine, because it's faster, easier, more repeatable, or redundant, then a person shouldn't have to do it. However, the inspection step is a part of the production process, does not involve a separate location or person to perform it, and automatically shuts off a machine when a problem arises. This prevents the mass production of defective parts.

Now contrast that with our operations. How long does it take us to find a problem, to convince somebody it's real, to get it solved, and to get the fix implemented? How much do we produce in the meantime that isn't any good?

Line shutdowns in Japan are encouraged to protect quality and because management has confidence in the individual worker. No one likes to see a line stopped, but Ohno suggests that a day without a single Jidoka drill can mean people aren't being careful enough.

Just-in-Time production. The Japanese system is based on a fundamental concept called Just-in-Time production. It requires the production of precisely the necessary units in the necessary quantities at the necessary time, with the objective of achieving plus or minus *zero* performance to schedule. It means that producing one extra piece is just as bad as being one piece short. In fact, anything over the minimum amount necessary is viewed as waste, since effort and material expended for something not needed now cannot be utilized now. (Later requirements are handled later.) Exhibit 15.5 highlights what Just-in-Time is, what it does, what is required, and what it assumes. That's another different idea for us, since our measure of good performance has always been to meet or exceed the schedule. It will be a most difficult concept for American manufacturing management to accept because it is contrary to our current practice, which is to stock extra material "just-in-case" something goes wrong.

The Just-in-Time concept applies primarily to a repetitive manufacturing process. It does not necessarily require large volumes, but is restricted to those operations that produce the same parts over and over again. Ideally, the finished product would be repetitive in nature. However, as a Westinghouse

EXHIBIT 15.5

Just-in-Time

WHAT IT IS	WHAT IT DOES
• Management philosophy • "Pull" system through the plant	• Attacks waste (time, inventory, scrap) • Exposes problems and bottlenecks • Achieves streamlined production
WHAT IT REQUIRES	**WHAT IT ASSUMES**
• Employee participation • Industrial engineering/basics • Continuing improvement • Total quality control • Small lot sizes	• Stable environment

Source: Adapted from Chris Gopal (of Price Waterhouse), "Notes on JIT."

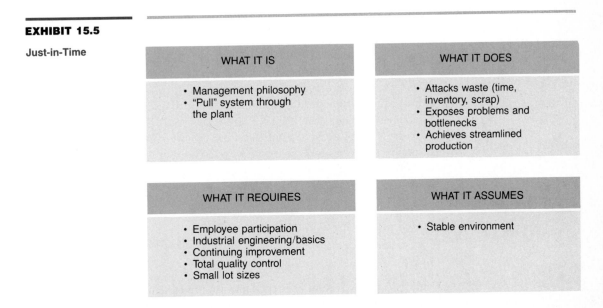

EXHIBIT 15.6 **Inventory Hides Problems**

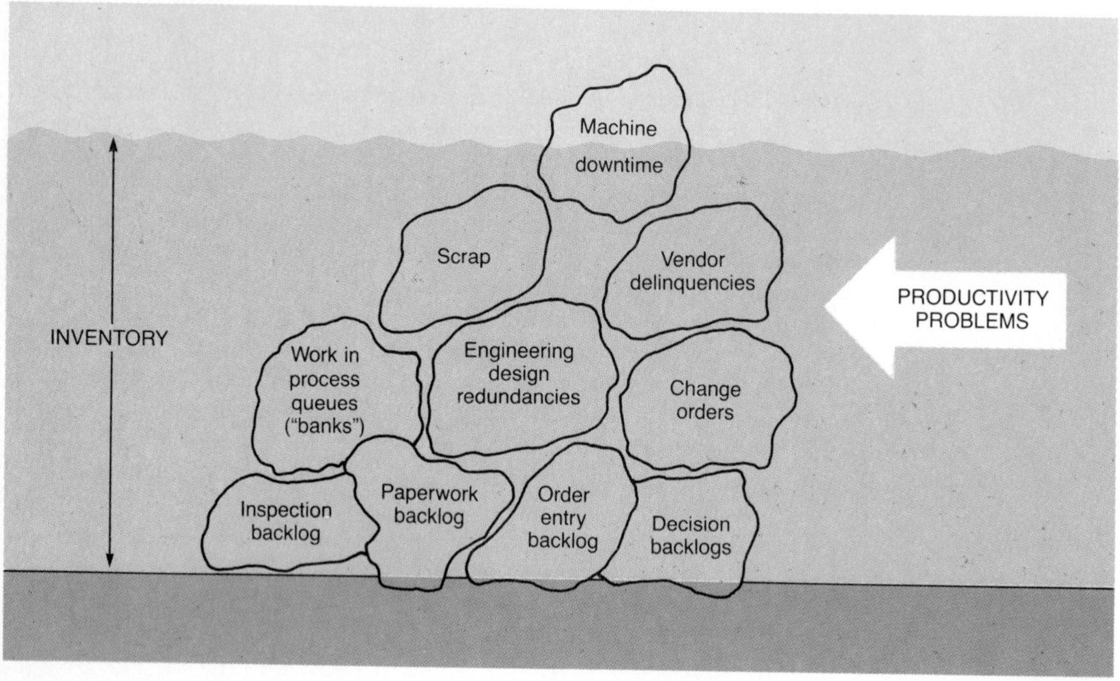

team learned during a visit to Mitsubishi Inazawa, a Japanese elevator manufacturer, the repetitive segments of the business may only appear several levels down the product structure. Even so, applying Just-in-Time concepts to a portion of the business produced significant improvements for them.

Under Just-in-Time, the ideal lot size is *one piece*. The Japanese view the manufacturing process as a giant network of interconnected work centers, where the perfect arrangement would be to have each worker complete his or her task on a part and pass it directly to the next worker just as that person was ready for another piece. The idea is to drive all queues toward zero in order to:

- Minimize inventory investment.
- Shorten production lead times.
- React faster to demand changes.
- Uncover any quality problems.

Exhibit 15.6 is a graphic that the Japanese use to depict the last idea. They look on the water level in a pond as inventory and the rocks as problems that might occur in a shop. A lot of water in the pond will hide the problems. Management will assume everything is fine. Invariably, the water level drops at the worst possible time, such as during an economic downturn. Management must then address the problems without the necessary resources to solve them. The Japanese say it is better to force the water level down on purpose (especially in good times), expose the problems, and fix them now, before they cause trouble.

The zeal with which the Japanese hammer at inventories is incredible. To begin with, inventory is viewed as a negative, not an asset. According to Toyota, "The value of inventory is disavowed." Auto air conditioner manufacturer Nippondenso's attitude is even more severe: inventory is "the root of all evil." Almost universally, the Japanese see inventory as a deterrent to product quality. Finally, since the shop floor is programmed to have very little inventory, the slightest aberration in the process that results in extra parts is readily visible and serves as a red flag to which immediate response is required.

Since it is impossible to have every worker in a complex manufacturing process adjacent to one another, and since the network also includes outside suppliers, the Japanese recognize that the system must allow for transit time between centers. However, transfer quantities are kept as small as possible. Typical internal lot sizes are one tenth of a day's production, vendors ship several times a day to their customers, and constant pressure is exercised to reduce the number of lots in the system.

Just-in-Time production makes no allowances for contingencies. Every piece is expected to be correct when received. Every machine is expected to be available when needed to produce parts. Every delivery commitment is expected to be honored at the precise time it is scheduled. Consequently, the Japanese heavily emphasize quality, preventive maintenance, and a high degree of mutual trust among all participants in the manufacturing enterprise. The process is gospel and everyone conscientiously adheres to it.

Uniform plant loading. To use the Just-in-Time production concept, it is necessary that production flow as smoothly as possible in the shop. The starting point is what the Japanese call *uniform plant loading*. Its objective is to dampen the reaction waves that normally occur in response to schedule variations. For example, when a significant change is made in final assembly, it creates changed requirements in feeder operations that are usually amplified because of lot sizing rules, setups, queues, and waiting time. By the time the impact is felt at the start of the supply chain, a 10 percent change at assembly could easily result in a 100 percent change at the front end.

The Japanese tell us the only way to eliminate that problem is to make the perturbations at the end as small as possible so that we get ripples going through the shop, not shock waves. Japanese companies accomplish it by setting up a firm monthly production plan for which the output rate is frozen. Most U.S. manufacturing people have been trying to achieve that for years, without success, because they've tried to freeze a specific, sequential configuration. The Japanese circumvent this issue by planning to build the same mix of products every day, even if the total quantities are small. For example, if

EXHIBIT 15.7

Toyota Example of Mixed-Model Production Cycle in a Japanese Assembly Plant

Model	Monthly Quantity	Daily Quantity	Cycle Time (minutes)
Sedan	5,000	250	2
Hardtop	2,500	125	4
Wagon	2,500	125	4

Sequence: Sedan, hardtop, sedan, wagon, sedan, hardtop, sedan; wagon, etc.

they're only building a hundred pieces a month, they'll build five each day. Since they expect to build some quantity of everything that's on the schedule daily, they always have a total mix available to respond to variations in demand.

Going even further, they'll take those five units and intermix them on the assembly line. An example of how Toyota would do this is shown in Exhibit 15.7. Presume three kinds of vehicles being made in an assembly plant: sedans, hardtops, and station wagons. The monthly rates shown are then reduced to daily quantities (presuming a 20-day month) of 250, 125 and 125, respectively. From this, the Japanese compute the necessary cycle times. *Cycle time* in Japan is the period of time between two identical units coming off the production line. The Japanese use this figure to adjust their resources to produce precisely the quantity that's needed, no more, no less.

The Japanese do not concern themselves with achieving the rated speeds of their equipment. In American shops, a given machine will be rated at 1,000 pieces per hour so if we need 5,000 pieces we'll run it five hours to obtain this month's requirement. The Japanese will produce only the needed quantity each day, as required. To them, cycle time is an indicator that defines how to assemble their resources to meet this month's production. If the rate for next month changes, the resources will be reconfigured.

Kanban production control system.[2] This kind of an approach calls for a control system that is simple and self-regulating and that will provide good management visibility. The shop floor/vendor release and control system is called *Kanban* (kahn-bahn), from the Japanese word meaning *card.* It is a paperless system, using dedicated containers and recycling traveling requisitions/cards, which is quite different from our old, manual shop-packet systems. This is referred to as a **Kanban pull system,** since the authority to produce or supply comes from downstream operations. While work centers

[2] Authors' note: The majority of factories in Japan don't use Kanban. Kanban is a Toyota Motor Company system, not a generic Japanese one. However, many companies in both the United States and Japan are pull systems with other types of signaling devices.

EXHIBIT 15.8

Flow of Two Kanbans

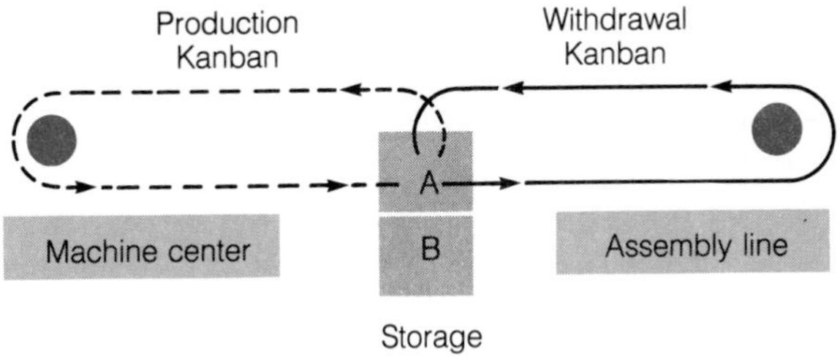

and vendors plan their work based on schedules, they execute based on Kanbans, which are completely manual.

There are two types of Kanban cards. The production Kanban authorizes the manufacturing of a container of material. The withdrawal Kanban authorizes the withdrawal and movement of that container. The number of pieces in a container never varies for a given part number.

When production rates change, containers will be added to or deleted from the system, according to a simple formula. The idea of safety stock is included in the basic calculation but is limited to 10 percent of a single day's demand. This gives the theoretical number of Kanban/containers required. In practice, efforts are made to reduce the number in circulation to keep inventories to a minimum.

The flow of Kanban cards between two work centers is shown in Exhibit 15.8. The machining center shown is making two parts, A and B, which are stored in standard containers next to the work center. When the assembly line starts to use Part A from a full container, a worker takes the withdrawal Kanban from the container and travels to the machining center storage area. He or she finds a container of Part A, removes the production Kanban, and replaces it with the withdrawal Kanban card, which authorizes him or her to move the container. The freed production Kanban is then placed in a rack by the machining center as a work authorization for another lot of material. Parts are manufactured in the order in which cards are placed on the rack (the Japanese call this the Kanban hanging), which makes the set of cards in the rack a dispatch list.[3]

[3] Many firms use withdrawal cards only. Under the simplest form of one-card system, the worker at the assembly line (or more likely a material handler) walks to the machine center with an empty container and a withdrawal Kanban. He or she would then place the empty container at a designated spot, attach the withdrawal card to a filled container, and carry it back to the assembly line. The worker at the machining center would know that a refill is required. This type of system is appropriate where the same part is made by the same people every day.

If it turns out that the demand for Part A is greater than planned and less than planned for Part B, the system self-regulates to these changes, since there can be no more parts built than called for by the Kanban cards in circulation. Mix changes of 10 to 20 percent can easily be accommodated because the shifts are gradual and the increments are small. The ripple effect upstream is similarly dampened.

The same approach is used to authorize vendor shipments. When both the customer and the vendor are using the Kanban system, the withdrawal Kanban serves as the vendor release/shipping document while the production Kanban at the vendor's plant regulates production there.

The whole system hinges on everyone doing exactly what is authorized and following procedures explicitly. In fact, the Japanese use no production coordinators on the shop floor, relying solely on supervisors to ensure compliance. Cooperative worker attitudes are essential to its success.

Results can be impressive. Jidosha Kiki, a Bendix breaking components affiliate in Japan, installed the Kanban/Just-in-Time system in 1977 with the help of its customer, Toyota. Within two years they had doubled productivity, tripled inventory turnover, and substantially reduced overtime and space requirements. Jidosha Kiki stated that this was a slow and difficult learning process for its employees, even considering the Japanese culture, because all the old rules of thumb had to be tossed out the window and deep-rooted ideas had to be changed.

Minimized setup times. The Japanese approach to productivity demands that small lots be run in production. This is impossible to do if machine setups take hours to accomplish. In fact, we use the economic order quantity (EOQ) formula in the United States to determine what quantity we should run to absorb a long and costly setup time.

The Japanese have the same formula, but they've turned it around. Instead of accepting setup times as fixed numbers, they fixed the lot sizes (very small) and went to work to reduce setup time.

That is a crucial factor in the Japanese approach. Their success in this area has received widespread acclaim. Many Americans have been to Japan and witnessed a team of press operators change an 800-ton press in 10 minutes. Compare those data with ours as shown in Exhibit 15.9. The Japanese aim for single-digit setup times (i.e., less than 10 minutes) for every machine in their factories. They've addressed not only big things, like presses, but small molding machines and standard machine tools as well.

Successful setup reduction is easily achieved when approached from a methods engineering perspective. The Japanese separate setup time into two segments: *internal*—that part that must be done while a machine is stopped, and *external*—that part that can be done while the machine is operating. Simple things, such as the staging of replacement dies, fall into the external category, which, on the average, represents half of the usual setup time.

EXHIBIT 15.9

Minimizing Setup Time—Hood and Fender Press Comparison (800-ton press)

	Toyota	USA	Sweden	W. Germany
Setup time	10 minute	6 hour	4 hour	4 hour
Setups/day	3	1	—	½
Lot size	1 day*	10 days	1 month	—

* For low-demand items (less than 1,000 month), as large as seven days.

EXHIBIT 15.10

Setup Reduction Results at JKC

Setup Time	1976	1977	1980
>60 minutes	30%	0	0
30–60 minutes	19%	0	0
20–30 minutes	26%	10%	3%
10–20 minutes	20%	12%	7%
5–10 minutes	5%	20%	12%
100 seconds–5 minutes	0	17%	16%
<100 seconds	0	41%	62%

Another 50 percent reduction can be achieved by the application of time and motion studies and practice. (It is not unusual for a Japanese setup team to spend a full Saturday practicing changeovers.) Time-saving devices like hinged bolts, roller platforms, and folding brackets for temporary die staging are commonly seen, all of which are low-cost items.

Only then is it necessary to spend larger sums, to reduce the last 15 percent or so, on things such as automatic positioning of dies, rolling bolsters, and duplicate tool holders. The result is that 90 percent or *more* of present setup times can be eliminated if we have a desire to do so.

Referring again to Jidosha Kiki Corporation, Exhibit 15.10 shows the remarkable progress the company made in just four years. These data relate to all the machines in the factory. It's interesting that while we are quite impressed that two thirds of their equipment can be changed over in less than 2 minutes, the company is embarrassed that 10 percent still takes more than 10 minutes!

The savings in setup time are used to increase the number of lots produced, with a corollary reduction in lot sizes. This makes the use of Just-in-Time production principles feasible, which in turn makes the Kanban control system practical. All the pieces fit together.

Respect for people

The second guiding principle for the Japanese, along with elimination of waste, is respect for people. This principle, too, has seven basic elements:

1. Lifetime employment.
2. Company unions.
3. Attitude toward workers.
4. Automation/robotics.
5. Bottom-round management.
6. Subcontractor networks.
7. Quality circles.

Lifetime employment. Much has been written about the Japanese concept of lifetime employment. When a Japanese worker is hired for a permanent position with a major industrial firm, he has a job with that company for life (or until retirement age) provided he works diligently. If economic conditions deteriorate, the company will maintain the payroll almost to the point of going out of business. We should understand, though, that these kinds of benefits apply only to permanent workers, who constitute about one third of the work force in Japan. What's important is that the concept is pervasive. When people can identify with the company as the place they're going to spend their working life, not just an interim place to get a paycheck, then they have a tendency to be more flexible and to want to do all they can do to help achieve the company's goals.

Company unions. When MacArthur introduced the union concept to Japan during the post-World War II reconstruction period, he undoubtedly had in mind trade unions, but the Japanese didn't think that way. Japanese workers at Toyota were concerned about Toyota. They really didn't identify with the other automobile manufacturing employees in the rest of the country. They identified not with the kind of work they were doing but rather with the company they were working for. So Toyota formed a union that included everybody who worked for Toyota, no matter what their skills were. The objective of both the union and management was to make the company as healthy as possible so there would be benefits accruing to the people in a secure and shared method. The resulting relationship was cooperative, not adversarial.

The Japanese system of compensation reinforces these goals because it is based on company performance bonuses. Everybody in a Japanese company, from the lowest employee to the highest, gets a bonus twice a year. In good times the bonus is high (up to 50 percent of their salaries), while in bad times there may be no bonus. As a result, the employees have an attitude that says, "If the company does well, I do well," which is important from the standpoint of soliciting the workers' help to improve productivity.

Attitude toward workers. The attitude of management toward the workers is also critical. The Japanese do not look at people as human machines. As a matter of fact, they believe that if a machine can do a job, then a person *shouldn't* do it because it's below his or her dignity. In the United States, we all believe in the value of human worth, but when it comes to the shop floor we don't necessarily practice it. A corollary concept says that if workers are really as important as people you must also believe that they can do much more than you are now giving them the opportunity to do. We normally have to see people in a job for some time before we accept their competence.

The Japanese say, "What workers are doing today is only tapping their capability. We must give them an opportunity to do more." Thus, a third and most significant attitude requires that the management system provide every worker with an opportunity to display his or her maximum capabilities. These concepts are practiced, not just discussed, and the Japanese spend more for employee training and education—at all levels—than any other industrial nation.

Automation robotics. When people feel secure, identify with the company, and believe that they are being given an opportunity to fully display their talents, then the introduction of automation and robotics is not considered staff-cutting moves. The Japanese feel that this is a way to eliminate dull jobs so people can do more important things, and they have been making major capital investments in these areas. Interestingly enough, Japan has invested one third of its gross national product in capital improvements for the last 15 years, compared to about 19 percent for the United States during the same period.

In automation, the Japanese have invested first in low-cost enhancements to existing or standard equipment, using some clever approaches. In the capital area they have been concentrating on programmable robots. A recent survey showed that Japan had approximately five times the number of programmable robots (some of them quite simple) as the United States. Most of those robots were built here. Again, we shipped our technology to Japan, where it was used to build products to compete with us. Today, Japan is building its own robots at a rapid pace and has become both the leading robot producer and robot user in the world. (A survey in the June 19, 1984, *Japan Economic Journal* gives the 1984 planned sales of the top 20 Japanese robot producers as around 100,000 units.)

Since the Japanese honestly believe that robots free people for more important tasks, there is little worker resistance to the robotics implementation. In fact, workers go out of their way to figure out how to eliminate their jobs, if they find them dull, because they know the company will find something better and more interesting for them to do.

Bottom-round management. This kind of mutual reliance is a manifestation of the management style the Japanese call *bottom-round management*. It's also been identified as *consensus management* or *committee management*. It is innate to the Japanese culture because they have grown up with the concept that the importance of the group supercedes that of the individual. Consider that in Japan more than 100 million people are crowded on a tiny island group about the size of California, 80 percent of which is mountainous, living very closely together in bamboo and paper houses. In those circumstances, citizens must have considerable respect for their neighbors, or social survival would be impossible. This cultural concept is ideal in a manufacturing facility because the process requires that people work together in a group to make a product. The individual cannot function independently, without concern for others, because he or she would only get out of synchronization with the rest of the group and disrupt the process.

Bottom-round management is a slow decision-making process. In attempting to arrive at a true consensus, not a compromise, the Japanese will involve all potentially interested parties, talk over a problem at great length, often interrupt the process, seek out more information, and retalk the problem until everyone finally agrees. While we have often criticized the slowness of this method, the Japanese have an interesting response.

They say, "You Americans will make an instant decision and then you'll take a very long time to implement it. The decision is made so quickly, without consulting many of the people it's going to affect, that as you try to implement it you begin to encounter all sorts of unforeseen obstacles. Now, in our system, we take a long time to make a decision, but it only takes a short time to implement it because by the time we've finally reached a conclusion, everybody involved has had their say."

A key to bottom-round management is that decisions are made at the lowest possible level. In essence, the employees recognize a problem, work out a potential solution with their peers, and make recommendations to the next level of management. They, in turn, do the same thing and make the next recommendation up the line. And so it goes, with everyone participating. As a result, top management in Japanese companies makes very few operating decisions, being almost totally devoted to strategic planning. It is important to note, though, that the use of bottom-round management makes it extremely difficult to manage a large, complex manufacturing organization. That's another reason why the Japanese build focused factories, which were discussed earlier.

Subcontractor networks. The specialized nature of Japanese factories has fostered the development of an enormous subcontractor network; most subcontractors have fewer than 30 employees. More than 90 percent of all Japanese companies are part of the supplier network, which is many tiers deep, because there is so little vertical integration in Japanese factories.

There are two kinds of suppliers: specialists in a narrow field who serve multiple customers (very much like U.S. suppliers), and captives, who usually make a small variety of parts for a single customer. The second kind is more predominant in Japan. Of course, the idea of sole-source suppliers is diametrically opposed to the U.S. multisource concept. Sole-source arrangements work in Japan because the relationships are based on a tremendous amount of mutual trust. They seek long-term partnerships between customer and supplier. Americans who do business with Japanese companies know that the very first stages of negotiation involve an elaborate ceremony of getting to know one another to determine whether there is a potential long-term relationship in the picture. Japanese businesspeople are rarely interested in a one-time buy, so it's a different way of doing business for us.

Suppliers in Japan consider themselves part of their customers' family. Very often key suppliers are invited to company functions such as picnics or parties. In return, suppliers deliver high-quality parts many times per day, often directly to the customer's assembly line, bypassing receiving and inspection. A typical scenario would have the supplier's truck arriving at a precise time of day, the driver unloading the truck, transporting the parts into the factory and delivering them to the assembly line at a given station, depositing the parts, picking up the empty containers, loading them in the truck, and leaving, without any interference. No receiving, no incoming inspection, no paper, no delays. It's an almost paper-free system, all built on mutual trust.

Trust is a two-way street. Because so many of the suppliers are small and undercapitalized, a Japanese customer will advance money to finance them, if necessary. Customer process engineers and quality personnel will help vendors improve their manufacturing system to meet the rigid quality and delivery standards imposed. Efforts will also be made to help vendors reduce their production process cost to help ensure their profitability. When there is an economic downturn, however, the customers will do more of the work in-house which they were previously buying from vendors. They do this to protect their own work force. Vendors are small and do not have the permanent, lifetime employment guarantees that the major companies do. However, this is known in advance and is an accepted risk to the suppliers.

Quality circles. Another interesting technique, with which many Americans are already familiar, is quality circles. The Japanese call them *small group improvement activities* (SGIA). A quality circle is a group of volunteer employees who meet once a week on a scheduled basis to discuss their function and the problems they're encountering, to try to devise solutions to those problems, and to propose those solutions to their management. The group may be led by a supervisor or a production worker. It usually includes people from a given discipline or a given production area, like Assembly Line A or the turning department. It can also be multidisciplined, for instance all material handlers who deliver materials to a department and the industrial engineers who work in that department. It does have to be led, though, by someone who is trained as a group leader. The trainers are facilitators, and each one may coordinate the activities of a number of quality circles. Westinghouse, for example, has 275 quality circles and about 25 facilitators.

In a full-blown company-wide system such as Westinghouse, quality circles can be an elaborate process to initiate. Circle members are taught brainstorming techniques, how to define a problem, how to evaluate solutions, how to prepare flowcharts, etc. They learn how to make a presentation to management so their proposals will sell. This takes time, effort, and money. Some companies do this all on company time, while others allow one half hour on company time and a half hour of personal time.

It really works because it's an open forum. It takes some skill to prevent it from becoming a "gripe" session, but that's where the trained group leaders keep the members on target. Interestingly enough, only about one third of the proposals generated turn out to be quality related. More than half are productivity oriented. It's really amazing how many good ideas these motivated employees can contribute toward the profitability and the improved productivity of their companies. Quality circles are actually a manifestation of the consensus, bottom-round management approach but are limited to these small groups.

Practical results have been impressive. In 1960, when Toyota had the equivalent of an American suggestion system, the company averaged one proposal per employee per year, about four times as good as the U.S. national average. Toyota subsequently initiated a quality circle program and 10 years later had increased the number of proposals to 2½ per employee; the acceptance rate jumped to 70 percent. This was a fivefold improvement in acceptable ideas in a 10-year span. In 1976, the program averaged 15 proposals per person per year with an 83 percent acceptance ratio.

On a small, introductory scale quality circles can be initiated quickly and can help set the stage for expansion into other areas and the introduction of other concepts. However, full realization of its benefits will take time (it took 10 years at Toyota) and should not be embarked upon as this year's catchy, "gee whiz" program.

Authors' Postscript: Applicability of Japanese Concepts to U.S. Manufacturers

Of the 14 techniques and concepts described in Wantuck's paper, some may be eliminated as inappropriate or impractical in the American environment:

- Lifetime employment, company unions, and subcontractor networks. These rely on the Japanese culture or economic relationships not prevalent in the United States.
- Attitude toward workers, bottom-round management, and quality circles. These are characteristics of Japanese management style, which will be appropriate only for some U.S. companies.
- Focused factory networks and automation/robotics. These are most definitely applicable to U.S. companies, but currently they are major strategic and investment decisions performed by top management. In short, few operations managers can influence these decisions in the short run.

What do we have left to import? According to Edward J. Hay, a consultant in Just-in-Time production,[4]

> We have left a group of six elements in which, in my opinion, are the most important elements of all. In addition to being most important they are the most appropriate and practical for the American environment and are well within our ability to implement. One of the main reasons why these techniques are so transferable is because, in one form or another, most of them had their origins in the United States. As a group, they make up a powerful set of manufacturing and quality control techniques, increasingly being referred to under the collective term, Just-in-Time production. For purposes of perspective, I have sorted these six elements under three labels:
>
> 1. Attitude.
>   Just-in-Time (philosophy).
>   Quality at the source.
> 2. Manufacturing engineering.
>   Minimized setup times.
>   Uniform plant load.
>   Group technology.
> 3. Production control.
>   Kanban system.
>
> The philosophy of Just-in-Time is the framework that gives organization and meaning to the other five elements. It requires:
>
> —Production of only the minimum necessary units in the smallest possible quantities at the latest possible time.
> —Elimination of inventories.

15.2 HOW TO ACCOMPLISH JIT PRODUCTION

In this section, our objective is to explain how to accomplish JIT production. To structure our discussion we will follow the steps given in Exhibit 15.11, expanding on some ideas given in the Wantuck paper and explaining selected features not previously discussed. In going through these steps, keep in mind that we are talking about *repetitive* production systems—those that make the same basic product over and over again. Also keep in mind that we are talking about features of a *total system,* which means that actions taken regarding any one of these features will have some impact on other features of the system. Finally, note that different companies use different terms to describe their JIT systems. IBM uses *continuous flow manufacture,* Hewlett-Packard uses *stockless*

[4] Edward J. Hay, "Just-in-Time Production, A Winning Combination of Neglected American Ideas," East Greenwich, R.I.: Edward J. Hay Associates, p. 2.

EXHIBIT 15.11 **How to Accomplish Just-in-Time Production**

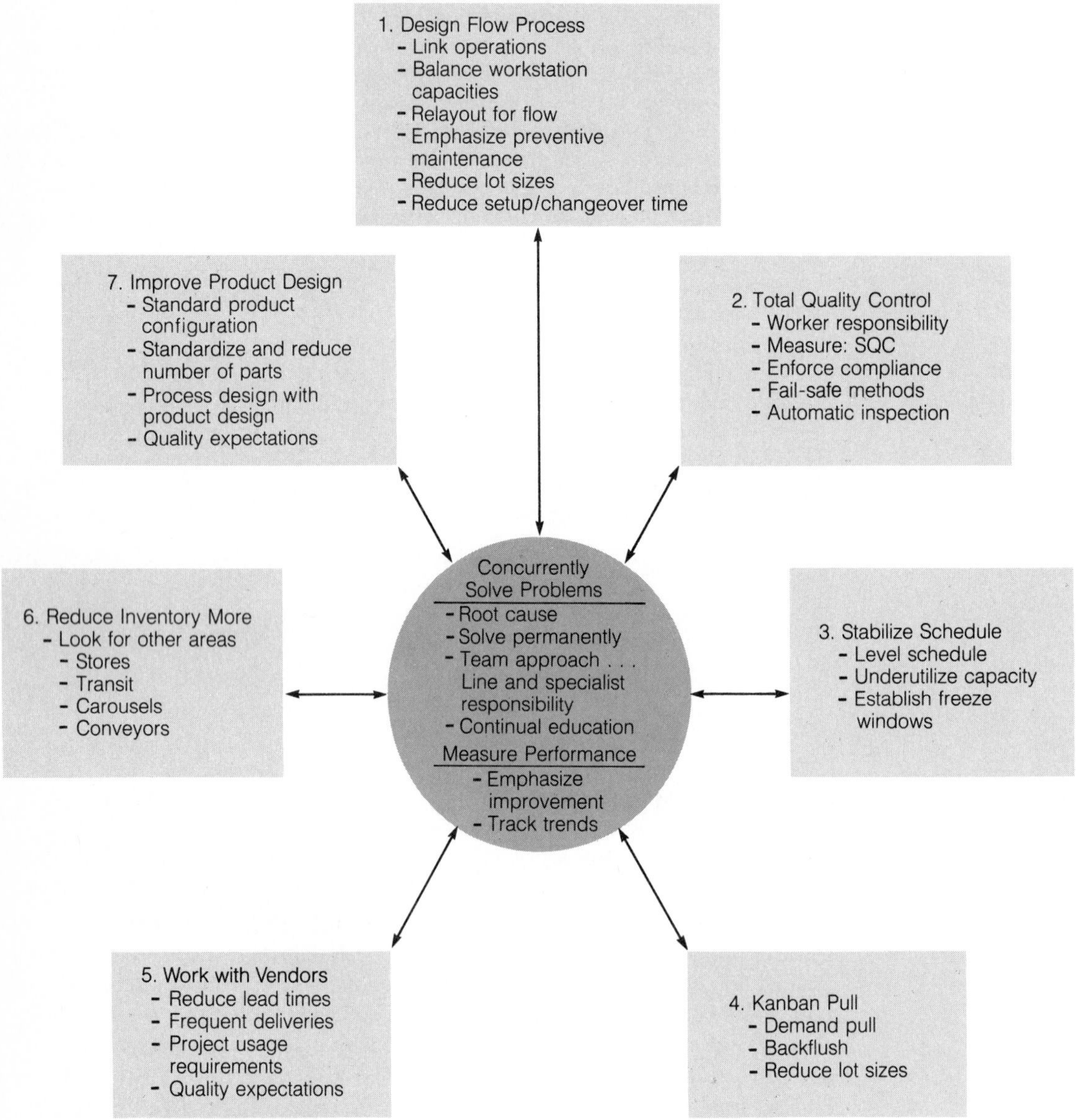

This diagram is modeled after the one used by Hewlett-Packard's Boise plant to accomplish its JIT program.

production at one plant and *repetitive manufacturing system* at another, while many Japanese firms use *Toyota system*.

Design Flow Process

JIT requires that the plant layout be designed to ensure balanced work flow with a minimum of work in process. This means that we must conceive of each workstation as part of a production line, whether or not a physical line actually exists. Capacity balancing is done using the same logic as for an assembly line, and operations are linked through a pull system (described below). This also means that the system designer must have a vision of how all aspects of the internal and external logistics system tie to the layout.

Preventive maintenance is emphasized to ensure that a continuous work flow is not interrupted by machine downtime or as a result of poor quality from malfunctioning equipment. Much of this maintenance is carried out by the operator, since he or she is responsible for the quality of products coming off the machine, and also because of his or her sensitivity to the idiosyncrasies of the machine as a result of working on it day in and day out. Finally, the fact that the JIT philosophy favors many simple machines rather than a few complex ones enables the operator to handle routine maintenance activities.

Reduction in setup/changeover time and lot sizes are interrelated and are key to achieving a smooth flow (and JIT success in general). Exhibit 15.12 illustrates the fundamental relationship between lot size and setup cost. Under the traditional approach, setup cost is treated as a constant, and the optimal order quantity is shown as six. Under the Kanban approach of JIT, setup cost is treated as a variable and the optimal order quantity, in this case, was reduced to two. This type of reduction can be achieved by employing setup time-saving procedures such as those described earlier in the chapter. *The ultimate goal of JIT from an inventory standpoint is to achieve an economic lot size of one.*

Total Quality Control

JIT and total quality control have become linked in the minds of many managers—and for good reason. **Total quality control** refers to "building in" quality and *not* "inspecting it in." It also refers to all plant personnel taking a responsibility for maintaining quality, not just "leaving it to the quality control department." When employees assume this responsibility, JIT is permitted to work at its optimal level, since only good products are pulled through the system. What results is having your cake and eating it too—high quality and high productivity. Exhibit 15.13 illustrates this subtle relationship.

Statistical quality control uses simple control methods (control charts, primarily) to monitor *all* aspects of a production system. If all aspects of a production process (raw materials, machine variability, etc.) are in control,

EXHIBIT 15.12 **Hypothetical Lot-Size Graphs under Traditional and Kanban Approaches**

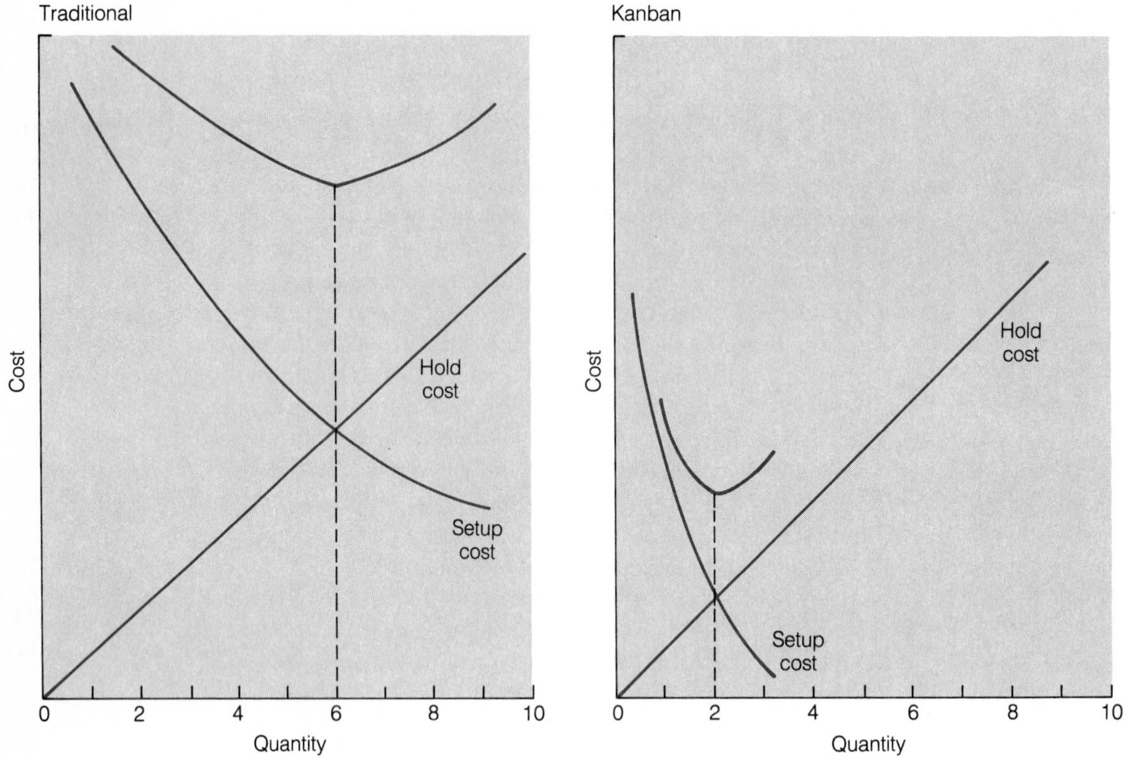

Source: C. Carl Pegels, "The Kanban Production Management Information System," in *Management by Japanese Systems*, eds. Sang M. Lee and Gary Schwendiman (New York: Praeger Publishers, 1982), p. 160.

then one can assume that the product coming out of that process is good. When items are produced in small lots, such as in the Kanban system, the inspection may be reduced to just two items—the first and the last. This is sometimes referred to as a sampling goal of $n = 2$. That is, inspect the first item of a batch and the last item; if they are perfect, assume that those produced in between are perfect as well.

Stabilize Schedule

Efficient repetitive manufacture requires a level schedule over a fairly long time horizon. (The actual length depends on many factors, but primarily two: whether the firm makes to order or makes to stock, and the range of product options it offers.) As Hall notes, "A level schedule is one that requires material

EXHIBIT 15.13

Relationship between JIT and Quality

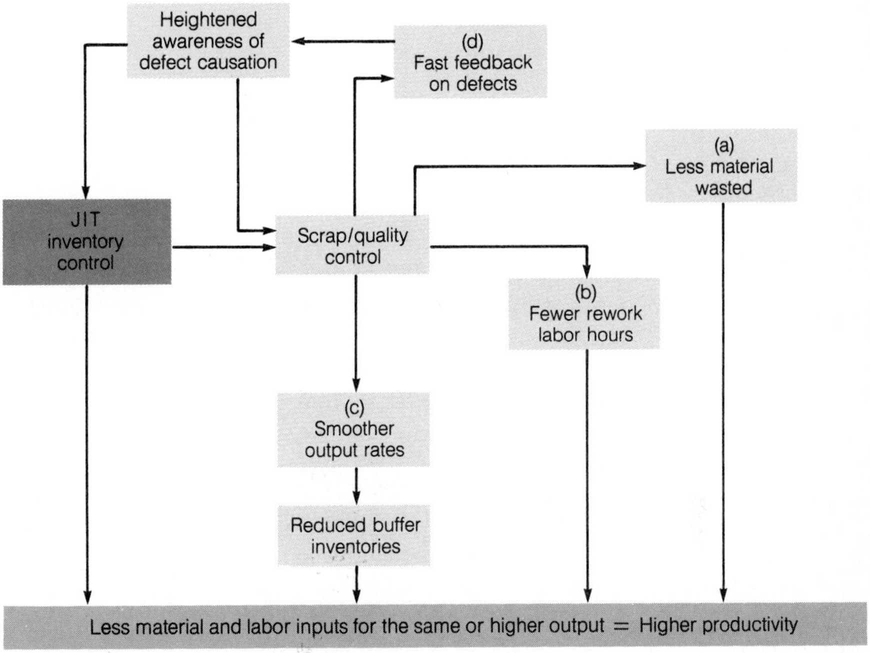

Source: Richard J. Schonberger, "Some Observations on the Advantages and Implementation Issues of Just-in-Time Production Systems," *Journal of Operations Management* 3, no. 1 (November 1982), p. 5.

to be pulled into final assembly in a pattern uniform enough to allow the various elements of production to respond to pull signals. It does not necessarily mean that the usage of every part on an assembly line is identical hour by hour for days on end; it does mean that a given production system equipped with flexible setups and a fixed amount of material in the pipelines can respond."[5] The term *freeze windows* refers to that period of time during which the schedule can't be changed.

Underutilization of capacity is probably the most controversial feature of JIT. Underutilized (or excess) capacity is really the cost incurred by eliminating inventories as a buffer in the system. In traditional manufacturing, safety stocks and early deliveries are used as a hedge against shortfalls in production from such things as poor quality, machine failures, and unanticipated bottlenecks. Under JIT, excess labor and machines provide the hedge. It should be emphasized, however, that excess capacity in the form of labor and equipment is generally far less expensive than carrying excess inventory. Moreover,

[5] Robert H. Hall, *Zero Inventories* (Homewood, Ill.: Dow Jones–Irwin, 1983), p. 64.

excess labor can be put to work on other activities during those periods when it is not needed for direct production. Further, the low idle-time cost incurred by the relatively inexpensive machines favored by JIT producers makes machine utilization a secondary issue for many firms. Finally, much of the excess capacity is by design—workers are expected to have time at the end of their shift to meet with their work groups, clean up their workstations, and ponder potential improvements.

Kanban Pull

Most people view JIT systems as pull systems, where the material is drawn or sent for by the users of the material as needed.[6] Production Kanbans are just one of many devices to signal the need for more parts. It is critical to note here that the signal sent is for a standard lot size conveyed in a standardized container, not just for a "bunch of parts."

Some typical Kanban-type signals used to initiate production are:

"Hey Joe, make me another widget."

A flashing light over a work center, indicating need for more parts.

A signal marker hanging on a post by the using workstation. (See Exhibit 15.14.)

Pull systems typically start with the master schedule specifying what the final assembly schedule will be. By referring to the final assembly schedule, materials schedulers and supervisors can see the days during the month when each part will be needed. They determine when to schedule supplier deliveries or internal parts manufacture by offsetting lead times from final assembly dates. Basically, then, the final assembly schedule exerts the initial pull on the system, with Kanbans controlling the flow. (See Exhibit 15.15. The flow of Kanbans is shown in Exhibit 15.8.)

Backflush is a term used to designate how component parts are accounted for in a pull system. Rather than keeping track of each individual part on a daily basis by job, JIT systems typically explode the bill of materials periodically, such as once a month, and calculate how many of each part must have gone into the final product(s). This eliminates a major shop-floor data collection activity, and thereby further simplifies the production management job.

Reducing lot sizes in a pull system means removing interstage inventory. This is accomplished in a variety of ways—by better balance of operations so that only two Kanban containers are used between two workstations rather than three, by moving workstations closer together to cut transit time, by automating processes that have high variability, and of course by Just-in-Time deliveries.

---

[6] As Hall notes, citing a no-nonsense plant supervisor, "You don't never make nothin' and *send* it no place. Somebody has to come and get it." Ibid., p. 41.

EXHIBIT 15.14

Diagram of Outbound Stockpoint with Warning Signal Marker

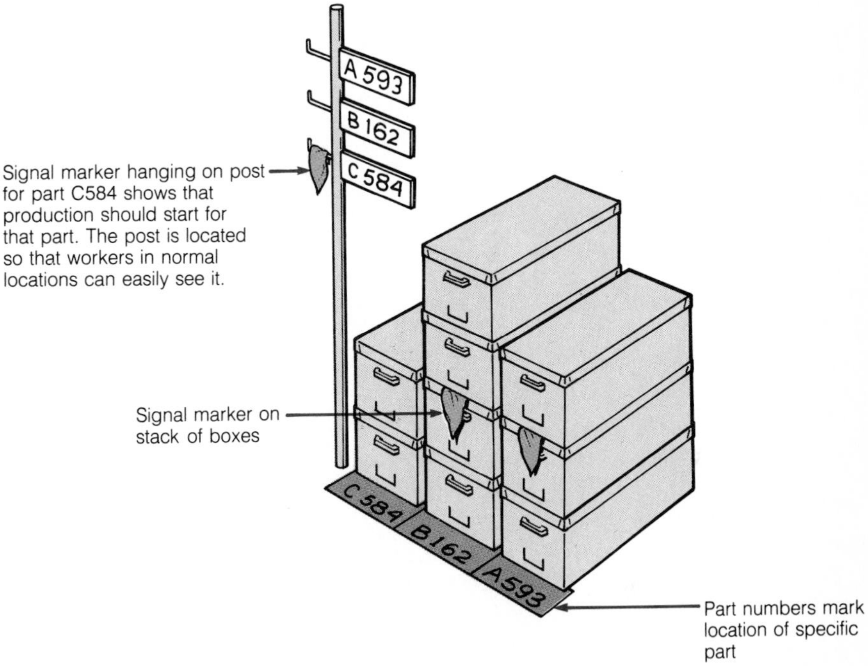
A593
B162
C584
Signal marker hanging on post for part C584 shows that production should start for that part. The post is located so that workers in normal locations can easily see it.
Signal marker on stack of boxes
C584
B162
A593
Part numbers mark location of specific part

Source: Robert Hall, *Zero Inventories* (Homewood, Ill.: Dow Jones-Irwin, 1983), p. 51.

Work with Vendors

All the items in this category of Exhibit 15.11 except "project usage requirements" have been discussed earlier. *Project usage requirements* means that the vendor is given a long-run picture of the demands that will be placed on his production and distribution system. This permits him to develop a level production schedule.

Reduce Inventory More

Stores, transit systems, carousels, and conveyors are places where inventory is held; thus, they are targets for inventory reduction efforts. Often there is heated debate when it comes to doing away with them. One reason is that such inventory locations are frequently the focus or result of a previous inventory improvement effort that has shown good results compared to the system used before that. The people involved in such an effort are unlikely to rush to support doing away with something that, at long last, works.

EXHIBIT 15.15 **Pull System**

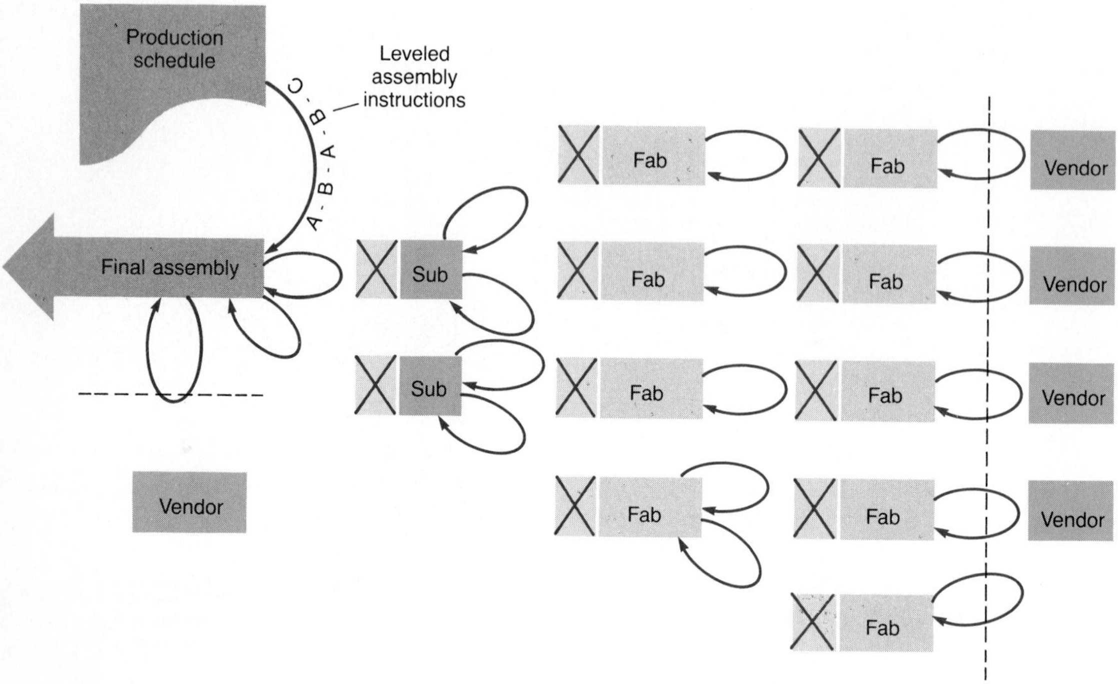

Source: Edward J. Hay, "Just-in-Time Production, A Winning Combination of Neglected American Ideas," East Greenwich, R.I.: Edward J. Hay Associates, 1983, p. 12.

Improve Product Design

Standard product configurations and fewer, standardized parts are important elements in good product design for JIT. When the objective is to establish a simple routine process, anything that reduces variability in the end item or the materials that go into it is worth careful consideration.

Process design with product design refers to the early involvement activities among product designers, process designers, and manufacturing discussed in Chapter 3. Besides improving the producibility of the product, such interaction facilitates the processing of engineering changes. Engineering changes (ECs) to a product can be extremely disruptive to the production process. They alter the specifications of the product, which in turn may call for new materials, new methods, and even new schedules. To minimize such disruptions, many JIT producers introduce their ECs in batches, properly sequenced with the production schedule, rather than one by one, as is common in traditional manufacturing. While batching sounds obvious and simple, it requires a great deal of coordination and a willingness to delay what may be significant changes in a product design in exchange for maintaining production stability.

Concurrently Solve Problems and Measure Performance

A JIT application is not an overnight, turnkey installation. Rather, it is an evolutionary system that is continually seeking ways of improving production. Improvement comes through looking at problems as challenges rather than threats—problems that can be solved with common sense and detailed, rigorous analysis.

The techniques for problem solving are primarily statistical methods we have discussed throughout the book. These are summarized in Exhibit 15.16. Effective problem solving means that the problem is solved permanently. Because JIT requires a team effort, problems are treated in a team context. Staff personnel are expected to be seen frequently on the shop floor, and in some companies are expected to arrive a half hour before production workers to ensure that things are in order, thus avoiding problems.

Continual education is absolutely essential if the system is to avoid stagnation. While JIT may cost little in the way of hardware, it requires a substantial investment in training people at all levels of the organization in what the system demands and how they fit into it.

Many performance measures emphasize the number of processes and practices changed to improve materials flow and reduce labor content, and the degree to which they do so. If the processes physically improve over time, lower costs will follow. According to Hall, a department head in a Japanese JIT system is likely to be evaluated on the following factors:

1. Improvement trends, including number of improvement projects undertaken, trends in costs, and productivity. Productivity is measured as:

$$P = \frac{\text{Measurement of department output}}{\text{Total employees (direct + indirect)}}$$

2. Quality trends, including reduction in defect rates, improvement in process capability, and improvement in quality procedures.
3. Running to a level schedule and providing parts when others need them.
4. Trends in departmental inventory levels, e.g., speed of flow.
5. Staying within budget for expenses.
6. Developing work force skills, versatility, participation in changes, and morale.[7]

[7] Ibid., pp. 254–55.

EXHIBIT 15.16

Techniques for Problem Solving

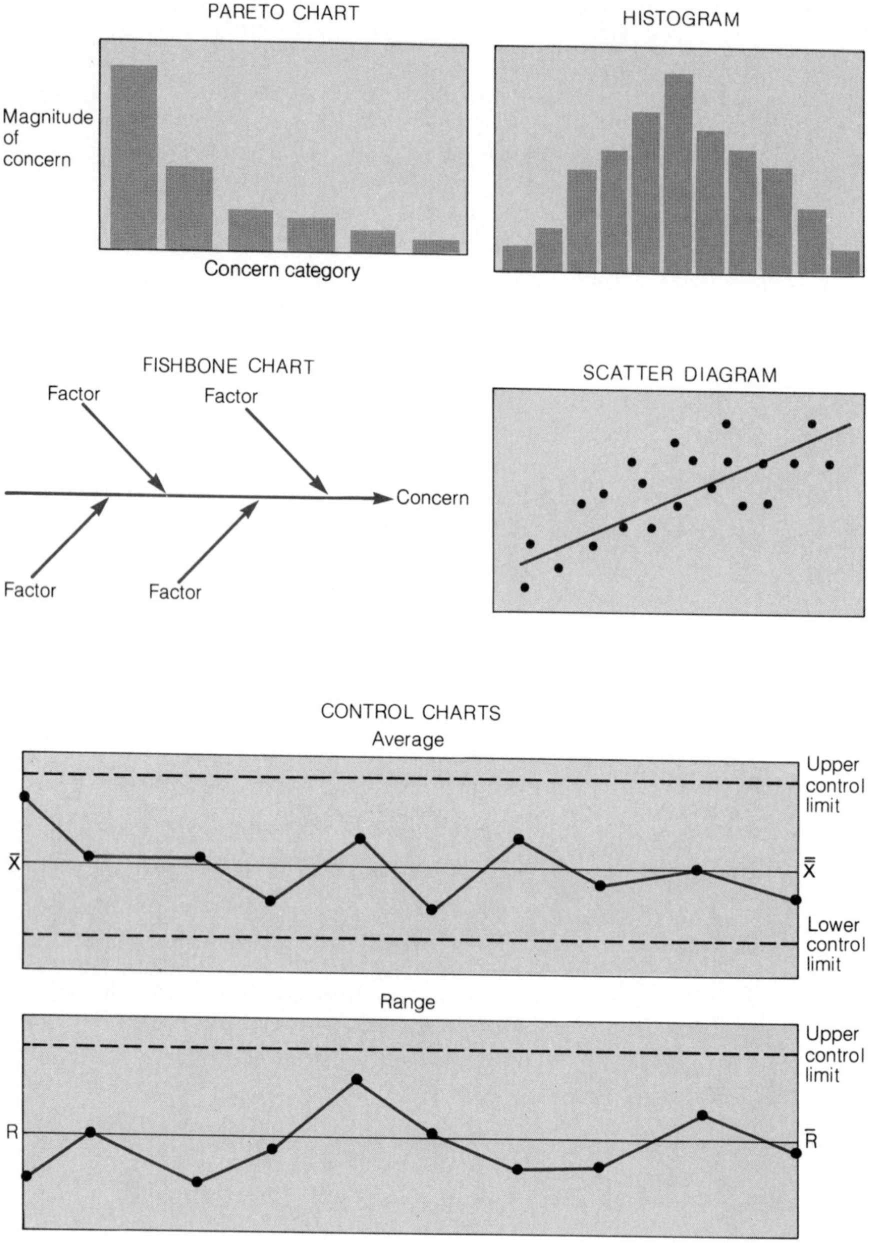

15.3 SOME TECHNICAL ISSUES ABOUT KANBAN

Kanban as a Fixed-Order Quantity/Reorder Point Inventory System

Both Kanban and the simple fixed-order quantity/reorder point system are reactive systems. Both systems are designed to replenish inventory, not in anticipation of future orders, but as soon as the inventory is depleted. Also, both assume continuous review, predetermined reorder points, and fixed replenishment quantities. The inventory behavior under the two systems is identical with the one exception that Kanban displays a lumpy usage pattern. The reason for this is that unlike the fixed-order quantity system where parts are withdrawn one at a time, Kanban withdraws a fixed number of them in standard sized containers. Such standardized containers, in turn, define the lot size, so each time one is withdrawn, a reorder point is reached.

In light of the basic similarity of the two systems, why has Kanban performed so well, while the fixed-order quantity system has generally failed? The answer is that Japanese management has been able to structure a manufacturing environment conducive to Kanban operation. The major contribution of Japanese management (relative to inventory control) lies in demand management and lead-time management, two features that are implicit in our discussion of JIT.

JIT and MRP

Exhibit 15.17 provides a general comparison between JIT and MRP. Although the exhibit suggests that an application is "either/or," current practice is to combine elements of both and link them together. That is, many companies use the basic MRP logic and procedures for ordering purposes and materials management, which are then executed under pull-system procedures. This has been referred to as *synchro-MRP*.

MRP is generally considered an excellent data support system, even when it is not used for its detailed scheduling capabilities. Many firms are realizing that the detail schedules and material requirements for a sequence of operations created by an MRP program can be simplified and JIT production procedures used instead. For example, a master production schedule shows when the finished product needs to be completed. A run through the MRP program produces detailed requirements stating order release dates, inventory requirements, and so on for the entire sequence. Suppose, however, that this sequence is located in the same productive area—that is, all the personnel, machines, and equipment are visible to each other. Further, suppose the entire series of operations is under the control of the same manager. In this case, it would be

EXHIBIT 15.17

Key Differences between JIT and MRP

Operating System Characteristics	JIT	MRP
Focus	Physical operations	Information system
Rates of output	Level schedule	Variable production plan
Work authorization	Kanban pull	Master schedule push
Data philosophy	Minimize data captured	Capture all data
Problem response	Resolve and fix	Regenerate
Clerical personnel	Decreased	Increased
Forms of control	Shop floor, visual, line workers	Middle management, reports, staff
Capacity adjustment	Visual, immediate	Capacity requirements planning, deferred

far more practical to tell the manager the required output and leave it up to his or her judgment as to how and when to produce it. The manager may elect to use JIT, which would then focus on the output at the last stage and draw from the previous stages to support that production and keep the amount of overall inventory low.

Spreadsheets, such as Lotus 1-2-3, are often used for local scheduling within specific production areas rather than using MRP output. For example, a department in a manufacturing firm may download the MRP requirements specified in the company MRP program to a spreadsheet on a personal computer located in that department. The department may then develop its own schedule and feed this back into the company's MRP program. Thus, while still interacting with the companywide MRP system, departments are able to retain local control, which often achieves better results than the detailed main system MRP program. Hewlett-Packard, for example, has software packages that use personal computers with spreadsheets and other software packages that allow interaction with its main MRP system.

JIT and Cost Accounting

Cost accounting systems have focused on direct labor since the Industrial Revolution. However, under JIT (and computer integrated management) overhead costs are dominant, often 20 times as high as direct labor. Moreover, with permanent employment, workers maintaining their own equipment, and other measures, the distinction between direct and indirect labor has become blurred for cost-allocation purposes. Hewlett-Packard has recognized this and has eliminated the cost category of direct labor, now using simply "labor" instead.

It appears at this time that the primary difference between traditional and JIT cost accounting is the application of overhead on the basis of product time in the system (cycle time) rather than direct labor or machine hours.[8]

15.4 COMPANY EXPERIENCES WITH JIT

Exhibit 15.18 summarizes the experiences of five major U.S. companies who have installed JIT (and TQC, total quality control). As can be seen, the impact on these companies' performance measures is overwhelmingly positive. Similar results have been reported in European and British firms. One study of 80 plants in Europe, for example, listed the following benefits from JIT:

1. An average reduction in inventory of about 50 percent.
2. A reduction in throughput time of 50 to 70 percent.
3. Reduction in setup times of as much as 50 percent without major investment in plant and equipment.
4. An increase in productivity of between 20 and 50 percent.
5. Payback time for investment in JIT averaged less than nine months.[9]

Additional success stories abound in the production-control journals. This is not to say that the implementation of JIT is trouble free, however. Exhibit 15.19 indicates that some problems just won't go away quickly.

15.5 JIT IN SERVICES

Service organizations and service operations within manufacturing firms present interesting opportunities for application of JIT concepts. In the following section we present an edited version of a paper by Randall J. Benson, a consultant for Coopers & Lybrand, that explains why JIT is not just for the factory.[10] Two additional cases describe successful use of JIT techniques at Midway Airlines and at a Japanese sushi house. The Midway Airlines case describes how total quality control techniques and some problem-solving tools mentioned in the Benson paper were used to solve this airline's late-departure problem. The Japanese sushi house article discusses how Just-in-Time techniques are applied to the operations of the sushi house.

How Does JIT Apply to Services?

While there are many differences between service and manufacturing, they also share the most basic attributes of production. Both manufacturing and

---

[8] Mohan V. Tatikonda, "Just-in-Time and Modern Manufacturing Environments: Implications for Cost Accounting," *Production and Inventory Management Journal* 28, no. 1 (1988), pp. 1–5.

[9] Amrik Sohal and Keith Howard, "Trends in Materials Management," *International Journal of Production Distribution and Materials Management* 17, no. 5 (1987), pp. 3–41.

[10] Randall J. Benson, "JIT: Not Just for the Factory," *Proceedings from the 29th Annual International Conference for the American Production and Inventory Control Society,* St. Louis, Missouri, October 20–24, 1986, pp. 370–74.

EXHIBIT 15.18 Summary of JIT/TQC Activities for Five U.S. Companies

Company Name (Division)	Product Category	Production Characteristics	Start/ Reporting Period	Who Initiated Action?	Why Started?	Where Started?	How Implemented	Problems Observed
Deere & Company	Heavy machinery Farm equipment Lawn-care equipment	Repetitive manufacturing	1980 1982–1984	CEO/ manufacturing managers (trip to Japan) Steering committee	Survival Foreign competition	Four plants	Visit to Japan Task force in plant Education Pilot projects Work-flow analysis	Initially, worker doubts Underestimated educational needs
Black & Decker (consumer power tools)	Electrical products	Repetitive manufacturing Floor space 385,000 sq. ft. Employees: 1,010	1982 1982–1984	Staff Production control committee	Large expenses in inventory carrying costs (high interest rates)	Assembly Purchasing	Education Balanced flow Rewrote work procedures Started to produce in weekly quantity	Vendor resistance Resistance to change
Omark Industries	Forestry equipment and sporting goods	Mostly repetitive 18 plants	1980 1981–1983	CEO (trip to Japan) Corporate task force Plant study terms	Corporate task force found JIT/ TQC/employee involvement as reason for success	Five pilot plants	Steering committee Plant study team Presentation by corporate staff Pilot projects	Middle management resistance Underestimated training needs Slowdown after first projects
Hewlett-Packard (Computer Systems division)	Computer and test systems	Forming/assembly/testing Many options	TQC: 3 years JIT: 1 year (1983–1984)	Steering committee	Questioned why overseas suppliers produced quality products	Assembly flow rearrangement	TQC first Employee training/ involvement Leveled schedule Process simplification	Cut WIP levels too quickly Major changes faster than could assimilate
FMC	Industrial equipment Defense Automotive Electrical	Multiple divisions with variety of products 50 manufacturing and mining operations	1982 1982–1984	Operations support staff Manufacturing vice president Controller	Survival Absence of patent protection Keen cost competition	Pilot projects Automotive and electrical: well-managed first operation	Seminars Pilot project Pilot plants Setup time Inventory target Positive reinforcement	Fine tuning Not enough manpower to implement ideas Occasional line stop from parts shortage

Company Name (Division)	Start/ Reporting Period	Labor Productivity Improvement	Setup Time (improvement)	Inventory Reductions	Quality Improvements	Space Savings	Production Lead Times	Effect on Corporate Culture	Comments
Deere & Company	1980 1982–1984	Subassembly: 19–35% Welding: 7–38% Manufacturing cost: 10–20% Materials handling 40%	Presses: 38–80% Drills: 24–33% Shears: 45% Grinders: 44% Avg. 45%	Raw steel: 40% Purchased parts 7% Crane shafts: 30 days → 3 days Average: 31%	Implemented process control charting in 40% of operations	Significant	Significant	Unexpected enthusiasm More responsive to all Increased employee participation	Japan's Yanmar Diesel's support Did not introduce TQC in the beginning
Black & Decker (Consumer power tools)	1982 1982–1984	Assembly: 24 operators → 6 operators Support: 7 → 5	Punch press: 1 hr. → 1 min. Drastic in many areas	Turns: 16 → 30	Reduced complaints in packaging 98% 100& customer service level	Significant	Products made in weekly lots 50% → 95%		Number of suppliers reduced by 40% Quality audit of suppliers
Omark Industries	1981/Jan. 1981–1983	Plant A: 30% Plant B: 30% Plant C: 20%	A: 165 → 5 min. B: 43 → 17 min. C: 360 → 17 min. D: 45 → 6 min.	Product A: 92% Product B: 29% Product C: 50%	Product A scrap and rework: 20% Product E Customer service cost: 50%	Parts travel distance: Product C: 24% Product E: 68%	A: 3 weeks → 3 days E: 21 days → 3 days	Hourly workers making decisions High employee involvement	JIT/TQC at the same time
Hewlett-Packard (Computer Systems Division)	TQC: 3 yrs. JIT: 1 yr. (1983–1984)	Standard hours: 87 hrs. → 39 hrs.	Not available	PC Assembly inventory $675,000 (100) → $190,000 (28)	Solder defects: 5000 PPM → 100 Scrap: $80,000/mo. → $5,000	PC Assembly: 8,500 → 5,750 sq.ft.	PC Assembly 15 days → 1.5 days	Corporate culture (H-P way) helped JIT Proud to be among first to implement JIT/TQC	Adopted TQC/JIT separately MRP did not support JIT
FMC	1982 1982–1984	Direct labor productivity: 13% (Automotive service equipment division)	Defense equipment group: 60%–75% Automotive/electrical: 80%	Turns: 1.9 → 4.0 (Automotive service equipment division)	Customer service: 88% → 98% Cost of quality: 3.5% → 2.1% (Auto. Svc. Eq. Div.)	Automotive/electrical: 25% Eliminated stockroom	Automotive/electrical: 1 mo. → 1 wk Suppliers: months → days	Grass-roots movement toward manufacturing excellence	Reduced suppliers by 50% Corporate plan to implement TQC/JIT at all plants by 1986

From Kiyoshi Suzaki, "Comparative Study of JIT/TQC Activities in Japanese and Western Companies," First World Congress of Production and Inventory Control, Vienna, Austria, 1985, pp. 63–66.

EXHIBIT 15.19

Implementation Problems

Problem Area	Was a Problem	Still a Problem	Now Under Control
Customer schedule changes	62.0%	57.4%	4.6%
Poor supplier quality	59.3	49.1	10.2
Poor production quality (internal)	57.4	43.5	13.9
Inability to change paperwork systems	57.4	46.3	11.1
Shortage of critical parts	57.4	44.4	13.0
Supplier inability to deliver JIT	56.5	49.1	7.4
Lack of employee commitment	49.0	30.5	18.5
Inability to reduce setup time	48.1	36.1	12.0
Inadequate equipment and tooling	45.4	30.6	14.8
Surplus of noncritical parts	43.5	33.3	10.2
Lack of top-management commitment	42.6	27.8	14.8
Labor contract problems	35.2	25.9	9.3

Source: Albert F. Celley, W. H. Gregg, A. W. Smith, and Ann A. Vondermbsc, "Implementation of JIT in the United States," *Journal of Purchasing and Materials Management* 22, no. 4 (Winter 1986), pp. 9–15.

services employ processes that add value to the basic inputs to create the end product or service.

JIT is commonly defined as an operating philosophy which has as its basic objective the *elimination of waste*. Waste, in the words of Cho, is "anything other than the *minimum* amount of equipment, materials, parts, space, and workers time, which are absolutely *essential*" to *add value* to the product or service." (Emphasis added.) *Value* is the functionality, usefulness, or importance as perceived by the customer.

JIT focuses on processes, not products. We can apply it to any group of processes, from manufacturing to service production. The JIT goal is approached by testing each step in the production process to determine if it adds value to the product or service. If the steps do not add value, then the process is a candidate for re-engineering. In this way, the production of processes will gradually and continually improve.

Both manufacturing and service production can be improved with JIT because both are systems of production processes and because JIT is essentially a process-oriented waste-elimination philosophy. The themes for JIT process improvement should apply equally in a service environment.

How Do the JIT Themes Fit Service?

The **JIT themes,** summarized in Exhibit 15.20, make no reference to manufactured products. These themes are applicable to all areas of JIT manufacturing, regardless of the specific technique being applied. Because they are process as opposed to product oriented, they should apply equally well to service production. Indeed, they lead to some interesting insights into service operations management.

EXHIBIT 15.20

The Themes of JIT

- Total visibility.
- Synchronization and balance.
- Respect for people.
- Flexibility.
- Continuous improvement.
- Responsibility for the environment.
- Holistic approach.
- Simplicity.

Total visibility

Total visibility means that the equipment, people, material, processes, process status, and process flows are visible to those participating in the production process. Visibility has a special marketing importance to service producers because the customer participates in the process. The service process is often the key tangible evidence of the value and quality of the service. The visibility inherent in a well-designed service production process favorably influences the customer's perception of the quality of the service.

Synchronization and balance

Synchronization and balance refers to the ability to match the sales cycle to the production cycle and the production cycle to the supply cycle. This is the concept that "If you don't need it now, don't make it now." A balanced operation runs at the same rate at every production stage because the processes are synchronized and extra inventory is eliminated. Synchronization and balance make smooth production possible without requiring complicated controls.

Service producers are typically required to synchronize sales and production almost perfectly because customers will not wait for service if they have other alternatives.

Respect for people

The people in the firing line are responsible for JIT production. They have huge, often untapped capacity to solve both simple and complex production problems. They must be allowed and expected to figure out how the system is supposed to work, identify and remove the obstacles, and refine the process by implementing their ideas. Focused improvement groups and quality circles allow employees to organize for continuous improvement. JIT producers hire people for their heads as well as their hands.

People play an extremely important role in service production. Each time a service employee interacts with a customer, a "moment of truth" takes place. It determines the customer's perception of the quality and value of the service. A negative moment of truth carries a much heavier weight in the customer's perception than a positive one. Service employees are often personally responsible for the quality, consistency, and value of the service. They are responsible for personally selling the service during each customer encounter. Respect for people is a matter of survival in the service industry.

Flexibility

Flexibility refers to the ability to rapidly adapt the process to produce what the customers want when they want it, without wasting production resources. Service producers must be especially flexible because they must produce a service instantaneously and tailor the service to the customer's expectations.

Continuous improvement

Because JIT is a philosophy, not a system, it doesn't end when an implementation project is completed. It is a vision of an absolute ideal that cannot be reached in actual practice. Continuous improvement involves moving always closer to the ideal by making many small improvements in the processes.

Because services tend to be labor intense, most of the improvements change the employees' activities. Many service firms have successfully used employee-centered improvement groups to improve the quality and value of the service.

Responsibility for the environment

JIT assumes that those who design, manage, and operate the production processes are totally responsible for the outcome. There is not room for Murphy's Law in a JIT operation. Problems are not inherent in the process. They can be eliminated, given an attitude of perfection and the time, attention, and creativity to experiment with process improvements.

Service operations have no more room for errors than manufacturing. In labor-intensive service industries, the employees have even more impact on the performance of the production process. Moreover, responsibility for the service environment means being totally responsible for the success or failure of the service. Every service employee must take full responsibility for each moment of truth that takes place during the customer contact and for improving the production processes.

Holistic approach

JIT is not a piecemeal approach to process improvement. Many JIT consultants can relate stories of clients who implemented JIT methods in a small area of their factory but have not seen the benefits in terms of substantial profit improvements. JIT works best when it is implemented as a company philosophy to eliminate waste, not just a technique to reduce inventory. All departments and all levels of operations get involved in eliminating waste. The piecemeal approach creates "islands of JIT," but falls short of achieving the companywide improvements that improve the firm's competitiveness.

In service firms the holistic approach is essential, because production and marketing cannot be separated. Service firms must approach production process changes as marketing needs change because the customers are influenced by the production process itself. A customer's perception of the quality and value of the service is largely determined by the production process.

Simplicity

JIT stresses simplicity over complexity and sophistication. Simplicity is necessary for control by the employees over the production processes. This self-control will improve the performance and reliability of the product or service. Simplicity is also required for understanding. The simplicity of the process allows people who run the process to identify opportunities for process improvements and to plan the process changes themselves.

Simplicity is no less important in the service sector. It may be even more important due to the worker-intensive nature of the service delivery system. Furthermore, customer participation will be more successful if the process is simple. Customers may not be frequent or experienced participants, yet their ability to perform their function will influence their satisfaction with the service. Simple processes, systems, and controls allow customers to easily engage, participate in, and disengage from the service delivery process.

The JIT themes described above are entirely appropriate for service firms. In fact, one could argue that the JIT improvements in manufacturing actually allow the manufacturer to operate more like a successful service firm. Isn't stockless production based on synchronization of fast-flow processes an excellent description of a service process?

The application of JIT techniques in service areas is consistent with the JIT themes. JIT has already been applied successfully in diverse service industries. This is a significant step for service firms because the service sector presently lacks a general and comprehensive approach to service operation improvements. A service version of JIT holds the promise to rationalize service operation across very dissimilar industries.

Which JIT Techniques Are Appropriate for Services?

Exhibit 15.21 lists some of the important techniques used to achieve the JIT philosophy in manufacturing firms. Many of them have been successfully applied by service firms. Just as in manufacturing, the suitability of each technique and the corresponding work steps depends on the characteristics of the firm's markets, production and equipment technology, skill sets, and corporate culture. Service firms are not different in this respect.

Organize problem-solving groups

Focused improvement groups and quality circles improve the quality and cost performance of manufacturing processes. In addition, they enhance com-

EXHIBIT 15.21

The JIT Techniques

- Organize problem-solving groups.
- Upgrade housekeeping.
- Upgrade quality.
- Clarify process flows.
- Revise equipment and process technologies.
- Level the facility load.
- Eliminate unnecessary activities.
- Reorganize physical configuration.
- Introduce demand-pull scheduling.
- Develop supplier networks.

munication and job satisfaction. The groups use methods such as group dynamics, brainstorming, Pareto analysis, and root-cause analysis to rethink manufacturing processes. Support for problem-solving groups demonstrates respect for the employees and a willingness to draw on everyone's potential to improve performance.

Honeywell is extending its quality circles from manufacturing into its service operations. Other corporations as diverse as First Bank/Dallas, Standard Meat Company, and Miller Brewing are using similar approaches to improve service. British Airways used quality circles as a fundamental part of its strategy to implement new service practices.

Upgrade housekeeping

Good housekeeping means more than winning the "clean broom award." It means that only the necessary items are kept in a work area, that there is a place for everything, that everything is clean and in a constant state of readiness. The employees clean their own area. Good housekeeping sets the stage for the other JIT techniques.

Service organizations like McDonald's, Disneyland, and Speedi-Lube have recognized the critical nature of housekeeping. Their dedication to housekeeping has meant that service processes work better, the attitude of the continuous improvement is easier to develop, and customers perceive that they are receiving better service.

Upgrade quality

Quality products and services are a function of the quality of the processes that produced them. The only cost-effective way to improve quality is to develop reliable process capabilities. Process quality is quality at the source—it guarantees first-time production of consistent and uniform products and services.

McDonald's is famous for building quality into its service delivery process. It literally "industrialized" the service delivery system so that part-time, casual workers could provide the same eating experience anywhere in the world. Quality doesn't mean producing the best, it means consistently producing products and services that meet the "fitness for use" criteria.

Clarify process flows

Clarification of the process flow usually involves redesign of the process routing, redesign of the work group, and development of flexible staffing. Process flows in factories usually center on the movement of manufactured items. In the service sector, process flows may involve information, materials, people (especially customers), ideas, and so on. Clarification of the flows, based on the JIT themes, can dramatically improve the process performance.

For example, Federal Express changed air flight patterns from origin-to-destination to origin-to-hub where the freight is transferred to an outbound plane for the destination. This revolutionized the air transport industry. The order entry department of a manufacturing firm converted from functional departments to customer-centered work groups and reduced the order processing lead time from 8 to 2 days. A county government used the JIT approach to cut the time to record a deed transfer by 50 percent. Supermaids sends in a team of house cleaners, each with her own responsibility, to clean the house quickly with parallel processes. Changes in process flows can literally revolutionize service industries.

Revise equipment and process technologies

This technique involves evaluation of the equipment and processes for their ability to meet the process requirements, process consistently within tolerance, and to fit the scale and capacity of the work group. Setup-reduction efforts take place at this stage. Routine maintenance procedures also begin here. Often the changes favor smaller machines, faster setups, simpler operation, and preventive maintenance.

Speedi-Lube converted the standard service-station concept to a specialized lubrication and inspection center by changing the service bays from drive-in to drive-through and by eliminating the hoists and building pits under the cars where the employees have full access to the lubrication areas on the vehicle.

A hospital reduced the operating-room setup time so that it had the flexibility to peform a wider range of operations without reducing the operation room availability.

Level the facility load

Factories develop uniform plant loads by synchronizing production with demand. They build a little of everything each period to meet demand rather than building large lots for inventory. The key concept is, "If you need it daily, build it daily." The production rate for final assembly sets the pace for the feeder operations.

Service firms also synchronize production with demand. They have developed unique approaches to leveling demand so they can avoid making the customer wait for service. They achieve more uniform loads by using reservation systems, complementary services, and incentives to use the service at off-peak times. The source sells time for less during the evening. McDonald's offers a special breakfast menu in the morning. Retail stores use take-a-number systems. The post office charges more for next-day delivery. These are all examples of the service approach for creating uniform facility loads.

Eliminate unnecessary activities

JIT manufacturers eliminate unnecessary activities by evaluating each step in the process flow for value added. If the step does not add value, it is a candidate for elimination. If the step does add value it may be a candidate for re-engineering to improve the process consistency or to reduce the time to perform the tasks.

A manufacturer analyzed its order-entry process and discovered that about 85 percent of the steps during booking, scheduling, and acknowledging a customer order involved moving, sorting, checking, correcting, copying, and filing, while only about 15 percent of the steps were actually analyzing the customer order. The company eliminated or redesigned many of the steps and reduced the order entry time by 75 percent.

A hospital discovered that a significant amount of time during an operation was spent waiting for an instrument that was not available when the operation began. It could develop a checklist of instruments required for each category of operation. Speedi-Lube eliminated steps, but it also added steps that didn't improve the lubrication process but did make the customer feel more assured about the work that was being performed.

Reorganize physical configuration

The work-area configurations frequently require reorganization during a JIT implementation. Often manufacturers accomplish this by setting up manufacturing cells to produce items in small lots, synchronous to demand. These cells, based on the principles of group technology, allow for a flexible number of workers per cell. Due to their compactness and lack of in-process inventory, manufacturing cells provide immediate feedback on quality. Separate operations are often consolidated in the cell. These cells amount to "micro-factories" inside the plant.

Most service firms are far behind manufacturers in this area. However, a few interesting examples do come out of the service sector. Some hospitals, instead of routing patients all over the building for tests, exams, X-rays, and injections are reorganizing their services into work groups based on the type of problem. Teams that treat only trauma are common, but other work groups have been formed to treat less immediate conditions like hernias. These amount to "micro-clinics" within the hospital facility.

Introduce demand-pull scheduling

The idea for the pull system was originally borrowed by Japanese manufacturers from the American service industry. The inspiration came while a Japanese business delegation was visiting the United States in the 1960s. Some of the delegation had visited a modern supermarket and they observed that the shelves were not replenished based on a set schedule, but rather when the customer removed the items from the shelf. This system required no complicated scheduling whatsoever because the shelf inventory level was visible and because the restocking process was designed to be very simple. They took the concept home to Japan and perfected it for manufacturing.

Due to the nature of service production and consumption, demand-pull (customer-driven) scheduling is necessary for operating a service business. Moreover, many service firms are separating their operations into "back room" and "customer contact" facilities. This approach creates new problems in coordinating the schedules between the facilities. The original Wendy's restaurants were set up so the cooks could see the cars enter the parking lot. They put a pre-established number of hamburger patties onto the grill for each car. This pull system was designed to have a fresh patty on the grill before the customer even placed an order.

Develop supplier networks

Supplier networks in the JIT context refer to the cooperative association of suppliers and customers working over the long term for mutual benefit. These relationships, free from the disruptions of bidding and selection, allow the customers and suppliers together to concentrate their efforts on better designs, process improvements, synchronization, and quality. The results have been high quality, elimination of incoming inspection, frequent production and deliveries, lower costs for the customer, and higher margins for the supplier.

Service firms have not emphasized supplier networks for materials because the service costs are often predominantly labor. Notable exceptions must include service organizations like McDonald's, one of the biggest food products purchasers in the world. A contract manufacturer recognized that it needed a cooperative relationship for temporary employees as well as for parts. It is considering a campaign to establish JIT-type relationships with a temporary employment service and a trade school to develop a reliable source of trained assemblers.

Summary

Theodore Leavitt eloquently summarized the need to apply manufacturing thinking to service:

> Until we think of service in more positive and encompassing terms, until it is enthusiastically viewed as manufacturing in the field, receptive to the same kinds of technological approaches that are used in the factory, the results are likely to be just as costly and idiosyncratic as the results of the lonely journeyman carving things laboriously by hand at home.[11]

Once we start thinking of services as an organized system of production processes, we can consider the use of JIT-type concepts to re-engineer service delivery operations. The result will be consistent services of high quality and excellent value, produced with high productivity.

15.6 MIDWAY AIRLINES PROBLEM-SOLVING GROUPS APPLY ANALYTICAL TOOLS TO DEPARTURE DELAYS

Midway Airlines is a small airline specializing in the frequent-traveler market.[12] Based on a customer survey, it was determined that a reduction in department delays was critical to the airline's survival.

Midway's front-line employees developed a fishbone diagram to determine the cause of the delays (see Exhibit 15.22). They then did a Pareto analysis, which revealed that nearly 90 percent of the departure delays for all airports other than the hub were accounted for by only four of the causes shown on the diagram. The actual causes of the late departures for one month of operation are displayed on the histogram in Exhibit 15.23. Obviously, accommodating late passengers was a major cause of flight delays. These passengers were not late from connecting flights; they were simply casual about getting to the airport. Individual gate agents had been making their own decisions about what was best for Midway in these circumstances. Most agents were anxious that Midway not lose the fares of the latecomers, and most agents were also sympathetic to the late passenger (although they forgot the inconvenience to the many passengers who had made the effort to arrive on time). Midway established a policy that it would operate on time and give top service to passengers who were ready to fly on schedule. This discipline was appreciated by the passengers, and the number of late passengers soon declined.

The delays in "pushback" (moving the aircraft away from the gate with motorized tugs) were reduced by better scheduling of tugs in some locations and by working more closely with subcontractors in other locations. Similar programs were initiated with cabin-cleaning contractors and fuel suppliers,

---

[11] Theodore Leavitt, "Production Line Approach to Service," *Harvard Business Review* 50, no. 5 (September–October 1972), p. 52.

[12] This example is taken from D. Daryl Wyckoff, "New Tool for Achieving Service Quality," *Managing Services: Marketing, Operations, and Human Resources,* C. H. Lovelock, ed. (Englewood Cliffs, N.J.: Prentice-Hall, 1988), pp. 226–39.

EXHIBIT 15.22 **Midway Airlines Fishbone Analysis—Causes of Flight Departure Delays**

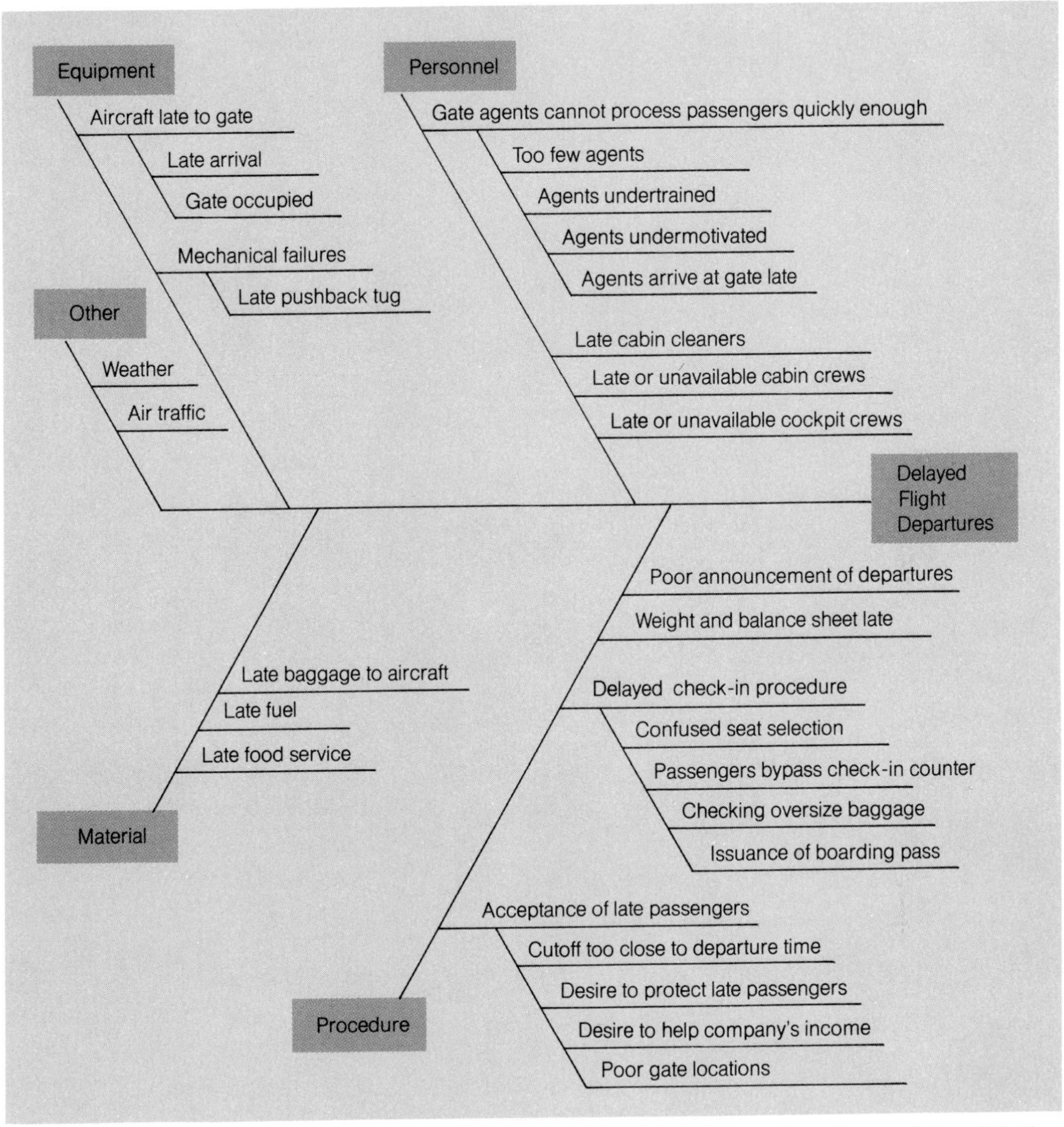

Source: D. Daryl Wyckoff, "New Tool for Achieving Service Quality," *Managing Services: Marketing, Operations, and Human Resources*, C. H. Lovelock, ed. (Englewood Cliffs, N.J.: Prentice-Hall, 1988), p. 236.

EXHIBIT 15.23

Pareto Histogram of Midway's Flight-Departure Delays

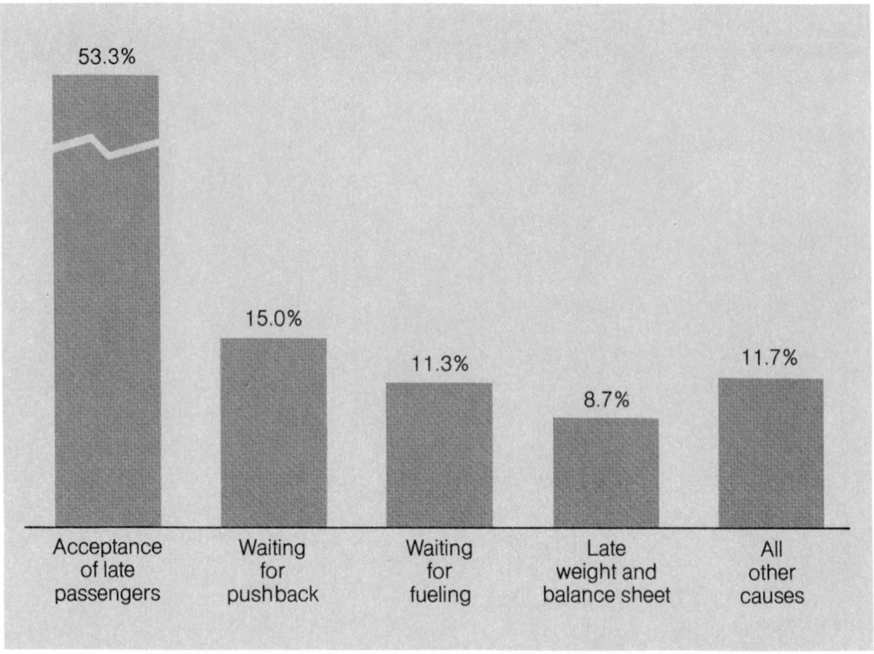

Source: D. Daryl Wyckoff, "New Tool for Achieving Service Quality," *Managing Services: Marketing, Operations, and Human Resources,* C. H. Lovelock, ed. (Englewood Cliffs, N.J.: Prentice-Hall, 1988). Data from table 3, p. 237.

EXHIBIT 15.24

Control Chart of Midway Airlines Departure Delays

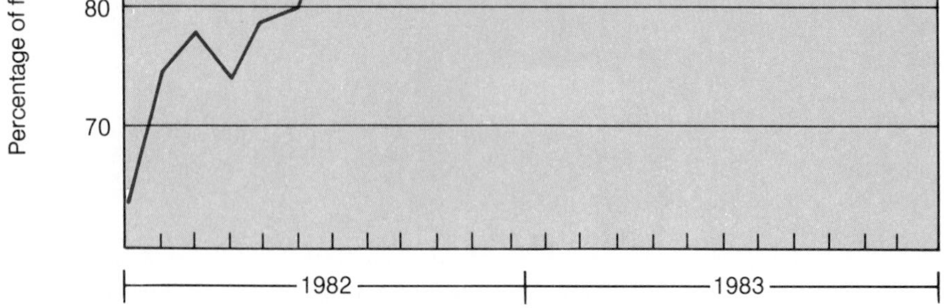

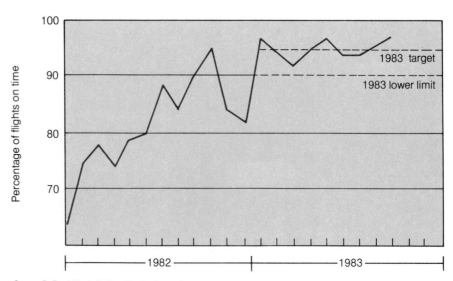

Source: D. Daryl Wyckoff, "New Tool for Achieving Service Quality," *Managing Services: Marketing, Operations, and Human Resources,* C. H. Lovelock, ed. (Englewood Cliffs, N.J.: Prentice-Hall, 1988), p. 236.

and the Midway staff placed greater priority on promptly supplying the plane's weight and balance calculations to the pilot.

In January 1983, once the flight-departure process was under control, the company set control limits. (See Exhibit 15.24.) At first, the minimum performance standard was set arbitrarily at 90 percent on-time flights. Soon there were data showing that this lower limit was too generous (but it was probably a good place to start). The company shortly decided that any month that the on-time record was more than three standard errors from the target of 95 percent, the process was out of control.

15.7 JAPANESE MANAGEMENT AND THE 100 YEN SUSHI HOUSE

The 100 Yen Sushi House is no ordinary sushi restaurant.[13] It is the ultimate showcase of Japanese productivity. As we entered the shop, there was a chorus of *"iratsai,"* a welcome from everyone working in the shop—cooks, waitresses, the owner, and the owner's children. The house features an ellipsoid-shaped serving area in the middle of the room, where three or four cooks were busily preparing sushi. Perhaps 30 stools surrounded the serving area. We took seats at the counters and were promptly served with a cup of "misoshiru," which is a bean paste soup, a pair of chopsticks, a cup of green tea, a tiny plate to make our own sauce, and a small china piece to hold the chopsticks. So far, the service was average for any sushi house. Then, I noticed something special. There was a conveyor belt going around the ellipsoid service area, like a toy train track. On it I saw a train of plates of sushi. You can find any kind of sushi that you can think of—from the cheapest seaweed or octopus kind to the expensive raw salmon or shrimp dishes. The price is uniform, however, 100 yen per plate. On closer examination, while my eyes were racing to keep up with the speed of the traveling plates, I found that a cheap seaweed plate had four pieces, while the more expensive raw salmon dish had only two pieces. I sat down and looked around at the other customers at the counters. They were all enjoying their sushi and slurping their soup while reading newspapers or magazines.

I saw a man with eight plates all stacked up neatly. As he got up to leave, the cashier looked over and said, "800 yen, please." The cashier had no cash register, since she can simply count the number of plates and then multiply by 100 yen. As the customer was leaving, once again we heard a chorus of *"Arigato Gosaimas"* (thank you), from all the workers.

The owner's daily operation is based on a careful analysis of information. The owner has a complete summary of demand information about different types of sushi plates, and thus he knows exactly how many of each type of sushi plates he should prepare and when. Furthermore, the whole operation is

---

[13] Sang M. Lee, "Japanese Management and the 100 Yen Sushi House," *Operations Management Review,* Winter 1983, Operations Management Association.

based on the repetitive manufacturing principle with appropriate Just-in-Time and quality control systems. For example, the store has a very limited refrigerator capacity (we could see several whole fish or octopus in the glassed chambers right in front of our counter). Thus, the store uses the Just-in-Time inventory control system. Instead of increasing the refrigeration capacity by purchasing new refrigeration systems, the company has an agreement with the fish vendor to deliver fresh fish several times a day so that materials arrive just in time to be used for sushi making. Therefore, the inventory cost is minimum.

In the Just-in-Time operation system, the safety stock principle is turned upside down. In other words, the safety stock is deliberately removed gradually, to uncover problems and their possible solutions. The available floor space is for workers and their necessary equipment but not for holding inventory. In the 100 Yen Sushi House, workers and their equipment are positioned so close that sushi making is passed on hand to hand rather than as independent operations. The absence of walls of inventory allows the owner and workers to be involved in the total operation, from greeting the customer to serving what is ordered. Their tasks are tightly interrelated and everyone rushes to a problem spot to prevent the cascading effect of the problem throughout the work process.

The 100 Yen Sushi House is a labor-intensive operation, which is based mostly on simplicity and common sense rather than high technology, contrary to American perceptions. I was very impressed. As I finished my fifth plate, I saw the same octopus sushi plate going around for about the thirtieth time. Perhaps I had discovered the pitfall of the system. So I asked the owner how he takes care of the sanitary problems when a sushi plate goes around all day long, until an unfortunate customer eats it and perhaps gets food poisoning. He bowed with an apologetic smile and said, "Well, sir, we never let our sushi plates go unsold longer than about 30 minutes." Then he scratched his head and said, "Whenever one of our employees takes a break, he or she can take off unsold plates of sushi and either eat them or throw them away. We are very serious about our sushi quality." As we laughed, he laughed, along with a 90-degree bow. As we were walking out of the sushi house, while *"arigato gosaimas"* was ringing in my ears, I was contemplating how to introduce the 100 Yen Sushi House concept to the States. Perhaps I can suggest the concept to the student union at the university for an experiment. Maybe McDonald's, Pizza Hut, Wendy's. . . .

15.8 CONCLUSION

The 1990s will see JIT as a dominant concept in both manufacturing and in services. This is primarily because of its simplicity in operation and its ability to preserve local control. It provides many benefits and few penalties when properly applied. "Little JIT" reduces inventory quantities and simplifies scheduling and control process by using the "pull" logic. "Big JIT" offers a broad view and philosophy of operations for the performance of the entire firm—not just product production, but also attitudes and beliefs about workers, management, company goals, etc.

15.9 REVIEW AND DISCUSSION QUESTIONS

1. Are there any aspects of the Japanese approach that you could apply to your own current school activities? Explain.
2. Do you believe that Fredrick W. Taylor, the father of scientific management, would be for or against the Japanese approach?
3. What objections might a marketing manager have against uniform plant loading?
4. What are the implications for cost accounting of JIT production?
5. What questions would you want to ask the president of Toyota about his operations management?
6. Explain how a one-card Kanban system operates.
7. In what ways, if any, are the following systems analogous to Kanban: returning empty bottles to the supermarket and picking up filled ones; running an automat at lunchtime; withdrawing money from a checking account; collecting eggs at a chicken ranch?
8. How does the old saying, "There's no such thing as a free lunch," pertain to the Japanese elimination of inventory?
9. Professor Chase is frustrated by his inability to make a good cup of coffee in the morning. Show how you would use a fishbone diagram to analyze the process he uses to make a cup of his evil brew.
10. Why do ECs cause so much trouble under JIT systems? How do the Japanese handle them?
11. Explain the relationship between quality and productivity under the JIT philosophy.
12. How does the Kinko's Copier operation, as described in the case at the end of Chapter 4, apply the techniques of JIT?
13. What JIT techniques would expedite the school registration process?
14. How does the use of automated teller machines incorporate JIT techniques?
15. Why is the respect for people concept, discussed in the Benson paper, crucial to the service industry?
16. How can the process of purchasing a new car through a dealership be improved using JIT techniques?

15.10 CASE: XYZ PRODUCTS COMPANY

XYZ Products Company is a supplier of gizmos for a large computer manufacturer located a few miles away. The company produces three different models of gizmos in production runs ranging from 100 to 300 units.

EXHIBIT 15.25

Gizmo Production Flow

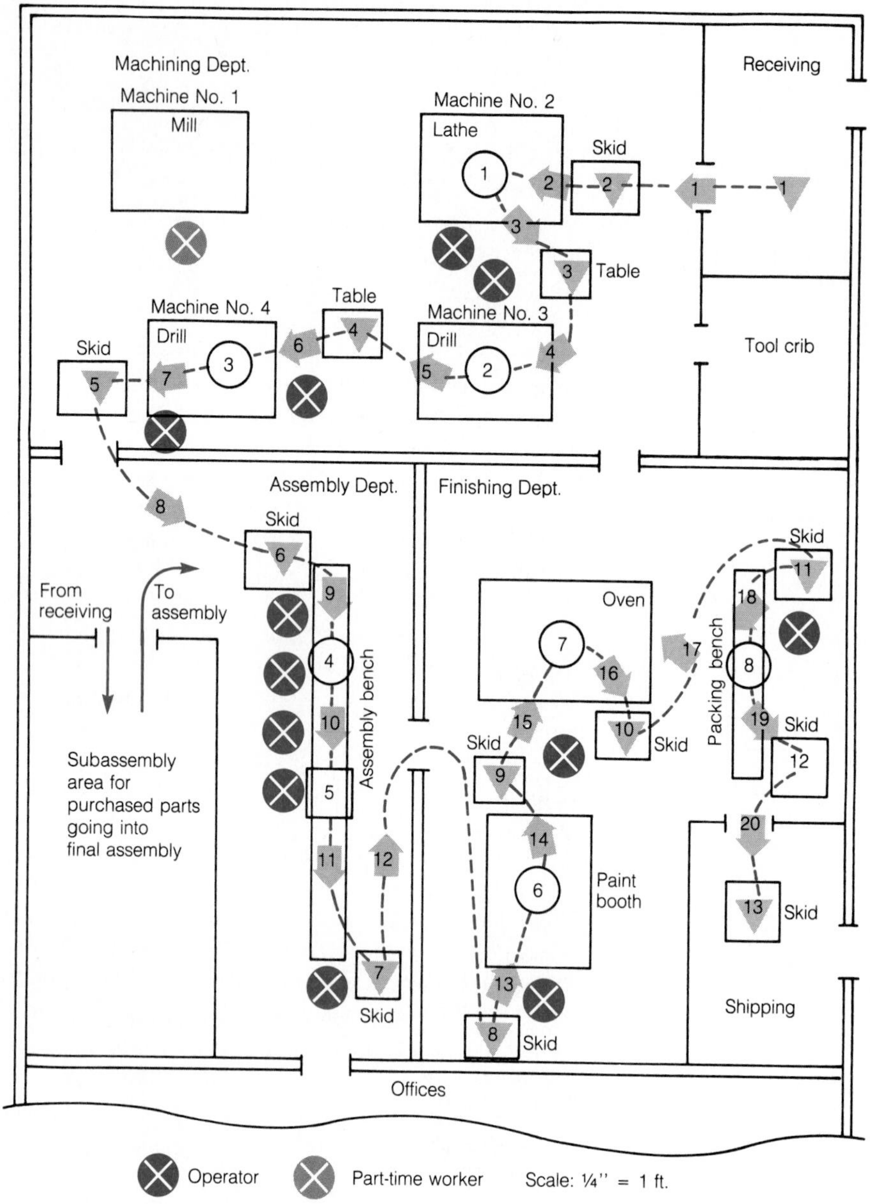

The production flow of Models X and Y is shown in Exhibit 15.25. Model Z requires milling as its first step, but otherwise follows the same flow pattern as X and Y. Skids can hold up to 20 gizmos at a time. Approximate processing times per unit by operation number and equipment setup times are shown below.

The demand for gizmos from the computer company ranges between 125 and 175 per month, equally divided among X, Y, and Z. Subassembly builds up inventory early in the month to make certain that a buffer stock is always available. Raw materials and purchased parts for subassemblies each constitute 40 percent of manufacturing cost of a gizmo. Both categories of parts are multiple sourced from about 80 vendors and are delivered at random times. (Gizmos have 40 different part numbers.)

Some other information: Scrap rates are about 10 percent at each operation, inventory turns twice yearly, employees are paid on day rate, employee turnover is 25 percent per year, and net profit from operations is steady at 5 percent per year. Maintenance is performed as needed.

The manager of XYZ has been contemplating installing an MRP system to help him control inventories and to "keep the skids filled." (It is his view that two days of work in front of a workstation motivates the worker to produce at top speed.) He is also planning to add three inspectors to clean up the quality problem. Further, he is thinking about setting up a rework line in order to speed up repairs. While he is pleased with the high utilization of most of his equipment and labor, he is concerned about the idle time of his milling machine. Finally, he has asked his industrial engineering department to look into high-rise shelving to store parts coming off Machine 4.

QUESTIONS

1. Which of the changes being considered by the manager of XYZ go counter to the JIT philosophy?
2. Make recommendations for JIT improvements in such areas as scheduling, layout, Kanban, task groupings, and inventory. Use quantitative data given above as much as possible; state necessary assumptions.
3. Sketch the operation of a pull system for XYZ's current system.
4. Outline a plan for the introduction of JIT at XYZ.

Operation Number	and Name	Operation Times (minutes)	Setup Times (minutes)
—	Milling for Z	20	60
1	Lathe	50	30
2	Mod. 14 drill	15	5
3	Mod. 14 drill	40	5
4	Assembly step 1	50	
	Assembly step 2	45	
	Assembly step 3	50	
5	Inspection	30	
6	Paint	30	20
7	Oven	50	
8	Packing	5	

15.11 CASE: McCALL DIESEL MOTOR WORKS REVISITED

The following questions relate to the McCall Diesel Motor Works case at the end of Chapter 14:

1. What changes in the product demand environment would have to take place in order for McCall to switch to JIT?
2. What JIT actions/concepts would you recommend for items *(a)* through *(l)* assuming that the demand environment is made suitable for JIT?

15.12 SELECTED BIBLIOGRAPHY

Cayer, Shirley. "Does Just-in-Time Have a Place in a Bank?" *Purchasing,* March 21, 1987, pp. 56–59.

Davidson, William H. *The Amazing Race: Winning the Technorivalry with Japan.* New York: John Wiley & Sons, 1984.

Edosomwan, Johnson A., and Carlena Marsh. "Streamlining the Material Flow Process for Just-in-Time Production." *Industrial Engineering,* January 1989, pp. 56–58.

Hall, Robert. *Zero Inventories.* Homewood, Ill.: Dow Jones–Irwin, 1983.

Hay, Edward J. "Any Machine Setup Time Can Be Reduced by 75%." *Industrial Engineering,* August 1987, pp. 62–66.

Henkoff, Ronald. "What Motorola Learns from Japan." *Fortune,* April 24, 1989, pp. 157–63.

Hohner, Gregory. "JIT-TQC: Integrating Product Design with Shop Floor Effectiveness." *Industrial Engineering,* September 1988, pp. 42–47.

Karmarkar, Uday. "Getting Control of Just-in-Time." *Harvard Business Review,* September–October 1989, pp. 122–31.

Lee, Sang M., and Gary Schwendiman, eds. *Management by Japanese Systems.* New York: Praeger Publishers, 1983.

Macbeth, Douglas K.; Lynne F. Baxter; Neil Ferguson; and George C. Neil. "Buyer-Vendor Relationships with Just-in-Time." *Industrial Engineering,* September 1988, pp. 38–42.

Monden, Yasuhiro. *Toyota Production System, Practical Approach to Production Management.* Atlanta, Ga.: Industrial Engineering and Management Press, 1983.

Nonaka, Ikujiro. "Toward Middle-up-Down Management." *Sloan Management Review,* Spring 1988, pp. 9–19.

Schonberger, Richard. *World Class Manufacturing Casebook: Implementing JIT & TQC.* New York: Free Press, 1987.

Welke, Helmut A., and John Overbeeke. "Cellular Manufacturing: a Good Technique for Implementing Just-in-Time and Total Quality Control." *Industrial Engineering,* November 1988, pp. 36–41.

Young, S. Mark; Michael D. Shields; and Gerrit Wolf. "Manufacturing Controls and Performance: an Experiment." *Accounting, Organizations and Society,* December 1988, pp. 607–16.

Chapter 16

Materials Management and Purchasing

EPIGRAPH

The lowest-cost item is not always the cheapest.

CHAPTER OUTLINE

KEY TERMS

Logistics

Materials Management

Value Analysis

Just-in-Time Purchasing

Automatic Storage and Retrieval Systems (AS/RS)

Value Density

The terms *materials management* and *logistics* are often used interchangeably, but there is a difference. **Logistics** more often means managing the flow of both information and the entire spectrum of materials—raw materials, components, subassemblies, and finished goods—from the source to the final consumer. This includes purchasing from the suppliers, shipping, receiving, manufacturing or service activities, inventory storages, and distribution to warehouses, retailers, and finally to the ultimate consumer. In common usage **materials management** is somewhat narrower and applies primarily to the manufacturing function, extending from the receipt of materials from the vendors, through the manufacturing process, and into finished goods within the facility. The front end of the total materials-flow system may be under the control of the purchasing department, flow within the manufacturing system itself left to the manufacturing manager, and the finished-goods storage and distribution left to the marketing manager. In other words, the overall control of materials flow is often divided among three managers, and this division has presented problems.

Many firms are taking a broader view of the entire flow, from purchasing to final delivery to the consumer, and are beginning to centralize the overall control. Some reasons for this include:

1. The trend toward minimizing all inventories brought on by the adoption of systems such as Just-in-Time (JIT).
2. The rapidly changing range of products and the need for speedy delivery to the market.
3. Shortened product life cycles, which necessitate knowledge and control of inventories in the various pipelines.
4. Trends in the legal system, which hold manufacturers liable for product failures even though causes may be outside the productive system itself.

The basic objective of logistics or materials management is to ensure that the right item is at the right place at the right time at a reasonable cost. Purchased materials and supplies constitute the major cost elements in most manufacturing firms and indeed a sizable working-capital investment in many service organizations. Thus, the importance of good materials management cannot be overstated.

In this chapter we will examine how materials are obtained (purchasing), how they are managed through the manufacturing system, and how they are distributed ultimately to the consumer.

16.1 OVERVIEW OF THE MATERIALS-FLOW PROCESS

Exhibit 16.1 provides an overview of the materials-flow process for a typical manufacturer. Orders for raw materials, parts, and components are placed with vendors by the purchasing department. The parts are shipped to the factory and placed in storage or transferred directly to production depart-

EXHIBIT 16.1 **Overview of the Materials Flow from Vendor to Consumer**

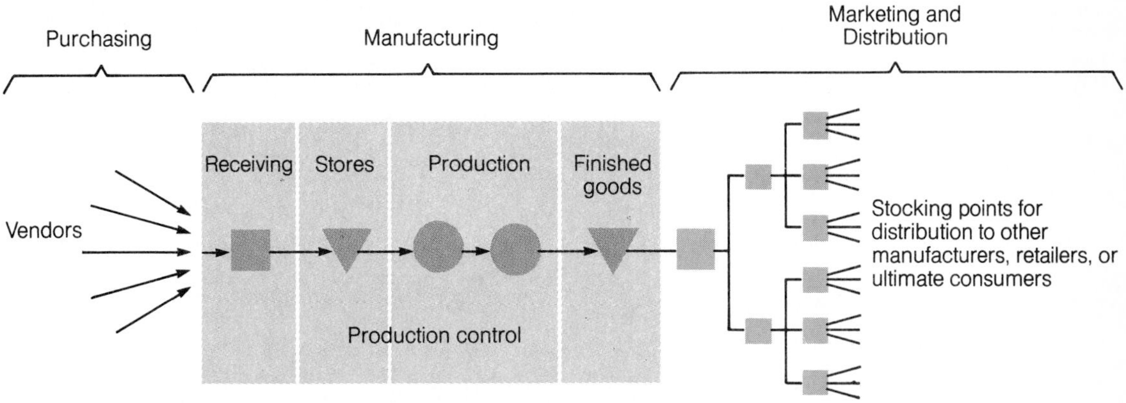

ments. Production-control personnel then distribute the parts according to the requirements given in the production schedule. Once completed, products are moved to finished-goods inventory by production control or internal traffic, where they are packed for shipping by the shipping department. Products are then sent to distribution centers, warehouses, or directly to the customer as prescribed in the shipping schedule and distribution policy. (Note that this system does not include automated materials handling or obvious provisions for Just-in-Time deliveries.)

Materials Management in Various Industries

Problems encountered in materials management differ from industry to industry.[1] This is because of the types and numbers of products or services being created, the variations among suppliers and customers, the nature of the raw materials and supply inputs, and economic factors such as the values of the individual units of product or service. Exhibit 16.2 shows typical materials flow in three different industries: services, marketing, and manufacturing.

Firms in the service industries are primarily concerned with procurement and material-input supplies. Their central focus is ordering, receiving, storing, and internally distributing the supplies needed to perform the service. Typical industries would be airlines, financial institutions, government agencies, and public utilities. The output tends to be a narrow range of services or products.

In marketing firms, the output products are about the same as the input products. The marketing firm essentially performs the function of change of ownership—purchasing products, storing, selling, order picking, shipping,

[1] John F. Magee, William C. Copacino, and Donald B. Rosenfield, *Modern Logistics Management, Integrating Marketing, Manufacturing and Physical Distribution* (New York: John Wiley & Sons, 1985), pp. 396–401.

EXHIBIT 16.2

Materials Flow in Service, Marketing, and Manufacturing Industries

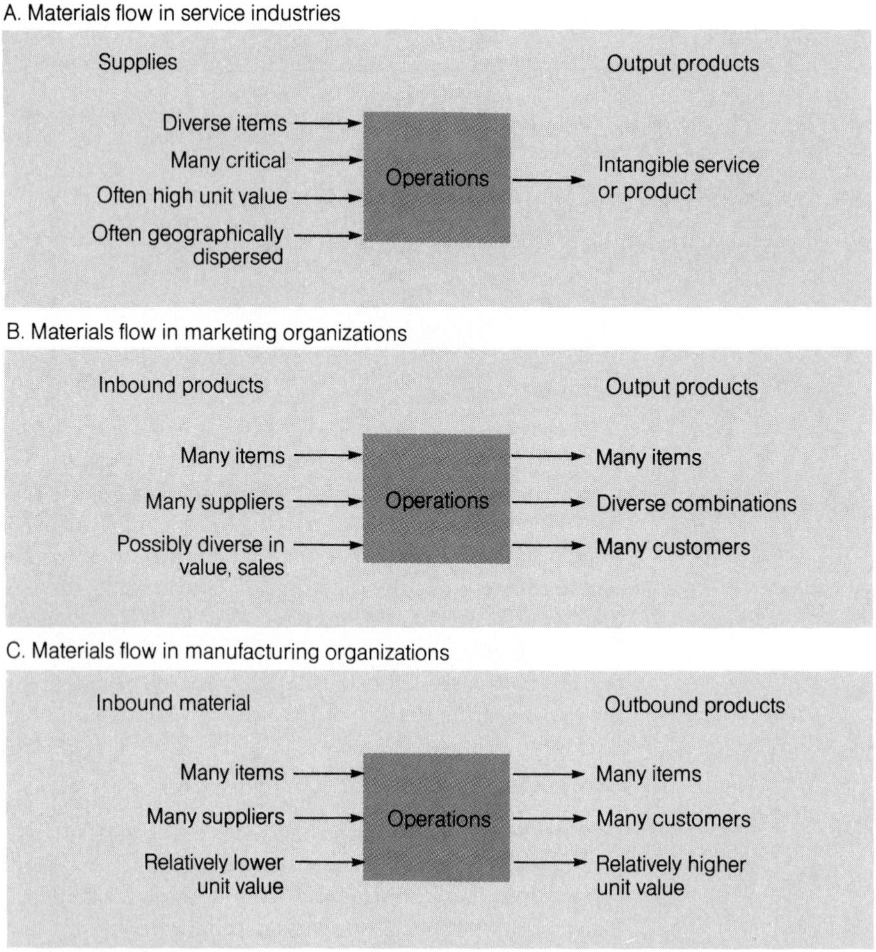

Source: John F. Magee, William C. Copacino, and Donald B. Rosenfield, *Modern Logistics Management, Integrating Marketing, Manufacturing and Physical Distribution* (New York: John Wiley & Sons, 1985), pp. 399–400.

and so forth. Wholesalers and retailers generally carry many items purchased from many suppliers with a wide range of costs. The items are sold essentially unchanged to many customers, who tend to buy a wide variety of items when they shop.

Manufacturing industries tend to look like marketing firms in that there are inputs of many items from many suppliers and outputs of many items to many customers, but the input materials are changed into very different output items. The changes can be physical (such as machining parts), chemical (such as a change in molecular structure), or cumulative, created by combining parts and components, such as an assembly process. Magee lists five activities that distinguish manufacturing logistics problems:[2]

1. There is a major flow of materials in and out of the activity.
2. Materials physically change form in the process.
3. The change of form takes time and effort. Therefore the conversion process occupies a great deal of the effort, capital, and managerial attention.
4. There is usually substantial internal materials management activity: flows of raw materials, parts, and products within the plants themselves, and to field distribution systems.
5. Logistic activities are concerned with maintaining the flow of product in and out of the operations activity, but tend to be subordinate to the manufacturing and marketing functions. Manufacturing tends to have responsibility and a stronger control of materials flow within the manufacturing system itself, and marketing has a strong control over finished goods and distribution.

16.2 ORGANIZATIONAL PLACEMENT OF MATERIALS MANAGEMENT

There is wide divergence of opinion about many aspects of materials management: where the function should be placed, what its responsibilities are, and whether it should be centralized or decentralized. While the final choice must always relate to the needs of the specific firm in question, the high cost of materials probably will support the current trend, which is to equate the materials management function with the other main functions of the organization. Such placement ensures executive-level attention to materials and gives the materials manager enough clout to be effective. A partial organization chart reflecting this placement is shown in Exhibit 16.3. Note the peculiar positioning of Production Planning and Control. This area is of utmost importance to manufacturing. As such, it may be assigned organizationally to Materials Management, but functionally to Manufacturing and physically located in the Manufacturing area. The following sections examine some of the materials management subfunctions in detail.

16.3 PURCHASING

Most senior executives think of purchasing as a reactive clerical function. But a few forward-looking managers at firms such as Hewlett-Packard, Polaroid, Motorola, GE, GM, and Xerox now look at purchasing as the orchestrator of

[2] Ibid., p. 400.

EXHIBIT 16.3

Organization Chart Showing Materials Management Functions

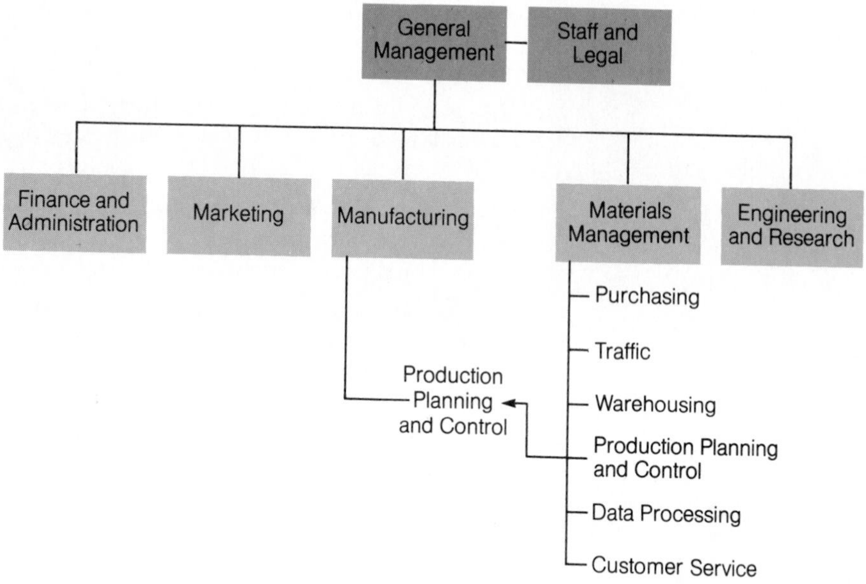

the system that spends 60 percent of the sales dollar and is also the source of half of the quality problems. The Insert shows some examples.

INSERT What Some Companies Are Doing with Purchasing

Ford and Buick Olds Cadillac Division of General Motors now involve purchasing and potential suppliers during product design.

The Purchasing Department at Eaton recently called its supplier in for design suggestions on aircraft switches. As a result, switch reliability went up, and costs went down.

At Cipher Data Products, quality assurance, purchasing, engineering, and manufacturing all review specifications, prints, and parts lists before production begins. The results are improved product and quality.

Design engineers and quality assurance engineers were once adversaries at an Allen-Bradley division. But a survey showed that 84 percent of all field failures were the result of materials failure and poor design. They now work together to assure that quality is designed into purchased materials.

Motorola, Xerox, and other leading manufacturers have assigned engineers to the purchasing and materials management departments to strengthen the teamwork between buyers and quality personnel. This has improved the quality of incoming material.

While many companies prequalify vendors, Hewlett-Packard and Tandem Computers also investigate suppliers for technological capabilities they may require years into the future.

Source: Excerpts from David N. Burt, "Managing Product Quality through Strategic Purchasing," *Sloan Management Review*, Spring 1989, pp. 39–48.

The purchasing (or procurement) department buys materials in amounts authorized by requisitions it receives from the production control and stores (e.g., stockroom) departments. A typical (large) purchasing department is staffed by a purchasing manager; assistant managers for buying, follow-up, and expediting, purchasing administration, data processing, and purchasing research; and purchasing agents for raw materials, capital equipment, and maintenance, repair, and operating supplies.

Ammer lists four basic purchasing activities:[3]

1. Selecting suppliers, negotiating the most advantageous terms of purchase with them, and issuing necessary purchase orders.
2. Expediting delivery from suppliers when necessary to assure delivery in time to meet schedules, and negotiating any changes in purchase schedules dictated by circumstances.
3. Acting as liaison between suppliers and other company departments, including engineering, quality control, manufacturing, production control, and finance, on all problems involving purchased materials.
4. Looking for new products, materials, and suppliers that can contribute to company profit objectives, and acting as the company's "eyes and ears" to the outside world and reporting on changes in market conditions and other factors that can affect company operations.

Selecting Suppliers

"The purchasing department must be able to locate dependable and progressive sources of supply and to secure and maintain their active interest and cooperation. All other purchasing contributions to the organization are secondary to the competent selection of suppliers."[4]

There are four stages of supplier selection:[5]

1. Survey, in which all possible sources for a product are explored.

[3] Dean S. Ammer, *Materials Management and Purchasing*, 4th ed. (Homewood, Ill.: Richard D. Irwin, 1980), p. 22.

[4] Michael R. Leenders, Harold E. Fearon, and Wilbur B. England, *Purchasing and Materials Management*, 7th ed. (Homewood, Ill.: Richard D. Irwin, 1980), p. 217.

[5] Stuart F. Heinritz and Paul V. Farrell, *Purchasing Principles and Applications*, 6th ed. (Englewood Cliffs, N.J.: Prentice-Hall, 1981), p. 231.

EXHIBIT 16.4 **An Illustrative Decision Hierarchy for Supplier Selection**

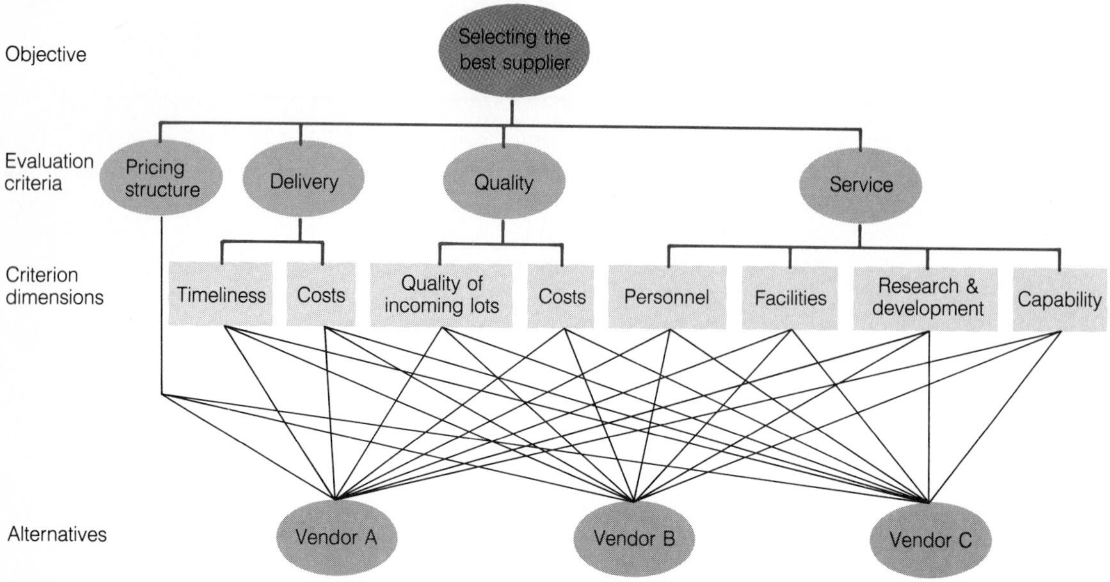

Source: Ram Narasimhan, "An Analytical Approach to Supplier Selection," *Journal of Purchasing and Materials Management*, Winter 1983, p. 28.

2. Inquiry, in which the relative qualifications and advantages of potential sources are analyzed.
3. Negotiation and selection, leading to the issue of an initial order.
4. Experience, in which a continuing vendor-supplier relationship is established or the earlier steps are reviewed in the search for a more satisfactory source.

Narasimhan provides a useful summary of the criteria used in choosing among suppliers (see Exhibit 16.4). Looking at the criterion dimensions, the items under Delivery and Quality are self-evident. The items under Service warrant some elaboration. Personnel denotes the abilities of the vendor's work force—both labor and management. Facilities refers to the quality and upkeep of the vendor's physical plant. Research and Development represents the technical resources of the vendor devoted to developing new products and helping customers solve problems related to the materials and vendor supplies. Capability refers to the existence of sufficient technical capability to perform the current job and flexibility to perform future work.

The process of certifying suppliers so that they can be placed on a firm's "approved list" may be quite extensive. Typically, this entails site visits, credit checks, contacting other customers of the vendor, and so on. Hewlett-Packard, for example, uses a nine-page Technical Sourcing Checklist to gather all the data required to determine if a vendor is good, adequate, or unacceptable.

Expediting Delivery

Just as in manufacturing, excessive expediting in purchasing is a sign of a poorly managed system. As McEneny notes, "Purchasing spends 80 percent of their time expediting and 15 percent solving vendor quality problems. That only leaves 5 percent of their time to evaluate and select vendors and reduce purchase prices. If these percentages could be reversed so buyers could spend 80 percent of their time selecting vendors and negotiating lower prices, the increase in company profits would be staggering.[6]

Several solutions to excessive expediting have been proposed. These include making sure that orders already late are rescheduled, not expedited further; and "preventive expediting," which means staying on top of the vendors as their due dates approach to ensure that the dates will be met. The rescheduling approach makes good sense and we would certainly support it. The shortcoming of preventive expediting is that the buyer must assume the vendor's responsibility for keeping on top of delivery commitments. This is the wrong way to do business—no vendor should make the approved list until that company can show it can meet scheduled due dates without being reminded by the customer.

Acting as Liaison

Of the various liaison activities, purchasing's interaction with engineering and quality functions are of particular current interest in manufacturing. The relationship with engineering revolves around keeping the bill of materials up to date. This means incorporating the latest engineering changes in the BOM file and making certain that purchasing is advised of these changes before placing orders with the vendor. The relationship with the quality control staff centers on developing a clear understanding of what constitutes acceptable quality from the vendor. This can be a real problem when a vendor delivers parts that function properly but have cosmetic defects such as slightly irregular paint color or scratches not readily visible. In such cases, QC may wish to reject the lot and pressure purchasing to find new vendors; purchasing may prefer to say that the parts work well and that the chosen vendor provided the best value for the price.

---

[6] Tim McEneny, *Up the Manufacturing Organization: The Modern Materials Manager's Guide to Survival* (Holmdel, N.J.: TSM Publishing, 1980), p. 141.

Value Analysis

An approach widely used by purchasing departments is **value analysis.** The basic idea is to compare the function performed by a purchased item with its cost in an attempt to find a lower-cost alternative. Exhibit 16.5 summarizes this approach.

Just-in-Time Purchasing

Just-in-Time purchasing is a major element of Just-in-Time (JIT) systems, as was discussed in Chapter 15. The basic idea behind Just-in-Time purchasing is to establish agreements with vendors to deliver small quantities of materials just in time for production. This can mean daily or sometimes twice-daily deliveries of purchased items. This approach contrasts with the traditional

EXHIBIT 16.5

The Value Analysis Approach: Comparison of Function to Cost

I. Select a relatively high cost or high volume purchased item to value analyze. This can be a part, material, or service. Select an item you suspect is costing more than it should.

II. Find out completely how the item is used and what is expected of it—its *function.*

III. Ask questions:
   1. Does its use contribute value?
   2. Is its cost proportionate to usefulness?
   3. Does it need all its features?
   4. Is there anything better, at a more favorable purchase price, for the intended use?
   5. Can the item be eliminated?
   6. If the item is not standard, can a standard item be used?
   7. If it is a standard item, does it completely fit your application or is it a misfit?
   8. Does the item have greater capacity than required?
   9. Is there a similar item in inventory that could be used?
   10. Can the weight be reduced?
   11. Are closer tolerances specified than are necessary?
   12. Is unnecessary machining performed on the item?
   13. Are unnecessarily fine finishes specified?
   14. Is commercial quality specified?
   15. Can you make the item cheaper yourself?
   16. If you are making it now, can you buy it for less?
   17. Is the item properly classified for shipping purposes to obtain lowest transportation rates?
   18. Can cost of packaging be reduced?
   19. Are you asking your supplier for suggestions to reduce cost?
   20. Do material, reasonable labor, overhead, and profit total its cost?
   21. Will another dependable supplier provide it for less?
   22. Is anyone buying it for less?

IV. Now:
   1. Pursue those suggestions that appear practical.
   2. Get samples of the proposed item(s).
   3. Select the best possibilities and propose changes.

Source: Michael R. Leenders, Harold E. Fearon, and Wilbur B. England, *Purchasing and Materials Management,* 7th ed. (Homewood, Ill.: Richard D. Irwin, 1980), p. 516.

approach of bulk buying items that are delivered far in advance of production. The critical elements of JIT purchasing are:

- Reduced lot sizes.
- Frequent and reliable delivery schedules.
- Reduced and highly reliable lead times.
- Consistently high quality levels for purchased materials.[7]

Each of these elements constitutes a major benefit to the purchasing firm, not the least of which is shortening the procurement cycle.

The ultimate objective should be a single reliable source for each item, and the consolidation of several items from each supplier. The result is that there will be far fewer suppliers in total. U.S. companies that have implemented JIT purchasing through fewer suppliers have obtained the following benefits:[8]

1. Consistent quality. Involving suppliers during the early stages of product design can consistently provide high quality products.
2. Savings on resources. Minimum investment and resources, such as buyer's time, travel, and engineering that are required when there is a limited number of suppliers.
3. Lower costs. The overall volume of items purchased is higher, which eventually leads to lower costs.
4. Special attention. The suppliers are more inclined to pay special attention to the buyer's needs, since the buyer represents a large account.
5. Saving on tooling. Total dollars spent to provide tooling to the suppliers is minimal, since the buyer concentrates on one source of supply.
6. The establishment of long-term relationships with suppliers, which encourages loyalty and reduces the risk of an interrupted supply of parts to the buyer plant; this may be the most important benefit of all.

JIT as an operating concept is a "hot" topic these days, but we must be careful not to become so captivated by the glamour of JIT's single-source philosophy that we overlook the many occasions when multiple sourcing is justified. It is often advantageous to have suppliers compete for a firm's business. In addition to possible lower prices, technical knowledge is gained from the vendor who has expertise in his area. Also, many materials, parts, and supplies are critical to a firm's continued operation, and any shutdown by a vendor—some sort of labor dispute or calamity such as a major fire or accident—can significantly hurt. The Department of Defense must purchase military and critical supplies from more than one source. This is done to

---

[7] Chan K. Hahn, Peter A. Pinto, and Daniel J. Bragg, "'Just-in-Time' Production and Purchasing," *Journal of Purchasing and Materials Management,* Fall 1983, p. 5.

[8] Sang M. Lee and A. Ansari, "Comparative Analysis of Japanese Just-in-Time Purchasing and Traditional U.S. Purchasing Systems," *International Journal of Operations and Production Management* 5, no. 4 (1985), pp. 5–14.

EXHIBIT 16.6

Characteristics of JIT Purchasing

Suppliers

Few suppliers
Nearby suppliers
Repeat business with same suppliers
Active use of analysis to enable desirable suppliers to become/stay price competitive
Clusters of remote suppliers
Competitive bidding mostly limited to new part numbers
Buyer plant resists vertical integration and subsequent wipeout of supplier business
Suppliers are encouraged to extend JIT buying to *their* suppliers

Quantities

Steady output rate (a desirable prerequisite)
Frequent deliveries in small lot quantities
Long-term contract agreements
Minimal release paperwork
Delivery quantities variable from release to release but fixed for whole contract term
Little or no permissible overage or underage of receipts
Suppliers encouraged to package in exact quantities
Suppliers encouraged to reduce their production lot sizes (or store unreleased material)

Quality

Minimal product specifications imposed on supplier
Help suppliers to meet quality requirements
Close relationships between buyers' and suppliers' quality assurance people
Suppliers encouraged to use process control charts instead of lot sampling inspection

Shipping

Scheduling of inbound freight
Gain control by use of company-owned or contract shipping, contract warehousing, and trailers for freight consolidation/storage where possible instead of using common carriers

Source: Richard J. Schonberger and James P. Gilbert, "Just-in-Time Purchasing: A Challenge for U.S. Industry," *California Management Review*, Fall 1983, p. 58.

reduce the risk of an enemy destroying the source of supply. Horowitz notes, "Management often purchases from two or more sources to assure a source of supply, reduce the firm's uncertainty, and reduce its vulnerability to supply shortages. This accounts for the reason why obtaining the lowest cost is not the sole objective."[9]

The most critical demands placed on the purchasing department to make JIT work are (1) the need to reduce the number of suppliers and (2) locating suppliers who are nearby (see Exhibit 16.6). The strategy of single sourcing is to purchase all parts of a given kind from a single vendor. Nearby suppliers are obviously necessary in order to allow frequent, piece-by-piece delivery. How well purchasing handles these demands depends on the type of relationship the firm establishes with its suppliers. As Hahn, Pinto, and Bragg note,

[9] Ira Horowitz, "On Two-Source Factor Purchasing," *Decision Sciences* 17, no. 2 (Spring 1986), pp. 274–79.

"Suppliers should be viewed as 'outside partners' who can contribute to the long-run welfare of the buying firm rather than as outside adversaries. The purchasing function should look at the new system as an opportunity to reaffirm its vital role in the formation and conduct of overall corporate strategy."[10]

16.4 MATERIALS MANAGEMENT AND MANUFACTURING

Internal to the manufacturing firm, materials management refers to the movement of materials from the receiving dock, through the productive system, and as completed goods to the loading dock. The following are of particular importance in this phase:

1. Where and in what form to store inventory.
2. The production-control system.
3. Materials handling and storage systems.

Inventory Stocking Level

In manufacturing, inventory can be stocked at several levels: assembly, subassembly, component, or part. Magee has listed some general principles to help determine whether items should pass through the production system and be stored as completed items, or whether storage is more appropriate before the production process:[11]

1. Value added. If little value is added during the manufacturing or assembly process (for example, a simple fast process or assembly), items might just as well be put through the process and carried as finished parts or goods inventory. If the opposite is true (for instance, long processing time, expensive tooling, or expensive material), the actual processing should be delayed closer to the time needed by holding the material at a lower level of the bill of materials.

2. Number of parts and finished goods. As the number of different products increases, the inventories needed to support the system increase. Therefore, if products have common parts, it would be better to stock the parts, which could be assembled later when the specific products needed have been identified, rather than stock the assembled items. This would greatly reduce the size and value of the total inventory.

3. Lead time. Inventories become more important as the time to process another batch of items lengthens. If the time to process another batch is short, it is not as vital to stock completed work.

---

[10] Hahn et al., "'Just-in-Time' Production," p. 10.
[11] Magee et al., *Modern Logistics Management,* pp. 97–98.

4. Market characteristics. The source and type of demand determine where to hold inventory. When a large number of expensive end items are made, the customer expects to wait for a custom order. When the product is a high-volume, low-cost standard item, the market expects immediate availability. In general, fast-selling products justify an inventory of completed items.

Bar Coding

The term *paperless factory* refers to the flow of product through a system without the accompanying paperwork that has traditionally been part of the flow. The computer was the initial major impetus making this possible, and the next major development was the increasingly widespread use of bar coding.

Several bar code schemes are in use today, all involving a scanner that reads and makes sense of a series of wide and narrow lines and spaces. Exhibit 16.7 shows the characters and bar code for Code 39, and the bar code for UPC (Universal Product Code). A total of nine binary bits per symbol are used in Code 39, with wide spaces and bars representing a 1 and narrow spaces and bars representing a 0. The bar code labeled CODE 39 is reproduced wider than normal to show the lines and spaces corresponding to C, O, D, E, space, 3, and 9. Generally, however, the bar code uses symbols, letters, and numbers to identify an item; this scheme is then interpreted by a computer and the correct item is identified. The bar coding for #4-D silk suture thread used during operations is coded as +H206453H1A, and the UPC for purified water is 2113007446. Code 39 is widely used in manufacturing, health care, and is the system used by the Department of Defense and General Services Administration. UPC is used by retailers and wholesalers of consumer products.

Bar coding has become very important for all industries, including both manufacturing and services, because it greatly simplifies inventory and production control. Using numbers to represent products allows the user to maintain a large block of information about each product—manufacturer, cost, price, order size, weight, etc. We've all experienced the greatly increased speed at which we can be checked out at a supermarket or department store using bar code reading. While the scanner identifies and prices our purchases, it is simultaneously updating inventory levels; it thus becomes part of the entire process from purchasing, receiving, stocking, moving, and distribution.

In a manufacturing environment, bar code labels attached to parts, subassemblies, and end items allow their continual monitoring. Information relayed as they pass through the process indicates where they have been and where they should go. Also, through this identification, each workstation can automatically display the processing instructions, record the processing and test results, and specify the next workstation.

In mechanized simple conveyers or more complex materials-handling systems, scanners can read the bar code and automatically route the item to its

EXHIBIT 16.7 Bar Code Characters

CHARACTERS	ASCII #	CODE 39
	32	
$	36	
%	37	
*	42	
+	43	
—	45	
.	46	
/	47	
0	48	
1	49	
2	50	
3	51	
4	52	
5	53	
6	54	
7	55	
8	56	
9	57	
A	65	
B	66	
C	67	
D	68	
E	69	
F	70	
G	71	
H	72	
I	73	
J	74	
K	75	
L	76	
M	77	
N	78	
O	79	
P	80	
Q	81	
R	82	
S	83	
T	84	
U	85	
V	86	
W	87	
X	88	
Y	89	
Z	90	

Start C O D E Space 3 9 Stop

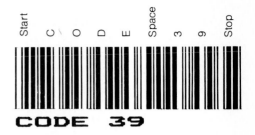

CODE 39

Code 39

SUTURE. SILK, #4-D

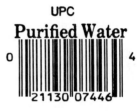

+H206453H1A

UPC

Purified Water

0 21130 07446 4

Source: Reprinted from James H. Todd, "Program Constructed for On-Demand Bar Code Printing," *Industrial Engineering* 18, no. 9 (September 1986), pp. 18–24. Copyright Institute of Industrial Engineers, 25 Technology Park/Atlanta, Norcross, Georgia 30092.

next location. The ultimate use (though expensive) can be a completely automated system, which can route a job through the entire manufacturing system, such as to work centers, ordering the required materials and tests, being physically moved through the use of automatic guided vehicles (AGV) or conveyers, and movement devices such as robots, mechanical diverters, and shuttle trucks—all computer controlled.

Bar code labels attached to each item can also allow automatic sorting and packaging of items flowing on a conveyer line. Even the package that then contains the sorted items can be bar coded for routing to the correct storage or shipping area.

Scanners to read bar codes can range from simple low-light-level probes to laser light-beam scanners that read the lines and spaces. Low-light-level probes, which use infrared or light-emitting diodes, need to touch the bar code to distinguish the line and space widths. More intense light sources do not require direct contact, but still must be a very short distance. The most effective scanners use laser light beams. These can be small and hand held, or they can be fixed such as positioned to read products moving along a conveyer (or products passing over it, as in a supermarket).

There are two types of laser scanners; one uses a fixed beam, which requires the operator to pass the beam over the bar code. The other type uses an oscillating or moving beam, which moves back and forth (even when the physical unit is held still) reading the bar code up to 600 times per second. In this way multiple readings of the same item increase the likelihood that the item will be read, and with a higher degree of accuracy.

Laser beam devices (a laser is a narrow beam of constant width), can read bar coding from a foot or so away. They can also read and interpret bar codes from any position—backward, forward, or sideways.

Materials Handling Systems

Apple and McGinnis[12] believe that the biggest challenge in designing materials handling systems is the development of an overall materials-flow concept, addressing the entire logistics network in both manufacturing and distribution. The equipment choice is fairly straightforward, once the requirements have been established.

Apple and McGinnis are specialists in designing materials handling systems. They state that a major problem today—especially in manufacturing—is that materials handling is an after-the-fact function, and not a "factory integrator," that is, it should be the thread which ties the system together. They argue that materials handling is charged with moving, storing, and tracking all material,

[12] James M. Apple, and Leon F. McGinnis, "Innovations in Facilities and Material Handling Systems: An Introduction," *Industrial Engineering* 19, no. 3 (March 1987), pp. 33–38.

which occurs as a result of someone else doing the process planning and production scheduling. They believe that material handling should be a factory integrator. Process planning and the production scheduling and control systems should incorporate materials handling system needs and limitations as part of their design. The final design of a materials handling system should include:[13]

1. Handling unit and container design.
2. Micromovement (within a production workplace).
3. Macromovement (between operations).
4. Staging or storage of material.
5. Control system for directing and tracking activity.

Each of these elements must also specify the level of technology, such as manual, mechanized, or fully automated.

Sanborn describes an automated conveyer system for routing the thermal conductor board used in IBM's top-of-the-line computer.[14] Each board weighs between 40 and 100 pounds as it passes through its processing steps.

At IBM's Poughkeepsie plant, several dozen operations are performed on the board. Some are done at workstations using simple tools, others use robots, and some operations are highly technical, such as involving sophisticated testing. Processing times vary from 10 minutes to 2 hours. Several workstations could perform similar processes while others could not. Also, the complexity of the board causes the routing to change as a result of testing or the need for rework. All this causes an almost random routing that could not be controlled manually.

A conveyer system was set up under the complete control of a computer. The complex computer system included bar code readers to identify the specific boards, a main conveyer line to move the boards through the center of the plant, load/unload devices to transfer the boards from the main line to spur cars for routing to main areas, shuttle cars to transfer between spurs, and movement devices and communications between the spur and the tools, operators, and waiting work.

Trends in materials handling

Two divergent trends seem to be taking place in the United States at the present time. At one extreme is the move toward simplicity with lesser mechanization. At the other extreme is the move toward highly complex materials handling and automated manufacturing systems. While there are specific areas within which each would be more appropriate, one school of

---

[13] Ibid., p. 38.

[14] Malcolm A. Sanborn, "Computer Control Strategy for a Flexibly Automated System," *Industrial Engineering* 20, no. 2 (February 1988), pp. 48–52.

thought believes that flexibility is possible through simplicity and little capital investment, while the opposing school sees flexibility as being built into the system through elaborate machinery, controls, and materials handling devices.

The demand for large-scale automated storage systems has been decreasing for the past few years, primarily for two reasons: (1) the trend toward reducing the quantities of inventories stored, and (2) the trend toward Just-in-Time systems, which reduces work in process. This has, however, increased the need for smaller and more flexible systems that can be disassembled and moved easily.

Even though the trend toward Just-in-Time systems has lessened the demand for large-scale automated storage systems, demand for finished-goods warehousing systems has held constant. At the same time, new types of materials handling and storage systems have been developed.

Hill describes some of the techniques:[15]

1. Unit-load ***automatic storage and retrieval systems*** (AS/RS). Major developments in this area include computer simulation programs that test various rules for handling materials to try to improve productivity. Also, older systems are being upgraded to enable automatic identification of items and interfacing with automatic guided vehicles (AGV).

2. Miniloads, microloads, and tote stackers. With the trend toward maintaining small inventories, control of parts and kits is critical. Users of these devices are the automotive, airline, and electronics industries.

3. Carousels. Vertical and horizontal carousels move the inventory storage system to the worker. Carousels have high potential because of their very low maintenance costs, as low as 0.1 percent of the original cost annually. Carousels are easily installed or, if need be, disassembled and moved to a new location.

4. Flow racks and paperless picking. When workers pick items in conventional warehouses for orders, the potential for error is high. To increase productivity and reduce errors, some companies have assigned workers to specific inventory areas and have sent information about orders directly to them, perhaps via a CRT screen. The worker collects the needed items that are in his work area and presses a button to send the order on to the next inventory location, where more items will be added. Results have shown error reductions of 90 percent or more, and up to 50 percent reduction in the average time to assemble the order.

The demand for the materials handling systems and controls described above is expected to increase rapidly.

The use of automatic guided vehicles (AGV) is growing at 30 percent per year, partly because of the ease of installation. They are also being used as transporting devices to move material from one workstation to the next.

---

[15] John M. Hill, "Changing Profile of Material Handling System," parts 1 and 2, *Industrial Engineering* 18, no. 11 (November 1986), pp. 68–73, and 18, no. 12 (December 1986), pp. 26–29.

Dependency on the Production-Control System

From the standpoint of materials handling, production-control systems that rigidly specify batch production merely complicate matters. An MRP system, for example, drives the materials handling system, which can only react to what the MRP specifies. Materials handling specialists, however, believe that much improvement can be made and would like to be part of the team that designs and controls the flow of materials and information throughout the plant. JIT systems on the contrary, are better suited for materials handling because of the more predictable movement time and routing, and because the number of items per movement is small.

16.5 MARKETING AND DISTRIBUTION

The final phase of materials management is distribution of the finished product to the field. The distribution function, variously termed *traffic, physical distribution,* or *logistics,* is responsible for arranging the means of shipping finished goods and controlling inventory levels at various stockkeeping points in the field. Stockkeeping points are typically viewed by level or echelons, and a multiechelon system for a major manufacturer would consist of factories, a main distribution center, regional warehouses, and retail outlets.

The major concerns in managing distribution systems are deciding how much inventory is to be kept at each stock point and determining appropriate policies for inventory replenishment. The basic objective is to meet the customer's delivery requirements at a low cost. This entails a trade-off between warehousing and inventory costs and transportation costs.

One firm may follow a strategy of having many warehouses and shipping in, say, carload lots. This keeps its transportation costs low, at the expense of relatively high warehousing and inventory costs. Another firm may follow a strategy of few warehouses, low field inventory, and frequent deliveries. This keeps its warehousing and inventory costs low, at the expense of relatively high transportation costs. In the terminology of distribution, companies with distribution centers are frequently operated as *pull systems.* A pull system exists when individual warehouses order independently, without regard to inventory levels at other warehouses. A pull system gets its name from the independent warehouses reaching out and pulling replenishment stocks from a central warehouse.

Besides high inventory costs, there are other drawbacks to using a pull system. Professor Jay Forrester of MIT showed that when different levels of replenishment operate in a pull system, very high oscillations can be caused.[16] He showed that a 10 percent increase in demand at the consumer level could cause a 100 percent increase at the factory: each level would not only order the

[16] Jay W. Forrester, *Industrial Dynamics* (Cambridge, Mass.: MIT Press, 1958).

increase noted, but also an additional amount for safety stock if it felt that the increase was actually an upward market trend rather than an unusual occurrence.

A *push distribution system* is characterized by a single level of remote warehouses, with the stock status of the total system being controlled by the factory. Using the forecast needs of the remote warehouses, the factory determines the quantity and time of shipments and "pushes" these units out to the warehouses. As implied by these strategies, the advantage of the push system is that it keeps inventories down, but it requires much tighter coordination than the pull system. Management must know what stocks exist at each warehouse at all times so that the total distribution system can react to shifts in retail demand.

To efficiently receive and distribute products, warehouses should be located in centers of transportation, preferably near the center of the product demand. Magee points out that, properly located, systems of 8 to 20 warehouses can service almost the entire United States with one-day delivery.[17]

It is important to note that there has been a significant change in the way many customers want deliveries. In manufacturing, Just-in-Time production is prompting firms to require smaller and more frequent deliveries of materials. Even in the wholesaling and retailing trade, large corporate buyers for store chains are requiring vendors to deliver to all their stores individually, rather than to a company-owned distribution warehouse.

Value Density (Value per Unit Weight)

While it may seem overly simplified, the value of an item per pound of weight—**value density**—is an important measure when deciding where geographically items should be stocked and how they should be shipped. In a classic Harvard case study,[18] the Sorenson Research Company must decide whether to stock inventory for shipment at major warehouses, minor warehouses, or "garage" warehouses, or whether to ship by Federal Express. Analysis shows that the time saved by shipping by air can be justified if the shipping cost is appropriate. The decision involves a trade-off: the savings of reduced transit time versus the higher cost to ship. Obviously, the solution involves a combination of methods.

We can approach the problem by examining a specific situation. Consider, for example, the cost for shipping from Boston to Tucson. Assume that the inventory cost is 30 percent per year of the product value (which includes cost of capital, insurance, decrease in warehouse costs, etc.), that regular United

---

[17] Magee et al., *Modern Logistics Management,* p. 159.

[18] W. Earl Sasser et al., *Cases in Operations Management* (Homewood, Ill.: Richard D. Irwin, 1982).

EXHIBIT 16.8 **Sorenson Research Company Shipping Cost Comparison**

Shipping Weight (pounds)	United Parcel (8 days to deliver)	Federal Express (2 days to deliver)	Cost Savings with UPS	Break-Even Product Value	Break-Even Product Value (per pound)
1	$1.91	$11.50	$ 9.59	$1,944.64	$1,944.68
2	2.37	12.50	10.13	2,054.14	1,027.07
3	2.78	13.50	10.72	2,173.78	724.59
4	3.20	14.50	11.30	2,291.39	572.85
5	3.54	15.50	11.96	2,425.22	485.04
6	3.88	16.50	12.62	2,559.06	426.51
7	4.28	17.50	13.22	2,680.72	382.96
8	4.70	18.50	13.80	2,798.33	349.79
9	5.12	19.50	14.38	2,915.94	323.99
10	5.53	20.50	14.97	3,035.58	303.56

Parcel shipments take eight days, and that we are considering second-day air service with Federal Express. We can set up a comparison table as shown in Exhibit 16.8.

The problem then becomes comparing the additional cost of transportation to the savings of six days. Logically we can make the general statement that expensive items can be sent by air from the factory warehouse, while lower-value items can be stocked at lower-level warehouses or shipped by a less expensive method.

$$\text{Regular shipment} - \text{Air shipping cost} = \text{Shipping cost savings}$$

At break-even,

$$\text{Cost savings} = \text{Inventory carrying cost}$$
$$= \frac{\text{Item value} \times 0.30 \times 6 \text{ days}}{365 \text{ days per year}}$$

Therefore,

$$\text{Item value} = \frac{365 \times \text{Savings}}{0.30 \times 6}$$

The last column in Exhibit 16.8 is the break-even based on the product value per pound for shipments of different weights. The exhibit indicates that any item whose value is greater than that amount should be sent by air. For example, a five-pound shipment of integrated circuits whose average value is $500 per pound should be shipped by air.

We have somewhat simplified this problem by ignoring other factors that might be present (such as quantity discounts, differences in pick-up policies, and so on), but the point is that the weight and cost of an item can justify centralized stocking with air shipping.

Warehouse Replenishment Systems

There are three basic approaches to warehouse inventory replenishment:

1. Reorder point/economic order quantity system.
2. Base stock system.
3. Distribution requirements planning.

EXHIBIT 16.9 **Distribution Requirements Planning**

Warehouse A

	Past due	Week 1	2	3	4	5	6	7	8
Gross requirements*		80	80	80	70	80	90	90	90
Scheduled receipts				500					
Projected on hand	204	124	44	464	394	314	224	134	44
Planned orders		500							

Warehouse B

	Past due	Week 1	2	3	4	5	6	7	8
Gross requirements*		30	30	30	20	30	35	35	35
Scheduled receipts					200				
Projected on hand	100	70	40	10	190	160	125	90	55
Planned orders		200							

Warehouse C

	Past due	Week 1	2	3	4	5	6	7	8
Gross requirements*		120	120	120	100	120	140	140	140
Scheduled receipts							700		
Projected on hand	600	480	360	240	140	20	580	440	300
Planned orders					700				

Direct sales

	Past due	Week 1	2	3	4	5	6	7	8
		50	50	50	50	50	50	50	50

Central supply

	Past due	Week 1	2	3	4	5	6	7	8
Gross requirements*		750	50	50	750	50	50	50	50
Scheduled receipts					1800				
Projected on hand	950	200	150	100	1150	1100	1050	1000	950
Planned orders		1800							

Order quantities and lead time

	Order quantity	Lead time (weeks)
Warehouse A	500	2
Warehouse B	200	3
Warehouse C	700	2
Central warehouse	1,800	3

*Forecast.

Source: Donald W. Fogarty and Thomas R. Hoffmann, *Production and Inventory Management* (Cincinnati: South-Western Publishing, 1983), p. 363.

The reorder point/economic order quantity system in distribution works the same way as for in-plant inventory control. The warehouse places an economic lot-size order when its inventory reaches the reorder point.

The base stock system works to scheduled shipment dates, and shipment size is equal to the actual usage in the previous period.

Distribution requirements planning (DRP) follows the logic of MRP. It converts a forecast of warehouse demand to a gross requirement, subtracts on-hand and on-order balances, and then places a replenishment order.

Of the three methods, DRP has the advantage of being based on projected demand rather than past sales. This avoids the risk of having a stockout at a central warehouse as a result of several branch warehouses reaching their reorder points simultaneously. An example of DRP calculations is shown in Exhibit 16.9.

16.6 CONCLUSION

This chapter has treated materials management in the context of manufacturing, but materials management is a vitally important function in service organizations as well. Hospitals and utilities of all kinds have major materials requirements under the category of supplies. Likewise, the military has billions of dollars invested in materials, and in fact the Navy publishes a major journal devoted to logistical issues (*Naval Logistics Research Quarterly*). Indeed, though materials management is one of those areas that historically has received little emphasis in business schools, how well it is performed can make or break an organization. Its importance and concern are rapidly growing.

16.7 REVIEW AND DISCUSSION QUESTIONS

1. What are the trade-offs in single-source versus multiple-source purchasing?
2. What skills and training are most important for a purchasing agent?
3. The following items have been taken from the purchasing section of an MRP II audit questionnaire:

   Purchasing people believe the schedules.
   Vendor lead time is 95 percent accurate.
   Vendor delivery performance is 95 percent or better.
   Vendor scheduling is done out beyond quoted lead times.

   Explain why these items are important to MRP II success.
4. Discuss the liaison activities of the purchasing department during the introduction of a new product.
5. "JIT purchasing is nothing more than a ploy to have vendors take over the burden of carrying inventory." Comment.

6. Distinguish between push and pull distribution systems. What are the pros and cons of each?
7. What is DRP? How does it work?
8. For the value density example given in Exhibit 16.8, what would the effect be if a competing firm offers you a similar service for 10 percent less than Federal Express's rates?

16.8 CASE: THOMAS MANUFACTURING COMPANY*

"Delivery of our 412 casting is critical. We can't just stop production for this casting every time you have a minor pattern problem," said Mr. Litt, engineer for Thomas Manufacturing.

"I'm not interested in running rejects," answered Mr. James of A&B Foundry. "I cannot overextend my time on these castings when the other jobs are waiting."

"If you can't cast them properly and on time, I'll just have to take our pattern to another foundry that can," retorted Mr. Litt.

"Go ahead! It's all yours. I have other jobs with fewer headaches," replied Mr. James.

Mr. Litt returned to Thomas Manufacturing with the 412 casting pattern. (A pattern is used in making molds in which the gray iron is formed. After cooling, the mold is broken off, leaving the desired casting.) He remembered that Mr. Dunn, vice president of manufacturing for Thomas (see Exhibit 16.10), had obtained a quote on his casting from Dawson, another gray-iron foundry, several months before. It seemed that Dawson had the necessary capabilities to handle this casting.

To Mr. Litt's surprise, Mr. Dunn was not entirely happy to find the 412 pattern back in the plant. Mr. Dunn contacted personnel at Dawson Foundry, who said that they could not accept the job because of a major facilities conversion that would take six months. Locating another supplier would be difficult. Most foundries would undertake complex casting only if a number of orders for simple casting were placed at the same time.

Mr. Dunn knew that gray-iron foundry capacity was tight. In general, foundries were specializing or closing down. Mr. Dunn had gathered some data on the gray-iron industry located within a 500-mile radius of his plant (see Exhibit 16.11), which highlighted the problems his company was facing. There were three gray-iron foundries located within 60 miles of Thomas Manufacturing. Thomas had dealt with one foundry until it suffered a 12-month strike. Thomas then moved most of its casting needs to A&B Foundry, but Mr. Dunn had given the occasional order to Dawson and requested quotes quite regularly from them. In the last four years all had gone well with A&B Foundry. Mr. Dunn had planned to share his business with both foundries. A&B was comparable to Dawson on price and had done an excellent job until now.

A telephone call back to A&B Foundry indicated to Mr. Dunn that Mr. James was adamant in his refusal to take the pattern back.

---

* From M. R. Leenders, H. E. Fearon, and W. B. England, *Purchasing and Materials Management,* 7th ed. (Homewood, Ill.: Richard D. Irwin, 1980), pp. 50–53.

EXHIBIT 16.10

Organization Chart of Thomas Manufacturing Company

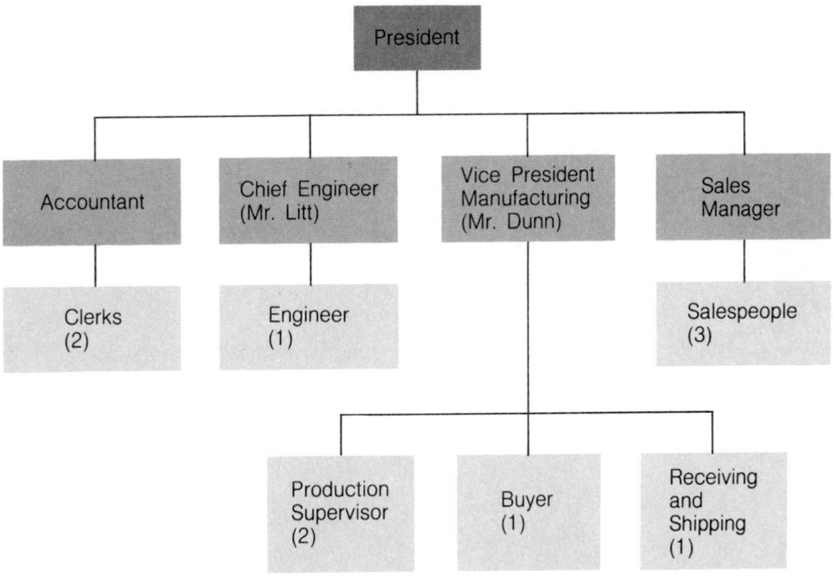

EXHIBIT 16.11

Foundry Data for Area within a 500-Mile Radius of the Thomas Plant

A. Shipments of Manufactured Goods

Gray Iron (commercial castings)	Quantity	Value
Previous year	280,000 tons	$65,000,000
Current year	243,000 tons	$54,000,000

B. Number of Establishments

									Current Year
140	133	131	134	137	134	134	128	126	116

Ten-Year History

THE 412 CASTING

Thomas Manufacturing Company was a portable generator manufacturer with sales above the $6 million level. Thomas employed approximately 160 people in a fairly modern plant. Many of its small portable generators were sold to clients all over North America.

The 412 casting was part of the most popular middle-of-the-line generator. The casting weighed 70 pounds and cost approximately $60, and its pattern was worth $8,000. A run normally consisted of 100 castings, and Thomas usually received 100 castings every month. The 412 represented about 15 percent of Thomas's casting needs.

Normal lead time was at least eight weeks. When the supply problem arose, Thomas held six weeks' inventory.

Mr. Litt, an expert in pattern work, explained that the pattern was tricky, but once the difficulties were ironed out and the job set up, a hand molder could pour 50 castings in two days without any problems.

QUESTIONS

1. What alternatives are open to Mr. Dunn to prevent disruption of his company's most popular generator?
2. Was it appropriate for Mr. Litt to repossess the 412 pattern?
3. From the data given, does it appear that the Thomas Company has any leverage in dealing with the foundries?

16.9 CASE: OHIO TOOL COMPANY (VENDOR SELECTION)*

The Ohio Tool Company designed a new machine, which it considered to be superior to anything else of its type on the market. Estimated sales were about $200,000 per year. The principal advantage of this machine over competition was a unique cam arrangement enabling the operator to adjust the unit very quickly.

To achieve the advantages offered by the design, it was necessary that the cam—of which two were required per unit—be manufactured to very close tolerances (see sketch below). Because of the difficulty of machining the several eccentric surfaces and the need for an integral locating key in the center bore, the part could not readily be made from solid bar stock.

---

* Source: Modified from P. E. Holden, F. E. Shallenberger, and W. E. Diehm, *Selected Case Problems in Industrial Management* (Englewood Cliffs, N.J.: Prentice-Hall, 1962), pp. 123–26.

Possible methods of manufacture rapidly narrowed down to some type of casting. The materials under consideration were aluminum, zinc, and iron. Aluminum and iron sand castings were excluded because the close tolerances on the finished part would require precise and very difficult secondary machining operations. Aluminum and zinc die castings could not be used because draft or taper on the cam surfaces, required to remove the part from the die, would also necessitate secondary machining operations to render the surfaces true again.

Another possibility for producing the part seemed to be through powder metallurgy, a process by which finely divided metal particles (in this case powdered iron) were formed to the desired shape by means of high pressure in a metal die, then "sintered" at high temperature to form a solid metal piece. The Ohio Tool Company located three possible powdered-metal sources and sent parts drawings to each.

Supplier A, located about 1,000 miles away, was one of the leaders in the powder metallurgy field. The Ohio Tool Company had purchased parts for another product from this supplier within the past year, and the supplier had failed to deliver on the agreed schedule. After many delivery promises via long-distance telephone and after a special trip to the plant by the purchasing manager, the parts arrived three months late. During this delay all other parts for the project had to be set aside and some workers laid off. In addition, the delay caused the Ohio Tool Company considerable loss of face with its customers because the product had been announced to the trade.

Supplier A submitted this quotation:

		Die cost—$1,968
5,000 pieces	$0.146 each	Delivery—Approximately 10 weeks, depending on the production schedule at the time order is entered.
10,000 pieces	$0.145 each	
20,000 pieces	$0.144 each	

The quotation did not include incoming freight cost of $0.012 each. Further, it was based on furnishing a cam with a slight projection on one of the surfaces, which would require a machining operation by the Ohio Tool Company at an estimated cost of $0.05 each.

Supplier B, located 300 miles away, was a relative newcomer to the powdered-metal field. The manager of the shop had been with this firm only a short time but had gained his experience from one of the old-line companies. The Ohio Tool Company's experience with this company had been very satisfactory. It had undertaken the job mentioned above at the same costs as Supplier A and had produced satisfactory parts in record time.

In reply to the request for a quotation, Supplier B suggested that, since it could not manufacture to specified tolerances, they be relaxed on several dimensions. However, the engineering department at Ohio Tool insisted that the critical function of this cam necessitated the tolerances as originally specified. When this information was passed along to Supplier B, it asked to be excused from quoting.

A third supplier, with whom the Ohio Tool Company had had no previous dealings, was asked to quote on the part. Supplier C was a subsidiary of one of the large automotive concerns and had an excellent technical reputation. It was understood, however, that the parent company was considering introducing several powdered-metal parts on its line of automobiles. The quotation of Supplier C was:

5,000 pieces	$0.186 each	Die cost—$890
10,000 pieces	$0.185 each	Delivery—10 weeks
20,000 pieces	$0.183 each	

Supplier C was located 900 miles from the Ohio Tool Company plant, and incoming freight would cost $0.012 per unit. The drawing accompanying the quotation indicated a projection on one of the cam surfaces, which would have to be machined by the Ohio Tool Company for the proper functioning of the part. Although special machining techniques would be required in this case, the Ohio Tool Company estimator felt the company could machine off the projection for about $0.06 each in quantities of 5,000 or more.

Because of the past performance record of Supplier B, the purchasing manager decided that he should make an effort to obtain a quotation. He made a personal visit to the plant to discuss the problem, and learned that the plant could hold the tolerances on the center hole closer than the engineering department required, making the cumulative tolerances on the outside diameter of the cam surfaces almost within the tolerance specified. The engineering department agreed to change the drawing accordingly and grant additional latitude on the cam surfaces. On this basis, Supplier B entered the following quotation:

5,000 pieces	$0.50 each	Die cost—$1,350
10,000 pieces	$0.40 each	Delivery—10 to 12 weeks
20,000 pieces	$0.32 each	
50,000 pieces	$0.275 each	

Freight in amounted to $0.005 each. The quotation was based on a part in exact accordance with the drawing, since the cost of secondary operations had been included in the quotation and would be performed by the supplier. By the time this quotation was received, manufacture of other parts of the product was assured and final assembly was scheduled for 12 weeks from that date.

Upon reviewing all the quotations, the relatively high cost of Supplier B was readily apparent. The purchasing manager decided to call Supplier B and ask him to review his costs again. The quotation was revised:

5,000 pieces	$0.45
10,000 pieces	$0.37

No change in 20,000 and 50,000 price

QUESTIONS

1. Which vendor would you select for the job? Why?
2. Should a purchasing agent enter into negotiations with one vendor after bids from competitors have been examined?
3. With reference to Question 2, prepare a policy statement that would guide the future actions of the purchasing department.

16.10 SELECTED BIBLIOGRAPHY

Apple, James M., Jr., and Leon F. McGinnis. "Innovations in Facilities and Material Handling Systems: An Introduction." *Industrial Engineering* 19, no. 3 (March 1987), pp. 33–38.

Batdorf, Leland, and Jay A. Vora. "Use of Analytical Techniques in Purchasing." *Journal of Purchasing and Materials Management,* Spring 1983, pp. 25–29.

Fogarty, Donald W., and Thomas R. Hoffmann. *Production and Inventory Management.* Cincinnati: South-Western Publishing, 1983.

Hahn, Chan K.; Peter A. Pinto; and Daniel Bragg. "'Just-in-Time' Production and Purchasing." *Journal of Purchasing and Materials Management,* Fall 1983, pp. 2–10.

Hill, John M. "Changing Profile of Material Handling System," parts 1 and 2. *Industrial Engineering* 18, no. 11 (November 1986), pp. 68–73, and 18, no. 12 (December 1986), pp. 26–29.

Lee, Sang M., and A. Ansari. "Comparative Analysis of Japanese Just-in-Time Purchasing and Traditional U.S. Purchasing Systems." *International Journal of Operations and Production Management* 5, no. 4 (1985), pp. 5–14.

McDonald, Richard A. "Bar Code Systems Enhance Productivity of Computer Systems with Real-Time Mode." *Industrial Engineering* 17, no. 11 (November 1985) pp. 70–74.

McEneny, Tim. *Up the Manufacturing Organization, The Modern Materials Manager's Guide to Survival.* Holmdel, N.J.: TSM Publishing, 1980.

Magee, John F.; William C. Copacino; and Donald B. Rosenfield. *Modern Logistics Management, Integrating Marketing, Manufacturing and Physical Distribution.* New York: John Wiley & Sons, 1985.

Narasimhan, Ram. "An Analytical Approach to Supplier Selection." *Journal of Purchasing and Materials Management,* Winter 1983, pp. 27–32.

Sanborn, Malcolm A. "Computer Control Strategy for a Flexibly Automated System." *Industrial Engineering* 20, no. 2 (February 1988), pp. 48–52.

Schonberger, Richard J., and James P. Gilbert. "Just-in-Time Purchasing: A Challenge for U.S. Industry." *California Management Review,* Fall 1983, pp. 54–68.

Taff, Charles A. *Management of Physical Distribution and Transportation,* 7th ed. Homewood, Ill.: Richard D. Irwin, 1984.

Vollmann, Thomas E.; William L. Berry; and D. Clay Whybark. *Manufacturing Planning and Control Systems,* 2nd ed. Homewood, Ill.: Richard D. Irwin, 1988, chap. 19.

Chapter 17

Synchronous Production

EPIGRAPH

The action you're proposing:
Will it increase throughput?
Will it decrease inventory?
Will it decrease operating expense?

Dr. Eliyahu A. Goldratt

CHAPTER OUTLINE

KEY TERMS

Synchronous Manufacturing
Hockey-Stick Phenomenon
Throughput
Inventory
Operating Expense
Productivity
Unbalanced Capacity
Bottleneck
Capacity-Constrained Resource
Backward/Forward Scheduling
Drum
Buffer
Rope
Time Buffer
Process Batch
Transfer Batches
Dollar Days
VAT Classification

MRP, covered in Chapter 13, is a push system because it schedules each operation in the sequence, forcing it through the system. JIT, covered in Chapter 15, is a pull system because only the end output is scheduled and all the intermediate stages pull from preceding stages as needed. A third way of controlling the production system, which we can term *synchronous production,* is to focus on the bottlenecks, or those operations that have the least capacity. These three techniques have been appropriately referred to as *push, pull,* and *squeeze.*[1]

In this chapter, we discuss "synchronous" production. **Synchronous production** refers to the entire production process working together to achieve the goals of the firm. All of the phases of the entire process work in step and in harmony. All temptations to use suboptimum performance measures are avoided (such as percent of labor or machine utilization) and total system performance is emphasized.

This approach to production deals with constraints. In order to correctly treat the topic, we must first discuss some basic issues about firms, such as purposes, goals, and performance measurements. We will then discuss where to position inventories for the best performance. Also presented is an interesting classification of manufacturing firms as V firms, A firms, and T firms, or VAT.

17.1 HOCKEY-STICK PHENOMENON

Just about every company faces a problem called the **hockey-stick phenomenon**—rushing to meet quotas at the *end* of the time period. If the time period is a month, then this is an end-of-the-month-syndrome; if the period is a quarter, it is an end-of-the-quarter syndrome (see Exhibit 17.1). It's called a hockey stick because it looks like a hockey stick—with a relatively flat bottom and a long rapid rise like a handle. The cause of the problem is that two sets of measurements are being employed: At the beginning of the period, cost-accounting *efficiency* measurements are used for utilizations and variances from standards. As the end of the month approaches, pressure mounts to meet a financial *performance.* These are global measurements stated in terms such as dollars of output shipped. As soon as the end of the month passes (with its frantic overtime and weekend work along with constant expediting and frequent setups aimed toward getting the product out), pressure decreases and everyone again looks at the efficiency measurements. And so the cycle repeats.

Note: Most of this chapter is based on the writings and teachings of Dr. Eliyahu M. Goldratt and Robert E. Fox. One of the authors of this text was a participant in several of their week-long seminars and courses. We express our thanks to Dr. Goldratt for his permission to freely use his concepts, definitions, and other material.

[1] Martin L. Ramsay, Steve Brown, and Kambiz Tabibzadeh, "Push, Pull, and Squeeze: Shop Floor Control with Computer Simulation," *Industrial Engineering,* February 1990, pp. 39–45.

EXHIBIT 17.1

Hockey-Stick Phenomenon—The End-of-the-Period Rush

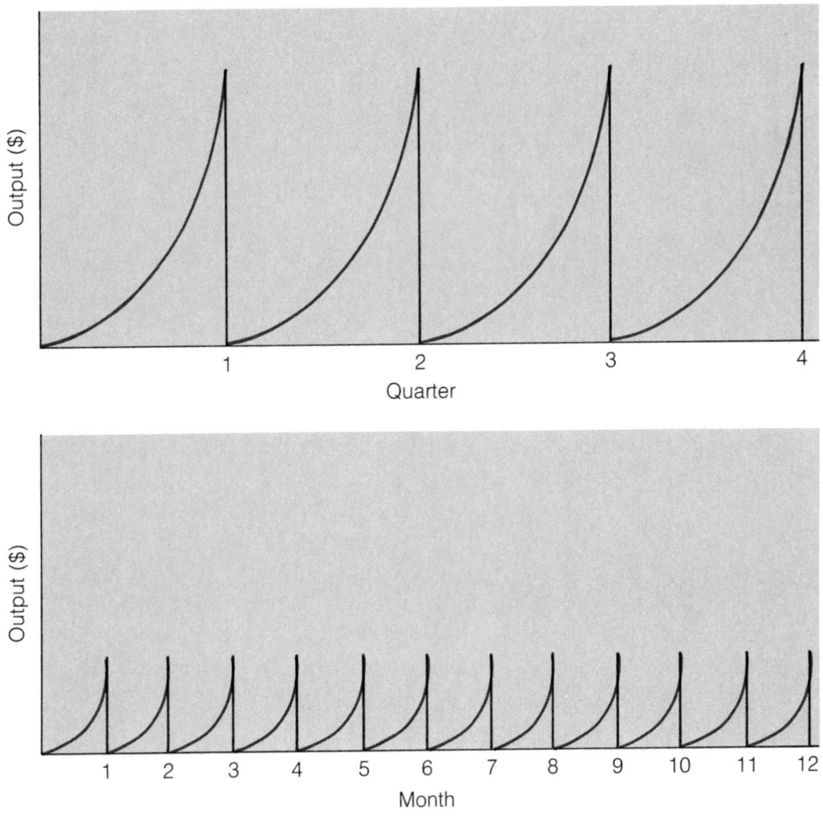

17.2 GOAL OF THE FIRM

Although many people disagree with him, Goldratt has a very straightforward idea of the goal of a firm.

THE GOAL OF A FIRM IS TO MAKE MONEY

Goldratt argues that while an organization may have many purposes—providing jobs, consuming raw materials, increasing sales, increasing share of the market, developing technology, or producing high-quality products—these do not guarantee long-term survival of the firm. They are means to achieve the goal, not the goal itself. If the firm makes money—and only then—it will prosper. When a firm has money, then it can place more emphasis on other objectives.

17.3 PERFORMANCE MEASUREMENTS

To adequately measure a firm's performance, two sets of measurements must be used: one from the financial point of view, and the other from the operations point of view.

Financial Measurements

How do we measure the firm's ability to make money? In financial terms, we keep track of:

1. Net profit, which is an absolute measurement in dollars.
2. Return on investment, which is a relative measure based on investment.
3. Cash flow, which is a survival measurement.

To accurately evaluate a firm's performance in financial terms, all three measurements must be used together. For example, a *net profit* of $10 million is important as one measurement, but it has no real meaning until we know how much investment it took to generate that $10 million. If the investment was $100 million, then this is a 10 percent *return on investment. Cash flow* is important since cash is necessary to pay bills for day-to-day operations; without cash, a firm can go bankrupt even though it is very sound in normal accounting terms. A firm can have a high profit and a high return on investment, but can still be short on cash if, for example, the profit is invested in new equipment or tied up in inventory.

Operational Measurements

Financial measurements cannot be used at the operational level. We need another set of measurements:

1. **Throughput**—the rate at which money is generated by the system through sales.
2. **Inventory**—all the money that the system has invested in purchasing things it intends to sell.
3. **Operating expenses**—all the money that the system spends in order to turn inventory into throughput.

Throughput is specifically defined as goods *sold*. An inventory of finished goods is not throughput, but inventory. Actual sales must occur. It is specifically defined this way to prevent the system from continuing to produce under the illusion that the goods *might* be sold.

Inventory includes all of the resources used for the production process, such as facilities and equipment, as well as materials and parts.

Operating expenses includes production costs, such as direct labor, indirect labor, inventory carrying costs, equipment depreciation, and administrative

EXHIBIT 17.2

Operational Goal

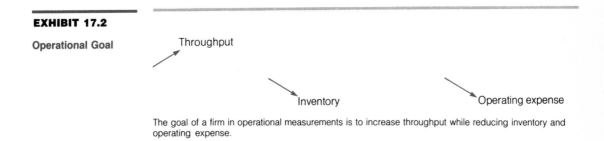

The goal of a firm in operational measurements is to increase throughput while reducing inventory and operating expense.

costs. The key difference here is that there is no need to separate direct and indirect labor.

As shown in Exhibit 17.2, the objective of a firm is to treat all three measurements simultaneously, and continually; this will achieve the goal of making money.

In these operational measurements, the goal of the firm is to

INCREASE THROUGHPUT WHILE SIMULTANEOUSLY REDUCING INVENTORY AND REDUCING OPERATING EXPENSE.

Productivity

Typically, **productivity** is measured in terms of output per labor hour. However, this measurement does not ensure that the firm will make money (for example, when extra output is not sold but accumulates as inventory). To test whether or not productivity has increased, we should ask these questions: Has the action taken increased throughput? Has it decreased inventory? Has it decreased operational expense? This leads us to a new definition:

PRODUCTIVITY IS ALL THE ACTIONS THAT BRING A COMPANY CLOSER TO ITS GOALS.

17.4 ATTEMPTS TO BALANCE CAPACITY

Historically (and still typically in most firms), manufacturers have tried to balance capacity across a sequence of processes, in an attempt to match capacity with market demand. Using systems manufacturing logic, however, this is the wrong thing to do—**unbalanced capacity** is better. Consider a simple process line with several stations, for example. Once the cycle time (or average output rate) of the line has been established, production people try to make the capacities of all stations the same. This is done by adjusting machines or equipment used, work loads, skill and type of labor assigned, tools used, overtime budgeted, and so on.

In synchronous production, however, making all capacities the same is a bad decision. Such a balance would be possible only if the output times of all stations were constant or had a very narrow distribution. A normal variation in output times causes downstream stations to have idle time when upstream stations take longer to process. Conversely, when upstream stations process in a shorter time, inventory builds up between the stations. The effect of the statistical variation is cumulative. The only way that this variation can be smoothed is by increasing work in process to absorb the variation (a bad choice, since we should be trying to reduce work in process), or increasing capacities downstream to be able to make up for the longer upstream times. The rule here is that capacities within the process sequence should not be balanced to the same levels. Rather, attempts should be made to balance the *flow of product* through the system. When flow is balanced, capacities will be unbalanced.

17.5 BOTTLENECKS, NONBOTTLENECKS, AND CAPACITY-CONSTRAINED RESOURCES

A **bottleneck** is defined as any resource whose capacity is less than the demand placed upon it. A bottleneck, in other words, is a process that limits throughput. It is that point in the manufacturing process where flow thins to a narrow stream. The bottlenecks may be a machine, scarce or highly skilled labor, or a specialized tool. Observations in industry have shown that most plants have very few bottleneck operations, usually just several.

Capacity is defined as the available time for production. This excludes maintenance and other downtime. A *nonbottleneck* is a resource whose capacity is greater than the demand placed on it. A nonbottleneck, therefore, should not be working constantly since it can produce more than is needed. A nonbottleneck contains idle time.

A **capacity-constrained resource** (CCR) is one whose utilization is close to capacity and could be a bottleneck if it is not scheduled carefully. For example, a CCR may be receiving work in a job-shop environment from several sources. If these sources schedule their flow in a way that causes occasional idle time for the CCR in excess of its unused capacity time, then the CCR becomes a bottleneck. This can happen if batch sizes are changed or if one of the upstream operations is down and starves the CCR for work.

17.6 COMPARING SYNCHRONOUS PRODUCTION TO MRP AND JIT

MRP uses **backward scheduling;** having been fed a master production schedule, it schedules production through a bill of materials explosion in a backward manner—working backward in time from the desired completion date. As a secondary procedure, MRP, through its capacity resource planning module, develops capacity utilization profiles of work centers. When work centers are overloaded, either the master production schedule must be adjusted or enough slack capacity must be left unscheduled in the system so that work can be smoothed at the local level (by work-center supervisors or the workers themselves). Trying to smooth capacity using MRP is so difficult and would require so many computer runs that capacity overloads and underloads are left to local decisions, such as at the machine centers. As a result, processing sequences for the product bill of materials usually are not followed and the MRP schedule becomes invalid just days after it was created.

The synchronous production approach uses **forward scheduling** since it focuses on the critical resources. These are scheduled *forward* in time, ensuring that loads placed on them are within capacity. The noncritical (or nonbottleneck) resources are then scheduled to support the critical resources. (This can be done backward to minimize the length of time inventories are held.) This procedure ensures a feasible schedule. To help reduce lead time and work in process, in synchronized manufacturing the process batch size and transfer batch size are varied—a procedure that MRP is not able to do.

Comparing JIT to synchronized manufacturing, JIT does an excellent job in reducing lead times and work in process, but it has several drawbacks:

1. JIT is limited to repetitive manufacturing.
2. JIT requires a stable production level (usually about a month long).
3. JIT does not allow very much flexibility in the products produced (products must be similar with a limited number of options).
4. JIT still requires work in process when used with Kanban so that there is "something to pull." This means that completed work must be stored on the downstream side of each workstation to be "pulled" by the next workstation.
5. Vendors need to be located nearby since the system depends on smaller and more frequent deliveries.

17.7 METHODS FOR CONTROL IN SYNCHRONOUS PRODUCTION

We will illustrate the way bottlenecks and nonbottleneck resources should be managed. Assume that Resource X has a market demand of 200 units of product per month and Resource Y has a market demand of 150 units per month, regardless of the building block configuration. Assume also that both X and Y have 200 hours per month available. To help understand our example, assume that each unit of product passing through X takes one hour of processing time and each unit passing through Y takes 45 minutes. With the available times, 200 hours of Resource X will produce 200 units of product and 200 hours of Resource Y can produce 267 units of product. Let's consider each of the four building blocks.

EXHIBIT 17.3

Product Flow through the Four Basic Building Blocks

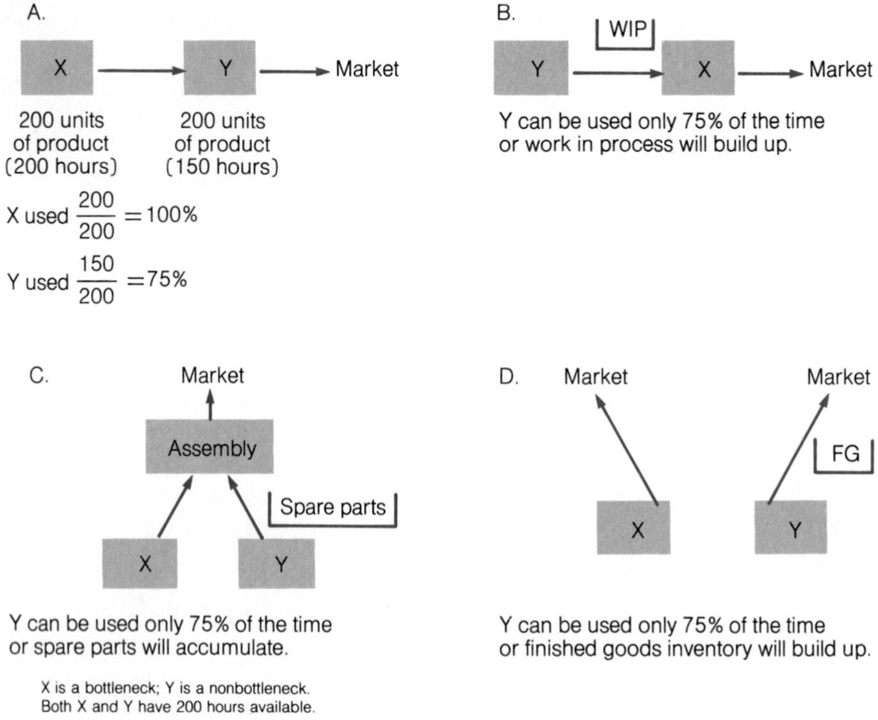
A.
X
Y
Market
200 units of product (200 hours)
200 units of product (150 hours)
X used 200/200 = 100%
Y used 150/200 = 75%
B.
WIP
Y
X
Market
Y can be used only 75% of the time or work in process will build up.
C.
Market
Assembly
Spare parts
X
Y
Y can be used only 75% of the time or spare parts will accumulate.
D.
Market
Market
FG
X
Y
Y can be used only 75% of the time or finished goods inventory will build up.
X is a bottleneck; Y is a nonbottleneck.
Both X and Y have 200 hours available.

In Exhibit 17.3A, the flow of product is in a dependent sequence, that is, it must pass through both Resource X (Machine X) and Resource Y (Machine Y). Resource X is the bottleneck since it has a capacity of 200 units whereas Y has a capacity of 267 units. Resource Y can be used only 75 percent of the time, since it is starved for work (X is not feeding it enough to allow it to work longer).

Section B of the exhibit is the reverse of Section A: a nonbottleneck is feeding a bottleneck. Since X can put through only 200 units, we must be careful not to produce more than 200 on Y, or inventory will build up as work in process.

Section C of the exhibit shows that the outputs from X (a bottleneck) and Y (a nonbottleneck) are assembled into a product. As a nonbottleneck, Y has more capacity than X, so it can be used only 75 percent of the time, otherwise spare parts will accumulate.

In Section D, market demands for X and Y are 200 units of each. Since 200 units from Y corresponds to only 75 percent of its capacity, Y can be used only

75 percent of the time or finished goods inventory will build up. (Current practice in industry is to consider utilization of resources as one of the measurements of performance. This encourages the overuse of nonbottleneck resources, resulting in excess inventories.)

Time Components

It is important to understand the various kinds of time that make up the production cycle time.

1. Setup time: the time that a part spends waiting for a resource to be set up to work on this same part.
2. Process time: the time that the part is being processed.
3. Queue time: the time that a part waits for a resource while the resource is busy with something else.
4. Wait time: the time that a part waits not for a resource but for another part so that they can be assembled together.
5. Idle time: the unused time: that is, the cycle time less the sum of the setup time, processing time, queue time, and wait time.

For a part going through a bottleneck, queue time is the greatest. For a nonbottleneck, wait time is the greatest (waiting for parts from a bottleneck).

Saving Time on Bottleneck and Nonbottleneck Resources

Recall that a bottleneck is a resource whose capacity is less than the demand placed on it. Since we focus on bottlenecks as restricting *throughput* (defined as *sales*), a bottleneck's capacity is less than the market demand. There are a number of ways in which we can increase throughput through the bottleneck (better tooling, higher quality labor, larger batch sizes, reducing setup times, etc.), but how valuable is this extra time?

AN HOUR SAVED AT THE BOTTLENECK ADDS AN EXTRA HOUR TO THE ENTIRE PRODUCTION SYSTEM.

Thus, the time saved is not just the operating expenses for the bottleneck, but the operating expenses and lost profit for the entire system!

How about time saved on a nonbottleneck resource?

AN HOUR SAVED AT A NONBOTTLENECK IS A MIRAGE AND ONLY ADDS AN HOUR TO ITS IDLE TIME.

Since a nonbottleneck has more capacity than the system needs for its current throughput, it already contains idle time. Implementing any measures to save more time does not increase throughput but only serves to increase its idle time.

Drum, Buffer, Rope

Every production system needs some control point or points to control the flow of product through the system. If the system contains a bottleneck, then the bottleneck is the best place for control. This control point is called the **drum,** for it will strike the beat that the rest of the system (or those parts which it influences) uses to function. Recall that a *bottleneck* is defined as a resource that does not have the capacity to meet demand. Therefore, a bottleneck will be working all the time and the reason for using it as a control point is to make sure that the operations upstream do not overproduce and build up excess work-in-process inventory that the bottleneck cannot handle.

If there is no bottleneck, then the next best place to set the drum would be a capacity-constrained resource (CCR). A capacity-constrained resource, remember, is one that is operating near capacity, but on the average has adequate capability as long as it is not incorrectly scheduled (for example, with too many setups, causing it to run short of capacity, or producing too large a lot size, thereby starving downstream operations).

If neither a bottleneck nor a CCR is present, the control point can be designated anywhere. The best position would generally be at some divergent point where the output of the resource is used in more than one downstream operation.

Dealing with the bottleneck is most critical, and our discussion will focus on protecting its operation. Exhibit 17.4 shows a simple linear flow. Suppose that Resource D, which is a machine center, is a bottleneck. This means that the capacities are greater both upstream and downstream from it. If this sequence is not controlled, we would expect to see a large amount of inventory in front of Machine center D and very little anywhere else. There would be little finished-goods inventory because (by the definition of the term *bottleneck*) all the product produced would be taken by the market.

EXHIBIT 17.4

Linear Flow of Product with a Bottleneck

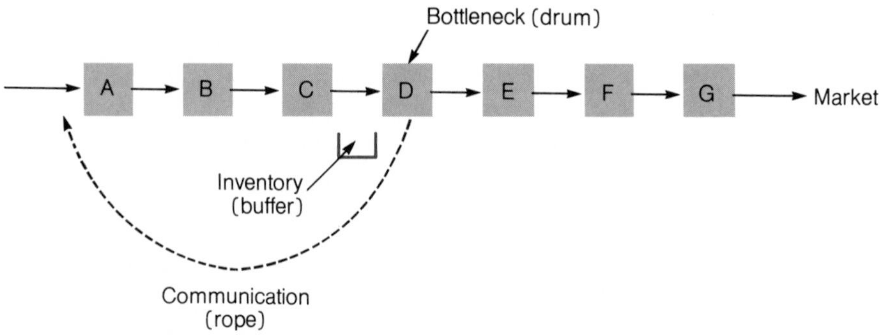

Product flows from Work centers A through G. Work center D is a bottleneck.

There are two things that we must do with this bottleneck:

1. Keep a **buffer** inventory in front of it to make sure that it always has something to work on. Because it is a bottleneck, its output determines the throughput of the system.
2. Communicate back upstream to A what D has produced so that A will provide only that amount. This will keep inventory from buiding up. This communication is called the **rope.** It can be formal, such as a schedule, or informal, such as daily discussion.

We might ask, How large should the buffer be? The answer: As large as it needs to be to ensure that the bottleneck continues to work. By examining the variation of each operation, we can make a guess. Precision is not critical. We could start with an estimate of the time buffer as one fourth of the total cycle time of the system. Say the sequence A to G in our example took a total of 16 days. We could start with a buffer of 4 days in front of D. If during the next few days or weeks the buffer runs out, we will need to increase the buffer size. We do this by releasing extra material to the first operation, A. On the other hand, if we find that our normal variation never drops below three days, we might want to hold back releases to A and reduce the time buffer to three days. Experience in the operation is the best determination of the final buffer size.

If the drum is not a bottleneck but a CCR (and thus it can have a small amount of idle time), then we might want to create two buffer inventories—one in front of the CCR and the second at the end as finished goods. (See Exhibit 17.5.) The finished-goods inventory will protect the market, and the time buffer in front of the CCR will protect throughput. For this CCR case, the market will not take all that we can produce, so we want to ensure that finished goods are available when the market does decide to purchase.

We need two ropes in this case: (1) a rope communicating from finished-goods inventory back to the drum to increase or decrease output, and (2) a

EXHIBIT 17.5

Linear Flow of Product with a Capacity-Constrained Resource

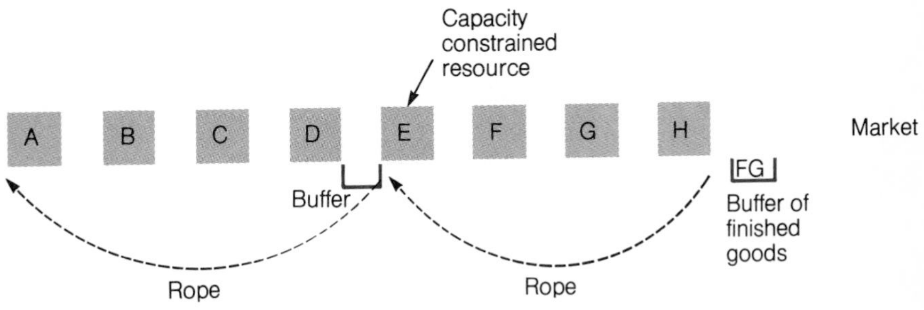

Product flows through Work centers A through H. Work center E is capacity constrained.

EXHIBIT 17.6

Network Flow with One Bottleneck

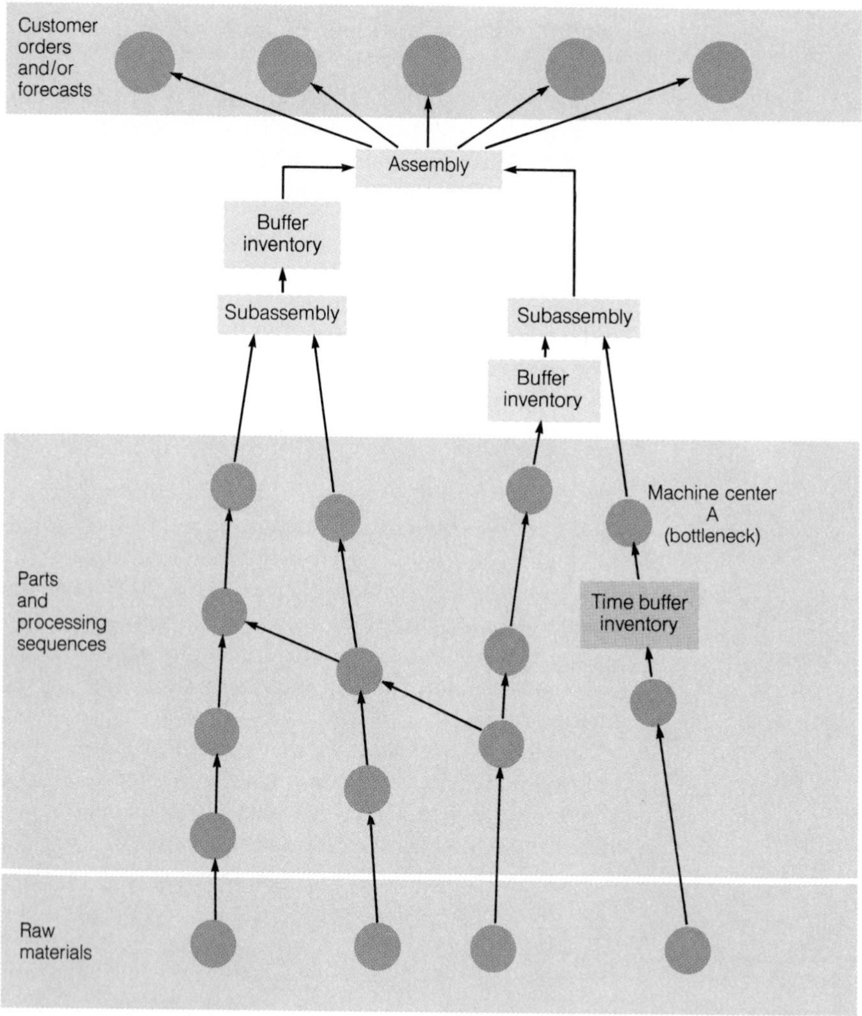

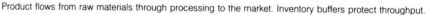

Product flows from raw materials through processing to the market. Inventory buffers protect throughput.

rope from the drum back to the material release point, specifying how much material is needed.

Exhibit 17.6 is a more detailed network flow showing one bottleneck. Inventory is provided not only in front of that bottleneck, but also after the nonbottleneck assembly to which it is assembled. This ensures that the flow of product after it leaves the bottleneck will not be slowed down by having to wait.

Importance of Quality

An MRP system allows for rejects by building a larger batch than actually needed. A JIT system cannot tolerate poor quality since JIT success is based on a balanced system. A defective part or component can cause a JIT system to shut down, thereby losing throughput of the total system. Synchronized production, however, has excess capacity throughout the system, except for the bottleneck. If a bad part is produced upstream of the bottleneck, the result is that there will be a loss of material only. Because of the excess capacity, there is still time to do another operation to replace the one just scrapped. For the bottleneck, however, extra time does not exist, so that there should be a quality control inspection just prior to the bottleneck to ensure that the bottleneck works only on good product. Also, there needs to be assurance downstream from the bottleneck so that the passing product is not scrapped—which means lost throughput.

Batch Sizes

In an assembly line, what is the batch size? Some would say "one," since one unit is moved at a time; others would say "infinity," since the line continues to produce the same item. Both answers are correct, but they differ in their point of view. The first answer, "one," in an assembly line focuses on the *part,* which is transferred one unit at a time. The second focuses on the *process;* from the point of view of the resource, the process batch is infinity since it is continuing to run the same units. Thus, in an assembly line, we have a **process batch** of infinity (or all the units, until we change to another process setup) and a **transfer batch** of one unit.

Setup costs and carrying costs were treated in depth in Chapter 12, Inventory Systems for Independent Demand. In the present context, setup costs relate to the process batch and carrying costs relate to the transfer batch.

A process batch is of a size large enough or small enough to be processed in a particular length of time. From the point of view of a resource, two times are involved: setup time and processing run time (ignoring downtime for maintenance or repair). Larger process batch sizes require fewer setups and therefore can generate more processing time and more output. For bottleneck resources, larger batch sizes are desirable. For nonbottleneck resources, smaller process batch sizes are possible (by using up the existing idle time), thereby reducing work-in-process inventory.

Transfer batches refer to the movement of part of the process batch. Rather than wait for the entire batch to be finished, work that has been completed by that operation can be moved to the next downstream workstation so that it can begin working on that batch. A transfer batch can be equal to a process batch but it cannot be larger.

The advantage of using transfer batches that are smaller than the process batch quantity is that the total production cycle time is shorter and therefore the amount of work in process is smaller.

Dollar days

A useful performance measurement is the concept of **dollar days,** which is a measurement of the value of inventory and the time it stays within an area. To use this measure, we could simply multiply the total value of inventory by the number of days, or we could establish a "normal" level of inventory and use dollar days as a penalty measurement on inventories over this norm.

Supposing Department X carries an average inventory of $40,000, and, on the average, the inventory stays within the department 5 days. In terms of dollar days then, Department X is charged with $40,000 times 5 days or $200,000 dollar days of inventory. At this point one cannot say the $200,000 is high or low, but it does show where the inventory is located. Management can then see where it should focus attention and determine acceptable levels.

Dollar-day measurements could also be used in other areas:

- Marketing, to discourage holding large amounts of finished-goods inventory. The net result would be to encourage sale of finished products.
- Purchasing, to discourage placing large purchase orders that on the surface appear to take advantage of quantity discounts. This encourages Just-in-Time purchasing.
- Manufacturing, to discourage large work in process and producing earlier than needed. This would promote rapid flow of material within the plant.

17.8 VAT CLASSIFICATION OF FIRMS

All manufacturing firms can be classified into one or a combination of three types designated V, A, and T, depending on the products and processes. Exhibit 17.7 shows all three types. The reason for using the letters **VAT** for classification is obvious when we note the actual appearance of the product flow through the system. In a "V" plant, there are few raw materials and they are transformed through a relatively standard process into a much larger number of end products. Consider a steel plant, for example: a few raw materials are converted into a large number of types of sheet steel, beams, rods, wire, etc.

An "A" plant is the opposite. In an "A" plant many raw materials, components, and parts are converted into few end products. Examples in aerospace would be making jet engines, airplanes, and missiles. In a "T" plant, the final product is assembled in many different ways out of similar parts and components. There are two stages in the production process: first, the basic parts and components are manufactured in a relatively straightforward way (the lower portion of the T) and are stored. Second, assembly takes place, combining these common parts into the many possible options to create the final product.

EXHIBIT 17.7 **VAT Classification of Firms**

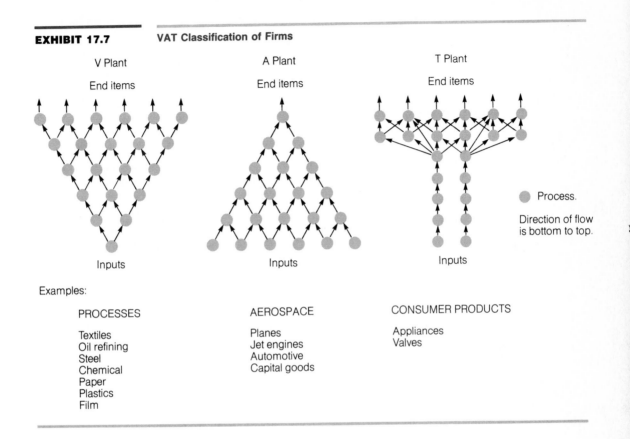

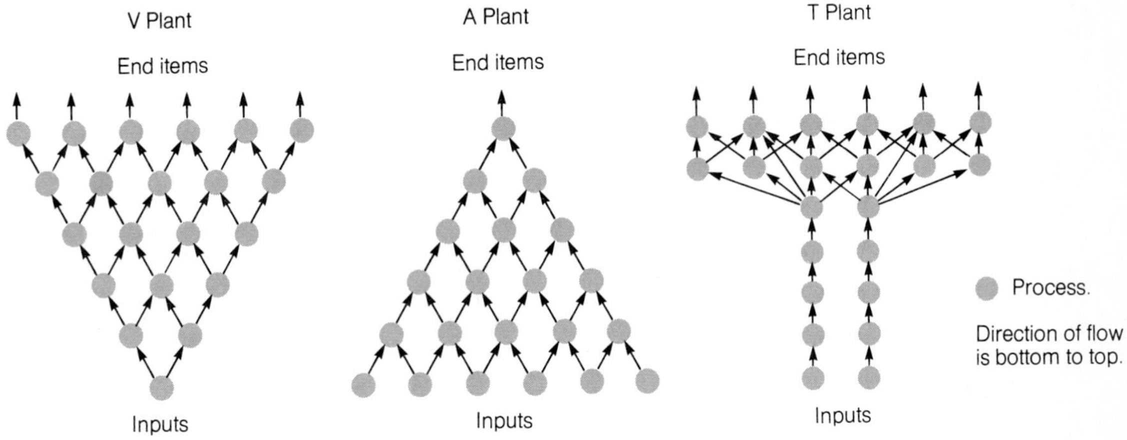

Examples:

PROCESSES	AEROSPACE	CONSUMER PRODUCTS
Textiles	Planes	Appliances
Oil refining	Jet engines	Valves
Steel	Automotive	
Chemical	Capital goods	
Paper		
Plastics		
Film		

"V" Plant

Problems that occur in a "V" plant show up as poor customer service, poor delivery, and high inventories of finished goods. The basic cause is generally a zealous effort to achieve high utilization levels, which instigates overly large process batch sizes.

"A" Plant

In an "A" plant, management areas of concern are low equipment utilization, high unplanned overtime, parts shortages, and lack of control of the production process. When the flow is controlled correctly, there is a better utilization of resources, overtime is reduced or eliminated, and inventory levels are greatly decreased.

"T" Plant

The main characteristic of a "T" plant is that the parts and components are common to many end items. The assembly of end products in a "T" plant is a combinatorial problem, with customers placing orders for different colors, features, or sizes, thus creating many possibilities. The lead time, as far as the customer is concerned, is the height of the cross bar of the T. This means that a customer's order is assembled from the standard parts and components that are stocked. Typically, management perceives the problem as a need for better forecasting, improved inventory control in warehouses, and reduced unit cost by controlling overtime and setups and by introducing automation and simplified designs.

The correct approach using synchronous production is to improve due-date delivery performance and to reduce operating expenses by:

1. Controlling the flow through the fabrication portion of the process.
2. Reducing batch sizes to eliminate the wavelike motion.
3. Stopping the "stealing" of parts and components at assembly.

"Stealing" parts is caused by the pressure from each supervisor in the assembly process to maintain high utilizations. When supervisors and workers are caught up on orders that are currently due, or when they cannot assemble a

EXHIBIT 17.8

Summary of VAT Plant Characteristics and Perceived Problems

SUMMARY

"V" Plant	Capital intensive Highly mechanized Dedicated Inflexible Specialization within the flow process
"A" Plant	Less capital intensive Versatile Flexible machines Can work at different levels of product flow
"T" Plant	Has fabrication and assembly areas Fabrication: Short routing Versatile machines Assembly area: Assembly is the predominant activity Short assembly lead time (days)

Management perceived problems

"V" Plant	Cost is the focus
"A" Plant	Need for control (constantly expediting, overtime, material availability, no idea of problem, wandering bottleneck)
"T" Plant	Due-date performance is usually bad and can't seem to be able to change it

product because parts are missing, they will reach ahead and assemble products for future orders. The result is that some other product in the assembly area will be short those items and therefore late.

In conclusion, the VAT classification can lead us to the source of the problem. Exhibit 17.8 shows a summary of plant characteristics and perceived problems. In a "V" plant, we would look for large inventories. In an "A" plant we would expect to find moving bottlenecks. In a "T" plant, we would suspect people are stealing parts to build ahead.

17.9 RELATIONSHIP WITH OTHER FUNCTIONAL AREAS

The production system must work closely with the other functional areas to achieve the best operating system. This section briefly discusses accounting and marketing—areas where conflicts can occur—and where cooperation and joint planning should occur.

Problems in Cost-Accounting Measurements

Cost accounting is used for performance measurement, cost determinations, investment justification, and inventory valuation. Two sets of performance measurements are used for evaluation: (1) global measurements, which are financial statements showing net profit, return on investment, and cash flow; and (2) local cost accounting measurements, or cost accounting showing efficiencies as variances from standard or utilization rate (hours worked/hours present).

From the cost-accounting (local measurement) viewpoint, then, the objective has traditionally been based on cost and full utilization. This logic forces supervisors to activate their workers all the time, which leads to excessive inventory. The cost-accounting measurement system can also instigate other problems. Any measurement system should support the objectives of the firm and not stand in the way. Fortunately, the cost-accounting measurement philosophy is now changing.

Marketing and Production

Marketing and production should communicate and conduct their activities in close harmony. In practice, however, they act very independently. There are many reasons for this. Marketing people are judged on the growth of the company in terms of sales, market share, and new products entered. Marketing is sales oriented. Manufacturing people are evaluated on cost and utilization. Therefore, marketing wants a variety of products to increase the company's position while manufacturing is trying everything to reduce cost. Data used for evaluating marketing and manufacturing are also quite different. Marketing data is "soft" (qualitative); manufacturing data is "hard" (quantitative). The orientation and experiences of marketing and production people also differ. Those in marketing management have likely come up through sales and a close association with customers. Top manufacturing managers have likely progressed through production operations and therefore have plant performance as a top objective.

Cultural differences can also be important in contrasting marketing and manufacturing personnel. Top managers in each can live quite differently since they have different motivations, goals, and hobbies as well. Marketing people tend to have a greater ego drive and are more outgoing. Manufacturing personnel tend to be more meticulous and perhaps more introverted (at least less of an extrovert than the marketing counterpart).

The solution to coping with these differences is to develop an equitable set of measurements to evaluate performance in each area, and to promote strong lines of communication so that they both contribute to reaching the firm's goals.

Consider the example in Exhibit 17.9, where different objectives and measurement criteria can cause several possible solutions to the same problem.

There are two workers on each of three shifts producing four products. The market demand is unlimited and will take all the product that the workers can produce. The only stipulation is that the ratio of products sold cannot exceed 10 to 1 between the maximum sold of any one product and the minimum of another. For example, if the maximum number sold of any one of the products is 100 units, then the minimum of any other cannot be less than 10 units. Workers 1 and 2, on each shift, are not cross trained and can only work on their operation. The time and raw material (RM) costs are shown in the exhibit, and a summary of the costs and times involved is on the lower portion of the exhibit.

The question is: What quantities of A, B, C, and D should be produced?

There are really three answers to this question, depending on each of the following objectives:

1. Paying sales personnel maximum commission.
2. Maximizing per-unit gross profit.
3. Maximizing the utilization of the constrained resource.

Objective 1: Maximizing sales commission on dollars sold

Sales personnel will prefer to sell B and D (selling price \$32) rather than A and C (selling price \$30). Weekly operating expenses are \$3,000.

The ratio of units sold will be: 1A : 10 B : 1 C : 10 D.

Worker 2 on each shift is the bottleneck and therefore determines the output.

5 days per week × 3 shifts × 8 hours × 60 minutes = 7,200 minutes per week available

Worker 2 spends these times on each unit:

EXHIBIT 17.9

Production Requirements and Selling Price for Four Products

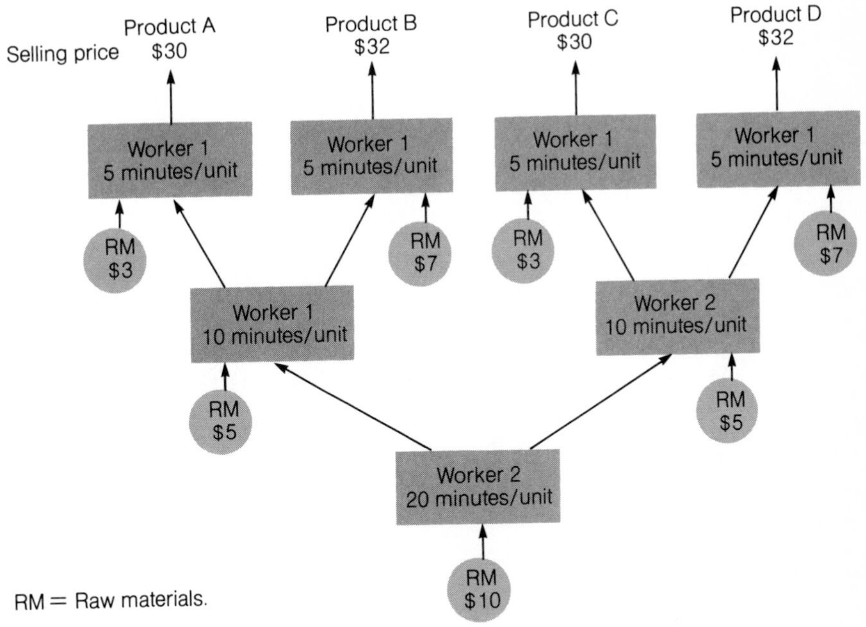

Product	Selling Price (each)	PROCESSING TIME REQUIRED PER UNIT		Raw Material Cost per Unit
		Worker 1	Worker 2	
A	$30	15 min.	20 min.	$18
B	32	15	20	22
C	30	5	30	18
D	32	5	30	22

One Worker 1 and one Worker 2 operate on each shift.
Three shifts.
Five days per week.
Eight hours per shift.
Operating expenses $3,000 per week.

A 20 minutes C 30 minutes
B 20 minutes D 30 minutes

Ratio of output units is 1 : 10 : 1 : 10. Therefore:

$$1x(20) + 10x(20) + 1x(30) + 10x(30) = 7{,}200$$
$$550x = 7{,}200$$
$$x = 13.09$$

Therefore the numbers of units produced is:

A = 13
B = 131
C = 13
D = 131

Gross profit (selling price less raw material, less weekly expenses) will be:

$$13(30 - 18) + 131\ (32 - 22) + 13(30 - 18) + 131(32 - 22) - 3{,}000$$
$$= 156 + 1{,}310 + 156 + 1{,}310 - 3{,}000$$
$$= (\$68)\text{ loss.}$$

Objective 2: Maximizing gross profit

	Gross Profit	=	Selling Price	−	Raw Material Cost
A	12	=	30	−	18
B	10	=	32	−	22
C	12	=	30	−	18
D	10	=	32	−	22

A and C have the maximum gross profit so the ratio will be 10 : 1 : 10 : 1 for A, B, C, and D. Worker 2 is the constraint and has

5 days × 3 shifts × 8 hours × 60 minutes = 7,200 minutes available per week

As before A and B take 20 minutes, C and D take 30 minutes. Thus

$$10x(20) + 1x(20) + 10x(30) + 1x(30) = 7{,}200$$
$$550x = 7{,}200$$
$$x = 13$$

Therefore the number of units produced will be:

A = 131
B = 13
C = 131
D = 13

Gross profit (selling price less raw material, less $3,000 weekly expense) will be:

$$131(30 - 18) + 13(32 - 22) + 131(30 - 18) + 13(32 - 22) - 3{,}000$$
$$= 1{,}572 + 130 + 1{,}572 + 130 - 3{,}000$$
$$= \$404\text{ profit}$$

Objective 3: Maximizing the use of the capacity-constrained resource—Worker 2

For every hour Worker 2 works, the following number of products and gross profit will result:

(1) Product	(2) Production Time	(3) No. Units Produced per Hour	(4) Selling Price Each	(5) Raw Material Cost Each Unit	(6) Gross Profit per Hour (3) × [(4) − (5)]
A	20 minutes	3	$30	$18	$36
B	20	3	32	22	30
C	30	2	30	18	24
D	30	2	32	22	20

Product A generates the greatest gross profit per hour of Worker 2 time, so the ratio would be 10 : 1 : 1 : 1 for A, B, C, and D.

Available time for Worker 2 is the same as before:

$$3 \text{ shifts} \times 5 \text{ days} \times 8 \text{ hours} \times 60 \text{ minutes} = 7{,}200 \text{ minutes}$$

Worker 2 should produce 10 A's for every 1B, 1C, and 1D, and his average production rate will be:

$$\begin{aligned} 10x(20) + 1x(20) + 1x(30) + 1x(30) &= 7{,}200 \\ 280x &= 7{,}200 \\ x &= 25.7 \end{aligned}$$

Therefore, the numbers of units that should be produced are:

A = 257
B = 25.7
C = 25.7
D = 25.7

And the gross profit (price less raw material, less $3,000 weekly expenses) will be:

$$\begin{aligned} &257(30 - 18) + 25.7(32 - 22) + 25.7\,(30 - 18) + 25.7(32 - 22) - 3{,}000 \\ &= 3{,}084 + 257 + 308.4 + 257 - 3{,}000 \\ &= \$906.40 \end{aligned}$$

In summary, using three different objectives to decide how many of each product to make gave us three different results:

1. Maximizing sales commission resulted in a $68 loss.
2. Maximizing gross profit gave us a profit of $404.
3. Maximizing the use of the capacity-constrained worker gave us the best profit—$906.40.

This example demonstrates that production and marketing need to interact. Marketing should sell the most profitable use of available capacity. However, in order to plan capacity, production needs to know from marketing what products could be sold.

17.10 ESTABLISHING A PROCESS OF ONGOING IMPROVEMENT

One of the great concerns in introducing change is that the system will stagnate once the changes have been made. Using the logic contained in this chapter requires continual effort in making changes. Revising the system becomes a way of life.

As part of his teaching, Goldratt uses a checklist to guide continual change. This checklist appears in Exhibit 17.10.

EXHIBIT 17.10

Establishing a Process of Ongoing Improvement

I. Analyze the business.
   A. Focus on weaknesses in competitive position.
      1. Environmental constraints.
         a. Market realities.
         b. Government regulation.
      2. Competitive position related to competition.
      3. Real versus perceived business problems.
      4. Business goals.
      5. Current performance against goals.
      6. Current programs aimed at goals.
   B. Focus on barriers to improvement, using constraint analysis.
      1. Process flow diagram.
      2. Logistical constraints (VAT framework).
         a. Capacity constraints (CCRs, bottlenecks).
         b. Other, such as material or transportation.
      3. Managerial constraints.
         a. Marketing strategy.
         b. Manufacturing policies.
         c. Performance measurements.
      4. Behavioral constraints.
         a. Practices that affect achievement of goals.
   C. Focus improvement efforts.
      1. Understand effect–cause–effect relationships of constraints to business problems.
      2. Set goals for improvement, tied to competitive position (A2 above).
      3. Determine which improvements will yield the most beneficial results.
      4. Estimate bottom-line benefits for two to three years.
         a. Increased throughput revenues.
         b. Little or no added operating expenses.
         c. Inventory-reduction effects on operating expenses, cash flow, future throughput.
         d. Net profit, return on investment, cash flow.
         e. "Order of magnitude" versus finely tuned calculations

EXHIBIT 17.10

Concluded

- II. Plan and educate for change.
  - A. Decide what must change, why, and ramifications.
    1. Logistical constraints, such as capacity investments, bottleneck utilization.
    2. Managerial constraints, such as possible need for new performance measures.
    3. Behavioral constraints, such as consensus of functional managers.
    4. Ramifications, such as capacity to handle increased throughput.
  - B. Educate for the changes at all organizational levels.
  - C. Decide how to accomplish the changes.
  - D. Develop detailed implementation plan.
- III. Synchronize for control.
  - A. Managerial: Adopt appropriate policies and performance measurements.
  - B. Logistical: Implement synchronized manufacturing.
    1. Identify bottlenecks and capacity-constrained resources (drum).
    2. Schedule capacity-constrained resources (CCR) forward (drumbeat).
    3. Protect throughput (buffers).
    4. Release material to support drumbeat (ropes).
    5. Schedule resources to support flow (ropes).
  - C. Behavioral: Establish a shop-floor policy and control points.
- IV. Process for ongoing improvement.
  - A. Logistical.
    1. Improve bottleneck/capacity-constrained resource utilization.
       - *a.* Squeeze idle time.
       - *b.* Reduce scrap before and after CCR.
       - *c.* Improve process.
       - *d.* Offload.
    2. Use buffer management to focus on competitive-edge improvements.
       - *a.* Analyze disruptions to buffers.
       - *b.* Locate and improve sources of disruption.
       - *c.* Reduce buffer/batch size.
       - *d.* Anticipate new CCRs and bottlenecks.
       - *e.* Break bottlenecks.
    3. Resynchronize as system changes.
  - B. Managerial: Use simulation to evaluate tradeoffs.
    1. Batch size implications: lead time versus mix.
    2. Product mix/pricing/bidding.
    3. Capacity investment.
    4. Manning policies.
  - C. Behavioral: Generate a climate for continuing improvement through education.

17.11 CONCLUSION

The measurement system within a firm should encourage the increase of net profits, return on investment, and cash flow. The firm can accomplish this if, at the operations level, it rewards performance according to the amount of throughput, inventory, and operating expense created. This is essential for the success of a firm.

To control throughput, inventory, and operating expense, the system must be analyzed to find the existence of bottlenecks and capacity-constrained resources. Only then can the company proceed to define a *drum* for control,

EXHIBIT 17.11

Goldratt's Rules of Production Scheduling

1. Do not balance capacity—balance the flow.
2. The level of utilization of a nonbottleneck resource is not determined by its own potential but by some other constraint in the system.
3. Utilization and activation of a resource are not the same.
4. An hour lost at a bottleneck is an hour lost for the entire system.
5. An hour saved at a nonbottleneck is a mirage.
6. Bottlenecks govern both throughput and inventory in the system.
7. Transfer batch may not and many times should not be equal to the process batch.
8. A process batch should be variable both along its route and in time.
9. Priorities can be set only by examining the system's constraints. Lead time is a derivative of the schedule.

buffers to assure throughput, and *ropes* for communicating the correct information to the correct locations, while minimizing work in process everywhere else. Without this focus, problems will not be correctly diagnosed and solution procedures will be impossible.

Goldratt defines nine rules (shown in Exhibit 17.11) to help guide the logic of an operating system and to identify the important points. These are basic to any operating system.

The underlying philosophy presented in this chapter—the vital importance of concentrating on system limitations imposed by capacity-constrained resources—has led Goldratt to broaden his view of the importance of system limitations and to develop his five-step "general theory of constraints":[2]

1. Identify the system constraints.
2. Decide how to exploit the system constraints.
3. Subordinate everything else to that decision.
4. Elevate the system constraints.
5. If, in the previous steps, the constraints have been broken, go back to Step 1, but don't let inertia become the system constraint.

In this context, Goldratt defines a constraint as "anything that limits a system from achieving higher performance versus its goal."

This general theory of constraints directs companies to find what is stopping them from moving toward their goal and finding ways to get around this limitation. If, in a manufacturing environment, the limitation is insufficient

[2] Eliyahu Goldratt, "Computerized Shop Floor Scheduling," *International Journal of Production Research* 26, no. 3 (1988), pp. 443–55; *The General Theory of Constraints* (New Haven, Conn.: Abraham Y. Goldratt Institute, forthcoming).

capacity, then ways to break the constraint might be overtime, specialized tools, supporting equipment, exceptionally skilled workers, subcontracting, redesigning product or process, alternate routings, and so on. Point 5 warns against letting biases in thinking prevent the search for and exploitation of constraints. For example, if a search and exploitation of a constraint has been conducted under the limitation of cost, make sure that this cost measure not be carried into the next search. Start clean each time.

One last comment in summary of this chapter: the firm should operate as a synchronized system, with all parts in harmony and supporting each other. Marketing, finance, production, and engineering (as well as all the other functional staff and administrative entities) are all necessary for achieving the goals of the firm.

17.12 REVIEW AND DISCUSSION QUESTIONS

1. State the global performance measurements and the operational performance measurements and briefly define each of them. How do these differ from the traditional accounting measurements?
2. Compare and contrast JIT, MRP, and synchronous production stating their main features, such as, where each is or might be used, amounts of raw material and work-in-process inventories, production lead times and cycle times, methods for control, etc.
3. Compare and contrast VAT type plants bringing in such points as where best applied, the main features of each (such as, product flow and equipment type), the major problems of each, the likely source of the problems, and the likely solutions to the problems.
4. Compare the importance and relevance of quality control in JIT, MRP, and synchronized manufacturing.
5. Discuss what is meant by forward loading and backward loading.
6. Define and explain the cause or causes of a moving bottleneck.

17.13 PROBLEMS

1. For the four basic configurations shown below, assume that the market is demanding product which must be processed by both Resource X and Resource Y for Cases I, II, and III. For Case IV, both resources supply separate, but dependent, markets; that is, the number of units of output from both X and Y must be equal.

   Plans are being made to produce a product which requires 40 minutes for each unit on Resource X, and 30 minutes on Resource Y. Assume that there is only one unit of each of these resources, and that market demand is 1,400 units per month.

   How would you schedule X and Y? What would happen otherwise in each Case?

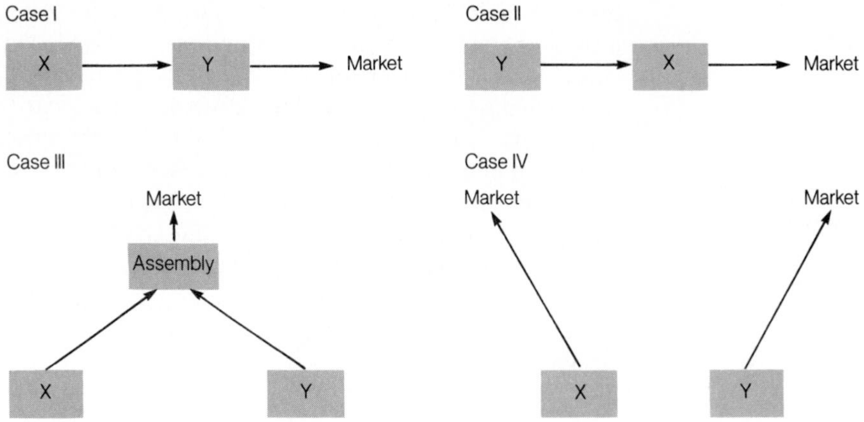

2. Following are the process flow sequences for three products: A, B, and C. There are two bottleneck operations—on the first leg and fourth leg marked with an X. Boxes represent processes, which may be either machine or manual.

   Suggest the location of the drum, buffer, and ropes.

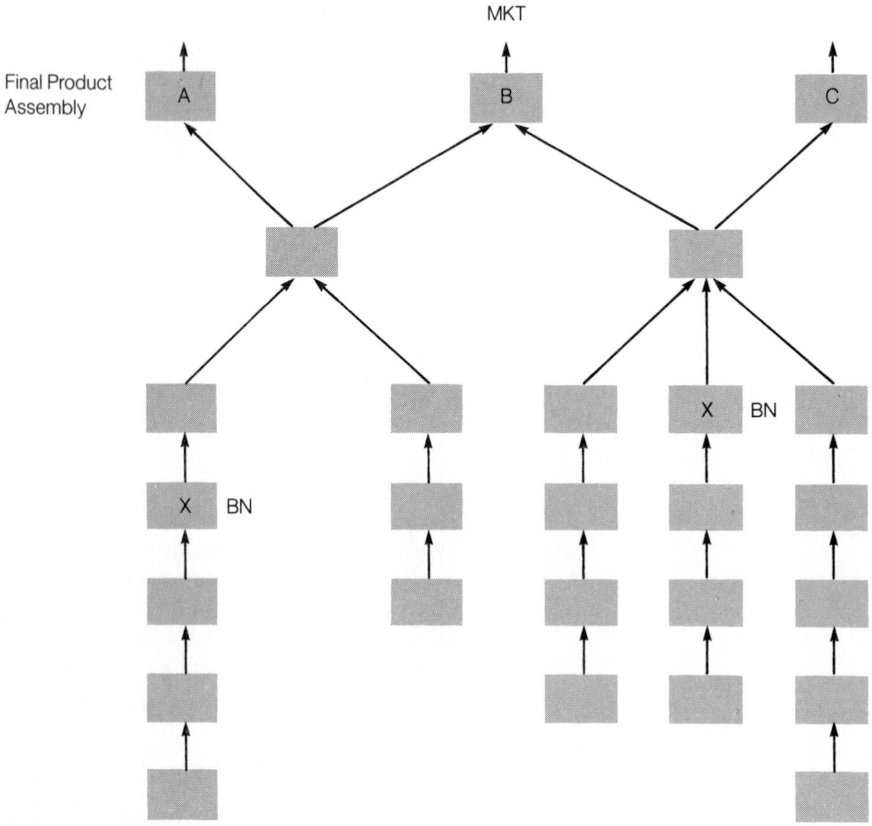

3. The figure below shows a production network model with the parts and processing sequences.

State clearly on the figure: (1) where you would place inventory; (2) where you would perform inspection; and (3) where you would emphasize high-quality output.

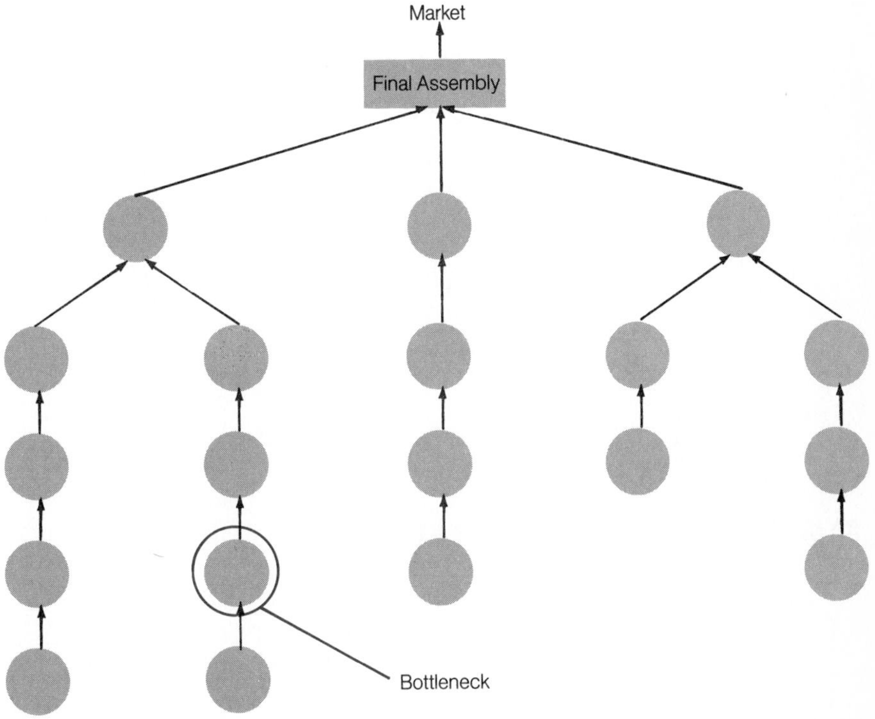

4. Following is the process flow for Products A, B, and C. Products A, B, and C sell for $20, $25, and $30, respectively. There is only one Resource X and one Resource Y which is used to produce A, B, and C for the numbers of minutes stated on the diagram. Raw materials are needed at the process steps as shown, with the costs in dollars per unit of raw material. (One unit is used for each product.)

The market will take all that you can produce.

a. Which product would you produce to maximize gross margin per unit?

b. If sales personnel are paid on commission, which product or products would they sell and how many would they sell?

c. Which and how many product or products should you produce to maximize gross profit for a one-week period?

d. From (*c*) how much gross profit would there be for the week?

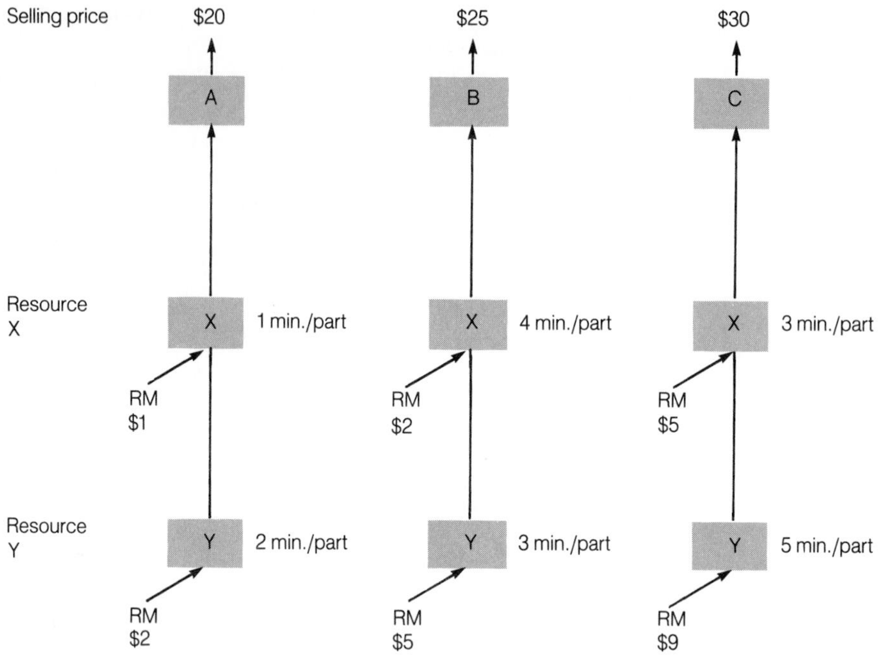

17.14 SELECTED BIBLIOGRAPHY

Adams, Joseph; Egon Balas; and Daniel Zawack. "The Shifting Bottleneck Procedure for Job Shop Scheduling." *Management Science* 34, no. 3 (March 1988), pp. 391–401.

Aggarwal, S. "MRP, JIT, OPT, FMS?" *Harvard Business Review,* September–October 1985, pp. 8–16.

Berlant, Debbie; Reese Brouning; and George Foster. "How Hewlett-Packard Gets Numbers It Can Trust." *Harvard Business Review,* January–February 1990, pp. 178–83.

Birk, Donald. "Increase Your Profits by Managing Your Constraints." *APICS, Conference Proceedings* (Falls Church, Va.: APICS, 1986), pp. 132–36.

Bylinsky, Gene. "An Efficiency Guru with a Brown Box." *Fortune,* September 5, 1983.

Faulhaber, Thomas A.; Fred A. Coad; and Thomas J. Little. "Building a Process Cost Management System from the Bottom Up." *Management Accounting,* May 1988, pp. 58–63.

Fox, Robert E. "MRP, Kanban, or OPT—What's Best?" *Inventories and Production,* July–August 1982.

———. "OPT: An Answer for America, Leapfrogging the Japanese, Part IV." *Inventories and Production* 3, no. 24 (March–April 1983).

———. "OPT vs. MRP: Thoughtware vs. Software." *Inventories and Production* 3, no. 6 (November–December 1983).

Frizelle, G. D. M. "A Classification and Measurement Structure for Manufacturing Plants." *International Journal of Computer Integrated Manufacturing* 6, No. 6 (1989), pp. 303–16.

Goldratt, Eliyahu E. "Computerized Shop Floor Scheduling." *International Journal of Production Research* 26, no. 3 (1988), pp. 443–55.

———. "Cost Accounting: The Number One Enemy of Productivity." *APICS, Conference Proceedings* (Falls Church, Va.: APICS, 1983), pp. 433–35.

Goldratt, Eliyahu M., and Jeff Cox. *The Goal: Excellence in Manufacturing.* Croton-on-Hudson, N.Y.: North River Press, 1984.

Goldratt, Eliyahu M., and Robert E. Fox. *The Race for a Competitive Edge.* Milford, Conn.: Creative Output, 1986.

Kaplan, Robert S. "Yesterday's Accounting Undermines Production." *Harvard Business Review,* July–August 1984, pp. 95–102.

———. "The Four Stage Model of Cost Systems Design." *Management Accounting,* February 1990, pp. 22–26.

Koziol, David S. "How the Constraint Theory Improved a Job-Shop Operation." *Management Accounting,* May 1988, pp. 44–49.

Krafik, John F. "Triumph of the Lean Production System." *Sloan Management Review,* Fall 1988, pp. 41–55.

Lippa, Victor. "Managing Performance with Synchronous Management. "*Management Accounting,* February 1990, pp. 54–60.

Main, Jeremy. "Under the Spell of Quality Gurus." *Fortune,* August 18, 1986, pp. 30–34.

Meleton, Marcus P. "OPT—Fantasy or Breakthrough?" *Production and Inventory Management,* second quarter 1986, pp. 13–21.

O'Guin, Michael. "Focus the Factory with Activity-Based Accounting." *Management Accounting,* February 1990, pp. 36–41.

Ostrenga. Michael R. "Activities: The Focal Point of Total Cost Management." *Management Accounting,* February 1990, pp. 42–49.

Plossl, George W. "Managing by the Numbers—But Which Numbers." *APICS, Conference Proceedings* (Falls Church, Va.: APICS, 1987), pp. 499–503.

Ramsey, Martin L.; Steve Brown; and Kambiz Tabibzadeh. "Push, Pull, and Squeeze: Shop Floor Control with Computer Simulation." *Industrial Engineering,* February 1990, pp. 39–43.

Rao, Vittal. "Total Quality: A Commitment to Excellence." *APICS, Readings in Productivity Improvement* (Falls Church, Va.: APICS, 1985), pp. 18–23.

Shapiro, Benson. "Can Marketing and Manufacturing Coexist?" *Harvard Business Review,* September–October 1977, pp. 416–27.

Srikanth, Mokshagundam L., and Harold E. Cavallaro, Jr. *Regaining Competitiveness: Putting the Goal to Work.* New Haven, Conn.: Spectrum Publishing Co., 1987.

"The Push for Quality." *Business Week* special report, June 8, 1987, pp. 130–44.

Thompson, O., and S. J. Connor. "Manufacturing Critical Resources: A Total Manufacturing Planning System." *Production Inventory Management Review,* March 1986, pp. 24–32.

Vollmann, Thomas E. "OPT as an Enhancement to MRP II." *Production and Inventory Management,* second quarter 1986, pp. 38–47.

Woods, Michael D. "How We Changed Our Accounting." *Management Accounting,* February 1989, pp. 42–46.

Chapter 18

Revising Operations Strategy

EPIGRAPH

Managers can no longer afford to view operations as a neutral apparatus for turning out goods. Every bit as much as, say, marketing, manufacturing has significant data to contribute to the broad process of strategic planning.

Alan M. Kantrow, "The Strategy-Technology Connection," *Harvard Business Review* (July–August 1980), p. 12.

CHAPTER OUTLINE

KEY TERMS

Strategy
Strategic Vision
Production Capabilities
Positioning Manufacturing
Focused Factory
Manufacturing Task
Strategic Business Units
Service Strategy

We have titled this chapter "*Revising* Operations Strategy" to reflect the fact that the long-run success of virtually every organization depends on its ability to alter its operations strategy in light of changes in its environment. Our emphasis in this chapter is on manufacturing strategy rather than service strategy, since the diversity of service businesses makes generalizations about them far more difficult. It should be noted, however, that strategy making in any context is still an art, and the proper course of strategic action is always contingent on the situation at hand.

18.1 MANUFACTURING'S ROLE IN CORPORATE STRATEGY

The development of manufacturing operations strategy has only recently been seen as worthy of the same scholarly research attention as corporate strategy, marketing strategy, and financial strategy. This is because, in the business world, manufacturing expertise was viewed as something that engineers and "shop-floor people" worried about, not senior executives and CEOs. In essence, manufacturing was treated as a support service, not a full partner in developing the strategy it had to implement. As a result of these attitudes, the best managers avoided manufacturing, and relatively few students studied manufacturing management. Moreover, through years of indifference to the manufacturing function (such as manufacturing executives not being invited to corporate strategy meetings), manufacturing executives failed to develop the external orientation necessary to make a positive contribution to corporate strategy. While marketing and finance executives spoke in terms of market share and return on equity, manufacturing executives talked about machine utilization rates and inventory control practices.

The end effect of all these factors is that many U.S. manufacturing firms were less competitive than they could be, and ultimately became vulnerable in many markets to foreign competition.

Strategy Defined

Strategy is a set of plans and policies by which a company aims to gain advantages over its competition. For the organization as a whole, strategy should be predicated on matching its *distinctive competence* (what it is good at) with its *primary task* (what it must do in light of competitive conditions). For the operations function (represented at the strategy level by the vice president of manufacturing or operations), operations strategy should provide clear, consistent operating policies and objectives that operations can reasonably achieve.

Hayes and Wheelwright list five characteristics of a strategy.[1]

[1] Robert H. Hayes and Steven C. Wheelwright, *Restoring Our Competitive Edge: Competing through Manufacturing* (New York: John Wiley & Sons, 1984), pp. 27–28.

1. *Time horizon.* Generally, the word *strategy* is used to describe activities that involve an extended time horizon, both the time it takes to carry out the activities and the time it takes to observe their impact.
2. *Impact.* Although the consequences of pursuing a given strategy may not become apparent for a long time, their eventual impact will be significant.
3. *Concentration of effort.* An effective strategy usually requires concentrating activity, effort, or attention on a fairly narrow range of pursuits. Focusing on these chosen activities implicitly reduces the resources available for other activities.
4. *Pattern of decisions.* Although some companies need to make only a few major decisions to implement their chosen strategy, most strategies require that a series of certain types of decision be made over time. These decisions must be supportive of one another, in that they follow a consistent pattern.
5. *Pervasiveness.* A strategy embraces a wide spectrum of activities ranging from resource allocation processes to day-to-day operations. In addition, the need for consistency over time in these activities requires that all levels of an organization act, almost instinctively, in ways that reinforce the strategy.

A Strategic Vision for Manufacturing

An effective manufacturing strategy requires manufacturing executives to have a **strategic vision** on how all the firm's productive resources relate to one another and to the environment. Exhibit 18.1 illustrates these general relationships using the notion of world-class manufacturing (WCM) to define the overarching goal of the firm's operations. As the exhibit suggests, achievement of this goal entails continual interactions with the customer and suppliers, and integrated manufacturing through appropriate blending of total quality control (TQC), computer-integrated manufacturing (CIM), and Just-in-Time production (JIT). Central to this integration is a system perspective, for as Gunn points out, "manufacturing consists of the entire range of activities from product and process design, through manufacturing planning and control, through the production process itself, through distribution, and through after-sale services and support in the field. This is one continuous spectrum. No activity can be performed along this spectrum without affecting some other part of it either upstream or downstream."[2]

With Gunn's model, it is important to bear in mind that the WCM vision is not the only one around, nor necessarily the best one for the firm as a whole.

[2] Thomas G. Gunn, *Manufacturing for Competitive Advantage: Becoming a World Class Manufacturer* (Cambridge, Mass.: Ballinger Publishing 1987), pp. 28–29.

EXHIBIT 18.1 **Manufacturing for Competitive Advantage Framework**

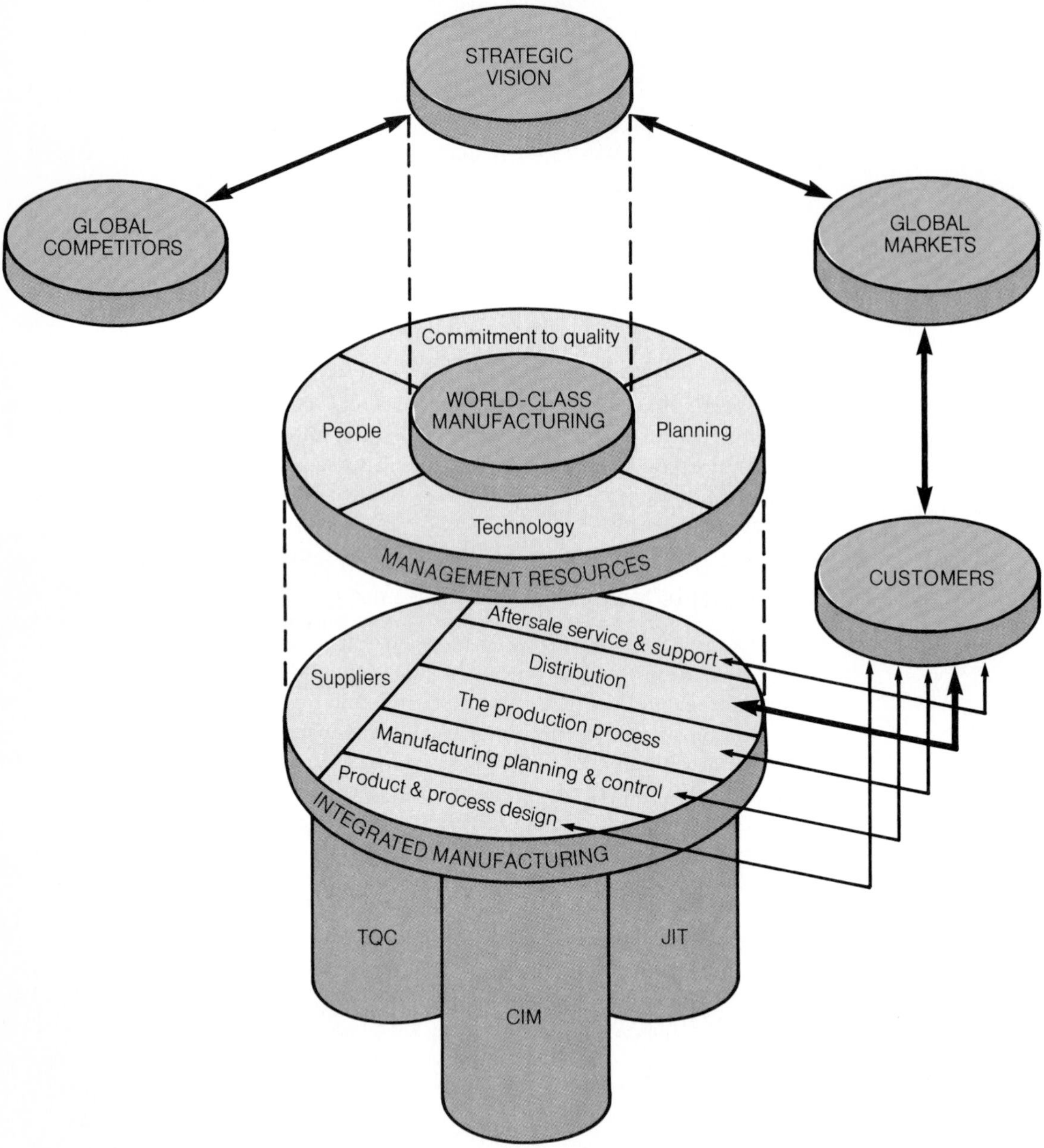

Source: From *Manufacturing for Competitive Advantage:* by Thomas G. Gunn, copyright © 1987 by Ballinger Publishing Company. Used by permission of Harper Business, a division of HarperCollins Publishers.

Recall the four-stage model of Wheelwright and Hayes from Chapter 2;[3] the important thing is to select the role that best supports the corporate strategy. Although it is unlikely that much support can be generated by manufacturing not being involved at all (Stages 1 and 2), it is not always desirable to adopt an offensive manufacturing posture involving major capital investment to become "world class" or to "out-Japanese the Japanese." Indeed, money may be more effectively spent in better marketing, better product design, or in just shaping up current manufacturing operations.

Production Capabilities as Competitive Weapons

The strategic vision should recognize specific production capabilities that can be used as competitive weapons. Some sample **production capabilities** and some current concepts or tools used to enhance them or "make them go" are:

Production Capabilities	*Supporting Concepts or Tools*
High quality	Total quality control
Adaptive production system	MRP, flexible manufacturing systems
Low-cost/high-volume production	Just-in-Time systems

The way these capabilities are used as a part of the firm's arsenal of weapons varies. Sometimes the capabilities have a particular marketing benefit. For example, E. T. Wright & Company, manufacturer of men's shoes for over 100 years, advertises its craftsmanship—as many as 17 days and 155 intricate steps, executed mostly by hand, go into making a pair of E. T. Wright shoes. In other instances, production capabilities have significant implications for corporate management in deciding what types of markets to enter. For example, Chaparral Steel of Texas uses the best production technology from around the world to produce over 350 products in its minimill. Finally, the capabilities of some companies lie in simply excelling in low-cost/high-volume manufacture. For example, the General Electric dishwasher manufacturing plant in Louisville has gone beyond manual JIT systems. The plant has adopted a "use

---

[3] Whybark summarizes this model:

> The four stages reflect increasing participation of manufacturing in the strategic planning process of the firm and perceptiveness in assessing developments in manufacturing technology. They range from "internally neutral" (meaning just don't screw up), through "externally neutral" (be as good, or bad, as the competition), to "internally supportive" (make sure that manufacturing strategy is not inconsistent with company goals) and, finally, to "externally supportive" (wherein manufacturing is a full partner in the strategic planning process and looks for ways of enhancing their capability to support company goals).

From D. Clay Whybark, "Strategic Manufacturing Management," IRMIS Working Paper #W601, School of Business, Indiana University, February 1986.

a part, make a part" approach: machines produce parts right next to the assembly line.[4]

Choosing which of these capabilities to use as a company's main competitive weapon is the basic purpose of the strategy development process.

18.2 DEVELOPING AND IMPLEMENTING A MANUFACTURING STRATEGY

The process of developing and implementing a manufacturing strategy is depicted in Exhibit 18.2. It starts with the customer needs as gathered by marketing and technical specialists, for example research and development staffs and engineers who are in contact with the customer. This information is fed to corporate-level managers, who make the determination of how to position manufacturing in light of corporate strategy and competition. Once positioning is decided, the manufacturing task is specified.

Implementation of the strategy entails all the features we have discussed throughout the book. In a firm's ongoing operations the general problem encountered in implementing a major shift in strategy is the management of change. Feedback from the marketplace completes the cycle.

Positioning Manufacturing

Positioning manufacturing might be thought of as the matching process between the firm's distinctive competence and its primary task. This process must take account of both product and production system life cycles and survey the market environment to determine the general direction manufacturing strategy must take over the next 5 to 10 years. We can identify two extreme types of manufacturing orientations that would be considered here: process focus and product focus. *Process focus* refers to systems that produce a wide variety of customized products. These systems must be flexible; hence, management must master flexible process technologies to compete effectively. *Product focus* refers to systems that produce standardized products in relatively high volume. These systems must be highly efficient; hence, management must master the coordination required to keep inventories flowing smoothly through the system. Examples of these two dimensions of positioning as they relate to finished-goods inventory policies are shown in Exhibit 18.3.

---

[4] The three example plants in this section have been identified as among the 10 best managed in a 1984 survey. See Gene Bylinsky, "America's Best-Managed Factories," *Fortune,* May 28, 1984, pp. 16–24.

EXHIBIT 18.2

The Manufacturing Strategy Development and Implementation Process

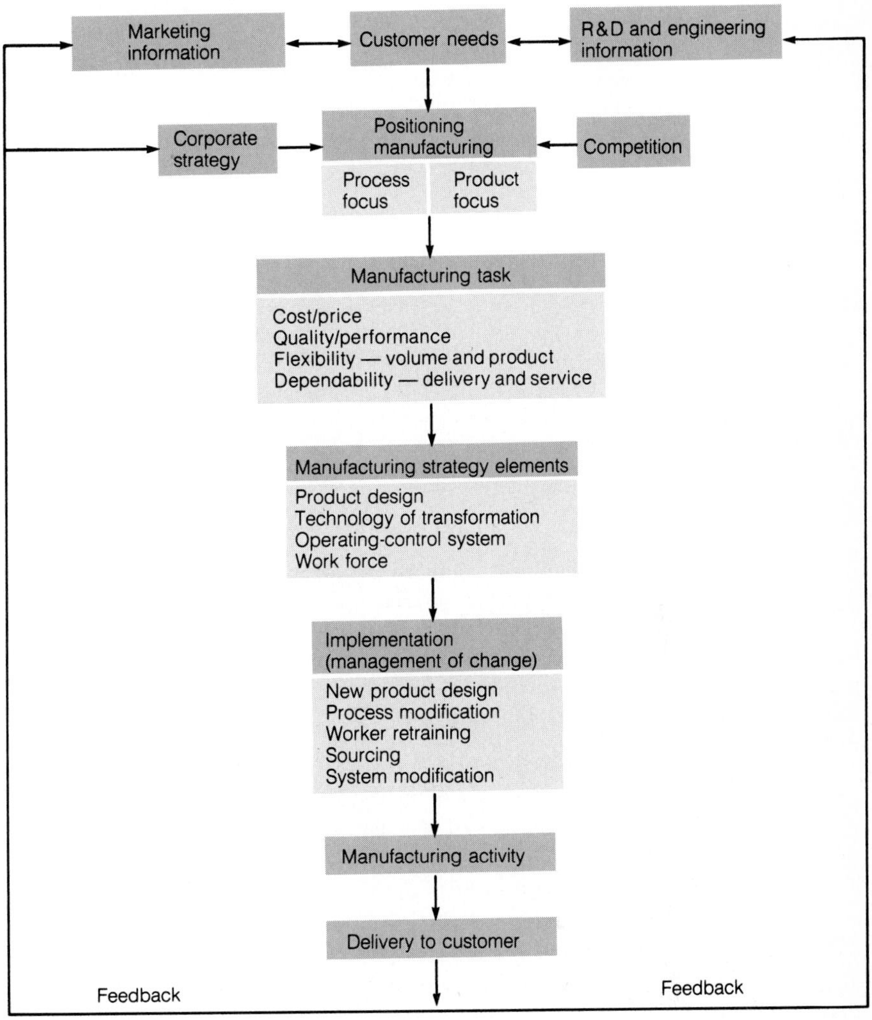

Factory Focus

Regardless of whether a firm follows a product or process positioning strategy, the factory which executes it should itself be focused. According to Skinner:

> A factory that focuses on a narrow product mix for a particular market niche will out-perform the conventional plant, which attempts a broader mission. Because its

EXHIBIT 18.3

Examples of the Two Dimensions of Positioning

Type of System	FINISHED GOODS INVENTORY POLICY	
	Make to Stock	Make to Order
Product-focused	Office copiers TV sets Calculators Gasoline	Construction equipment Buses, trucks Experimental chemicals Textiles Wire and cable Electronic components
Process-focused	Medical instruments Test equipment Electronic components Some steel products Molded plastic parts Spare parts	Machine tools Nuclear pressure vessels Electronic components Space shuttle Ships Construction projects

Source: Elwood S. Buffa, *Meeting the Competitive Challenge* (Homewood, Ill.: Richard D. Irwin, 1984), p. 51.

> equipment, supporting systems, and procedures can concentrate on a limited task for one set of customers, its costs and especially its overhead are likely to be lower than those of the conventional plant. But, more importantly, such a plant can become a competitive weapon because its entire apparatus is focused to accomplish the particular manufacturing task demanded by the company's overall strategy and marketing objective.[5]

As we noted in Chapter 15 the **focused factory** concept can be applied not only to a single plant but to departments within a plant. This pertains when a company has a diversity of products, technologies, and market requirements that must be served by a single facility. Called the *plant within a plant* (PWP) concept, it divides the plant both organizationally and physically into separate units, each with its own manufacturing task, its own work force, production control system, and processing equipment. Engineering, materials handling, and so forth are specialized as needed.

An example of separating a company's total manufacturing capability into specialized units is provided by the Lynchburg Foundry, a subsidiary of the Mead Corporation. This foundry has five plants in Virginia. One plant is a job shop, making mostly one-of-a-kind products. Two plants use a decoupled batch process and make several major products. A fourth plant is a paced assembly line operation that makes only a few products, mainly for the

[5] William Skinner, "The Focused Factory," *Harvard Business Review* (May–June 1974), p. 115.

automotive market. The fifth plant is a highly automated pipe plant, making what is largely a commodity item.

While the basic technology is somewhat different in each plant, there are many similarities. However, the production layout, the manufacturing processes, and the control systems are very different. This company chose to design its plants so that each would meet the needs of a specific segment of the market in the most competitive manner. Its success would suggest that this has been an effective way to match manufacturing capabilities with market demand.[6]

The Manufacturing Task

The output of the positioning process is the general identification of those tasks that the manufacturing function must do well. The specific formalization of these requirements is collectively referred to as the **manufacturing task,** or *manufacturing priorities*. These consist of the factors we've discussed throughout the book—low cost/price, high quality/performance, high flexibility, and high dependability.

According to Hill, choosing which task is most important depends on what "wins orders" in the marketplace.[7] As we saw in Chapter 2, U.S. manufacturing executives saw consistent quality as the top competitive priority, so we would assume that all firms would choose to compete on quality. On the other hand, Japanese executives listed low price as their top priority so they aren't competing on quality, right? Wrong. They have *already* achieved consistent quality, so they are going after the next class of customer—the one who is price sensitive. Using another one of Hill's terms, quality has become just a *qualifying criterion* to enter the market—it lets you play but won't necessarily win orders since the other guy has high quality too.

In one sense, this interpretation of task priorities runs counter to the generally held view that a manufacturing organization can't do everything well, and hence tradeoffs among priorities must be made. A closer look, however, suggests that there is no inconsistency, providing we recognize that acceptable performance that permits qualification for a market is a given, not a priority. In our view, not doing everything well does not always mean that a firm is doing poorly on a task priority; it simply means that it is doing better on some than on others. The key is that the firm excels on those tasks that are critical to supporting corporate strategy, and keeps working to improve on other dimensions.

---

[6] Ibid., p. 114.

[7] T. J. Hill, "Teaching Manufacturing Strategy," *International Journal of Operations & Production Management* 6, no. 3 (1986), pp. 10–20.

EXHIBIT 18.4

Application of Manufacturing Criteria by Corporate Manufacturing Staff

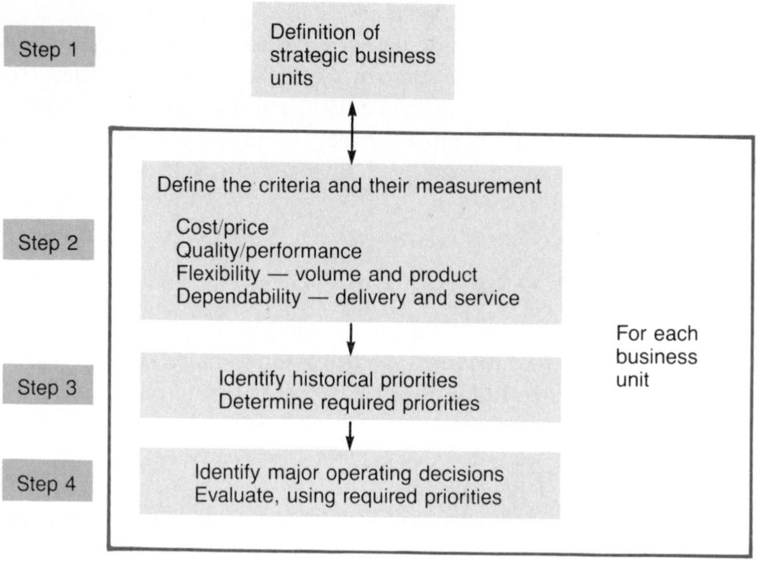

Source: Steven C. Wheelwright, "Reflecting Corporate Strategy in Manufacturing Decisions," *Business Horizons,* February 1978, p. 63.

Evaluating Manufacturing Task Priorities

A systematic approach to evaluating the priority of specified task elements has been proposed by Wheelwright.[8] As Exhibit 18.4 shows, this approach starts by identifying **strategic business units** (SBUs), which are essentially homogenous product-market groupings within, say, a division of a company. (Such a grouping might be large home appliances for the consumer market, which is part of a general appliance division.) The next step is defining the task elements ("criteria and measurement"), which can be done through structured discussions or brainstorming. The third step is identifying, through a series of conferences, historical priorities and determining required priorities.

The results of this third step are shown in the table in Exhibit 18.5. This particular table was developed by a vice president of manufacturing to see how his peers (vice presidents) and subordinates (marketing managers) perceived current and required task element priorities. The task elements (cost, quality, dependability, and flexibility) are given across the top of the table. The numerical entries in the table reflect the point totals (from 0 to 100) assigned by

[8] Steven C. Wheelwright, "Reflecting Corporate Strategy in Manufacturing Decisions," *Business Horizons,* February 1978, pp. 57–66.

EXHIBIT 18.5

Current and Required Priorities as Assessed by Vice Presidents (VP)* and Manufacturing Managers (MM)*

	COST		QUALITY		DEPENDABILITY		FLEXIBILITY	
	VP	MM	VP	MM	VP	MM	VP	MM
Product 1								
As is	42	44	17	15	25	26	16	15
Should be	28	46	24	16	31	26	17	12
Needs more (less)	(14)	2	7	1	6	0	1	(3)
Product 2								
As is	26	20	37	43	24	22	13	15
Should be	26	30	36	38	26	20	12	12
Needs more (less)	0	10	(1)	(5)	2	(2)	(1)	(3)
Product 3								
As is	34	36	27	28	23	19	16	17
Should be	34	38	29	24	24	20	13	18
Needs more (less)	0	2	2	(4)	1	1	(3)	1
Product 4								
As is	24	34	30	22	19	17	27	27
Should be	39	44	20	25	23	15	18	16
Needs more (less)	15	10	(10)	3	4	(2)	(9)	(11)
Product 5								
As is	45	37	21	14	18	31	16	18
Should be	22	31	24	13	35	35	19	21
Needs more (less)	(23)	(6)	3	(1)	17	4	3	3

* Criteria totals for VP and MM for each priority = 100.

Source: Steven C. Wheelwright, "Reflecting Corporate Strategy in Manufacturing Decisions," *Business Horizons*, February 1978, p. 65.

nonmanufacturing vice presidents (VP) and manufacturing managers (MM) to each product and task combination. "As is" refers to the current priority weighting for a task element relative to a given product; "should be" refers to what weighting should actually be applied in light of the mission of manufacturing in the corporate strategy; and "needs more (less)" refers to the numerical difference between "as is" and "should be."

The final step of the process is to make changes in operating decisions in light of the evaluation exercise.

Some of the actions indicated from an analysis of the table (Exhibit 18.5) were:

Product 1 should have modest increases in quality and dependability at the expense of manufacturing cost efficiencies.

Products 2 and 3 should have no significant changes in manufacturing.

Product 4 should have a significant improvement in manufacturing cost efficiencies at the expense of quality and flexibility.

Product 5 should have a significant increase in dependability at the expense of manufacturing cost efficiencies.

Developing the task statement

The following seven guidelines for specifying the production task have been recommended by Skinner.[9] An illustrative task statement is presented in the Insert.

1. The task must be written in sentences and paragraphs, not merely outlined.
2. It must explicitly state the demands and constraints on manufacturing relative to corporate strategy, marketing policy, financial policy, industry and firm economics, and industry and firm technology.
3. It must state how production can be a competitive weapon and how performance can be judged.
4. It must identify what will be especially difficult ("the name of the game").
5. It must explicitly state priorities, including what may have to suffer.
6. It must explicitly state the requirements on the production control system, quality control system, production work force, and production organization structure.
7. It should be boiled down to a symbol, slogan, or cartoon to communicate it to all members of the production organization and managers in other parts of the organization.

INSERT Illustrative Task Statement for an Automobile Manufacturer

Our task is to be number one in the production of economy cars within the next five years. We recognize that our tooling may not be as efficient as we would like and we expect many engineering change orders (ECOs) in our new models. Nevertheless, we will scramble to meet this objective, understanding full well that competitive pressures force us off our historical production and development sequence. We will be judged by how quickly we can adapt our methods and technology to a competitive car design and by how our product performs under rigorous testing. The name of the game is quality output in a hurry. Cost reduction through productivity improvements will have to come later. We will structure our production organization as a project team with QC, production inventory control, and union representatives working closely with the project manager. Our slogan will be "40 MPG and quality."

---

[9] Modified from Wickham Skinner, *Manufacturing in the Corporate Strategy* (New York: John Wiley & Sons, 1978), pp. 107–8.

Manufacturing Strategy Audit

The task statement will lead to evaluation of the four categories of strategy elements shown in Exhibit 18.2. This evaluation is commonly preceded by a manufacturing audit. A complete manufacturing audit is very involved, but the questionnaire presented in Exhibit 18.6 conveys the essence of the problem. It can be used in two ways:

1. To compare current and required policies ("as is" versus "should be"). In this application, managers of a company can derive a percentage score to obtain an estimate of the degree of alignment between "where we are" and "where we should be" (see bottom of Exhibit 18.6).
2. As a checklist for examining major operations areas for purposes of problem solving or improvement.

Implementation

Implementation of a revised strategy should be managed basically like any other project. That means establishing a plan of action, allocating decision responsibility, and developing the coordination and control mechanisms to ensure that the job gets done.

A particularly useful tool in clarifying who will be responsible for different parts of strategy implementation is the *linear responsibility chart*. Exhibit 18.7 is an example of such a chart developed by manufacturing management personnel of a large appliance manufacturer as a basis for implementing JIT. This identifies which function has decision authority (Z), is consulted (C), or is informed (I), regarding different aspects of JIT introduction. Once the responsibilities are clearly understood, project scheduling techniques such as the critical path method can be readily employed.

The major problem in implementing a major change, such as a new manufacturing strategy, is obtaining employee support. The following guidelines are useful here:

1. Communicate the logic and philosophy behind the change, and clearly specify the employee's role in it.
2. Where possible, hold the disturbance of existing customs and informal relationships to a minimum.
3. Provide information about the change in advance.
4. Encourage employee participation in instituting the change.
5. Attempt to minimize the cost to the employee of making the change.
6. Provide the opportunity for the employee to register personal concern about the change.

EXHIBIT 18.6 **Manufacturing Audit Questionnaire**

Product	
A. Design	
1. Breadth of product line (standardized / mixed / customized)	A B C
2. Allowable variability in component specifications (little / some / much)	A B C
3. Coordination among engineering, marketing, and manufacturing (little / some / much)	A B C
4. Design from scratch rather than around existing components (usually / sometimes / rarely)	A B C
5. Concern for producibility (little / some / much)	A B C
B. Introduction	
6. Use of specialized startup procedures (little / some / much)	A B C
7. Stability of design after production release (little / some / much)	A B C
Technology of transformation	
8. Degree of mechanization of product assembly (little / some / much)	A B C
9. Degree of automatic inspection and testing (little / some / much)	A B C
10. Degree of mechanization of materials handling (little / some / much)	A B C
11. Degree of equipment specialization (little / some / much)	A B C
12. Flexibility of equipment to meet changes in volume, run length, and product mix (little / some / much)	A B C
13. Number of plants (one / few / many)	A B C
14. Plants located to be near (suppliers / markets / labor pools)	A B C
15. Plants specialized by (product / both / process)	A B C
16. Extent of production-related R&D (little / some / much)	A B C
17. Extent of subcontracting (little / some / much)	A B C
Operating control system	
18. Investment in production and inventory control system (low / medium / high)	A B C
19. Use of inventory to decouple production stages (little / some / much)	A B C
20. Production to order versus production for stock (order / mixed / stock)	A B C
21. Production strategy (level production / mixed / adjust with demand)	A B C
22. Emphasis on quality control (little / some / much)	A B C
23. Amount of inspection throughout the manufacturing process (little / some / much)	A B C
24. Organization of manufacturing (functional / project / product)	A B C
25. Number of supervisory levels in manufacturing (few / several / many)	A B C
26. Number of staff departments to support manufacturing (few / several / many)	A B C
Work force	
27. Range of worker skills (narrow / medium / broad)	A B C
28. Job content of most jobs (short cycle / medium / long)	A B C
29. Extent of worker control over workpace (little / some / much)	A B C
30. Extent of worker or group discretion in work planning (little / some / much)	A B C
31. Wage payment system (salary / salary + output / output)	A B C

Instructions for scoring

1. Circle either A, B, or C to identify what you believe to be the *correct* policy alternative (A, B, and C correspond to the order of the descriptive terms in the parentheses).
2. Place an X over either A, B, or C to identify what appears to be the policy *currently* being used.
3. Calculate the percentage of items in agreement out of the total items that you were able to score (i.e., the items that have both a circle and an X associated with them). This gives an alignment percentage.

   General scoring guide: 90–100% = excellent; 80–89% = good; 70–79% = fair; 60–69% = poor; below 60% = very poor.

Source: This questionnaire is based upon a questionnaire entitled "Choices and Alternatives in Production System Design," developed by Wickham Skinner and his associates at the Harvard Graduate School of Business Administration.

EXHIBIT 18.7

Linear Responsibility Chart

	Departments											
Project Activities	Manufacturing	Production Control	Quality Control	Industrial Engineering	Computer Systems	Manufacturing Engineering	Design Engineering	Distribution	Training	Purchasing	Cost Accounting	Maintenance
Floor organization	Z	C		C				I		I		
Re-layout	C	C		Z		C		I				
Level schedule	C	Z			C			C		C	I	
WIP planning	C	Z			I					I	I	
Maintenance schedule	Z											C
Supplier quality			Z				C			C		
Supplier delivery	C	Z								C	I	
Pull system design	Z	C	I	C	I	C	I			I	I	I
Material handling	C	Z	C	C		C						
MRP interface	C	Z			C					I		
Equipment experiment	Z						C					
Receiving area	C	Z								I		
Costing		Z			C						C	
Supervisor training	C								Z			
Worker training	C	C							Z			

Z = Responsible for activity.
C = Consulted on activity.
I = Informed about activity.

18.3 OPERATIONS STRATEGY IN SERVICES

Operations strategy development in a service organization is analogous to that followed in manufacturing. However, since most services are characterized by simultaneous production and marketing, identifying a distinct production task is difficult. On the other hand, we can discern at least some of the adjustments required of the production system when a corporate **service strategy** changes. A sampling of these in several types of service organizations is given in Exhibit 18.8. A questionnaire for auditing service systems is given in Exhibit 18.9.

EXHIBIT 18.8

Production System Adjustments as a Result of Strategic Change in Several Service Systems

Service Organization	Strategic Change	Production System Adjustments
Fast-food restaurant	Broaden product by addition of health foods and salad bar	Retraining, re-layout, handle increased inventory
Bank	Adding services such as pay-by-phone accounts and automatic lines of credit	Additional workers, reprogramming of computers, paper-flow adjustments
Hospital	Adding a burn center	Purchase specialized equipment, add specialized staff
Accounting firm	Broadened to include management services	Add new division and personnel
Auto agency	Improve quality of repair service	Purchase new testing equipment, change procedures, quality-based incentive programs
Emergency medical service (e.g., ambulance, fire department, rescue squad)	Broaden medical capabilities	Add equipment (e.g., cardiac defibrillator) on mobile units, upgrading paramedic skills

A Methodology for Service Branch Strategy Determination

Chase, Northcraft, and Wolf developed the following six-step methodology for strategy determination and implementation for branches of a savings and loan.[10] Exhibit 18.10 illustrates the decision-making process involved.

1. *Identify the mission of the branch of service unit.* Environmental factors (such as the presence or absence of competitors) and the overall corporate strategy combine to define a mission or optimal goal for a particular branch of the service organization. This mission should take into account the role of the service unit in the service network of the parent organization and will include both efficiency (production) and effectiveness (marketing) goals.

2. *Identify the contact requirements.* A definition of the contact requirements necessary for the service unit to accomplish the goals set out in the mission is needed. The four contact features shown provide a framework for thinking about and identifying a branch's requirements. For instance, if a

[10] R. B. Chase, G. Northcraft, and G. Wolf, "Design of High Contact Services: Application to Branches of a Savings and Loan," *Decision Sciences* 15, no. 4 (Fall 1984), p. 551.

EXHIBIT 18.9 **Service Systems Audit Questionnaire**

Product	
1. Ratio of customer direct contact time with system to service creation time (low / medium / high)	A B C
2. Extent of direct labor input in creating service product (small / medium / large)	A B C
3. Primary service is viewed as (professional / trade / artistic)	A B C
4. Breadth of service (standard / mixed / customized)	A B C
5. Variability of customer service demands (low / medium / high)	A B C
6. Number of major elements defining service product (few / some / many)	A B C
7. Range of supplementary services (narrow / medium / wide)	A B C
8. Uniqueness of service relative to regional competition (little / some / much)	A B C
9. Introduction of major new services (rare / occasional / frequent)	A B C
10. Concern with legal restrictions in performing service (little / some / much)	A B C
Technology of transformation	
11. Capability to alter service capacity rapidly (little / some / much)	A B C
12. Degree of mechanization of service (little / some / much)	A B C
13. Amount of preparatory work prior to providing a unit of service (little / some / much)	A B C
14. Average number of processing stages customer goes through in obtaining service (few / several / many)	A B C
15. Emphasis on efficiency in layout of facility (little / moderate / major)	A B C
16. Emphasis on aesthetics in layout of facility (little / some / much)	A B C
17. Extent of equipment specialization (little / some / much)	A B C
18. Number of service centers (one / few / many)	A B C
19. Size of service center relative to direct competitors (small / medium / large)	A B C
20. Specific service centers located primarily for (convenience of customer / convenience of owner / other)	A B C
21. Reliance upon suppliers (little / some / much)	A B C
Operating-control system	
22. Investment in inventory control system (low / medium / high)	A B C
23. Extent of use of supplies to produce service (little / some / much)	A B C
24. Primary inventory viewed as (space / people / supplies)	A B C
25. Service strategy (level / mixed / adjust with demand)	A B C
26. Allowed variability in service scheduling (little / some / much)	A B C
27. Ability to backlog service orders (little / some / much)	A B C
28. Number of supervisory levels (few / several / many)	A B C
29. Number of staff departments to support service (none / some / many)	A B C
30. Method of assignment of service personnel (customer selects / mixed / system selects)	A B C
Work force	
31. Size of work force relative to competition (small / medium / large)	A B C
32. Required range of worker skills (narrow / medium / broad)	A B C
33. Use of certified professionals in creating service product (none / some / much)	A B C
34. Job content of most jobs (short cycle / medium / long cycle)	A B C
35. Work pace controlled by (customer / worker / system)	A B C
36. Wage payment system based primarily on (fees / hourly / output or sales)	A B C

Instructions for scoring

1. Circle either A, B, or C to identify what you believe to be the *correct* policy alternative (A, B, and C correspond to the order of the descriptive terms in the parentheses).
2. Place an X over either A, B, or C to identify what appears to be the policy *currently* being used.
3. Calculate the percentage of items in agreement out of the total items that you were able to score (i.e., the items that have both a circle and an X associated with them). This gives an alignment percentage.

   General scoring guide: 90–100% = excellent; 80–89% = good; 70–79% = fair; 60–69% = poor; below 60% = very poor.

EXHIBIT 18.10

General Decision-Making Framework for Service System Strategy Determination

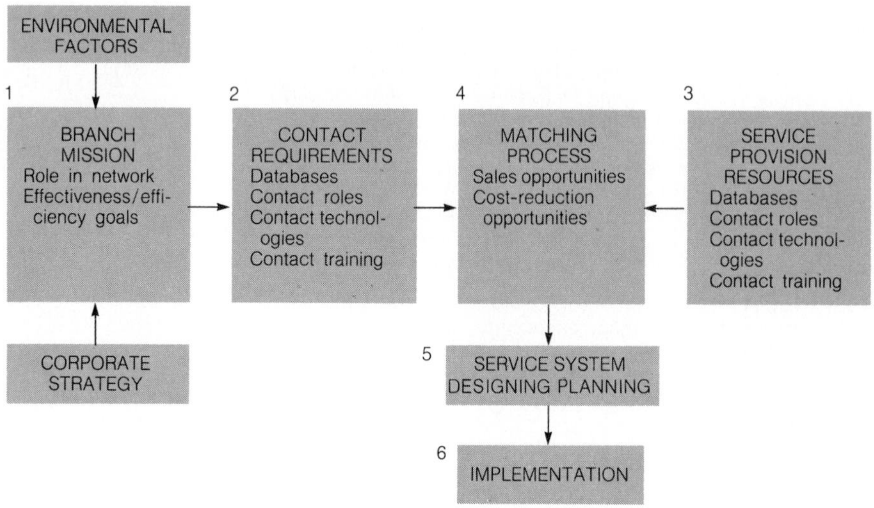

Source: R. B. Chase, G. Northcraft, and G. Wolf, "Design of High Contact Services: Application to Branches of a Savings and Loan," *Decision Sciences* 15, no. 4 (Fall 1984), p. 551.

service unit has the goal of acquiring a reputation for personal service, contact training may be an important dimension for that service unit to consider.

3. *Identify the service provision resources available.* After identifying the contact requirements, the service unit needs to think about what resources are available to fill the needs or requirements specified in Step 2.

4. *Search for a match between contact requirements and resources available.* The service-provision resources and the contact requirements derived from the mission are input into a matching process. The outcomes of the matching process should pair requirements to possibilities (resources) for dealing with the requirements.

5. *Develop a revised contact strategy.* The match is turned into plans for the design of service production and delivery in the service unit. This revised strategy should take into account any trade-offs among conflicting goals of the mission, rather than generate a series of actions that service particular goals at the expense of the unit's overall mission.

6. *Implement the revised contact strategy.* For this, databases provide a means for keeping track of customer accounts and demographics to help the sales mission. *Contact roles* are the specific skills needed (sales or word processing, for example), and *contact technologies* are the means by which services are actually delivered.

18.4 THE SERVICE FACTORY[11]

In the prior sections of this chapter, we presented manufacturing strategy and service strategy as separate entities. It has become quite evident that successful competitors in both domestic and global markets are those manufacturers who provide good service with their products. Customers want not only low prices and high quality, they demand short lead times and wide variety as well. They also look for outstanding field support when product repairs, upgrades, or modifications are needed. Furthermore, industrial customers particularly want the manufacturer's factories to be "user friendly"—readily accessible, easy to communicate with, and responsive to needs and complaints. In short, starting with the factory, customers want service throughout each stage of the production-distribution process.

What Is a "Service Factory"?

A *service factory* is the concept that a manufacturing firm, in addition to its products, produces a blend of services as well, which are integral to each of its products. How then can a manufacturing firm become a service factory?

Redefining the factory mission as a service concept
Most contemporary manufacturers prominently feature a customer orientation in their mission statements. These statements tend to focus solely on product attributes such as functional capabilities and quality levels rather than the product's benefits to the customer. On the other hand, service businesses, because they deal with intangible processes, are usually benefit oriented. This subtle, but important, distinction is reflected in Heskett's definition of the service concept: "What are important elements of the service to be provided in terms of results produced for the customers?" The answer to this question must be the central element of the mission statement for the service factory.

An open systems logic
The traditional approach to manufacturing is to seal off the core production technology from outside disturbances so that production may be accomplished without disruption. Happiness for the production manager is the production of one kind of product, all of one color, with infinitely long production runs. This is done by placing organizational buffers (marketing, product design, etc.) between the customer and the production system. There are, however, fewer and fewer markets that can be effectively serviced by this closed system philosophy. What is needed today is quite the opposite—an open system that

---

[11] This section has been adapted from R. B. Chase, and W. J. Erikson, "The Service Factory," *The Academy of Management Executive* 2, no. 3 (1988), pp. 191–96. For additional information on the topic, see also Richard B. Chase and David A. Garvin, "The Service Factory." *Harvard Business Review* 67, no.4 (July–August 1989), pp. 61–69.

includes the customer—one that can gather and act on information from the marketplace in real time. This is more than Just-in-Time production; it is Just-in-Time service across the entire spectrum of the firm's encounters with customers.

A well-managed customer-system interface

An effective service process requires that information exchanges between the system and the customer are handled smoothly, quickly, and inexpensively. Interorganizational systems (IOS) is emerging as an approach to achieving these objectives. An IOS, in contrast to a distributed data processing system, crosses company boundaries rather than being under the control of a single organization. IOSs are common in the service industry (for example, the CIRRUS nationwide network of automated teller machines that perform banking services for a variety of banks). IOSs are just now being introduced into manufacturing, linking manufacturers with their suppliers (who should be viewed as an extension of the service factory). Where appropriate, such as in non sole sourcing situations, a firm will be able to have its computer "shop" among suppliers and automatically initiate purchase orders to ensure timely and low-cost meeting of customer needs. Saturn, the new GM division, is planning to link electronically dealers' showrooms to the factory so that orders may be made in real time.

Decoupled production facilities

The four walls of the factory no longer limit the domain of manufacturing. Manufacturing can be done at the customer's plant, in the repairshop, and even in transit. For many manufacturers the service factory will consist of multiple production units as small as one technician in the field and as large as a satellite assembly complex adjacent to a customer's plant. (This may seem like a radical notion, but companies who sell liquid oxygen and nitrogen have been installing production equipment on or next to customer sites for years.) The extension of production throughout the value-added chain will call for closer coordination of field/factory operations, which may require enlarging factory management's job to include field production planning as well as internal operations. Widespread employee rotation through service positions may become a necessity as well.

Flexible capacity

Managers of service factories need to select workers and equipment that can adapt to overnight changes in the market. Flexible manufacturing systems—computer controlled machine tools capable of handling a wide variety of parts and tasks—are "have it your way" equipment, explicitly designed for this purpose. The "zero changeover-time plant" is now becoming a reality through movable equipment, knock-down walls, easily accessible and re-routable utilities, etc. An analogy to one kind of service captures the flavor quite well: "Automation that is easy to install and easy to tear down—similar to Ringling Bros.-Barnum and Bailey Circus in the old tent-circus days."

Customer-oriented factory personnel

Service factory managers and supervisors should be far more inclined to interact with the customers than similar personnel of the traditional plant. This means they must be adept at communication and sensitive to customer needs, in addition to possessing technical knowledge. Like the typical service supervisor, the service factory supervisor will be a visible representative of the organization, who can make or break a relationship with a customer. Of course, not all shop-floor employees will or should interact with the customer. As a practical matter, jobs of service factory personnel can be differentiated as being high customer contact or low customer contact, as is common in service businesses.

Adoption of refined service quality measures

The typical cost of quality report used in manufacturing covers prevention costs, appraisal costs, internal failure costs, and external failure costs. The first three items are internally oriented and pertain only to tangible products. External failure costs include warranty costs, out-of-warranty repairs and replacement, customer complaints and lost future sales, product liability, and transportation costs. Of these, only customer complaints is a direct measure of service quality. We suggest that adoption of a service perspective on quality calls for a new type of report explicitly for factory management. This might be termed a "factory customer service report," including such service measures as response time of engineering and production control to customer information requests, user's manual accuracy, completeness of the database on each customer's product needs, speed of emergency modifications and emergency repairs, perhaps even courtesy. It is interesting to note that while many manufacturers pride themselves on responding to these service needs, few routinely measure their performance to the level of detail that service organizations do.

Goods and service marketing blended with goods production

A well-run factory is a powerful marketing tool, yet some major manufacturing firms still do not recognize this point and discourage all customers from visiting the plant. In fact, we know of a company that requires its own managers from outside the manufacturing function to go through an elaborate request and sign-off process before they are allowed to visit the shop floor! From a service perspective, this not only presents a curious image to the customer but it clearly violates a basic precept of any marketing campaign: "Gain access to the customer to show off your wares." The service factory, by recognizing its sales mission as well as its production mission, should be expressly designed to maximize the sales opportunity that exists when the customer is in the system. This is done by extending and refining the growing practice of making quality visible, highlighting work force skills, and demonstrating the capabilities of the technology. For many companies in the production control and engineering software business as well as manufacturing, the plant should be viewed as a showroom where their own systems can be sold along with the main product. This process, however (which can be referred to as "modeling your own clothes"), has not been exploited to its full potential. Computer manufacturers, for example, sell state-of-the-art MRP systems, yet many don't use these products to run their plants. Despite the fact that there may be good reasons (software was developed by other divisions of the company, they have older systems that do the job, and so on) viewing the factory as a selling tool might well justify a change in strategy.

Has Anybody Used the Service Factory Concept?

A number of manufacturers have included aspects of the service factory in their operations, although none that we know of has used the service factory notion as a unifying concept. Some examples of plants that excel in particular features follow.

Chaparral Steel and Worthington Mills are clearly adherents of an open system philosophy. They encourage customers not only to visit plants, but to work on site with factory personnel on the full range of production issues. In addition, they have production people spend time at their customers' and suppliers' facilities to gain insight into how the factory can be of service. Hewlett-Packard is well known for its customer-oriented factory personnel who, in addition to just being friendly, can spin out the technical features of HP's Just-in-Time production system at the drop of a hat.

IBM's Lexington typewriter plant and GE's Louisville dishwasher plant were designed to show off their technologies to visitors as well as to make products. Carrying this point further, Yamazaki Machinery UK's Worcester plant, which opened last year, was designed with two objectives: One objective is to be the most advanced CNC machine tool factory in the world. The second goal is to be ". . . a showplace designed to impress the industrialists and engineers of Western Europe with the capabilities of the worldwide Yamazaki Corporation." An intensive publicity effort brought in 2,200 visitors during the first week of operation.

Shape Inc. of Biddeford, Maine, is beating firms from *both* Japan and Taiwan on price, quality, and service. Shape's performance is particularly surprising since they manufacture computer disks, audiocassettes, videocassettes, and similar items that most people consider to be the exclusive domain of overseas manufacturers. The key to success at Shape is the explicit recognition that the service dimension of their business is central to success. They compete not only on price and quality but on their ability to meet customer delivery and support requirements and, in addition, to do all this for small lot sizes as well as large.

The Kelly-Springfield Tire Co., another example, increased market share in an industry characterized by overcapacity and intensive price competition. Their approach was to provide better service while simultaneously reducing cost. The service issue that seemed most critical to management was shipping delays. Directly addressing this problem resulted in raising the number of units shipped within 24 hours of receipt of order from 78.8 to 85.3 percent. Costs did not rise as a result of this focus on service: they went down. The average inventory level was reduced from 94.7 days to 78.8 days sales (resulting in annual savings of $2.2 million). It seems obvious they could have reduced inventory further if they had kept service at the same 78.8 percent level instead of raising it to 85.3 percent. It is unlikely, however, they would have increased market share without a focus on *both* service and price.

Finally, there is Allen-Bradley's connector plant, which "models its own clothes," while achieving two central objectives of the service factory—flexibility and speed. The factory uses its commercially available CIM (computer integrated manufacturing) system to provide 24-hour delivery on a virtually unlimited variety of contractors and relays.

One common theme running through these examples is that service, as delivered by the service factory, is a multidimensional concept. It can refer to doing something for the customer, to doing something with the customer, or (as was the case in the new factory examples) it can refer to providing a service to another function of the business such as the marketing arm. By blending customer service needs into factory operations, these organizations found that service is not a cost factor to be controlled, but the key to increasing market share.

Service Factory Concept

The service factory concept implies that the service characteristics and the product characteristics be considered as a unit. The service dimension is not an "add on" feature; it must be addressed at the design stage, the manufacturing stage, and the support stage. This idea is conveyed in Exhibit 18.11, along with references to service firms that exemplify particular service actions.

Suggestions for Manufacturing Executives

Manufacturing executives have several related roles to play in helping their organizations blend service into their operations. The dominant issue, of course, is to ensure that the service dimension is included in the mission of manufacturing. Some suggestions on how to do this are as follows.

Define factory output as a service package

This is a fundamental first step in changing the factory's mission. It operationalizes the service factory concept by explicitly recognizing how the intangible service must interact with the tangible product. This requires some

EXHIBIT 18.11

Building the Factory Service Package

Production Steps		Service Actions
Design	Design what ⟷ the customer wants	Bring customers on site ▪ Codesign product ▪ Codesign service Like Kinko's Copy Centers
Manufacturing	Build what ⟷ they want when they want it	Design plant to facilitate ▪ Fast production ▪ Quality checks ▪ Modifications ▪ Status reporting in real time Like LensCrafters
Support	Support ⟷ what they bought	Game plan for effective response ▪ Guarantees ▪ Warranties ▪ Who to contact ▪ When to contact ▪ How to contact Like American Express

creative thinking, of course. However, there is at least one very successful "manufacturer" that can be used as a role model: McDonald's. Its hamburger manufacturing process is perfectly integrated with its service process to provide a "service factory" in the field.

Specify the service goals

The service goals must be defined in as much detail as possible. It is not sufficient to say that "service comes first." It is more meaningful to state that customer orders will be shipped within 24 hours of receipt, and that response time for customer service requests will not exceed two hours. Added to this of course is TLC—which includes the usual "tender loving care," but goes on to include "thinking like a customer."

Measure service performance

Organizational performance on service goals must be measured, not just to correct deviations but to foster the further improvement mentioned above. Mechanisms for this include the standard service industry tools of focus groups and surveys, which here would be applied to industrial customers. Such approaches should explicitly probe service effectiveness and their findings should be given boardroom attention.

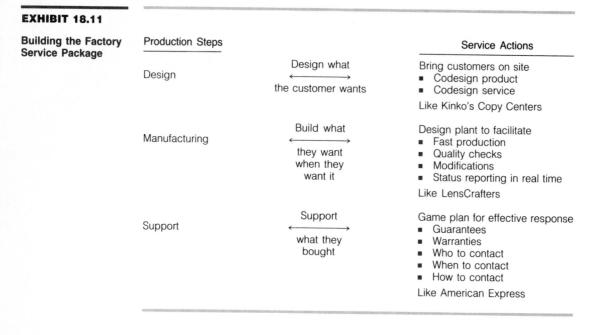

Include the customer in the service design process

Measuring customer satisfaction with service performance is but one way of involving the customer. Why not go further and have the customer help with designing the services as well? This is more than just negotiating shipment amounts and delivery times. It gets into such questions as: "What forms of contact would the customer like with the factory?" "How much service customization is necessary?" And, "How can factory operations make life easy for your customers?" Working through these questions with customers can enhance their loyalty, generate additional sales, and provide valuable public relations, which attracts new customers.

Include the employee in the service design process

The service factory requires greater participation on the part of the employees than is typical in the excessively compartmentalized factory of today. Therefore, we would suggest that manufacturing executives consider creating a permanent program to ensure that all employees are involved in the service design process.

This brief list of suggestions is a starting point. As any executive knows, it is impossible to excel in every performance measure all the time. Successful executives (and successful organizations) are aware of which performance measures are most important. We believe the service factory concept provides a framework that will enhance the executive's ability to solve the right problems at the right times and to improve continuously the competitive posture of the organization.

18.5 CONCLUSION

It is appropriate to conclude this book with the topic of strategy because it is here that operations management has an expanded and critical role to play. In the past several years American industry has been characterized as being good at financing and selling products, but somewhat less than world class at making them. While we do indeed have some of the best companies in the world in manufacturing, the fact is that far more companies need major upgrading in their operations management to remain competitive with foreign producers in their industry niche.

Recently, we have seen a veritable explosion in the thinking, writing, and most important, in the actions by companies directed toward achieving excellence in manufacturing. We believe that the next step is to include the services that a company provides as an integral part of its manufactured products and operate as a service factory. This would suggest including customer service within its "bill of materials," along with raw materials, parts, and subassemblies. This organization should blend the best practices of manufacturing with operating logic commonly found in effective service organizations. The net result will be a factory that excels both in producing goods and in providing the associated services that make these goods the premier choice of customers.

18.6 REVIEW AND DISCUSSION QUESTIONS

1. What particular production capabilities are included in the arsenals of the following firms?
   a. Volkswagen.
   b. Rolls-Royce.
   c. Chrysler.
2. Which characteristics of strategy are evident in obtaining a college education?
3. Explain the positioning concepts of process focus and product focus. How would they pertain to services such as a gourmet restaurant and an automobile agency?
4. Using your college or university as an example, refute or support the assertion that a production system cannot excel on every measure of performance.
5. How might a company president use the Wheelwright approach to establishing task priorities and a linear responsibility chart in strategic planning?
6. Briefly describe how you would use the methodology for service branch strategy determination in setting up a travel agency.
7. Give an example of how the strategy decision of automating through the use of robots would affect the personnel function and the finance function of an organization.

18.7 CASE: MEMPHIS TOY COMPANY

The Memphis Toy Company (MTC) views its primary task as making for stock a standardized line of high-quality, unique toys that "last from pablum to puberty." As a rule, MTC introduces one or two new toys a year. In August 1984, the owner and manufacturing manager, Dwight Smith-Daniels, has been informed by his toy inventors that they have designed a Michael Jackson doll. This doll will stand two feet high and is capable of break dancing and singing via an electronic voice synthesizer. One of the company's three manufacturing staff departments, design engineering, states that the product can be made primarily from molded plastic using the firm's new all-purpose molders (now used for making small attachments to the firm's wooden toys). MTC, in its previous initial production of new toys, has relied heavily on its skilled work force to "debug" the product design as they make the product and to perform quality inspections on the finished product. Production runs have been short runs to fill customer orders.

If the Jackson doll is to go into production, however, the production run size will have to be large and assembly and testing procedures will have to be more refined. Currently, each toymaker performs almost all processing steps at his or her workbench. The production engineering department believes that the assembly of the new toy is well within the skill levels of the current work force but that the voice synthesizer and battery-operated movement mechanism will have to be subcontracted. (The company is not sure about subcontracting the sequined glove that goes with the doll.) MTC has always had good relations with subcontractors, primarily because the firm has placed its orders with sufficient lead time so that its vendors could optimally sequence MTC's orders with those of some larger toy producers in Memphis. Dwight Smith-Daniels has always favored long-range production planning so that he can keep his 50 toymakers busy all year. (One of the reasons he set up the factory in Memphis was so that he could draw upon the large population of toymakers from the "old country" who lived there.) Smith-Daniels believes the supervisors of the firm's three production departments—castles, puppets, and novelties—are favorable to the new product. The novelty department supervisor, Fred Avide, has stated, "My workers can make any toy—you give us an output incentive, and we'll produce around the clock."

The marketing department has forecast a demand of 5,000 Michael Jackson dolls for the Christmas rush. The dolls should sell for $29.50. A preliminary cost analysis from the process engineering department is that they will cost no more than $7 each to manufacture. The company is currently operating at 70 percent capacity. Financing is available and there is no problem with cash flow. Dwight Smith-Daniels is wondering if he should go into production of Michael Jackson dolls.

QUESTIONS

1. Indicate the correct and current policy choices on the manufacturing policy questionnaire. Calculate the percentage of items that are in agreement.
2. Based on your findings, should MTC introduce the Michael Jackson doll? Explain.

18.8 CASE: BIG JIM'S GYM

Big Jim has been in the body-building business for many years in Glendale, California. His gymnasium, originally built for men, now consists of separate facilities for men and women located beneath a pizza parlor in downtown Glendale. Jim views the primary task of his business as "providing a full range of body-building and weight-reduction services for upper- and middle-class men, women, and children in the Glendale area."

Currently, he has 20 employees who work with the customers in designing their health programs. His gym has separate weightlifting and exercise rooms for men and women, a pool, a sauna bath, and a small running track behind the building. While Jim states that every customer is different, he makes men go through his 23-step conditioning course and women follow the diet in "Big Jim's Energy Diet" pamphlet. (Customers are usually enrolled in a 10-week introductory course and then left to advance at their own pace.)

The gym is modeled after the one Jim first managed on an army base in Pennsylvania, "right down to the olive-drab walls." Jim maintains that the spartan atmosphere is necessary "to build mental and physical toughness." With some pride, Jim notes that he has all the latest barbells and slant-board apparatus. Jim has always viewed his major inventory items as liniments and bandages, which are ordered periodically from a wholesaler or purchased from a nearby drugstore if stockouts occur. (Other items are purchased from a local sporting goods store.)

Jim is very concerned about keeping all his staff busy and keeping the equipment in constant use, so he requires that customers follow a specific hour-by-hour schedule on equipment use. If the equipment is scheduled to capacity, he requests that his customers come at slow periods during the day or evening. (This procedure has met with some resistance from customers, but Jim tells them that that is the price they must pay if he is to provide the most up-to-date health center services.)

Jim has done a survey of the prices charged by the other four health centers in the area and his fees are about average.* The other health centers have about the same number of employees, although two of them use licensed beauty consultants. Jim considers this an "unnecessary frill" and tells all his customers that anybody who works for him is an expert on all aspects of body maintenance. Jim has instituted a policy of job rotation whereby each member of the staff, with the exception of the clerk-typist, changes activities each hour. Employees are paid by the hour and are primarily college graduates who are interested in athletics. Turnover has not been a problem, even though Jim pays only slightly more than the minimum wage.

Although Jim's capacity is fully utilized, the number of memberships has dropped off from 500 to about 300 in the last six months, and profits have dropped proportionately. His accountant is looking into the possibility of raising membership fees.

QUESTIONS

1. Develop a new primary task for Big Jim's Gym.
2. Use the service systems audit questionnaire (Exhibit 18.9) to determine the alignment percentage between current policy and correct policy in light of the primary task you have proposed.
3. Based on your analysis, what steps do you recommend Jim take to reverse the trend in memberships?

18.9 SELECTED BIBLIOGRAPHY

Chase, Richard B., and David A. Garvin. "The Service Factory." *Harvard Business Review,* July–August 1989, pp. 61–69.

Hayes, R. H., and R. W. Schmenner. "How Should You Organize Manufacturing?" *Harvard Business Review*, January–February 1978, pp. 105–18.

Hayes, R. H., and S. C. Wheelwright. "Link Manufacturing Process and Product Life Cycles." *Harvard Business Review,* January–February 1979, pp. 133–40.

———. *Restoring Our Competitive Edge: Competing through Manufacturing*. New York: John Wiley & Sons, 1984.

Heskett, J. L. *Managing in the Service Economy*. Cambridge, Mass.: Harvard University Press, 1986.

Hill, T. J. "Manufacturing Implications in Determining Corporate Policy." *International Journal of Operations & Production Management* 1, no. 1 (1980), pp. 3–11.

---

* Within this market segment, Jim is competing with, among others, Vicki's Athletic Club. VAC's facilities include 10 handball-racquetball courts, 8 tennis courts, a 50-meter pool, sauna and steam rooms, a weight room with five $5,000 Nautilus weightlifting machines, and a fully equipped health bar. VAC's staff includes a trainer, 5 masseuses, 5 instructors, and 10 other staff members.

Kantrow, Alan M. "The Strategy-Technology Connection." *Harvard Business Review*, July–August 1980, pp. 6–8, 12.

Kumpe, Ted, and Peit T. Bolwijn. "Manufacturing: the New Case for Vertical Integration." *Harvard Business Review*, March–April 1988, pp. 75–82.

Peters, T. *Thriving on Chaos: Handbook for a Management Revolution*. New York: Alfred A. Knopf, 1987, pp. 158–171.

Schonberger, R. J. *World Class Manufacturing: The Lessons of Simplicity Applied*. New York: The Free Press, 1986, pp. 169–71.

________. "The Rationalization of Production." *Proceedings of the 50th Anniversary of the Academy of Management*, 1986, pp. 64–70.

Skinner, W. "Manufacturing—Missing Link in Corporate Strategy." *Harvard Business Review*, May–June 1969, pp. 136–45.

________. "The Focused Factory." *Harvard Business Review*, May–June 1974, pp. 113–21.

________. *Manufacturing in the Corporate Strategy*. New York: John Wiley & Sons, 1979.

Thomas, D. R. "Strategy Is Different in a Service Business." *Harvard Business Review*, July–August 1978, pp. 158–65.

Wheelwright, S. "Reflecting Corporate Strategy in Manufacturing Decisions." *Business Horizons*, February 1978, pp. 57–66.

Appendixes

OUTLINE

APPENDIX A Uniformly Distributed Random Digits

56970	10799	52098	04184	54967	72938	50834	23777	08392
83125	85077	60490	44369	66130	72936	69848	59973	08144
55503	21383	02464	26141	68779	66388	75242	82690	74099
47019	06683	33203	29603	54553	25971	69573	83854	24715
84828	61152	79526	29554	84580	37859	28504	61980	34997
08021	31331	79227	05748	51276	57143	31926	00915	45821
36458	28285	30424	98420	72925	40729	22337	48293	86847
05752	96045	36847	87729	81679	59126	59437	33225	31280
26768	02513	58454	56958	20575	76746	40878	06846	32828
42613	72456	43030	58085	06766	60227	96414	32671	45587
95457	12176	65482	25596	02678	54592	63607	82096	21913
95276	67524	63564	95958	39750	64379	46059	51666	10433
66954	53574	64776	92345	95110	59448	77249	54044	67942
17457	44151	14113	02462	02798	54977	48340	66738	60184
03704	23322	83214	59337	01695	60666	97410	55064	17427
21538	16997	33210	60337	27976	70661	08250	69509	60264
57178	16730	08310	70348	11317	71623	55510	64750	87759
31048	40058	94953	55866	96283	40620	52087	80817	74533
69799	83300	16498	80733	96422	58078	99643	39847	96884
90595	65017	59231	17772	67831	33317	00520	90401	41700
33570	34761	08039	78784	09977	29398	93896	78227	90110
15340	82760	57477	13898	48431	72936	78160	87240	52710
64079	07733	36512	56186	99098	48850	72527	08486	10951
63491	84886	67118	62063	74958	20946	28147	39338	32109
92003	76568	41034	28260	79708	00770	88643	21188	01850
52360	46658	66511	04172	73085	11795	52594	13287	82531
74622	12142	68355	65635	21828	39539	18988	53609	04001
04157	50070	61343	64315	70836	82857	35335	87900	36194
86003	60070	66241	32836	27573	11479	94114	81641	00496
41208	80187	20351	09630	84668	42486	71303	19512	50277
06433	80674	24520	18222	10610	05794	37515	48619	62866
39298	47829	72648	37414	75755	04717	29899	78817	03509
89884	59651	67533	68123	17730	95862	08034	19473	63971
61512	32155	51906	61662	64430	16688	37275	51262	11569
99653	47635	12506	88535	36553	23757	34209	55803	96275
95913	11085	13772	76638	48423	25018	99041	77529	81360
55804	44004	13122	44115	01601	50541	00147	77685	58788
35334	82410	91601	40617	72876	33967	73830	15405	96554
57729	88646	76487	11622	96297	24160	09903	14047	22917
86648	89317	63677	70119	94739	25875	38829	68377	43918
30574	06039	07967	32422	76791	30725	53711	93385	13421
81307	13114	83580	79974	45929	85113	72268	09858	52104
02410	96385	79067	54939	21410	86980	91772	93307	34116
18969	87444	52233	62319	08598	09066	95288	04794	01534
87863	80514	66860	62297	80198	19347	73234	86265	49096
08397	10538	15438	62311	72844	60203	46412	65943	79232
28520	45247	58729	10854	99058	18260	38765	90038	94209
44285	09452	15867	70418	57012	72122	36634	97283	95943
86299	22510	33571	23309	57040	29285	67870	21913	72958
84842	05748	90894	61658	15001	94005	36308	41161	37341

APPENDIX B Normally Distributed Random Digits

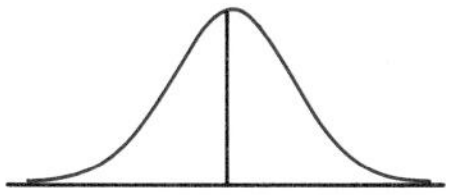

0

An entry in the table is the value *z* from a normal distribution with a mean of 0 and a standard deviation of 1.

1.98677	1.23481	−.28360	.99217	−.87919	−.21600
−.59341	1.54221	−.65806	1.08372	1.68560	1.14899
.11340	.19126	−.65084	.12188	.02338	−.61545
.89783	−.54929	−.03663	−1.89506	.15158	−.20061
−.50790	1.14463	1.30917	1.26528	.09459	.16423
−1.63968	−.63248	.21482	−1.16241	−.60015	−.55233
1.14081	−.29988	−.48053	−1.21397	−.34391	−1.84881
−.43354	−.32855	.67115	.52289	−1.42796	−.14181
.05707	.35331	.20470	.01847	1.71086	−1.44738
.77153	.72576	−.29833	.26139	1.25845	−.35468
−1.38286	.04406	−.75499	.61068	.61903	−.96845
1.60166	−1.66161	.70886	−.20302	−.28373	2.07219
−.48781	.02629	−.34306	2.00746	−1.12059	.07943
−1.10632	1.18250	−.60065	.09737	.63297	1.00659
.77000	−.87214	−.63584	−.39546	−.72776	.45594
−.56882	−.23153	−2.03852	−.28101	.30384	−.14246
.27721	−.04776	.11740	−.17211	1.63483	1.34221
−.40251	−.31052	−1.04834	−.23243	−1.52224	.85903
1.27086	−.93166	−.03766	1.21016	.13451	.81941
1.14464	.56176	.89824	1.54670	1.48411	.14422
.04172	1.49672	−.15490	.77084	−.29064	2.87643
−.36795	1.22318	−1.05084	−1.05409	.82052	.09670
1.94110	1.00826	−.85411	−1.31341	−1.85921	.74578
.14946	−2.75470	−.10830	1.02845	.69291	−.78579
.32512	1.11241	.45138	.79940	−.91803	−1.35919
.66748	−.55806	.27694	.80928	−.18061	1.26569
−1.23681	−.49094	.34951	1.66404	.30419	−1.32670
−.57808	−.04187	2.01897	.92651	.10518	−.34227
1.24924	−.98726	−.24277	−.48852	1.14221	−.43447
.38640	−.26990	−.21369	.65047	.27436	−2.30590
.47191	.52304	−1.16670	1.11789	−.10954	1.17787
−1.12401	.24826	.03741	−.72132	−.44131	−1.10636
−.04997	−1.19941	−.63591	1.27889	.69289	−.27419
−.08265	1.08497	.12277	−.61647	−2.74235	1.10660
.28522	.04496	−1.53535	.42616	−.54092	−1.99089
−.60318	−.00926	−1.57852	−.68966	−1.07899	−2.26274
1.66247	−.94171	−1.84672	.14506	−1.79616	−.03350
−.06993	.82752	−1.79937	−.58224	.38834	1.17421
.22572	−.23812	1.38760	.97453	−.48264	.42092
2.12500	.18124	.22034	1.06353	−.84988	−1.40673
−.51185	−1.35882	1.34636	−.03440	.31133	−1.63670
.35724	−1.45402	.16793	1.16726	−.76094	−.38834
−1.29352	−.28185	.86607	.68714	2.16262	1.82108
.34521	1.16515	−.11361	−1.35778	.16051	.93119
−1.33783	−.28278	−.09756	1.38268	−1.74537	.76566

APPENDIX C Areas of the Standard Normal Distribution

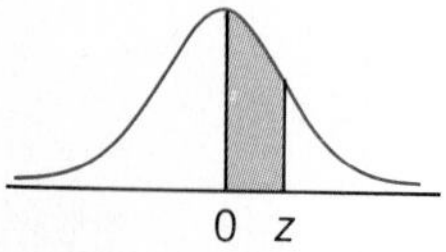

An entry in the table is the proportion under the entire curve which is between $z = 0$ and a positive value of z. Areas for negative values of z are obtained by symmetry.

z	*.00*	*.01*	*.02*	*.03*	*.04*	*.05*	*.06*	*.07*	*.08*	*.09*
0.0	.0000	.0040	.0080	.0120	.0160	.0199	.0239	.0279	.0319	.0359
0.1	.0398	.0438	.0478	.0517	.0557	.0596	.0636	.0675	.0714	.0753
0.2	.0793	.0832	.0871	.0910	.0948	.0987	.1026	.1064	.1103	.1141
0.3	.1179	.1217	.1255	.1293	.1331	.1368	.1406	.1443	.1480	.1517
0.4	.1554	.1591	.1628	.1664	.1700	.1736	.1772	.1808	.1844	.1879
0.5	.1915	.1950	.1985	.2019	.2054	.2088	.2123	.2157	.2190	.2224
0.6	.2257	.2291	.2324	.2357	.2389	.2422	.2454	.2486	.2517	.2549
0.7	.2580	.2611	.2642	.2673	.2703	.2734	.2764	.2794	.2823	.2852
0.8	.2881	.2910	.2939	.2967	.2995	.3023	.3051	.3078	.3106	.3133
0.9	.3159	.3186	.3212	.3238	.3264	.3289	.3315	.3340	.3365	.3389
1.0	.3413	.3438	.3461	.3485	.3508	.3531	.3554	.3577	.3599	.3621
1.1	.3643	.3665	.3686	.3708	.3729	.3749	.3770	.3790	.3810	.3830
1.2	.3849	.3869	.3888	.3907	.3925	.3944	.3962	.3980	.3997	.4015
1.3	.4032	.4049	.4066	.4082	.4099	.4115	.4131	.4147	.4162	.4177
1.4	.4192	.4207	.4222	.4236	.4251	.4265	.4279	.4292	.4306	.4319
1.5	.4332	.4345	.4357	.4370	.4382	.4394	.4406	.4418	.4429	.4441
1.6	.4452	.4463	.4474	.4484	.4495	.4505	.4515	.4525	.4535	.4545
1.7	.4554	.4564	.4573	.4582	.4591	.4599	.4608	.4616	.4625	.4633
1.8	.4641	.4649	.4656	.4664	.4671	.4678	.4686	.4693	.4699	.4706
1.9	.4713	.4719	.4726	.4732	.4738	.4744	.4750	.4756	.4761	.4767
2.0	.4772	.4778	.4783	.4788	.4793	.4798	.4803	.4808	.4812	.4817
2.1	.4821	.4826	.4830	.4834	.4838	.4842	.4846	.4850	.4854	.4857
2.2	.4861	.4864	.4868	.4871	.4875	.4878	.4881	.4884	.4887	.4890
2.3	.4893	.4896	.4898	.4901	.4904	.4906	.4909	.4911	.4913	.4916
2.4	.4918	.4920	.4922	.4925	.4927	.4929	.4931	.4932	.4934	.4936
2.5	.4938	.4940	.4941	.4943	.4945	.4946	.4948	.4949	.4951	.4952
2.6	.4953	.4955	.4956	.4957	.4959	.4960	.4961	.4962	.4963	.4964
2.7	.4965	.4966	.4967	.4968	.4969	.4970	.4971	.4972	.4973	.4974
2.8	.4974	.4975	.4976	.4977	.4977	.4978	.4979	.4979	.4980	.4981
2.9	.4981	.4982	.4982	.4983	.4984	.4984	.4985	.4985	.4986	.4986
3.0	.4987	.4987	.4987	.4988	.4988	.4989	.4989	.4989	.4990	.4990

Source: Paul G. Hoel, *Elementary Statistics* (New York: John Wiley & Sons, 1960), p. 240.

APPENDIX D Answers to Selected Problems

SUPPLEMENT TO CHAPTER 4 Waiting Line Theory

1. Quick Lube Inc.

   $\lambda = 3,\ \mu = 4$

   a. Utilization $(\rho) = \dfrac{\lambda}{\mu} = \dfrac{3}{4} = 75\%.$

   b. $\bar{n}_1 = \dfrac{\lambda^2}{\mu(\mu - \lambda)} = \dfrac{3^2}{4(4-3)} = \dfrac{9}{4} = 2.25$ cars in line.

   c. $\bar{t}_1 = \dfrac{\lambda}{\mu(\mu - \lambda)} = \dfrac{3}{4(4-3)} = \dfrac{3}{4} = 45$ minutes in line.

   d. $\bar{t}_s = \dfrac{1}{\mu - \lambda} = \dfrac{1}{1} = 1$ hour (waiting + lube).

2. American Vending Inc.
   Case I: One worker.

   $\lambda = 3/\text{hour Poisson},\ \mu = 5/\text{hour exponential}$

   There is an average number of machines in the system of:

   $$\bar{n}_s = \frac{\lambda}{\mu - \lambda} = \frac{3}{5-3} = \frac{3}{2} = 1\tfrac{1}{2} \text{ machines}$$

   Downtime cost is \$25 × 1.5 = \$37.50 per hour; repair cost is \$4.00 per hour; and total cost per hour for 1 worker is \$37.50 + \$4.00 = \$41.50.

Downtime (1.5 × \$25)	=	\$37.50
Labor (1 worker × \$4)	=	4.00
		\$41.50

   Case II: Two workers.

   $\lambda = 3,\ \mu = 7$

   $$\bar{n}_s = \frac{\lambda}{\mu - \lambda} = \frac{3}{7-3} = .75 \text{ machines}$$

Downtime (.75 × \$25)	=	\$18.75
Labor (2 workers × \$4.00)	=	8.00
		\$26.75

   Case III: Three workers.

   $\lambda = 3,\ \mu = 8$

   $$\bar{n}_s = \frac{\lambda}{\mu - \lambda} = \frac{3}{8-3} = \frac{3}{5} = .60 \text{ machines}$$

Downtime (.60 × \$25)	=	\$15.00
Labor (3 workers × \$4)	=	12.00
		\$27.00

Comparing the costs for one, two, or three workers, we see that Case II with two workers is the optimal decision.

CHAPTER 5 Design of the Quality Control System

1. Should Part A be inspected?

   .03 defective with no inspection.
   .02 defective with inspection.

   a. This problem can be solved simply by looking at the opportunity for 1 percent improvement.

   Benefit = .01(\$4.00) = \$0.04
   Cost of inspection = \$0.01

   Therefore, inspect and save \$0.03 per unit.

   b. A cost of \$0.05 per unit to inspect would be \$0.01 greater than the savings, and therefore, inspection should not be performed.

CHAPTER 6 Forecasting

1. *a.* Simple moving average, 4-week.

$$\text{Monday} \quad \frac{2{,}400 + 2{,}300 + 2{,}400 + 2{,}200}{4} = \frac{9{,}300}{4} = 2{,}325 \text{ doz.}$$

$$\text{Tuesday} \quad = \frac{8{,}500}{4} = 2{,}125 \text{ doz.}$$

$$\text{Wednesday} \quad = \frac{9{,}500}{4} = 2{,}375 \text{ doz.}$$

$$\text{Thursday} \quad = \frac{7{,}500}{4} = 1{,}875 \text{ doz.}$$

$$\text{Friday, Saturday, and Sunday} \quad = \frac{19{,}200}{4} = 4{,}800 \text{ doz.}$$

b. Weighted average with weights of .40, .30, .20, and .10.

	(.10)		(.20)		(.30)		(.40)		
Monday	220	+	480	+	690	+	960	=	2,350
Tuesday	200	+	420	+	660	+	880	=	2,160
Wednesday	230	+	480	+	690	+	1,000	=	2,400
Thursday	180	+	380	+	540	+	800	=	1,900
Friday, Saturday, and Sunday	470	+	900	+	1,530	+	1,960	=	4,860
	1,300	+	2,660	+	4,110	+	5,600	=	13,670

c. $F_t = F_{t-1} + \alpha(A_{t-1} - F_{t-1})$
$= 22{,}000 + 0.10(21{,}000 - 22{,}000)$
$= 22{,}000 - 100$
$= 21{,}900$ loaves

d. $F_{t+1} = 21{,}900 + \alpha(22{,}500 - 21{,}900)$
$= 21{,}900 + .10(600)$
$= 21{,}960$ loaves

CHAPTER 7 Capacity Planning and Location

1. Art Fern.

Lease decision

@D	Revenue for 8 years = 8[.5(700,000) + 0.3(500,000) + 0.2(300,000)]		$4,480,000
	Lease cost for 8 years = 8(250,000)	$2,000,000	
	Operating cost for 8 years = (200,000)	1,600,000	3,600,000
	Net income		$ 880,000
@E	Revenue for 8 years = 8[.5(700,000) + 0.3(500,000) + 0.2(300,000)]		$4,480,000
	Lease cost 30 percent greater or 1.30(250,000)	$ 325,000	
	Lease for 8 years = 8(325,000)	2,600,000	
	Operating cost for 8 years = 8(200,000)	1,600,000	4,200,000
	Net income		$ 280,000

@C Net income = 0.5(880,000) + 0.5(280,000) = 580,000

@B Net income = Revenue for 2 years − Operating cost for 2 years − Lease cost for 2 years + Value of node C
= 2[.5(700,000) + 0.3(500,000) + 0.2(300,000)] − 2(250,000) − 2(200,000) + $580,000
= $800,000

Build Inglewood

@F	Revenue for 10 years = 10[0.5(400,000) + 0.3(300,000) + 0.2(200,000)]	$3,300,000
	Operating costs for 10 years = 10(200,000)	−2,000,000
	Plus salvage value	–0–
		1,300,000
@A	Less cost to build	−1,000,000
	Net income	$ 300,000

The best decision is to lease, with a net income of $800,000; building would produce a net income of only $300,000.

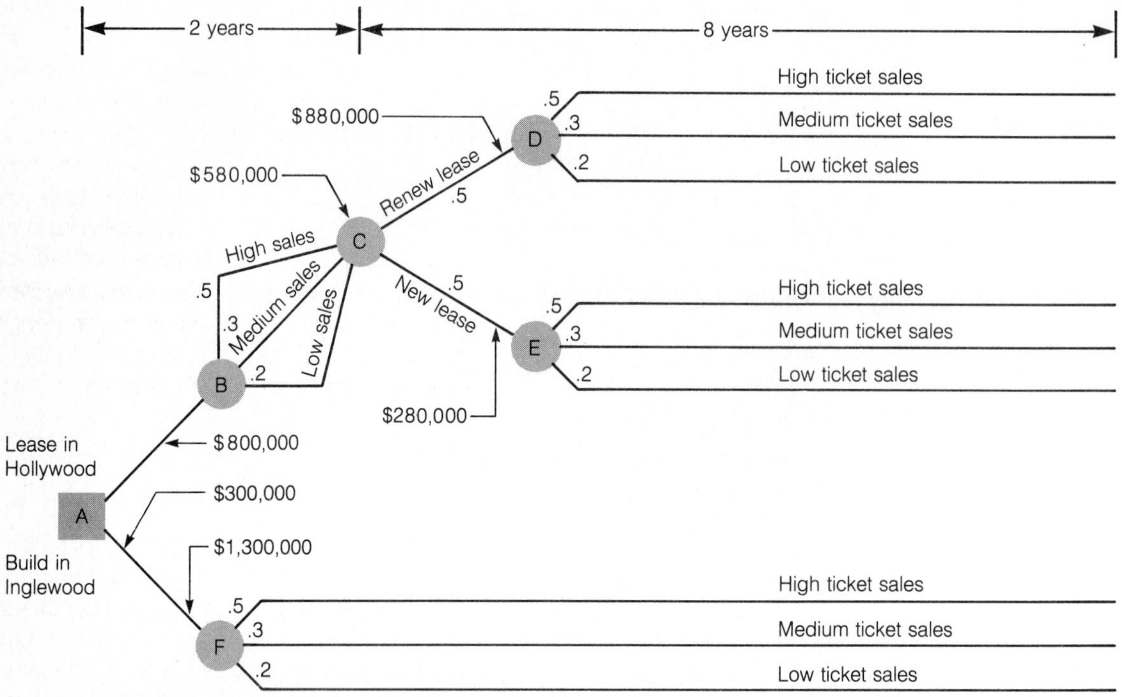

SUPPLEMENT TO CHAPTER 7 Linear Programming

1. The optimal point, as shown on the next page, is $X = 67$ and $Y = 133$. Profit at this point would be $10(67) + 5(133) = \$1,335$.

   $X + Y \leq 200$
   $4X + Y \leq 400$

   Maximize $10X + 5Y$

   (1) $X + Y = 200$
   $@X = 0 \quad Y = 200$
   $@Y = 0 \quad X = 200$

   (2) $4X + Y \leq 400$
   $@X = 0 \quad Y = 400$
   $@Y = 0 \quad X = 100$

   Assume:

   $10X + 5Y = 500$
   $@X = 0 \quad Y = 100$
   $@Y = 0 \quad X = 50$

To fit the graph scale and area of interest double the values to $Y = 200$, $X = 100$.

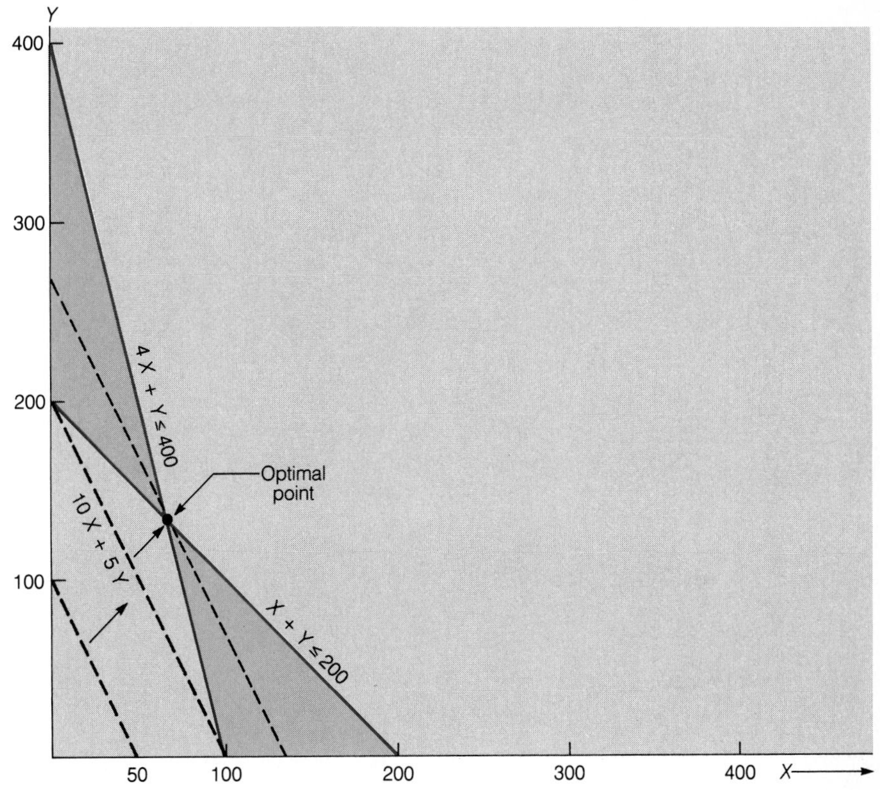

2. Simplex solution to Problem 1.

	$10 X	$5 Y	0 S_1	0 S_2	
S_1	1	1	1	0	200
S_2	4	1	0	1	400
	$10	$5	0	0	
S_1	0	3/4	1	−1/4	100
X	1	1/4	0	1/4	100
	0	2.50	0	−2.50	
Y	0	1	4/3	−1/3	133
X	1	0	−1/3	1/3	67
			$−3.33	$−1.66	

With $X = 67$ and $Y = 133$, the value of the objective function would be $Z = 10(67) + 5(133) = \$1,335$.

CHAPTER 8 Facility Layout

1. University office layout.
   a. Evaluate this layout according to one of the methods in the chapter.

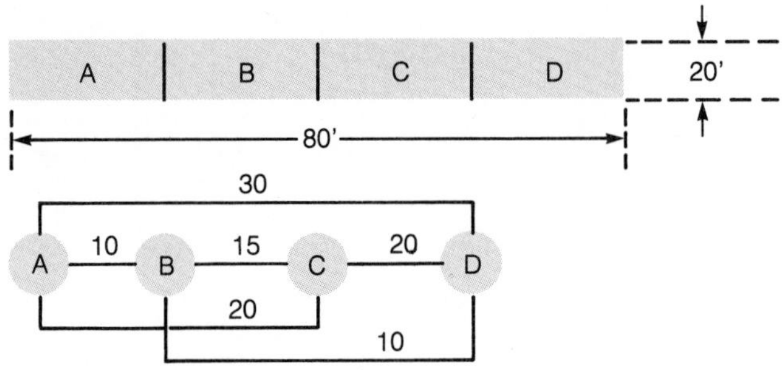

Using the material handling cost method shown in the toy company example we obtain the following costs, assuming that every nonadjacency doubles the initial cost/unit distance:

$AB = 10 \times 1 = 10$
$AC = 20 \times 2 = 40$
$AD = 30 \times 3 = 90$
$BC = 15 \times 1 = 15$
$BD = 10 \times 2 = 20$
$CD = 20 \times 1 = 20$
Current cost = 195

   b. Improve the layout by exchanging functions within rooms. Show your amount of improvement using the same method as in (*a*). A better layout would be BCDA.

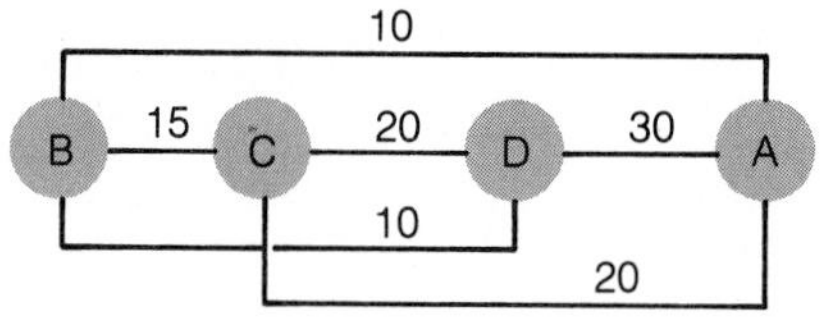

$AB = 10 \times 3 = 30$
$AC = 20 \times 2 = 40$
$AD = 30 \times 1 = 30$
$BC = 15 \times 1 = 15$
$BD = 10 \times 2 = 20$
$CD = 20 \times 1 = 20$
Improved cost = 155

2. Assembly line balancing.
   a. Draw the schematic diagram.

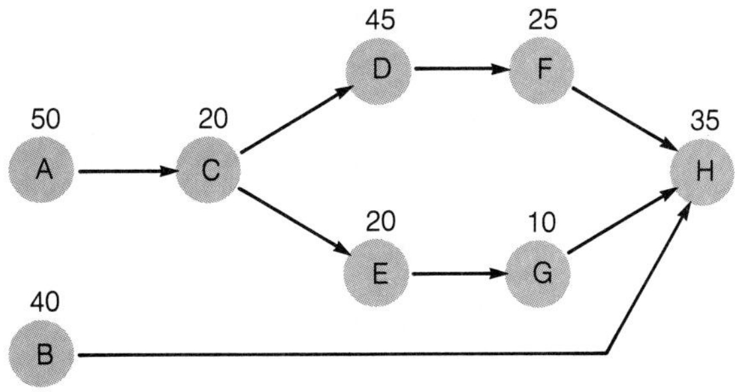

   b. Theoretical minimum number of stations to meet D = 400 is:

$$N_t = \frac{T}{C} = \frac{245 \text{ seconds}}{\left(\dfrac{60 \text{ seconds} \times 480 \text{ minutes}}{400 \text{ units}}\right)} = \frac{245}{72} = 3.4 \text{ stations}$$

   c. Use the longest operating time rule and balance the line in the minimum number of stations to produce 400 units per day.

	Task	Task Time (seconds)	Remaining Unassigned Time	Feasible Remaining Tasks
Station 1	A	50	22	C
	C	20	2	None
Station 2	D	45	27	E, F
	F	25	2	None
Station 3	B	40	32	E
	E	20	12	G
	G	10	2	None
Station 4	H	35	37	None

SUPPLEMENT TO CHAPTER 8 Simulation

1. Assign random numbers to the balls to correspond to the percentage present in the urn.

	Random Number
10 green balls	00–09
40 red balls	10–49
50 spotted balls	50–99

Many possible answers exist, depending on how the random numbers were assigned and which numbers were used from the list provided in the problem.

For the random number sequence above and using the first two numbers of those given we obtain the following:

RN	Color
26	Red
42	Red
95	Spotted
95	Spotted
66	Spotted
17	Red
3	Green
56	Spotted
83	Spotted
55	Spotted

For the 10 there were 1 green, 3 red, and 6 spotted balls—a good estimate based on a sample of only 10!

2. Demand for blood.

DELIVERY			NUMBER OF PATIENTS			PATIENT DEMAND		
Pints	Frequency	Random Number	Blood	Frequency	Random Number	Pints	Frequency	Random Number
4	.15	00–14	0	.25	00–24	1	.40	00–39
5	.20	15–34	1	.25	25–49	2	.30	40–69
6	.25	35–59	2	.30	50–79	3	.20	70–89
7	.15	60–74	3	.15	80–94	4	.10	90–99
8	.15	75–89	4	.05	95–99			
9	.10	90–99						

Week No.	Beginning Inventory	QUANTITY DELIVERED		Total Blood on Hand	PATIENTS NEEDING BLOOD		QUANTITY NEEDED			Number of Pints Remaining
		RN	Pints		RN	Patients	Patient	RN	Pints	
1	0	74	7	7	85	3	First	21	1	6
							Second	06	1	5
							Third	71	3	2
2	2	31	5	7	28	1		96	4	3
3	3	02	4	7	72	2	First	12	1	6
							Second	67	2	4
4	4	53	6	10	44	1		23	1	9
5	9	16	5	14	16	0				14
6	14	40	6	20	83	3	First	65	2	18
							Second	34	1	17
							Third	82	3	14
7	14									

At the end of 6 weeks, there were 14 pints on hand.

CHAPTER 9 Job Design and Work Measurement

1. Felix Unger time study (assume minutes).

	ST	$\bar{T}$	Performance Rating	*NT*
Get shoeshine kit	.50	.50/2 = .25	125%	.31
Polish shoes (2 pair)	3.40	3.40/2 = 1.70	110	1.87
Put away kit	.75	.75/2 = .375	80	.30
Normal time for one pair of shoes				2.48

Standard time for the pair = 2.48 × 1.05 = 2.61 minutes.

2. Work sampling of head baker.

To calculate the number of observations, use the formula at the bottom of Exhibit 9.14, since the 95 percent confidence is required (i.e., $Z \cong 2$).

$$p = \text{"Doing"} = 6/15 = 40\%$$
$$E = 5\% \text{ (given)}$$
$$N = \frac{4p(1-p)}{E^2} = \frac{4(.4)(1-.4)}{(.05)(.05)} = \frac{.96}{.0025} = 384$$

CHAPTER 10 Project Planning and Control

1. CPM problem.

The answers to *(a)*, *(b)*, and *(c)* are shown in the diagram below.

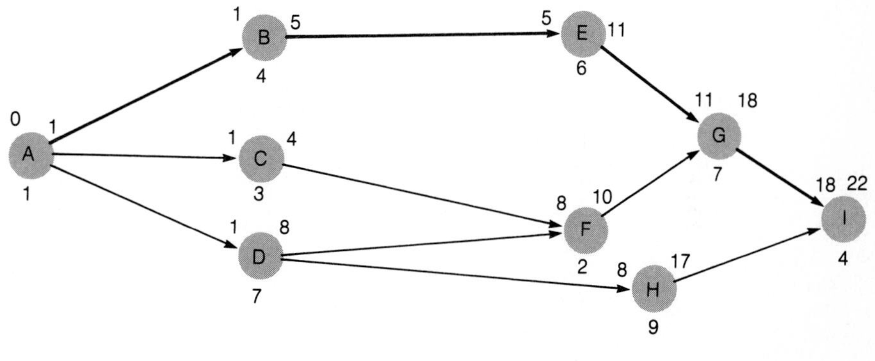

d. New critical path: A, D, F, G, I. Time of completion = 23 days.

2. PERT problem.

Using the estimated time as $ET = \frac{a + 4m + b}{6}$, the PERT network is as follows:

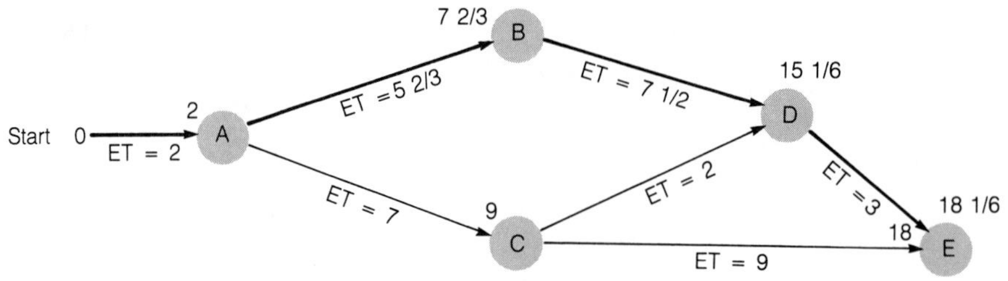

a. 18⅙ weeks.

b. Critical path is Start, A, B, D, E.

c. $$\sigma_{cp} = \sqrt{\left(\frac{3-1}{6}\right)^2 + \left(\frac{11-3}{6}\right)^2 + \left(\frac{12-5}{6}\right)^2 + \left(\frac{4-2}{6}\right)^2}$$
$= 1.8$ weeks

d. $$Z = \frac{D - T_e}{\sigma_{cp}} = \frac{20 - 18\frac{1}{6}}{1.8} = 1.02$$
From Appendix C at $Z = 1$, the probability is .8413, or ≈ 84%.

SUPPLEMENT TO CHAPTER 10 Learning Curves

1. Computing the price for two additional subs for the Loch Ness Monster search team.

The solution is found by applying learning curve (LC) values to labor costs for the 11th and 12th subs and adding these amounts to the material requirements. A 10 percent markup is then added to the sum. LC of the 11th is estimated as the average of the 10th and 12th.

Cost of the 11th sub:	
Materials	$200,000
Labor: 300,000 (.3058 + .2784) ÷ 2	87,630
	$287,630
Cost of the 12th sub:	
Materials	$200,000
Labor: .2784 × 300,000	83,520
	$283,520
Selling price: 1.10 × (287,630 + 283,520)	$628,265

6. *a.* Learning rate $= \dfrac{9 \text{ minutes}}{10 \text{ minutes}} = 90\%$

From Exhibit S10.4, the time for the 1,000th unit is .3499 × 10 minutes = 3.499 minutes.

Yes, hire the person.

b. From Exhibit S10.4, unit 10 at 90% is .7047. Therefore, time for 10th unit = .7047 × 10 = 7.047 minutes.

CHAPTER 11 Aggregate Planning

1. *Plan 1: Exact production; vary work force* (assume 10 in work force to start).

Month	(1) Production Required	(2) Production Hours Required (1) × 4	(3) Hours/Month per Worker 22 × 8	(4) Workers Required (2) ÷ (3)	(5) WORKERS Hired	(6) Fired
January	300	1,200	176	7	0	3
February	600	2,400	176	14	7	0
March	650	2,600	176	15	1	0
April	800	3,200	176	19	4	0
May	900	3,600	176	21	2	0
June	800	3,200	176	19	0	2

Month	(7) Hiring Cost (5) × $50	(8) Layoff Cost (6) × $100	(9) Straight-Time Cost (2) × $12.50
January	0	$300	$ 15,000
February	350	0	30,000
March	50	0	32,500
April	200	0	40,000
May	100	0	45,000
June	0	200	40,000
	$700	$500	$202,500

Total cost for plan:

Hiring cost	$ 700
Layoff cost	500
Straight-time cost	202,500
Total	$203,700

Plan 2: Constant work force; vary inventory and stockout only.

Month	(1) Cumulative Production Requirement	(2) Production Hours Available 22 × 8 × 10	(3) Units Produced (2) ÷ 4	(4) Cumulative Production
January	300	1,760	440	440
February	900	1,760	440	880
March	1,550	1,760	440	1,320
April	2,350	1,760	440	1,760
May	3,250	1,760	440	2,200
June	4,050	1,760	440	2,640

Month	(5) Units Short (1) − (4)	(6) Shortage Cost (5) × $20	(7) Units Excess (4) − (1)	(8) Inventory Cost (7) × $10	(9) Straight-Time Cost (2) × $12.50
January	$ 0	0	140	1,400	$ 22,000
February	20	400	0	0	22,000
March	230	4,600	0	0	22,000
April	590	11,800	0	0	22,000
May	1,050	21,000	0	0	22,000
June	1,410	28,200	0	0	22,000
		$66,000		$1,400	$132,000

Total cost for plan:

Shortage cost	$ 66,000
Inventory cost	1,400
Straight-time cost	132,000
Total	$199,400

Plan 3A: Constant work force of 10; vary overtime only; inventory carryover permitted.

Month	(1) Production Requirement	(2) Standard-Time Production Hours Available 22 × 8 × 10	(3) Standard-Time Units Produced (2) ÷ 4	(4) Overtime Required in Units (1) − (3)
January	300	1,760	440	0
February	460*	1,760	440	20
March	650	1,760	440	210
April	800	1,760	440	360
May	900	1,760	440	460
June	800	1,760	440	360
				1,410

*600 − 140 units of beginning inventory in February.

Month	(5) Overtime Required Hours (4) × 4	(6) Overtime Cost (5) × $18.75	(7) Straight-Time Cost (2) × $12.50	(8) Excess Inventory Costs (3) − (1) × $10
January	0	$ 0	$ 22,000	$1,400
February	80	1,500	22,000	
March	840	15,750	22,000	
April	1,440	27,000	22,000	
May	1,840	34,500	22,000	
June	1,440	27,000	22,000	
		$105,750	$132,000	$1,400

Total cost for plan:

Straight-time cost	$132,000
Overtime cost	105,750
Inventory cost	1,400
Total	$239,150

Plan 3B: Constant work force of 10; vary overtime only; no inventory carryover.

Month	(1) Production Requirement	(2) Standard-Time Hours Available 22 × 8 × 10	(3) Standard-Time Units Produced Min. [(2) ÷ 4; (1)]	(4) Overtime Required in Units (1) − (3)
January	300	1,760	300	0
February	600	1,760	440	160
March	650	1,760	440	210
April	800	1,760	440	360
May	900	1,760	440	460
June	800	1,760	440	360

Month	(5) Overtime Required in Hours (4) × 4 Hours	(6) Overtime Cost (5) × $18.75	(7) Standard-Time Cost (2) × $12.50	(8) Excess Inventory Cost (3) − (1) × $10
January	0	$ 0	$ 22,000	$1,400
February	640	12,000	22,000	
March	840	15,750	22,000	
April	1,440	27,000	22,000	
May	1,840	34,500	22,000	
June	1,440	27,000	22,000	
		$116,250	$132,000	$1,400

Total cost for plan:

Straight time cost	$132,000
Overtime cost	116,250
Excess inventory cost	1,400
	$249,650

Summary.

Plan Description	Hiring	Layoff	Straight Time	Shortage	Excess Inventory	Total Cost
	COSTS					
1 Exact production; vary work force	$700	$500	$202,500	—	—	$203,700
2 Constant work force; vary inventory and shortages		—	132,000	$66,000	$1,400	199,400
		Overtime				
3A Constant work force; vary overtime with carryover of inventory	—	105,750	132,000	—	1,400	239,150
3B Constant work force; vary overtime (carryover not permitted)	—	116,250	132,000	—	1,400	249,650

CHAPTER 12 Inventory Systems for Independent Demand

1. The quantity to be ordered each time is:

$$Q = \sqrt{\frac{2DS}{H}} = \sqrt{\frac{2(1{,}000)5}{4}} = 50 \text{ units}$$

   a. The total ordering cost for a year is:

$$\frac{D}{Q}S = \frac{1{,}000}{50}(\$5) = \$100$$

   b. The storage cost for a year is:

$$\frac{Q}{2}H = \frac{50}{2}(\$4) = \$100$$

2. $$\sigma_{T+L} = \sqrt{(14 + 7)(30)^2} = \sqrt{18{,}900} = 137.5$$

$$E(z) = \frac{120(14)(1 - .99)}{137.5} = 0.122$$

   From Exhibit 12.5, $z = .80$;

$$\begin{aligned} q &= \bar{d}(T + L) + z\sigma_{T+L} - I \\ &= 120(14 + 7) + .80(137.5) - 130 \\ &= 2{,}500 \text{ units} \end{aligned}$$

CHAPTER 13 Inventory Systems for Dependent Demand: Material Requirements Planning

1. *a.*

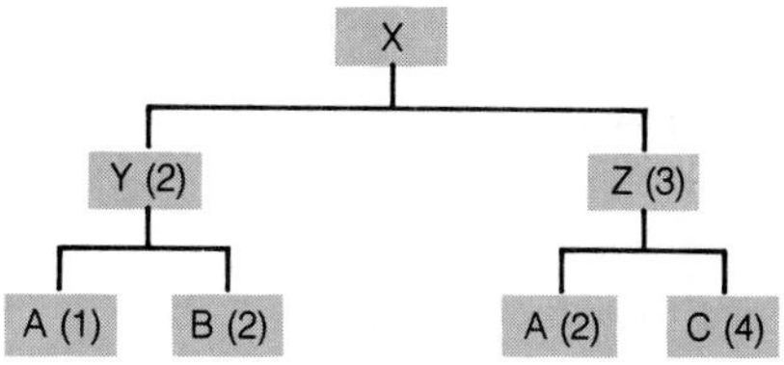

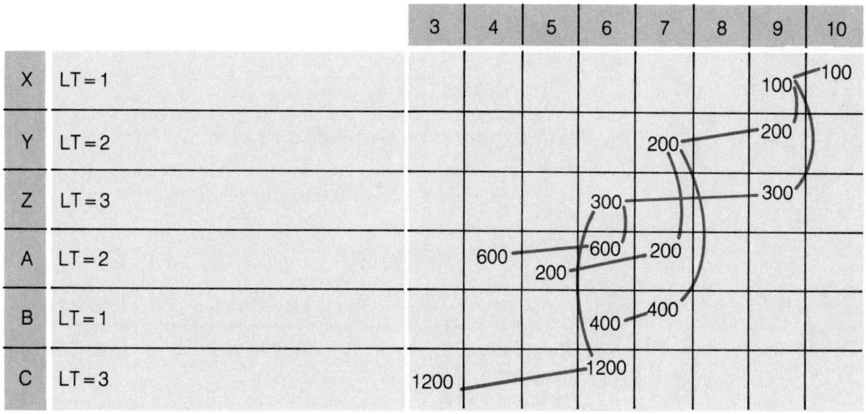
3
4
5
6
7
8
9
10
X LT=1
Y LT=2
Z LT=3
A LT=2
B LT=1
C LT=3
100
100
200
200
300
300
600
600
200
200
400
400
1200
1200

2. *a.*

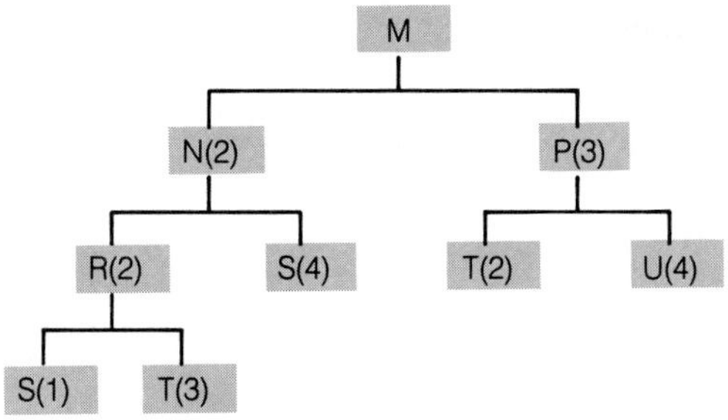

b. M = 100
N = 200
P = 300
R = 400
S = 800 + 400 = 1,200
T = 600 + 1,200 = 1,800
U = 1,200

c.

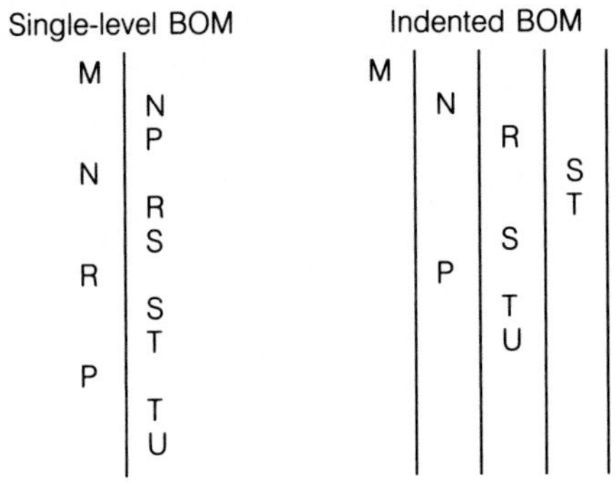

CHAPTER 14 Operations Planning and Control—Job Shops

1. Runout problem on allocating expense money.

	(1) Expense Money on Hand	(2) Daily Expenses
Eldest son	$3.20	$1.95
Daughter	2.40	1.65
Youngest son	1.80	.55
	$7.40	$4.15

$$\text{Aggregate runout time} = \frac{\text{Inventory on hand} + \text{New amount}}{\text{Daily demand}}$$

$$= \frac{7.40 + 20}{4.15} = 6.60 \text{ days}$$

	(3) Total Expense Money Required (2) × 6.60	(4) Net Amount to Be Allocated (3) − (1)
Eldest son	$12.87	$ 9.67
Daughter	10.89	8.49
Youngest son	3.63	1.83
	$27.39	$19.99

The allocations are $9.67, $8.49, and $1.83. Rounding accounts for the 1 cent difference between the $20 and $19.99 allocated.

2. This problem can be viewed as a two-machine flow shop and can be easily solved using "Johnson's method."

Original Data			Johnson Method	
Car	Refitting Time (hours)	Repainting Time (hours)	Order of Selection	Position in Sequence
A	6	3	4th	3rd
B	0	4	1st	1st
C	5	2	3rd	4th
D	8	6	5th	2nd
E	2	1	2nd	5th

Graph of Johnson solution:

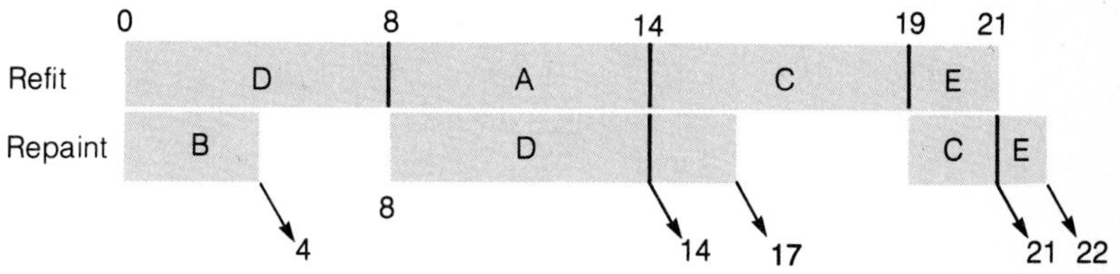

Name Index

I–J

K

L

M

N

O

P

Q–R

S

T

U–V

W

Y–Z

Subject Index

D

E

F

G

H

I

J–K

L

M

N

O

P

Q

R

S